ACADEMIC LEADERSHIP AND GOVERNANCE OF HIGHER EDUCATION

ACADEMIC LEADERSHIP AND GOVERNANCE OF HIGHER EDUCATION

A Guide for Trustees, Leaders, and Aspiring Leaders of Two- and Four-Year Institutions

James T. Harris, Jason E. Lane, Jeffrey C. Sun, and Gail F. Baker

Foreword by Nancy L. Zimpher

Foreword to the First Edition by Stan Ikenberry

SECOND EDITION

STERLING, VIRGINIA

Published by Stylus Publishing, LLC.
22883 Quicksilver Drive
Sterling, Virginia 20166-2019

Library of Congress Cataloging-in-Publication-Data
Names: Harris, James T., 1958- author. | Lane, Jason E., author. | Sun, Jeffrey C., author. | Baker, Gail Frances author.
Title: Academic leadership and governance of higher education: a guide for trustees, leaders, and aspiring leaders of two- and four-year institutions / James T. Harris, Jason E. Lane, Jeffrey C. Sun, and Gail F. Baker ; Foreword by Nancy L. Zimpher ; Foreword to the First Edition by Stan Ikenberry.
Description: Second edition. | Sterling, Virginia : Stylus Publishing, LLC, [2022] | Includes bibliographical references and index. | Summary: "The purpose of this new edition, published a turbulent decade after the first, is to provide institutional leaders with a broad understanding of the academic enterprise, strategic guidance, and key principles, to assist them in navigating the future and drive the success of their institutions as they confront the unimagined"-- Provided by publisher.
Identifiers: LCCN 2022011537 (print) | LCCN 2022011538 (ebook) | ISBN 9781642674088 (cloth) | ISBN 9781642674095 (paperback) | ISBN 9781642674101 (pdf) | ISBN 9781642674118 (epub)
Subjects: LCSH: Universities and colleges--United States--Administration--Handbooks, manuals, etc. | College administrators--United States--Handbooks, manuals, etc. | Educational leadership--United States--Handbooks, manuals, etc.
Classification: LCC LB2341 .H433 2022 (print) | LCC LB2341 (ebook) | DDC 378.1/01--dc23
LC record available at https://lccn.loc.gov/2022011537
LC ebook record available at https://lccn.loc.gov/2022011538

13-digit ISBN: 978-1-64267-408-8 (cloth)
13-digit ISBN: 978-1-64267-409-5 (paperback)
13-digit ISBN: 978-1-64267-410-1 (library networkable e-edition)
13-digit ISBN: 978-1-64267-411-8 (consumer e-edition)

Printed in the United States of America

All first editions printed on acid free paper
that meets the American National Standards Institute
Z39-48 Standard.

Bulk Purchases

Quantity discounts are available for use in workshops and for staff development.

Call 1-800-232-0223

Second Edition, 2022

To our family members and friends whose love and support have made it possible for us to advance the missions of the remarkable institutions we have had the privilege to serve.

To future leaders who are called to advance the democratic ideals of higher education.

CONTENTS

PART THREE: THE BOUNDARY SPANNERS

PART FOUR: THE ACADEMIC CORE

PART FIVE: IMPLEMENTATION OF THE ACADEMIC MISSION

16   PLANNING, ASSESSMENT, AND BUDGETING   437

     THE WRITING TEAM   459

     INDEX   463

What Is Your Theory of Leadership?
Higher education is entering a period of unprecedented change. I've heard this phrase many times throughout my career—as you probably have as well; but I believe that it is truer now than ever before. As a sector, we are facing an impending demographic cliff as the number of students graduating high school plummets. The debt crisis among student graduates has raised significant concerns about the value of higher education. Polls reveal that public opinion regarding higher education—particularly across middle America—is waning. Local, state, and national politics have reached a point where it is near impossible to agree on anything across the aisle.

All of these challenges may make an academic leader wonder if it's worth it. I would argue it is. A line from a column by *New York Times* columnist David Leonhardt summarizes what continues to drive me: "Education—educating more people and educating them better—appears to be the best bet any society can make."

I would argue that it is more than a bet—it's a necessary investment that all societies should make. And, there is reason for hope ahead. While the high school graduation numbers may be declining, we are seeing an increasing number of youth from historically underrepresented backgrounds coming into higher education. That same population still believes that education is a "smart investment." There are also millions of Americans who need to be reskilled and upskilled as jobs become more advanced. The higher education sector remains the backbone of the nation's innovation ecosystem and our colleges and universities are community anchors that foster economic development and quality of life.

What we need are knowledgeable and engaged academic leaders who are prepared to guide the nation's colleges and universities into a tomorrow that is very different than the time when I began to study leadership. And, this handbook does just that—it provides novice and experienced leaders with a broad overview of higher education as well as what leaders need to know to be successful.

The volume is guided by four key principles.

1. Be *mission*-centric by making all key decisions based on a core mission and set of values.
2. Be able to *adapt* to environmental change in alignment with the mission and core values.
3. Be committed to *democratic* ideals by seeking to promote them and modeling democratic practices on and off campus.
4. Be models for *inclusion*, equity, and positive social change.

The first three principles guided the first edition and remain as important today as they did nearly a decade ago. The fourth principle is new, and I commend the authors for their careful reflection and openness to evolving their framework. Issues of equity and inclusion have been part of the academic leadership discourse for many years, but the events of the last few years have brought forth increased energy and effort such that it has become central to the work of academic leaders.

Referencing Dr. Martin Luther King, the authors rightly observe that "the 'arc' of U.S. colleges and universities has bent toward greater inclusion, equity, and social justice" (see chapter 3, this volume). I appreciate this framing as it rightly highlights that higher education is in a perpetual state of betterment. There are lots of reasons to criticize higher education over the centuries and there is still plenty of work to be done to expand access, close achievement gaps, and increase completion rates. But, these are not problems that can be addressed overnight—the role of good academic leaders is to keep pushing their institutions forward—hopefully, leaving them better than how they found them.

In fact, I have long argued that we should not be focused on achieving some form of an ideal state; rather our ultimate goal as a sector should be to the *best at getting better*. There are tools for doing this—quality improvement circles, improvement science, six sigma, and I'm sure others that will be developed. For leaders, though, it is not as much about the tools as it is about the mindset. Leaders need to challenge their organizations to confront their shortcomings and find a path forward.

To do this, you need a theory of leadership that can guide your thinking and actions. I don't mean that you align with a particular theoretical framework. Rather, how do you think about your role as a leader? For me, my theory of leadership has six key components: creating vision, involving many stakeholders, taking action (or do something), tracking outcomes, telling the story, and creating a sustainability strategy. To be certain, a theory of leadership is not necessarily static—mine evolved over time. For example, I used to talk about accountability; now I talk about outcomes. As a leader, I want to see my organization move forward and that is about achieving outcomes—which is more than simply holding each other accountable. The point is that you need to be willing to change and learn from the situations you encounter and the new knowledge you gain.

As you read this insightful volume, I would ask that you keep these questions in the back of your mind:

- What is my theory of leadership?
- How does what I learn conform with or challenge my theory?
- What might I need to do differently based on what I'm learning?

This book is one of the best that I have read at providing the reader with a broad understanding of how higher education works and helping leaders see their role in dealing with different aspects of the enterprise—from student development to working with the governing board. Yet, its real impact should be on how it helps you evolve as a leader.

I firmly believe that higher education remains one of the more important sectors in the American society and we need great leaders to ensure that it remains that way.

—Nancy L. Zimpher
Chancellor Emeritus of The State University of New York
Senior Fellow, National Association of System Heads
Cofounder of StriveTogether

FOREWORD TO THE FIRST EDITION:
ACADEMIC LEADERSHIP AND ITS CONSEQUENCES

If academic institutions functioned in a stable environment, the demands for leadership would be modest. Vision, mission, programs, and policies could simply be put on automatic pilot. For colleges and universities, however, automatic pilots don't work. The environment is in continual flux, and the implications and consequences of these changes for the future of colleges and universities are often profound. Sound, authentic, creative, empowering leadership is indispensable, and it spells the difference between healthy, productive, sustainable, academic institutions and programs and ones that are in constant crisis—vulnerable and failing.

One need only reflect on the change that has come about in higher education over the last century. The very mission and scale of colleges and universities have been transformed. Institutions are altering the very ways and means of teaching and learning. New directions in research and service to society are evolving. The costs and benefits of the academic enterprise are in continual fluctuation and open to challenge. The roles of faculty are different, as are campus cultures. The very definition of precisely who is served and touched by academic institutions is in transition. Amid this whirlwind, the authors of this handbook on academic leadership make a conscious effort to think afresh about the challenges and opportunities of leadership. The main themes of the book are grounded in the argument that successful higher education institutions embrace three essential qualities:

1. Sound institutional decisions must be based on a clearly articulated mission and set of core values.
2. Successful institutional adaptation to a changed environment must be grounded and aligned with the fundamental mission and core values.
3. Successful academic leaders must be able to create and foster partnerships, bringing diverse individuals and interests together around a shared vision and mission grounded in common values.

Each of these three themes surfaces throughout the book, and for good reason. Every decision and the very definition of each issue and problem is based on and defined by core values. The issue of access, for example, is embedded in fundamental human values that touch on equality of opportunity, notions of fairness, human rights, and our aspirations for our democracy and society. The issue of college costs must be understood as a never-ending contest among competing interests and values, including the tensions between costs and quality, costs and vested interests, and costs and opportunity. The very meaning of quality itself can only be grasped in the context of a clearly understood and widely shared sense of mission and purpose. Defining, articulating, testing, promulgating, and applying these core values and sense of mission is the most fundamental job of any academic leader.

Leading and managing change is clearly the most difficult and taxing challenge faced by academic leaders. Occupying a position of leadership and exercising the role of leader are entirely different. The first requires only a title. Too many positions of academic leadership are filled by those who occupy the chair and carry the title but fail to lead academic institutions in ways that enable them to adapt to a demanding environment, optimize their mission, align with values, and produce a lasting contribution to society. This handbook does not speak to the position of leadership, to title, or to mere survival skills; rather it speaks to the creative act, the behavior, the hard work and courage, the art and skill of academic leadership.

The third theme that appears here and in the life of every effective academic leader is the notion of teamwork, collaboration, empowerment of others, and the art of coalition and team building. This is the essence of academic leadership and is indispensable to bringing about successful and enduring institutional change. Leadership is a team sport. It involves working with and inspiring other people. It involves effective and authentic communication grounded in the integrity of core values and clarity of mission.

Too often we think of the leader as reaching down to empower and bring along the followers, forgetting that communication and team building is a two-way street in which leaders almost always learn and receive more from the team than they give. Thinking of leadership as reaching down also fails to recognize that effective academic leaders reach out and reach up. Team building and collaboration doesn't begin and end in a department, program, or an institution. It involves reaching out and building coalitions across department, program, and institutional boundaries. And truly creative leadership involves reaching up, building coalitions, and aligning with the larger forces of the institution's operation, and ultimately society itself.

Sound academic leadership is more important than ever before. At many higher education institutions mission is no longer obvious. Core values are no longer so obvious as to be self-executing. Change—in whatever form— is viewed as threatening. Regaining a clear vision and crafting consensus around core values is not easy when the larger environment is in a whirl, and individual interests and programs are threatened. Strengthening academic quality and performance while containing and reducing costs is a trick few institutions have mastered, and yet it is precisely the challenge facing all of U.S. higher education.

This book addresses the basic building blocks of 21st-century higher education. There is no easy three-step cookbook recipe, nor are there any pat answers to be found in the back of the book. Academic leadership is difficult. Almost always the way forward is ambiguous. Still, asking honest questions, defining and prioritizing the options, and gathering, valuing, and using evidence in decision-making are the qualities that served successful leaders in the past, and those same habits will sustain those who lead in the future.

One fundamental fact merits repetition: Colleges and universities touch more lives more profoundly than any social institution in society. The strength of America's democracy, economic competitiveness, and quality of life, and the health of our communities, our culture, and the arts—all of this and more—rests on the quality and performance of academic institutions. U.S. higher education will be profoundly different in the 21st century. Bringing about the change and understanding and managing the consequences will be the overriding challenges of academic leaders going forward. How well American higher education responds and performs will turn on the quality of leadership it receives.

—Stanley O. Ikenberry
100th President of the American Council on Education
14th and 17th President of the American Council on Education

ACKNOWLEDGMENTS

"This book has been a labor of love." These are the opening words in the original acknowledgments page of the first edition of this book when it was published in 2013. The writing may have been a labor of love, but it was also a dream come true. The initial idea for this book came from Robert M. Hendrickson, who for 3 decades taught a graduate course titled "Administration in Higher Education." It was his dream that we would write a book that would provide graduate students, busy academic leaders, external stakeholders, and lay board members an overview of American higher education. Based on the results, it appears we did accomplish that goal. The first edition of *Academic Leadership and Governance of Higher Education* became a Stylus bestseller and today is used in classrooms and boardrooms across the country.

When Stylus approached us to complete a second edition of this book, two of the original authors, Richard Dorman and Robert Hendrickson, were retired and decided that since they were no longer active scholars or administrators that it would be best if we found other authors to assist in this new edition. While they did not participate in this edition, their words are throughout this book, and we are indebted to them for their contributions.

If the first edition was a labor of love, the second edition felt like a call to action. At the time we were approached to write this edition, the world was in the middle of a global pandemic, the United States was embroiled in a national reckoning with regard to race relations, and the democratic underpinnings of our nation seemed under siege. Perhaps most importantly for this book is that American higher education is more often viewed today as a commodity primarily used for individual gain rather than as a key element in the promotion of democracy or the advancement of society. Through the publication of this book, we hope to help restore the dialogue on the important and vital role higher education plays in American society by educating current and future higher education leaders.

Two of the original authors, James T. Harris, DEd, president of the University of San Diego, and Jason E. Lane, PhD, dean of the College of Education, Health, and Society at Miami University, contributed to the second edition. We were joined by two incredibly gifted scholars and practitioners: Gail F. Baker, PhD, an Emmy award–winning documentarian and provost at the University of San Diego, and Jeffrey C. Sun, JD, PhD, a professor of higher education and law and associate dean at the University of Louisville. Collectively, we have worked for numerous private and public colleges and universities as well as system administrations, serving as faculty members, directors, chairs, deans, provosts, and president. In addition, we have served on and staffed boards of trustees, worked for state-level departments of higher education and federal agencies, and served in leadership roles in several national associations. Through all these experiences, we recognized that very limited resources exist to help academic leaders, external stakeholders, and lay board members understand the complexities of the academic organization and how it interacts with various aspects of society.

This book is the culmination of decades of practice and study. In conceiving and writing this volume, we spent countless hours debating various issues. One of the major decisions we made was to expand our original three guiding principles to four by including a principle grounded in the importance of diversity, inclusion, and equity to American society and the role higher education plays in promoting those values. While we underestimated the amount of work involved in producing a second edition, the discussions and debates that occurred during our online meetings and many conference calls have greatly enriched our own understanding of the academy and, we believe, have enriched the volume.

We owe a great debt of gratitude to many individuals who helped us in this process. As with any project such as this, our thinking has been influenced by a wide array of students, colleagues, mentors, and friends. There is no way to thank all who have in some small or large way helped with the development of this book or our own understanding of academic leadership.

Specifically, we were fortunate to benefit once again from the editorial work of Sarah Fuller Klyberg, PhD, a higher education professional, researcher, and writer. Sarah essentially took the writings of six authors with disparate voices and created a volume that provides a unity of voice. Her knowledge of higher education as a field of study, attention to detail, sense of humor, organizational skills, patience, and flow of writing resulted in a publication that fosters the reader's acquisition of knowledge and understanding.

For this edition we were fortunate to attract other talented individuals to support our efforts. Gabriel Nuñez-Soria, who has 2 decades of experience working in secondary education and is a PhD student in the Education for Social Justice program at the University of San Diego, contributed much to our work. In addition to helping the authors search for and include new data and research on myriad topics, his expertise in and knowledge of diversity, inclusion, and equity had a big impact on how we ultimately framed the four principles that guide this book. Rob Woodward, a PhD student in educational policy and leadership at the State University of New York (SUNY) at Albany, was also critical for updating key data and trends that had changed since the first edition was published and for establishing the digital structure to keep us organized. We also wish to recognize the work of Katherine E. Crooks, MSc, and Victoria Crooks, MSA, for their contributions to the chapter on diversity, equity, and inclusion, as well as Heather Turner, PhD, at the University of Louisville for gathering new literature for several chapters. Liz Kodela of Capital District Design provided the design work for all of the new imagery in this edition, David Prout handled the indexing and Kristin Sciabllaba provided assistance on the final edits.

We would like to thank John von Knorring and the staff at Stylus. From the very beginning when John proposed that it was time for another edition, he made it clear that a second edition would not be a simple matter of editing but rather would require a substantial rewrite if we wanted to complete a book that was relevant for the times. He was right, and we are grateful for his sage counsel and advice.

Finally, we wish to thank Nancy L. Zimpher, PhD, chancellor emeritus of the SUNY system, for authoring the foreword for this edition. As a president of two major research universities and the largest comprehensive system of higher education in the country, she knows well both the challenges of leadership and the need to more develop and support these leaders. Her words offer critical reflection and inspiration for readers. Stanley O. Ikenberry, former president of the American Council on Education and the University of Illinois system, provided the foreword to the first edition, which we have included in this edition as his words on leadership remain timely and inspirational.

It is our hope that this second volume will provide a useful guide and reference for many people who seek answers to complex questions concerning American higher education. The book is intended for a wide audience of seasoned professionals, graduate students in the field, and laypeople alike. We recognize that as soon as a book is published it is placed in a moment of time, and over time it may lose some of its relevance. However, we also believe firmly that the guiding principles we provide are timeless, have served American higher education well for centuries, and will continue to do so in the future.

The U.S. higher education sector is the most diverse in the world. It is characterized by a wide array of institutions—private and public, secular and faith-based, not-for-profit and for-profit—and includes institutions as varied as community colleges, research universities, and liberal arts colleges. These colleges and universities can be found in rural communities and major urban centers, while others exist by offering their academic content almost entirely in an online or virtual environment. Every higher education institution believes it has a specific mission and educational philosophy that make it unique in the marketplace. As much value as each of these colleges and universities has provided to society, in the 21st century, an ever-changing, volatile, and globally competitive environment; shifting demographics; and the demand for more social mobility through education will place pressures on these institutions unlike any other time in history. To prosper and thrive in this new global environment, U.S. higher education will need to adapt, innovate, and evolve once again, as it has during every major societal change over the past 4 centuries. The purpose of this book is to provide institutional leaders with a broad understanding of the academic enterprise and assist them in knowing what principles are likely to drive institutional success.

Since the dawn of the 21st century, significant transformation has occurred in the operating environment of higher education institutions. Within the United States, major demographic changes have occurred, from a sudden drop-off in birth rates to rising numbers of retirees to increases in populations traditionally underserved by higher education. The United States has been engaged in multiple military conflicts, and the world economy has experienced the worst recession in a century. The financial crisis brought on by the Great Recession was followed by a global pandemic that disproportionately affected lower-income populations and made institutions of higher education reimagine their own operating models.

During this same time, democratic reform movements swept across the globe only to be replaced in some countries with extreme nationalistic and autocratic movements that have threatened democratic ideals. The U.S. electorate has been divided on the future direction of the nation, electing two Republican and two Democratic presidents in a span of 20 years. The election of the first U.S. president of color and then the first woman and person of color as U.S. vice president led some to believe that the country had risen above its historical struggles with racial injustice. Yet we have come to realize that as a nation we have not lived up to our founding democratic ideals, and institutions of higher education have often fallen short in their roles to promote inclusion and equity and to be beacons of social justice. At the same time, college campuses have gained a reputation to some as bastions of liberal thought that are not open to conservative ideas and where free speech is not truly embraced. These societal tensions manifest on college campuses every day, and the pressures on institutional leaders to find common ground necessitate a new level of sophistication and a balanced approach to personal communications and leadership that were not expected of college leaders at the beginning of the century.

Leading in this environment has become more complicated through advances in artificial intelligence, information technology, and the growth of social media platforms, which have forever changed the way people communicate and share information. In addition, an assault on the value of scientific inquiry and the integrity of scientific data has challenged the very nature of open discourse on issues (ranging from climate change to the efficacy of wearing masks to stop the spread of airborne diseases) on campuses across the United States.

While adapting to change has been a struggle for higher education, in recent years the pace of change has accelerated so rapidly that academic leaders face new and unprecedented demands, making it difficult to manage these challenges and adapt to new realities. In this context, academic leaders must not only understand how to manage, but also how to lead their institutions.

To be successful, academic leaders need to develop a broad appreciation of how their college or university is structured and how it functions and engages with the external environment, while simultaneously understanding the locus of decision-making on institutional issues. They must also learn to cultivate relationships with myriad stakeholders including faculty, students, alumni, parents, elected officials, foundations, and philanthropists by taking advantage of new communication tools such as social media. New environmental forces, such as changing demographics, expanding global competition, emerging technologies, additional government regulations, reduced government funding for education, increasing discount rates, and incivility in public discourse make leading these institutions more difficult than ever. For instance, cyberattacks that originate overseas continue to challenge institutions that are seeking to safeguard student records, research data, and intellectual property. Similarly, artificial intelligence and the use of big data present potentially promising opportunities and perilous developments as institutional leaders explore the use of predictive analytics on students, personalized learning modules, and research opportunities in which control over the innovation may be commercialized and transferred.

While the challenges are many, the need to redefine an institution's purpose and foci to adapt and stay ahead of emerging trends is necessary to thrive. We believe that academic leaders who acquire new knowledge and skills on how to adapt will enhance their ability to thrive rather than simply survive in tough times. In other words, academic leaders must be more knowledgeable than ever about the effects of external pressures on their institutions, the levers for change that they have within their institutions, and the strategies needed to adapt to new external influences.

A vast literature exists on administration, management, and leadership in higher education, and it tends to focus primarily on the impact that the environment, external forces, and internal issues have on research-intensive universities. The hallmark of higher education in the United States, however, is the diversity of institution types, each of which is affected differently by external and internal influences. As such, this book uses examples and information from a range of institutional contexts to provide background and knowledge of the environment, organization, and management of U.S. colleges and universities in the not-for-profit sector. Moreover, instead of focusing only on one level of academic leadership, this book addresses management and leadership issues facing board members, presidents, provosts, vice presidents, deans, and department chairs, placing those issues in organizational and environmental contexts.

Four Essential Principles

Colleges and universities have the potential to be the most influential institutions in society. Higher education's civic purpose, societal role, and extraordinary possibility for promoting the common good and social mobility provide it with a unique opportunity to contribute powerfully to meaningful change in a global society. In the first edition of this book the authors argued that if institutions wished to be successful in the future, they should embrace three basic principles. In the foreword from the first edition of this book, Stanley O. Ikenberry, former president of the American Council on Education and president emeritus of the University of Illinois, provided this guidance about how academic leaders need to think about decision-making: "Every decision and the very definition of each issue and problem is based on and defined by core values" (pp. xiii–xiv, this volume). The purpose of this book is to assist institutional leaders by reminding them that defining core values and following essential principles will be the key to success in the 21st century.

In this edition we continue to suggest that the leaders of the colleges, universities, and systems who have been most successful in advancing the academy, as well as society as a whole, have embraced common principles that have distinguished them within a crowded sector and helped them navigate an ever-changing and volatile environment. In addition to the original three principles found in the first edition, we have added a fourth, which grew out of the third principle on democratic ideals. We believe this expansion of democratic ideals into two distinct principles better represents the unique purpose of U.S. higher education and, in conjunction with the other principles, will characterize colleges and universities that will prosper and thrive in the 21st century:

1. Be **mission** centric by making all key decisions based on a core mission and set of values.
2. Be able to **adapt** to environmental change in alignment with the mission and core values.
3. Be committed to **democratic** ideals by seeking to promote them and modeling democratic practices on and off campus.
4. Be models for **inclusion**, equity, and positive social change.

It is important to note that leaders of institutions that have flourished over time have practiced all four principles because no one element guarantees success on its own. In the first chapter we provide the reasoning and rationale for each principle, and we carry these four principles throughout the book.

While higher education institutions today are diverse, global, and ever changing, the resiliency of U.S. colleges and universities compared to other organizations over time is remarkable. As Kerr (1987) noted:

> About 85 institutions in the western world established by 1520 still exist in recognizable forms, with similar functions and with unbroken histories, including the Catholic church, the Parliaments of the Isle of Man, of Iceland and of Great Britain, several Swiss cantons and seventy universities. (p. 184)

Moreover, in the United States none of the original 30 industries listed on the Dow Jones Industrial Average in 1928 are on the list today, and many no longer exist at all, yet all 30 of the top universities in the country in 1928 still exist, and most of them would still be considered among the best (Geiger, 2004).

This record is important because a plethora of business articles suggest to the average reader that business and industry leaders understand their missions as well or better than college and university administrators do because the primary mission of a business is to bring value to its shareholders. This focus on shareholder value makes the mission of these organizations seem straightforward and easy to understand. However, a simple focus on shareholder value does not appear to be enough to guarantee success over time or be supportive of the goals of a democratic society. Similarly, engagement in teaching, research, and service does not guarantee a college or university's success, as is evidenced by the hundreds of higher education institutions that have closed over the centuries. Rather, it is the combination of focusing on a specific mission; adapting to a changing milieu while maintaining that mission; promoting democratic ideals; and embracing a focus on inclusion, diversity, and social justice that has allowed institutions of higher learning to become arguably the most respected organizations in society today.

Organization of This Book

This book is intended to serve as a reference for scholars as well as a useful guide for professionals in the field of higher education. To make the subject matter more accessible, the book is divided into five parts. Part One introduces the reader to the scholarly field of higher education and establishes the contextual framework for the rest of the book. Part Two investigates the multifaceted and often complex relationships that exist between institutions of higher learning and the external constituencies they encounter. Part Three focuses on how college and university presidents and their boards of trustees keep an institutional mission focus while adapting to changes in the environment, and Part Four analyzes how colleges and universities fulfill their core mission through shared democratic partnerships and a commitment to inclusion. Part Five describes how effective academic leaders implement their institution's academic mission.

We recommend that all readers review the Introduction and Part One before reading the rest of the book, as it sets the stage for the remaining chapters. The chapters in Parts Two through Five do not have to be read in successive order. They are designed as self-contained modules to provide the reader with a greater understanding of specific topics. Throughout the book, examples of certain colleges and universities and their leaders are cited as models of the application of theory to practice.

Moreover, we should emphasize again that this book draws specifically on the context of the not-for-profit higher education sector in the United States. Institutions around the world, in developing and developed countries, could benefit from learning about and adopting the four principles: being mission driven, adaptable, democratic, and inclusive. However, the contexts in which higher education institutions operate vary by country and state. Not embedding a book such as this in a specific context risks creating a volume so general in nature that it provides very little value its readers. As much as possible, though, we have sought to structure this book in such a way that readers in other national contexts could distill lessons for their own work. Throughout the book, we use the terms *U.S.* and *American* interchangeably to refer to the U.S. context and not to the broader continental contexts of North and South America.

Welcome to the remarkable and resilient world of higher education in the United States. We humbly offer this book in the hope of contributing something of value to current and aspiring leaders of colleges and universities as they navigate the challenges and opportunities of the 21st century.

References

Geiger, R. L. (2004). *Knowledge and money: Research universities and the paradox of the marketplace.* Stanford University Press.

Kerr, C. (1987). A critical age in the university world: Accumulated heritage versus modern imperatives. *European Journal of Education, 22*(2), 183–193. https://doi.org/10.2307/1503216

I

PRINCIPLES OF
ACADEMIC LEADERSHIP

In 1994 a group of new college and university presidents from around the world gathered at Harvard University to discuss their roles as academic leaders. During that meeting, a small group of those presidents (James T. Harris was among them) had the opportunity to meet with the distinguished American sociologist David Riesman. The purpose of the meeting was to expose these recently hired presidents to some of the research Riesman and his colleagues at Harvard had been conducting on successful academic institutions and the people who lead them.

After a brief presentation of the data he had collected and the conclusions he had drawn from his research, Riesman asked if there were any questions. At first there was silence, but then one president raised his hand and asked if there was any one thing he could do as the leader of his university to guarantee he would be successful in his new role. Riesman paused, looked directly at the man, and said, "Become the living embodiment of the mission of the institution you serve." He went on to describe how a successful institution, and the people who lead it, understand the institution's basic purpose or mission and make decisions in alignment with that specific mission. Riesman added that while there were no guarantees, mission-driven and democratic institutions and leaders are more likely to weather tough times successfully and adjust to challenges than those with less clear direction and purpose.

In many ways, Riesman's advice to the new president seems obvious and logical. It makes sense that leaders at institutions that have a clear sense of purpose and direction make better decisions about how to use scarce resources and face changes in the environment with greater resiliency. Or does it?

Conflicting Goals, Ambiguous Aims

Many scholars would have us believe that the basic purpose or mission of any institution of higher education could be described as having three essential components: teaching, research, and service. In *How Colleges Work*, Birnbaum (1988) stated that these three elements are interrelated and mutually reinforcing, and to some extent they broadly describe the work of individual faculty members and the primary goal of the academy as a whole. Furthermore, he noted that as institutions of higher learning have become more diverse and complex, missions have not become more clear. Rather, they have also become more complex, creating greater tensions between competing constituencies. These tensions can be best characterized by the decades-old conflict between teaching and research, that is, which one is the most prized activity within the academy.

Other scholars have proposed similar ideas, mainly that the problem is not that college and university officials are unable to identify their goals and direction (e.g., Gross & Grambsch, 1974). Rather, they embrace too many conflicting goals, which causes more tension and leads to confusion about an institution's mission. Cohen and March (1974) were more direct when they stated that institutions of higher learning, specifically American universities, were really "organized anarchies" (p. 2) with ill-defined goals, ambiguous organizational processes, and ever-changing boundaries.

With the increased complexity of higher education since the second half of the 20th century, one may be led to believe that focusing on an institutional mission is not as important as identifying and clarifying the roles and responsibilities of various constituents within the academy—primarily the board, administration, and faculty. Much has been written on the subject, and several major higher education accrediting bodies and associations, including the Association of Governing Boards of Universities and Colleges (AGB, 1996) and the American Association of University Professors (AAUP, n.d.), have issued statements on the importance of shared governance in the successful management of the academy. These statements speak to the difficulty of managing a complex organization and subscribe to the notion that good governance, however it may be applied at any particular institution, is the key to success in higher education—and is perhaps even a viable substitute for being mission driven. Indeed, with the predominance of literature on academic governance models, one could almost be led to believe that a good organizational structure is at the heart of institutional success, regardless of whether an organization is producing something desirable to the marketplace or in alignment with its mission and values.

The notion that since institutions of higher learning are too complex to lead, and that the best we can do is hope for collaboration and effective power sharing within wisely devised governance structures is myopic and one-dimensional. A highly effective shared governance model is as much the product of an institution whose administrators and faculty understand its purpose or mission as healthy enrollments, strategic planning, and clear budgeting and management. In other words, leaders of healthy, thriving institutions clearly understand their mission, values, and niche in the broader higher education community, and because of this alignment, their institutions are better governed and positioned to succeed in tough times.

As discussed in the introduction, this volume is guided by four mutually reinforcing principles (see Figure 1.1):

1. Be **mission** centric by making all key decisions based on a core mission and set of values.
2. Be able to **adapt** to environmental change in alignment with the mission and core values.
3. Be committed to **democratic** ideals by seeking to promote them and modeling democratic practices on and off campus.
4. Be models for **inclusion**, equity, and positive social change.

These four principles are weaved throughout the entirety of the volume. In this chapter, we discuss these four principles in more depth.

Importance of Being Mission Centric

What exactly does it mean to be mission centric? The literature is full of examples why clear purpose or a set of core values that drives decision-making at an institution is so critical. Welzenbach (1982) described mission as the "broad, overall, long term purpose of the institution" (p. 15). That broad purpose may be based on religious or philosophical tenets or may be driven by an institution's relationship to the state or federal government (Davies, 1986; Dewey, 1916; Kerr, 1964). Handy (1997) proposed that because of the growing complexity of life in a virtual world, organizations are not necessarily tied in tangible ways to a campus with buildings or a specific location. Under these conditions, the work of the academic leader is to help people in the institution understand how their work contributes to the mission regardless of the location, time, or place in which it is fulfilling its educational purpose. That task requires the college or

Figure 1.1. Four principles of academic leadership and governance.

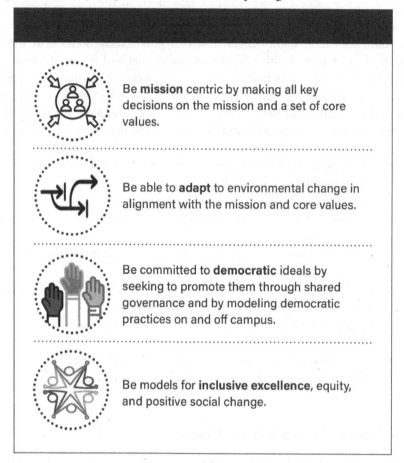

Be **mission** centric by making all key decisions on the mission and a set of core values.

Be able to **adapt** to environmental change in alignment with the mission and core values.

Be committed to **democratic** ideals by seeking to promote them through shared governance and by modeling democratic practices on and off campus.

Be models for **inclusive excellence**, equity, and positive social change.

university to have a distinctive mission, one that helps to differentiate it from others.

Institutional leaders who clearly identify their mission and articulate in unequivocal terms what they value have a greater opportunity to claim a distinctive position in the marketplace and have the greatest impact on society. Geiger (2011) chronicled the history of several colleges and universities that could trace their history back for more than 2 centuries and discovered that the relative success of an institution is associated with a few key factors—including a clear understanding of mission, which emanates from the historical and societal traditions of its founders (Geiger, 2011). In his book on strategic planning, Keller (1983) emphasized the importance of an organizational charter in developing a clear mission for an institution that would help drive decision-making at all levels. Maurrasse (2001) believed an institution's mission should address the overall reason for its existence and establish a set of norms and expectations of a "way of doing business" (p. 6).

For this book, the word *mission* refers to the purpose, philosophy, and educational aspirations of a college or university. A college or university's educational philosophy or mission statement should direct an institution and its leaders. It should provide a rationale for the way a college or university leader approaches decisions about every aspect of the institution, from whom the board selects to lead to how the curriculum should be structured to how resources should be distributed. In the end, it should provide the glue that binds the organization together as well as offer the core values that guide the institution's decision-making. In other words, a mission statement should help college and university administrators determine not only what the institution will do, but equally importantly, what it will not do. As was pointed out earlier, the lack of a clear and distinguishing mission can diminish an institution's focus and lead to unclear goals and objectives, which in turn can create problems internally and externally.

BoardSource's (2010) authors outlined 12 principles of governance that they believe power exceptional boards. Among the 12 recommendations for board members are remaining strategic in their thinking, creating an ethos of transparency, and being results-oriented. Most important, however, is the underlining theme that all decisions—from selecting new leadership to budgeting—must "ensure the congruence between decisions and core values" (p. 23). That is, exceptional board members recognize that their primary role is to mold and uphold the mission of the institution they serve.

The value of mission statements is exemplified by the fact that all major accrediting bodies require that an institution demonstrate that its mission is appropriate and achievable in some reasonable manner. For example, the authors of the WASC Senior College and University Commission's (2018) *2013 Handbook of Accreditation* (revised) state that each institution seeking accreditation or reaffirmation be compliant with a specific set of standards, and that under standard 1, "Defining Institutional Purposes and Ensuring Educational Objectives," each institution's "formally approved statements of purpose are appropriate for an institution of higher education and clearly define its essential values and character" (p. 1). The authors also explained that an institution must clearly demonstrate how it "contributes to the public good" (p. 1). Furthermore, the commission reinforced the idea that the main purpose of shared governance is to realize fully the stated mission of the college or university.

The mission of an institution has long been believed to be important in the creation of the academic curriculum and the promotion of democratic ideals. For example, in 1977 the Carnegie Foundation for the Advancement of Teaching published a report in which it asserted that "governing boards have a responsibility for making the institutional mission an explicit instrument of educational policy" (p. 258). In 1987, Boyer wrote a report on the state of undergraduate education in which he noted that several things reduce its quality. To Boyer (1987), the main problem was a lack of a clear understanding of the goals and purposes of higher education. In other words, he discovered that while some colleges and universities do reasonably well in helping students understand and even become competent in specific fields, most higher education institutions lack a clear sense of direction or purpose, which ultimately diminishes an undergraduate's education. The implication is clear: Colleges and university leaders who understand their institution's core purpose and tie it to their educational outcomes provide the richest learning environments for their students.

A clear sense of mission not only improves a college or university's ability to obtain important accreditations, has a positive impact on student learning outcomes, and promotes civic education; it also helps institutions' trustees to assess leadership. In an essay by Colgan and deRussy (2006), sponsored by the Institute for Effective Governance in Higher Education, the authors argued that it is imperative for trustees to tie the assessment of a president to the institution's three most critical documents: its mission statement, strategic plan, and corresponding budget.

Adapting to an Ever-Changing and Volatile Environment

Being mission driven is no guarantee that an institution will enjoy success, however. In fact, Chait et al. (2005) suggested that institutions will suffer if their board members assume that being mission driven insulates them from threats outside the academy. Their research shows that administrators who have chosen to ignore environmental factors such as changes in technology or enrollment trends because they believe they are mission driven have done so at their own peril. Therefore, boards and institutions that have found ways to engage continuously in boundary-spanning assessment and planning are better able to adjust to their ever-changing and volatile environment and ensure that the mission of the institution remains relevant.

A focus on mission does not mean that an organization cannot adapt to change. Instead, being mission driven allows an institution to use its mission as a lens to interpret changes in the environment and connect institutional aspirations with what is happening in the world. For example, most early colonial liberal arts colleges emphasized the classics for all students, which included language training in Greek, Latin, and Hebrew. As Rudolph (1962) stated in his history of U.S. higher education, these languages served as "tools with which teacher and student found their way" (p. 25) through ancient texts. Today those languages, while still offered at some institutions, are not required because of the broad access everyone has to translations of those texts. Although core language requirements may have changed in response to a major environmental shift, no one would suggest that those same institutions are not fulfilling their mission as liberal arts colleges because they no longer require those texts to be taught in their original languages.

The ability of academic leaders to understand and adjust to changes in the external environment while remaining in alignment with the core values of their college or university requires the discipline to interpret change through the lens of their institution's mission. For example, when developing a strategic plan, leaders must scan the external landscape as well as the internal workings of their institution to ensure that the future direction of their institution will be in alignment with its core values. However, this discipline is easy to ignore when colleges and universities face environmental threats, and such disregard has led many higher education administrators to neglect their core mission in favor of making their institutions more like those that are ranked more highly, or that they believe are more prestigious or perceive to have an advantage.

A risk of emulating other colleges and universities in the hope of acquiring resources and prestige is *mission creep* (Lane, 2005). A particular problem with mission creep is not that schools have added new programs or services to enhance their mission, but rather that these additions make them more closely resemble other institutions in the marketplace. In a 2001 letter to the California legislature, Clark Kerr described mission creep as "a phenomenon in which one segment of higher education redefines its mission to include the responsibility already being performed by another" (as cited in Lane, 2005, pp. 4–5). In their book on innovation in higher education, Christensen and Eyring (2011) pointed out that the trend toward imitation is not by mistake. Rather, they asserted that "the roots of the problems are genetic, and the DNA is fundamentally Harvard's" (Christensen & Evring, 2011, p. 197). In other words, with such an emphasis and focus on places like Harvard, many institutions wrongly believe they need to be more like Harvard to be successful. This is a fool's errand because society neither needs nor should desire another Harvard. What society needs are distinctive institutions that understand their mission and excel at what it is they are uniquely positioned to do. Beyond diminishing the diversity of higher education institutions, this mimicking of another mission to attain additional resources or prestige rarely results in a sustainable model of education and often moves an institution away from its original purpose and makes it less able to adapt to environmental changes. "To the extent that pluralism is a guiding value in public policy deliberations, we need to discover new forms of intersectoral coordination that will encourage diversification rather than hastening homogenization" (DiMaggio & Powell, 1983, p. 158).

The practice of imitation as a means to advance a college or university's reputation differs significantly from the historical tradition of major shifts through which new institution types emerged. For example, the Morrill Act of 1862 facilitated the development of land-grant institutions, which advanced the American priority of agricultural and industrial education. The emergence of the German research university in the late 19th century had a tremendous impact on higher education in Europe as well as in the United States, and the creation of community college systems in the 20th century expanded access to higher education to many more Americans. Over the years, individual states have expanded the missions of particular higher education sectors to meet societal demands, but in these cases expansion of mission did not mean copying other institutions. Rather, through these reforms new institutions with distinct missions were developed in response to societal change.

Administrators of colleges and universities that are mission driven yet responsive to societal change do not allow their institutions to creep into an area that is incongruent with what they are or what they aspire to be. Rather they only add programs, services, or responsibilities that advance their basic purpose and are in harmony with their core values. Deciding what to add (or eliminate) is best completed through a rigorous, systematic, and ongoing planning and assessment process that leads to institutional renewal. Such a process is a sign of institutional vigor and sustainability and typically leads to better decision-making and resource allocations. Institutional renewal in alignment with the mission is enhanced when the process has transparent aims and is inclusive of myriad constituents. In other words, the process of institutional renewal and growth is imbued with and guided by basic democratic decision-making principles that view participants as partners in the process.

Importance of Democratic Ideals in Advancing the Academy

So far, we have made the case that alignment with mission is paramount in all decision-making in higher education. Moreover, we have argued that institutional renewal and change should be tied to a systematic assessment process in harmony with the core values of the organization. We will now turn our attention to the important role higher education in the United States plays in the promotion of democracy by engaging the local community, producing engaged citizens, and ensuring that all decision-making is congruent with democratic principles.

One of the core purposes of colleges and universities is to promote democratic ideals such as freedom of inquiry and speech, inclusion, equality, and social justice. In fact, evidence suggests that the broad support our colleges and universities have enjoyed over the centuries is because of an implicit understanding that higher education exists in part to help our democracy flourish. Several researchers who have investigated the role of higher education in advancing democracy have argued that openness to change and adaptation is a critical element within any institution that wishes to pursue social justice as its aim (Clift, 1948; Josephson, 2020).

It is not enough, however, for college and university administrators, faculty, and staff to encourage students to develop into responsible citizens equipped to work collaboratively in a global society. Rather, they—both as individual scholars and as a collective group—must model the same behavior. Institutions and their leaders can exemplify this aspect of their mission through their interactions with students and through their shared governance processes. They can also model democratic values and responsible citizenship through the creation of reciprocal, democratic alliances with other organizations outside the academy.

In their discussion on civic education, Colby et al. (2003) argue that the schools that are most successful in promoting a democratic agenda have a core institutional commitment that is "intentional and holistic" (p. 9) and shapes most, if not all, aspects of a student's experience while in school. In describing the more successful models of civic education, they reaffirm that the mission of an institution is the starting point for the creation of a unique learning environment.

It is important to recognize that ultimate responsibility for any institution of higher learning, and therefore its promotion of democratic ideals, rests with its governing board. Governing boards are required to have authority over all matters pertaining to the operation of the organization including academic, administrative, financial, and compliance issues. Although they retain ultimate authority, governing boards delegate their responsibilities to the president or chancellor through a shared governance model that is tied to the institutional mission and reflects democratic principles in its implementation. While all shared governance models have unique characteristics, it is not the model that matters so much as whether the institution has developed a democratic way to share governance that gives appropriate decision-making authority to those most able to successfully execute particular decisions.

Colleges and universities that are mission driven and have developed a process for institutional renewal also need to develop ways to engage their diverse constituencies. Such engagement requires time for appropriate discourse, appreciates the distinctive role of each constituent group, and fosters an environment of mutual understanding and respect. To accomplish these goals, leaders of an institution must view each constituent as a partner in the shared governance process and adhere to basic values such as transparency, inclusiveness, and accountability. Engaging with these values does not mean that everything is open to debate and a vote. Instead, it ensures a mechanism for civil and rational discourse to occur, and that in the end the appropriate people in the governance structure are held accountable for the decisions that are made.

For many, this matter of accountability is the sticking point in governance. Board members and senior administrators have fiduciary and legal responsibilities that could make them personally liable for damages. In contrast, faculty members typically have neither fiduciary responsibility nor career accountability for the decisions in which a typical governance structure allows them to participate. Fortunately, at most colleges and universities the majority of faculty members involved in governance understand these issues and participate with the best interests of the institution at heart.

Abraham Flexner (1930), an early 20th-century educator, described colleges and universities as organisms, and Kerr (1964) believed the various components of those organisms are "inextricably bound" (p. 20). If an institution of higher learning is an organism, to remain robust and healthy, the various components within it must discover ways to function in unison and recognize that no single element is predominant. In real terms, this realization requires a balance among and between an institution's various constituencies. While the ultimate responsibility for an institution rests with its governing board, it would be unrealistic to think that any board could manage every aspect of an organization as complex as a college or university. Institutions that create democratic processes to share this management fare better over time.

Unfortunately, shared governance often is only thought of as an internal mechanism for ensuring that an institution can continue to function successfully. In highly effective institutions, however, the same principles and practices used inside the academy also apply to dealings with external groups and issues. Colby et al. (2003) asserted that commitment to reasoned and honest discourse and respect for others are two basic values all colleges and universities should uphold, and those same values should guide decision-making when dealing with issues outside the academy. The very notion that what is considered good democratic practice within an institutional governance structure is what should be modeled when dealing with people and organizations outside of it is an idea that has been part of the lexicon of higher education for centuries, but only recently has it emerged as a leading indicator of institutional strength and rigor.

If the academy desires to maintain its exalted place in a democratic society, the sharing of authority through thoughtfully designed and institutionally appropriate democratic processes cannot simply be an ideal practiced by colleges and university administrators within their own walls; it must be an imperative in their work outside the academy as well. Moreover, if institutions of higher learning do not engage their students in democratic and responsible ways, how can leaders of colleges and universities expect their students to behave as responsible members of society? Over the years, many universities have decided that one way to demonstrate their commitment to acting in a democratic and responsible way is by incorporating these principles into the learning environment. Service learning, community-based learning, and other forms of experiential learning—in which faculty lead students in the "active construction of knowledge" (Colby et al., 2003, p. 2)—require the teacher and the student to consider the impact of their work on others and engage in democratic practices that advance democratic partnerships, scholarship, and learning.

Being a Catalyst for Inclusion, Equity, and Social Justice

Dr. Martin Luther King, Jr., the great American civil rights leader, once stated that the "arc of the moral universe is long, but it bends toward justice" (King, 1968). With this statement Dr. King was attempting to provide a description of our nation's history that recognizes that while the founders excluded a significant percentage of the population from actively participating in and benefitting from our democracy, over time our nation has moved in a direction that is more inclusive of diverse peoples, opinions, and ideas. If we were to paraphrase Dr. King in the context of American higher education, we would propose that while the original colonial colleges may not have had inclusion and equity in mind when they were founded, the "arc" of U.S. colleges and universities has bent toward greater inclusion, equity, and social justice.

Several authors have argued that, over time, institutions of higher education have served as a catalyst for the advancement of democratic ideals and, more specifically, as champions for preparing citizens for active participation in our democracy. Colleges and universities gradually recognized that greater inclusion of populations traditionally underserved by higher education would be necessary if they were to fulfill their mission of promoting democratic ideals. The early colonial colleges, however, did not begin as models of democracy.

In his book on the history of U.S. colleges and universities, historian Fredrick Rudolph (1962) stated, "While exerting a profound influence on such an environment through the civil and religious leaders it trained, the colonial college failed to establish itself as a popular institution intimately affecting the lives of the people" (p. 19). Rudolph observed that the idea that colleges should serve the purpose of promoting democratic ideals really did not take hold until after the American Revolution. He noted that in the first 20 years after the revolution "more than twice as many colleges as had been founded during the almost 150 previous years," and they all had at their core some component of promoting democracy and the preparation of citizens for the new nation (Rudolph, 1962, p. 35–36).

As American higher education expanded over the next 2 centuries, institutions adopted two beliefs that ultimately became part of the ethos of the sector: belief in the importance of providing access to diverse populations traditionally underserved by higher education, and belief that one of the core purposes of a college was to uphold and promote democratic ideals. These ideas had gained so much traction by the end of the 19th century that the president of the University of Chicago, William Rainey Harper, declared in an 1899 address that the university was the "Messiah" of democracy and that "education is the basis of all democratic progress" (Harper, 1905, pp. 12, 32).

One early example of a higher education sector created to educate a diverse population was the establishment of faith-based colleges to help meet the educational needs for the increasing number of children of immigrants to the United States, many of whom settled in urban areas across the country. Rudolph (1962) observed that the "Catholic Church needed no prodding to follow the counsel of Saint Ignatius to place colleges in cities" (p. 94). The mission of the early Roman Catholic institutions was clear: to educate the next generation of Catholics to assume their roles as productive members of American society. Originally, these institutions focused on educating a specific demographic. For example, Boston College's original charter, established in 1863, was to serve Boston's predominantly poor, Irish Catholic population. Boston College's focus on educating first-generation, poor immigrants provided one of the first examples of expanding the reach and scope of higher education beyond the realm of the wealthy in the United States.

Prior to the American Civil War access to higher education for people of color was practically nonexistent. While a few Black colleges were established in the first half of the 19th century, it was not until the second Morrill Act of 1890 when states, who wished to use federal funds to establish segregated schools for Blacks, were provided funding and support to establish what later became known as historically Black colleges and universities (HBCUs). Many of these institutions still exist today and continue to offer equal access and opportunity to education for all students.

The inclusion of women in U.S. higher education also took many generations to develop. In the 18th century a few institutions were dedicated to training women for "domestic" life, but it was not until 1837 that Oberlin College in Ohio became the first "coed" institution when four women were admitted (Rudolph, 1962). That same year a teaching seminary for women, now Mount Holyoke College, was established specifically for the education of women, and throughout the 19th century dozens of colleges were chartered for the education of women. In addition, during the 19th and early 20th centuries numerous colleges, both public and denominational, were established to serve coed student populations. However, during this period women's access to higher education was generally limited to schools designated specifically for women and to professions traditionally occupied by women. It was not until the middle of the 20th century, as many larger public institutions across the nation opened their doors to women, that women secured true access to higher education. Today, women make up the majority of students enrolled in institutions of higher learning.

The creation of new higher education institutions at other points in U.S. history provided greater access for students traditionally underserved in society as well. It can be argued, for example, that no movement in history has had a greater impact on providing access to higher education than the creation of community college systems across the nation during the 20th century. When we consider other higher education developments of the past century, such as the passage of the Servicemen's Readjustment Act of 1944 (commonly known as the GI Bill), which provided access to higher education for millions of veterans returning from World War II; the emergence of tribal colleges and universities (TCUs) in the 1960s; and the introduction of the Hispanic-serving institution (HSI) designation in the 1990s, it is clear that throughout American history the arch of higher education has been for greater access, inclusion, and a drive toward social justice.

In this book we do not assert that the U.S. higher education sector sought to become more diverse and inclusive entirely on its own. We fully acknowledge that for most of American history the journey toward greater access and inclusion has been difficult. Over time, external factors, including state and federal governments, faith-based organizations, and philanthropic supporters, have influenced the direction that colleges and universities have taken, and those paths have not always led toward justice. Indeed, a good part of this journey has come at a significant cost to those advocates who have demanded greater inclusion.

Clearly there is much work to be done before fully realizing our potential and agency as institutions for positive social change. What we do propose is that inclusion, equity, and social justice have become the sine qua non of the U.S. higher education sector in the 21st century, and institutions that fail to adapt to changing norms, refuse to embrace the national movement for greater access, and do not believe inclusion and belongingness are key to their identity will struggle and likely not survive.

Application of the Four Principles Throughout This Book

In this book, we assert that higher education institutions that have committed to four essential principles—being mission centric; being adaptable to environmental changes; perpetuating democratic principles; and serving as models for inclusion, equity, and positive social change—have consistently fared better than those institutions that have not adhered to these ideas and are better positioned for the future. Therefore, administrators should consider them as key building blocks for success in the 21st century. In the chapters that follow, these four principles are applied to the study and practice of effective academic administration and provide a framework for the reader to comprehend the nuances of the complex organizations that are colleges and universities.

References

American Association of University Professors. (n.d.). *1940 statement on principles of academic freedom and tenure with 1970 interpretive comments.* http://www.aaup .org/AAUP/pubsres/policydocs/contents/1940statement.htm

Association of Governing Boards of Universities and Colleges. (1996). *Renewing the academic presidency: Stronger leadership for tougher times.* Author.

Birnbaum, R. (1988). *How colleges work: The cybernetics of academic organization and leadership.* Jossey-Bass.

BoardSource. (2010). *The handbook of nonprofit governance.* Jossey-Bass.

Boyer, E. L. (1987). *College: The undergraduate experience in America.* HarperCollins.

Carnegie Foundation for the Advancement of Teaching. (1977). *Missions of the college curriculum: A contemporary review with suggestions.* Jossey-Bass.

Chait, R., Ryan, W. P., & Taylor, B. E. (2005). *Governance as leadership: Reframing the work of nonprofit boards.* Wiley.

Christensen, C. M., & Eyring, H. J. (2011). *The innovative university: Changing the DNA of higher education from the inside out.* Jossey-Bass.

Clift, V. A. (1948). The role of higher education in transmitting democratic ideals into behavior patterns. *Journal of Negro Education, 17*(2), 134–140. https://doi .org/10.2307/2966054

Cohen, M. D., & March, J. G. (1974). *Leadership and ambiguity: The American college president.* McGraw-Hill.

Colby, A., Ehrlich, T., Beaumont, E., & Stephens, J. (2003). *Educating citizens: Preparing America's undergraduates for lives of moral and civic responsibility.* Jossey-Bass.

Colgan, C., & deRussy, C. (2006). *Essays in perspective: Assessing the university president.* Institute for Effective Governance in Higher Education.

Davies, G. K. (1986). The importance of being general: Philosophy, politics, and institutional mission statements. In J. C. Smart (Ed.), *Higher education: Handbook of theory and research* (Vol. 2, pp. 85–102). Agathon.

Dewey, J. (1916). *Democracy and education: An introduction to the philosophy of education.* The Free Press.

DiMaggio, P. J., & Powell, W. W. (1983). The iron cage revisited: Institutional isomorphism and collective rationality in organizational fields. *American Sociological Review, 48*(2), 147–160. https://doi.org/10.2307/2095101

Flexner, A. (1930). *Universities: American, English, German.* Oxford University Press.

Geiger, R. L. (2011). The ten generations of American higher education. In R. O. Berdahl, P. G. Altbach, & P. J. Gumport (Eds.), *Higher education in the twenty-first century* (3rd ed., pp. 37–68). Johns Hopkins University Press.

Gross, E., & Grambsch, P. V. (1974). *Changes in university organization, 1964–1971.* McGraw-Hill.

Handy, C. (1997). Unimagined futures. In F. Hesselbein, M. Goldsmith, & R. Beckhard (Eds.), *The organization of the future* (pp. 377–383). Jossey-Bass.

Harper, W. R. (1905). The university and democracy. *The trend in higher education* (pp. 1–34). The University of Chicago Press.

Josephson, J. J. (2020). Higher education and democratic public life. *New Political Science, 42*(2), 155–170. https://doi.org/10.1080/07393148.2020.1773726

Keller, G. (1983). *Academic strategy: The management revolution in American higher education.* Johns Hopkins University Press.

Kerr, C. (1964). *The uses of the university.* Harvard University Press.

King. M. L., Jr. (1968, March 31). *Remaining awake through a great revolution* [Speech]. The National Cathedral, Washington, DC. https://seemeonline.com/history/mlk-jr-awake.htm

Lane, J. E. (2005, November 17–19). *Politics of mission creep: A framework for understanding the phenomena* [Paper presentation]. Association for the Study of Higher Education 30th Annual Conference, Philadelphia, PA, United States.

Maurrasse, D. J. (2001). *Beyond the campus: How colleges and universities form partnerships with their communities.* Routledge.

Morrill Act of 1862, 7 U.S.C. 301 et seq. (1862)

Morrill Act of 1890, 26 Stat. 417, 7 U.S.C. § 321 et seq. (1890)

Rudolph, F. (1962). *The American college and university: A history.* Random House.

WASC Senior College and University Commission. (2018). *2013 handbook of accreditation* (revised November 2021). https://www.wscuc.org/resources/handbook-accreditation-2013

Welzenbach, L. F. (Ed.). (1982). *College and university business administration.* National Association for College and University Business Officers.

PART ONE

HISTORICAL, CONTEXTUAL, AND THEORETICAL UNDERPINNINGS

2

THE CHANGING CONTEXTS
FOR HIGHER EDUCATION

Higher education is an integral part of society, both influencing and being influenced by what happens around it. In fact, no academic leader can be effective in their role without at least some understanding of the dynamics of the contexts beyond the fuzzy boundaries of the institution they lead. Even the curriculum, which is at the heart of the academic enterprise, is tied to the context in which it exists. In his history of the college curriculum, Rudolph (1977) noted:

> [T]he curriculum has been an arena in which the dimensions of American culture have been measured, an environment for certifying an elite at one time and facilitating the mobility of an emerging middle class at another. It has been one of those places where we have told ourselves who we are. (p. 1)

Of course, the college curriculum is embedded in the institution that offers it. It lives and evolves within the college environment, controlled by the college faculty, challenged by the students, and protected by the administrative structure that surrounds it.

The context of higher education is always in flux, which is why the curriculum has continued to evolve over the centuries. That which is offered within the curriculum at Harvard today is very different than what was first offered at its founding in 1636. What has also changed, however, are the administrative structures of our colleges and universities and higher education systems. These changes in administrative structures mean that the expectations of the leaders within those structures have evolved as well. Throughout this volume, we provide readers with insights into the operations, the opportunities, and the challenges within these structures.

In this chapter we attempt to look into the proverbial crystal ball to see what challenges might lie ahead for academic leaders. We approach this activity with a note of caution, as there is no way for us to fully know what will happen in the future. Had this edition come out in 2019, we would have entirely missed the impact of the pandemic, which transformed higher education. Seemingly overnight, nearly all curricular delivery was shifted to remote instruction, students were sent home from residence halls, financial models crumbled, and enrollment planning became unworkable. Even now, it is impossible to know the long-term effects of the pandemic, which exacerbated existing challenges and created new opportunities.

The Greek philosopher Heraclitus said, "Change is the only constant in life." If academic leaders take away nothing else from this chapter, it should be that our contexts will continue to evolve, and we have a responsibility to lead our institutions through those changes. The rapidity of change has also caused a major shift in how higher education organizations are structured. In fact, many current senior higher education leaders developed their skill sets when domestic and international demand for higher education was strong, public funding more stable, and tuition increases more palatable. If public funding declined, tuition could be increased. If domestic student enrollment fell, an institution would recruit more international students.

For many institutions, those simple tradeoffs are no longer options. A declining U.S. birth rate will lead to fewer high school graduates. Concerns about student debt make tuition increases more difficult to implement and have led to an increase in tuition discount rates. State funding continues to ebb and flow, and public scrutiny of the academy may be at an all-time high. International student enrollment plummeted during the pandemic, and growing international competition and nationalistic rhetoric may discourage international students from returning.

The purpose of this chapter is to provide the reader with insights into key trends that are affecting and may continue to affect higher education. We do not have space to explore each topic in depth—even if we did, it is not clear what information might be the most relevant in the long term. We are also not able to cover all the most pressing issues facing higher education in this volume, but we have dedicated entire chapters to some. For example, in chapter 3 we discuss the changing context of social justice, the disparate treatment of certain communities, and the need for higher education to advance its excellence through boarder inclusiveness. Chapter 5 provides insights into changing global dynamics such as increased competition for international students and the impact of heightened Chinese–U.S. tensions. We have structured this chapter to first provide a very brief historical overview and then summarize current issues. Many of these topics are discussed (or at least referenced) throughout this edition. We encourage readers to seek out additional information, both scholarly and in the media, to learn more.

Historical Development of the Academic Institution in the United States

The emergence and evolution of colleges and universities in America since the early 17th century is largely a study of the American spirit itself, for few social institutions so harmoniously reflect the ideals, aspirations, beliefs, and competitive spirit of the United States and its people as the growth and development of its higher education organizations. Today's panoply of over 4,400 institutions includes, but is not limited to, two-year community colleges, traditional four-year liberal arts colleges, regional and state universities, large research universities, universities devoted only to professional preparation (such as medical, maritime, or engineering schools), proprietary institutions, seminaries and rabbinical colleges, and a host of universities that exclusively provide online education.

Modern colleges and universities were born from an organizational and evolutionary lineage that ranks among the most enduring of humanity's intellectual and social creations. In addition to its longevity, when compared with corporate organizations, as mentioned in chapter 1, the modern academy continues to enjoy high regard by the public at large and is viewed as one of the United States' most important social institutions, although some of that esteem has waned in recent years, particularly along political party lines. These institutions' status and longevity are all the more noteworthy since, over the centuries, colleges and universities have taken a plethora of forms, and complex decision-making structures have emerged within them to accommodate the various internal and external constituencies that compete for authority and legitimacy. Three main factors have contributed to this current condition: (a) historical antecedents that established strong intellectual traditions, (b) the application of democratic principles that has encouraged individualism in the expression of educational ideals, and (c) the richness of diversity among those who claim legitimacy in the execution of the organizations' missions. An appreciation of these three factors is important to render more informed management and administration of higher education organizations, which is why they deserve mention here.

The endurance of the nation's colleges and universities rests in part on the many historical traditions that have followed their development. In his narrative on the history of U.S. higher education, Lucas (2006) noted that the precursors of the modern college and university essentially began in the medieval period, between the 11th and 15th centuries. Individuals with shared common interests in learning about specific disciplines collectivized into guilds governed by representatives elected from within the organizations. Often, those elected to oversight responsibilities were reluctant to assume such managerial duties because of the tension it caused among and between them and their peers. Vestiges of those early tensions continue to exist today among contemporary faculties and administrations. As organized entities, these shared social relationships developed into intellectual collectives exhibiting an organizational autonomy legitimized through the unique knowledge possessed by the organizations' members. Lucas (2006) suggested that the strongest resemblance between medieval universities and academic institutions of today rests "in the sense of corporate, institutional identity, together with an elaborate system of rights, privileges, prerogatives, and special forms of academic authority" (p. 68). This authority was exercised even in the earliest centuries of higher education, when "once securely established, universities did not hesitate to intervene in public affairs, to air grievances before kings and popes alike, to offer advice, and to pass upon a variety of important legal and religious questions" (p. 69).

The relative autonomy enjoyed by the medieval guilds provided a historical foundation for new forms of higher education to emerge in the earliest years of the United States. Although the earliest American colleges barely resemble any of the higher education organizations of today, the European model of individualism and independent guilds provided a historical template for creativity and individuality that permitted highly varied organizational interpretations of what higher education should look like in the development of a learned society.

As a new U.S. society itself was emerging, these fledgling institutions responded to a variety of environmental influences to help shape and sustain them. They were able to do so in part because of their independence and their ability to adapt through that independence. In his history of U.S. higher education, Thelin (2004) noted that the richness of diversity in U.S. higher education emerged as much from influences of local, state, and regional factors as from any national trends that mirrored the development of America from the time of the founding of Harvard College in 1636. Much like the rise of entrepreneurism that characterized the new American spirit, higher education became America's "cottage industry" (p. 41). Especially during 1785–1860, Thelin (2004) argued, higher education witnessed

> a period of extreme innovation and consumerism, with virtually no government accountability or regulation. Yet, it was not a period of chaos for higher education, because the college displayed a pattern of both initiation and response that was very much in tune with the nation's changing geographic, demographic, and economic character. (p. 41)

The factors of historical and intellectual autonomy born of a rich and embedded European medieval tradition, coupled with creative adaptation demanded by the necessities of adjusting to the societal needs of an emergent nation, produced a level of higher education organizational diversity that would later become the hallmark of U.S. higher education.

Geiger (2005) chronicled 10 generations of development in the historical evolution of the U.S.'s colleges and universities, each lasting about 30 years from the founding of Harvard College in 1636 to the beginning of the 21st century. He charted these generations from two perspectives: (a) student origins that traced the diversity of students, and (b) destinations that defined the outcomes sought for those students as a result of their education. This origins and destinations perspective is particularly useful when examining the diversity and uniqueness of academic organizations because it speaks to the multiple forces of individuals, religious bodies, governments, and foundations, among others, that exercised significant influence in the formation of today's wide array of institution types as well as illustrates how higher education has continued to become more accessible and diverse. Speaking to the democratic principles that guided this evolutionary process, Geiger (2005) stated, "Underlying the fortunes of individual institutions . . . lay fundamental questions stemming in large measure from the . . . putative republican model: Who owned the colleges? What was their mission? What should students be taught? And how could they be controlled?" (p. 45). As the societal needs of a growing United States expanded and matured, new institutions of higher education emerged throughout this generational progression, but, just as important, existing institutions adapted to a changing environment in a fashion typical of the entrepreneurial spirit of the nation. A noteworthy irony about U.S. higher education has been its ability to adapt and conform to the external influences that created and shaped it over the centuries while possessing an organizational essence often steeped in inflexible tradition and a codified set of fixed rights and organizational privileges that hearken to its earliest European roots.

The implications of these historical and developmental factors for the manner in which colleges and universities should ultimately be managed and administered are significant. Basic to any managerial function within the academy is a firm understanding of the particular mission of one's institution, which often emanates from the societal and historical traditions on which it was founded. "The key to being effective and the ability to make change begins first with an accurate assessment of the type of organization in which you work" (Julius et al., 1999, p. 114).

The Pandemic

The pandemic illustrated both how quickly our context can change and just how nimble higher education leaders, faculty, staff, and students can be. In spring 2020, the coronavirus spread quickly across the world. As of this writing, no one fully understands the long-term implications of the virus on education, or on the world at large. Right around the time of most U.S. higher education institutions' spring break, public health officials began issuing stay-at-home orders. The result was that when students left campus for spring break, they would not physically return for the rest of the semester (although in the beginning of the crisis most academic leaders operated under the assumption that students would be back before the semester ended). The result was that nearly all college classes had to shift to remote delivery in a matter of a few days. For some, this switch was fairly easy. At the time, however, most U.S. college faculty had little to no experience teaching online.

But they did it. The members of the faculty, Luddites and all, shifted quickly to delivering their courses online. It is important to note that this transition was no easy shift. Colleges and universities made quick, significant, and expensive investments in technology and training. Accreditors and government officials waived policies that regulate the delivery of online courses and programs. Substitute experiences were developed for clinical requirements such as student teaching and counseling services, which could no longer happen in person. All these changes happened within a matter of a few short weeks.

For at least the next 2 years, academic leaders managed an ever shifting (and sometime frightening) reality as they sought to continue learning, keep employees healthy, and preserve the financial stability of their institutions. Throughout this time, the most successful academic leaders had to be nimble, insightful, and comforting. Terms such as *flexibility* and *empathy* led the way as everyone encountered new challenges. The pandemic led to the closure of a few institutions, although the crisis likely accelerated what was already inevitable. Many institutions had to lay off or furlough faculty and staff and/or go through academic reorganization. Others tightened their belts, but significant changes were forestalled due to federal pandemic recovery funds. At this time of this writing, the early 2022 COVID surge was receding, campuses were beginning to lift mask mandates, countries were reopening borders to international students, and society was beginning to explore the switch from pandemic to endemic.

This discussion is not intended as a sort of assessment of the pandemic. Rather, it illustrates both how quickly the environment can change and how academic leaders need to be prepared help their institution navigate what may have once been the unthinkable.

Changing Demographics

The demographics of higher education have always been in transition, often influenced by expanding access to new students who have not previously had the opportunity to attend college. Sometimes these shifts happen quickly, such as the jump in the percentage of female college students from 42% in 1970 to 50% in 1980 (it now stands at around 57%) (de Brey et al., 2021). However, some demographic changes are more predictable. In 2018, Grawe predicted that higher education was facing a demographic storm that would result in decreasing college enrollments across the United States. The Northeast and Midwest were already in decline due to outmigration, but Grawe warned that the entire nation should be bracing for what he called the "birth dearth." Essentially, the birth rate dropped after the Great Recession, and that trend would start to be seen 18 years later, in the number of high school graduates in 2026. Specifically, there were approximately 400,000 fewer births in 2012 than in 2007 (Kearney & Levine, 2021), meaning approximately 400,000 fewer students graduating high school and potentially looking at college.

Grawe (2018) was not the first to see the looming drop in high school graduates, but his book was what finally caught the attention of senior academic decision makers. Of course, as with all predictions, nothing is certain. More recent data from the Western Interstate Commission for Higher Education (WICHE), which has predicted high school graduation rates for more than 20 years in their regular report "Knocking at the College Door," found that more students of color graduated high school than projected (Bransberger et al., 2020). WICHE has asserted that this trend will lead to a 10% higher graduation rate in 2025 than originally predicted, which means that the number of high school graduates in 2026 will also be higher than originally predicted. Even with increases in graduation rates among certain groups, however, the overall decline in births is still expected to lead to annual declines in the total number high school students starting in 2026—a caveat being that these trends will vary by state and region. And, a similar drop in the birthrate has occurred during the pandemic, portending another significant decline in a generation from now.

While the overall number of high school students declines, the cohort itself is becoming more diverse. WICHE predicts that by 2036, White students will be 43% percent of high school graduates, with students of color comprising the majority of graduates in 24 states (Bransberger et al., 2020). The birth dearth will bring uncertain changes to higher education, as the sector has been used to expanding high school enrollments, and institutions will need to be responsive to the market to continue to attract students. At the same time, forward-looking academic leaders are positioning their institutions to serve more diverse, first-generation, low-income, and adult students.

In addition, the overall U.S. population is aging. The total number of adults over the age of 65 is predicted to double to 80 million between 2020 and 2040. At that time, roughly one in five Americans will be over the age of 65 compared to one in eight in 2000. The full effect of this shift on higher education is not clear. It will certainly present funding challenges as governments have to divert additional resources to support programs for senior citizens such as Social Security and Medicare. It could also present opportunities should colleges and universities develop more programs aimed at lifelong learners. Some institutions have even created senior living communities on or near campus in response to this trend.

Demographics have and will continue to have a major effect on higher education.

Shifting Enrollment Patterns

In fall 2019, approximately 19.6 million students enrolled in some form of postsecondary education (de Brey et al., 2021). This figure was part of a 10-year slide in overall enrollments, having peaked at 21 million in academic year (AY) 2010–2011 (see Figure 2.1). The decline was due in part to a strong economy, as education has been considered a countercyclical industry in which enrollments tend to increase when the economy weakens and vice versa (Pissarides, 2011; Stewart, 1978).

By the end of AY 2020–2021 (the 1st full academic year after the pandemic started), however, overall postsecondary enrollments were down 4.2% from a year prior, with declines occurring across all racial/ethnic groups. This decrease masked sublevel trends at degree level, such as a 4.4% increase in graduate education and a nearly 11% drop in associate degree enrollments (National Student Clearinghouse, 2021). Unlike in previous economic downturns, during the pandemic higher education did not come to the fore as a countercyclical industry, despite the efforts of faculty members and enrollment management professionals' efforts to leverage online learning environments to recruit and retain students. How enrollments will fare in the future remains to be seen; this decline may continue given the falling birth rate discussed previously.

About 16.5 million undergraduate students were enrolled in 2019, down significantly from a high of 18 million in 2010 (de Brey et al., 2021). Around 60% of these students were enrolled full-time, 57% were female, and nearly 80% were matriculated in public colleges and universities. Forty-three

Figure 2.1. U.S. higher education enrollment trends.

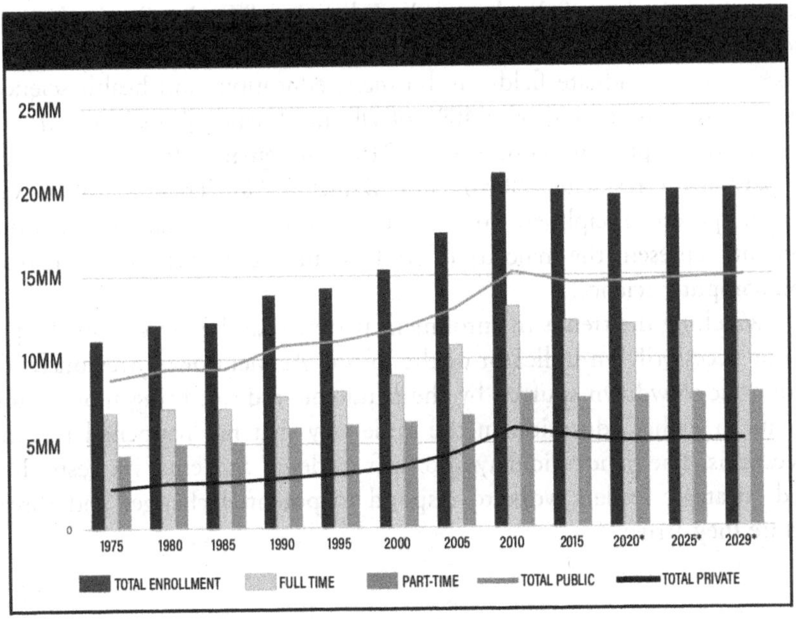

* Projected.

percent of undergraduate students in 2019 were non-White, with the largest numbers of those students coming from Latinx, Black, and Asian/Pacific Islander backgrounds (in that order). In 2010, more than 3 million Black students were enrolled in college, making them the largest minority group in higher education; but their numbers have declined since that time, while Latinx enrollments have increased.

For many years, higher education has experienced an increasing (though slow) push toward online and hybrid instructional modalities. The pandemic accelerated this change, as stay-at-home orders necessitated the shift of nearly all educational delivery to remote formats for anywhere from a few weeks to a full academic year. Prior to the start of the pandemic toward the end of AY 2019–2020, around 15% of undergraduate students took courses exclusively at a distance, and 36% took at least one course at a distance (de Brey et al., 2021). That said, within the private, for-profit sector a majority of students were already exclusively enrolled in distance education, and some public and not-for-profit universities, such as Arizona State, Liberty, Southern New Hampshire, and Purdue, had also begun to significantly expand their online enrollments.

At the graduate level, more than 3 million students were enrolled in certificate, master's, doctoral, and other postgraduate professional degree programs in 2019 (de Brey et al., 2021). A yearly survey sponsored by the Council of Graduate Schools and the Educational Testing Service has provided some insights into these enrollments (Okahana et al., 2020). The three most popular graduate fields are business, education, and health sciences, collectively representing over 40% of all enrollments. A majority of first-time graduate program enrollees in 2019 were female (59%), U.S. citizens or permanent residents (80%), and White (75%). These numbers vary within specific disciplines, however. For example, men and international students represent the majority of students in engineering as well as math and computer science.

Watching the trends in enrollment patterns can be useful, but the past is not necessarily an indicator of the future. As mentioned previously, the economic slowdown spurred by the pandemic did not bring more enrollments to higher education in the same way that has happened in other recessions. The pandemic may also shift students' academic interests. That said, strategic leaders work to respond to potential changes and threats before they arrive.

Funding and Financial Models

The finances of higher education are complicated and vary by institution type. For the vast majority of colleges and universities, the primary source of revenue tends to be tuition and fees paid by the student (or family) or via financial aid from the state or federal government. Public institutions tend to receive some not insignificant portion of their budget from state appropriations, separate from the aid allocated to students directly. Both public and not-for-profit institutions have come to rely increasingly on private gifts, grants, and contracts to offset the cost of tuition and to fund special initiatives. In the 2017 American College President Study, 85% of respondents believed that private fundraising would comprise a larger share of their budget in the next 5 years, while 41% believed state funding would decrease (American Council on Education [ACE], 2017). These findings suggest that presidents may have more confidence in the financial levers on which they have more direct influence (e.g., fundraising).

The two primary sources of funding for public higher education are state appropriations and tuition revenue. Over the last 40 years, there has been a major shift in the financing of public higher education from state appropriation to tuition revenue (State Higher Education Executive Officers Association [SHEEO], 2021). In 1980, net tuition revenue accounted for almost 21% of funding for public higher education; in 2020 that number had risen to 44%. In fact, in half of all states in 2020, net tuition revenue account for at least 50% of the share of an institution's budget. Overall, net tuition revenue per full-time equivalent (FTE) has increased 61.7% between 2000 and 2020; at the same time state student financial aid per FTE has increased as well.

In terms of direct state support for higher education, prior to the pandemic the sector was still seeking to recover from the cuts taken during the Great Recession. Nationally, education appropriations in FY 2020 remained 6% below prerecession levels in 2008 (SHEEO, 2021). State-by-state recovery varied widely, however. As of 2020, 18 states had recovered to at least prerecession levels, while 12 states remained at least 20% below those levels. Amid the pandemic, higher education finances were significantly disrupted as many institutions refunded millions of dollars in room and board after students were sent home at the end of AY 2019–2020, uncertainty about enrollments in AY 2020–2021 raised questions about tuition revenue, and a sudden decrease in tax funding cut state support for higher education (Yuen, 2020).

In terms of private institutions, their revenue typically comes primarily from net tuition revenue. In that space, there has been a significant rise in what is called tuition discounting, which is the amount of money institutional financial aid a student receives—effectively discounting the total cost below the published tuition rate. For example, if the tuition sticker price were $40,000 and a student received $20,000 in institutional aid, the discount rate would be 50%. According to a study by the National Association of College and University Business Officers (NACUBO, 2021), the discount rate for all undergraduates at private institutions increased from 38.6% in FY 2012 to 48.1% in FY 2021. For first-time undergraduates the discount rate first surpassed the 50% mark in FY 2018, and it was 54% in FY 2021. As a group, incoming students are paying less than half the published tuition rate, which can significantly affect the revenue available to the institution.

At the time of this writing, higher education funding remains in flux. However, as of the spring 2021, Moody's, the bond rater, raised the outlook on higher education from negative to stable because institutions were committing to having students back on campus in fall 2021, federal relief included additional help for higher education, state funding appeared to have stabilized, and investment returns were quite strong (Seltzer, 2021). The report did note, however, that some institutions will continue to struggle financially because of long-term demographic changes and shifts in student preferences. This experience illustrates why academic leaders need to continue to monitor what is happening in the external environment and position their campuses to be able to manage these changes.

The Rise of Data-Informed Decision-Making for Student Success

An analytics revolution is overtaking many colleges and universities and is transforming institutional efforts to improve efficiency of operations, enhance assessment, and increase student success in college (Gagliardi et al., 2018). This revolution is not focused on finding new ways to measure learning outcomes. Instead, the effort concerns drawing from the increasing digital cloud that each person generates every day to better understand the individualized experiences of each learner. Lane (2014) has come to refer to this practice as "building a smarter university."

Beyond basic descriptive data that institutional research offices have historically captured and reported to the federal government, these new data are being drawn from a variety of places, such as learning management systems, student ID card usage, and student financial accounts (Parnell, 2018). Taken together, these data can help us better understand each student through their own experience as well as by digitally comparing them to students with similar data profiles.

What can be fully realized from this new era of data is yet to be known. The use of such data is still fairly nascent, but colleges and universities across the United States are investing in new technologies to capture, transform, and analyze these data. The intention is to identify students who may be at risk of dropping out before they do so, as well as to understand what structural barriers in the design and delivery of the curriculum may detract from a student's ability to complete a degree (Denley, 2022).

The result of much of this work has been to develop guided pathways (Jenkins et al., 2018), real-time interventions to support students to complete courses (Essa & Ayad, 2012), and digital nudges that use learning from the data to help students to stay on track (Wildavsky, 2013). For example, text messages with reminders about registering for classes or filling out key forms can reduce the likelihood that students from "at-risk" backgrounds fail to matriculate in the fall. Austin Peay State University developed an analytics system, Degree Compass, to predict which courses a student may want to take based on the course selections of previous students (similar to "you may also like this" recommendations on Amazon or Netflix) (Denley, 2022).

Such knowledge, though, remains relatively useless unless our faculty and staff—the individuals who work with students and the curriculum on a regular basis—understand how these strategies work; what they mean for their practice as advisors, teachers, and curriculum designers; and how they can be used to positively impact students' academic pursuits.

Public Perceptions of Higher Education

Americans' views of higher education have historically been quite positive, with colleges and universities among the most trusted social institutions in the country. Kerr (1994), however, identified the 1990s as the beginning of "times of trouble" for higher education (p. 11). In preceding decades, higher education was viewed as an important part of the changing social fabric of the country—from educating veterans after the World War II to inspiring a national cultural awakening and revolution in the 1960s, to contributing to the United States' success in the Cold War. The 1990s, Kerr argued, witnessed a shifting relationship between higher education and society, one that moved from collaborative to transactional. The reasons for this shift were threefold: Few resources were available from the government, more individuals and organizations were fighting for those resources, and society presented unprecedented expectations that higher education support the economy.

Americans' view of higher education would become increasingly mixed in subsequent decades. In 2003, reporting on public opinion of higher education, Selingo wrote that while there was wide "mistrust [in] corporations and Congress and . . . little confidence in their public schools, . . . faith in American higher education remains at extraordinary levels" (p. A10). This belief may have been tied to the importance Americans placed on the college degree for an individual's professional success. A regular survey by Public Agenda found that from 2000 to 2009, the percentage of Americans who believed a college degree was necessary to compete in the working world grew from 31% in 2000 to 55% in 2009, which would be the peak (Schleifer & Silliman, 2016).

Menand (2011) explored the different purposes of higher education, including the various personal and social benefits associated with a college degree. He noted that in popular culture there are generally three theories of why people go to college. Theory 1 states that education is meritocratic, a social stratifier that effectively sorts individuals based on their willingness and ability to demonstrate a range of competencies: "Society needs a mechanism for sorting out its more intelligent members from its less intelligent ones" (para. 6). Theory 2, the democratic approach, holds that education provides an enlightened citizenry reflective of the skills, attributes, and characteristics that distinguish humankind at its best: "College exposes future citizens to material that enlightens and empowers them, whatever careers they end up choosing" (para. 8). Theory 3 asserts that higher education should be vocationally oriented, specifically designed to train and equip the student with skills relevant to a job: Since "advanced economies demand specialized knowledge and skills, and since high school is aimed at the general learner, college is where people can be taught what they need in order to enter a vocation" (para. 3). Behind these three distinct theories rest fundamental questions about what constitutes higher education and what students should learn from it. Additional questions exist regarding the cognitive and affective outcomes shown to result from acquiring higher education and whether those outcomes have proven beneficial and worthy of the time and expense of obtaining them.

Public confidence in higher education has declined significantly in the years between the first and second editions of this book. By 2016, the belief that college is necessary dropped to 42% of Public Agenda survey respondents (Schleifer & Silliman, 2016). A 2019 poll by the Pew Research Center found that only about half of respondents believed colleges and universities were having a positive effect on the way things were going in the United States (Doherty & Kiley, 2019). In a 2018 Gallup poll, 48% of U.S. adults expressed "a great deal" or "quite a lot" of confidence in higher education—a decrease from 57% in 2015 (Jaschik, 2018). A drop in confidence was seen across Democrats, Republicans, and Independents, although confidence in higher education dropped far more among Republicans (17 points) than other groups, illustrating an overall trend in alignment of political affiliation with views on higher education.

One of the long-standing differences in poll results has been how individuals of different races view the value of higher education. A 2000 survey by the National Center for Public Policy and Higher Education revealed that while two thirds of White high school parents believed there were ways to succeed in the world without higher education, one third of Latinx high school parents and less than half of African American high school parents thought so (Immerwahr, 2000). Fast forward to 2017, when more than half of White working-class citizens who responded to a New America survey believed higher education was a "risky gamble," while a majority of Black (56%) and Latinx (68%) respondents saw college as a "smart investment" (Fishman et al., 2017).

It is important for those who read any survey or poll data to be careful in how they interpret the results. That said, there does appear to be an overall trend toward greater skepticism of the value of higher education, which is coinciding with a greater overall skepticism of societal institutions from the church to the state. The data show noteworthy and long-standing differences based on political affiliation and race, which may provide insights into the need to tailor messages to the needs of different groups. And it is not yet clear how the pandemic will further shape public opinion of higher education.

Murray (2008) highlighted this rising debate over the value of higher education in a controversial essay that reflected our society's growing disenchantment with the benefits of a college education. He argued that with the exception of engineering and some of the sciences, a "bachelor's degree tells an employer nothing except that the applicant has a certain amount of intellectual ability and perseverance" (para. 5). He proposed that the traditional bachelor's degree be replaced with a certification process in which students complete a rigorous course of study in a specific discipline. Murray's opinion centered on the belief that the primary role of higher education should be preparation for a specific job or career. As utilitarian as this perspective may be, one should also ask whether preparation for employment is the *only* reason one should seek learning beyond high school. It is this vocational education view that prompted Presidents George W. Bush and Barack Obama to propose federal programs to enhance associate degree programs at community colleges (NBC News, 2005; Smith, 2012). What other purposes exist for higher education, and what outcomes can and should be expected from the experience of attending college?

An early indication may come from a national survey of college students that was administered three times during AY 2020–2021 (Klebs et al., 2021). It revealed that two thirds of respondents did not believe higher education was worth the cost. This number increased across the three administrations of the survey. The immediate effects of the pandemic and looming concerns about the pace of economic recovery may have influenced their responses, but it likely would not be wise for institutional leaders to ignore students' growing concern about college debt and the overall return on investment of a college education.

The Future of Work and the Credential

While the purposes of higher education are many, one cannot ignore the connection between higher education and employment, and the world of work continues to change. The tension between providing students with a broad-based liberal education and preparing them for specific vocational pursuits dates back more than 200 years (and is explored in more depth in chapter 15). Automation, artificial intelligence, machine learning, and remote work are trends that are causing disruption in work, from displacing workers from traditional jobs to transforming how we educate students. For some institutions, this situation may present an opportunity to upskill and reskill adult learners; for others, the curriculum will need to be revised to meet the shifting landscape (Wingard & Farrugia, 2021).

A study by McKinsey and Company identified 56 foundational skills most workers will need in the future (Dondi et al., 2021). These skills fell into four broad areas: cognitive (e.g., critical thinking, planning, communication, and mental flexibility), interpersonal (e.g., mobilizing systems, developing relationships, and teamwork), self-leadership (e.g., self-awareness, entrepreneurship, and goals achievement), and digital (e.g., digital fluency, software use and development, and understanding digital systems). These areas all cut across fields of work, and many of the skills, such as critical thinking and communication, are long-standing components of most college curricula, although areas such as entrepreneurship and digital fluency are more nascent in their integration into the learning experience.

Developing skills is just one aspect of a degree program, but with questions about the basic return on investment of a college education being at the forefront of the public's mind, higher education leaders must address how their institutions prepare their graduates for the workforce—no matter their major. At the time of this writing, media headlines were proclaiming, "The future of work won't be about college degrees" (Kasriel, 2018), and asking, "Is this the end of college as we know it?" (Belkin, 2020). However, a 2018 national survey of employers revealed that the value of the college degree remains quite strong in the hiring ecosystem, with more than three quarters of respondents indicating that the value of the degree had increased or remained the same over the last 5 years (Gallagher, 2019). Moreover, over half of all job openings have consistently preferred at least a bachelor's degree, and the average college graduate with just a bachelor's degree earns $78,000 annually compared to $45,000 for workers with only a high school diploma (Abel & Deitz, 2019). Assuming that the $30,000 college wage premium holds fairly consistently over the 30 to 40 working years of the average adult, this difference would translate into around a $1 million premium.

An increased focus on skill development has spurred growth in micro-credentials, which seek to document the specific skills or knowledge someone gains through workshops or a handful of courses. Entities like EdX and Coursera were among the first to develop these initiatives, providing a range of short-term learning opportunities and providing a digital credential (e.g., badge) to evidence the learning that occurred. Increasingly, colleges and universities have begun to develop such credentials, either as part of continuing education offerings or as part of a degree. Similar trends have spurred development of stackable credentials, meaning that components of a larger degree (e.g., associate, bachelor, or master) could be truncated into smaller blocks of learning and credentials, such as certificates, that are awarded along the way (Marcus, 2020). The idea is that such offerings allow students to advance their learning without having to commit to an entire degree program, and the learning will "stack" into a larger degree (Bailey & Belfield, 2017).

This section provided a high-level overview of some of the major themes regarding work and the credential, and readers are encouraged to explore these issues in more depth. How work changes will continue to affect the college degree, from curricular design to the structure of credentials. If colleges and universities do not adjust appropriately, they risk being viewed as less relevant in the long term.

Social Media

Over the past decade, social media has emerged as a major component of the higher education ecosystem. From Facebook to Twitter to LinkedIn, students, faculty, campus leaders, and their institutions have come to both use and be influenced by social media. But what is social media? Many definitions exist, and they all roughly resemble the following: "Social media is understood as the different forms of online communication used by people to create networks, communities, and collectives to share information, ideas, messages, and other content, such as videos" (Jones, 2015, para. 5).

Social media was once nearly the sole domain of students. However, in 2021, nearly 4 billion people across the globe were reported to use some formal of social media, with most of those individuals logging on daily (Dean, 2021). Today, parents, friends, elected officials, faculty, academic leaders, and a vast array of offices within higher education institutions have social media accounts, and many use them for both personal and professional forms of communication. In many ways, the advent of social media has led to an increase in direct communication to and among students and other constituencies. For example, presidents and other leaders use social media to provide insight into their lives, communicate priorities, and connect with various constituencies. It is not uncommon to see some leaders posting selfies during opening week or sharing information about initiatives about which they want more people to be aware.

Social media can be a double-edged sword, as it can generate criticism from the public, particularly as the forum continues to develop, and expectations for using it are still not fully formed and differ based on the user (e.g., as a university president versus as a student). Take, for example, Santa Ono, the president of the University of British Columbia (UBC) and a frequent user of social media. In 2018, he was criticized by the UBC student newspaper for how he used Twitter—interspersing personal opinions, institutional policy statements, and UBC promotional materials, which made it difficult to discern what was an official UBC pronouncement or Ono's personal belief (McKenzie, 2018). Forums that allow more direct engagement with followers can also lead to more criticism when mistakes are made or when they do not agree with a particular perspective.

The emergence of social media has also meant that colleges and universities have less control over the flow of information, which is a particular concern during a crisis. As a result, information, both accurate and not, can flow quickly. Asselin (2012) illustrated how social media can distort and accelerate campus crises through the uncontrolled creation and sharing of information. At one time, the standard crisis management plan sought to control how and when information was shared. Social media has weakened this approach, and if college or university leaders do not communicate quickly, others will fill the void—often with inaccurate information.

Social media networks have become important tools for colleges and universities, from recruiting students to sharing faculty accomplishments. They have also become a more frequent forum for leaders to interact with the various constituencies they serve. At the same time, more open and rapid networks for communication can lead to more criticism of leaders and institutions as well as a more rapid spread of misinformation. The social media landscape will continue to evolve and reshape itself, and leaders would be wise to be aware of its possibilities, positive and negative, and develop strategies to take advantage of its opportunities and mitigate its threats.

Preparing for the (Un)Foreseen Crisis

Since higher education contexts are changing so rapidly, colleges and universities have had to develop more structures to help buffer them from those changes. For example, increasing reliance on tuition has led to expansion of strategic enrollment management and the addition of staff to recruit and retain students. The uncertainty (and importance) of government funding has often led to the addition of governmental relations officials to support the president in building and maintaining political relationships. The increase in social media has resulted in the expansion of media and marketing offices to manage information flows and leverage those new mediums to raise awareness of the institution. The associated risks of all these changes generated the establishment of risk management offices, where personnel focus on reducing the institution's risks and liabilities.

Some crises, however, will simply occur unexpectedly, such as floods, fires, pandemics, or shootings. Still others may be outside any reasonable expectation. For example, one of the authors worked at an institution where a custodian knocked over an old safe, probably not opened for decades, in a storage room. Inside was a forgotten vial of americium, a synthetic radioactive chemical element, which broke. The liquid began to spill out of the safe. The custodian, not knowing what the liquid was, began to clean it up, moving it all over the building and potentially exposing others. A faculty member soon realized something was amiss and alerted authorities to the situation. Fortunately, exposure was limited, and no one, including the custodian, was believed to be unduly injured. The point, though, was that the institution had no way to plan for that specific situation, but the established crisis management plan guided the institutional response.

Online advice and plenty of consultants can assist an institution in developing a crisis management plan. The basic concept is that the plan guides the institution in how to respond should a crisis occur. A crisis typically has three phases: precrisis, during the crisis, and postcrisis. The more time spent preparing in the precrisis phase, the more likely the institution will navigate the crisis well. The plan is an attempt to design the process for engaging in a crisis and is likely to determine members of the crisis management team; identify the spokesperson (to control the message); and develop notification processes, procedures for assessing and responding to threats, and strategies for communicating with stakeholders—including via social media. Most plans also include processes for testing and updating the plan to ensure it remains up-to-date. The key is planning ahead so that the institution is as prepared as possible if (likely when) a crisis occurs.

Conclusion

In the midst of changing social, political, and economic contexts and dynamic public opinion, colleges and universities must continually consider what they teach, how they teach, and whom they teach. Some changes are slower and more predictable, such as demographic shifts. Others, such as a worldwide pandemic, are more rapid and unexpected (at least for most of us). How higher education stakeholders and observers respond to academic leaders' handling of change can be unpredictable as well, and with the emergence of social media, it is more difficult to regulate. Academic leaders need to constantly scan the horizon to understand how their institutional context is changing, as well as work to ensure that their institution is responding to change in ways that ensure its long-term sustainability.

References

Abel, J. R., & Deitz, R. (2019). *Despite rising costs, college is still a good investment.* Federal Reserve Bank of New York. https://libertystreeteconomics.newyorkfed.org/2019/06/despite-rising-costs-college-is-still-a-good-investment.html

American Council on Education. (2017). *American college president study.* https://www.acenet.edu/Research-Insights/Pages/American-College-President-Study.aspx

Asselin, M. J. (2012). *Utilizing social networks in times of crisis: Understanding, exploring, and analyzing critical incident management at institutions of higher education* (Publication No. 3518565) [Doctoral dissertation, University at Albany]. ProQuest Dissertations.

Bailey, T., & Belfield, C. R. (2017). *Stackable credentials: Awards for the future?* (CCRC Working Paper No. 92). Teachers College, Columbia University. https://ccrc.tc.columbia.edu/publications/stackable-credentials-awards-for-future.html

Belkin, D. (2020, November 12). Is this the end of college as we know it? *Wall Street Journal.* https://www.wsj.com/articles/is-this-the-end-of-college-as-we-know-it-11605196909

Bransberger, P., Falkenstern, C., & Lane, P. (2020, December). *Knocking at the college door: Projections of high school graduates.* Western Interstate Commission for Higher Education. https://knocking.wiche.edu/wp-content/uploads/sites/10/2020/12/Knocking-pdf-for-website.pdf

Dean, B. (2021, October 10). *Social network usage and growth statics: How many people uses social media in 2021?* https://backlinko.com/social-media-users

de Brey, C., Snyder, T. D., Zhang, A., & Dillow, S. A. (2021). *Digest of educational statistics, 2019.* National Center for Education Statistics, U.S. Department of Education. https://nces.ed.gov/pubs2021/2021009.pdf

Denley, T. (2022). Predictive analytics and choice architecture and their role in system scale student success: Empowering a mobile advising tool across campuses. In J. Gagliardi and J. Lane (Eds.), *Higher education systems redesigned: From perpetuation to innovation to student success.* State University of New York Press.

Doherty, C., & Kiley, J. (2019). *Americans have become much less positive about tech companies' impact on the U.S.* Pew Research Center. https://www.pewresearch.org/fact-tank/2019/07/29/americans-have-become-much-less-positive-about-tech-companies-impact-on-the-u-s/

Dondi, M., Klier, J., Panier, F., & Schubert, J. (2021). *Defining the skills citizens will need in the future world of work.* McKinsey & Company. https://www.mckinsey.com/industries/public-and-social-sector/our-insights/defining-the-skills-citizens-will-need-in-the-future-world-of-work

Essa, A., & Ayad, H. (2012). Improving student success using predictive models and data visualisations. *Research in Learning Technology, 20,* 58–70. https://doi.org/10.3402/rlt.v20i0.19191

Fishman, R., Ekowo, M., & Ezeugo, E. (2017, August). *Varying degrees: New America's annual survey on higher education.* New America. https://na-production.s3.amazonaws.com/documents/Varying-Degrees.pdf

Gagliardi, J. S., Parnell, A., & Carpenter-Hubin, J. (Eds.). (2018). *The analytics revolution in higher education: Big data, organizational learning, and student success.* Stylus.

Gallagher, S. (2019, September 20). How the value of educational credentials is and isn't changing. *Harvard Business Review.* https://hbr.org/2019/09/how-the-value-of-educational-credentials-is-and-isnt-changing

Geiger, R. L. (2005). The ten generations of American higher education. In P. G. Altbach, R. O. Berdahl, & P. J. Gumport (Eds.), *American higher education in the twenty-first century: Social, political, and economic challenges* (pp. 38–69). Johns Hopkins University Press.

Grawe, N. D. (2018). *Demographics and the demand for higher education.* Johns Hopkins University Press.

Immerwahr, J. (2000). *Great expectations: How the public and parents—White, African American, and Hispanic—view higher education.* National Center for Public Policy and Higher Education. https://eric.ed.gov/?id=ED444405

Jaschik, S. (2018, October 9). Falling confidence in higher ed. *Inside Higher Ed.* https://www.insidehighered.com/news/2018/10/09/gallup-survey-finds-falling-confidence-higher-education

Jenkins, D., Lahr, H., Fink, J., & Ganga, E. (2018, April). *What we are learning about guided pathways.* Community College Research Center, Teachers College, Columbia University. https://ccrc.tc.columbia.edu/media/k2/attachments/guided-pathways-part-1-theory-practice.pdf

Jones, M. (2015, June 16). *The complete history of social media: A timeline of the invention of social networking.* History Cooperative. https://historycooperative.org/the-history-of-social-media/

Julius, D. J., Baldridge, J. V., & Pfeffer, J. (1999). A memo from Machiavelli. *Journal of Higher Education, 70*(2), 113–133. https://doi.org/10.2307/2649124

Kasriel, S. (2018, October 31). *The future of work won't be about college degrees, it will be about job skills.* CNBC. https://www.cnbc.com/2018/10/31/the-future-of-work-wont-be-about-degrees-it-will-be-about-skills.html

Kearney, M. S., & Levine, P. (2021, May 24). *Will births in the US rebound? Probably not.* Brookings Institution. https://www.brookings.edu/blog/up-front/2021/05/24/will-births-in-the-us-rebound-probably-not/

Kerr, C. (1994). American society turns more assertive: A new century approaches for higher education in the United States. In P. G. Altbach, R. O. Berdahl, & P. J. Gumport (Eds.), *Higher education in American society* (pp. i–xi). Prometheus.

Klebs, S., Fisham, R., Nguyen, S., & Hiler, T. (2021). *One year later: COVID-19's impact on current and future college students.* Third Way. https://www.thirdway.org/memo/one-year-later-covid-19s-impact-on-current-and-future-college-students

Lane, J. E. (2014). *Building a smarter university: Big data, innovation, and analytics.* State University of New York Press.

Lucas, C. J. (2006). *American higher education: A history.* Palgrave Macmillan.

Marcus, J. (2020, June 2). *Urgency of getting people back to work gives new momentum to "microcredentials."* The Hechinger Report. https://hechingerreport.org/more-students-start-earning-stackable-credentials-on-their-way-to-degrees/

McKenzie, L. (2018, June 15). A college president's Twitter strategy. *Inside Higher Ed.* https://www.insidehighered.com/news/2018/06/15/drawing-line-between-policy-and-personality-twitter

Menand, L. (2011, June 6). Live and learn: Why we have college. *New Yorker.* https://www.newyorker.com/magazine/2011/06/06/live-and-learn-louis-menand

Murray, C. (2008, August 13). *For most people, college is a waste of time.* American Enterprise Institute. https://www.aei.org/articles/for-most-people-college-is-a-waste-of-time/

National Association of College and University Business Officers. (2021). *2020 tuition discounting study.* Author.

National Student Clearinghouse. (2021, October 26). *COVID-19: Stay informed with the latest enrollment information.* https://nscresearchcenter.org/stay-informed/

NBC News. (2005, March 2). *Bush boosts nation's community colleges.* https://www.nbcnews.com/id/wbna7067604

Okahana, H., Zhou, E., & Gao, J. (2020). *Graduate enrollment and degrees: 2009–2019.* Council of Graduate Schools and ETS GRE. https://cgsnet.org/ckfinder/userfiles/files/CGS_GED19_Report_final2.pdf

Parnell, A. (2018). Data analytics for student success. In J. S. Gagliard, A. Parnell, & J. Carpenter-Hubin (Eds.), *The analytics revolution in higher education: Big data, organizational learning, and student success* (pp. 43–54). Stylus.

Pissarides, C. A. (2011). Regular education as a tool of counter-cyclical employment policy. *Nordic Economic Policy Review, 1,* 209–232. https://www.fpr.se/download/18.6c09f59d1287ef288f9800077954/1606374821307/100527_6_Pissarides.pdf

Rudolph, F. (1977). *Curriculum: A history of the American undergraduate course of study since 1636.* Jossey-Bass.

Schleifer, D., & Silliman, R. (2016, October). *What's the payoff? Americans consider problems and promises of higher education.* Public Agenda. https://files.eric.ed.gov/fulltext/ED591331.pdf

Selingo, J. L. (2003, May 2). What Americans think about higher education. *Chronicle of Higher Education, 49*(34), A10.

Seltzer, R. (2021, March 23). Moody's raises higher ed outlook to stable. *Inside Higher Ed.* https://www.insidehighered.com/quicktakes/2021/03/23/moodys-raises-higher-ed-outlook-stable

Smith, A. A. (2015, September 9). Obama steps up push for free community college. *Inside Higher Ed.* https://www.insidehighered.com/news/2015/09/09/obama-unveils-new-push-national-free-community-college

State Higher Education Executive Officers Association. (2021). *State higher education finance: FY 2020.* https://shef.sheeo.org/wp-content/uploads/2021/05/SHEEO_SHEF_FY20_Report.pdf

Stewart, C. D. (1978). Countercyclical education and training. *New Directions for Education and Work, 1978*(3), 89–98.

Thelin, J. R. (2004). *A history of American higher education*. Johns Hopkins University Press.

Wildavsky, B. (2013, September 10). *Nudge nation: A new way to prod students into and through college*. Education Sector. https://www.air.org/sites/default/files/publications/Nudge.pdf

Wingard, J., & Farrugia, C. A. (Eds.). (2021). *The great skills gap: Optimizing talent for the future of work*. Stanford University Press.

Yuen, V. (2020, June 11*)*. *Mounting peril for public higher education during the coronavirus pandemic*. Center for American Progress. https://www.americanprogress.org/issues/education-postsecondary/reports/2020/06/11/485963/mounting-peril-public-higher-education-coronavirus-pandemic/

3

DIVERSITY, EQUITY, AND INCLUSION

The value of diversity in higher education has been hotly debated for decades, with progress being interpreted differently depending on one's perspective. What is undeniable is the fact that U.S. demographics are changing—the country is becoming more diverse, and students and other higher education stakeholders expect institutions to engage with them in more equitable and inclusive ways. Colleges and universities, guided by their leaders, must reflect on their own values and adapt to this change if they are to remain relevant.

Few topics are more clearly aligned with the four principles of academic leadership set forth in this book than are the values of diversity, equity, and inclusion (DEI). Two of our guiding principles specifically inform this chapter. First, democratic ideals are at the heart of advancing American higher education. Second, higher education has served as a catalyst for inclusion, equity, and social justice in American society. Both principles took centuries to germinate and take root in U.S. higher education, as there has been—and continues to be—resistance to these ideals. However, no matter how long it has taken U.S. higher education to embrace these principles, as we asserted in chapter 1, the "arc" of U.S. colleges and universities still "bends toward justice," consistent with the vision of Dr. Martin Luther King, Jr., regarding the moral universe.

The original colonial colleges in America were neither democratic nor diverse. Rudolph (1962) wrote that the colonial colleges were "shaped by aristocratic traditions and they served the aristocratic elements of colonial society, a society which was being subjected to the stresses of New World conditions" (pp. 18–19). The "conditions" to which he referred included a new set of norms that "encouraged individual effort" and looked "with jealousy and hostility at privilege" (Rudolph, 1962, p. 19). Ellis (2007) argued that the democratic ideals that took hold in America were rooted in the classical education many of the founders received at these distinctly American colleges during the Enlightenment in the 17th and 18th centuries, and these educational experiences were a key element in sparking the American Revolution.

The democratic ideals of the American Revolution would shape the future of U.S. higher education, but it was not until the late 19th century that colleges and universities began to include in a more systematic way those who were denied access in the past. In this chapter we highlight some of the significant historical and cultural movements that led to the democratization of U.S. higher education, which in turn has led to greater access and inclusion and a commitment to social justice as a guiding principle at most higher education institutions across the nation. What has emerged from a troubled past has been the creation of the most diverse set of colleges and universities in the world.

It is important to note that this chapter was written during a time of significant societal upheaval, which affects the environment in which DEI issues exist. As U.S. colleges and universities entered the 2020s, they suddenly and dramatically faced the challenges of the COVID-19 pandemic, as well as a national surge in social activism ignited by reactions to several well-publicized tragedies and led in large measure by the Black Lives Matter (BLM) social movement. It is also being written while some of the democratic ideals that have governed this nation and have been the foundation of U.S. higher education are being challenged, including attacks on free speech, voting rights, and the legitimacy of free elections. By the end of 2020, a new U.S. president was elected who promised widespread changes in the country—particularly in enhancing access to higher education.

This chapter provides an overview of the theoretical and historical underpinnings of DEI in U.S. higher education; discusses various issues pertaining to DEI and higher education; highlights how some colleges and universities have addressed these concerns; and looks to the future with a review of the Biden administration's DEI-related higher education agenda and several recommendations for academic leaders who aspire to promote DEI more fully at their institutions. We acknowledge that additional issues that fall under the heading of DEI are not covered in this chapter—not because they are unimportant, but because of the vast depth and breadth of the topic and the limited scope of this book. DEI is ever evolving as new concerns emerge, demographics shift, and more voices rise. We encourage readers to remain current on and increase their understanding of these matters through engagement with their campus community and by accessing more information from scholarly publications and the media.

Theoretical and Historical Underpinnings

Understanding the current situation requires an understanding of both the past and present. In this section we first seek to problematize common definitions and use of terminology as well as proivde an overview of both historical and theoretical contexts.

Problematizing Definitions and Purposes

Working definitions of diversity, equity, and inclusion differ perhaps as widely as the disparate attitudes and passions that exist toward these concepts as they relate to higher education (Jaschik, 2021; Kamarck, 2019). For the purposes of our discussion, we orient toward the terms' combined purpose of ensuring that access to higher education is democratic in nature and available to all who seek it, and that these benefits reflect a quality that provides significant utility and enriching experiences to all who engage in the pursuit of academic and professional outcomes. In short, the promise of an outstanding, accessible, high-quality education system has served as a cornerstone of American heritage, and this chapter discusses the ongoing effort to achieve that promise for all.

The facets that comprise DEI vary with the individuals and their respective roles within the education system. All bring to the table their own backgrounds, personalities, and perspectives. While ideally a system of education would be customized to each individual who seeks its benefits, at this stage such an approach is not technically possible. In fact, DEI efforts will vary by state and territory due to the centrality of those governments in determining educational experiences. But it is possible—and crucial—that the entire system be sufficiently flexible to be useful to all, and responsive and responsible to each. For higher education to be accessible and productive for all individuals who seek its services, and for society as a whole, those who have historically been denied these services or could not achieve equal benefits from them must be provided a passage toward such achievement (Mayhew et al., 2005; O'Donovan, 2010).

It is also important to note that the labels often used to describe a set of individuals can hide important differences within groups. The difference between the cultures, histories, and needs of the thousands or millions of people within typical groupings can be as diverse as human imagination. For example, the term *Native American* lumps together hundreds of tribal cultures spread across the United States and often displaced because of colonists and settlers. Even within the subcategories, there tends to be a media bias toward referencing the Lakota, Navajo (Diné), or Apache (Qureshi, 2016).

Another racially, ethnically, linguistically, geographically, and otherwise diverse group within U.S. society and thus U.S. higher education is Asian Americans/Pacific Islanders (AAPI). The AAPI designation is problematic for a variety of reasons, including that this "panethnicity" is "detrimental to indigenous self-determinations, a central issue among Pacific Islanders" (as cited in Poon et al., 2016, p. 471). Hall (2015) echoed and lamented this sentiment in a piece on Pacific Islander issues regarding demographic framing and research. Some have assumed Asians and Asian Americans are "overrepresented" in U.S. higher education, thus ignoring many of the challenges individuals encounter in this overly generalized demographic. In a literature review on "model minority myth" (MMM), Poon et al. (2016) asserted that this narrative is an attempt to create "racial wedge politics" and complicate discussions about racial disparities in higher education (p. 469). Further, Poon et al. argued that the MMM label defines Asian Americans as a "middleman minority"—a buffer between the White majority and the country's other racial minority populations, particularly Black, Indigenous, and Latinx populations. This status results in some economic advantages, but it also means that Asian Americans encounter "hostility" from both the majority population and other minority groups (Poon et al., 2016, p. 5). Indeed, some studies have suggested that the idealization of Asian American success has created a counter thesis to claims of racial oppression from other racial/ethnic minorities (Poon et al., 2016).

As with Native Americans and Alaska Natives and Asian Americans and Pacific Islanders, each Latinx/Hispanic individual may come from any location from a continental or intercontinental span (V. Torres, 2004). Latina/o Critical Theory (LatCrit) scholars have distilled issues of this massive aggregate into areas they feel are salient concerns: "immigration, language rights, bilingual schooling, internal colonialism, sanctuary for Latin American refugees, and census categories for Latinos" (Delgado & Stefancic, 2017, p. 93). However, there may be a shifting sense of association among subgroups within the larger group. Natural disasters such as violent Caribbean hurricanes may bond those from that region within the Gulf area and Florida residents rather than Latinx from Colombia or Central Mexico. In Texas, for example, a Hispanic student's local heritage may well predate the Battle of the Alamo, or the student may be a "DREAMer" (an informal recognition conveyed by the yet-to-be-approved Development, Relief, and Education for Alien Minors Act seeking to recognize undocumented residents who were brought to the United States as children and grew up in the country—see DREAM Act of 2017). Distinguishing various groups from a main segment of the population and the population as a whole is not intended to create a wall between them, but to better understand each group of individuals in turn so that the parts can be reassembled to benefit all and do justice to each (Hall, 2015).

In this volume we at times use the term *Latinx*. Some have argued for the pan-ethnical label *Latin** (Salinas, 2020) and/or using a person's country of origin (Noe-Bustamante et al., 2020), when possible. Previously, the literature and practice within higher education identified pan-ethnic labels for persons of Latin origin or descent often using the government categorization of "Hispanic" or the broader ethnic identity of "Latinos" (Salinas & Lozano, 2021; Scharrón-del Río & Aja, 2020; Vidal-Ortiz & Martinez, 2018). As a pan-ethnic label, it has been argued that *Latinos* fails to include a broader recognition of gender and sexual identities within the English language (Cardemil et al., Salinas & Lozano, 2021). Academics and activists presented a solution by referencing the pan-ethnic group as Latinx, which is inclusive and avoids gender references (Salinas & Lozano, 2021). Stated another way, "Latinx acts as a new frame of inclusion, while also posing a challenge for those used to having androcentric terms serve as collective representational proxies" (Vidal-Ortiz & Martinez, 2018, p. 384). Although the Latinx identity reference presents an inclusive and neutral approach (rather than Latino, Latina, Latina/o, Latin@, or Latin descent), its usage is still under debate and we acknowledge not preferred by some persons represented within the pan-ethnic group. For instance, a Gallup poll asked Latinx respondents about their preferred pan-ethnic term. A majority (57%) indicated that it did not matter, but respondents favored Hispanic (23%) over Latinx (4%). A Pew Research Center study (Noe-Bustamante et al., 2020) reported that 23% of Latinx persons sampled heard of the Latinx reference, yet only 3% use it with other studies expressing that the term seems to appeal to academics more than the broader persons impacted (Salinas, 2020; Scharrón-del Río & Aja, 2020). Persons sampled prefer identifying with their country of origin such as Mexican, Cuban, or Bolivian as opposed to pan-ethnic labels like Latinx. For lack of better options at the time of this writing, Latinx was chosen as the preferred term for this volume.

Further complicating this issue within higher education has been a movement to allow students to identify as more than one racial/ethnic subgroup, acknowledging that many students are now descendants of multiple groups—not just one. As we discuss in chapter 15, this practice has led the multiracial group to be the fastest growing group among U.S. higher education students.

Theoretical Underpinnings

When examining facets of the DEI environment, it is helpful to review how researchers have framed the very nature of potential and actual inequalities within the social system. Historians, communication researchers, and linguists have long examined the phenomenon of ethnocentrism, introduced into the vernacular by Sumner (1906/1940), who described it as the "view of things in which one's own group is the center of everything, and all others are scaled and rated in reference to it" (p. 13). Sumner offered several examples of this pervasive trait, such as Romans' labeling outsiders as "barbarians" and Caribs' answering queries regarding their origins as "we alone are people" (p. 14). In 1974, Peng identified ethnocentric linguistics as communication that displays degrees of distance between the speaker and the listener of another culture and saw the increasing degrees of distance as being "indifference, avoidance, and disparagement," with the last overtly displaying hostility (as cited in Lukens, 1976, p. 11). In the introduction to *The Native Americans: An Illustrated History*, Josephy (1993) lamented that Eurocentrism, an offshoot of ethnocentrism, is the "fundamental problem" (p. 16) in the forced removal of Native Americans from their lands. Recent research into the development, persistence, and dissolving of ethnocentric traits has suggested that group identity is not so much inherited, but rather the groups with which people identify are "fluid." Concluded one research team, "Ethnocentrism might be viewed as merely one possible expression of inherent groupishness, but not a long term evolved [phenomenon]" (Hales & Edmonds, 2019, p. 1).

The rather ethnocentric viewpoint in the collective eyes of many members of the United States' majority population gave rise to a body of scholarship dedicated to answering why such self-inflicted blinding persisted well beyond the days of slavery and the American Civil War. Beginning in the 1970s, a group of legal and feminist scholars and lawyers (e.g., D. Bell, 1992; Crenshaw, 1989; Delgado, 1984; Ladson-Billings & Tate, 1995; P. J. Williams, 1991) began to "interrogate" the processes within U.S. society, exposing the role of racism within these structures.

From its intellectual root structure, research in a variety of disciplines and fields uncovered a set of entrenched attitudes and behaviors that barely allowed any non-Western thought or non-European perspectives to earn any oxygen (George, 2021). Many pedagogical theories of practice have addressed the material and existential conditions of students of color and serving marginalized student populations by focusing educational experiences on equity and social justice. Some of these theories and practices include critical pedagogy (Freire, 1970/2018); culturally relevant, sustaining, and revitalizing pedagogies (Ladson-Billings, 1995, 2014; Paris & Alim, 2014), and community responsive pedagogy (Tintiangco-Cubales & Duncan-Andrade, 2021). These theories, in their own ways, support the cultivation of critical consciousness in students by centering, valuing, and empowering their narratives, cultures, and assets within educational institutions that strive to respond directly to the needs of the communities they serve.

Beyond the Eurocentric view of life and its environment that these pedagogies have challenged, there was something pervasive about the basic interrelationship of people where so many saw their very existence as depending on winning their share of a perceived zero-sum game for life's riches. Researchers found that it mattered little which way they turned or which corner they explored—the White American advantage held true (George, 2021). This observation evolved into Critical Race Theory (CRT) and through it was coined the phrase "White privilege" (Delgado & Stefancic, 2017, pp. 3–4, 89–90). While semantically useful for identifying areas of inequality, this term invoked pushback, especially from some White Americans who individually did not see themselves as privileged (Greenfield, 2021)—further evidencing how the individual does not always see themselves in the collective. And, so long as many in each political party see advantages gained by one group as equally a loss by another, the result seems to be a hardening of political positions aligned with perceptions of CRT's findings and assertions (Delgado & Stefancic, 2017; Newkirk, 2020).

Rather than treating higher education as a zero-sum game, researchers have provided evidence that diversity benefits everyone in a community, although here we limit our discussion to the higher education context. Mayhew et al. (2005), for example, argued that promoting racial diversity in higher education is not only a way to promote better access for historically underserved and marginalized populations; it is also a means to promote a better, more stimulating academic and intellectual environment for all students. Levine and Stark (2015) found that members of homogenous groups were more easily influenced by their group members and more likely to "fall for wrong ideas" based on mimicking or copying their group members (p. A35), whereas individuals in racially diverse groups engaged in more robust critical thinking, error detection, and more accurate calculations. Levine and Stark asserted,

> Ethnic diversity is like fresh air: It benefits everybody who experiences it. By disrupting conformity it produces a public good. To step back from the goal of diverse classrooms would deprive all students, regardless of their racial or ethnic background, of the opportunity to benefit from the improved cognitive performance that diversity promotes. (p. A35)

Despite evidence of the opportunities and benefits that diverse learning environments provide for all members of a learning community, such remains controversial within some constituencies within U.S. society.

Historical Context

Advancement of fair and equal access to the opportunities available through higher education has made DEI a necessity for many U.S. colleges and universities in the 21st century. Given the political, social, and economic disparities that emerged during the COVID-19 pandemic and the changing demographics of the U.S. population, institutions that do not accept and address this responsibility are likely to not succeed. While over time U.S. higher education has moved toward greater diversity and inclusion, especially since the civil rights movement of the 1960s, the progress has not been linear. Past events, however, highlight historical inequities and explain the need for colleges to take action. In this section, we provide an overview of the evolution of U.S. higher education, from its exclusive and inequitable roots to the present, using a DEI lens to explore the ways in which colleges and universities have engaged in—or resisted—the promotion of diversity and inclusion.

Higher Education Before the Civil War

From its beginning, the U.S. education system was thought to be a model of human advancement through equal opportunity—except, of course, for females, enslaved Africans, Native Americans, the poor, or those children otherwise engaged in other sunrise-to-sunset duties and chores. In colonial America, the lack of widespread interest in educating the mass population of youth meant that no standard system and few resources existed to support this enterprise. With the possible exception of Dartmouth College, the American colleges founded before the 19th century were institutions for White male elites who had access to primary and secondary education (Thelin, 2011). Indeed, Dartmouth College was initially chartered in 1769 as a school for Native Americans, but graduation rates of Native Americans were abysmal (Lee, 2019).

The primary focus of higher education in the colonial period was on producing men who could serve as leaders with the congregations and other societal institutions that often sponsored their colleges. Starting with the Protestant establishment of the colonial colleges, higher education in America has been strongly buttressed by support from organized religion, which continues to influence many institutions' functions and philosophies (Marsden, 1994). To an extent, this religious background has also influenced the bend toward greater access—though in fits and starts. After the American Revolution, numerous faith-based colleges were founded to help educate the increasing number of children of immigrants to the United States, many of whom migrated to urban areas. Rudolph (1962) observed that the "Catholic Church needed no prodding to follow the counsel of Saint Ignatius to place colleges in cities" (p. 94) to educate the next generation of Catholics to assume their roles as productive members of U.S. society. These institutions usually focused on educating a specific demographic. Georgetown College (now University) in Washington DC was founded in 1789 to foster "an education that would combine the best of the Catholic and republican cultures" (Curran, n.d.). Boston College, founded in 1863, served Boston's predominantly poor, Irish Catholic population—one of the first examples of expanding the reach and scope of higher education beyond the realm of the wealthy in the United States.

In the 1820s, the first recorded graduations of Black students occurred in the United States, all from colleges in the Northeast: Middlebury, Amherst, and Dartmouth (Slater, 1994). Oberlin College in Ohio was founded in 1833 with a mission to serve a broader range of students, especially Blacks and women, and would enroll Rebecca Lee, the first recorded Black female U.S. college graduate, in 1862. However, expanded access for Black students during the 19th century mostly came through the development of a separate and unequal system that segregated students. The first higher education institutions for Black students were established in the Philadelphia, Pennsylvania, area prior to the Civil War (Thelin, 2011). Founded by a Quaker philanthropist, the Institute for Colored Youth (now Cheyney University) opened in 1837, and the Ashmun Institute (now Lincoln University) was established by Presbyterians in 1854. In 1856, African Americans from the African Methodist Episcopal Church founded Wilberforce University in Ohio.

Other Christian benefactors led the creation of institutions to serve ethnic minorities, people of color, and women long before it became a mandate in the public sector (Slater, 1994). For example, Berea College (n.d.) in Kentucky was founded by abolitionist John Gregg Fee in 1855 as a Christian, coeducational institution and enrolled both Black and White students during its 1st full year after the Civil War, and Benedict College (n.d.) in South Carolina was founded in 1870 by Baptists to educate "recently freed people of African descent." Before the end of the Civil War, however, approximately 40 Blacks had graduated from U.S. colleges, all in the North (Slater, 1994).

The Morrill Act of 1862 established land-grant postsecondary institutions and opened access to higher education for children of the industrial and agricultural classes. Like most colleges established before them, however, land-grant institutions almost exclusively benefited White students. Moreover, it is a troubling heritage of the Morrill Act of 1862 (and its successor act in 1890), that almost 11 million acres of land whose sale financed the land-grant institutions were wrested from nearly 250 Native tribal nations with negligible or no compensation (Ahtone & Lee, 2020; Nash, 2019). The legacy of this land-grant land grab is a treasure of invaluable academic programs and resources, but benefits have been minimal for the Native people whom these institutions displaced (Ahtone & Lee, 2020; Nash, 2019). (See also chapter 7, this volume.)

Higher Education After the Civil War

In the post–Civil War Reconstruction period, the Freedmen's Bureau opened hundreds of schools for Black children across the South (Bentley, 1955). During Reconstruction and beyond, ex-slaves' relationship to education was one of knowing the liberatory power of literacy, primarily due to the multigenerational experience of having it withheld from them at the cost of life and limb (Anderson, 1988). Schools were segregated, but the pursuit of education was an opportunity for the ex-enslaved to exercise self-determination in both excelling at learning and at establishing and sustaining their own institutions of learning and leadership development with minimal to no interference from outside entities. During this period Blacks in the South attended school at much higher rates than their White counterparts (Anderson, 1988).

In 1890, Congress attempted to expand access to higher education through the second Morrill Act, which restricted funding to states "when a distinction of race or color is made in the admission of students." (Morrill Act, 1890, §323). However, the act also allowed that "the establishment and maintenance of such colleges separately for white and colored students shall be held to be in compliance with the provisions of this act if the funds are received in such State or Territory be equitably divided" (Morrill Act, 1890, §323). The result was the establishment of 19 land-grant colleges and universities for Black students, primarily in former slave states, and establishment of the legal doctrine "separate but equal" (see *Plessy v. Ferguson*, 1896).

While the second Morrill Act resulted in an increase in the number of Black college students, Black leaders did not agree on what education should look like for the Black community. Booker T. Washington advocated for Blacks to accept segregation and learn trades rather than participate in academic studies and careers, while W.E.B. Du Bois encouraged members of the Black community to engage in intellectual pursuits from primary through postsecondary education. Ultimately, though, the efforts of freed slaves and free Blacks during Reconstruction created the ideologies and institutions in the South that have propelled universal education to the status it occupies to this day—a narrative in complete contrast to one of Black cultural inferiority in relation to education (Aiello, 2016).

Higher Education in the Early 20th Century
The 20th century brought to light tension between efforts to expand access and who was eligible for that access. For example, federal policies such as the land-grant movement expanded access to higher education across the country, but ongoing legal struggles challenged what constituted equitable access to those institutions. Again, toward the end of World War II, a similar tension emerged as the Servicemen's Readjustment Act of 1944 greatly expanded funding for higher education, although local implementation of the GI Bill left a sizeable portion of eligible students behind—particularly potential Black students in the South (Blakemore, 2021).

One major impediment to expanding access to higher education was lack of access to elementary and secondary education (Warder, 2015). In the early 1900s, government reforms and community activism began to address this issue, leading to every state requiring children to finish at least elementary school (although it would be decades before this goal was actually realized). Despite limited federal support, Southern Black children's access to public education was maintained in large part by resources provided by Black community members. For instance, the vast majority of resources provided to source and build thousands of new schools from 1914 to 1935 were provided by members of the Black community in the South, demonstrating a continued fight for access to public education for their children through the Jim Crow era (Anderson, 1988).

High school enrollments exploded during the middle of the century. In 1940, less than half of the adult age population in the United States had earned a high school diploma (U.S. Census Bureau, 2017). At the end of that decade, about 2.4 million students were enrolled in higher education—about 15% of 18- to 24-year-olds at the time. By the end of the 1950s, half the young adults in the United States had completed high school, and approximately 30% of these graduates were women, and while other demographics are not known, the number of non-White students is believed to be quite low and largely in those institutions predominantly serving minority students (Snyder, 1993).

The Latter 20th Century: The Era of Desegregation
While segregation's demise began following the Civil War, it only became a dominant component of the U.S. educational ecosystem in the latter half of the 20th century. The major turning point in expanding access for African American and other underrepresented communities came in the *Brown v. Board of Education* decision of 1954, in which the U.S. Supreme Court ruled that segregation of students according to racial identity was unconstitutional—separate could not be equal. This ruling, we know, would not

be the end of the struggle by people of color to access education in the United States. (See chapter 8 for a legal discussion of the ruling.)

In the tumultuous decade that followed, higher education was part of an overall effort to seek greater equality in society. In 1960, students from the North Carolina Agricultural and Technical College (now North Carolina A&T University) launched a sit-in movement at a segregated Woolworth's lunch counter in Greensboro. Four years later, as part of what would become known as Freedom Summer, members of civil rights organizations, such as the Student Non-Violent Coordinating Committee (SNCC), trained hundreds of volunteers at the Western Women's College (now part of Miami University) in Ohio to conduct voter registration drives across the South and influenced the creation of the Voting Rights Act of 1965 (McAdam, 1988).

Other legislation that supported President Lyndon Johnson's Great Society initiative, including the Higher Education Act (HEA) of 1965, established federal scholarships and low-interest loans for college students and expanded the number of community colleges across the country. The Higher Education Act of 1965 also formally designated HBCUs as any "college or university that was established prior to 1964, whose principal mission was, and is, the education of black Americans" (HEA 1965, §322). The history of expanding access continues to be written, and this section only provides a limited overview of what has occurred to date. From the flap copy of Hubert Humphrey's (1968) publication, "The whole modern movement for human rights in America is one continuous struggle—that is still going on, and if we are to maintain a free society, it must continue." And while we have limited our discussion to race and ethnicity, as it has been the dominant historical narrative thus far, important steps have been taken to expand access to other groups based on, for example, gender, sexual orientation, or disability.

Contemporary Issues in Higher Education

While the number of Black and Latinx students entering U.S. colleges and universities has increased over the past 2 decades, higher education remains a highly racially divided and inequitable space. National data demonstrate that White and Asian students are overrepresented at resource-rich institutions, while Black, Latinx, and Indigenous students are primarily enrolled at universities with fewer resources (Hamilton & Nielsen, 2021). Cuts to public support for higher education in recent decades have coincided with increases in enrollment by students of color (Hamilton & Nielsen, 2021).

Clearly much is yet to be done. The divide between what is possible for improving DEI for underrepresented students is still a chasm away from reality. Wealth inequality and educational attainment between most minority groups and the national average is an issue that prevents any meaningful closure of the racial gap in higher education. Until this disparity is solved, the inequity will persist (Hanks et al., 2018; McCormack & Novello, 2019).

In 2019, the National Center for Education Statistics (NCES) revealed stark information regarding "educational progress and challenges students face in the United States by race/ethnicity," which affects the opportunities for those students to access and complete higher education (de Brey et al., 2019, p. iii). For example, the percentage of school-age Native Americans/Alaska Natives in the total national population of that category was 1%, with only the percentage of Pacific Islanders being less. The percentage of children living with both parents was highest for Asian American families at 84%, compared to 45% for Native American/Alaskan Natives families. For AY 2015–2016, 17% of Native American/Alaska Native students received services through the Individuals With Disabilities Education Act (NCES, 2019), while "Black and White students followed with 16% and 14%, respectively, and 7% of Asian American students received services" (de Brey et al., 2019, p. iv).

Further, once on campus, closing success gaps and meeting retention-to-graduation targets requires a quiver full of supporting arrows, not the least of which are faculty and staff mentors with whom students can gain a thorough understanding of their field and the whole educational process (Haring, 2009; Hinton et al., 2020). Whittaker et al. (2015) highlighted the crucial role mentoring plays for improving retention of Black students and faculty, a conclusion that applies to nearly all minority groups. Meanwhile, the entire system needs a self-audit to fully examine every facet of the learning environment. Students who demonstrate the passion that forges a strong understanding of a chosen field and a commitment to engage in a global environment should not have to overcome obstacles that serve no purpose except the deterioration of the learning experience (Chun & Evans, 2019).

It is not difficult to argue that among minority groups on any campus, individuals with disabilities often need the most support from their college or university to achieve their academic and professional goals, often because institutional structures have not been designed to support those with challenges to their physical or mental health. Many campuses now have dedicated offices to support students with disabilities, although unlike in previous levels of education, college students must actively work with their institution to determine appropriate accommodations in courses and beyond.

Disabilities present similar, but also different, challenges for faculty and staff members than for students. While various requirements of the Americans With Disabilities Act (ADA), enacted in 1990, and other regulations provide essential, enforceable guidance on how best to serve and support people with disabilities, there is no regulatory substitute for proactive organizational emphasis and individual empathy in creating an equitable and inclusive environment for persons with disabilities. (See chapter 8 for additional information about ADA's mental health accommodations.)

LGBTQ+ students have likely always been present on college campuses, although they have come to the forefront as students demand recognition, acceptance, services, and safety. In 2012, Blumenfeld found that the lived experience for LGBTQ+ students remained difficult. In the ensuing decade, campuses have responded with designated offices and meeting spaces and recognition of and support for organizations, events, and programs. Because of a strong ally movement, students who do not identify as LGBTQ+ support the rights of all students to be treated with equity and respect, yet as with all other issues around diversity, attitudes can be stubborn, and change can be slow. Popular media reports continue to indicate that LGBTQ+ students still encounter unacceptable levels of harassment and violence as part of their college experience.

Often students have intersectional identities that can further isolate them (Postsecondary National Policy Institute, 2021). In fact, while we often discuss DEI based on particular group membership, awareness is rising of the *intersectionality* of identities—a term coined by Crenshaw (1989, 1991). For example, the relationship of one's gender and race can influence how one interacts with one's surroundings. Similarly, sexual and gender identities can construct one's experience differently than simply one's gender. Crenshaw demonstrated discriminatory employment effects on Black women. Similarly, Byrd et al. (2019) have aggregated examples of how examining a single identity feature (e.g., race) offers insufficient analysis of the effects of identity on support mechanisms, resources, curricular offerings, and enrollment concerns in higher education. They illustrated how recognizing intersectionality of student identities helps campus leaders address identity and inequality in ways that are appropriately responsive and solution oriented.

Minority-Serving Institutions

Within the United States, several sets of institutions, by design or default, have come to serve specific groups of students. These minority-serving institutions (MSIs) include HBCUs, HSIs, and TCUs. Although HBCUs were formally recognized in the 1965 HEA they have been the mainstay of higher education access for Black students for decades. In 1991, the Office for Civil Rights at the U.S. Department of Education reported that 75% of Black people with doctorates at that time had received their undergraduate degrees at HBCUs, as did 75% of all African American officers in the U.S. Armed Forces and 80% of Black federal judges.

More recently, the Thurgood Marshall College Fund reported that HBCUs produced 22% of bachelor's degrees awarded to Black students, and 40% of Black members of Congress, 40% of Black engineers, 12.5% of Black CEOs, and 50% of Black doctors and lawyers graduated from HBCUs (Gaillot, 2018). While these statistics provide evidence of the past effectiveness of HBCUs, a lack of funding, a lack of national visibility through grants and athletics, and the recruitment of Black students to predominantly White institutions (PWIs) changed how these institutions were perceived in terms of their academic rigor and societal relevance (Harper, 2019). In fact, in 1968, the Kerner Commission warned of an American "apartheid" through which education disparities were creating separate Black and White societies (Darling-Hammond, 2018). Actions inspired by Kerner Commission recommendations addressed some of these inequalities, but while "the Black-White achievement gap was cut by more than half during the 1970s and early 1980s," this momentum stalled, as federal support for poor urban and rural schools and college access plummeted (Darling-Hammond, 2018, para. 7). At the time of this writing, however, HBCUs have been gaining renewed and positive attention through increased philanthropic support and the hiring of high-profile and influential leaders in the African American community.

During this same period, recognition has also emerged of the need to address disparities imposed on the Native American population. Some 90% of Native Americans perished as European settlers, and their "Old World" diseases, swept over the continent (Diamond, 1999, p. 375). While Native Americans had practiced their own forms of education, with great richness and spirituality, survivors were subjected to a European model of education that transformed education in the "New World" into a system based on Greek philosophy, Judeo-Christian religion, Oxbridge traditions, and Scots-Irish work ethic (Diamond, 1999, p. 375), leaving little space for Native customs and beliefs to flourish in the mainstream. Until the 19th and 20th centuries, though, Native Americans' access to the education system was very limited, and when they did participate, Western-style education often came at the price of their cultures—and worse (Tani, 2013). Specifically, regarding higher education, Newkirk (2020) asserted that the Kerner Commission "overlooked . . . the haunting invisibility of Native Americans" (p. 3), but in the wake of Native activism of the 1960s, Great Society reforms, and rise of the concept of Native self-determination (Crum, 2007; Ridingin et al.,

2008) the American Indian Higher Education Consortium was established in 1973. It was not until 1978, however, that the federal government provided financial support to TCUs in the United States (see also chapter 6).

Akin to HBCUs and TCUs are colleges and universities that are designated as HSIs. This designation was established in the early 1990s and is reserved for institutions where Latinx/Hispanic students comprise at least 25% of FTE students at both the undergraduate and graduate levels. The Latinx/Hispanic categorization is extremely broad. Individuals in this generalized group may trace their roots to places as geographically diverse as the Andes, the Amazon, and the Caribbean. They may also identify with multiple races; national origins; and languages, as Spanish is only one language spoken within this category. Other languages spoken by a Latinx student may include French, Portuguese, Dutch, English, any number of Indigenous tongues, or a highly localized mixture of languages. In sum, Latinx cultures vary greatly and dramatically, so while generalized statistics may offer some insights into overall trends, the factors behind the numbers may vary to such a degree that assumptions drawn from data regarding this group are as likely to be as wrong as right.

While 17% of all public and not-for-profit U.S. colleges and universities are HSIs, 67% of all Latinx undergraduate students are enrolled at HSIs (Brownlee, 2021). The HSI designation makes an institution eligible for certain federal funding, but Garcia (2018) asserted that many of these colleges are not yet effectively structured to support Latinx students' needs and ways of knowing and being.

Diversity Within the Faculty

The demographics of the full-time faculty within U.S. higher education are not consistent with the demographics of the population of the United States. This disparity is of concern because, as Taylor et al. (2010) stated, "All students are better educated and better prepared for leadership, citizenship and professional competitiveness in multicultural America and the global community when they are exposed to diverse perspectives in the classroom."

Among full-time full professors, in 2020 roughly 53% were White males, and 8% were Asian/Pacific Islander males. In contrast, within the all-ages general population, White, non-Hispanic males constituted 30% of the population, and Asian/Pacific Islander males are 3% (Hussar et al., 2020). The difference narrows incrementally at the full-time assistant professor rank. At this level in 2020, 34% of full-time assistant professors were White males, 39% were White females, 7% were Asian/Pacific Islander males, and 7% were Asian/Pacific Islander females, while 5% were Black females. Black males, Latinx males, and Latinx females each made up 3% of full-time assistant professors. Native Americans, including Alaskan Natives, accounted for 1% or less of full-time assistant professors, as did those who identified as "two or more races" (Hussar et al., 2020, p. 151).

M. P. Bell et al. (2020) noted that while many colleges and universities profess a desire to increase faculty diversity, many lack cultures and practices that address discrimination and other negative experiences that underrepresented faculty members often encounter. They emphasized that the absence of Black faculty on college campuses is not due to lack of qualifications or interest of those faculty. Rather, some departments have never hired a Black faculty member, some have a revolving door through which Black faculty pass year after year, and still others will go for a long period after a Black faculty member leaves before hiring another Black faculty member (M. P. Bell et al., 2020).

Similarly, a 2019 study identified an "uneven playing field" for faculty of color, finding that faculty of color perceive they need to work harder than their White counterparts to gain legitimacy (Stolzenberg et al., 2019). Among interview participants, 70.2% of Black faculty, 70.2% of Asian faculty, 70.6% of Latinx faculty, and 66.7% of Native American faculty reported that extensive stress and longer hours contribute to their feelings of discrimination and job insecurity (Stolzenberg et al., 2019).

The challenges that faculty, staff, and students of color face in the predominantly White ecosystems typical of academia include tokenism, marginalization, racial microaggressions, and a dissonance between the culture of the academy and their own racial/ethnic identity. For example, an interview study of 118 faculty of color[1] at a PWI examined how institutional evaluation systems and individual biases toward faculty of color paint them as illegitimate scholars, devaluing their scholarship and creating epistemic exclusion (Settles et al., 2019). The researchers found that the formal hierarchies of evaluation and metrics that ostensibly assess the quality of scholarship tend to value quantitative over qualitative research and theory-based over practical studies. The informal processes that devalue the scholarship of faculty of color include lack of recognition, legitimacy, and comprehension by their White counterparts. Some of the coping mechanisms employed by faculty of color included seeking validation, support, and valuation of their work from outside their institution (Settles et al., 2019). Settles et al. (2019) contend that epistemic exclusion is a form of gatekeeping in the academy that negatively affects the recruitment, promotion, and retention of faculty of color and suggest three ways in which PWIs can reduce the effects of epistemic exclusion on faculty of color: heightened awareness of epistemic exclusion, realignment of values and practices, and accountability.[2]

In terms of the LGBTQ+ status of faculty, Tilcsik et al. (2015) concluded that while prior studies have indicated that "lesbian and gay workers are often found in occupations that are traditionally associated with the opposite sex" (p. 447), other factors appear to influence career aspirations of individuals in these two groups. Specifically, Tilcsik et al. identified the promise of task independence, the occupation's requirement for individuals to be socially perceptive, or both factors as influences on gay and lesbian individuals' gravitation to academia. The authors described "task independence" as "the worker's ability to perform . . . tasks with limited dependence on the work activities of others" (p. 453). Faculty job descriptions tend to correspond to this form of task independence. Moreover, according to the authors, lesbian and gay individuals tend to be more perceptive of their social surroundings due to heightened coping skills forged by the need to perceive threats of stigmatization in early adolescence (Tilcsik et al., 2015). This acquired skill is an asset in positions where it is valued, including teaching.

Indeed, Tilcsik et al.'s (2015) analysis of survey data regarding occupations in which lesbian and gay individuals are well represented revealed that college faculty ranked ninth of 15 occupations with the highest proportion of gay and lesbian workers. In their analysis they controlled for a variety of factors such as levels of education, urban and non-urban settings, race, and age (Tilcsik et al., 2015). As faculty composition relates to mentorship and role modeling, lesbian and gay students may have access to faculty empathy and support from lesbian and gay faculty members who are comfortable providing such guidance. At most U.S. colleges and universities, many faculty and staff members, representing diverse sexual and gender identities, indicate through rainbow logos on their office doors a promise of support and sanctuary to LGBTQ+ students (American Psychological Association, 2015).

While we have discussed aspects of specific groups, another important consideration is that an individual's experience within higher education is not dependent on a single characteristic. In fact, an expanding area of research has identified the importance of the intersectionality of multiple characteristics, such as race, gender, and sexual orientation. The Settles et al. (2019) study revealed that variability in experiences of epistemic exclusion existed between disciplines and due to the intersectionality of race, gender, and nationality. Rangel (2020) illustrated through a qualitative study "that academic freedom—the ostensible bedrock of the U.S. university system—is in fact a stratified freedom drawn across academic-rank lines, reflecting the racial and gender hierarchies of larger society, and that the culture of the academy encourages conformity rather than ethical risk-taking" (p. 365). For many academic leaders it can be too easy to think of our students or employees according to how they are described on a demographic data sheet, overlooking the uniqueness each individual brings to our campus community through their particular set of characteristics and experiences.

Current Political Considerations

Over the last decade, DEI issues have become increasingly controversial within local, state, and national politics. After efforts by the Obama administration to address issues of structural racism within the federal government, an executive order by the Trump administration in 2020 banned federal agencies and contractors from conducting diversity and inclusion training that promoted "divisive concepts" (Executive Order No. 13950, 2020). CRT—perhaps because of its name—emerged as the synonym for any topic involving race. Education administrators, scholars, and organizations such as the American Bar Association came forward in defense of CRT as a construct for understanding the current state of race relations in the nation. However, many parents, legislators, and activists also objected to the use of CRT (or any teaching of racial issues) in schools out of concern that it heightened racial tensions. The executive order was overturned in 2021 by the Biden administration (Guynn, 2021); though it remains a controversial topic within some states. Some legislatures have banned the teaching of CRT in public schools, claiming that learning about race creates division (Impelli, 2021).

President Biden issued five executive orders during the 1st week of his presidency that specifically addressed racial equity and social justice. The first order was a general order calling on all federal government departments and agencies to address racial equity in policy and practice. The other orders (a) directed the Department of Housing and Urban Development (HUD) to address racial disparities, (b) ended the use of private prisons by the federal government, (c) committed the federal government to strengthening its relationship with tribal nations and their sovereignty, and (d) opposed anti-Asian and Pacific Islander discrimination (The White House, 2021). Additional executive orders by President Biden addressed issues that disproportionately affected people of color, such as COVID-19 relief, hunger and food insecurity (affecting almost 25% of Black families and 20% of Latinx families), and the student loan debt freeze (The White House, 2021). These efforts have not been without objection by some in the Republican party, however.

It is against this ever-shifting backdrop that U.S. colleges and universities must determine how best to approach matters of DEI, as many of their past, present, and future stakeholders, including students, alumni, boards, and legislators, may hold limited—if not negative—perceptions of these issues and the role of higher education in addressing them.

Supporting Diversity on Campus

U.S. colleges and universities have struggled to address the structural inequities faced by students, faculty, and staff whose experiences do not necessarily fit within the White male cultural foundations on which American higher education has been built. As more individuals with diverse racial/ethnic, sexual, and gender identities and physical abilities have arrived on campus, however, pressures have mounted to provide equitable quality teaching, learning, and working experiences to all. Academic leaders who wrestle with this responsibility have looked to theories and frameworks to help shape institutional policies—with limited success. These inequities are among the challenges that U.S. colleges and universities are seeking to address through DEI initiatives.

One effort that has become increasingly widespread is the hiring of senior diversity officers as a means of ensuring a coordinated and executive-level approach to fostering more equitable and inclusive campuses and cultures (Wilson, 2007). A report from the American Council on Education identified three primary models for this role (D. A. Williams & Wade-Golden, 2007). The *collaborative* officer model is typically a single person (possibly with some administrative support) who focuses on building relations and coordinating efforts across the institution. The *unit-based* model includes a senior officer, supported by one more professional staff. The *portfolio* model adds additional diversity units that report directly to the senior diversity officer. These roles have also become cabinet-level positions, with direct access to the president.

This work must involve more than creating a new position, however. In 2019, Chun and Evans asserted that "too often diversity is seen as an add-on to the educational process—nice to have, but a luxury" (p. 1). Written in the year preceding the BLM movement's rise and the COVID-19 pandemic, this statement may have been accurate when it was published, but the ensuing years have lent new urgency and necessity to higher education's engagement with DEI initiatives. Indeed, patience for change is a condition now past. To address institutional stakeholders' concerns and create a more diverse, equitable, and inclusive campus environment, academic leaders might consider using Chun and Evans's (2019) framework for conducting an effective, meaningful DEI self-examination. The "dimensions" of their approach are:

1. Developing a common definition of *diversity* and *inclusion*
2. Defining the academic/mission-centered case for diversity and inclusion

3. Assessing compositional and relational demography
4. Evaluating strategic diversity infrastructure
5. Implementing systemic diversity strategic planning based on data analytics, collaborative input, accountability metrics, and benchmarking
6. Creating an asset inventory of diversity education and professional development programs for faculty, administrators, staff, and students
7. Evaluating the climate, culture, and readiness for diversity transformation (p. xii).

In the summer of 2020, amid the COVID-19 pandemic, a highly publicized series of police–Black citizen tragedies inflamed the passions of the nation. When a police officer pinned down George Floyd by a knee to his neck long enough for Floyd to die—with the event captured on an ubiquitous camera phone—it set off a national outcry. Floyd's murder accelerated movement toward resolving DEI-related issues on college campuses. The pandemic had already locked down or limited access to these institutions, and meetings by administrators were often through immediate internet-based audiovisual conferencing programs such as Zoom. As a result, higher education administrators could confer immediately with colleagues—without having to confront students protesting and performing sit-ins at their office. Instant communication demanded quick response time, but COVID-19 allowed physical distance for easier reflection as well as the ability to caucus quickly to get the response right. While some administrators' initial statements were somewhat tone deaf and required revisions, in all, U.S. college and university responses to these crises bent toward justice, in line with the predominant and ongoing national sentiment regarding these issues. Colleges and universities often followed their statements with programs that were greatly assisted by virtual technology, such as free conferences that brought DEI issues and potential solutions to wide audiences (Bryan, 2020).

The pandemic also highlighted a significant rise in hate crimes against the AAPI community. Prior to 2016, hate crimes against these segments of the U.S. population had decreased for 2 consecutive decades, but they spiked during the pandemic. The top five states where hate crimes have occurred have been California, New York, Washington, Texas, and Illinois (Chitkara et al., 2021). In May 2021, a panel of Asians and Asian Americans from universities in California and Florida offered various suggestions in how higher education institutions could address the issues specifically related to anti-Asian hate crimes, although the suggestions could apply to dealing with hate crimes in general. The suggestions included celebrating the democratic ideals of America; telling a broader and more inclusive history in K–12 schools; promoting organizations, including one's own, that engage in clear and positive actions to embrace DEI initiatives; highlighting achievers within an organization who are from minority groups; sharing stories from representatives of various minority groups throughout social media; and conducting audits of the organization's commitment and action to meet DEI goals, including asking the tough questions (Chitkara et al., 2021). Panelists emphasized the role of leadership and especially mentorship in providing a safe and enriching educational and human development environment. For institutions of higher education, active and highly supportive mentorship is an essential pillar of the education process—whether for students, faculty, or staff.

Much can be (and probably should be) learned from MSIs, that specifically focus on supporting underrepresented populations in higher education. For example, one institution with a majority Latinx student population, Florida International University in Miami, recently published a study on how its Cuban American community viewed U.S.–Cuba relations, seeking to inform national and local leaders and policymakers on this issue of international and domestic relations (Steven J. Green School of International & Public Affairs, 2019). Such research demonstrates how HSIs can provide insights into vital issues of subgroups within the Latinx community. These activities are particularly important as more PWIs are becoming HSIs due to shifting demographics. Earning HSI status should be intentional and strategic, as these students—like all others from diverse backgrounds—bring their own expectations to the campus. Administrators should prepare the campus to be truly Hispanic serving and not merely Hispanic enrolling or Hispanic dwelling (Brownlee, 2021).

Many colleges and universities, including those once built on native lands, have begun to actively recognize their intertwined histories with native peoples (see chapter 7). Miami University in Ohio may have one of the most long-standing relationships with the tribe upon which their university is build and with which they share a name (Weingartner, 2021). In 1972, the chief of the Miami Tribe visited the university unannounced and struck up a relationship with the university president. That visit gave birth to a 50-year relationship, shepherded by the Myaamia Center, a joint initiative of the tribe and the university, which conducts research to preserve the tribe's culture and language and to expose members of the Miami university community to the tribe and its culture. The relationship also supports members of the tribe to pursue their college education at the University, while receiving tailored financial and academic supports – with nearly 40 students now enrolled and graduation rates well exceeding the national average (Weissman, 2021).

Strategic and thoughtful supports should be available to groups within a college or university, regardless of the size of the student population. For example, beyond federal and state requirements, a robust program to assist faculty, staff, and students with disabilities must begin with the institution's unwavering recognition of the contributions that members with disabilities make, as well as aggressive and relentless provision of innovative solutions to the challenges they face. Access to services should be as easy and direct as possible, such as at the University of Pennsylvania, which includes a contact link for health and wellness support on the first page of its website.[3] Resources provided elsewhere include the Accessibility Resource Center at the University of New Mexico (n.d.) and a Q&A page for students with disabilities regarding services at Brigham Young University's University Accessibility Center (n.d.).

Building on our forced migration to online meetings and instruction during the pandemic, colleges and universities can make online opportunities for engagement in DEI activities available to all who are willing to participate and navigate their virtual meeting portal. For example, in 2021, The Ohio State Office of Diversity and Inclusion, in its Education for Citizenship Discussion Series, held forums on "Becoming Weavers in a Divided Nation" and "Race and Democracy in America," featuring its new president (Office of Diversity and Inclusion, The Ohio State University, n.d.). The Texas A&M University School of Law, almost immediately upon changing to online instruction, began a series of legal forums on solving pandemic-related legal issues, including immigration concerns and legal remedies related to the Coronavirus Aid, Relief, and Economic Security Act (Helge et al., 2020). The Massachusetts Institute of Technology took its DEI planning directly to its stakeholders—all of them. In the "Composition" folder of its DEI@MIT website, MIT published a draft plan for improving its DEI efforts and asked members of the MIT community to provide feedback by editing the document as they saw fit (Institute Community and Equity Office, MIT, n.d.).

With the pandemic-cloistered world more attuned to the news cycle as a way to stay connected with the outside world, colleges and universities were compelled to be responsive to DEI issues. At the University of Minnesota, for example, the Office for Equity and Diversity recognized that it was the "epicenter" following George Floyd's death. Office staff immediately produced statements on the case and trial of the Minneapolis police officer charged with his murder, as well as publishing a message from the university's president. Through these messages, the University of Minnesota not only presented its leadership's collective opinion on the tragedy but also used the moment to present, again, its numerous DEI-related resources and programs (Office for Equity and Diversity, University of Minnesota, n.d.). The university also made its position clear regarding the rise of violence against Asians and Asian Americans since the beginning of the COVID-19 pandemic.

Concern about violence toward the Asian population was echoed throughout U.S. colleges and universities, including a very pointed and thorough message by the associate chancellor and chief diversity officer of the

University of California, Merced. This message included links to antiracism resources, a "radical healing session," and an electronic mailing list for ongoing DEI initiatives (University of California, Merced, n.d.). Higher education institutions should continue to assess their environment. At the time of this writing, antisemitic activity is rising throughout the country and is likely to seep onto college campuses—again (Kogen, 2021).

College and university leaders cannot allow lag times when stakeholders raise concerns regarding DEI issues in their campus community. No longer can these concerns be overshadowed by other matters. Leaders who fail to incorporate DEI themes into programs, policies, and activities can expect pushback by those individuals who are seeking a more inclusive institution.

Conclusion

In this book we submit that there are four key principles of academic leadership and governance: being mission centric; adapting to environmental changes; committing to democratic ideals; and modeling inclusive excellence, equity, and positive social change. DEI efforts support each of these principles. All institutions, regardless of their individual missions, have a responsibility to prepare their students to be productive members of a diverse global society.

Likewise, institutional sustainability and viability are dependent on the ability to respond to the demographic and societal shifts discussed in this chapter. A commitment to democratic ideals is at the core of the push for a more diverse and equitable educational system. Colleges and universities can and should be models for the inclusivity and positive social change we would like others to emulate.

While this chapter is wide ranging, it is certainly not comprehensive. As we noted at the beginning, the evolving landscape of diversity in higher education simply does not permit a definitive work on the topic. Despite what is here, there is plenty that is not, such as the mental health challenges diverse students face; the obstacles people of faith (especially non-Christians) face in institutions of higher education; the sordid politics surrounding the initial application of the GI Bill as it pertained to Black veterans; effective communication to stakeholders who do not see the value of diversity; and, along those lines, coping with the backlash leveled at administrations who do establish DEI as a priority for their institution. This chapter does not address improving the pipeline for diverse leaders in higher education, and for that matter how best to increase the pool of diverse faculty members, particularly in such areas as women in STEM fields. New concerns arise daily. As demand increases for senior administrators with responsibilities for DEI priorities on campuses across the country, how does any institution help establish them for success? Turnover is also likely to become an issue.

Leadership in higher education is a practical, task-oriented duty, but it is also an acceptance of a moral responsibility. For any number of compelling reasons, providing chairs at the higher education table for all sectors of our society not only taps into key insights and perspectives to advance the mission of an academic institution—it is simply the right thing to do. Understanding the issues behind the drive for DEI within higher education is the first step toward enhancing DEI's mission and purpose. The second step is the effective implementation of a plan to bring an institution's DEI vision to fruition. The days of posting slogans and unfulfilled promises have passed. The success of any college or university leader will, from this time forward, be measured by the degree to which every member of the campus community shares in the institution's measurements of success.

Notes

1. The composition of respondents was 47% Asian, 25% Black, 22% Latinx, and 5% Native (Settles et al., 2019).

2. For additional information, we encourage readers to explore the expansive academic and professional literature on this topic. As a starting place, Abel and Gonzalez (2020) suggested a social justice framework to better support faculty of color, and hence students; Pecci et al. (2020) developed a literature review of culturally competent leadership in higher education; and L. Torres (2019) proposed a framework for retention of faculty of color.

3. See https://www.upenn.edu for details.

References

Abel, Y., & Gonzalez, I. (2020). Using a social justice continuum to better support faculty of color in higher education settings. In C. A. Mullen (Ed.), *Handbook of social justice interventions in education* (pp. 1–26). Springer. https://doi.org/10.1007/978-3-030-29553-0_117-1

Ahtone, T., & Lee, R. (2020, May 7). Ask who paid for America's universities. *The New York Times.* https://www.nytimes.com/2020/05/07/opinion/land-grant-universities-native-americans.html

Aiello, T. (2016). *The battle for the souls of Black folk.* Praeger.

American Psychological Association. (2015). *Proud and prepared: A guide for LGBT students navigating graduate training.* https://www.apa.org/apags/resources/lgbt-guide.pdf

Americans With Disabilities Act, 42 U.S.C. §§ 12132 et seq. (2021)

Anderson, J. (1988). *The education of Blacks in the South, 1860–1935*. University of North Carolina Press.

Bell, D. (1992). *Faces at the bottom of the well: The permanence of racism*. Basic Books.

Bell, M. P., Berry, D., Leopold, J., & Nkomo, S. (2020). Making Black lives matter in academia: A Black feminist call for collective action against anti-blackness in the academy. *Gender, Work & Organization, 28*(S1), 39–57. https://doi.org/10.1111/gwao.12555

Benedict College. (n.d.). *History*. https://www.benedict.edu/about-benedict/history/

Bentley, G. R. (1955). *A history of the Freedmen's Bureau*. University of Pennsylvania Press. https://doi.org/10.9783/9781512814330

Berea College. (n.d.). *Berea College early history*. https://www.berea.edu/about/history/

Blakemore, E. (2021, April 20). *How the GI Bill's promise was denied to a million Black WWII veterans*. History. https://www.history.com/news/gi-bill-black-wwii-veterans-benefits

Blumenfeld, W. J. (2012). LGBTQ campus climate: The good and the still very bad. *Diversity & Democracy, 15*(1), 20–21. https://www.aacu.org/publications-research/periodicals/lgbtq-campus-climate-good-and-still-very-bad

Brown v. Board of Education, 347 U.S. 483 (1954)

Brownlee, M. I. (2021, April 19). *The rise of Hispanic-serving institutions and the path forward*. EdSurge. https://www.edsurge.com/news/2021-04-19-the-rise-of-hispanic-serving-institutions-and-the-path-forward

Bryan, J. (2020, September 11). *How 2020 accelerated conversations on diversity, equity and inclusion*. Smarter With Gartner. https://www.gartner.com/smarterwithgartner/how-2020-accelerated-conversations-on-diversity-equity-and-inclusion/

Byrd, W. C., Brunn-Bevel, R. J., & Ovink, S. M. (Eds.). (2019). *Intersectionality and higher education: Identity and inequality on college campuses*. Rutgers University Press.

Cardemil, E. V., Millán, F., & Aranda, E. (2019). A new, more inclusive name: [Editorial]. *Journal of Latinx Psychology, 7*(1), 1–5. https://doi.org/10.1037/lat0000129

Chitkara, A., Spector, S., & Tanaka, P. (2021). *Stop AAPI hate: The role of communicators*. Museum of Public Relations. https://www.youtube.com/watch?v=WWmT_p87sHc

Chun, E., & Evans, A. (2019). *Conducting an institutional diversity audit in higher education: A practitioner's guide to systematic diversity transformation*. Stylus.

Crenshaw, K. (1989). Demarginalizing the intersection of race and sex: A Black feminist critique of antidiscrimination doctrine, feminist theory and antiracist politics. *University of Chicago Legal Forum, 1989*(1), Article 8. https://chicagounbound.uchicago.edu/uclf/vol1989/iss1/8/

Crenshaw, K. (1991). Mapping the margins: Intersectionality, identity politics, and violence against women of color. *Stanford Law Review, 43*(6), 1241–1299. https://doi.org/10.2307/1229039

Crum, S. J. (2007). Indian activism, the Great Society, Indian self-determination, and the drive for an Indian college or university, 1964–71. *American Indian Culture and Research Journal, 31*(1), 1–20. https://doi.org/10.17953/aicr.31.1.l0l0653114863637

Curran, R. E. (n.d.). *Georgetown University: A brief history*. 2021–2022 undergraduate bulletin, Georgetown University. https://bulletin.georgetown.edu/about/guhistory/

Darling-Hammond, L. (2018, April 11). Kerner at 50: Educational equity still a dream deferred. *LPI Blog*. https://learningpolicyinstitute.org/blog/kerner-50-educational-equity-still-dream-deferred

de Brey, C., Musu, L., McFarland, J., Wilkinson-Flicker, S., Diliberti, M., Zhang, A., Branstetter, C., & Wang, X. (2019). *Status and trends in the education of racial and ethnic groups 2018*. National Center for Education Statistics, U.S. Department of Education. https://nces.ed.gov/pubs2019/2019038.pdf

Delgado, R. (1984). The imperial scholar: Reflections on a review of civil rights literature. *University of Pennsylvania Law Review, 132*(3), 561–578. https://doi.org/10.2307/3311882

Delgado, R., & Stefancic, J. (2017). *Critical race theory: An introduction* (3rd ed.). New York University Press.

Diamond, J. (1999). *Guns, germs, and steel: The fates of human societies.* Norton.

DREAM Act of 2017, S.1615, Sec.3(b)(1)(B), and H.R.3440, Sec.3(b)(1)(B) (2017)

Ellis, J. J. (2007). *American creation: Triumphs and tragedies at the founding of the republic.* Knopf.

Exec. Order No. 13950, 85 Fed. Reg. 60683 (2020)

Freire, P. (2018). *Pedagogy of the oppressed: 50th anniversary edition* (M. B. Ramos, Trans.). Bloomsbury Academic. (Original work published 1970)

Gaillot, A.-D. (2018, February 14). *How historically Black colleges transformed America* [Interview with S. Nelson, Jr.]. The Outline. https://theoutline.com/post/3395/tell-them-we-are-rising-stanley-nelson-jr-interview

Garcia, G. A. (2018). Decolonizing Hispanic-serving institutions: A framework for organizing. *Journal of Hispanic Higher Education, 17*(2), 132–147. https://doi.org/10.1177/1538192717734289

George, J. (2021, January 11). *A lesson on critical race theory*. American Bar Association. https://www.americanbar.org/groups/crsj/publications/human_rights_magazine_home/civil-rights-reimagining-policing/a-lesson-on-critical-race-theory/

Greenfield, N. M. (2021, January 9). So is critical race theory poisonous or illuminating? *University World News*. https://www.universityworldnews.com/post.php?story=2021010810452697

Guynn, J. (2021, January 20). President Joe Biden rescinds Donald Trump ban on diversity training about systemic racism. *USA Today*. https://www.usatoday.com/story/money/2021/01/20/biden-executive-order-overturns-trump-diversity-training-ban/4236891001/

Hales, D., & Edmonds, B. (2019). Intragenerational cultural evolution and ethnocentrism. *Journal of Conflict Resolution, 63*(5), 1283–1309. https://doi.org/10.1177/0022002718780481

Hall, L. K. (2015). Which of these things is not like the other: Hawaiians and other Pacific Islanders are not Asian Americans, and all Pacific Islanders are not Hawaiian. *American Quarterly, 67*(3), 727–747. https://doi.org/10.1353/aq.2015.0050

Hamilton, L., & Nielsen, K. (2021, March 2). Op-ed: Is it possible to fix the UC's system of haves and have-nots? *Los Angeles Times*. https://www.latimes.com/opinion/story/2021-03-02/university-california-riverside-merced-state-funding

Hanks, A., Solomon, D., & Weller, C. E. (2018, February 21). *Systematic inequality*. Center for American Progress. https://www.americanprogress.org/issues/race/reports/2018/02/21/447051/systematic-inequality/

Haring, M. J. (2009). The case for a conceptual base for minority mentoring programs. *Peabody Journal of Education, 74*(2), 5–14. https://doi.org/10.1207/s15327930pje7402_2

Harper, B. E. (2019). African American access to higher education: The evolving role of historically Black colleges and universities. *American Academic, 3*, 109–128. http://co.aft.org/files/article_assets/F3AFCF46-AB7A-29CF-CA9E1AE-AC8FA4F78.pdf

Helge, T., Lucas, G., & Probasco, B. (2020, April 6). *Individual incentives under the CARES Act: What's in it for me?* [Video]. Texas A&M University School of Law. https://info.law.tamu.edu/cares-act-webinar-series

Higher Education Act of 1965, Pub. L. No. 89-329 (1965)

Hinton, A. O., Jr., Vue, Z., Termini, C. M., Taylor, B. L., Shuler, H. D., & McReynolds, M. R. (2020). Mentoring minority trainees. *EMBO Reports, 21*(10), e51269. https://doi.org/10.15252/embr.202051269

Humphrey, H. H. (1968). *Beyond civil rights: A new day of equality*. Random House.

Hussar, B., Zhang, J., Hein, S., Wang, K., Roberts, A., Cui, J., Smith, M., Bullock Mann, F., Barmer, A., & Dilig, R. (2020). *The condition of education 2020*. National Center for Education Statistics, U.S. Department of Education. https://nces.ed.gov/pubs2020/2020144.pdf

Impelli, M. (2021, May 11). North Carolina seventh state set to ban critical race theory in schools. *Newsweek*. https://www.newsweek.com/north-carolina-seventh-state-set-ban-critical-race-theory-schools-1590620

Institute Community and Equity Office, Massachusetts Institute of Technology. (n.d.). *DEI@MIT: Composition*. https://deiactionplan.mit.edu/composition

Jaschik, S. (2021, April 13). Is diversity moral? Educational? *Inside Higher Ed.* https://www.insidehighered.com/news/2021/04/13/study-suggests-american-colleges-explain-diversity-way-appeals-white-not-black

Josephy, A. M., Jr. (1993). Introduction. In B. Ballantine & I. Ballantine (Eds.), *The Native Americans: An illustrated history* (pp. 14–21). Turner.

Kamarck, K. N. (2019, June 5). *Diversity, inclusion, and equal opportunity in the armed services: Background and issues for Congress* (CRS Report No. R44321). Congressional Research Service. https://crsreports.congress.gov/product/pdf/R/R44321

Kogen, S. (2021, February 2). It's time we taught anti-semitism. *Inside Higher Ed.* https://www.insidehighered.com/views/2021/02/02/anti-semitism-major-problem-campuses-and-students-must-be-educated-about-it-opinion

Ladson-Billings, G. (1995). Toward a theory of culturally relevant pedagogy. *American Educational Research Journal, 32*(3), 465–491. https://doi.org/10.3102/00028312032003465

Ladson-Billings, G. (2014). Culturally relevant pedagogy 2.0: A.k.a. the remix. *Harvard Educational Review, 84*(1), 74–84. https://doi.org/10.17763/haer.84.1.p2rj131485484751

Ladson-Billings, G., & Tate, W. (1995). Toward a critical race theory of education. *Teachers College Record, 97*, 47–68.

Lee, G. (2019, October 11). Native American education at Dartmouth develops over time. *The Dartmouth.* https://www.thedartmouth.com/article/2019/10/native-american-education-at-dartmouth-develops-over-time

Levine, S. S., & Stark, D. (2015, December 9). Diversity makes you brighter. *The New York Times*, A35.

Lukens, J. G. (1976, April 13–17). *Ethnocentric speech: Its nature and implications* [Paper presentation]. Annual Meeting of the International Communication Association, Portland, Oregon. https://files.eric.ed.gov/fulltext/ED140378.pdf

Marsden, G. M. (1994). *The soul of the American university*. Oxford University Press.

Mayhew, M., Grunwald, H., & Dey, E. (2005) Curriculum matters: Creating a positive climate for diversity from the student perspective. *Research in Higher Education, 46*, 389–412.

McAdam, D. (1988). *Freedom summer*. Oxford University Press.

McCormack, M., & Novello, A. (2019, November 26). *The true state of the U.S. economy*. Century Foundation. https://tcf.org/content/report/true-state-u-s-economy/

Morrill Act of 1862, 7 U.S.C. § 301 et seq. (1862)

Morrill Act of 1890, 26 Stat. 417, 7 U.S.C. § 321 et seq. (1890)

Nash, M. A. (2019). Entangled pasts: Land-grant colleges and American Indian dispossession. *History of Education Quarterly, 59*(4), 437–467. https://doi.org/10.1017/heq.2019.31

National Center for Education Statistics. (2019, February). *Indicator 9: Students with disabilities*. https://nces.ed.gov/programs/raceindicators/indicator_rbd.asp

Newkirk, P. (2020). *Diversity, Inc.: The fight for racial equality in the workplace*. Bold Type Books.

Noe-Bustamante, L., Mora, L., & Lopez, M. H. (2020). *About one-in-four U.S. Hispanics have heard of Latinx, but just 3% use it*. Pew Research Center. https://www.pewresearch.org/hispanic/wp-content/uploads/sites/5/2020/08/PHGMD_2020.08.11_Latinx_FINAL.pdf

O'Donovan, M. M. (2010). Cognitive diversity in the global academy: Why the voices of persons with cognitive disabilities are vital to intellectual diversity. *Journal of Academic Ethics, 8*(3), 171–185. https://doi.org/10.1007/s10805-010-9116-x

Office for Civil Rights. (1991, January 3). *Historically Black colleges and universities and higher education desegregation*. U.S. Department of Education. https://www2.ed.gov/about/offices/list/ocr/docs/hq9511.html

Office for Equity and Diversity, University of Minnesota. (n.d.). *Welcome to OED.* https://diversity.umn.edu/

Office of Diversity and Inclusion, The Ohio State University. (n.d.). *Education for citizenship events: 2021 discussion series.* https://odi.osu.edu/education-citizenship-events

Paris, D., & Alim, H. S. (2014). What are we seeking to sustain through culturally sustaining pedagogy? A loving critique forward. *Harvard Educational Review, 84*(1), 85–100. https://doi.org/10.17763/haer.84.1.982l873k2ht16m77

Pecci, A., Frawley, J., & Nguyen, T. (2020). On the critical, morally driven, self-reflective agents of change and transformation: A literature review on culturally competent leadership in higher education. In J. Frawley, G. Russell, & J. Sherwood (Eds.), *Cultural competence and the higher education sector: Australian perspectives, policies and practice* (pp. 59–81). Springer. https://doi.org/10.1007/978-981-15-5362-2_5

Plessy v. Ferguson. (1896). 163 U.S. 537 (more) 16 S. Ct. 1138, 41 L. Ed. 256, 1896 U.S. LEXIS 3390

Poon, O., Squire, D., Kodama, C., Byrd, A., Chan, J., Manzano, L., Furr, S., & Bishundat, D. (2016). A critical review of the model minority myth in selected literature on Asian Americans and Pacific Islanders in higher education. *Review of Educational Research, 86*(2), 469–502. https://doi.org/10.3102/0034654315612205

Postsecondary National Policy Institute. (2021, June 12). *LGBTQ students in higher education.* https://pnpi.org/lgbtq-students-in-higher-education/

Qureshi, F. (2016, February 10). Native Americans: Negative impacts of media portrayals, stereotypes. *The Journalist's Resource.* https://journalistsresource.org/race-and-gender/native-americans-media-stereotype-redskins/

Rangel, N. (2020). The stratification of freedom: An intersectional analysis of activist-scholars and academic freedom at U.S. public universities. *Equity & Excellence in Education, 53*(3), 365–381. https://doi.org/10.1080/10665684.2020.1775158

Ridingin, L., Longwell-Grice, R., & Thunder, A. (2008, December 1). In our own best interest: A (brief) history of tribal colleges in America. *Academic Advising Today.* https://nacada.ksu.edu/Resources/Academic-Advising-Today/View-Articles/In-Our-Own-Best-Interest-Tribal-Colleges-in-America.aspx

Rudolph, F. (1962). *The American college and university: A history.* Random House.

Salinas, Jr., C. (2020). The complexity of the "x" in *Latinx*: How Latinx/a/o students relate to, identify with, and understand the term *Latinx. Journal of Hispanic Higher Education, 19*(2), 149–168. https://doi.org/10.1177/1538192719900382

Salinas, C., & Lozano, A. (2021). The history of the term Latinx. In E. G. Murillo et al. (Eds.), *Handbook of Latinos and education.* Routledge.

Scharrón-del Río, M. R., & Aja, A. A. (2020). Latinx: Inclusive language as liberation praxis. *Journal of Latinx Psychology, 8*(1), 7–20. https://doi.org/10.1037/lat0000140

Servicemen's Readjustment Act of 1944, Pub. L. No. 78-346, 58 Stat. 284m (1944)

Settles, I. H., Buchanan, N. T., & Dotson, K. (2019). Scrutinized but not recognized: (In)visibility and hypervisibility experiences of faculty of color. *Journal of Vocational Behavior, 113*, 62–74. https://doi.org/10.1016/j.jvb.2018.06.003

Slater, R. B. (1994). The Blacks who first entered the world of White higher education. *Journal of Blacks in Higher Education, 4*, 47–56. https://doi.org/10.2307/2963372

Snyder, T. D. (Ed.). (1993). *120 years of American education: A statistical portrait.* National Center for Education Statistics, U.S. Department of Education. https://nces.ed.gov/pubsearch/pubsinfo.asp?pubid=93442

Steven J. Green School of International & Public Affairs. (2019). *2018 FIU CUBA-poll: How Cuban Americans in Miami view U.S. policies toward Cuba.* Florida International University. https://cri.fiu.edu/research/cuba-poll/2018-fiu-cuba-poll.pdf

Stolzenberg, E. B., Eagan, K., Zimmerman, H. B., Lozano, J. B., Cesar-Davis, N. M., Aragon, M. C., & Rios-Aguilar, C. (2019). *Undergraduate teaching faculty: The HERI faculty survey 2016–2017.* Higher Education Research Institute, University of California, Los Angeles. https://www.heri.ucla.edu/monographs/HERI-FAC2017-monograph.pdf

Sumner, W. G. (1940). *Folkways: A study of the sociological importance of usages, manners, customs, mores, and morals.* Ginn and Company. (Original work published 1906)

Tani, K. (2013, November 5). The long history of the Indian Child Welfare Act [Review of the article "Remember the 'forgotten child': The American Indian child welfare crisis of the 1960s and 1970s," by M. D. Jacobs]. *Journal of Things We Like (Lots).* https://legalhist.jotwell.com/the-long-history-of-the-indian-child-welfare-act/

Taylor, O., Apprey, C. B., Hill, G., McGrann, L., & Wang, J. (2010). Diversifying the faculty. *Peer Review, 12*(3). https://www.aacu.org/publications-research/periodicals/diversifying-faculty

Thelin, J. (2011). *A history of American higher education.* Johns Hopkins University Press.

Tilcsik, A., Anteby, M., & Knight, C. R. (2015). Concealable stigma and occupational segregation: Toward a theory of gay and lesbian occupations. *Administrative Science Quarterly, 60*(3), 446–481. https://doi.org/10.1177/0001839215576401

Tintiangco-Cubales, A., & Duncan-Andrade, J. (2021). *Still fighting for ethnic studies: The origins, practices, and potential of community responsive pedagogy* [Unpublished manuscript].

Torres, L. (2019). *Retention of faculty of color.* Marquette Immersive Leadership Experience. https://www.marquette.edu/diversity/documents/retention-faculty-of-color-toolkit.pdf

Torres, V. (2004). The diversity among us: Puerto Ricans, Cuban Americans, Caribbean Americans, and Central and South Americans. *New Directions for Student Services, 2004*(105), 5–16. https://doi.org/10.1002/ss.112

University Accessibility Center, Brigham Young University. (n.d.). *Services offered.* https://uac.byu.edu/content/services-offered

University of California, Merced. (n.d.). *Office of equity, diversity and inclusion.* https://diversity.ucmerced.edu/

University of New Mexico. (n.d.). *Accessibility resource center.* https://arc.unm.edu/

U.S. Census Bureau. (2017, December 14). *High school completion rate is highest in U.S. history* [Press release]. https://www.census.gov/newsroom/press-releases/2017/educational-attainment-2017.html

Vidal-Ortiz, S., & Martinez, J. (2018). Latinx thoughts: Latindad with an x. *Latino Studies, 16,* 384–395. https://doi.org/10.1057/s41276-018-0137-8

Warder, G. (2015). *Horace Mann and the creation of the common school.* Disability History Museum. https://www.disabilitymuseum.org/dhm/edu/essay.html?id=42

Weingartner, T. (2021, December 10). *How neepwaantiinki has led to 50 years of partnership between Miami University and the Miami Tribe.* WVXU. https://www.wvxu.org/education/2021-12-10/miami-university-miami-tribe-mark-50-years-of-partnership.

Weissman, S. (2021, November 19). A relationship from a rocky past. *Inside HigherEd.* https://www.insidehighered.com/news/2021/11/19/miami-university-ohio-attracts-native-american-students.

The White House. (2021, January 26). *Fact sheet: President Biden to take action to advance racial equity and support underserved communities.* https://www.white-house.gov/briefing-room/statements-releases/2021/01/26/fact-sheet-president-biden-to-take-action-to-advance-racial-equity-and-support-underserved-communities/

Whittaker, J. A., Montgomery, B. L., & Martinez Acosta, V. G. (2015). Retention of underrepresented minority faculty: Strategic initiatives for institutional value proposition based on perspectives from a range of academic institutions. *Journal of Undergraduate Neuroscience Education, 13*(3), A136–A145. https://www.ncbi.nlm.nih.gov/pmc/articles/PMC4521729/

Williams, D. A., & Wade-Golden, K. (2007). *The chief diversity officer: A primer for college and university presidents.* American Council on Education.

Williams, P. J. (1991). *The alchemy of race and rights.* Harvard University Press.

Wilson, J. L. (2007). Emerging trend: Chief diversity officer phenomenon in higher education. *Journal of Negro Education, 82*(4), 433–445. https://doi.org/10.7709/jnegroeducation.82.4.0433

4

UNDERSTANDING
ACADEMIC ORGANIZATIONS

Among the most notable features of U.S. higher education are the rich diversity of institution types and the inherent complexity that accompanies their administration and management. This diversity has arisen not from any purposeful design but through a centuries-long evolutionary process that reflects the educational aspirations of myriad religious, individual, social, and governmental entities independently seeking to express their higher education ideals within a democratic society that permitted and encouraged organizational individuality and creativity.

Given this rich organizational diversity, how can the subject of administration and management be approached to account for the vast differences that exist? Leadership and decision-making by academic administrators, regardless of institution type, become more informed when they are accompanied by a basic understanding of the uniqueness of academic organizations on several levels: typological, organizational, and contextual.

Typological differences among higher education organizations are largely a function of historical development and institutional mission. Organizationally, colleges and universities share certain internal normative behaviors and processes that differentiate them from nonacademic organizations. Finally, each college or university must be understood within its own institutional context. Every institution of higher learning in the United States is idiosyncratic. Each possesses a unique history and organizational culture resulting from etiological circumstances determined by its founding; mission; level and source of resources; structure; and, most significantly, the institution's organizational ethos, which characterizes how its stakeholders have come to interact and behave collectively.

This chapter provides the reader with a broad overview of the academic organization and its internal operations. It addresses several important questions: How and why are academic organizations different from other organization types? What are the central characteristics and defining features of all academic organizations? Through what perspectives can the academic organization best be understood? What theories of leadership help understand these complex organizations? What decision-making models are effective in achieving institutional goals? A fundamental understanding of the challenges inherent in the administration and management of higher education organizations can best be achieved by addressing these key questions.

Defining College and University

What is a college? How does it differ from a university? These are deceptively simple questions, as there are often no clear answers. In the most basic sense, a university is an organization that offers advanced education (e.g., postsecondary or tertiary) and awards degrees based on completion of requirements in various academic disciplines. What then distinguishes a university from a college? Historically, in Europe, colleges operated under the umbrella of a university, with the university coordinating across multiple colleges and officially granting degrees. Many colleges were then semi-autonomous entities with responsibility for the teaching and development of their students. In fact, in England, it used to be not unusual for a college to leave one university and join another. In some ways, we still have such structures within larger universities in the United States. Universities are comprised of academic colleges and/or schools, but it is unlikely one would move between universities (despite the desires of some deans).

Today in the United States, the terms *university* and *college* are often used interchangeably when referring to standalone postsecondary degree-granting institutions, although a general distinction is often that colleges tend to be smaller and offer a more focused set of undergraduate academic degrees and maybe a handful of graduate degrees. Universities usually offer a more comprehensive set of academic programs, including doctoral programs. A few states, though not all, do not regulate the use of the term *university*. New York, which may have the most specific and stringent regulations, defines a university as

a higher educational institution offering a range of registered undergraduate and graduate curricula in the liberal arts and sciences and doctoral programs registered in at least three of the following discipline areas: agriculture, biological sciences, business, education, engineering, fine arts, health professions, humanities, physical sciences, and social sciences. (§224(1)(a); 8 NYCRR 3.29)[1]

Educational entities in New York that do not meet this definition are not permitted to use the term in their name.

While these definitions focus on the legal definitions and types of degrees offered, others have taken separate approaches. In *The Idea of a University* in 1852/1893, Cardinal John Henry Newman described the university as "the high protecting power of all knowledge and science, of fact and principle, of inquiry and discovery, of experimentation and speculation; it maps out the terrain of the intellect" (p. 459). Abraham Flexner (1930) shared similar lofty ambitions, stipulating that the modern university

> is not outside, but inside the general fabric of our era. It is not something apart, something historic, something that yields as little as possible to forces and influences that are more or less new. It is, on the contrary . . . , an expression of the ages, as well as an influence operating upon both present and future. (p. 3)

According to Kerr (1963), the 20th century witnessed the birth of the "multiversity," a conglomeration of the following communities:

> the community of the undergraduate and the community of the graduate; the community of the humanist, the community of the social scientist, and the community of the scientist; the communities of the professional schools; the community of all the nonacademic personnel; the community of the administrators. (p. 14)

In fact, Kerr's focus on the communities found within the multiversity illustrates our pillar of building democratic partnerships and also holds to the etymological origins of the word *university*. The Latin origin, *universitas magistrorum et scholarium,* translates to "community of teachers and scholars" and emphasizes the importance of higher education institutions being a shared community among faculty, staff, and students, who collectively work together to advance learning and engage in effective shared governance of the community.

Henry Tappan (1858), the president of the University of Michigan in the 1800s, summarized the university in this way:

> How simple the idea of a university! An association of eminent scholars in every department of human knowledge; together with books embodying the results of human investigation and thinking, and all the means of advancing and illustrating knowledge. How simple the law which is to govern this association!—That each member as a thinker, investigator, and teacher shall be a law unto himself, in his own department. (p. 7)

Kerr (1963), not quite as idealistic, wrote, "I have sometimes thought of [the modern university] as a series of individual faculty entrepreneurs held together by a common grievance over parking" (p. 15).

The uniqueness of colleges and universities resides both in their authority to provide and certify advanced levels of study and in their responsibility to determine how that authority is fulfilled by a professionalized core of academic experts. Any leader in the enterprise benefits from understanding the history of their institution as well as the centuries of history that have led to the modern university. The leader needs also to understand and help those within the university to understand that the institution has always evolved and will continue to grow and change. To reiterate Flexner's words, the university is "an expression of the ages, as well as an influence operating upon both present and future."

In many ways, these few words illustrate the connection between the pillars of being mission driven and adapting to change. They also implicitly demonstrate the tension that has existed in terms of restricting and expanding access to higher education: Some institutions reflected the restrictive nature of the times, while others led the way to build a more inclusive society. (See chapter 3, this volume, for a more detailed discussion of DEI).

The Components of Academic Organizations

We live in a world of organizations. Businesses, civic groups, churches, and other charitable entities are all organizations. Because of the ubiquity of organizations, for more than a century, scholars have been trying to answer the question "How does an organization go about doing what it does and with what consequence for its people, processes, products, and persistence?" (Weick, 1976, p. 1). According to Scott and Davis (2016), "Most analysts have conceived of organizations as *social structures created by individuals to support the collaborative pursuit of specified goals*" (p. 11, emphasis added).

The academic organization, however, often stands apart from other organizational types. James Perkins (1972), the former president of Cornell College, framed the complexity of the academic organization this way:

> Organizationally, the university is, in fact, one of the most complex structures in modern society; it is also increasingly archaic. It is complex because its formal structure does not describe either actual power or responsibilities; it is archaic because the functions it must perform are not and cannot be discharged through the formal structure provided in its charter. (p. 679)

This tension between the formal structure and the actual operation of the academic organization can be attributed, at least in part, to higher education institutions' long evolution and to the fact that an institution's focus of power lies, at least in part, within a guild of self-governing scholars. Indeed, this tension has fostered a great deal of theoretical exploration.

The study of organizations considers the production of knowledge relevant to problem-solving or decision-making within organizations; it serves as the foundation for much of this book, and it is at the core of a substantial portion of higher education study and research (see, e.g., Bastedo, 2012; Bess & Dee, 2007; and Manning, 2018, for more in-depth explorations of organizational theory as applied to higher education). Attempts to understand and characterize organizations, academic and otherwise, focus on seven common elements: strategy and goals, work, decision-making, formal structures, informal structures, people, and environment (Scott & Davis, 2016). How these elements are described here applies to a vast majority of higher education institutions in the United States, and they may not be as applicable to for-profit institutions or colleges and universities outside the United States.

Strategy and Goals

At their core, organizations are entities designed to accomplish certain goals. Goal setting determines what an organization intends to accomplish, and strategy defines how it will go about achieving its ambitions. However, most organizations must deal with goal complexity. That is, there is often a difference between the stated goals of an organization and the real goals that motivate individuals within the organization. In addition, support goals are necessary for maintaining the organization (Perrow, 1970). More than just setting goals, organizations also develop strategies to achieve those goals. Leaders make decisions about where they will operate, the type of product or service they will produce, and whom they will hire to perform the work.

Educational institutions, particularly those in the public sector, are often constrained in their ability to define their own goals and develop strategies to achieve them because their leaders do not control institutional budgets and have limited flexibility to adjust their workforce because of tenure and union rules. Yet within whatever constraints that exist, leaders must determine how best to define and achieve institutional goals. In fact, constraints can themselves drive strategy. For example, some public colleges and universities have begun to offer courses in other states, as it is easier to expand outside their home state because of fewer regulatory constraints elsewhere (Lane et al., 2013). Being able to operate in the midst of goal complexity and strategize within constraints is a key characteristic of successful academic leaders.

Whereas most bureaucratic organizations operate with high degrees of organizational rationality—that is, they are focused on the attainment of a specific goal or goals—academic organizations possess significant goal ambiguity. Do these organizations exist to teach or to perform research and create new knowledge? Do they provide services to the community, the state, or the nation? What goals are ascribed to the organization by its administration, faculty, trustees, alumni, students, parents, and community? Because of the diverse expectations that different constituencies place upon colleges and universities, higher education institutions are susceptible to myriad purposes that may be consigned to them by organizational stakeholders. This circumstance causes situations in which "not only do they often try to be all things to all people but they rarely have a single mission. Because their preferences are unclear, they also find it hard to decline additional goals" (Baldridge et al., 1978, p. 21).

Work

Work can mean many things, but for organizations, "*work* describes the tasks that the organization needs to accomplish in order to achieve the goals that it has set for itself" (Scott & Davis, 2016, p. 21). Analysis of work considers a variety of different factors, such as the amount of interdependence among different parts of the organization, which affects how the work is accomplished and how actors interact. As Wiener (1954) explained, "Organizations we must consider as something in which there is an interdependence between the several organized parts but in which this interdependence has degrees" (p. 322). This notion of degrees of interdependence led to the concept of organizational coupling, which describes how tightly or loosely connected two components are. For example, units in academic affairs tend to be much more independent of each other than units in student affairs, often resulting in a higher degree of interaction among student affairs administrators in different units than among faculty members in different departments.

It is also important to understand that the work of the academic organization requires a balance between professionalism and bureaucracy. Central to the concept of professionalism are individual autonomy and creativity to exercise one's unique professional knowledge. The question for any campus leader is how to maintain organizational control and direction without imposing undue influence on these embedded professional values. As Etzioni (1964) explained:

> Only if immune from ordinary social pressures and free to innovate, to experiment, to take risks without the usual social repercussions of failure, can a professional carry out his work effectively. It is this highly individualized principle which is diametrically opposed to the very essence of the organizational principle of control and coordination by superiors—i.e., the principle of administrative authority. (pp. 76–77)

Noted sociologist Blau (1974) focused on the inherent conflict between bureaucracy and professionalism when addressing the issue of authority in organizations:

> The various components of professionalism must be distinguished in analyzing its implications for hierarchical authority in organizations. Full-fledged professionalization entails not only expert skills but also a body of abstract knowledge underlying them, a self-governing association of professional peers, professional standards of workmanship and ethical conduct, and an orientation toward service. Some of these factors may easily come into conflict with the discipline required by bureaucratic authority. (p. 247)

In his research specific to academic organizations, Blau (1973) described colleges and universities as organizations bifurcated into two spheres, the bureaucratic and the academic, and outlined the organizational tension that arises between these centers of authority. Noting that academics claim exclusive authority over their own work, insist on professional independence, and set their own standards for competence in their disciplines, Blau (1973) stated:

> These claims to professional autonomy and self-regulation create potential conflicts with the bureaucratic authority of administrators, since administrative and professional considerations are often at variance, for example, when budgetary requirements conflict with optimum professional service to clients, or when administrative demands infringe upon the specialized responsibilities of experts. (p. 159)

Since the time of Blau's scholarship, however, substantial changes have arisen within college and university employment structures that further complicate the relationship between the bureaucratic and academic spheres.

More recently, scholars have problematized the relationship between the bureaucratic and academic realms of colleges and universities. They have called attention to the unbundling of the academic profession, which includes separating tasks to more defined expertise (Gehrke & Kezar, 2015; Rhoades & Torres-Olave, 2015). For example, more technical aspects of academic advising such as course scheduling and financial aid compliance have been shifting from faculty to professional advisors, though often with the idea that faculty should retain an active role in mentoring students. While the academic sphere of Blau's (1973, 1974) time was comprised primarily of full-time, tenure-track professors, colleges and universities now rely heavily on contingent part-time faculty to instruct their classes (Kezar & Dizon, 2019; U.S. Department of Education, 2020). This shift in faculty roles has generated increasing conflict between the bureaucratic and academic spheres, as the division of the faculty has raised new issues that did not exist when the faculty was more homogeneous. Although studies have shown that engaging contingent faculty in shared governance leads to more just and equitable decision-making (Kezar & Sam, 2014), their inclusion is frequently prohibited by their employment contracts, which usually do not compensate them for additional labor (e.g., serving on committees) beyond their contractual teaching requirements (Kezar & Dizon, 2020). Thus, current labor conditions complicate the relationship between the bureaucratic and academic spheres, as administrators, tenure-track faculty, and contingent faculty continue to attempt to create structures that allow their institutions to achieve their goals.

Decision-Making Processes

So messy is decision-making in academic organizations that it has been described as resembling a garbage can (Cohen et al., 1972). In their study of universities as organized anarchies, Cohen et al. (1972) suggested that academic organizations are collections of solutions looking for problems, issues, and feelings looking for decision opportunities to be vented, and decision makers looking for something to do. Thus, decision-making in academic organizations can be construed as a set of problems, solutions, and participants who move from one decision-making opportunity to another. The outcome of a decision is influenced by the availability of solutions, the people involved in the process, and the nature of the process. In such organizations, solutions are often uncoupled from decisions. While decision-making is believed to be a process to find a solution for a given problem, Cohen et al. (1972) averred, it is more like a complicated dance to align problems, solutions, and decision makers to allow action to occur.

Decision-making in all organizations is a complex process, but in higher education, leaders face decision-making challenges that are not frequently faced in other organizational types. Colleges and universities operate within a shared governance model, which is a system through which members of the campus community come together to make collective institutional decisions. Traditionally, shared governance primarily entailed faculty, administrators, and trustees working together to make decisions (Rhoades, 2005), but as higher education has evolved, the number of stakeholder groups included within shared governance systems has grown. At some institutions, shared governance now also includes accrediting agencies, alumni, employers, higher education councils and coordinating boards, legislators, contingent faculty, staff, and students (Bejou & Bejou, 2016). The inclusion of these stakeholders remains the exception, rather the norm, however (Kezar & Dizon, 2020; see chapter 11, this volume, for a full discussion of shared governance).

Regardless of the specific stakeholders involved, individuals will approach decision-making with differing priorities and views on the issues, and it is important to consider the levels of power that each constituent within shared governance brings to the decision-making process. As Gonzales et al. (2018) explained, "When organizations are filled with people from diverse histories, social locations, and otherwise differentially positioned groups, relations of power cannot be ignored, particularly if one wants to administer an organization that is committed to justice and inclusion" (p. 527). Understanding the differential effects of power and considering the needs of diverse stakeholders are key challenges for higher education leaders as they strive to advance the goals of their institutions.

To account for power differentials, Posselt et al. (2020) provided a reimagined framework for equitable decision-making. This framework begins with the premise that evaluation processes and criteria directly affect the equity and justice of the outcomes. Yet these processes and criteria are nested within micro (individual decision makers, individual colleges and universities, decision-makers' positionality and biases, institutional policies and practices) and macro (academia and disciplines, society, state and federal policies, racialization and other intersectional systems of stratification) contexts. All aspects of the decision-making process are affected by the variable power of the groups involved, and Posselt et al. explained that power manifests in their model in two ways. First, "power flows explicitly and implicitly from macro processes like racialization down to micro actions like decisions" and, second, power "builds as an accumulation of micro actions through time and space, whether intentionally or not, to reinforce or transform our wider social conditions" (p. 48).

Clearly, leadership and decision-making in a college or university is a highly fluid and dynamic process, which assumes different characteristics depending on the particular role one holds in the organization. For example, decision-making for department chairs is significantly different from that of a dean or provost, whose decision circumstances in turn are quite unlike the decision-making conditions faced by an institution's president. Though all operate within a shared governance environment in which spheres of influence and responsibility are allocated according to one's function, acceptance of a decision is determined by the legitimacy and authority ascribed to the decision maker by others inside and outside the institution. For example, one of the most challenging and precarious administrative positions on today's campuses is that of the provost. Having most often risen to the position from within the professoriate, a provost must straddle serving as an advocate for the faculty and their interests and serving at the pleasure of the president in an executive administrative capacity. Provosts must deftly support faculty autonomy through shared governance while firmly asserting administrative accountability:

> As trust is the cornerstone of academic leadership, the chief academic officer (CAO) must be vigilant about not letting faculty go around their department chairs or deans, must avoid sharing information with just one dean or having a backdoor for negotiations, and must be consistently evenhanded in all matters. The CAO cannot undercut the authority of deans and department chairs by publicly second-guessing them or getting involved in matters for which the deans and chairs are responsible. At times, this means supporting those to whom one delegates daily responsibility for academic affairs even if the CAO disagrees with their actions. (Ferren & Stanton, 2004, pp. 13–14)

Because academic organizations are structured according to principles of shared governance—a system in which authority is divided between bureaucratic and academic spheres of responsibility—differences in the perception of roles within each sphere or at various levels within a sphere often exist and can create tension. Effective leadership and decision-making in academic organizations therefore requires congruence among and between members of these different spheres regarding how different organizational roles are perceived and exercised. Role theory explores the consistency between one's assigned organizational role and the perception of that role by others. Especially in academic organizations in which authority and decision-making are widely distributed throughout the institution, and levels of participation in shared governance vary widely based on organizational roles, successful leadership requires an understanding of role differences between and across the institution's multiple spheres of authority. Appreciation of these distinctions is a prerequisite to effective administration and management.

People

At their core, organizations are composed of people. This detail is no less true for academic organizations, which are comprised of students, faculty, staff, administrators, and alumni. One of the difficulties in understanding this aspect of the academic organization, however, is identifying which people are part of the organization and which are not. Students are not (necessarily) employees, but it is difficult to imagine an educational institution without students. Alumni are neither employees nor students, but they are often active on alumni councils, provide substantial resources to the organization, and sometimes exercise influence over institutional decision-making. Beyond understanding who is involved, it is also important to know what induces people to participate in the organization (see Barnard, 1938; Simon, 1997). In addition, identity characteristics and personal backgrounds (e.g., age, gender, race, knowledge, skills) can affect how people interact with each other and perform on behalf of the organization.

As organizations designed for and intended as agencies of knowledge production and educational transformation, colleges and universities are client-serving in their purpose. Academic organizations serve a diverse collection of clients, including students, governments, foundations, businesses, and local community organizations. It can also be argued that they serve parents, alumni, and donors. Because of their focus on multiple clients, academic organizations are often pulled in multiple directions, and the services they provide are often complicated and require highly professionalized staff. For example, the educational process is highly complex, based on the nature of the content to be taught, the pedagogical skills of the teacher, the learning styles of the student, and how that learning can be empirically assessed. Unlike manufacturing organizations, which employ static processes and machinery to yield a given product, colleges and universities grapple with often unclear and uncertain processes as they attempt to generate educational outcomes or products (i.e., graduates). The plethora of programs and approaches to improve teaching and learning that have been attempted at the local, state, and federal levels for decades still have not yielded a consistent and broadly accepted teaching template suitable for application in all educational circumstances, which is likely due, at least in part, to the reality that "serving clients is difficult to accomplish, to evaluate, and show short-term successes. Considering the entire person is a holistic task that cannot be easily separated into small, routine technical segments" (Baldridge et al., 1978, p. 22).

Environment

One cannot fully understand an organization without also recognizing the environment in which it operates, as no organization is self-sufficient.

Just as a seed must interact with its environment for nutrients, sunlight, and water to grow, the growth and development of a college or university is both dependent on and reflective of its environment and where it obtains resources.

The complexity of their environments fosters the creation of great colleges and universities. This assertion is based on the law of limited variety put forth by Pondy and Mitroff (1979): "A system will exhibit no more variety than the variety to which it has been exposed in its environment" (p. 7). Hall (1977) suggested that organizations vary in the extent to which they are vulnerable to environmental pressures, and the level of environmental influence is correlated to an organization's dependency on external resources.

For colleges and universities, the environment significantly affects how they operate. Whether an institution is located in Oxford, Ohio, or San Diego, California, the location will affect whom it serves, how it serves, and the types of academic programs it offers. Moreover, how and where resources are obtained will have an impact on the ways the organization structures itself (Pfeffer & Salancik, 1978). For example, whether an institution's budget is derived from tuition, state appropriations, or donations will affect the emphasis the organization places on such functions as student recruitment, lobbying, and fundraising.

These factors have important implications for the manner in which an organization is managed since its structure and processes will be required to conform to the expectations and resource opportunities placed on it by its environment. This arrangement is especially true in the case of academic organizations, which can vary in their susceptibility to environmental pressures, depending on their reliance on external factors:

> When professional organizations are well insulated from the pressures of the outside environment, then professional values, norms, and work definitions play a dominant role in shaping the character of the organization. On the other hand, when strong external pressure is applied to colleges and universities, the operating autonomy of the academic professionals is seriously reduced. (Riley & Baldridge, 1977, p. 6)[2]

Torres (2020) echoed the work of Riley and Baldridge (1977), arguing that for many organizations "external and internal influences create a constant topsy-turvy environment that can create confusion or disorder, yet most administrators adapt to this by understanding the difference between the desired and the real outcomes within the institution" (p. 82). Adept administrators must continually negotiate between the ideals for which they strive and the current norms, which are heavily influenced by environmental factors.

A challenge often presented to students of higher education and college and university employees alike is to identify where the organization ends, and the environment begins:

> [Organizations] do, of course, [have boundaries] and must expend energy in boundary maintenance. But it is of equal importance that energies be devoted to activities that span and, more recently, redraw boundaries. Because of the openness of organizations, determining their boundaries is always difficult and sometimes appears to be a quite arbitrary decision. Does a university include its students within its boundary? Its alumni? Faculty during the summer? The spouses of students in university housing? (Scott & Davis, 2016, p. 95)

These conditions led Kerr (1963) to refer to a higher education institution as "an inconsistent institution. It is not one community but several. . . . Its edges are fuzzy" (p. 14).

While boundaries do exist between institutions of higher education and their environments, identifying their exact location can be quite difficult. A useful approach presented by Pfeffer and Salancik (1978) is to consider individuals not as unitary actors who have to be on one side of the organizational boundary or the other. Rather, a certain subset of their actions exists within the boundary. While this approach is helpful, it does not provide total clarity. As Scott and Davis (2016) noted, some actions can affect more than one system. For example, students who depart one institution may be viewed as newly admitted students at the school to which they are transferring, or students who earn their bachelor's degrees at one college may enroll in different institutions for graduate school.

To understand organizational boundaries, scholars have also drawn from postcolonial and decolonial work to call attention to the socially constructed nature of organizational boundaries. That is, because many colleges and universities exist on land that was colonized from Indigenous and Native people and communities, the boundaries that comprise these organizations at the local, state, and national levels are not naturally occurring (Gonzales et al., 2018; Wilder, 2013). Further complicating this issue, Shahjahan and Kezar (2013) called attention to how higher education's boundaries are "normatively discussed using the nation-state as a presupposition for society" (p. 20), yet such discussions discount the socially and politically constructed nature of the nation-state and the effects of globalization on U.S. higher education. In short, many factors complicate the notion of boundaries in higher education, and our understanding of boundaries is likely to become even more complex as U.S. higher education becomes increasingly aware of its connections to its colonial past and globally connected future.

Organizational Culture and Climate in Higher Education

Academic organizations possess a distinct culture compared to other organizational types. Although the higher education literature on administration and management tends to focus heavily on the role of institutional leadership in shaping and directing an organization—especially as it pertains to the role of the president—the distinctive cultural aspects of academic organizations rest primarily in the value system of the faculty, which has evolved over many centuries. While academic organizations tend to share common cultural characteristics, the culture and climate of a specific college or university often are a function of the relationship between its faculty and its administration, in which there is an inherent natural tension flowing from the incompatibility of professionalization and formalization. Moreover, campus culture is also heavily influenced by the characteristics of the student body. For example, whether an institution primarily enrolls full-time traditional students or part-time nontraditional students can have a significant influence on campus culture.

Culture is different from climate, and we employ the definitions of both provided by Austin (1994) to distinguish between the two: "Whereas culture pertains to the embedded and stable beliefs, values and norms of a group, climate refers to members' assessment, views, perceptions, and attitudes toward various aspects of organizational life" (p. 52). Austin underscored the need for academic administrators to understand fully the notion of institutional culture, but as importantly, to recognize that organizational culture is not monolithic. Rather, it is fragmented, as subcultures exist within and beyond the academy at multiple levels. In discussing the various cultures related to faculty, Austin noted,

> Faculty cultures include the culture of the academic profession, the culture of the academy as an organization, the cultures of particular disciplines, the cultures of institutional types, and the culture of the particular department or unit where the faculty member has a position. Deans, department chairpersons, and institutional researchers seeking to support the work of department and college leaders must understand the values of each of these cultures. (p. 48)

By understanding faculty culture, institutional leaders can better understand their own faculty, and faculty members can better understand one another. Administrator sensitivity to faculty culture yields a more informed and astute leader who is capable of better decision-making since one can more accurately project the consequences of future decisions based on the values and norms already embedded in the organization. In other words, "the key to being effective and the ability to make change begins first with an accurate assessment of the type of organization in which you work" (Julius et al., 1999, p. 114).

But how does one culturally assess the type of organization one helps to lead? It is first important to distinguish between the culture of the academy and the culture of the institution because each operates at different levels and exhibits different characteristics. The culture of the academy is present throughout U.S. higher education and is based on a concept we call *collective individualism*, whereby the values of personal independence and professional autonomy—held by individual faculty members and legitimized and protected through the doctrine of academic freedom—are juxtaposed with a broader social and institutional value of shared intellectual collegiality, forming an academic community that exhibits a socially cohesive body in appearance but in actuality is a loosely aligned confederation of independent scholars.

The concept of faculty as an amalgamation of independent contractors is not an inaccurate depiction when one considers variations in remuneration patterns among faculty members even at the same institution. For instance, faculty roles and pay can vary widely based on such variables as scholarly discipline, academic rank, course load, overloads to the normal teaching load, additional compensation for nonteaching duties, ability to attract external grant sources, and a variety of other factors all negotiated through individual contractual relationships or collective bargaining agreements. Understanding the concept of collective individualism requires higher education leaders to balance the group identity of the faculty with the individual professional values held by each member of that body. This tension between the individualism of faculty members and the collective interests of the faculty as a group was highlighted by Gumport (2000), who noted the "chasm" that exists between faculty self-interest and a broader concern for the common good, and that "at the most basic operating level, the tension appears when faculty members try to get what they can from their institutions rather than puzzling over how best to serve them" (p. 9).

The culture of an institution is specific to the organization itself and is reflective of the idiosyncratic nature of each college or university. It is the ethos or personality of an organization, built from a sense of shared accomplishment and distinctive purpose. This topic was addressed by Clark (1972), who examined the psychosocial determinants of a group's collective embrace of its organization's history and achievements as an institution's "saga." He defined saga as "a collective understanding of a unique accomplishment based on historical exploits of a formal organization, offering strong normative bonds within and outside the organization" (p. 178). Central to Clark's definition of saga are the themes of history, the uniqueness of the organiza-tion itself, and the shared value placed on that uniqueness by the organiza-tion's members.

While the concept of saga is useful in understanding the distinctive nature of individual academic organizations, other factors affect the culture of an institution. One is the collective personality of the institution's faculty. The existence of tenure and its role as a protector of academic freedom are important factors in shaping that personality. Though the merits of tenure are increasingly debated as financial pressures and a need for more insti-tutional fiscal flexibility rise, the presence of tenure has provided continu-ity and stability within each institution's faculty and has contributed to the emergence of a particular group dynamic unique to that institution. This phenomenon is widely overlooked in debates over the benefits or challenges of tenure. Imagine how the culture of an institution would change if all its faculty members were free agents, unbound by tenure and institutional loyal-ties, to ply their intellectual skills competitively in an open market. Such a scenario would result in a significant loss of institutional memory and a less coherent student learning experience, as well as contribute to a fluid, rather than stable, organizational personality.

Another factor that affects the culture of nearly every contemporary college and university in the United States is the prevalence of neoliberal-ism. Scholars usually trace the rise of neoliberalism to the 1960s and 1970s, arguing that it rose out of the economic crises and civil rights movements of those decades. The effects of neoliberalism within higher education have been widely discussed (see, e.g., Giroux, 2002, 2010; Saunders, 2010; Slaughter & Rhoades, 2004), and Museus and LePeau (2020) drew from this work to categorize the five elements of neoliberalism. According to Museus and LePeau, neoliberalism is built from *consumerism*, which leads to an emphasis on revenue generation in higher education. Closely related to consumerism is the shift toward *competitive individualism*, wherein cam-pus members advance self-interest above all else. At the same time, neolib-eralism relies heavily on *surveillance* (e.g., monitoring, reporting) and places individuals in *precarious* employment situations (e.g., contingent faculty). These factors combine to cause *declining morality*, as the emphasis on profits subsumes other institutional values.

Given these elements, it is perhaps unsurprising that scholars who study neoliberalism have spoken strongly of its deleterious effects on campus cul-ture. For Museus and LePeau (2020), the greatest and most profound effects come from the decline in social justice orientations, as they see neoliberal values and agendas being antithetical to equity and inclusion. Museus and LePeau proposed four strategies to circumvent the barriers to social justice created by neoliberalism. First, external forces that control higher education (e.g., boards of trustees, external funders, donors) should be minimized if they are not oriented toward social justice. They did not necessarily recommend that the power of boards of trustees should be reduced, but rather that boards should include social justice advocates. Similarly, they argued that many institutions are not upholding the values of their mission statements, and a return to core values, supported through funding and programming, would help institutions to realign with their stated missions. Museus and LePeau's final two suggestions focus on embracing protest and resistance to problematize and examine current operational structures.

Regardless of the factors affecting institutional culture, a new higher education administrator will benefit from early, strong communication between and among constituents. Strengthening communication allows campus leaders to conduct an expansive inventory of the attitudes and perceptions of the organization by those within their oversight. In turn, this process allows administrators to determine not only the issues or concerns most important to the group but the collective mindset as well. Such dialogue should include a thorough understanding of the organization's history, its norms, and the nature of its influential relationships and power structures. If constituent compliance to decision-making actions is to occur effectively, leaders must be perceived by others as having a working knowledge of the organization, its history, and its constituents beyond the administrative issues at hand. The concept of *institutional fit* is appropriate to this discussion. Many failures in academic leadership occur when the incumbent is unable or unwilling to incorporate; adapt to; or, at a minimum, understand an academic or institutional culture that has been shaped over decades or even centuries.

Having examined the typological, organizational, and contextual differences that exist in higher education organizations, and having given added attention to cultural factors that influence administrative decision-making, we can now examine the theoretical models that have emerged to characterize colleges and universities as unique organizational types. Specific to this examination are issues of legitimacy and authority in matters of institutional governance and decision-making, as various stakeholders, internal and external to the institution, stake claims to their spheres of influence.

Models of Academic Governance

Organizational theory attempts to provide insight into the structure and process of organizations. Given the various differentiating and unique features of academic organizations previously described, a major challenge for higher education theorists over the decades has been how to adequately characterize these features in prevailing theoretical models of governance. Older models of organizational understanding largely rooted in traditional bureaucratic theories were deemed inadequate for application to higher education. Academic organizations' highly complex structures and processes, with their multiple centers of decision-making authority, prompted the creation of new models.

Three theoretical models of governance now dominate the literature. These distinct perspectives view authority and decision-making in the academy through structural (bureaucratic), relational (collegial), and legislative (political) frameworks. These governance models provide useful perspectives to understand the interrelationship between and among the organizational participants based on such factors as power, persuasion, or legislative influence. In reality, considerations of all three models are appropriate and helpful when attempting to understand the administration and management of colleges and universities.

The Bureaucratic Model

In his seminal book on bureaucratic theory, Weber (1915/1947) described an organization as a system of hierarchical roles and formal chains of command acting in concert toward the realization of a set of defined goals. Central to Weberian bureaucratic theory are the linear and vertical relationships among decision makers that are based on their roles and ranks in the organization and the formalization of the rules and policies that they follow. In an early attempt to apply existing bureaucratic theory to higher education, Stroup (1966) sought to characterize academic organizations against these bureaucratic features. To do so was understandable since the bureaucratic paradigm appropriately conformed to many of the processes and structures found in colleges and universities.

It is not surprising that one would attribute traditional bureaucratic descriptors to contemporary higher education organizations given their enormous complexity. Yet for all the applicability of the bureaucratic model to academic organizations, significant weaknesses exist. According to Riley and Baldridge (1977), the bureaucratic model focuses more on formal power and the hierarchical structures that define it than the informal power relationships that often exist in organizations and that frequently change over time, depending on the issue or policy under debate. Another weakness in the bureaucratic model can be its preoccupation with policy execution over policy formulation. The model also tends to minimize the role of multiple interest groups and political struggles that exist among them in campus settings.

The Collegial Model

A second way academic organizations can be viewed is as a community. This thesis was first introduced by Millett (1962), who believed that the application of hierarchical principles to colleges and universities failed to account for the internal decision-making pluralism that exists in higher education institutions. Millett argued that a focus on hierarchy emphasized the role that absolute authority plays within an organization since the concept of bureaucracy implies formal power structures and a system of superior and subordinate relationships:

> In terms of their own internal organization our colleges and universities have sought arrangements which would equally reflect [a] concern to avoid absolute authority. In this endeavor the colleges and universities have built up a practice of community as the fundamental basis of organization. (p. 61)

Millett highlighted the various institutional constituencies that participate to varying degrees in institutional decision-making processes, citing the roles that students, alumni, and faculty all play in academic governance. As Millet was serving as president of Miami University of Ohio when he published his book, he likely was reflecting on the administrative challenge of accommodating multiple interests in a spirit of group accommodation.

One central theme of the collegial model is the values that members of the faculty share as they relate to the academic profession itself and their role within the decision-making structure of their institution. Implied in the model is a strong sense of collegiality within the professoriate. In her discussion of the culture of the academic profession, Austin (1994) noted how faculty members share a commitment to intellectual honesty and fairness, as well as a commitment to the concept of a community of scholars whose collegiality guides their interactions and their involvement in institutional decision-making. Yet it is important to remember that "these values are expressed in different ways depending on institutional and disciplinary contexts" (Austin, 1994, p. 49).

While the collegial model accurately portrays a higher education organization's need to accommodate multiple constituencies in a harmonious—we hope—fashion, the weakness of the model rests in its failure to account adequately for the decision-making processes themselves, during which multiple constituencies compete within the decision-making environment. Decision-making is a consequence of authority, and the collegial model is largely silent on the issue of which constituencies hold primacy over certain issues in the governance of colleges and universities. This weakness was later addressed in research that explored the authority structures of the academic enterprise and how competing interest groups influence organizational decision-making through the exercise of political influence. This line of inquiry produced the third model of academic governance.

The Political Model

The paradigm of viewing academic governance as a political process and colleges and universities as independent political systems was first proposed by Baldridge (1971). In this model, the campus is made up of a set of competing interest groups whose participation in the decision-making process is fluid, depending on the nature of the issue at hand. Policy formation serves as a focal point since the creation and adoption of policy is directly related to institutional mission and direction and the various operational decisions that flow from it. As a consequence, conflict among organizational interest groups is inherent. Such interest groups are not limited to those constituencies in the institution itself but extend to external parties that may hold vested interests in the organization as well.

The fragmented and complex decision-making processes found within colleges and universities lend the political model much credibility in the study of academic governance. The reality of academic governance is that decisions most often are not made unilaterally by a central authority. Instead, they follow prescribed systems of review and consultation with a variety of individuals or entities, depending on the nature of the decision to be made:

> When the very life of the organization clusters around expertise, decision-making is likely to be diffuse, segmentalized, and decentralized. A complex network of committees, councils, and advisory bodies grows to handle the task of assembling the expertise necessary for reasonable decisions. Decision-making by the individual bureaucrat is replaced with decision-making by committee, council, and cabinet. Centralized decision-making is replaced with diffuse decision-making. The process becomes a far-flung network for gathering expertise from every corner of the organization and translating it into policy. (Baldridge, 1971, p. 190)

The involvement of different interest groups in academic decision-making by virtue of their roles and expertise provides the legitimacy for the concept of shared governance developed by Mortimer and McConnell (1978). We include shared governance in our discussion of the political model because decision-making in a shared governance environment is performed through the exercise of influence rather than formal position. Matters of shared governance are largely an issue between faculty and administration (and to a lesser extent trustees and students) because of the tensions between professional authority (the faculty) and formal authority (the administration) that were identified in earlier organizational models. The notion of shared governance involves the acceptance of the authoritative rights possessed by certain constituencies based on their expertise or formal position. A central question in the discussion of shared authority is "How is authority distributed in recognition of the legitimate expertise ascribed to a particular incumbent or group?" According to Mortimer and McConnell (1978):

> A full account of governance should cover four basic questions: (1) *What* issue is to be decided? (2) *Who*—what persons or groups—should be involved in the decision? (3) *When* (at what stage of the decision-making process) and *how* should such involvement occur? (4) *Where*—at what level in the organizational structure—should such involvement occur? (p. 13, emphasis added)

While Mortimer and McConnell's (1978) work established a foundational understanding of shared governance, more recent scholars have reconceptualized our understanding of shared governance to account for changes in higher education. Kezar and Dizon (2020), for instance, have offered a social justice and equity-based model for shared governance. As they explain, contemporary models of shared governance must account for "the complexity of college campuses today that face more regulation, greater external pressures, declining funding, and [the] need to adjust to integrating new technologies, a more diverse student body, and a multitude of new challenges" (p. 26). Borrowing from the work of Byrne-Jiménez and Orr (2013), Kezar and Dizon's model includes four elements aimed at reconceptualizing shared governance: (a) conscious public commitment by campus stakeholders; (b) widening the circle of participation; (c) transformative discourse to foster collaborative dialogue and problem-solving; and (d) dynamic institutionalization, or the ability to continually revise and rethink policies and practices. All elements are focused on including diversity of thought and experiences in the decision-making process, while also ensuring that the stakeholders who are most affected by policies and practices have a voice in shaping and approving such measures.

Aside from a lack of attention to social justice, the political model has several additional weaknesses. First, the model was developed in an era that predated the creation of the for-profit education sector and the emergence of institutions that specialize in online learning modalities. The missions of some for-profit institutions and online campuses often bear little resemblance to their more traditional academic counterparts in their structures and relationships between faculty, employees, and management. Second, the rise of collective bargaining and the role of faculty unions have significantly altered decision-making processes on campuses where unions exist, substituting functional authority by virtue of expertise with formal authority that is legislatively and legally derived. Finally, the political model focuses predominantly on the internal organizational relationship between faculty and administration but fails to account sufficiently for the rise in external environmental factors that substantially affect college and university governance today. Diminishing federal and state resources designated for higher education, coupled with governmental efforts to exact greater accountability from colleges and universities, are leading to the encroachment of governmental entities into institutional decisions concerning how precious resources should be expended, as well as what society should expect in the way of outcomes from those investments.

In an evaluation of the future challenges facing higher education governance, Kezar and Eckel (2004) provided a thorough review of 40 years of research. They concluded that the primary models of academic governance focus on structural and political theories of governance but provide limited explanation of how academic governance could be improved. An important theme that Kezar and Eckel highlighted is that the structural and political models that have guided understanding of shared governance in recent decades will be inadequate for understanding and accommodating rapid organizational change in the coming years as colleges and universities must adapt to new internal and external constraints. The authors cited three factors that will make governance more difficult: (a) an increase in imposed accountability requirements and competition from an increasingly challenging and competitive external environment (e.g., uncertainty in state funding and fewer high school graduates); (b) the changing nature of the faculty, as significant numbers of rather homogeneous professors retire and are replaced with more diverse faculty members; and (c) a need to expedite decision-making to accommodate rapid change (Kezar & Eckel, 2004).

While these issues continue today, the everchanging landscape of higher education has presented additional challenges to the future of governance. For instance, the COVID-19 pandemic affected many facets of higher education, including increasing the prevalence of online education, reducing the number of faculty and staff, and leading to decreases in enrollment and funding. At the same time, in 2020 and 2021 many colleges and universities adopted policies to respond to growing concerns about the effects of structural racism, such as revising curricula, working to hire more diverse faculty and staff, rethinking student services and support, and implementing more training on issues related to DEI. While it is too early to know the full effects of these changes, chief academic officers have reported that the coming years will bring more changes, such as further expansion of online education, increases in collaboration between colleges and universities, alignment of funding with institutional mission, elimination of underperforming academic programs, dismissal of underperforming faculty, and incentives for older faculty members to retire (Jaschik & Lederman, 2021). These factors complicate issues of shared governance, as they involve changes in faculty structures, funding models, and institutional priorities.

Conclusion

In chapter 1, we outlined several principles that serve as a foundation to our study of academic leadership and governance in U.S. higher education: the understanding of the importance of institutional mission; the need for institutional adaptation to changing environmental and societal circumstances; the value of democratic partnerships in the formation and operation of colleges and universities; and the role of institutions of higher education as catalysts for inclusion, equity, and social justice. Those individuals entrusted with governance responsibilities as either fiduciaries or administrators in U.S. higher education institutions cannot effectively lead without embracing those principles and appreciating how each affects management decisions on an ongoing basis. This chapter suggests how issues of institutional mission and democratic partnerships have evolved over the centuries into a dynamic and complex array of thousands of separate and unique organizations, each requiring of its leadership a separate set of understandings and strategies that are equally unique to the organization. It is not nearly enough to understand how colleges and universities differ markedly from other organizational types. More important, informed campus leaders can excel by understanding how their institution distinguishes itself from every other, as well as by acknowledging what they, as leaders, understand (or do not understand) about their role as an academic leader and about those whom they lead and/or serve.

Notes

1. This definition, adopted in 2021, comes from section 50 of New York State's Education Law §224(1)(a); 8 NYCRR 3.29. It amended the previous definition adopted in 1969: "University means a higher educational institution offering a range of registered undergraduate and graduate curricula in the liberal arts and sciences, degrees in two or more professional fields, and doctoral programs in at least three academic fields."

2. Mintzberg (1979) similarly argued that when the resource base shifts from stable to unstable, such as when state appropriations fluctuate or student tuition dollars become more scarce, the academic organization shifts from a professional bureaucracy to an adhocracy as power and influence within the organization shifts from the academic core to those offices and functions that help the institution manage the instability in the environment, such as admissions and government relations.

References

Austin, A. E. (1994). Understanding and assessing faculty cultures and climates. *New Directions for Institutional Research, 1994*(84), 47–63. https://doi.org/10.1002/ir.37019948406

Baldridge, J. V. (1971). *Power and conflict in the university.* Wiley.

Baldridge, J. V., Curtis, D. V., Ecker, G., & Riley, G. L. (1978). *Policy making and effective leadership.* Jossey-Bass.

Barnard, C. I. (1938). *The functions of the executive.* Harvard University Press.

Bastedo, M. N. (2012). *The organization of higher education: Managing colleges for a new era.* Johns Hopkins University Press.

Bejou, D., & Bejou, A. (2016). Shared governance: The key to higher education equilibrium. *Journal of Relationship Marketing, 15*(1–2), 54–61. https://doi.org/10.1080/15332667.2015.1091630

Bess, J. L., & Dee, J. R. (2007). *Understanding college and university organization: Theories for effective policy and practice.* Stylus.

Blau, P. M. (1973). *The organization of academic work.* Wiley.

Blau, P. M. (1974). *On the nature of organizations.* Wiley.

Byrne-Jiménez, M., & Orr. M. T. (2013). Evaluating social justice leadership preparation. In L. C. Tillman & J. J. Scheurich, *Handbook of research on educational leadership for equity and diversity* (pp. 670–702). Routledge. https://doi.org/10.4324/9780203076934

Clark, B. R. (1972). The organizational saga in higher education. *Administrative Science Quarterly, 17*(2), 178–184. https://doi.org/10.2307/2393952

Cohen, M., March, J., & Olsen, J. (1972). A garbage can model of organizational choice. *Administrative Science Quarterly, 17*(1), 1–25. https://doi.org/10.2307/2392088

Etzioni, A. (1964). *Modern organizations.* Prentice Hall.

Ferren, A. S., & Stanton, W. W. (2004). *Leadership through collaboration: The role of the chief academic officer.* Praeger.

Flexner, A. (1930). *Universities: American, English, German.* Oxford University Press.

Gehrke, S., & Kezar, A. (2015). Unbundling the faculty role in higher education: Utilizing historical, theoretical, and empirical frameworks to inform future research. In M. B. Paulsen (Ed.), *Higher education: Handbook of theory and research* (Vol. 30, pp. 93–150). Springer. https://doi.org/10.1007/978-3-319-12835-1_3

Giroux, H. M. (2002). Neoliberalism, corporate culture, and the promise of higher education: The university as a democratic public sphere. *Harvard Educational Review, 72*(4), 424–463. https://doi.org/10.17763/haer.72.4.0515nr62324n71p1

Giroux, H. M. (2010). Neoliberalism as public pedagogy. In J. A. Sandlin, B. D. Schultz, & J. Burdick (Eds.), *Handbook of public pedagogy: Education and learning beyond schooling* (pp. 486–499). Routledge.

Gonzales, L. D., Kanhai, D., & Hall, K. (2018). Reimagining organizational theory for the critical study of higher education. In M. B. Paulsen (Ed.), *Higher education: Handbook of theory and research* (Vol. 33, pp. 505–559). Springer. https://doi.org/10.1007/978-3-319-72490-4_11

Gumport, P. J. (2000). *Academic governance: New light on old issues* (Occasional Paper No. 42). Association of Governing Boards of Universities and Colleges.

Hall, R. H. (1977). *Organizations: Structure and process.* Prentice-Hall.

Jaschik, S., & Lederman, D. (2021). *2021 Survey of college and university chief academic officers: A study by Inside Higher Ed and Hanover Research.* Inside Higher Ed and Hanover Research.

Julius, D. J., Baldridge, J. V., & Pfeffer, J. (1999). A memo from Machiavelli. *Journal of Higher Education, 70*(2), 113–133. https://doi.org/10.2307/2649124

Kerr, C. (1963). *The use of the university.* Harvard University Press.

Kezar, A., & Dizon, J. P. M. (2020). Renewing and revitalizing shared governance: A social justice and equity framework. In A. Kezar & J. Posselt (Eds.), *Higher education administration for social justice and equity: Critical perspectives for leadership* (pp. 21–42). Routledge.

Kezar, A., & Eckel, P. D. (2004). Meeting today's governance challenges. *Journal of Higher Education, 75*(4), 371–399. https://doi.org/10.1080/00221546.2004.11772264

Kezar, A., & Sam, C. (2014). Governance as a catalyst for policy change: Creating a contingent faculty friendly academy. *Educational Policy, 28*(3), 425–462. https://doi.org/10.1177/0895904812465112

Lane, J. E., Kinser, K., & Knox, D. (2013). Regulating cross-border higher education: A case study of the United States. *Higher Education Policy, 26*(2), 147–172. https://doi.org/10.1057/hep.2012.23

Manning, K. (2018). Organizational theory in higher education (2nd ed.). Routledge.

Millett, J. D. (1962). *The academic community: An essay on organization.* McGraw-Hill.

Mintzberg, H. (1979). *The structure of organizations: A synthesis of the research.* Prentice Hall.

Mortimer, K. P., & McConnell, T. R. (1978). *Sharing authority effectively.* Jossey-Bass.

Museus, S. D., & LePeau, L. A. (2020). Navigating neoliberal organizational cultures. In A. Kezar & J. Posselt (Eds.), *Higher education administration for social justice and equity: Critical perspectives for leadership* (pp. 209–224). Routledge.

Newman, J. H. (1893). *The idea of the university*. Longmans, Green, and Co. (Original work published 1852)

Perkins, J. A. (1972). Organization and function of the university. *The Journal of Higher Education, 43*(9), 679–691. https://doi.org/10.2307/1978999

Perrow, C. (1970). *Organizational analysis: A sociological view*. Wadsworth.

Pfeffer, J., & Salancik, G. R. (1978). *The external control of organizations: A resource dependence perspective*. Harper & Row.

Pondy, L. R., & Mitroff, I. I. (1979). Beyond open systems models of organization. In B. M. Staw (Ed.), *Research in organizational behaviors* (Vol. 1, pp. 3–29). JAI Press.

Posselt, J., Hernandez, T., & Villarreal, C. D. (2020). Choose wisely: Making decisions with and for equity in higher education. In A. Kezar & J. Posselt (Eds.), *Higher education administration for social justice and equity: Critical perspectives for leadership* (pp. 43–66). Routledge.

Rhoades, G. (2005). Capitalism, academic style, and shared governance. *Academe, 91*(3), 38–42. https://doi.org/10.2307/40252785

Rhoades, G., & Torres-Olave, B. M. (2015). Academic capitalism and (secondary) academic labor markets: Negotiating a new academy and research agenda. In M. B. Paulsen (Ed.), *Higher education: Handbook of theory and research* (Vol. 30, pp. 383–430). Springer. https://doi.org/10.1007/978-3-319-12835-1_9

Riley, G. L., & Baldridge, V. J. (1977). *Governing academic organizations: New problems new perspectives*. McCutchan.

Scott, W. R., & Davis, G. F. (2016). *Organizations and organizing: Rational, natural, and open system perspectives*. Routledge.

Saunders, D. B. (2010). Neoliberal ideology and public higher education in the United States. *Journal for Critical Pedagogy Education Policy Studies, 8*(1), 41–77. http://www.jceps.com/archives/626

Shahjahan, R. A., & Kezar, A. J. (2013). Beyond the "national container" addressing methodological nationalism in higher education research. *Educational Researcher, 42*(1), 20–29. https://doi.org/10.3102/0013189X12463050

Simon, H. A. (1997). *Administrative behavior: A study of decision-making processes in administrative organizations* (4th ed.). Macmillan.

Slaughter, S. A., & Rhoades, G. (2004). *Academic capitalism and the new economy: Markets, state, and higher education*. Johns Hopkins University Press.

Stroup, H. (1966). *Bureaucracy in higher education*. The Free Press.

Tappan, H. P. (1858). *The university; its constitution, and its relations, political and religious: A discourse*. Regents of the University of Michigan.

Torres, V. (2020). Working in topsy-turvy higher education environments. In A. Kezar & J. Posselt (Eds.), *Higher education administration for social justice and equity: Critical perspectives for leadership* (pp. 82–90). Routledge.

U.S. Department of Education (2020). *Condition of education*. National Center for Education Statistics, U.S. Department of Education.

Weber, M. (1947). *The theory of social and economic organizations* (T. Parsons, Trans.). The Free Press. (Original work published ca. 1915)

Weick, K. E. (1976). Educational organizations as loosely coupled systems. *Administrative Science Quarterly, 21*(1), 1–19. https://doi.org/10.2307/2391875

Wiener, N. (1954). *The human use of human beings: Cybernetics and society.* Doubleday.

Wilder, C. S. (2013). *Ebony and ivy: Race, slavery, and the troubled history of America's universities.* Bloomsbury.

PART TWO

POLITICAL, LEGAL, AND GLOBAL CONSIDERATIONS

5

GLOBAL ENGAGEMENT OF COLLEGES AND UNIVERSITIES

The world is changing rapidly, and the role of higher education has never been more important. As the knowledge economy gives way to the information economy, colleges and universities need to adjust to ensure their curriculum design and delivery models remain relevant to local audiences, but higher education has also become an increasingly important player in the economic competitiveness of nations. The rise of nationalism calls for institutions to be even more purposeful in cultivating global perspectives and intercultural understanding. Issues such as climate change, social justice, energy production, migration, and water scarcity are globally relevant, and higher education institutions facilitate and lead collaborations of scientists and scholars around the world to work on such challenges. Indeed, governments have become more purposeful in leveraging higher education to advance national purposes. All these trends call for engaged academic leaders who can lead their institutions to adapt to these changes in equitable and democratic ways that are in line with their mission.

Scholars and students have long crossed international borders in the pursuit of new experiences, new people, new jobs, and new knowledge (Rait, 1931; Rashdall, 1895). Even before the internet, knowledge could hardly be limited to national borders. Books, academic journals, students, and scholars moved between nations, bringing new knowledge from one country to another. The increasing interconnectedness of economies, governments, and cultures has made it even more important for students to acquire the skills and knowledge necessary to be internationally engaged. Moreover, higher education institutions are now viewed broadly as economic drivers, critical for nations to maintain or expand their economic competitiveness (Lane, 2012).

For the past 2 decades, internationalization of U.S. higher education has focused on attracting students from other countries, transforming curricula, providing opportunities for students to study abroad, and hiring faculty members with degrees from institutions outside the United States. More recently, though, many colleges and universities have been aggressively expanding their global footprint through engagements in joint partnerships with institutions in other nations, building research capacity abroad, and running offices and campuses in multiple countries. For some institutions, the movement of students, faculty, and campuses across international borders is transforming the ways they operate.

At the same time, external influences have required the international education sector to recalibrate a great deal, with the pandemic being the latest source of destabilization for many assumptions and activities. For example, in 2020, international student enrollments at U.S. colleges and universities plummeted by 43% from the year before (Baer & Martel, 2020). International student numbers began to rebound, though many unknowns remain from the impact of new variants of the Coronavirus to renewed travel bans to shifting student preferences. Such shocks to the higher education system are not new, but it can take institutions a while to recover from them. U.S. higher education experienced a similar a decline following the 9/11 attacks in 2001, and it took 6 years for international student enrollments in the United States to reach their pre-9/11 level. An important difference, though, was that international student numbers were increasing prior to 9/11—they were declining before the pandemic.

The geopolitical landscape has also shifted significantly. At the time of this writing, China remains by far the largest sender of international students to the United States, yet China–U.S. relations are at a near historic low, driven by disagreements over a range of issues from trade tariffs to cybersecurity to intellectual property to human rights. The U.S. government is pressuring universities to close their China-supported Confucius Institutes and is prosecuting U.S. researchers for not disclosing ties to the Chinese government or Chinese funders. Chinese government officials have publicly sought to dissuade students from studying in the United States, warning about safety risks inherent to living and studying there. In spring 2021, the Chinese foreign minister warned the Biden administration to stop "harassing Chinese students, restricting Chinese media outlets, shutting down Confucius Institutes and suppressing Chinese companies" (Bloomberg, 2021).

The importance of global awareness becomes even more significant when considered from a national perspective. Colleges and universities provide students with formative experiences that can affect their perspectives of other countries, their willingness to engage with them, and the ways in which they engage (James, 2005; see also chapter 3, this volume). International experiences are important for increasing appreciation of other cultures, learning languages, and encouraging long-term willingness to travel abroad. A U.S. report about the national importance of study abroad experiences began with this passage:

> On the international stage, what nations don't know can hurt them. In recent generations, evidence of that reality has been readily available. What we did not know about Vietnam hurt the United States. What we did not understand about the history and culture of the former Ottoman Empire has complicated our efforts in the Middle East for decades. Mistakes involving the Third World and its debt have cost American financiers billions of dollars. And our lack of knowledge about economic, commercial, and industrial developments in Japan, China, and India, successively, has undermined American competitiveness. Global competence costs, but ignorance costs far more. (Commission on the Abraham Lincoln Study Abroad Program, 2005, p. 3)

The Lincoln commission's argument was that study abroad is much more than an institutional imperative. It is of national importance. The argument is that all American undergraduate students should have the opportunity to study abroad, and that such experiences should be the norm on college campuses—not an exception limited to the rich or privileged. The reason is that society benefits in multiple ways if it is more globally engaged and aware. This chapter provides an overview of the changing global contexts in which higher education operates, which campus leaders can use to help their institutions be successful in this space.

The Global Higher Education Student Landscape

Around the world, demand for higher education is growing. In 2018, approximately 250 million students were pursuing some form of higher education, and that number is projected to grow to nearly 600 million by 2040 (Calderon, 2018). For comparison purposes, around 20 million students are enrolled in U.S. higher education institutions annually, and that figure is predicted to remain about the same in the near future (with a caveat that these predictions were made before the pandemic) (NCES, 2019).

Of these 250 million students, the Organisation for Economic Co-operation and Development (OECD, 2020) has estimated that more than 5.5 million study outside their home country each year.[1] Approximately

4 million of these students are from OECD countries, but mobility of students from both OECD and non-OECD countries is growing. Nearly 60% of all international students are from Asia, with India and China combined accounting for almost one third of all students who study abroad. The most popular academic majors for international students tend to be in the areas of business, engineering, and construction.

The leading destination for international students is the United States, which accounts for 18% of the market (OECD, 2020). Prior to the pandemic, the United States hosted more than 1 million international students each year, although the country's global market share has continually dropped over the last 20 years. The next leading receivers of international students are Australia, the United Kingdom, and Germany. For many of these countries, international education has become a major contributor to their economy. For example, education is the sixth largest service export in the United States, valued at more than $40 billion (U.S. International Trade Administration, n.d.). In Australia, education is the third largest export overall, valued at more than $35 billion (Tehan, 2019).[2]

The growth in the international education sector's economic impact has been spurred partially by increasing demand for tertiary education, particularly in developing countries where access to and need for higher education historically have been limited (Levy, 2006). Increasing need is being driven by rising numbers of secondary school graduates in those countries; heightened demand for educational opportunity among females; and changing workforce demands fostered by movement toward an information-based economy, which has led to greater global connectivity and competition.

Rankings and World-Class Universities

Rankings now dominate the policy and practice of higher education around the globe. While academic leaders in the United States still largely look to domestic rankings such as those produced by *U.S. News & World Report*, most of the rest of the world has become consumed by global rankings of institutions such as the *Times Higher Education World University Rankings* or Shanghai Jiao Tong University's *Academic Ranking of World Universities*. These rankings have emerged as big business for those who produce them, and they influence how higher education stakeholders operate around the world (Hazelkorn, 2015). In fact, rankings now influence where students apply to study, with which institutions a university seeks to partner, and even national funding strategies (see Hazelkorn & Mihut, 2021 for a review of research on rankings).

In part the dominance of rankings is tied to institutional and national pursuits to develop so-called "world-class universities," which are those institutions that are able to attract and retain the best and brightest students and scholars around the world (Salmi & Altbach, 2016). The rankings have become surrogates for assessing the relative standing of countries' higher education institutions. Whether for pride or competitiveness, many nations have now adopted public policies explicitly linked to these global rankings. For example, Russia adjusted its funding models to try to move five of its universities into the top 100 in the international rankings (Grove, 2015), and in 2014 Hong Kong adopted a policy limiting its financial support to students who study abroad, restricting them to top-ranked institutions outside Hong Kong (Education Bureau, Hong Kong, 2021).

The whole situation is fraught, however. "Everyone wants a world-class university. No country feels it can do without one. The problem is that no one knows what a world-class university is, and no one has figured out how to get one" (Altbach, 2004, p. 5). A major criticism of the pursuit of a world-class university is that nations are throwing money after an unclear concept to realize some unclear set of gains. Yet for many academic leaders,

> winning a higher position in these [rankings] is perceived as one of the ultimate goals in running universities since a higher ranking might bring with it world-wide reputation, better staff and students, and a greater capacity to attract public resources and private donations. (Mok & Cheung, 2011, p. 234)

Our purpose here is not to unpack this complicated issue, but it is a major driver of activity in the global higher education landscape, and academic leaders need to understand just how important rankings are in this context.

Geopolitics and Higher Education

We often do not think about the relationship between geopolitical activities and higher education initiatives, yet the two are often intractably linked, for better or for worse. Take for example a situation in which one of the authors oversaw global affairs for the State University of New York (SUNY) system. At the time, SUNY had two outreach offices in Russia, one of which was opened in the 1970s and was the first such U.S. educational outpost in what was then the Soviet Union. When Russia annexed Crimea from Ukraine in 2014, the U.S. government called for business and governmental leaders to pull back from their engagements with Russia. An inquiry to the U.S.

Department of State about whether SUNY's offices in Russia should be suspended or closed was met immediately with a negative reaction. The rationale was that while the U.S. government was playing economic hardball with Russia, it wanted to sustain the United States' educational and social ties as means to balance the relationship.

The point here is that governments in the United States and beyond view higher education as a strategic national asset, even if this priority is not overtly clear to those who lead and operate the colleges and universities. While government engagements in internationalization have intensified of late, they have existed for at least a century. Following World War I, the Institute of International Education was created in the United States; Akademischer Austauschdienst, the predecessor to Deutcher Akademischer Austauschdienst (DAAD) was established in Germany, and the United Kingdom formed the British Committee for Relations with Other Countries, which would evolve into today's British Council. These entities serve a variety of purposes, such as facilitating student and faculty exchanges, fostering multi-institutional academic partnerships, and expanding understanding (and possibly acceptance) of different cultures.

In a 2015 paper, Lane explored why governments care about higher education internationalization. He identified three primary areas where governments and higher education activities intersect: economic competitiveness, public diplomacy, and national security. The following sections provide an overview of these areas.

The Great Brain Race: Economic Competitiveness

The emergence of the knowledge-based society has elevated higher education as a critical component in modern cultural, political, and economic development. Indeed, the title of Wildavsky's (2010) book proclaimed his belief about the importance of higher education: *The Great Brain Race: How Global Universities Are Reshaping the World*. This concept is not new, however. Clark Kerr (1963), the former chancellor of the University of California system, wrote more than 50 years ago, "We are just now perceiving that the university's invisible product, knowledge, may be the most powerful single element in our culture, affecting the rise and fall of professions and even of social classes, or regions, and even nations" (pp. vii–viii). More recently, Wildavsky explained how countries such as China and India are increasingly investing in higher education to prevent brain drain and to attract the best and brightest students from other nations.

When Porter (1990) published *The Competitive Advantage of Nations,* he posited that countries' economic prosperity would be created, not inherited.

His premise challenged more traditional economic notions that a nation's economic prosperity was tied to access to natural resources and labor as well as effective regulation of the marketplace. Instead, Porter argued that economies would be driven by innovators. Today, the World Economic Forum describes the importance of higher education in the advancement of national economies this way:

> Although less-advanced countries can still improve their productivity by adopting existing technologies or making incremental improvements in other areas, for those that have reached the innovation state of development, this is no longer sufficient for increasing productivity. Firms in these countries must design and develop cutting-edge products and processes to maintain a competitive edge. This requires an environment that is conducive to innovative activity, supported by both the public and private sectors. In particular, it means sufficient investment in research and development (R&D), especially by the private sector; the presence of high-quality scientific research institutions; extensive collaboration in research between universities and industry; and the protection of intellectual property. (Schwab, 2011, p. 7)

The intersection of higher education and the economy has manifested in many ways. In several countries, such as Australia, the United Kingdom, and the United States, higher education has itself emerged as a leading service export (Lane et al., 2015). In the United States, international students are often core components of the innovation ecosystem, contributing to research projects and patents developed by the research universities in which they enroll (W. Kerr, 2018; Nager et al., 2016) and supporting local economies through the payment of rent and the purchase of supplies to support their living and learning needs (Lane, 2012). Many of these students stay in the United States after graduation and continue to contribute culturally and economically.

Observers often do not realize how important foreign-born individuals, many of whom come to the United States as undergraduate or graduate students, are to innovation in this country. According to a report from the National Foundation for American Policy, international students make up large portions of the U.S. graduate student population in key areas of innovation: 81% in electrical engineering, 79% in computer science, and 75% in industrial engineering (Redden, 2017). A 2016 study of innovators, primarily award-winning inventors and international patent holders, in the United States revealed that 35.5% were born abroad (Nager et al., 2016). Indeed, Watney (2020) warned that the more restrictive immigration rhetoric and regulations of the Trump administration, along with the pandemic's curtailing of the circulation of people and ideas, has led to a major damaging of "the engine of American innovation."

Around the world—illustrating Wildavsky's (2010) argument—other countries are now seeing these benefits and are investing in their own higher education infrastructure to gain similar advantages. Countries that once exported students abroad are now building education hubs to attract students to their shores (Knight, 2013). In fact, in places such as the United Arab Emirates, Qatar, and Malaysia, governments are importing branch campuses of U.S. institutions to build their educational capacity and recruit students from other countries (Lane, 2011). The result is that colleges and universities, and their leaders, are increasingly involved in a complex and competitive race to attract and retain brains.

Public Diplomacy and Soft Power

Public diplomacy is an "ideological battle for the hearts and minds of people around the world" (Gilboa, 2008, p. 55). The U.S. Department of State (n.d.) describes the role of the undersecretary of the state for public diplomacy and public affairs in this way:

> to support the achievement of U.S. foreign policy goals and objectives, advance national interests, and enhance national security by informing and influencing foreign publics and by expanding and strengthening the relationship between the people and Government of the United States and citizens of the rest of the world. (para. 1)

Building soft power through the establishment of relationships is the aim of public diplomacy. From a global perspective, the goal of public diplomacy is to create a more stable and peaceful world through the development of greater mutual understanding among different countries and cultures and the generation of positive change in public attitudes toward different communities and identities.

It is difficult to pinpoint exactly when international education began to play an active role in national public diplomacy efforts, although one could argue that World War II activated unprecedented interaction between governments and international education programming with an explicit focus on public diplomacy. These activities, which ranged from student mobility to economic development projects, built the foundation on which many international education partnerships rest today.

The end of World War II and the onset of the Cold War led to the formation of several multinational organizations, including the North Atlantic Treaty Organization (NATO), the Soviet Bloc, and the European

Economic Community (the European Union's predecessor). These organizations quickly turned toward leveraging international education as part of their efforts to build intercultural understanding, funding programs, and making available scholarships for students to study in other member nations (Klineberg, 1976). National governments also saw the benefits of supporting international study. The United States created the Fulbright program in 1946, and in the postwar period the United Kingdom and France both established scholarships to bring students from their former colonies to study in their higher education institutions (Güriz, 2008). In 1960, the Soviet Union opened the Patrice Lumuba Peoples' Friendship University, with a mission to spread Soviet culture and beliefs among developing nations by bringing students from those countries to study there.

Academics were also very active in reconstruction projects in Europe and Asia following World War II. U.S. academics were instrumental in reconstruction in Europe and later in Japan (Krige, 2006). The Colombo Plan, initiated in 1950, led to the engagement of universities in Australia and New Zealand in the development of countries across Southeast Asia (Oakman, 2004). An ancillary result of these efforts was significant increases in the number of students coming to Australia, the United States, and New Zealand to pursue their studies.

Today, higher education institutions' global engagement is expansive. From study-abroad programs for students to research sites deep in jungles, to offices and campuses around the world, many universities have emerged as truly multinational organizations (Lane & Kinser, 2011). It is not uncommon for academic presidents to meet with foreign dignitaries and be part of signing ceremonies with overseas partners. In fact, the concept of public diplomacy has become even more nuanced with international collaborations of researchers and athletes evoking terms such as *science diplomacy* and *sport diplomacy* (Fedoroff, 2009; Nygård & Gates, 2013).

What is important for academic leaders is to be aware of connections—existing and potential—between their institution's activities and the public diplomacy efforts of their country, as well as similar activities abroad.

National Security

While internationalization has always been linked to national security, the connection between the two has received increased attention over the last few years. As noted, efforts such as the Fulbright program have promoted positive relationships around the world, which in turn can enhance or diminish national security. In this section, we focus on issues of border security and safety, export control, and the rise of nationalism.

By its very nature, international education often involves the crossing of borders by students and scholars. Most countries now have specific visa categories for students, which allow those individuals to enter the country to pursue their studies. In the United States, the process for obtaining a student visa was significantly revised following the 9/11 terrorist attacks as several of the attackers entered the country on student visas. These revisions resulted in higher education institutions' having to assume more responsibility for monitoring international students at their schools as well as the creation of the Student and Exchange Visitor Information System (SEVIS), a web-based system to track international students and scholars who are in the United States on temporary, nonimmigrant visas to participate in U.S. education. All postsecondary educational institutions in the United States are required to comply with SEVIS reporting requirements. For example, upon the start of an international student's study in the United States, the college or university becomes responsible for tracking and reporting any changes in the student's address, course of study, or funding situation.

Until the pandemic, the number of international students in the United States had been on the rise for more than a decade, topping 1 million annually. That number declined precipitously during the pandemic, however. From fall 2019 to fall 2020, the number of international students fell by 13%, and the number of new international students dropped by 43% (Baer & Martel, 2020). These declines were partly due to travel limitations caused by the pandemic, but they were also exacerbated by the effects of the Trump administration's aggressive efforts to limit immigration, including among foreign-born students and scholars, through a combination of travel bans, rule changes, and court battles (Dickler, 2020; Kanno-Youngs, 2020; Redden, 2020). It is unclear how long it will take international student enrollments to rebound, but based on the post-9/11 experience and ongoing challenges of the pandemic, it will likely be a few years (Lane, 2021).

Other areas of national security related to higher education that have gained public attention concern foreign influence and intellectual property security. Around 2020, heightened awareness emerged regarding foreign entanglements among U.S. colleges and universities. Under Section 117 of the Higher Education Act (HEA) of 1965 all U.S. higher education institutions are required to report to the U.S. Department of Education all foreign gifts and contracts totaling more than $250,000. A comprehensive investigation of the phenomenon revealed that many institutions underreported or completely failed to report these transactions for many years (Ellis & Baumann, 2020). In a more extreme example, the chair of Harvard's Department of Chemistry and Chemical Biology was arrested for not revealing his relationships with the Chinese government, a requirement for receiving National Science Foundation (NSF) and National Institutes of Health (NIH) funding (U.S. Department of Justice, 2020). These rules have existed for decades, although they often were not aggressively monitored or enforced, which resulted in some significant lapses in compliance and potentially severe illegal activity.

One area of federal involvement in cross-border education that is not often discussed, but that may increase in importance and thus be more relevant for higher education leaders, is the country's export control laws. These laws regulate the disbursement of information, products, and services deemed "protected" because of foreign trade policy and national security concerns to foreign nationals and nation-states. An export is any item that leaves the United States, and imparting knowledge to international students, whether in the United States or abroad, is classified as exporting.[3] For U.S. colleges and universities, most teaching and research activities are exempted from export control laws.[4] However, a U.S. campus located in another country does not receive the same exemptions as its home campus. It does not matter if an item is leaving permanently or temporarily, nor does it matter if it is being transferred to an organization wholly owned by a U.S. entity (such as a branch campus) located outside the United States.

An important takeaway from this discussion is that as international activities of colleges and universities grow, so too does the need for institutional oversight of those activities and assurance that governmental rules and regulations are being met. Both in the United States and abroad, issues of immigration and intellectual property are undergoing greater scrutiny, and academic leaders need to stay abreast of these changes and be prepared to discuss institutional activities and how they are affected by changes in rules.

Internationalization of Higher Education Institutions

The term *internationalization* has been used since the 1980s to indicate a "process of integrating an international, intercultural, and global dimension into the purpose, functions (teaching, research, services) and the delivery of post-secondary education" (Knight, 2003, p. 2). Academic leaders should take note of several important components of this definition. First, as a process, efforts in this arena should be ongoing and evolving—not static. The international scene continues to change, and institution officials who desire to be involved in such a dynamic environment should be prepared to respond to those changes. Second, the process involves international, intercultural, and global dimensions. *International* emphasizes the concept of nations as distinct entities from which we can learn and that we can understand in a comparative fashion. *Intercultural* decouples the concept from being solely about nations by highlighting the role of people and their cultural traditions. The international and intercultural themes address the comparative aspect of internationalization. This comparative perspective helps those engaged in the process to understand people who are different from them, but it also provides opportunities to reflect on their own nation and culture. Culture is not necessarily restricted by geopolitical boundaries; groups of people and their cultures can transcend such borders. Indeed, Knight's (2003) use of the word *global* was intended to "provide the sense of worldwide scope" of internationalization (p. 3).

Next we describe additional aspects of internationalization with which academic leaders should have some familiarity.

Cultural Intelligence

A key component of internationalization efforts is to build the cultural intelligence of students. It is also an important trait for effective faculty members and academic leaders. Cultural intelligence (CQ) is understood as an extension of intelligence quotient (IQ), and emotional intelligence (EQ) helps individuals better understand and advance the ways in which their mental framing affects how they see the world and interact with others (Middleton, 2014). We often consider cultural phenomena as things we encounter when crossing borders, although Middleton (2014) has argued, "It is about crossing all kinds of cultural borders, learning to operate effectively in unfamiliar surroundings and finding a way to break down barriers that may well not be geographical at all" (p. 11). In fact, one of the important attributes of internationalization is that it not only has the capacity to improve how we see the world beyond our shores—it can also improve how we interact with those around us on a daily a basis.

At CQ's foundation is the development of *intercultural understanding*, which is centered on understanding individuals' social position and status (e.g., age, religion, disability, employment, etc.) and cultural history, and the power dynamics that shape interactions between dominant and nondominant cultures (Pope et al., 2004). As discussed in chapter 3 of this volume, these differences and the intersections of different identities have come to dominate the discourse in both politics and academia in the United States, but they extend across the world. Effectively navigating these issues takes more than simple understanding, however, which is where cultural intelligence comes into play.

One of the strengths of higher education is that is has always been a crossroads of cultures and interconnectivity. The interaction of different groups is intensifying due to globalization and efforts to confront inequities and other forms of discrimination inside and outside our organizations. Academic leaders today need skills that enable them to work successfully with and across diverse cultures as well as to be champions for mutual respect and building cultures of belonging on campus. Colleges and universities also need to purposefully provide opportunities to prepare their students to be leaders in a world that seems increasingly fractured by cultural divides.

Internationalization at Home

In the last 2 decades, higher education leaders have been encouraged to expand their notions of internationalization to focus on how to internationalize the campus and the curriculum. The phrase *internationalization at home* (IAH) represents the idea that an institution can undertake activities to internationalize its campus in ways beyond or separate from hosting international students and scholars (Crowther et al., 2000; Leask, 2009). IAH often includes development of intentional activities within curricular and cocurricular spaces "to ensure that all students have opportunities to engage in global, international, and intercultural learning in classrooms and across campuses" (Agnew & Kahn, 2014, p. 31). With fewer than 10% of U.S. college students studying abroad (and half of those who travel doing so for less than a semester), IAH has become an important way to ensure all students have opportunities to expand their perspectives beyond their local context.

IAH is often associated with transforming the curriculum to incorporate more international perspectives as well as building out cocurricular activities that engage students in learning about different cultures. For example, within the general education curriculum at Miami University (n.d.) in Oxford, Ohio, undergraduate students are required to take courses in intercultural understanding. This public ivy's program, the Miami Global Plan, is designed to provide "intensive focus on global inquiry and intercultural consciousness" through "a deeper understanding of self and others (e.g. biases, norms) in a multilingual and multicultural world," (para. 7). The University at Albany, an urban public research institution within the SUNY system, developed a Global Distinction (Center for International Education and Global Strategy, University at Albany, n.d.) milestone to allow students "to acquire the necessary knowledge, skills, and perspectives to succeed in a globalized world—to become Globally Competent" (para. 1) and receive a special designation on their transcript.

Another IAH model that has become particularly popular in the wake of the pandemic is virtual mobility. This type of IAH allows students to engage with overseas locations and students without leaving home. One of the more sophisticated models, collaborative online and international learning (COIL), enables faculty members in two different countries to coteach a single course.[5] This innovative format allows faculty to collaborate with international colleagues and students to engage with international peers in class discussions and group projects without having to leave their campuses, thereby connecting them with the broader world and enhancing their cultural intelligence.

Comprehensive Internationalization

Internationalization of an institution is about more than the curriculum. Hudzik (2015) argued that colleges and universities should adopt *comprehensive internationalization*, which is "the means by which higher education institutions respond to the widening and more complex expectations to connect globally across all missions to better serve students, clientele, and society in the twenty-first century context" (p. 1). The idea is that international perspectives and engagements should be integrated throughout the institution, including into the three core activities of teaching, research, and service.

No single path toward comprehensive internationalization exists; it is not a strategy so much as a mindset or way of operating. The goal, though, is to reorient the operations of the institution so that international perspectives become part of the core discourse, and international engagement is approached strategically, rather than being driven by the whim and will of individual faculty members and idiosyncratic interests. As noted previously, the world is changing rapidly, and the role of higher education institutions is becoming more important. To be effective in engaging and competing in this world, college and university leaders should consider how they want their institutions to approach international activities: Are international students welcome on campus? Does the curriculum reflect international perspectives? Are institutional policies designed to facilitate international activities in teaching and research? Are there international service opportunities for students? Comprehensive internationalization is intended to push an institution toward naturally incorporating international perspectives into all aspects of how the institution operates.

Four Forms of Mobility: Students, Faculty, Programs, and Institutions

A key aspect of internationalization is mobility across borders. While traditionally we think of students and faculty as the primary participants in educational travel, programs and institutions are all now mobile as well. The following sections provide an overview of these four core types of mobility.

Students

Study-abroad programs can be divided into three general types, which can last a few days or an entire semester. In faculty-led endeavors, students accompany a professor to another country, usually to study a particular issue as part of an academic course. The faculty member works with local entities (e.g., businesses, governmental agencies, and not-for-profit organizations) to provide students with opportunities to talk with local leaders, visit specific places, engage in a service project, and participate in other activities. These activities extend the theoretical aspects of the course and allow students to experience more fully the challenges confronted by people in other countries.

Another type of study abroad is institutional exchange. In these situations, historically, an institution establishes an agreement with a counterpart in another country to allow its students to enroll in the partner institution for a period of time, often a semester. Recently some such arrangements have become part of multi-institutional agreements or are run by larger organizations that broker the relationships. These exchanges allow students to obtain a more in-depth cultural experience and engage in another country's academic system by living and learning with the students in the local community.

A third set of study abroad experiences, short-term internship, research, and service programs, has become popular in the past decade. These types of study abroad allow students to engage in a work or internship experience, although it is important to ensure that these experiential learning programs are designed responsibly and in collaboration with local partners (see chapter 9, this volume, for a discussion of engaging effectively with internship development and community engagement). During AY 2018–2019, more than 38,000 students in 428 U.S. institutions engaged in noncredit work, volunteer engagements, internships, or research activities in another country (Baer & Martel, 2020). Institutions are now tapping their alumni to help place students in international internships. Levin (2008), for example, noted that Yale University had developed an alumni infrastructure to support summer internships in 17 cities: Shanghai, Hong Kong, Singapore, Delhi, Accra, Cape Town, Kampala, Montreal, Monterrey, Buenos Aires, João Pessoa, Brussels, Budapest, Istanbul, London, Madrid, and Athens.

Faculty

The faculty is the core of the academic enterprise. Internationalization activities such as IAH, faculty-led study abroad, and research collaborations cannot succeed without faculty members' participation (Klyberg, 2012). While the faculty has always been an international profession—as intellectual curiosity and scientific inquiry rarely end at national borders—to encourage faculty investment in campus-wide internationalization, leaders must ensure that these policies are developed and implemented in ways that adhere to the principles of this book. That is, they are democratic, adaptable, inclusive, and consistent with their institution's mission.

Beyond campus internationalization, an increasing number of faculty members appear to be pursuing international careers. Where they obtain their graduate degrees may differ from the country in which they grew up, and they may take a position in yet another country. Moreover, research is an increasingly internationalized pursuit as scholarly societies, academic journals, and research programs broaden to a more global focus. Indeed, many of today's most pressing research problems transcend borders and require international and interdisciplinary collaboration between scholars and higher education institutions.

Unlike students, however, information about the international mobility of faculty is very limited. No international organization collects these data in a systematic way. That said, the NSF does track a variety of statistics related to faculty in the fields of science, technology, engineering, and mathematics. It reported that in 2017 nearly 20% of all full-time faculty members with science, engineering, and health doctorates who were employed by U.S. colleges and universities received their doctorate abroad (National Science Board, 2020).

Research on the international engagement of faculty is also limited. In a 14-nation study, Altbach and Lewis (1996) found that U.S.-based academics were the least interested in reading scholarship by authors in other countries, engaging with international scholars, and internationalizing their curricula. Similarly, results of a 2007 survey of respondents from 17 nations showed that U.S.-based faculty were among the least likely to collaborate or coauthor a publication with international researchers in other countries (Finkelstein et al., 2009). That said, Finkelstein et al.'s (2009) study did find that U.S. faculty reported above-average integration of international perspectives in teaching and research activities.

Academic Programs

While some students cross borders to pursue an education, a number of institutions are now moving their academic programs across borders to increase their availability to students in other countries. Knight (2005) defined *cross-border program mobility* as

> the movement of individual education/training courses and programs across national borders through face-to-face, distance, or a combination of these modes. Credits toward a qualification can be awarded by the sending foreign country provider or by an affiliated domestic partner or jointly. (p. 10)

These types of programs, which can include a range of activities, from franchise agreements to joint- or dual-degree programs, are on the rise. However, data about their prevalence are limited. A study of 285 institutions in 28 countries revealed that almost all respondents (95%) saw such programs as part of their internationalization strategy, although only 55% had a clear policy related to joint- or dual-degree program development (Obst et al., 2011). The United States offered the most dual-degree programs, preferring them over joint-degree programs, and France was the top provider of joint-degree programs. While most dual-degree programs globally are at the master's level, a majority of these programs in the United States are at the undergraduate level. Moreover, according to the survey, U.S. institutions (along with those in China, France, India, and Germany) were among the most desired collaborators. We note that these data are now more than a decade old, and trends are likely to have shifted, particularly with a rise in interest and engagement from higher education institutions in Asia.

Institutions

Over the past 2 decades the number of higher education institutions with branch campuses in more than one country has rapidly increased. An international branch campus (IBC) is an

> entity that is owned, at least in part, by a foreign education provider; operated in the name of the foreign education provider; engages in at least some face-to-face teaching; and provides access to an entire academic program that leads to a credential awarded by the foreign education. (Lane, 2011, p. 5)

According to the Cross-Border Education Research Team (2020), more than 300 international campuses are operating in nearly 40 countries. China is now the largest importer of such campuses, followed by the United Arab Emirates, Singapore, Malaysia, and Qatar. The United States is by far the largest exporter of such campuses, followed by the United Kingdom, France, Russia, and Australia. Of note, China has become increasingly involved in exporting its universities overseas as well.

IBCs may be wholly owned by the home campus, operated in partnership with a foreign investor, or subsidized by the host government (Garrett et al., 2016). IBCs are not study-abroad locations. They tend to serve students from the IBC's local environment and are increasingly involved in activities that advance the host country's public agenda. While primarily teaching focused, Pohl and Lane (2018) found that about one third of the institutions are engaged in research activity. IBCs in Qatar and Malaysia contribute significantly to the innovative ecosystems of those countries.

Conclusion

The international environment is changing quickly, and college and university leaders need to be aware of these changes and consider how they affect their institutional mission. Some institutions, such as Northeastern University, may find ways to extend traditional services and activities into the international domain. Others may seek out new frontiers, such as New York University's decision to build degree-granting campuses in Abu Dhabi and Shanghai. In addition, intensifying international pressures may force some institutions to reinvest in their traditional mission, embracing it as a means to confront the growing interconnectedness discussed in this chapter. Regardless of the direction an institution takes, its leaders need to be aware of changing international dynamics and, with the faculty and other stakeholders, make purposeful decisions on the appropriate response.

Notes

1. These figures often do not include displaced and undocumented students, whose numbers have surged since 2015 due to economic conditions, political conflicts, and war (Bhandari et al., 2018).

2. The United States has a larger overall economy than Australia, so as a proportion of the economy, international education plays a larger role in Australia than in the United States.

3. According to the U.S. Department of Commerce (2018), "'Items' include commodities, software or technology, such as clothing, building materials, circuit boards, automotive parts, blue prints, design plans, retail software packages and technical information" (p. 2). See http://www.bis.doc.gov/licensing/exportingbasics.htm for updated guidelines.

4. Campus leaders should be aware of three primary aspects of export regulations. First, the International Traffic in Arms Regulations (ITAR, 1976) controls military- or defense-related articles, technologies, and services. Except under special exemption or with authorization from the U.S. Department of State, information about items listed on the U.S. Munitions List may only be shared with U.S. people. Second, the Bureau of Industry and Security in the U.S. Department of Commerce enforces export administration regulations, which control commercial and dual-use products and technologies (Commerce and Foreign Trade, 1982). Some items require a license before they can be exported, and export administration restrictions on items may vary among destinations, based on the nature of the relationship between the United States and the importing country. Third, the Office of Foreign Assets Control in the U.S. Department of the Treasury prohibits transactions with countries subject to boycotts, trade sanctions, and embargoes.

5. For an example of a COIL initiative, see the SUNY COIL Center's website: https://coil.suny.edu/.

References

Agnew, M., & Kahn, H. E. (2014). Internationalization at home: Grounded practices to promote intercultural, international, and global learning. *Metropolitan Universities, 25*(3), 31–46. https://journals.iupui.edu/index.php/muj/article/view/20580

Altbach, P. G. (2004). The costs and benefits of world class universities. *Academe, 90*(1), 20–23. https://doi.org/10.2307/40252583

Altbach, P. G., & Lewis, L. (1996). The academic profession in international perspective. In P. G. Altbach (Ed.), *The international academic profession: Portraits of fourteen countries* (pp. 3–48). Carnegie Foundation for the Advancement of Teaching.

Baer, J., & Martel, M. (2020). *Fall 2020 international student snapshot.* Institute of International Education. https://www.iie.org/Research-and-Insights/Open-Doors/Fall-International-Enrollments-Snapshot-Reports

Bhandari, R., Robles, C., & Farrugia, C. (2018). *International higher education: Shifting mobilities, policy challenges, and new initiatives.* UNESCO. https://unesdoc.unesco.org/ark:/48223/pf0000266078

Bloomberg. (2021, February 1). *China diplomat's "red line" warning points to U.S. tensions.* https://www.bloomberg.com/news/articles/2021-02-02/china-s-top-diplomat-warns-biden-not-to-touch-internal-affairs

Calderon, A. (2018). *Massification of higher education revisited.* RMIT University. https://www.academia.edu/36975860/Massification_of_higher_education_revisited

Center for International Education and Global Strategy, University at Albany. (n.d.). *Global distinction.* https://www.albany.edu/international/globaldistinction.php

Cross-Border Education Research Team. (2020, November 20). *C-BERT international campus listing* [Data originally collected by K. Kinser and J. E. Lane]. http://cbert.org/resources-data/intl-campus/

Commerce and Foreign Trade, 15 C.F.R. 300 et seq., 700 et seq. (1982)

Commission on the Abraham Lincoln Study Abroad Program. (2005). *Global competence & national needs: One million Americans studying abroad.* https://www.nafsa.org/policy-and-advocacy/policy-resources/report-commission-abraham-lincoln-study-abroad-fellowship-program

Crowther, P., Joris, M., Otten, M., Nilsson, B., Teekens, H., & Wächter, B. (2000). *Internationalisation at home: A position paper.* EAIE.

Dickler, J. (2020, July 14). *Trump administration reverses course on foreign student ban.* CNBC. https://www.cnbc.com/2020/07/14/fight-heats-up-over-foreign-student-ban-as-more-than-200-schools-join-in.html

Education Bureau, Hong Kong. (2021, May 27). *Hong Kong scholarship for excellence scheme.* https://hkses.edb.gov.hk/en/index.html

Ellis, L., & Baumann, D. (2020, March 6). "Moving the goal posts": What you need to know about DeVos's closer scrutiny of foreign gifts. *The Chronicle of Higher Education, 6*(24).

Fedoroff, N. V. (2009). Science diplomacy in the 21st century. *Cell, 136*(1), 9–11. https://doi.org/10.1016/j.cell.2008.12.030

Finkelstein, M. J., Walker, E., & Chen, R. (2009). The internationalization of the American faculty: Where are we, what drives or deters us? *Report of the International Conference on the Changing Academic Profession project, 2009* (RIHE International Seminar Report No. 13, pp. 113–142). Research Institute for Higher Education, Hiroshima University. https://rihe.hiroshima-u.ac.jp/publications/en/others/ap_en/

Garrett, R., Kinser, K. Lane, J. E., & Merola, R. (2016). *International branch campuses: Trends and developments, 2016.* Observatory for Borderless Higher Education and Cross Border Education.

Gilboa, E. (2008). Searching for a theory of public diplomacy. *Annals of the American Academy of Political and Social Science, 616*(1), 55–77. https://doi.org/10.1177/0002716207312142

Grove, J. (2015, January 22). Russia's universities: Rebuilding "collapsed stars." *Times Higher Education,* https://www.timeshighereducation.com/features/russias-universities-rebuilding-collapsed-stars/2018006.article

Gürüz, K. (2008). *Higher education and international student mobility in the global knowledge economy.* State University of New York Press.

Hazelkorn, E. (2015). *Rankings and the reshaping of higher education: The battle for world-class excellence* (2nd ed.). Palgrave Macmillan.

Hazelkorn, E., & Mihut, G. (eds). (2021). *Research handbook on university rankings: Theory, methodology, influence, and impact.* Edward Elgar Publishing.

Higher Education Act, Pub. L. No. 89-329 (1965)

Hudzik, J. K. (2015). *Comprehensive internationalization: Institutional pathways to success.* Routledge.

International Traffic in Arms Regulations, 22 C.F.R. 121.1 et seq. (1976)

James, K. (2005). International education: The concept and its relationship to intercultural education. *Journal of Research in International Education, 4*(3), 313–332. https://doi.org/10.1177/1475240905057812

Kanno-Youngs, Z. (2020, January 31). Trump administration adds six more countries to travel ban. *The New York Times.* https://www.nytimes.com/2020/01/31/us/politics/trump-travel-ban.html

Kerr, C. (1963). *The uses of the university.* Harvard University Press.

Kerr, W. R. (2018). *The gift of global talent: How migration shapes business, economy, and society.* Stanford University Press.

Klineberg, O. (1976). *International student exchange: An assessment of its nature and its prospects.* Mouton.

Klyberg, S. G. F. (2012). *The faculty experience of internationalization: Motivations for, practices of, and means for engagement* (Publication no. 3534672) [Doctoral dissertation, Pennsylvania State University]. ProQuest Dissertations Publishing.

Krige, J. (2006). *American hegemony and the postwar reconstruction of science in Europe.* The MIT Press.

Knight, J. (2003). Updated definition of internationalization. *International Higher Education,* (33), 2–3. https://doi.org/10.6017/ihe.2003.33.7391

Knight, J. (2005). *Cross-border education: Programs and providers on the move* (Millennium Research No. 10). Canadian Bureau for International Education. https://files.eric.ed.gov/fulltext/ED549966.pdf

Knight, J. (2013). Education hubs: International, regional and local dimensions of scale and scope. *Comparative Education, 49*(3), 374–387. https://doi.org/10.108 0/03050068.2013.803783

Lane, J. E. (2011). Importing private higher education: International branch campuses. *Journal of Comparative Policy Analysis, 13*(4), 367–381. https://doi.org/ 10.1080/13876988.2011.583106

Lane, J. E. (2012). Higher education and economic competitiveness. In J. E. Lane & D. B. Johnstone (Eds.), *Colleges and universities as economic drivers: Measuring higher education's role in economic development* (pp. 221–252). State University of New York Press.

Lane, J. E. (2015). Higher education internationalization: Why governments care. In E. Ulberg (Ed.), *New perspectives on internationalization and competitiveness* (pp. 17–30). Springer.

Lane, J. E. (2021, April 29). *Four reasons international student numbers in the US are unlikely to rebound quickly*. The PIE News. https://thepienews.com/the-view-from/four-reasons-international-student-numbers-in-the-us-are-unlikely-to-rebound-quickly/

Lane, J. E., & Kinser, K. (Eds.). (2011). *Multinational colleges and universities: Leadership, administration, and governance of international branch campuses* (New Directions for Higher Education, no. 155, pp. 5–17). https://doi.org/10.1002/ he.440

Lane, J. E., Owens, T. L., & Kinser, K. (2015). *Cross border higher education, international trade, and economic competitiveness: A review of policy dynamics when education crosses borders*. ILEAP, CUTS International Geneva, & CARIS. http://www .cuts-geneva.org/pdf/TAF087_cross-border-education-and-trade-policy.pdf

Leask, B. (2009). Using formal and informal curricula to improve interactions between home and international students. *Journal of Studies in International Education, 13*(2), 205–221. https://doi.org/10.1177/1028315308329786

Levin, R. C. (2008, May 6). *The internationalization of the university* [Speech transcript]. Yale University. https://president.yale.edu/about/past-presidents/levin-speeches-archive

Levy, D. (2006). The unanticipated explosion: Private higher education's global surge. *Comparative Education Review, 50*(2), 217–240. https://doi.org/10.1086/500694

Miami University. (n.d.). *Global Miami plan*. https://miamioh.edu/academics/core-curriculum/index.html

Middleton, J. (2014). *Cultural intelligence: The competitive edge for leaders crossing borders*. Bloomsbury.

Mok, K. H., & Cheung, A. B. L. (2011). Global aspirations and strategising for world-class status: New form of politics in higher education governance in Hong Kong. *Journal of Higher Education Policy and Management, 33*(3), 231–251. https://doi.org/10.1080/1360080X.2011.564998

Nager, A., Hart, D. M., Ezell, S. J., & Atkinson, R. D. (2016). *The demographics of innovation in the United States*. Information Technology & Innovation Foundation. http://www2.itif.org/2016-demographics-of-innovation.pdf

National Center for Education Statistics. (2019). *Digest of educational statistics, 2018*. U.S. Department of Education. https://nces.ed.gov/fastfacts/display.asp?id=98

National Science Board. (2020). *Science and engineering indicators 2020*. National Science Foundation. https://ncses.nsf.gov/pubs/nsb20201

Nygård, H. M., & Gates, S. (2013). Soft power at home and abroad: Sport diplomacy, politics and peace-building. *International Area Studies Review, 16*(3), 235–243. https://doi.org/10.1177/2233865913502971

Oakman, D. (2004). *Facing Asia: A history of the Colombo plan*. Pandanus.

Obst, D., Kuder, M., & Banks, C. (2011). *Joint and double degree programs in the global context: Report on an international survey*. Institute of International Education. http://www.iie.org/Research-and-Publications/Publications-and-Reports/IIE-Bookstore/~/media/Files/Corporate/Publications/Joint-Double-Degree-Survey-Report-2011.ashx

Organisation for Economic Co-operation and Development. (2020). *Education at a glance 2020: OECD indicators*. https://www.oecd-ilibrary.org/education/education-at-a-glance-2020_69096873-en

Pohl, H., & Lane, J. E. (2018). Research contributions of international branch campuses to the scientific wealth of academically developing countries. *Scientometrics, 116*(3), 1719–1734. https://doi.org/10.1007/s11192-018-2790-y

Pope, R. L., Reynolds, A. L., & Mueller, J. A. (2004). *Multicultural competence in student affairs*. Jossey-Bass.

Porter, M. E. (1990). *The competitive advantage of nations*. The Free Press.

Rait, R. S. (1931). *Life in the medieval university*. Cambridge University Press.

Rashdall, H. (1895). *The universities of Europe in the Middle Ages*. Henry Frowde.

Redden, E. (2017, October 11). Foreign students and graduate STEM enrollment. *Inside Higher Ed*. https://www.insidehighered.com/quicktakes/2017/10/11/foreign-students-and-graduate-stem-enrollment

Redden, E. (2020, September 25). Major changes to student visa rules proposed. *Inside Higher Ed*. https://www.insidehighered.com/news/2020/09/25/trump-administration-proposes-major-overhaul-student-visa-rules

Salmi, J., & Altbach, P. G. (2016). World-class universities. In P. N. Teixeira & J.-C. Shin (Eds.), *Encyclopedia of international higher education systems and institutions*. https://doi.org/10.1007/978-94-017-9553-1_37-1

Schwab, K. (2011). *The global competitiveness report, 2011–2012*. World Economic Forum. http://www3.weforum.org/docs/WEF_GCR_Report_2011-12.pdf

Tehan, D. (2019, November 22). *International education makes significant economic contribution* [Press release]. Department of Education, Skills and Employment, Government of Australia. https://ministers.dese.gov.au/tehan/international-education-makes-significant-economic-contribution?utm_source=miragenews&utm_medium=miragenews&utm_campaign=news

U.S. Department of Commerce. (2018). *Introduction to commerce department export controls.* https://www.bis.doc.gov/index.php/documents/regulations-docs/142-eccn-pdf/file

U.S. Department of Justice. (2020, January 28). *Harvard University professor and two Chinese nationals charged in three separate China related cases* [Press release]. https://www.justice.gov/opa/pr/harvard-university-professor-and-two-chinese-nationals-charged-three-separate-china-related

U.S. Department of State. (n.d.). *About us—Under secretary for public diplomacy and public affairs.* https://www.state.gov/about-us-under-secretary-for-public-diplomacy-and-public-affairs/

U.S. International Trade Administration. (n.d.). *U.S. education service exports.* https://www.trade.gov/education-service-exports

Watney, C. (2020, July 19). America's innovation engine is slowing. *The Atlantic.* https://www.theatlantic.com/ideas/archive/2020/07/americas-innovation-engine-slowing/614320/

Wildavsky, B. (2010). *The great brain race: How global universities are reshaping the world.* Princeton University Press.

6

FEDERAL ENGAGEMENT
IN HIGHER EDUCATION

The federal government casts a long shadow over higher education. While the states retain primary authority over most of the nation's colleges and universities, the federal government has used its legislative power and purse strings to influence higher education's development, expansion, operations, and innovation. From providing billions of dollars in student financial aid each year to subsidizing research and development (R&D) to investigating issues from athletics to foreign funding, the federal government has become inextricably linked to higher education, with the extent of its influence often aligned with an institution's mission.

The relationship between our four pillars and federal engagement with higher education is likely very evident when one considers the multiple roles in which federal policy interacts with colleges and universities—whether public or private. As discussed throughout this chapter, the federal government has long viewed higher education as an important partner in advancing our democratic society, supporting the economy, and protecting the nation. Its support has directly shaped institutional missions, such as the creation of land-grant colleges and the chartering of military academies. Through direct funding and legislative engagement, the federal government has also taken an active role in expanding access to higher education and supports to encourage success among students who have traditionally be underserved, as well as for providing legal protections for different groups of individuals. College and university leaders also have responded quickly to changes in federal policy, such as when the Trump administration unexpectedly enacted travel restrictions on international students and changed visa requirements. In fact, the federal government's influence has become so expansive that many institutions now employ staff who deal directly with federal relations.

The sprawling character of the federal government's involvement in higher education can make it difficult to understand the nature of such involvement. Generally, though, federal interaction with higher education can be grouped into five primary areas (see Figure 6.1).

While most of the federal government's initiatives can be classified under one or more of these areas, the exact nature of federal involvement in higher education can vary significantly based on the interests and initiatives of

Figure 6.1. Five primary areas of federal involvement in higher education.

Access and Success: Programs and initiatives focused on increasing enrollments and providing supports for success in specific programs as well as across all institutions

Accountability and Transparency: Initiatives meant to ensure compliance with institutional reporting and other federal protections, requirements, and expectations

Research and Innovation: Programs pertaining to building the nation's research capacity and fostering innovation

Institutional Development: Initiatives designed to develop specific types of institutions such as land-grant institutions and minority-serving institutions

International Engagements: Programs and regulations that focus on the movement of individuals, programs, and institutions and funds across international borders

elected officials and other environmental factors. For example, national service initiatives supported by Presidents George H. W. Bush and Bill Clinton encouraged the widespread engagement of colleges and their students in community service. President George W. Bush's interest in accountability brought about the No Child Left Behind Act and a subsequent national discussion about accountability in higher education. During President Barack Obama's administration, health-care reform changed how institutions dealt with student health insurance, a focus on urban renewal involved institutions in the redevelopment of major metropolitan areas, and new regulations curtailed for-profit college development. President Donald Trump's administration launched investigations into foreign funding of higher education, Chinese theft of U.S. intellectual property, and the use of race in college admission. In addition, the Trump administration rolled back Obama-era regulations pertaining to for-profit colleges, sexual assault, and protections for undocumented immigrants—many of whom had enrolled in college. At the time of this writing, President Joe Biden's administration appears to be focused on tackling affordability, possibly expanding loan forgiveness and direct aid to reduce the cost of college. Each of these agendas have long-standing ripple effects across higher education that can last well beyond the end of the particular administration.

The Evolution of Federal Engagement in Higher Education

For many academic administrators, the federal government is viewed as a source of research funding, student aid, campus disclosures, and protection for civil rights and other freedoms. Few may realize that the federal government plays a secondary, or supportive, role to state governments, which bear primary responsibility for education at all levels. The country's founders, including George Washington, James Madison, and Alexander Hamilton, favored the creation of a federal university, but the vote to give the U.S. Congress the power to create such an institution was narrowly defeated in 1798 (Rainsford, 1972). While this early attempt to grant the federal government some participation in the nation's postsecondary education sector failed, the federal government's involvement would not be forestalled for long.

Only a few short years after the failed vote to create a national university, the federal government took a new interest in the postsecondary sector. The first major federal foray into higher education occurred with the creation of the U.S. Military Academy at West Point in 1802, and although the institution was not allowed to offer collegiate-level degrees until 1933,

Francis Wayland, president of Brown University, noted its importance in 1850 when he suggested that every engineered bridge and highway in the United States to that point had been designed by West Point graduates (Babbidge & Rosenzweig, 1962). While a truly national university was never created, the federal government continues to sponsor several military academies that provide undergraduate education and leadership development for commissioned officers in the U.S. military.[1]

The first recorded significant congressional committee debate regarding higher education occurred on December 7, 1818, when Congressman John Floyd of Virginia suggested that the Public Lands Committee of the House of Representatives investigate the appropriation of federal lands to each state to endow a university (U.S. House Journal, 1818). While the committee did not immediately adopt the suggestion, Floyd started a several-decades committee debate about the role of the federal government in higher education that culminated in 1862 with the passage of the Morrill Act, also called the Land-Grant College Act, named after Representative Justin Morrill of Vermont (a second Land-Grant College Act was passed in 1890 and is discussed later in the chapter). Indeed, the act spurred the creation of some of the nation's most productive research universities and thrust the federal government into becoming the most significant sponsor of agricultural research in the world.[2]

With the passage of the land-grant acts, Congress also established a precedent of involving itself in higher education when it needed the nation's colleges and universities to help with specific social or economic problems. The land-grant acts helped revolutionize agricultural production, manufacturing, and infrastructure development at a time when the industrial revolution was transforming many developed economies. The federal government's engagement in higher education was mostly limited to land-grant institutions until World War I, when institutions became militarized to help support the war effort. Indeed, during times of war, the United States' colleges and universities have often played a significant role in the nation's story, serving as incubators for critics and protestors, trainers of military professionals, and providers of new research in national defense (Rudy, 1996). The years surrounding World War I were among the most active in the development of the relationship between higher education and the federal government.

In 1915 Congress authorized the creation of the Coast Guard Academy (following the creation of West Point and the Naval Academy). A year later in 1916, the National Research Council was established to coordinate the federal government's support of R&D. The following year, the Smith-Hughes Act of 1917 provided money for vocational training below the college level. Other federal policies affecting colleges and universities during this time included rehabilitation policies for disabled veterans, military training through the Students' Army Training Corps (SATC) and the Reserve Officer Training Corps (ROTC; permanently established in 1920), and disposal of surplus military items (much of which was given to educational institutions).

At the start of World War I, the academic enterprise was largely insular, focused inward, and inadequate to support the needs of the modern military (Kolbe, 1919). In 1918, however, when the United States entered the war, the ACE was created by a group of college presidents to "coordinate the services which educational institutions and organizations could contribute to the Government in the national crisis brought on by World War I" (Quattlebaum, 1960, p. 41). Ultimately, the nation's colleges and universities mobilized to support national defense efforts:

> In fact, the doctrine of "preparedness" had become a watchword in educational circles as the danger of war loomed nearer. With the actual outbreak the universities saw the horizon of their pre-war opportunities for useful cooperation infinitely widened, and their whole activity suddenly elevated from the plane of every-day education to that of national defense. (Kolbe, 1919, p. 21)

During World War I, U.S. colleges and universities forged a new union with society through their demonstrated usefulness in research, the training of military personnel, and the education of young men. These same institutions, however, confronted a number of challenges during the nation's war effort, including declining enrollments, shrinking budgets, and an increasingly militaristic social and academic culture (Levine, 1986). Despite the changes that occurred in higher education,

> the subsequent proliferation of "reserve-officer training" and service academies themselves was but an extension of the principle established early in the Union, namely, that the expenditures of federal funds for educational purposes and the use of educational institutions were justified in the effort to produce highly or uniquely trained personnel to meet identifiable needs of the national government. Much of the subsequent history of Federal involvement in American higher education constitutes nothing more than a broadening of the definition embodied in this concept. (Babbidge & Rosenzweig, 1962, p. 7)

Indeed, for several more decades, the federal government continued to engage in using higher education to achieve other national goals (Morse, 1966; Russell, 1951). During the 1930s, President Franklin Delano Roosevelt turned to higher education as one of the mechanisms to implement his New Deal programs to lift the nation out of the Great Depression. In 1935 the Emergency Relief Appropriation Act funded many education-related programs, including the National Youth Administration, which provided funding to more than 620,000 students between the ages of 16 and 25 to continue their education. This program was the first time the federal government would support private higher education institutions during peacetime.

While World War I transformed the relationship between the federal government and higher education, World War II transformed higher education. First, the federal government took a leadership role in funding scientific inquiry, relying heavily on the nation's research institutions to support a number of R&D programs, such as the Manhattan Project, which created the first atomic bomb. Second, the passage of the Servicemen's Readjustment Act of 1944 (commonly known as the GI Bill) greatly expanded higher education access, and institutions soon burgeoned with new enrollments as veterans returned to civilian life and could not find employment in the postwar economy. Research has evidenced that the GI Bill had a positive impact on the educational attainment of White and Black men overall; but the ongoing discrimination and educational segregation meant that Black veterans did not benefit in the same way that White men did. (Turner & Bound, 2002). For the 1.2 million Black American veterans of World War II, they faced numerous barriers to accessing their GI benefits. Southern Congressman insisted the bill's benefits be distributed by states instead of the federal government in order to localize control. Discrimination of distributing benefits covered a range of intended benefit areas, from unemployment support to housing loans, to educational access. It has been reported that the systemic discrimination ran deep, with some mail carriers in the South failing to deliver the forms needed for these veterans to access benefits and the VA actively encouraging Black veterans to apply for vocational training as opposed to university-level programs (Herbold, 1995). During the 1940s, when the bulk of veterans accessed these benefits, Black enrollment in higher education across the North and West never exceed 5,000 individuals, while 20,000 eligible Blacks could not find an academic institution to attend in 1947 alone; and around 95% of those who were admitted to higher education attended one of the all-Black segregated colleges in the South (Taylor, 2008).

The 1950s witnessed continued expansion of federal engagement in higher education, primarily because of the growing power of the Soviet Union. The Cold War fostered a national interest in the advancement of science and engineering, and the federal government wanted to build on the positive working relationship it had established with institutions of higher education during World War II. Indeed, in 1950 the NSF was created, and an excerpt from its first annual report (1950–1951) indicated the importance of the nation's higher education institutions in helping to win the war:

> Penicillin, the proximity fuse, the atom bomb, among a host of other scientific contributions to American victory in the Second World War, brought home to many citizens the value of scientific research. In the continuing crisis after the war, there were few who opposed the proposition that sustained Federal support of science and research was essential to the defense and welfare of the United States. (NSF, 1951, p. 1)

The report goes on to state that Congress approved the creation of the NSF for such purposes as promoting science; advancing the nation's health, prosperity, and welfare; and securing the national defense.

The launch of Sputnik in 1957 intensified fears that U.S. scientists were falling behind their Soviet counterparts, and Congress passed the National Defense Education Act in 1958. The act provided general funding through the National Defense Student Loan program to increase the number of students enrolled in higher education. In addition, the act provided targeted funding to support foreign language studies, engineering students, and area study centers.

Not all federal involvement in higher education has stemmed from the legislative and executive branches. One significant action by the federal judiciary in the 1950s had long-reaching effects. In 1954 the U.S. Supreme Court ruled in *Brown v. Board of Education* that separate educational facilities for members of different races could not be considered equal. This ruling (discussed in more depth in chapter 8, this volume) caused dramatic changes in many public institutions, particularly in those states that had established separate land-grant institutions for Black and White students. Seemingly overnight, the federal judiciary set aside decades of institutionalized practice and case law supporting segregation and declared such practices illegal.

In the 1960s the federal government began to move away from interventions exclusively motivated by a desire to meet national needs. *Brown v. Board of Education* (1954) served as the foundation for the Civil Rights Act of 1964, which banned discrimination against minorities, such as Blacks and women. The act applied not just to higher education, but it specifically required the desegregation of public colleges and universities and authorized the federal attorney general to file lawsuits to enforce those provisions of the law.

Separately, Congress passed the Higher Education Act (HEA) of 1965, which created the Federal Student Aid Program, which has provided millions of students with grants or low-interest loans to help offset the cost of their postsecondary education. These funds eventually supported the educational pursuits of hundreds of thousands of students each year. The HEA included a sunset clause, which meant that it needed to be reauthorized by Congress periodically. Thus, there have been nine reauthorizations. At the time of this writing, the HEA's 2008 reauthorization has been temporarily extended to allow Congress to prepare an update.

Under the 1968 and 1972 reauthorizations, Congress worked to consolidate many of the federal government's higher education roles under one act. However, only about 25% of all federal engagements now fall under the HEA. While the HEA may not have consolidated all the federal government's higher education initiatives, it has served as a focal point for congressional interest in the topic. Indeed, in the past 4 decades, Congress's engagement with higher education issues occurred most frequently around the time of the authorization of the HEA (Lane & Lefor, 2007).

The HEA started a new era in the federal government's relationship with higher education. Higher education emerged as an important social institution in its own right, not merely a mechanism to help the federal government achieve other policy goals. For example, over the next several decades, the federal government became the most significant provider of financial aid to assist students with the cost of pursuing a college degree. It also continued to fund research, expanding existing sources and creating new ones. By the beginning of the 21st century, however, several members of Congress had begun to question (and challenge) the extensive support the federal government was giving to higher education.

The remainder of this chapter provides readers with an overview of important federal policies and current engagements with higher education. These activities are so vast and diffuse that any treatment is certain to fail to provide a complete picture. As Knight (1960) noted in the introduction of a book in which he undertook a similar task:

> The temerity of writing a brief book on this subject is exceeded only by the necessity of it. None of us would pretend for a moment that we could do justice to that common ground of [federal] government and higher education, which is so confused and yet so critical a part of our national life. . . . Too many plans are in part the result of political expediency and compromise to allow us the comfort of knowing where the relationships of federal government and higher education are headed. We realize that a large amount of federal income is being invested in higher education of one kind or another; but we know surprisingly little beyond this fact. (p. 1)

Sixty years later, this passage remains remarkably relevant. While there is now greater understanding of the various involvements of the federal government with higher education, it remains practically impossible to inventory their full depth and breadth because of their scope across multiple departments and agencies.

Primary Areas of Federal Engagement

While the states retain primary financial and regulatory responsibilities for higher education, the importance of the nation's colleges and universities continues to attract the attention of the federal legislative, executive, and judicial branches. Moreover, one of the main means of support for U.S. higher education comes from federal financial aid programs, which provide students and families with loans and grants to offset the cost of attending a college or university. Various U.S. presidents have initiated their own institutional development programs and executive orders related to higher education, such as Educational Excellence for Hispanic Americans (Executive Order No. 12900, 1994), Improving American Indian and Alaska Native Educational Opportunities and Strengthening Tribal Colleges and Universities (Executive Order No. 13592, 2011), and the White House Initiative to Promote Excellence and Innovation at Historically Black Colleges and Universities (Executive Order No. 13779, 2017). Federal agencies support a range of programs that focus on research, international exchanges, and graduate-level training, among others. Congress, in addition to fulfilling its responsibility for creating and passing laws, engages in various monitoring activities that may not directly force change but can bring new attention to issues of concern. Finally, the federal courts have been involved in a range of cases covering issues such as discrimination, student privacy, academic freedom, and state sovereignty (most of these issues are discussed in chapter 8).

Since primary responsibility for education falls to state governments, no central federal authority ever emerged. Consequently, the federal government's involvement with higher education is diffused across several federal departments and agencies. The decentralized nature of federal engagement makes the task of describing it particularly difficult. In many nations, one national agency has primary responsibility for the affairs of higher education—not so in the United States. While there is a federal Department of Education, the federal government engages in the funding and oversight of higher education through a cadre of additional departments and agencies such as the Departments of Agriculture, Defense, Energy, Health and Human Services, State, Transportation, and Veteran Affairs, as well as the NSF, the National Endowment for the Arts (NEA), and the National Endowment for the Humanities (NEH), among others. These engagements usually involve either oversight of federal mandates and laws (e.g., compli-ance) or providing funding to institutions or individuals (e.g., federal finan-cial aid). For example, the Department of Education oversees more than $115 billion in its grant, loan, and work-study programs designed to aid stu-dents in their pursuit of their postsecondary studies; the Department of State supports the international exchange of students and faculty; the Department of Homeland Security oversees the nation's student visa program; and the NSF, NEA, NEH, NIH, and others provide funding for R&D. In addition, millions of federal dollars have been earmarked for institutions to address a range of programmatic and capital projects.

As previously mentioned, federal involvement with higher education can be grouped into five primary areas: (a) access and success, (b) accountability and oversight, (c) research and innovation, (d) institutional development, and (e) international engagements. The following discussion provides an overview of each of the areas and describes relevant legislation, regulations, and federal agencies.

Access and Success

One of the primary goals of the federal government regarding higher educa-tion is to increase access and success of college students. The federal govern-ment is the primary provider of financial aid, which is a complex system meant to help students pay for their education. While some aid programs target specific groups of individuals based on their background (e.g., military service) or academic interest, most aid is allocated to students based on need, regardless of their academic program or other characteristics. The HEA (1965) was originally passed "to strengthen the educational resources of our colleges and universities and to provide financial assistance for students in postsecondary and higher education" (para. 1) and was designed to expand access to higher education through the provision of various grant and loan programs for students from lower- and middle-income families. It also cre-ated programs (now known as the TRIO programs) to help at-risk students pursue undergraduate degrees.

Data from 2020 indicate that the percentage of full-time undergradu-ates at four-year institutions who are receiving financial aid is rising (Hussar et al., 2020). Specifically, the percentage of financial aid awards for first-time, full-time degree- or certificate-seeking undergraduate students at four-year colleges moved from 75% of students in 2000–2001 to 86% in 2017–2018. A parallel rise occurred with the percentage of full-time undergradu-ates at two-year institutions who receive financial aid. At two-year colleges in 2000–2001, 62% of first-time, full-time degree- or certificate-seeking undergraduate students at two-year colleges were awarded financial aid, and by 2017–2018 that percentage increased to 78%. At the federal level, students may be eligible for three general types of aid: grants, loans, and work study.

The general federal student aid programs are administered by the Department of Education. To qualify for federal student aid, a student must complete the Free Application for Federal Student Aid (FAFSA).[3] When the HEA was originally passed in 1965, most of the aid was allocated through grants to increase access to low-income students. For example, Pell grants, which have been awarded annually since 1973–1974, support students with financial need by helping to defray the cost of college and do not need to be repaid. Pell grants have been an important component in expanding access to underrepresented students in higher education. In 2015–2016, 58% and 48% of Black and Latinx students, respectively, in higher education received a Pell grant, whereas about a third of White students did (NCES, 2019a). Over the past several decades, however, loans have emerged as the largest source of federal aid for students. The Stafford Loan Program makes low-interest loans to students to assist them with covering college costs. Students are required to repay these loans after they graduate or stop attending college. Work-study programs are by far the smallest of all the general aid programs. They provide funding to higher education institutions to subsidize the cost of employing student workers from underrepresented backgrounds.

Support for the nation's veterans to attend college comes through the Department of Veteran Affairs.[4] The 1944 GI Bill provided education and other support to veterans of World War II. While the law eventually transformed higher education by significantly expanding access, it almost did not survive congressional debates. One of the primary concerns was whether it was appropriate to send hardened veterans to college, a place historically reserved for societal elites. While the GI Bill bolstered college enrollments, it also helped forestall a potential economic recession similar to the one that followed World War I (Patterson, 1997). The GI Bill provided veterans with numerous benefits, including unemployment payments, inexpensive housing loans, and grants to cover tuition and other education-related expenses. The law had an immediate impact, with veterans accounting for almost half of all college enrollments in 1947 (Geiger, 2004). When the original GI Bill ended in 1956, nearly half (7.8 million) of the 16 million veterans of World War II had pursued education or training programs through the bill, though the early benefits were unequally realized due to the segregation of the South (Turner & Bound, 2002). Updated versions of the GI Bill were subsequently authorized for veterans of the Korean and Vietnam Wars.[5]

The GI Bill was reauthorized in 1984 under the leadership of Representative Gillespie V. Montgomery of Mississippi, and it became known as the Montgomery GI Bill. The expanded law provides the opportunity for educational benefits to all who enlist in the U.S. Armed Forces as well to some members of the Selected Reserve. The level of benefits is determined by length of service, type of service, and other requirements. Generally, veterans have up to 10 years after the completion of their service to take advantage of the benefits. A new benefit program, the Post-9/11 Veterans Educational Assistance Act of 2008 (often referred to as the Post-9/11 GI Bill), further expanded options for veterans. The number of veterans who are taking advantage of these higher education benefits continues to grow, and the complexity of facilitating the distribution of benefits has required many higher education institutions to create offices dedicated to handling their veteran students' affairs.

As the GI Bill represents workforce development and educational opportunities for service members and veterans, the federal government has developed other workforce preparation and transition programs. For instance, both secondary and postsecondary education rely on the Carl D. Perkins Career and Technical Education Act (Perkins) to advance career preparation in fields such as agriculture, computer science, construction, engineering technology, family and consumer science, health science, and manufacturing. First authorized in 1984 and most recently reauthorized as the Strengthening Career and Technical Education for the 21st Century Act of 2018 (Perkins V), the goal of Perkins is to align employer needs; industry requirements, including certifications and other defined competencies, local/regional area gaps; and educational offerings. In addition, it offers career and technical education alignment between secondary and postsecondary education. Perkins is administered by the Department of Education, and its focus is on providing holistic services to learners so that they are ready for the workforce.

These policy design linkages (i.e., connecting educational providers, employers, industry standards, local/regional labor needs) at the federal level also exist under the Workforce Innovation and Opportunity Act (WIOA, 2015), which is administered by the Department of Labor. The Department of Labor has been instrumental in leading education and training for adult learners who are seeking reentry into the workforce, unemployed or displaced workers who need career supports, and incumbent workers who are employed individuals seeking to upskill to meet evolving employer or labor demands. Under WIOA, however, the focus is more about providing holistic services to advance the worker into the workforce, which likely includes education and training. Accordingly, under WIOA, states have been able to combine services with the Departments of Education and Health and Human Services to map career service supports, identify education and training needs, and create action plans. In addition, states have established, with the collaboration of their community and technical colleges, regional workforce development centers and programming, which include nondegree workshops, certifications, or degree tracks, sometimes at no cost to the individual.

Institutional Development

As discussed previously, one of the federal government's earliest engagements with higher education was in institutional development through the Morrill Acts of 1862 and 1890, which transformed the nation's higher education landscape. In addition to creating some of the nation's greatest research universities, the 1890 act was also instrumental in developing several HBCUs. Moreover, under the Elementary and Secondary Education Reauthorization Act of 1994, 32 of the nation's tribal colleges were granted land-grant status, making them eligible for funding designated for land-grant colleges and universities.[6] These efforts have also been instrumental in expanding access to higher education.

In the middle of the 19th century, several members of Congress believed the nation's economy was in the process of changing and that higher education could play an important role in creating that new economy. The Morrill Act of 1862 was an attempt to foster innovation in the agricultural and mechanical sciences as well as facilitate the private development of federal lands. Land-grant institutions,

> without excluding other scientific and classical studies and including military tactics . . . [were to] teach such branches of learning as are related to agriculture and the mechanic arts, in such manner as the legislatures of the States may respectively prescribe, in order to promote the liberal and practical education of the industrial classes in the several pursuits and professions in life. (Morrill Act, 1862)

Each state was allocated a certain number of acres of federal land in the Western territories.[7] The states could then use the revenues produced by that land (usually through its sale) to support the development of a higher education institution dedicated to the advancement of the agricultural and mechanical arts as well as the liberal arts. Most states used the money to support the development of new or existing public institutions, such as Pennsylvania State University, Michigan State University, and North Carolina State University. Two notable exceptions were New York and Massachusetts, which designated Cornell University and Massachusetts Institute of Technology (as well as the University of Massachusetts) as their land-grant institutions.

Two subsequent acts expanded the number of institutions designated as land-grant colleges or universities. The second Morrill Act was passed in 1890 with the intention of providing additional support for land-grant institutions. This act required that if race were considered as part of the admission criteria for a land-grant institution, a second land-grant institution had to be created to serve those students excluded by those admission policies. The act created many of today's public HBCUs, such as Lincoln University (Missouri), South Carolina State University, and Prairie View A&M University (Texas).

In addition to the Morrill Acts, the federal government has undertaken several other initiatives designed to help build the nation's institutions of higher education. For example, in the 1950s, during a time of severe shortage of health-care professionals, Congress allocated funds to build the capacity of medical and nursing schools. The National Defense Education Act of 1958 provided federal support for institutions to build foreign language and international studies programs.

Many current institutional development initiatives fall under the Department of Education. The undersecretary oversees the President's Advisory Board on Tribal Colleges and Universities and the President's Advisory Board on Historically Black Colleges and Universities, which extend the institutional development work started under the land-grant acts. The department is also responsible for most of the development programs authorized under the HEA, including the Fund for the Improvement of Postsecondary Education; institutional development programs aimed at the nation's HBCUs and Alaska Native and Native Hawaiian institutions; programs designed to support Hispanic-serving and other minority-serving institutions; and TRIO programs, which support students from disadvantaged backgrounds.

The Department of Education also plays an important role in institutional development through the collection of data. NCES collects data about the nation's education system and provides research and analysis for public use. All institutions that accept federal financial aid are required to submit information to NCES's Integrated Postsecondary Education Data System,[8] which provides basic data about student enrollments, staff demographics, and institutional characteristics. These data, along with others collected by NCES, are important for understanding the development of the nation's higher education system and are often used by institutions for benchmarking and other purposes. A criticism of NCES, however, is that Congress has restricted its ability to collect student-level data, leaving the focus of data on institutions rather than on students. This shortcoming was partly addressed in 2009 with the American Recovery and Reinvestment Act's (ARRA) designation of federal funding for states to build student longitudinal data systems (SLDSs) (Gagliardi et al., 2018). (See chapter 7, this volume, for more information about SLDSs and state accountability.)

Accountability and Transparency

The members of the U.S. Congress, comprised of the Senate and House of Representatives, serve an important role in defining and developing the relationship between the federal government and higher education. While federal agencies and departments are often the primary intermediary between the government and institutions, Congress establishes the parameters of the interactions through the federal budget, legislation for programs, and definition of responsibilities of entities that receive federal aid. Beyond these basic legislative functions, Congress has also assumed responsibility for oversight of federal actors and others engaged in activities of national interest, such as higher education. This section provides an overview of Congress's role in the oversight of higher education and describes four key federal laws related to higher education.

Higher education serves a central function in the development of the nation's communities and economy, and the federal government directly contributes billions of dollars each year for research, student access, and a variety of other projects. Consequently, higher education now captures significant interest from many members of Congress. This interest, while sometimes resulting in legislation affecting higher education, often manifests itself through congressional hearings (Cook, 1998; Hannah, 1996; Parsons, 1997).

Congressional oversight hearings, while not always resulting in legislation, have led to altered institutional behavior. In one example of a congressional committee's oversight activities, the Senate Finance Committee's chairman, Charles E. Grassley of Iowa, "announced an investigation of American University and called the [governing] board a 'poster child for why review and reform are necessary' for governing boards of nonprofit organizations" (Fain, 2006, p. A25). The committee's investigation was a response to a financial scandal at American University in 2005 in which the institution's president was alleged to have misspent hundreds of thousands of dollars, and the institution's trustees were accused of not providing adequate oversight of the president's activities (Fain & Williams, 2005; Kinzie & Strauss, 2006). The scandal resulted in the firing of the president and the resignation of four trustees. While Congress did not pursue any governance reforms for colleges or universities in response to this scandal, many observers feared that such an action could have been the next step for Congress had American University's leaders not responded in the way they did.

Occasionally, legislative committees investigate alleged federal abuses, such as the Veterans Administration's overpayments to higher education institutions during the 1950s and institutions' purposeful defrauding of the government through federal financial aid programs during the 1980s and 1990s. A *The New York Times* article about possible academic integrity concerns at Auburn University resulted in a congressional investigation of that institution's athletic program (Wolverton, 2006). In line with an investigation of the tax-exempt status of several nonprofit organizations, the House Ways and Means Committee also explored the commercialization of college athletics (Wolverton, 2006). Hearings since 2015 have focused on the role of accreditation in quality assurance, freedom of speech on college campuses, expanding federal financial aid, and reauthorization of the HEA.[9] In many cases, these hearings are designed to give attention to an issue of national importance or of importance to the constituents of a particular member of Congress, not to influence new legislation.

Beyond congressional oversight and funding for higher education, the federal government assumes an active role in the protection of the public. For instance, Congress mandated college tuition affordability and transparency efforts so consumers, particularly prospective students and parents, can have a better understanding of the college's net price (Transparency in College Tuition for Consumers, 2021). Further, the federal government has led the efforts to protect human and animal subjects used in research (LaFollette, 1994). Most colleges and universities now have an office of regulatory research compliance, which includes an institutional review board (IRB) of academics and is intended to regulate research projects to ensure the safety and privacy of human and animal subjects. The genesis of most of these offices comes from federal initiatives in the 1970s to provide additional protections for subjects of research projects. The protections arose from concerns about reports of unethical research practices, including the Tuskegee Syphilis Study, a 40-year experiment conducted by the U.S. Public Health Service. The participants in the study, poor African American men, thought they were receiving free health services, but they were actually the subjects of a study tracking the untreated development of syphilis (Jones, 1981).

In response to the concerns raised by such projects, the National Research Act, passed in 1974, created the National Commission for the Protection of Human Subjects of Biomedical and Behavioral Research. In 1979 the commission released the "Belmont Report: Ethical Principles and Guidelines for the Protection of Human Subjects of Research." The report set forth the foundation of research protections in the United States, describing three fundamental ethical principles:

1. Respect for people: Researchers should protect the autonomy and self-direction of all individuals, giving particular consideration to participants with diminished capacities. Participants should have to give informed consent, and researchers should be truthful in all matters.
2. Beneficence: Research should be guided by the principle of "do no harm" and seek to maximize the benefits of the project while minimizing potential harm to participants.
3. Justice: Distribution of benefits and costs should be fair so that those who participate in the research are not denied the benefit of such research.

The commission was part of the U.S. Department of Health, Education, and Welfare (HEW, later renamed Health and Human Services [HHS]), which adopted a series of research regulations in the 1970s and 1980s that pertained to research funded by HEW. Most federal agencies have since adopted HHS's regulations, placing the burden of proof on higher education institutions to ensure that research conducted by their faculty members and students conforms to these guidelines. Indeed, most institutions now require all research projects, not just those funded by the federal government, to follow these rules, and the *Belmont Report* remains an important reference item for many IRBs.

Research and Innovation

The federal government is the largest supporter of basic research in the United States (Congressional Research Service, 2020), which means that the R&D enterprise within higher education is largely dependent on financial and other support provided by federal agencies. Thus, higher education research productivity is largely tied to this funding, which according to the American Association for the Advancement of Science, a primary tracker of federal support of R&D, has ebbed and flowed significantly over the last 2 decades (Hourihan, 2021).

Federal funding of R&D increased significantly from 1997 to 2004, then plateaued until 2010. The increase was largely fueled by congressional efforts to double the budget for NIH, although the NSF and the Department of Energy's Department of Science also saw significant increases (Hourihan, 2021). At that point, federal deficits incurred after the Great Recession led to a decline in R&D funding, largely in line with declines in other discretionary funding in the federal budget. Since that time, however, federal funding for R&D has steadily risen with bipartisan support in Congress, even during the Trump administration, when the White House questioned and reduced public confidence in science (Hourihan, 2021). In fact, appropriations for R&D in fiscal year (FY) 2018 were the largest in 15 years. Yet as Sun (2020) observed when reviewing the data, the Trump administration shifted funding to more applied activities such as 5G technology, cybersecurity, artificial intelligence, and quantum information science, while the NIH's biomedical research fund was slashed by 7%, and the NSF's budget was cut by 6.5%.

According to the NSF, in FY 2018, 12 departments and eight agencies provided more than $37 billion in R&D funding to the nation's colleges and universities. Most of this money came in the form of direct grants to institutions, although around 10% was allocated directly to federally funded R&D centers (FFRDC) located in universities. For example, MIT runs the U.S. Air Force's Lincoln Laboratory, the University of California oversees the Department of Energy's Lawrence Livermore National Laboratory, and the California Institute of Technology is responsible for the National Aeronautics and Space Administration's (NASA) Jet Propulsion Laboratory.

The federal government is one of the primary funders of academic research, and much of the federal funding is allocated through a competitive process in which individuals or institutions apply for support. Interested parties are usually required to submit an application to the relevant program area or in response to a call for proposals. While some program officers retain discretion over small pools of funding, most proposals are reviewed and rated by a panel of experts. Those evaluations are then used to determine which projects receive funding. Grant proposals usually include direct and indirect costs. The direct costs go to support the researcher and the project.

Indirect costs are those expenses that cannot be directly associated with a project but that pay for services an institution provides to support the work of that project. Such costs can include utilities, janitorial support, and building depreciation. (In general, direct costs are those that can be clearly associated with the research or sponsored project.) An institution recovers indirect costs, sometimes referenced as facilities and administration (F&A), through a general surcharge on externally sponsored projects. The indirect cost rate is negotiated by each institution with HHS or the Office of Naval Research. The exact classification of costs is determined by the Office of Management and Budget's (2004) Circular A-21.[10]

As previously discussed, the federal government began to invest significant amounts of money in research following World War II. During much of this time, there was no unified policy regarding patents on new products that resulted from this federal support, although most patents ended up under the control of federal departments and agencies, which accumulated as many as 30,000 patents prior to 1980. However, only about 5% of these patents were commercially licensed, suggesting that much of the research output funded by the government was not being developed in ways that could broadly benefit the nation.

In 1980, Congress passed the Patent and Trademark Law Amendments Act, often referred to as the Bayh–Dole Act, which allowed many recipients of federal research funding, including higher education institutions, to retain the patents on their research discoveries. It is widely believed that the passage of Bayh–Dole Act sparked the creation of institutions' current emphasis on the development and marketing of inventions by their faculty members (Lane & Johnstone, 2012). Many institutions not only support the research of their faculty but have also created innovation centers, research parks, and incubation sites designed to help faculty and students commercialize and market the results or products of their research. Of course, institutions often retain control of the intellectual property and share in the profits of successful inventions, designs, software, literary works, and other creations.

International Engagements

Another area in which the federal government can take a clear leadership role is international engagements, although like many other initiatives at this level, relevant policy and practices are spread across several agencies, and no coherent set of national policies and expectations related to internationalization has emerged. As discussed in chapter 5, the involvement of governments in international education tends to focus on economic development, public diplomacy, and national security (Lane, 2015).

Historically, the U.S. Department of State has served as the primary federal intermediary between U.S. higher education institutions and individuals and institutions in other countries. The practice of using higher education as part of the nation's public diplomacy efforts began in 1946 after Congress created the Fulbright program, which used the sale of surplus war property to support the international exchange of students to promote goodwill among nations. Through its Bureau of Educational and Cultural Affairs (ECA), the State Department now oversees numerous exchange programs for students and scholars, including the Fulbright program, and through its EducationUSA centers abroad[11] it has become involved in promoting U.S. higher education overseas as well as in encouraging domestic students to study abroad. Primary financial support for the Fulbright program comes from an annual appropriation to ECA. In addition to the more than $270 million allocated by Congress annually (as of 2020), Fulbright also receives support from private foundations and foreign governments that help fund the binational commissions that support the program in other countries. The program is administered by cooperating organizations such as the Institute for International Education.

In addition to the public diplomacy efforts of the Department of State, the United States Agency for International Development (USAID) is an independent agency designed to provide developing nations with support in the areas of health, economic growth, agriculture, and conflict prevention. It is intended to support capacity development in foreign countries and advance the foreign policy agenda of the United States. Many of the capacity-building projects supported by USAID involve higher education institutions and their staffs and work to build cooperative relationships among the involved nations. As President Joe Biden (2021) commented, "When we invest in the economic development of countries, we create new markets for our products and reduce the likelihood of instability, violence, and mass migrations" (para. 57).

While the international engagements of U.S. colleges and universities have primarily focused on international exchanges of students and scholars, higher education has also emerged as one of the nation's leading service exports amid a hypercompetitive global market (Lane et al., 2015). Beyond attracting students from overseas, more institutions are participating in the export of educational services through the development of international branch campuses, joint degree programs, and foreign research sites. In fact, around the world, higher education has emerged as part of many countries' economic competitiveness strategies as they compete in the "great brain race" (Wildavsky, 2010). These increasing international engagements, along with the growing importance of higher education in domestic economic development, have begun to capture the interest of the U.S. Department of Commerce, which is more frequently including the sector in its trade development initiatives. However, the United States remains one of the only top providers of higher education in the world without a national strategy for advancing the sector.

Federal interaction with higher education as it relates to national security has increased significantly in the past decade and covers five primary areas:

Immigration. More than 1 million students traveled annually from foreign countries to study at U.S. colleges prior to the pandemic. Their ability to come to the United States is regulated by the Department of Homeland Security and federal immigration regulations, which determine how long students and scholars can stay in the country and how long they will be able to legally work in the United States after the completion of their degree.

Export control. The federal government regulates the export of sensitive scientific advances, such as technology, software, and equipment, as part of protecting national security and advancing foreign policy agendas. These regulations are largely part of the Export Administration Regulations (EAR) and the International Traffic in Arms Regulations (ITAR). Since higher education produces a significant proportion of the nation's basic and applied research, higher education leaders need to ensure their institutions comply with these regulations.

Systems security. The federal government includes higher education institutions in cybersecurity and other risk assessments in three capacities. First, they are parties to be protected from ransomware and other cybercriminals. Second, they are parties to engage in research, curriculum development, and instruction with organizations such as the NSF and the National Security Agency (NSA) with opportunities to establish an NSA National Center of Academic Excellence in Cybersecurity. Third, colleges and universities may be parties subject to the compliance standards such as the Cybersecurity Maturity Model Certification (CMMC), which will be required for all U.S. Department of Defense grants and contracts (Kelly et al., 2021).

Workforce development. The linkage between education and workforce development to address national security has been at the forefront of the federal government. It is seeking ways to reduce dependence on H-1B employment visas and expand employment capacity among learners in two- and four-year postsecondary institutions. To those ends, federal agencies have sought to stimulate education and workforce development in gap areas, especially in manufacturing, health care, information technology, energy, and transportation. For instance, from 2011 to 2018, the U.S. Department of Labor awarded nearly $2 billion for the Trade Adjustment Assistance Community College and Career Training (TAACCCT) grant program to support community and technical colleges in developing and enhancing workforce-ready programs that are aligned with industry. Similarly, programs in career and technical education, primarily funded through Perkins and WIOA, have invested billions annually to connect education to the workforce through coordinated efforts at the local and state levels.

Foreign funding. Foreign funding of higher education is supposed to be reported to U.S. Department of Education per a requirement in the HEA (Green, 2019), and in recent years these sources have come under increasing scrutiny. Federal guidelines require colleges and universities to report funding, including gifts and contracts, of more than $250,000 from foreign sources.

Primary Departments and Agencies for Federal Engagement

As discussed previously, federal involvement with higher education cuts across many departments and agencies. The following discussion describes of some of the agencies that provide significant research support to higher education institutions, which results in many innovations.

Department of Agriculture

Upon passage of the Morrill Acts in 1862 and 1890, many U.S. colleges and universities contributed to the transformation of the agricultural industry and made the United States the leading food producer in the world. The agricultural research and service work of these institutions continues to be supported primarily through funding from the U.S. Department of Agriculture (USDA), which was created in 1862, the same year as the first land-grant act. Through an array of grants and programs, the USDA works to bring together farmers, ranchers, higher education institutions, and other public and private partners to advance agricultural production in the United States and abroad. Much funding comes through the Hatch Act (1887) and the Smith-Lever Act (1914), which provide financial support for the development and operation of agricultural experimentation stations and cooperative extension services in each state. The funding provided through these two acts is allocated to land-grant universities by the USDA, and states are expected to provide matching funds for much of the federal support.

Department of Education

The former federal Department of HEW split into the Department of Education and the Department of HHS in 1979. The Department of Education establishes and enforces many of the federal policies and regulations for the nation's schools and colleges; administers some federal financial support for education, including the $115 billion postsecondary student aid program; and prohibits discrimination and ensures equal access to education across the country.

Data about the U.S. educational system is collected by the NCES, which makes most of its data publicly available on its website. The Integrated Postsecondary Education Data System (IPEDS) collects annual data on all colleges and universities that participate in the federal student aid programs. NCES also administrators a series of longitudinal surveys, such as the National Postsecondary Student Aid Study (NPSAS), Beginning Postsecondary Students (BPS), and Baccalaureate and Beyond (B&B).

NCES is part of the Institute for Educational Sciences (IES), which is an independent and nonpartisan entity charged with collecting data on the nation's educational system, evaluating programs, and funding and advancing evidence-based research about education. IES provides statistical reports about the status of education in the country, conducts large-scale evaluation of federal educational policies and programs, funds rigorous research on improving student learning outcomes, and advances the use of data in educational decision-making.

In addition, the secretary of education is responsible for granting government recognition to nongovernmental accreditation organizations that are responsible for quality assurance of colleges and universities. While accreditation in the United States is not formally a governmental responsibility like it is in most other countries, institutions must receive recognition from an accreditor recognized by the secretary of education for their students to qualify for Title IV federal financial aid. The National Advisory Committee on Institutional Quality and Integrity (NACIQI), constituted under the Higher Education Opportunity Act of 2008, provides recommendations to the secretary regarding governmental recognition of accrediting agencies.

Department of Energy

During World War II, the federal government created the Manhattan Project, which employed many university faculty members and graduate students in the development of the atomic bomb. At the end of World War II, Congress established the Atomic Energy Commission to oversee research into atomic energy. The commission eventually evolved into the Department of Energy, which was established in 1977 to oversee energy-related programs, production, and regulation, including supervision of the nation's nuclear energy research facilities and power plants. Throughout the 1940s and 1950s, the commission created a network of laboratories, many of which were located in the nation's top universities.

Today, the R&D efforts of the Department of Energy are overseen by its Office of Science, which is the largest federal sponsor of physical science research, supporting about 27,000 investigators at nearly 300 academic institutions and department research laboratories. In addition, the Office of

Science provides funding to academic programs that educate undergraduate and graduate students in the physical sciences. In FY 2019, the Department of Energy allocated more than $4.5 billion to R&D at the nation's colleges and universities (NCES, 2019b).

Department of Defense

Compared to many other federal agencies, the Department of Defense provides only a fraction of the federal dollars that support scientific research, but it has been one of the primary sources of funds for research in areas such as computer science and electrical engineering. Moreover, although the department's financial contributions to research at higher education institutions is not as high as that provided by NIH and NSF, it does signal a rather rare partnership between the nation's military establishment and its colleges and universities. Notably, Defense commits over $2.4 billion annually for higher education learning, including for ROTC, active-duty personnel, and service academies. Indeed, the U.S. military has long relied on the nation's higher education institutions for research and planning support. Price (1954) noted:

> The United States is the only nation that has ever been willing to support and create private institutions to make studies on problems combining scientific and military considerations—problems of a sort that would elsewhere be considered the very heart of general staff planning. The private institutions . . . [receiving] military funds are the most important sources of independent, skeptical, and uninhibited criticism of military thinking today. (pp. 143–144)

The Department of Defense's support for higher education initiatives ranges from developing new research related to national defense to fostering advanced foreign language skills and knowledge about critical regions. For example, the National Security Education Program provides support for undergraduate and graduate students wanting to study languages and regions critical to national security. It also grants funding for institutional development of language and area study programs. In addition, the Multidisciplinary University Research Initiative (MURI) funds interdisciplinary basic research projects and in 2021 announced $179 million to fund research efforts in this area (U.S. Department of Defense, 2021).

Department of Homeland Security

The Department of Homeland Security (DHS) provides primary oversight and enforcement of the nation's immigration policies, including issuance of visas and compliance with visa provisions. International students and scholars, who regularly travel to the United States to study and research at the nation's colleges and universities, are among those noncitizens who fall under DHS's oversight. The Student and Exchange Visitor Program (SEVP) manages the presence of international students and other educational visitors through SEVIS (see chapter 5 for further discussion). The actual issuance of visas happens at U.S. embassies and consulates, which operate under the Department of State, but receipt of a student visa is dependent upon admission to an accredited U.S. institution and entry of accurate information about the visa applicant into SEVIS. Once a student arrives in the United States, institutions are required to ensure student compliance with immigration rules and update SEVIS on changes in student status and progress toward a degree.

Department of State

In addition to responsibility for issuing visas to international students and scholars, the Department of State oversees most federally supported international exchange programs, which serve both citizens and noncitizens. The flagship exchange program is the Fulbright program, which provides about 8,000 awards annually for U.S. citizens to study or teach overseas and for noncitizens to engage in academic activities in the United States. The Peace Corps, another exchange program, supports U.S. citizen volunteers who engage in community development in other countries. These exchange programs are overseen by ECA, which is responsible for fostering mutual understanding between the people of the United States and other countries.

National Institutes of Health

The NIH, part of HHS, was created in the 1880s and is the federal agency primarily responsible for biomedical and public health–related research. It invests nearly $42 billion in medical research annually. The NIH campus is located outside Washington DC, in Bethesda, Maryland. The agency comprises 27 separate institutes, such as the National Institute for Allergy and Infectious Disease, which led much of the nation's response to COVID-19. NIH provides extramural funding for research, mostly awarded through competitive processes to researchers at the nation's colleges and universities. In addition, parts of NIH, such as the National Institute of Aging, the National Institute on Drug Abuse, the National Institute of Environmental Sciences, and the National Institute of Allergy and Infectious Diseases, engage in their own research projects.

National Science Foundation

The NSF, founded in 1950 by an act of Congress, provides support for research and education in a broad range of scientific and engineering fields (except for medical-related research, which is funded through the NIH). In FY 2021 the NSF had an operating budget of nearly $8.5 billion, which accounted for about 20% of all federally supported research conducted by U.S. colleges and universities. The leadership of the NSF (i.e., its director, deputy director, and the National Science Board) is appointed by the president and confirmed by the Senate. About 10% of the NSF's staff members are academics who take leaves of absence from their faculty positions to work in its various program areas.

Prevailing Challenges

While federal funding has increased college access and success, led to accountability and oversight, shaped research and innovation, contributed to institutional development, and facilitated international engagements, the funds that support these forms of participation include stipulations beyond federal government compliance that transcend the discussion in the accountability and transparency section of this chapter. That is, the federal government uses its funding and programming as opportunities to weigh in and compel many postsecondary institutions to act in accordance with federal policies. Notably, many laws—such as Title VI of the Civil Rights Act of 1964 (prohibiting discrimination on the basis of race or national origin in any program or activity that receives federal financial assistance), Title IX of the Education Amendments of 1972 (prohibiting discrimination based on sex within any education program or activity that receives federal financial assistance), and the Jeanne Clery Disclosure of Campus Security Policy and Campus Crime Statistics Act (mandating that campuses that participate in student federal aid programs report certain crimes)—place compliance requirements onto campuses that receive federal financial assistance such as grants or student financial aid. It should be noted that some private colleges do not accept federal funds, not even student financial aid, and those institutions are not subject to these compliance requirements, as they intentionally want autonomy from federal requirements (Caputo & Marcus, 2016). Nonetheless, most colleges and universities are subject to the many federal compliance measures.

According to the Higher Education Compliance Alliance (HECA, n.d.), which maintains a repository of key federal laws and regulations applicable to the sector, as of October 2019, there were more than 250 federal statutes that postsecondary institutions must follow, yet its updated site lists more than 60 other regulations, data requests, and rulemaking considerations. Federal regulatory compliance requirements are not minor commitments. Based on an analysis of 13 higher education institutions of different sizes and types (e.g., private not-for-profit, private for-profit, public two-year and four-year, HBCUs and PWIs, primarily online, primarily residential, commuter, rural, suburban, urban, enrollments ranging from 1,615 to nearly 40,000 students), federal compliance expenditures ranged between 3% and 11% of each institution's entire operating expenditures for FY 2014, with the median cost at 6.4% of an institution's overall operating expenditures.

When estimated for the entire higher education sector, the study output suggested the total cost of federal regulatory compliance was $27 billion for FY 2014 (HECA, n.d.). Translating that amount into more contemporary dollars, the amount in 2022 was expected to be well over $30.3 billion. What is notable is that research activities are a significant source of compliance expenditures. Disaggregating the data, institutions' compliance expenditures for research compliance reach as high as 25% of research expenditures for one university. In short, although education is not one of the enumerated areas for the federal government and falls by default within states' rights, federal engagement is quite broad and impactful. Moreover, institutional participation in federal programs requires a significant commitment as the trade-off for the many opportunities provided through federal funding.

Conclusion

It is uncertain how the federal government's relationship with higher education will evolve. At the time of this writing, the U.S. public is increasingly interested in a federal solution to the rising cost of higher education, and the government is looking for ways to reduce the federal deficit. Meanwhile, higher education's importance for the United States' global competitiveness continues to grow. How federal leaders meet these competing demands will likely have an important effect on U.S. higher education's development and competitive edge.

Notes

1. In addition, because Washington DC is controlled by the U.S. Congress, institutions within that territory have an unusually direct connection with the federal government.

2. The Morrill Act of 1890, also called the Agricultural College Act, was the second land-grant act and was intended to extend the provisions of the 1862 act to the former Confederate states, so long as they could prove that race was not a factor in admissions. Providing separate institutions for Blacks and Whites was permissible in meeting this requirement.

3. See https://studentaid.gov/ for application information.

4. This discussion is intended to provide readers with a basic understanding of the requirements and benefits of the GI Bill. Readers are encouraged to contact the U.S. Department of Veterans Affairs for more detailed information regarding these matters, including additional programs, exemptions, and requirements.

5. These updates were the Veterans' Readjustment Assistance Act of 1952, the Veterans' Readjustment Benefits Act of 1966, and the Post-Vietnam Era Veterans' Educational Assistance Act of 1977.

6. The Elementary and Secondary Education Reauthorization Act of 1994 was not the first time the federal government involved itself in the affairs of tribal colleges. The Tribally Controlled Community College Assistance Act of 1978 was the first time the federal government provided funding assistance for these institutions.

7. A state received 30,000 acres for each of its members of Congress. Thus, if a state had two representatives and two senators, it received 120,000 acres. More information about the Morrill Act of 1862 can be found in Sorber (2018) and Williams (1991).

8. See http://nces.ed.gov/ipeds/ for more information.

9. This list is drawn directly from a review of congressional committee activity as recorded in the Congressional Information Service Abstracts passim.

10· While the indirect rate is set by the institution with the federal government, most institutions establish a policy that all sponsored projects include indirect costs as part of all projects' budgets. These costs now often exceed 50% of the project's direct costs. However, some private foundations will not pay indirect costs or place a smaller cap on such costs than federally negotiated rates. Also, some federal programs pay lower indirect rates than those otherwise negotiated with the federal government. For example, many training grants will only pay an indirect rate of 8%. Most institutions will allow researchers to pursue grants with lower indirect cost rates, but they first need to obtain institutional permission to do so.

11. See https://educationusa.state.gov/ for details.

References

Babbidge, H. D., Jr., & Rosenzweig, R. M. (1962). *The federal interest in higher education*. McGraw-Hill.

Bayh–Dohl Act, 37 C.F.R. 401 (1980)

Biden, J. R., Jr. (2021, February 4). *America's place in the world* [Remarks transcript]. https://www.whitehouse.gov/briefing-room/speeches-remarks/2021/02/04/remarks-by-president-biden-on-americas-place-in-the-world/

Brown v. Board of Education, 347 U.S. 483 (1954)

Caputo, I., & Marcus, J. (2016, July 7). The controversial reason some religious colleges forego federal funding. *The Atlantic*. https://www.theatlantic.com/ducation/archive/2016/07/the-controversial-reason-some-religious-colleges-forgo-federal-funding/490253/

Carl D. Perkins Vocational and Technical Education Act, Pub. L. No. 98-524 (1984)

Civil Rights Act, Pub. L. No. 88-352, 78 Stat. 241 (1964)

Congressional Research Service. (2020, December 17). *Federal research and development (R&D) funding FY 2021*. https://crsreports.congress.gov/product/pdf/R/R46341

Cook, C. E. (1998). *Lobbying for higher education: How colleges and universities influence federal policy*. Vanderbilt University Press.

Elementary and Secondary Education Reauthorization Act, Pub. L. No. 103-382, 108 Stat. 3518 (1994)

Emergency Relief Appropriation Act, Pub. Res. 11, 74th Cong. (1935)

Exec. Order No. 12900, 59 Fed. Reg. 9061 (1994)

Exec. Order No. 13592, 76 Fed. Reg. 76603 (2011)

Exec. Order No. 13779, 82 Fed. Reg. 12499 (2017)

Fain, P. (2006, June 2). American University's chastened trustees approve wide-ranging reforms. *The Chronicle of Higher Education*, p. A25.

Fain, P., & Williams, G. (2005, November 11). U.S. Senate probe begun at American U. *The Chronicle of Higher Education*, p. A30.

Gagliardi, J. S., Parnell, A., & Carpenter-Hubin, J. (2018). *The data analytics revolution in higher education: Big data, organizational learning, and student success*. Stylus.

Geiger, R. L. (2004). *Research and relevant knowledge: American research universities since World War II*. Transaction.

Green, E. (2019, August 30). Universities face federal crackdown over foreign financial influence. *The New York Times*, p. A17.

Hannah, S. B. (1996). The Higher Education Act of 1992: Skills, constraints, and the politics of higher education. *Journal of Higher Education*, *67*(5), 498–527. https://doi.org/10.2307/2943866

Hatch Act, 7 U.S.C. § 361a et seq. (1887)

Herbold, H. (1995). Never a level playing field: Blacks and the GI Bill. *The Journal of Blacks in Higher Education*, *6*, 104–108.

Higher Education Act, Pub. L. No. 89-329 (1965)

Higher Education Compliance Alliance. (n.d.). *Compliance matrix*. https://www.higheredcompliance.org/compliance-matrix/

Hourihan, M. (2021). *A primer of federal R&D budget trends*. American Association for the Advancement of Science. https://www.aaas.org/news/primer-federal-rd-budget-trends

Hussar, B., Zhang, J., Hein, S., Wang, K., Roberts, A., Cui, J., Smith, M., Bullock Mann, F., Barmer, A., & Dilig, R. (2020). *The condition of education 2020*. National Center for Education Statistics, U.S. Department of Education. https://nces.ed.gov/pubsearch/pubsinfo.asp?pubid=2020144

Jeanne Clery Disclosure of Campus Security Policy and Campus Crime Statistics Act, Pub. L. No. 101-542 (1990)

Jones, J. (1981). *Bad blood: The Tuskegee syphilis experiment.* The Free Press.

Kelly, B., McCormack, M., Reeves, J., Brooks, D. C., & O'Brien, J. (2021). *EDU-CAUSE horizon report: Information security edition.* EDUCAUSE. https://library .educause.edu/-/media/files/library/2021/2/2021_horizon_report_infosec.pdf

Kinzie, S., & Strauss, V. (2006, May 18). Senator questions school's governance. *The Washington Post*, p. B2.

Knight, D. M. (Ed.). (1960). *The federal government and higher education.* Prentice Hall.

Kolbe, P. R. (1919). *The colleges in war time and after.* Appleton.

LaFollette, M. C. (1994). The politics of research misconduct: Congressional oversight, universities, and science. *Journal of Higher Education, 65*(3), 261–285. https://doi.org/10.1080/00221546.1994.11778500

Lane, J. E. (2015). Higher education internationalization: Why governments care. In E. Ullberg (Ed.), *New perspectives on internationalization and competitiveness: Integrating economics, innovation, and higher education* (pp. 17–30). Springer.

Lane, J. E., & Johnstone, D. B. (Eds.). (2012). *Colleges and universities as economic drivers: Measuring higher education's role in economic development.* State University of New York Press.

Lane, J. E., & Lefor, D. (2007, November 9). *Federal oversight of higher education: An analysis of congressional committees, 1944–2004* [Paper presentation]. Association for the Study of Higher Education 32nd Annual Conference, Louisville, KY.

Lane, J. E., Owens, T. L, & Kinser, K. (2015). *Cross border higher education, international trade, and economic competitiveness: A review of policy dynamics when education crosses borders.* ILEAP, CUTS International Geneva, & CARIS. http://www .cuts-geneva.org/pdf/TAF087_cross-border-education-and-trade-policy.pdf

Levine, D. O. (1986). *The American college and the culture of aspiration, 1915–1940.* Cornell University Press.

Montgomery GI Bill, Pub. L. No. 78-346, 58 Stat. 284m (1984)

Morrill Act, 7 U.S.C. § 301 et seq. (1862)

Morrill Act, 26 Stat. 417, 7 U.S.C. § 321 et seq. (1890)

Morse, J. F. (1966). The federal government and higher education: Old answers breed new questions. In W. J. Minter (Ed.), *Campus and capitol: Higher education and the state* (pp. 49–62). Western Interstate Commission for Higher Education.

National Center for Education Statistics. (2019a). *Trends in Pell grant receipt and the characteristics of Pell grant recipients: Selected years, 2003–04 to 2015–16.* U.S. Department of Education. https://nces.ed.gov/pubs2019/2019487.pdf

National Center for Education Statistics. (2019b). *Federal on-budget funds for education, by level/educational purpose, agency, and program: Selected fiscal years, 1970 through 2019.* U.S. Department of Education. https://nces.ed.gov/programs/ digest/d19/tables/dt19_401.30.asp

National Commission for the Protection of Human Subjects of Biomedical and Behavioral Research. (1979). *The Belmont report: Ethical principles and guidelines for the protection of human subjects of research.* Office for Human Research

Protections, U.S. Department of Health and Human Services. http://www.hhs.gov/ohrp/humansubjects/guidance/belmont.html

National Defense Education Act, Pub. L. No. 85-864, 72 Stat. 1580 (1958)

National Research Act, Pub. L. No. 93-348 (1974)

National Science Foundation. (1951). *The first annual report of the National Science Foundation: 1950–51.* https://www.nsf.gov/about/history/ann_report_first.pdf

Office of Management and Budget. (2004). *Circular A-21: Revised 05/10/04.* https://obamawhitehouse.archives.gov/omb/circulars_a021_2004/

Parsons, M. D. (1997). *Power and politics: Federal higher education policy making in the 1990s.* State University of New York Press.

Patent and Trademark Law Amendments Act, Pub. L. No. 96-517, 94 Stat. 3015 (1980)

Patterson, J. T. (1997). *Great expectations: The United States, 1945–1974.* Oxford University Press.

Post-9/11 Veterans Educational Assistance Act, Pub. L. No. 110-252, Title V (2008)

Post-Vietnam Era Veterans' Educational Assistance Act, 38 U.S.C. § 1642 (1977)

Price, D. K. (1954). *Government and science.* New York University Press.

Quattlebaum, C. A. (1960). Federal policies and practices in higher education. In D. M. Knight (Ed.), *The federal government and higher education* (pp. 35–52). Prentice Hall.

Rainsford, G. N. (1972). *Congress and higher education in the nineteenth century.* University of Tennessee Press.

Rudy, W. (1996). *The campus and a nation in crisis: From the American Revolution to Vietnam.* Associate University Presses.

Russell, J. E. (1951). *Federal activities in higher education after the Second World War: An analysis of the nature, scope, and impact of federal activities in higher education in the fiscal year 1947.* King's Crown Press.

Servicemen's Readjustment Act, Pub. L. No. 78-346, 58 Stat. 284m (1944)

Smith-Hughes Act, Pub. L. No. 64-347, 39 Stat. 929 (1917)

Smith-Lever Act, 7 U.S.C. § 343 (1914)

Sorber, N. M. (2018). *Land-grant colleges and popular revolt: The origins of the Morrill Act and the reform of higher education.* Cornell University Press.

Strengthening Career and Technical Education for the 21st Century Act, Pub. L. No. 115-224 (2018)

Sun, J. C. (2020, November 10). *Advancing higher education through the 2020 presidential term* [Panel presentation]. Association for the Study of Higher Education 45th Annual Conference, New Orleans, LA/Virtual, United States.

Taylor, J., III. (2008). War. In N. L. M. Brown & B. M. Stentiford (Eds) *The Jim Crow encyclopedia: Greenwood milestones in African American history* (pp. 594–595). Greenwood.

Transparency in College Tuition for Consumers, 20 U.S.C. § 1015a (2021)

Tribally Controlled Community College Assistance Act, Pub. L. No. 95-471 (1978)

Turner, S. E., & Bound, J. (2002). *Closing the gap or widening the divide: The effects of the G.I. Bill and World War II on the educational outcomes of Black Americans*

(Working Paper No. 9044). National Bureau of Economic Research. https://www
.nber.org/papers/w9044

U.S. Department of Defense. (2021, February). *DoD announces fiscal year 2021
university research funding awards* [Press release]. https://www.cto.mil/2021-muri/

U.S. House Journal. (1818, December 7). 15th Cong., 2nd sess.

Veterans' Readjustment Assistance Act of 1952, 38 U.S.C. § 997 (1952)

Veterans' Readjustment Benefits Act of 1966, Pub. L. No. 89-358 (1966)

Wildavsky, B. (2010). *The great brain race: How global universities are reshaping the
world.* Princeton University Press.

Williams, R. L. (1991). *The origins of federal support for higher education: George W.
Atherton and the land-grant college movement.* Pennsylvania State University Press.

Wolverton, B. (2006, September 22). Congress broadens an investigation of college
sports. *Chronicle of Higher Education*, p. A36.

Workforce Innovation and Opportunity Act of 2015, Pub. L. No. 113-128 (2015)

7

STATE AND LOCAL GOVERNMENTS' RELATIONSHIP WITH HIGHER EDUCATION

State and local governments play a key role in the development and oversight of colleges and universities in the United States. The U.S. Constitution designates state governments, as opposed to the federal government, as the primary governmental actor in relation to education.[1] As such, each state (and territory) has its own regulatory and funding environment. State governments, through their constitutions, laws, and regulations, determine which higher education institutions can operate within their borders, how they are governed, how they are funded, how academic programs are approved and reviewed, who has access to pursue a degree, and what protections are provided for students.

It is not surprising, then, that state and local governments play a critical role in how colleges and universities deal with the four themes of this book. States recognize and invest in higher education institutions, public and independent, under the premise that such institutions will support the public policy goals of the state. In some states, the state government plays an active role in determining the mission of institutions and approving the types and scope of academic programs offered. State governments can be key players in expanding access to higher education, as well as influencing how college and university leaders address various aspects of DEI. Finally, as states are instrumental in changing economic environments, institutions have to respond to the ways their state governments fund and regulate the higher education sector.

In this chapter we explore the nexus of the relationship between state government and the higher education sector—both individual institutions and the sector as a whole. To be successful, higher education leaders need to be aware of their contexts, particularly in the state(s) where their institutions operate. The discussion here is intended to provide readers with a framework with which to better understand fundamental aspects of how states interact with higher education. Readers are encouraged to investigate more about their particular state contexts.[2]

Institutional Licensure: The Core of the State–Higher Education Relationship

A primary characteristic of colleges and universities that distinguishes them from other organizations is their ability to confer an academic degree. Rarely has the ability to grant this credential been an act self-acquired by a college or university; throughout history that authority has typically come from an external entity such as a government or church (Duryea, 2000; Kinser & Lane, 2017). Even Harvard, founded in 1636 and now considered an independent institution, was created by the Massachusetts Bay Colony government and could not have a commencement "without the procession led by the Sheriff of Middlesex County, and no degree could be awarded without approval of a board whose membership included the governor of the Massachusetts Bay Colony" (Thelin, 2011, p. 33; see also Morison, 1986). This external authorization is both an historic and an important, though often overlooked, component of the role of the state in regulating higher education.

The idea of degree authorization raises a question: What is a degree? A degree is widely recognized but sometimes difficult to define, particularly in terms of what it confers upon its recipient. The Supreme Court of Vermont stated:

> In practical affairs, [a degree] introduces its possessor to the confidence and patronage of the general public. Its legal character gives it moral and material credit in the estimation of the world, and makes it thereby a valuable property right of great pecuniary value. (*Townshend v. Gray*, 1890, p. 636)

In many ways, the value of the degree is tied to the legitimacy of the institution that grants it and to the entity that authorizes the institution to grant it. In the case of the states, many educational agencies even go so far as to define what constitutes a degree, such as the minimum number of credit hours required and, for certain regulated professions, the type of knowledge and training to be included, which may be defined by a state agency or a state-recognized professional group.

While the primacy of state governments in regulating educational institutions is widely acknowledged, their legal authority to license educational institutions has been little explored. In an overview of this issue, Contreras (2009) argued there are three legitimate sources of degree-granting authority in the United States: tribal, state, and federal governments. Because of their semi-sovereign status in the United States, tribal governments have licensed numerous tribal colleges, mostly providing educational offerings to Native Americans.[3] At the federal level, a handful of institutions, such as the nation's military academies, received their degree-granting authority from the U.S. Congress.

Nearly all postsecondary educational institutions, public and private, in the United States receive their degree-granting authority from their state government, however.[4] That authority comes in three basic forms:

- public institutions owned or operated by the state government or a subunit of the government (such as a community college taxing district)
- institutions exempted from state regulation on religious grounds
- nonpublic (not-for-profit and for-profit) institutions with formal authorization to operate in the state

The authority for public institutions to grant degrees comes directly from a state government when it authorizes an institution. Public institutions are generally created (or recognized) through either statutory or constitutional provision.[5] In some states, public institutions were created prior to statehood, so their mention in their state's constitution or statutes reflects recognition of their special relationship with the state rather than an actual chartering of the institution. Many others were created after statehood was granted, and their existence was authorized through some form of state approval, typically via statute. Institutions that are enshrined in a state constitution tend to have more autonomy from state government than peers mentioned in state statutes (Blackwell, 1961). Legislators and governors have power over statutes, but it typically takes broad approval by a state's citizens to amend the constitution.

While roughly 75% of all college students in the United States attend a public college or university, approximately 60% of colleges and universities are nonpublic.[6] The authorization of nonpublic colleges and universities comes in two primary forms. First, many institutions, particularly the oldest in the United States, were authorized through some form of state-issued charter or "some other kind of *sui generis* state action that approves specific schools by name" (Contreras, 2009, p. 6). Many of the colonial colleges, for example, were authorized by royal decree. These charters define the relationship between the institution and the state and in some cases grant special rights to the institution, such as freedom from paying property taxes. Second, some states delegate licensing authority to a regulatory agency charged with insuring compliance with state rules. In most states, authorization is regulated by a set of policies enforced by a state agency. If an institution meets the necessary requirements, then a license to operate is issued. Many agencies make a distinction between not-for-profit and for-profit higher education, administering a more active licensing review of for-profit institutions.

The courts have largely held that states have the right to regulate all degree-granting institutions within their borders. (See, e.g., *New Jersey State Board of Higher Education v. Board of Directors of Shelton College* [1982] and *State ex rel. McLemore v. Clarksville School of Theology* [1982].) This largely esoteric legal issue became a major public policy concern when the U.S. Department of Education released regulations in 2010 that required institutions to evidence they have appropriate approval to provide an education to students located in other states (State Authorization, 2019). This language reinforced the idea that state governments had the authority to regulate both in-person and distance higher education modalities that serve students who reside within their borders, and it required institutions to seek state approval for distance education offerings. Thus, at the same time as many colleges and universities were beginning to expand their online and distance delivery, they had to be careful to ensure they met the state rules where their students were located. Although these regulations began in 2010, numerous legal questions were sorted out over the next decade, leading to several federal cases and modifications to the regulations, which did not go into full effect until 2020 (WICHE Cooperative for Educational Technologies, n.d.).

To address the resulting patchwork of state regulations, an innovative solution was created: the National Council for State Authorization Reciprocity Agreements (NC-SARA). This voluntary approach to state oversight of distance education allows state governments to join a consortium of states that agree to abide by a common set of rules and regulations for handling out-of-state distance education delivery. Institutions in a state that is a member of NC-SARA can operate in any other member state so long as they abide by the established rules. At the time of this writing, 49 states and most U.S. territories belong to NC-SARA (n.d.), effectively covering the United States. This collaboration is an example of effective coordination between higher education leaders and state policymakers to advance policy solutions that meet state responsibilities for authorization and accountability while also supporting colleges and universities in their efforts to broaden their educational reach.

Accountability

In addition to licensure, states have assumed a larger role in holding colleges and universities accountable on a range of public policy issues from affordability to completion.[7] The advent of more centralized coordinating boards and public university multicampus systems since the 1970s has led some state governments to assume a more active role in advancing accountability efforts related to higher education (Berdahl, 1971; McGuiness, 2013). At the same time, leaders of both public and nonpublic colleges and universities have increasingly become key actors in many local and state-level policy circles. At the state level, such engagements, which in many instances apply to both public and private institutions, are commonly referred to as *accountability measures* (Burke, 2005). Many states' accountability efforts have moved beyond an academic focus to include financial and regulatory issues. Institutions, particularly those in the public realm, are now often required to submit a host of reports to their state government as well as comply with an array of regulations and oversight meant to hold the institution accountable to the state government (Lane, 2007).

The term *accountability* has become so common that it means everything and nothing. Public officials use the term to describe vaguely defined notions such as trustworthiness, fidelity, and justice (Bovens, 2006). Neither scholars nor policymakers have been able to develop a common definition (Dubnick, 2005), and attempts to do so have only resulted in a proliferation of models, typologies, analogies, and the like. For example, in his review of the higher education literature, Burke (2005) identified multiple models of accountability: bureaucratic, professional, political, managerial, market, and managed market. Higher education accountability has been represented as a triangle (Clark, 1983), a sphere (Behn, 2001), and a diamond (Middlehurst, 2011). It also has been described as facing upward, downward, inward, and outward (Vidovich & Slee, 2000). Lane (2007) referred to multiple types of state accountability mechanisms as a spider web that comes to envelop an institution.

Although difficult to define, accountability is an increasingly pressing concern for both public and nonpublic colleges and universities. The growing focus on accountability can be attributed to three trends in higher education: (a) the increasing cost of tuition, (b) an inability of public funding to match rising tuition costs, and (c) overarching concerns about the quality of U.S. higher education (Kelchen, 2018). Yet state accountability measures extend far beyond the cost of tuition or the quality of education provided. Adelman and Carey (2009), for instance, defined 21 categories of state accountability measures. Some of these categories focus on processes and outcomes within the institution (e.g., student learning outcomes, faculty scholarship, student engagement), while others identify ways in which states measure the quality and results of higher education institutions (e.g., governance, funding, public information). More recently, Brown (2018) has argued that accountability can be categorized into seven "accountability silos," including assessment, accreditation, institutional research, institutional effectiveness, educational evaluation, educational measurement, and higher education public policy (p. 30).

State-level accountability processes can take passive and active forms. Many states now have sunshine laws designed to allow the public broad access to higher education information and meetings (McLendon & Hearn, 2004). Consequently, most governing board meetings, except those that deal with personnel or other exempted matters, must be announced in advance and be held in a public forum. Salaries, reports, and other documents are usually covered by freedom of information laws, which require public educational institutions and other governmental entities to allow outsiders access to their work products and other data. The idea behind such laws is to increase transparency and therefore improve accountability. With these initiatives, institutions tend to be mostly passive participants, facilitating the public's access to their meetings and documents.

States have also instituted many more active accountability requirements. These programs require institutions to report their performance to their state governments, and at times to the general public. These initiatives have been called *performance reporting, performance funding,* and *performance budgeting* (Burke & Associates, 2002). Performance reporting requires institutions to report performance outcomes along a range of common measures. Increasingly, these measures are being made available to the public via the internet. Performance funding and performance budgeting tie financial allocations to performance reporting (see Dougherty et al., 2016; Ortagus et al., 2020). Performance funding is intended to reward institutions financially for their performance on predetermined measures, while performance budgeting allocates money to institutions as an enticement for them to engage in new initiatives aligned with their state's policy agenda.

Further, part of the move to increased accountability entails access to current and detailed state-level educational data. To facilitate the management, analysis, and use of these data, many states maintain student longitudinal data systems (SLDSs). The goals of these systems are to improve educational outcomes, inform administrative decision-making, promote actionable research, and contribute to workforce development. SLDS data include four core areas: early learning, K–12, postsecondary, and workforce. Although every state can connect the data from these core areas, not all states currently use these connections. According to Education Commission of the States, as of 2019, only 16 states have a full "P20W" system that connects data across the four core areas, from early childhood through workforce, while 41 states connect at least two of the four core areas (Keiley, 2019). The future will likely bring further emphasis on data-driven decision-making at the state level.

State Actors and Institutions

Those working in higher education know that multiple actors, many not directly involved with the academy, influence policy and administrative decisions. Even those associated with these decisions, however, are not often aware of the full breadth of actors engaged in (or how they are engaged in) higher education, which Lane (2007) referred to as a "spider web of oversight" (p. 639). This section introduces readers to some of the relevant actors. Their activities are reviewed briefly, and readers are encouraged to explore additional information about the role of these actors in their particular states.[8]

Government Actors

As noted, state and local governments are key players in the higher education landscape, and we review them here. (Issues pertaining to higher education and the judicial branch of government are covered in chapter 8.)

Executive Branch

In each state, the governor heads the executive branch of government, which typically includes most of the administrative functions within the government. Depending on their institutional power and interest in education, governors can play an influential role in their state's higher education sector. Many governors have the authority to appoint members of institutional and system governing boards as well as statewide coordinating bodies. In most states, the state higher education executive officer is also appointed by the governor, and that position is occasionally considered part of the governor's cabinet. In addition, some states grant the governor power to propose the initial state budget to the legislature, giving that office substantial influence over higher education appropriations. If higher education is a significant policy interest, a governor may champion legislation or governance reform, in addition to using the bully pulpit to influence institutional behavior such as keeping tuition as low as possible or focusing institutional efforts on workforce development. For example, the movement in the past decade toward free college tuition was led initially by the governors of Tennessee and

New York, who successfully advocated for programs to support variations of free college in their states.[9]

The power of the governor depends on a variety of factors, and state constitutions can either constrain or empower those who hold the position. According to Fowler (2000), "The strongest governors are elected to serve a four-year term and can be reelected at least once, have the power to appoint numerous state officials, have considerable control over the state budget, and can veto legislation" (p. 147). Not all governors have such expansive powers, however. For example, Texas has been frequently regarded as having a constitutionally weak governor. While the Texas governor has the power to make numerous appointments, the position has limited influence over the budget and policy processes. In that state, the lieutenant governor is viewed as the most powerful statewide elected leader, particularly in influencing higher education, as that person is the head of the state senate and has the power to appoint committees and their chairs (Bracco, 1997).

The executive branch also comprises numerous state agencies with roles in higher education. The state's education department (or the equivalent that oversees higher education) tends to have the largest influence on the higher education sector, at times having the power to approve the type, level, and focus of degrees an institution can award. Many agencies may also have limited direct oversight of (or engagement with) specific aspects of higher education, but their collective engagement creates a web of oversight that can be quite burdensome and constraining to institutions (Lane, 2007). Other agencies often engaged with higher education include those focused on areas such as P–12 education; workforce development; economic development; R&D; and, as demonstrated during the pandemic, public health.

Legislative Branch

State legislatures are similar across the nation. Each state has a bicameral legislative system. That is, they have two houses or chambers, largely based on the model established by the U.S. Congress. The only exception to this system is Nebraska, which has a unicameral, or one-house, system. The primary responsibilities of a legislature involve developing state statutes; passing resolutions; allocating state resources; and providing some oversight of state entities, including colleges and universities.

A legislature engages with higher education in multiple ways. Occasionally, a legislature will involve itself in such concerns as educational governance structures, quality assurance, curriculum design, transfer of credit, faculty workload, student conduct, and workforce and economic development. Beyond such core policy issues, legislatures, or more often a legislator or group of legislators, may engage in inquiries of specific institutional activities, such as controversial student-sponsored events or salaries of executives or coaches. Such oversight is often sparked by media reports or constituent correspondence, and an institution is forced to defend itself before legislative committees or through written responses to legislative inquiries (Heller, 2004; Lane, 2007). The primary entanglement with the legislature relates to state funding of higher education (discussed later in this chapter).

While state legislatures are often quite influential on higher education policy, individual legislators can be even more powerful (Marshall et al., 1989). The most prominent tend to be members of budget and higher education committees (sometimes higher education is subsumed under other committees that deal with broader mandates such as education from early childhood through graduate degrees or workforce development). These committees hold hearings and draft legislation related to higher education policy or budgeting. Thus, the committee members, particularly the committee chairs, can exert a great deal of influence on the higher education sector.

Many state legislators now have professional support staff who play an important role in the development of policy and directing the focus of the legislators for whom they work. Historically, state legislators were part-time and had limited access to staff. However, as expectations of state legislatures have increased, efforts have been taken to professionalize the role of legislators by increasing their salaries, providing office space, and funding staff for legislative offices (Bowman & Kearney, 1988). Thus, in many states, legislators are now full-time public servants with their own staffs helping support the work of the legislative office. It is important to note, though, that in some states, mostly in the western United States, legislatures remain nonprofessional, with part-time legislators (a small number of state legislatures only meet for one session every 2 years) and without dedicated staff, instead sharing centralized staffing pools (Patterson, 1996).

Local Governments

Higher education's relationship with local governments such as those at the county and city/town level are important, extensive, and often overlooked. In 29 states, state support for higher education is supplemented by local appropriations (SHEEO, 2020). In many cases this funding is directed at community and technical colleges, which play a significant role in expanding access to traditionally underserved populations. County and city governments also provide a range of supports such as fire and police, which may be called upon quite frequently to address both on- and off-campus activities. At the same time, public and private universities may be exempted from paying property taxes—a key revenue source of many local governments. In recognition of the lack of direct tax revenue, some locales have negotiated payments in lieu of taxes (PILOTS), whereby the institution agrees to pay a certain amount to the local government to offset some of the costs incurred by the institution.

As discussed in chapter 9, many colleges and universities are increasingly engaged in their local communities as part of their education, research, and service missions. Examples vary widely from the creation of community schools that link higher education and P–12 in the training of teachers and the education of primary and secondary students to providing interns to community-facing organizations, to conducting publicly engaged research intended to improve the conditions of local communities (Jacoby & Associates, 2009). In addition, these colleges and universities tend to be anchor institutions, often serving as one of the area's largest employers and adding value for attracting and retaining educated employers and workers, who also attract students who frequent local businesses (Lane & Johnstone, 2012).

Tribal Governments

The relationship between tribal governments, state governments, the federal government, and higher education is complicated and often fraught. In fact, the relationship of these three governments has long been structured, at least in part, around education (Reyhner & Eder, 2004). In the 1800s, the U.S. government and religious organizations created boarding schools where young Native Americans were sent, often against their will, to be educated. This so-called education was intended to assimilate the students into the dominant White, European American culture and leave behind their families, cultures, and heritage (Davis, 2001; Pratt, 2004). In the 1920s, the Institute for Government Research (which eventually became the Brookings Institution), commissioned a report with financial support from the Carnegie Foundation on the condition of Native Americans across the country. What would come to be called the Meriam Report (1928) criticized the treatment of Native Americans by the federal government and the overall condition of reservations and the boarding schools. After several decades of debate, the U.S. Senate released a report, "Indian Education: A National Tragedy—A National Challenge," which called for more local control of education by tribal governments (S. Rep. No. 91-501, 1969).

The movement for local control led to the development of what are now known as tribal colleges. The first tribal college, Navajo Community College (renamed Diné College in 1997) was created in 1968 in Arizona to expand postsecondary educational access to a traditionally underserved population and to provide a culturally relevant curriculum. The movement has an overall goal of "protecting and enhancing their own [tribal] cultures and at the same time embracing many of the tools of standard postsecondary education" (Stein, 2009, p. 18). More than 30 such institutions operate today, primarily across the western United States. These colleges, many of which provide two-year programs, are critical to addressing the significant underrepresentation of Native Americans in higher education, particularly in states with large Native American populations (Brayboy et al., 2012). In the last 50 years, fewer than one of every 100 college students has identified as Native American (de Brey et al., 2021), which is due in part to the lack of postsecondary access on reservations. Tribal colleges now serve approximately 10% of all Native Americans enrolled in colleges and universities.

Even though tribal colleges are located within states, they largely exist outside their state's higher education regulatory ecosystem. State governments have no obligation to fund tribal colleges, and most do not, with the exceptions of North Dakota, Montana, and Arizona (Nelson & Frye, 2016). Tribal colleges, while accredited by a federally recognized accreditor to be eligible for federal student financial aid, are not subject to the oversight or accountability mechanisms of the state. Indeed, their authority to grant degrees is derived from the tribal government and not the state. That said, there is increasing interest in integrating tribal colleges into states' higher education ecosystems as a means to strengthen these institutions, as well as to provide students in two-year programs with pathways to earn bachelor's degrees (Crazy Bull et al., 2020).

A number of public colleges and universities have also come to publicly recognize that their campuses are built on the lands once inhabited by native peoples. Institutions, such as Miami University in Ohio have issued land acknowledgments, which are often read at public meetings. In the case of Miami University, which occupies the land once inhabited by the Myaamia people, it was developed in collaboration with the leadership of the Miami Tribe in Oklahoma and reads, in part:

> Miami University is located within the traditional homelands of the Myaamia and Shawnee people, who along with other indigenous groups ceded these lands to the United States in the first Treaty of Greenville in 1795. The Miami people, whose name our university carries, were forcibly removed from these homelands in 1846. (Miami Tribe and Miami University, n.d., para. 3)

Such land acknowledgments are important steps forward in the broader panoply of higher education institutions recognizing their interrelated history with native peoples and working to build more inclusive environments. The U.S. Department of Arts and Culture (n.d.) suggests, "Acknowledgment is a simple, powerful way of showing respect and a step toward correcting the stories and practices that erase indigenous people's history and culture and toward inviting and honoring the truth" (para. 3).

Nongovernmental Actors

In addition to the governmental actors, numerous state-level nongovernmental actors also influence the relationship between the state and the higher education sector. The media tend to hold a great deal of sway over setting agendas, as well as the perceptions of local and state civic leaders (McCombs et al., 2014; McCombs & Shaw, 1972). In a review of state oversight of higher education, Lane (2007) found that state policymakers' perceptions of higher education were heavily influenced by the media. The attention of the media can be a double-edged sword. It can serve as a means for highlighting successful endeavors, outstanding students and faculty, and exciting new programs. Such coverage, casting the institution in a positive light, can influence legislators, prospective students, and alumni. Media attention can quickly turn critical, though, particularly when an incident is likely to cause controversy with the local population. This other form of coverage can result in increased scrutiny from external stakeholders.

While the media seem to hold great influence over policymakers and others, institutional leaders need to be aware of the drawbacks of such coverage. McLendon and Peterson (1999) expressed concerns about the legitimacy of the media in informing higher education policy-making because of the press's reliance on partisan sources and tendencies to create "realities that appear singular, objective, and certain, although they are, in fact, multiple, subjective, and permeable" (p. 242). Such concerns have become even more prevalent with the rise of the internet, intensifying political polarization, and increasing public skepticism of both the media and academia. Now news websites and quasinews sites report on campus events, particularly potentially controversial or negative ones, sometimes with very little fact checking. Blogs and social networking sites allow nearly anyone to provide commentary about campus activities or policy decisions. The advent of such "news" outlets has made it more difficult for institutions to influence media messages and has fed into the enhanced accountability expected by external stakeholders.

Various interest groups also influence a state's relationship with higher education. Trade organizations represent and lobby on behalf of independent, proprietary, and religious institutions. In some states, agricultural groups such as the farm bureau can be quite active in lobbying on behalf of agricultural education efforts, which are usually undertaken by the state's land-grant universities. Labor unions have also become increasingly engaged in both negotiating contracts on behalf of their members and lobbying the government on various issues affecting the sector.[10] In fact, public institutions, more than their private counterparts, tend to be covered by union contracts. According to a report from the National Center for the Study of Collective Bargaining in Higher Education, more than 600 bargaining units represent faculty in public colleges and universities, and the number of bargaining units is on the rise (Herbert et al., 2020). In addition to bargaining for a legally binding labor agreement, these groups sometimes also engage in lobbying over other education-related policy issues, such as state funding and state regulation of higher education institutions.

State Governance of Higher Education

U.S. higher education has evolved in such a way that authority for institutions commonly rests in a corporate board. Essentially, a multitude of lay individuals assume responsibility for a college or university (Duryea, 2000). Particularly in the public sector, however, not all institutions have their own boards. Indeed, while most governing boards in the United States oversee one institution, most students in the United States attend a college or university that shares its governing board with other institutions (MacTaggart, 1998). (This chapter focuses primarily on issues pertaining to state governance of higher education. Chapter 10 includes further discussion of the role of governing boards.)

How colleges and universities are governed varies in each state, and there are occasional efforts to restructure those governance arrangements. In the decade prior to the publication of this edition, Oregon disbanded its system of higher education, allowing institutions to opt for single institutional governing boards; Tennessee essentially separated the four-year campuses from the governance of the Tennessee Board of Regents, leaving that board to oversee only the state's 40 community and technical colleges; and the Pennsylvania State System of Higher Education moved to consolidate several of its campuses to create a more financially viable system. This ebb and flow of centralization and decentralization is basically what former SUNY Chancellor D. Bruce Johnstone (2013) referred to as the "apportionment of authority and autonomy" (p. 76).

Public higher education is generally overseen by two types of boards: *governing* and *coordinating*. Governing boards assume operational authority for an institution or a group of institutions and oversee a single institution or a system of institutions (Kerr & Gade, 1989). These boards, commonly referred to as a *board of regents* or a *board of trustees*, assume authority for hiring (and, if needed, firing) the chief executive officer (e.g., president or chancellor), ensuring the financial integrity of the institution, and establishing policies.

Coordinating boards, however, are designed to perform functions on behalf of the entire sector or a large segment of the sector, such as limiting the duplication of degree programs, coordinating institutional budget requests to the state government, licensing educational institutions, overseeing quality assurance mechanisms, dispersing state-supported student aid, and approving institutional missions.[11] Unlike governing boards, the role of these entities is not to oversee the operational aspects of educational institutions. Rather, they are meant to ensure coordination and collaboration among a state's educational institutions and ensure that those institutions operate in a way that is aligned with state priorities and advance a public agenda.

States vary markedly in how they design their governing and coordinating structures. In some states, governing boards operate separately from coordinating boards. In others, a combined board serves both functions, having operational authority for several institutions and responsibility for coordinating operations among them. In New York, for example, SUNY, with 64 campuses, and the City University of New York (CUNY), with 25 campuses, each has its own governing board that also coordinates among its constituent campuses. New York's board of regents then serves as a statewide coordinating board that approves all academic programs at both public and independent colleges and universities.

In fact, the majority of all public colleges and universities are a part of the approximately 60 multicampus university systems of higher education operating in 44 states. These systems serve a large majority of all students in public higher education and yet have been largely overlooked in the academic literature (Lane, 2013). That said, these systems also played a significant leadership role in supporting higher education institutions and their states in responding to and recovering from the COVID-19 pandemic, often coordinating the shift to online learning and enabling campuses to serve as vaccine distribution sites (Gagliardi & Lane, 2022).

In terms of membership, the composition of public boards has remained fairly homogeneous. According to a 2015 survey by the AGB (2016), public board membership remained mostly male (68%) and White (83%). As the South Carolina Statehouse Report headline read, "Whites, males" account for most of the board member slots in that state (Street, 2019). Forty percent of members had a background in business (AGB, 2016). The Campaign for College Opportunity (2018) also reported that California's public higher education systems fall short of reflecting the state and its students' diversity. In some states, efforts have been made to increase the diversity of board membership, but the makeup is often dependent on how membership is determined, such as by appointments by the governor or other selection processes. Nonetheless, fewer than half of board members who responded to a national survey supported the idea that diversifying their board by race, gender, or occupational background was very important to them (AGB, 2020).

While structures differ across the states, the members of public institutions' governing boards are generally either appointed or elected, with a few serving ex officio. Members typically come from the state, and it is likely many are "beholden to external political interests" (Kerr & Gade, 1989, p. 40). Increasingly, membership also includes individuals who represent internal stakeholders, such as students and faculty. Those who study governing boards suggest, however, that all members should view themselves as guardians of the institution rather than champions of particular groups or interests (Chait et al., 1996).

Beyond who constitutes the membership of a governing board, how a board is structured can influence its operations. Toma (1990) found,

> The structure of the boards is important because it helps to define the constraints on the board members and on the internal agents of the universities. . . . Public universities can be made to function more like private ones by placing them under separate governing boards. (p. 7)

Whether one of these approaches is more effective than the other is a matter of debate and perspective. Increasingly, the multicampus model is seen as a mechanism for ensuring that public higher education is advancing the public good and may be an important structure to realize economies of scale to buffer against rising costs, as well as rethinking higher education in a postpandemic environment (Gagliardi & Lane, 2022; Zimpher, 2021). Moreover, a board's scope of responsibility can affect how it relates to the institution or institutions under its control. For example, while a board of a single institution can focus all its efforts on advancing that institution, multicampus boards must make decisions about how to balance institutional needs and distribute resources. As Johnstone (2013) observed, "As multicampus system governing boards and system administrations act on behalf of state government and as agents of the statewide public interest, tensions between systems and member institutions—generally seeking maximum autonomy—are inevitable" (p. 82).

How members are selected can also influence board operations. Elected and appointed members often see their roles differently. Most appointments are made by the governor, while some come directly from the legislature. Appointments are generally favored over elections, as the vetting process tends to be more involved to ensure that dedicated and knowledgeable individuals are appointed, although numerous examples exist of political appointments based on cronyism rather than relevant characteristics or skills (Kerr & Gade, 1989). Elected board members, however, may wield more political influence and have greater opportunity to challenge unfriendly politicians, but they may also take a similar approach toward institutional leaders (Kerr & Gade, 1989). The selection process may not only affect how members interact with others, but it may also influence their priorities. Empirical studies in this area are quite limited, but Lowry (2001) found that elected rather than appointed boards generally result in lower tuition rates at public institutions. The reason may be that elected boards are more attuned to the demands of the public, which often are focused on keeping tuition low.

Community College Governance

Most community colleges developed along a separate path than four-year institutions, resulting in different governance arrangements. Some institutions were created as two-year branch campuses affiliated with four-year institutions, so they are generally governed by the same board as the four-year institutions. These institutions were initially meant to serve as feeder schools so that the students would complete some of their early coursework at the branch before attending the larger institution. Alternatively, many two-year institutions were founded by school districts or local communities to provide technical and vocational training beyond high school as well as to provide access to those historically underserved by four-year campuses. Today, regardless of their origins, most two-year institutions have evolved into comprehensive community colleges that provide an array of vocational programs, transfer programs, continuing education courses, and other services (Cohen & Brawer, 2009).

Although community colleges exist in every state, they share no common governance structure. While in some states two-year colleges are included in a comprehensive public system, in others community colleges are governed separately. For example, the Illinois Community College Board serves as the coordinating entity for 48 community colleges. Each community college has its own board of trustees, whose members are elected from the local community college district. Less frequently, the governance remains entirely local with a school board or local tax district retaining control over an institution (Tollefson et al., 1999). Regardless of the specific structure, community college governance is influenced by a number of factors, including board composition, articulation agreements, collective bargaining agreements, and historical values and customs (Fletcher & Friedel, 2017).

State Funding

States and localities play a significant role in the funding of public (and some private) higher education institutions. While the federal government provides substantial loans to students and research grants to faculty, the amount of federal funds directly allocated for institutional support is limited. States and localities provide funds to higher education in three primary ways: operating funds, capital funds, and student aid. In FY 2019 state and local governments allocated more than $100 billion to support higher education, an increase of nearly 20% from the decade before (SHEEO, 2020). A vast majority of the funding comes from state tax appropriations, which accounted for around 85% of state and local funding during the 2010s. About 11% comes from local sources, and about 4% from nontax sources such as lottery sales.[12] These funding sources typically have not provided incentives for institutions to improve student outcomes, but the increased focus on accountability has led many states to adopt performance-based funding policies.

Broadly, performance-based funding (PBF) ties state funding for public colleges and universities to performance indicators, such as degrees conferred and job placement rates. Although the movement began in the United States with Tennessee's adoption of a PBF policy in 1979 (Hillman et al., 2018), it was reconceptualized and became more widely adopted in the late 2000s and early 2010s. There are five primary differences between the PBF of the 20th and early 21st centuries (PBF 1.0) and the redesigned PBF of the late 2000s and 2010s (PBF 2.0): (a) increased emphasis on degree production and the emerging economy; (b) state-specific workforce development; (c) desires to strengthen connections between institutional missions, measures, and incentives; (d) the addition of throughput success indicators, such as gateway course completion rates; and (e) financial and political pressures placed on the higher education sector (McLendon & Hearn, 2013). These changes likely influenced many states that did not adopt PBF 1.0 to adopt

PBF 2.0; as of 2020, 41 states maintain some form of PBF policy (Ortagus et al., 2020).

Although the benefits of PBF have been widely promoted and supported by advocacy groups such as the Lumina Foundation and the Bill and Melinda Gates Foundation (Gandara et al., 2017), recent research has questioned the efficacy of these models. Umbricht et al. (2017), for example, found in a study of Indiana's PBF policies that not only did PBF not increase the number of degrees conferred, it led to declining admission rates and increased selectivity at Indiana's public universities. The inefficacy of PBF policies is further illustrated by the work of Ortagus et al. (2020), who conducted a systematic synthesis of studies on PBF with strong causal inference designs published between 1998 and 2019. In this review, they found that PBF policies have null or only modest positive effects on desired outcomes, such as graduation rates and credit hours conferred. More troubling, Ortagus et al. (2020) found substantial evidence that PBF policies have deleterious effects, such as a reduction in educational access and manipulation of PBF systems. Moreover, they found that these negative outcomes are more likely to affect underserved student groups and underresourced institution types, although PBF policies that tie funding to serving underrepresented students offset some of these negative effects.

While most states have not historically provided state aid directly to students, as such aid has been a primary funding role of the federal government, this trend has changed in the past few decades. As of 2020, New Hampshire was the only state that did not provide state aid directly to students (SHEEO, 2020). States use a variety of methods to distribute aid, such as grants, loans, scholarships, work study, and tuition waivers, although the most common approach is grants (National Association of State Student Grant and Aid Programs [NASSGAP], 2020). Aid policies differ in two primary ways. First, in terms of how much money is allocated to student aid programs, all states except New Hampshire now appropriate at least a small amount of money to student aid programs, but the amounts vary significantly, from less than $100 per FTE student in Michigan, Arizona, Montana, Hawaii, and Iowa to more than $2,200 per FTE in Tennessee (SHEEO, 2020). A number of reasons explain these differences, including direct state and local support to institutions, state fiscal culture, institutional tuition levels, and the number of students in each system. Overall state aid to students increased 30.4% from 2009 to 2019, with wide variations among states. Michigan, for example, experienced a 96.8% decrease in state aid between 2001 and 2019 (Pew, 2019).

The second difference concerns how eligibility for aid is determined. Eligibility is often defined in terms of merit or need, although states vary markedly in their aid policies, which directly affects who benefits. Merit-based aid is allocated to students according to their previous academic performance or other types of exceptional achievements. Need-based aid is intended for students with financial need. Eligibility for need-based aid, even at the state level, is usually determined by the federal FAFSA. Most states support undergraduate students with a need-based component, and 24 states also have aid programs exclusively based on merit. Out of all aid awarded to undergraduates in the 2018–2019 AY, exclusively need-based aid accounted for 44%; exclusively merit-based aid accounted for 19.8%; and the remaining 36.2% was accounted for by other programs, including programs that provide both need and merit components (NASSGAP, 2020).

The shift to spending more on need-based aid over merit-based aid is a relatively recent development in state-funded student aid. Although politically popular, merit-based aid has been shown to disproportionately advantage the dominant class of affluent White students at the expense of minority students and students from low socioeconomic backgrounds (Burd, 2020; Pew, 2019), so this shift may be driven by concerns over equity and educational access. Examples of shifts to need-based aid include Georgia and Utah, which both added need-based grants in 2018. Utah in particular appears to be making large strides toward need-based aid. In 2019, the Utah State Board of Regents moved to eliminate two merit-based scholarships that monopolized 90% of the state's financial aid spending. The board proposed replacing these scholarships with need-based grants that would be funded by 70% of the state's $20 million annual student aid budget (Quinton, 2019).

In a few states, appropriations are allocated to support nonpublic institutions. These states are primarily east of the Mississippi River, and the funding is relatively small compared to that provided to public institutions. Only in seven states (Indiana, Iowa, Kentucky, New Jersey, New York, Pennsylvania, and South Carolina) does support to independent institutions exceed 5% of all higher education funding in the state. This funding is primarily allocated via student aid programs to students, although a small handful of states also provide limited operational funding (SHEEO, 2020).

Another major policy shift has been the bipartisan effort toward free college. At the time of this writing, Tennessee, New York, and Rhode Island had state-supported, last-dollar programs to cover the costs of attending public colleges and universities. The Tennessee Promise, the first such policy in the country, supports a student's attendance at the state's community and technical colleges. New York's Excelsior Scholarship provides 4 years of support to eligible students at any public college and some private institutions in New York. The Rhode Island Promise provides eligible state residents with 2 years of free tuition at the Community College of Rhode Island.

Future Issues

States are the primary organizing structure for the nation's higher education sector. State governments retain primary responsibility for licensing and regulating a state's colleges and universities. In addition, state governments have historically served as the principal funders of their public institutions. The relationship between higher education and the state is often debated, particularly during times of great political or financial upheaval, but the fundamental connections usually remain intact. When we wrote the first edition of this book following the Great Recession in 2008, there was great deliberation about the future of funding of higher education. Some observers wondered whether state divestiture from higher education might lead to less government oversight. While funding has only recently begun to return to prerecession levels, state governments are as engaged as ever in oversight and accountability activities. At the time of this writing, the COVID-19 pandemic appears to be recalibrating higher education from enrollment patterns to governance structures, and nothing suggests that states are looking to step away from their engagement in higher education. Given that other instances of economic turbulence have led states to expand access to education (Boggs, 2018), the pandemic may lead states to more involvement in higher education governance.

In fact, as noted previously, higher education has become part of larger political platforms. Some polls suggest unprecedented questioning of the value of higher education, as part of broader distrust of the integrity of the nation's social institutions such as the media, the courts, and elections. At times, these attitudes have led some elected state officials to question the value of state funding of higher education and advocate for reductions to state appropriations. However, state leaders on both sides of the aisle have also advocated for increasing state support of higher education, particularly recognizing its role in supporting state economies and communities. Indeed, members of populations historically underrepresented in higher education, such as African American and Latinx communities, continue to see higher education as an important mechanism for social mobility. The effort to increase college affordability through a combination of loan forgiveness and increased state funding is likely to be part of the political landscape for the foreseeable future. Efforts to limit tuition rates, however, may lead to another crisis of college funding, which will lead to more discussions about state support and institutional financial structures.

Another topic that is beginning to gain attention across states is workforce development. Over the past several years, states have increasingly begun to consider and enact legislation that builds connections between the higher education and workforce sectors. Such legislation typically falls into four broad categories: (a) developing programs that lead to specific job and career pathways; (b) strengthening partnerships between P–12, postsecondary, and workforce organizations; (c) providing financial incentives to institutions and students to promote attainment of career-focused degrees and credentials; and (d) compiling data related to workforce development to inform postsecondary programs and policies (Keily, 2019). More specifically, in the 2020 state legislative sessions, the majority of states reviewed bills related to using postsecondary education to meet workforce development needs, and 16 bills were enacted into law. Kentucky, for instance, passed HB 419, which requires the Council on Postsecondary Education to collect and publish data on the most in-demand jobs in the commonwealth and their associated salaries, as well as data on the affordability and graduation outcomes of postsecondary institutions in Kentucky. Similarly, Virginia passed HB 1276, which requires school boards to create detailed career plans for career and technical education programs that compare workforce needs with degree programs and graduation outcomes of postsecondary institutions in the commonwealth. Taking a more focused approach, Louisiana's SB 79 allocates state funding for the development of degree and certificate programs in cybersecurity fields (National Conference of State Legislatures [NCSL], 2020).

Much of the conversation around workforce development centers on building work-based learning (WBL) into postsecondary curricula. WBL is a form of experiential learning that typically pairs classroom instruction with on-the-job training in the form of apprenticeships and internships; students may also be paid for the on-the-job training they receive. Although many states began considering WBL programs prior to 2020, the pandemic has likely accelerated the rate at which states will implement these initiatives. Due to the pandemic, 25% of individuals between the ages of 16 and 24 became unemployed, an increase from 8% in February 2020, before the pandemic began in the United States (Kochar, 2020).

WBL frequently allows students to earn an income while pursuing their degrees, presenting a potential solution to alleviate high unemployment rates through direct targeting of workforce needs. However, implementing high-quality WBL programs that meet student and workforce needs raises several areas of concern for state policymakers. Drawing from specific instances of WBL policy issues across the United States, Altstadt et al. (2020) argued that WBL policy concerns center around five key areas: (a) strengthening partnerships between P–12 systems, postsecondary institutions, and employers; (b) enabling the innovative use of technology, without restricting access to certain groups; (c) providing WBL experiences at the secondary school level; (d) creating variety in WBL experiences, such as microcredentials, pre-apprenticeships, and apprenticeships; and (e) using preexisting structures and systems to implement WBL experiences. To help facilitate navigation of these and other emerging issues, the National Governors Association (NGA) has developed a state-to-state mentoring program in which states that are more advanced in WBL will participate in learning labs with states that desire to expand their WBL offerings (NGA, 2020).

Another issue surrounding the implementation of WBL is the tendency of many WBL programs to use competency-based education (CBE). CBE is a curricular format that reconceptualizes the process of earning academic credits, as it awards credits to students based on their demonstrated mastery of certain skills or competencies. Although development of CBE programs remains slow, a wide variety of colleges and universities have recently begun to adopt this practice. Indeed, a recent survey showed that CBE programs span all institution types, although most institutions that implement CBE do so in a piecemeal way (Mason & Parsons, 2019). Many challenges remain for the future of CBE, such as incompatibility with existing institutional processes and regulations surrounding federal financial aid. Despite these challenges, many leaders in higher education are optimistic about the future of CBE and anticipate that CBE offerings will grow within their institutions in the coming years (Mason & Parsons, 2019).

Even as some states are seeking to disrupt the traditional recognition of academic credits, another effort by states and multicampus systems seeks to improve the transfer of credits between institutions. The transfer of credit has been an area of institutional and policy concern for several decades, and a report from the U.S. Government Accountability Office (2017) revealed that transfer students "lose" 43% of their credits when they transfer. The focus historically has been on designing articulation agreements to facilitate the movement of credits from two-year institutions to four-year institutions under a 2 + 2 model. The problem with this approach is that it is largely based on what works for institutions rather than students. Data from SUNY revealed that one third of transfers in their systems transferred *to* community colleges (Lane, 2018). Moreover, a report from the Community College Resource Center (Jenkins & Fink, 2016) found that just over 60% of baccalaureate completers transferred from a two-year institution before completing an associate degree, and less than 10% followed a formal 2 + 2 model. These trends have led several state systems and some state legislatures to adopt policies designed to improve the transfer experience of students and likely shift higher education toward more multidirectional and multicampus networks that more effectively use technology to automate and streamline credit mobility (Lane et al., 2021).

While these matters represent some of the key issues that will occupy the attention of policymakers in states for some time, the years ahead are likely to yield new and unforeseen concerns. What is important is that higher education leaders stay attuned to these topics as well as develop relationships with political leaders and policymakers to ensure that higher education can be part of the discussion that ultimately yields useful policy outcomes.

Notes

1. As discussed in chapter 5, amendments to the U.S. Constitution give control of education to state governments. The federal government, however, has always maintained some interest in these affairs.

2. Readers may find additional information about their state context from their state education department and the local media. In addition, these organizations track issues related to state policy and funding: National Association of Systems Heads (NASH), National Conference of State Legislatures (NCSL), National Governors Association (NGA), and SHEEO.

3. According the American Indian Higher Education Consortium, there are more than 30 tribal colleges. The federal government has been involved with tribal colleges. For example, the Tribally Controlled Community College Assistance Act of 1978 provides federal funding to tribal colleges, and the Equity in Educational Land-Grant Status Act of 1994 designated them as federal land-grant institutions, making them eligible for additional funding. More information about tribal colleges can be found in chapter 6 and at http://www.aihec.org.

4. The Education Commission of the States maintains a list of state licensure agencies on its website: http://www.ecs.org.

5. A handful of institutions also attained public status after first operating as private entities. For example, Temple University and the University of Pittsburgh were created as private institutions, but when they became financially troubled, the Commonwealth of Pennsylvania began to provide them with annual appropriations because of the important roles they played in Philadelphia and Pittsburgh. Though these institutions fought to maintain their private status, the Supreme Court of Pennsylvania ruled that "a symbiotic relationship between the institution and the Commonwealth exists," so "action taken by those institutions are, therefore, actions taken under of color of state law" (*Krynicky v. University of Pittsburgh*, 1984, n.p.).

6. According to the *Digest of Education Statistics* (de Brey et al., 2021), as of 2019–2020, 3,982 accredited institutions in the United States were awarding associate degrees or higher. Of this number, 1,625 were public; 1,660 were private, not-for-profit; and 697 were private, for-profit institutions.

7. In this section we discuss accountability as distinct from quality assurance efforts undertaken by nongovernmental accreditation agencies (see chapter 16).

8. The section draws on and adapts the typology developed by Fowler (2000).

9. Republican Governor Bill Haslam of Tennessee advanced free community college for all state residents under the Tennessee Promise initiative in 2014. In 2017, New York initiated Democratic Governor Andrew Cuomo's Excelsior Scholarship, a last-dollar initiative designed to cover the tuition at any state college or university for 4 years for families making up to $125,000.

10. National groups such as AFT Higher Education, the American Association of University Professors, and the National Education Association are the primary representation of public-sector faculty and staff. The United University Professions, an affiliate of AFT, represents the faculty and professional staff at the four-year campuses of SUNY and is the largest single higher education union organization.

11. The idea of statewide coordination attracted great interest during the 1960s and 1970s and was widely adopted during the 1980s and 1990s. Berdahl (1971) found that some states had almost no coordination, or the coordination occurred voluntarily. The formal coordinating bodies that did exist focused on master planning and budgeting for their state's institutions, often with a particular focus on facilities planning. Moving into the 1980s and 1990s, the focus of coordinating boards began to evolve into more "market-driven 'strategic investment' approaches" designed to influence institutional behavior (MacTaggart, 1998, p. 12).

12. Funding sources vary across the states. For a majority of all states, the largest source of public support is state taxes. Arizona, Kansas, Michigan, and Oregon are the only states where more than 20% of higher education funding comes from local appropriations; 21 states do not provide local appropriations to higher education (SHEEO, 2020).

References

Adelman, C., & Carey, K. (2009). *Ready to assemble: Grading state higher education accountability systems.* Education Sector.

Altstadt, D., Barrett, L., Cahill, C., Cuevas, E., & Maag, T. (2020). *Expanding high quality work-based learning.* Education Commission of the States. https://www .ecs.org/expanding-high-quality-work-based-learning/

Association of Governing Boards of Universities and Colleges. (2016). *Policies, practices, and composition of governing boards of public colleges, universities, and systems.* AGB Press.

Association of Governing Boards of Universities and Colleges. (2020, January 29). *The AGB 2020 trustee index: Concern deepens for the future of higher education.* https://agb.org/reports-2/the-agb-2020-trustee-index/

Behn, R. D. (2001). *Rethinking democratic accountability.* Brookings Institution Press.

Berdahl, R. O. (1971). *Statewide coordination of higher education.* American Council on Education.

Blackwell, T. E. (1961). *College law: A guide for administrators.* American Council on Education.

Boggs, B. G. (2018). *Challenges facing legislatures and postsecondary education.* National Conference of State Legislatures. https://www.ncsl.org/research/education/a-legislator-s-toolkit-for-the-new-world-of-higher-education.aspx

Bovens, M. (2006). *Analysing and assessing public accountability: A conceptual framework.* https://ideas.repec.org/p/erp/eurogo/p0005.html

Bowman, A. O., & Kearney, R. C. (1988). Dimensions of state government capability. *Western Political Quarterly, 41*(2), 341–362. https://doi.org/10.1177/106591298804100208

Bracco, K. R. (1997). *State structures for the governance of higher education: Texas case study summary.* California Higher Education Policy Center. https://eric.ed.gov/?id=ED412870

Brayboy, B. M., Fann, A. J., Castagno, A. E., & Solyom, J. A. (2012). Postsecondary education for American Indian and Alaska Natives: Higher education for nation building and self-determination. *ASHE Higher Education Report, 37*(5), 1–154. https://doi.org/10.1002/aehe.v37.5x

Brown, J. T. (2018). Leading colleges & universities in a new policy era: How to understand the complex landscape of higher education accountability. *Change: The Magazine of Higher Learning, 50*(2), 30–39. https://doi.org/10.1080/0009 1383.2018.1483175

Burd, S. (2020). *Crisis point: How enrollment management and the merit-aid arms race are derailing public higher education.* New America.

Burke, J. C. (2005). The many faces of accountability. In J. C. Burke (Ed.), *Achieving accountability in higher education* (pp. 1–24). Jossey-Bass.

Burke, J. C., & Associates. (2002). *Funding public higher education for performance: Popularity, problems, and prospects.* Rockefeller Institute Press.

Campaign for College Opportunity. (2018). *Left out: California's higher education governing boards do not reflect the racial and gender diversity of California and its student body.* https://collegecampaign.org/portfolio/left-out-governance/

Chait, R., Holland, T. P., & Taylor, B. E. (1996). *The effective board of trustees.* Oryx.

Clark, B. R. (1983). *The higher education system: Academic organization in cross-national perspective.* University of California Press.

Cohen, A., & Brawer, F. (2009). *The American community college* (5th ed.). Wiley.

Contreras, A. L. (2009). *The legal basis for degree-granting authority in the United States.* State Higher Education Executive Officers.

Crazy Bull, C., Lindquist, C., Burns, R., Vermillion, L., & McDonald, L. (2020). Tribal colleges and universities: Building nations, revitalizing identity. *Change: The Magazine of Higher Learning, 52*(1), 23–29. https://doi.org/10.1080/0009 1383.2020.1693819

Davis, J. (2001). American Indian boarding school experiences: Recent studies from Native perspectives. *OAH Magazine of History, 15*(2), 20–22. https://doi.org/10.1093/maghis/15.2.20

de Brey, C., Snyder, T. D., Zhang, A., & Dillow, S. A. (2021). *Digest of education statistics 2019.* National Center for Education Statistics, U.S. Department of Education. https://nces.ed.gov/pubs2021/2021009.pdf

Dougherty, K. J., Jones, S. M., Lahr, H., Natow, R. S., Pheatt, L., & Reddy, V. (2016). *Performance funding for higher education.* Johns Hopkins University Press.

Dubnick, M. J. (2005). Accountability and the promise of performance: In search of the mechanisms. *Public Performance & Management Review, 27*(3), 376–417.

Duryea, E. D. (2000). *The academic corporation: A history of college and university governing boards.* Falmer.

Equity in Educational Land-Grant Status Act, Pub. L. no.103-382, 108 Stat. 4048 (1994)

Fletcher, J. A., & Friedel, J. N. (2017). Typology of state-level community college governance structures. *Community College Journal of Research and Practice, 41*(4–5), 311–322. https://doi.org/10.1080/10668926.2016.1251355

Fowler, F. C. (2000). *Policy studies for educational leaders: An introduction.* Prentice Hall.

Gagliardi, J., & Lane, J. E. (2022). *Higher education systems redesigned: Shifting from perpetuation to innovation to student success.* State University of New York Press.

Gandara, D., Rippner, J. A., & Ness, E. C. (2017). Exploring the "how" in policy diffusion: National intermediary organizations' roles in facilitating the spread of performance-based funding policies in the states. *Journal of Higher Education, 88*(5), 701–725. https://doi.org/10.1080/00221546.2016.1272089

Government Accountability Office. (2017, August 14). *Students need more information to help reduce challenges in transferring college credits.* https://www.gao.gov/products/gao-17-574

Heller, D. E. (2004). State oversight of academia. In R. G. Ehrenberg (Ed.), *Governing academia: Who is in charge at the modern university?* (pp. 49–68). Cornell University Press.

Herbert, W. A., Apkarian, J., & van der Naald, J. (2020). *Supplementary directory of new bargaining agents and contracts in institutions of higher education, 2013–2019.* National Center for the Study of Collective Bargaining in Higher Education. http://www.hunter.cuny.edu/ncscbhep/assets/files/SupplementalDirectory-2020-FINAL.pdf

Hillman, N. W., Hicklin Fryar, A., & Crespín-Trujillo, V. (2018). Evaluating the impact of performance funding in Ohio and Tennessee. *American Educational Research Journal, 55*(1), 144–170. https://doi.org/10.3102/0002831217732951

Jacoby, B., & Associates. (2009). *Civic engagement in higher education: Concepts and practices.* Jossey-Bass.

Jenkins, D., & Fink, J. (2016). *Tracking transfer: New measures of institutional and state effectiveness in helping community college students attain bachelor's degrees.* Community College Resource Center.

Johnstone, D. B. (2013). Higher education autonomy and the apportionment of authority among state governments, public multi-campus systems, and members of colleges and universities. In J. E. Lane & D. B. Johnstone (Eds.), *Higher education systems 3.0: Harnessing systems, delivering performance* (pp. 75–100). State University of New York Press.

Keily, T. (2019). *Postsecondary workforce development policies.* Policy Snapshot. Education Commission of the States. https://eric.ed.gov/?id=ED600045

Kelchen, R. (2018). *Higher education accountability.* Johns Hopkins University Press.

Kerr, D., & Gade, M. (1989). *The guardians: Boards of trustees of American colleges and universities.* Association of Governing Boards.

Kinser, K., & Lane, J. E. (2017). *Authorization and quality assurance of higher education institutions: A global overview.* UNESCO. https://unesdoc.unesco.org/ark:/48223/pf0000259561

Kochar, R. (2020, June 11). *Unemployment rose higher in three months of COVID-19 than it did in two years of the Great Recession.* Pew Research Center. https://pewrsr.ch/2UADTTZ

Krynicky v. University of Pittsburgh, 742 F.2d 94 (3rd Cir. 1984)

Lane, J. E. (2007). The spider web of oversight: An analysis of external oversight of higher education. *Journal of Higher Education, 78*(6), 1–30. https://doi.org/10.1080/00221546.2007.11772074

Lane, J. E. (2013). Higher education systems 3.0: Adding value to states and institutions. In J. E. Lane & D. B. Johnstone (Eds.), *Higher education systems 3.0: Harnessing systems, delivering performance* (pp. 3–26). State University of New York Press.

Lane, J. E. (2018). Data analytics, systemness, and predicting student success in college: Examining how the data revolution matters to higher education policy makers. In Gagliardi, J., Parnell, A., Carpenter-Hubin, J. (Eds.). *The Analytics Revolution in Higher Education: Big Data, Organizational Learning, and Student Success.* Stylus.

Lane, J. E., & Johnstone, D. B. (Eds.). (2012). *Colleges and universities as economic drivers: Measuring higher education's role in economic development.* State University of New York Press.

Lane, J. E., Khan, M. I., & Knox, D. (2021). *Transfer student success: Higher education systems' five top policy levers.* National Association of System Heads. https://ts3.nashonline.org/transfertopfive/

Lowry, R. C. (2001). Government structures, trustee selection, and public university process and spending: Multiple means to similar ends. *American Journal of Political Science, 45*(4), 845–861. https://doi.org/10.2307/2669328

MacTaggart, T. J. (1998). *Seeking excellence through independence: Liberating colleges and universities from excessive regulation.* Jossey-Bass.

Marshall, C., Mitchell, D., & Wirt, F. (1989). *Culture and education policy in the American states.* Falmer.

Mason, J., & Parsons, K. (2019). *State of the field: Findings from the 2019 national survey of postsecondary competency-based education.* American Institutes for Research. https://www.air.org/project/national-survey-postsecondary-competency-based-education

McCombs, M. E., & Shaw, D. L. (1972). The agenda-setting function of the mass media. *Public Opinion Quarterly, 36*(2), 176–187. https://doi.org/10.1086/267990

McCombs, M., Shaw, D., & Weaver, D. (2014). New directions in agenda-setting theory and research. *Mass Communication and Society*, *17*(6), 781–802. https://doi.org/10.1080/15205436.2014.964871

McGuiness, A. C., Jr. (2013). The history and evolution of higher education systems in the United States. In J. E. Lane & D. B. Johnstone (Eds.), *Higher education systems 3.0: Harnessing systems, delivering performance* (pp. 45–74). State University of New York Press.

McLendon, M. K., & Hearn, J. C. (2004). Why "sunshine" laws matter: Emerging issues for university governance, leadership, and policy. *Metropolitan Universities*, *15*(1), 67–83. https://journals.iupui.edu/index.php/muj/issue/view/1109

McLendon, M. K., & Hearn, J. C. (2013). The resurgent interest in performance-based funding for higher education. *Academe*, *99*(6), 25–30. https://www.aaup.org/article/resurgent-interest-performance-based-funding-higher-education#.YJCYgrVKiM8

McLendon, M. K., & Peterson, M. W. (1999). The press and state policy making for higher education. *Review of Higher Education*, *22*(3), 223–245. https://doi.org/10.1353/rhe.1999.0013

Meriam, L. (1928). *The problem of Indian administration: Report of a survey made at the request of Honorable Hubert Work, secretary of the interior, and submitted to him, February 21, 1928.* https://eric.ed.gov/?id=ED087573

Miami Tribe and Miami University. (n.d.). *Land Acknowledgement.* Miami University Office of Diversity & Inclusion. https://miamioh.edu/diversity-inclusion/land/index.html.

Middlehurst, R. (2011). Accountability and cross-border higher education: Dynamics, trends, and challenges. In B. Stensaker & L. Harvey (Eds.), *Accountability in higher education: Global perspectives on trust and power* (pp. 179–202). Routledge.

Morison, S. E. (1986). *Three centuries of Harvard, 1636–1936.* Belknap.

National Association of State Student Grant and Aid Programs. (2020). *50th annual survey report on state-sponsored student financial aid: 2018–2019 academic year.* https://www.nassgapsurvey.com/survey_reports/2018-2019-50th.pdf

National Conference of State Legislatures. (2020, December 2). *Higher education legislation in 2020.* https://www.ncsl.org/research/education/higher-education-legislation-in-2020.aspx

National Council for State Authorization Reciprocity Agreements. (n.d.). *About NC-SARA.* https://nc-sara.org/about-nc-sara

National Governors Association. (2020, January 21). *National Governors Association names 6 states to mentor peers on work-based learning* [Press release]. https://www.nga.org/news/press-releases/national-governors-association-names-6-states-to-mentor-peers-on-work-based-learning/

Nelson, C., & Frye, J. R. (2016). *Tribal college and university funding: Tribal sovereignty at the intersection of federal, state, and local funding.* American Council on Education.

New Jersey State Board of Higher Education v. Board of Directors of Shelton College, 90 N.J. 470, 448 A.2d 988 (1982)

Ortagus, J. C., Kelchen, R., Rosinger, K., & Voorhees, N. (2020). Performance-based funding in American higher education: A systematic synthesis of intended and unintended consequences. *Educational Evaluation and Policy Analysis, 42*(4), 520–550. https://doi.org/10.3102/0162373720953128

Patterson, S. C. (1996). Legislative politics in the states. In V. Gray & H. Jacob (Eds.), *Politics in the American states* (6th ed., pp. 159–206). Congressional Quarterly Press.

Pew. (2019, October 15). *Two decades of change in federal and state higher education funding: Recent trends across levels of government.* [Issue Brief]. https://www.pewtrusts.org/en/research-and-analysis/issue-briefs/2019/10/two-decades-of-change-in-federal-and-state-higher-education-funding

Pratt, R. H. (2004). *Battlefield and classroom: Four decades with the American Indian.* University of Oklahoma Press.

Quinton, S. (2019, December 10). *Some states move toward financial aid based on need rather than merit.* Pew. https://www.pewtrusts.org/en/research-and-analysis/blogs/stateline/2019/12/10/some-states-move-toward-financial-aid-based-on-need-rather-than-merit

Reyhner, J. A., & Eder, J. M. O. (2004). *American Indian education: A history.* University of Oklahoma Press.

S. Rep. No. 91-501 (1969)

State Authorization, 34 CFR § 600, 2019

State ex rel. McLemore v. Clarksville School of Theology, 636 S.W.2d. 706 (Tenn. 1982)

State Higher Education Executive Officers Association. (2020). *State higher education finance: FY 2019.* https://shef.sheeo.org/wp-content/uploads/2020/04/SHEEO_SHEF_FY19_Report.pdf

Stein, W. J. (2009). Tribal colleges and universities: Supporting the revitalization in Indian country. In L. S. Warner & G. E. Gipp (Eds.), *Tradition and culture in the millennium: Tribal colleges and universities* (pp. 17–34). Information Age.

Street, L. (2019, July 19). *Whites, males comprise majority of state university governing boards.* Statehouse Report. https://www.statehousereport.com/2019/07/19/big-story-whites-males-comprise-big-majority-of-state-university-governing-boards/

Thelin, J. R. (2011). *A history of American higher education* (2nd ed.). Johns Hopkins University Press.

Tollefson, T. A., Garrett, R. L, Ingram, W. G., & Associates. (1999). *Fifty state systems of community colleges: Mission, governance, funding, and accountability.* Overmountain.

Toma, E. F. (1990). Boards of trustees, agency problems, and the university output. *Public Choice, 67*(1), 1–9. https://doi.org/10.1007/BF01890153

Townshend v. Gray (1890) 62 Vermont 373. *Atlantic Reporter, 19,* 635–637.

Tribally Controlled Community College Assistance Act of 1978. 25 U.S.C. 1802 et seq. (1978)

Umbricht, M. R., Fernandez, F., & Ortagus, J. C. (2017). An examination of the (un)intended consequences of performance funding in higher education. *Educational Policy, 31*(5), 643–673. https://doi.org/10.1177/0895904815614398

U.S. Department of Arts and Culture. (n.d.). *Honor Native land: A guide and call for acknowledgement.* https://usdac.us/nativeland/.

Vidovich, L., & Slee, R. (2000, December). *The unsteady ascendancy of market accountability in Australian and English higher education* [Paper presentation]. Australian Association for Research in Education Conference, Sydney University, NSW, Australia.

WICHE Cooperative for Educational Technologies. (n.d.). *History: Oversight of education is a function of the state.* Western Interstate Commission for Higher Education. https://wcetsan.wiche.edu/resources/history

Zimpher, N. L. (2021, March 8). Higher education systems and the big rethink. *Inside Higher Ed.* https://www.insidehighered.com/views/2021/03/08/reimagining-new-post-pandemic-roles-university-systems-can-play-opinion

8

THE COURTS AND
HIGHER EDUCATION

Across higher education, college leaders spend a significant amount of time on legal issues, whether addressing unpredictable developments around the "pandemic, protests, and politics" at the presidential level (Storbeck, 2021) or issues of the curriculum and academic freedom, equity and structural racism, health and safety, faculty tenure, and sexual harassment—which are among the reported key concerns that keep chief academic officers and their deans awake at night (Jaschik & Lederman, 2021). The rise in the number of cases and complexity of the legal environment within higher education are often attributed to social changes driven by the courts. Notably, in May 1954, the U.S. Supreme Court took a bold step. In *Brown v. Board of Education*, it overturned the "separate but equal" doctrine, making it a federal constitutional violation to operate separate public schools, with drastically different resources, and consider that separation fair under the law. Put simply, educational segregation and unequal resources in public education were declared illegal. That case, however, represented more than a dismantling of educational segregation; it started a movement in which society recognized civil rights as applicable to educational settings.

As greater demands for rights and calls for fairness increased following the *Brown v. Board of Education* case, litigation in higher education grew. According to Donoso and Zirkel (2008), overall litigation involving colleges rose from 158 to 340 cases between the 1950s and the 1960s. Also during that time, and through much of the 1970s, societal mindsets started to challenge higher education. Courts in particular held colleges as the responsible party for injuries sustained to students, recognizing *in loco parentis* in which a college acted in the place of a parent. Not surprisingly, when colleges became increasingly more responsible for harms their students experienced, litigation in higher education increased. Donoso and Zirkel (2008) reported that the number of cases grew quite substantially, from 340 in the 1960s to 1,360 in the 1970s, which represented a 300% increase.

The courts' expectations of colleges changed during the 1980s. Judges and legislators, via court cases and policy, started to relieve universities in many instances from liability for student injuries, particularly from accidents caused by third parties (i.e., persons beyond the college and the injured party) and taking place outside the classroom. A federal appellate court case, *Bradshaw v. Rawlings* (1979), started this trend by declaring that colleges and universities are not an insurer of student safety. This outcome was unlike many past cases. The court ruled that the college did not owe a duty to protect students from harm even though the drunk driver who caused an accident got drunk at a college-sponsored event. In this case and subsequent cases that followed the same logic, the courts made clear that a university's scope of responsibility could not continue to extend beyond its campus and when the institution could not control the situation (see, e.g., Bickel & Lake, 1999). Presumably that logic would have reduced the number of cases for higher education, but while the courts reduced college liability in one area (i.e., acts of a third party in which the college had no control), legislators and courts started to hold higher education institutions accountable in many more areas to help change behaviors of their students and other community members—especially in terms of providing safety on campus, advancing equity in admissions, upholding fairness in disciplinary proceedings, and reaffirming employment rights. Given these changes in the legal environment, several higher education professional associations now include legal awareness, compliance, and college policy development as part of their core competencies to qualify for professional roles in higher education (e.g., Farr & Cunningham, 2017; Professional Competencies Task Force, 2015).

Although legal awareness (e.g., new court rulings, legislation, and regulations) is important for campus leaders, the law does not operate in a vacuum within an institution. Instead, college leaders must consider the law within their institution's mission, adaptable approach, democratic partnerships, and commitment to social change. Specifically, when addressing the legal environment in higher education, college leaders should recognize how the mission drives policies and practices—especially key decisions. In addition, as colleges learn to navigate court rulings and new laws, they must adapt in ways that are compliant and mission focused. Further, when operating in the legal environment, colleges should focus on democratic partnerships that ensure that shared governance and institutional systems support each other. And equally significant, the courts and legal policies illustrate how colleges must model inclusion, equity, and positive social change so that policies and practices have meaningful impacts throughout our institutions and society.

To those ends, this chapter focuses on the key legal policies, which are driven by the courts, that college administrators either reference often as top matters that occupy their time or that reflect an emerging concern for our campuses (Gregory et al., 2020; Turk et al., 2020; White, 2015). Specifically, we offer an overview of legal issues about campus protests and free speech; campus safety and supports; student due process; race-conscious admissions; amateurism and safety in athletics; and employment rights, particularly faculty tenure and academic freedom.

Campus Protests and Free Speech

Higher education is often associated with its support of free speech. Historically, campus free speech has been an avenue to stimulate debate, advance civil rights, and further civil liberties. Researchers on campus free speech have documented how student activism has furthered women's equal rights, increased access and combated discrimination for students and scholars of color, heightened awareness and changed campus climate to advance an antisexual assault priority on campuses, divested financial connections to companies harming the environment, advocated for tuition fairness regardless of immigration status, established collective bargaining and fair wage campaigns, and adopted rights for the LGBTQ+ community (Rhoads, 2016; Sun & McClellan, 2019). Nonetheless, what is permissible free speech under the First Amendment tends to be murky for campus leaders because of at least three factors: confusion about the legal differences between public and private colleges, lack of knowledge about basic First Amendment principles, and a mistaken belief that hate speech is prohibited under the law.

Distinction Between Public and Private Colleges

When a student or employee at a private college claims, "I have free speech rights and the college administration cannot stop me from expressing my political views," that claim may not be entirely true.[1] Free speech law is complicated, but a significant lesson is that it differs greatly between public and private institutions. Significantly, the legal sources between public and private colleges lead to very different outcomes. The First Amendment states, "Congress [or government] shall make no law . . . abridging the freedom of speech." In other words, the laws pertaining to free speech under the First Amendment generally apply only to public entities such as state universities, not private universities.

By contrast, policies at private colleges are treated like contracts, so the contract language governs what is permissible. At private colleges, free speech or campus activism policies, which are often covered with the student code of conduct or employee handbook, may limit what students and employees may express inside and outside the classroom. Private colleges may place more restrictions or parameters than public colleges. They may block expressions, including words, images, or artistic expressions that do not adhere to the college's mission, values, or community standards of civility and respect. These policies often include prohibiting offensive, demeaning, and childish expressions, as well as presenting disciplinary consequences for violators.

At public colleges, these policies would be considered too broad and too restrictive because public institutions cannot restrict all offensive, demeaning, and childish expressions. For instance, offensive skits are generally permissible at public colleges as artistic expressions deserving of heightened protections. Also, political speech against a targeted population of students (e.g., race or gender identity) may be protected speech even though they present hurtful words to students and harm campus climate. Because the First Amendment applies to public colleges, they have more at stake regarding campus protests. If leaders at public colleges make a mistake and impermissibly block students from exercising their free speech, that error may lead to a constitutional violation, and the financial judgment for inhibiting students' free speech may be quite significant when compared to private colleges.

Private colleges can adopt policies resembling the First Amendment's free speech clause, which gives a fair amount of rights to students and other persons protesting. For instance, a private university can express in general terms that it firmly supports academic freedom and free speech on campus. To those ends, it may adopt language such as the following:

> Because the University is committed to free and open inquiry in all matters, it guarantees all members of the University community the broadest possible latitude to speak, write, listen, challenge, and learn. Except insofar as limitations on that freedom are necessary to the functioning of the University, the University fully respects and supports the freedom of all members of the University community to discuss any problem that presents itself. (University of Chicago, 2015, para. 1)

While a private college can adopt a rather explicit commitment to First Amendment ideals, it can also adopt a code of conduct that prohibits hate speech and bans sexually suggestive images and demeaning skits and events that marginalize certain identities. Because private colleges' policies are treated as contracts, the legal concern about "free speech" at private colleges is whether the institution breached the contract, and if so, what damages, such as monetary loss, resulted when it blocked permissible speech. That loss is typically rather insignificant. Whereas when public colleges are challenged, the legal consequences are whether the public college deprived persons of their constitutional rights—a far more significant problem. The financial penalties under the law may be quite severe because the persons who were deprived of their constitutional rights may recover in monetary damages more than the direct loss in a contract case. The persons may also recover, when applicable, reduced earning capacity, pain and suffering, loss of liberty, punitive damages (i.e., additional amounts to deter a public college from acting reprehensibly in the future), and attorneys' fees.

First Amendment Principles

First Amendment policies are complex, and at times, administrators at public colleges assert the wrong legal principles, which they should have known as an administrator, leading them to be personally liable (Sun, 2015). A review of several core concepts and rules is useful for campus leaders, so they do not inadvertently deprive a person's constitutional rights. Administrators at public colleges should keep in mind that the law is intended to allow for as much speech as possible to continue uninhibited from government intrusion, but the law has a liking to certain types of expressions. Sun and McClellan (2019) noted that the law places a metaphorical forcefield and a presumptive protection for political, social, ideological, religious, scientific, and artistic expressions. When speech arises into one of those categories, the basic presumption is that government actors, such as public university staff, cannot take actions that would censor or limit the speech absent certain behaviors that turn the speech into a less protected expression (e.g., threat of imminent harm, harassment, substantial disruption to the university mission).

An example of students' expressions that warrant metaphorical forcefield protection is when college students sought to wear an empty holster as a symbolic protest against laws prohibiting concealed-carry firearms. That expression arose to symbolic political speech. Specifically, the empty holster represented students who are "unarmed and potentially defenseless against a gunman" (*Smith v. Tarrant County College District*, 2010, p. 613). However, the college administration informed the protestors that such an effort outside the free speech zone (i.e., the designated area on campus to protest or disseminate materials about one's perspective) would be prohibited. The administration also declared wearing the empty holster would arise to disruptive activity, which the college defined as an event that "interrupts scheduled activities or the process of education" (*Smith v. Tarrant County College District*, 2010, p. 613). The court disagreed with the college, ruling that the college policy prohibiting students from wearing empty holsters in the classroom and hallways was unconstitutional as applied. Students were free to engage in the policy debate around permitted on-campus concealed carry when the protest did not present violating behaviors such as disruption or harassment.

Although the First Amendment grants special protection over political, social, ideological, religious, scientific, and artistic expressions, the law does allow public colleges to adopt certain restrictions to free speech (Sun & McClellan, 2019). Generally, public institutions can adopt reasonable rules around time, place, and manner (Sun, 2015). In addition, the law grants differing rights regarding the spaces in which free speech may be exercised. Courts examine the college's policies and practices, and they check for consistency on how the college treats each space or "forum" (Sun, 2015; Sun & McClellan, 2019). Public colleges may open selected sections of campus, such as all outdoor spaces at least 150 feet from academic buildings, for the campus community and the public to exercise free speech during certain times. Further, public colleges may place even greater limits on certain areas. For instance, they may designate certain areas for student groups only and bar off-campus community members from using those spaces. The student groups may be limited to their use for meetings, protests, and related activities (Sun, 2015). However, once a public college makes the space or resource available to one group, it cannot discriminate based on the content (e.g., barring signs critical about campus policies around COVID-19) or viewpoint (e.g., prohibiting ideological positions on vaccines).

First Amendment Principles and Hate Speech

First Amendment principles derive from a variety of settings involving public entities, and the rules established from these cases do not always align well with educational values and principles. Notably, a mythical presumption exists that hate speech overcomes free speech arguments (Sun, 2015). The reality is that hate speech is often protected speech. Keeping in mind that First Amendment laws are not specific rules only applicable to higher education, a case about picketers at a military funeral illustrates the types of expressions permitted under the constitution (*Snyder v. Phelps*, 2011). The protestors chanted and displayed placards stating inflammatory messages such as "America is doomed," "You're going to hell," "God hates you," "Fag troops," and "Thank God for dead soldiers." Although the expressions at issue would be harmful to a college campus, the protestors, who included members of Westboro Baptist Church in Kansas, were protected under the First Amendment. According to church representatives, God is angry at the nation and is killing military service members to punish America for condoning homosexuality. The father of the deceased service member whom the funeral was honoring had to endure the hateful chant outside his son's funeral. Based on that experience and the physical manifestations that followed, such as vomiting and severe depression, the father sued the protestors under Maryland's tort law of an intentional infliction of emotional stress. He lost the case. The expressions at issue would no doubt be harmful to a college campus, but hate itself is not an exemption to free speech.

Although hate speech is generally permissible, the law does not protect all forms of expression. Speech and behavior arising to obscenity, true threat, harassment, libelous remarks, disruptive speech, or intellectual property protections would not be protected. To that end, potentially harassing conduct intending to instill fear or intimidate others through symbols with targeted messages would typically not be protected under the First Amendment. For instance, a swastika or noose may be posted to convey a political message about injustice or characterizations of past treatments, but if those symbols are placed to target a student, perhaps on a Jewish student's residence hall door with a message stating "kill them all," that expression could arise to a hostile environment harassment or a true threat (i.e., message meant to frighten or intimidate the targeted person into believing that they will be seriously harmed by the speaker or by someone acting at the speaker's behest, and the speaker intended such meaning).

Beyond such expressions as obscenity, true threat, and harassment, the law recognizes penalties for hate crimes. Hate crimes are criminal offenses motivated in whole or in part by the perpetrator's bias against an identity feature that is covered by the law such as race, religion, disability, sexual orientation, ethnicity, gender, or gender identity. The U.S. Supreme Court has upheld laws that either criminalize these acts or impose harsher punishment when it can be proven that the perpetrator targeted the victim based on the protected identity. Other forms of hate that the law does not protect include illegal behaviors such as vandalism or setting school property on fire that is designated for a protected group.

As this discussion illustrates, the First Amendment is based on constitutional doctrine that does not always align well with educational principles. For instance, when institutions have tried to protect minoritized voices by demonstrating a clear, urgent, and supportive response by establishing a bias response or campus climate response team, Speech First, a not-for-profit group asserting free speech protections, has challenged these policies as vague and overly broad coverage of prohibited actions or other chilling effects (see, e.g., *Speech First, Inc. v. Fenves,* 2020; *Speech First, Inc. v. Killeen,* 2020; *Speech First, Inc. v. Schlissel,* 2019). So far, Speech First has primarily been targeted as having adverse effects on free speech public college policies that are intended to create equitable and inclusive environments.

Despite the laws backing some expressions, many equity and inclusion practitioners have questioned the effect of asserting the First Amendment as the justification for a public institution's actions when confronted with conflicting values between free speech and educational inclusion. As a recent article captured, "Whether hateful speech occurs on campus or on social media . . . , students want to see peers [who] engage in it disciplined, including with suspension or expulsion" (Anderson, 2020, para. 5). This perspective is consistent with college students' growing interest in protecting diversity and inclusion efforts. In 2018, a national survey by Gallup and the Knight Foundation asked if diversity and inclusion or free speech is more important. College student respondents placed the diversity and inclusion priority slightly higher than free speech rights, 53% to 46%, respectively. In 2020, a follow-up study, also by Gallup and the Knight Foundation, reported that 76% of college students believed that actions taken to foster diversity and inclusion clash with free speech rights either frequently (27%) or occasionally (49%). These perspectives display shifts in college students' values, demonstrating greater concern for equity and inclusion. Further, they call us to pause and consider our model (i.e., mission, adaptability, democratic ideals, and inclusion), as we respond to campus incidents of marginalization and hate. One news article summed up thoughts from campus informants, suggesting, "The First Amendment is important, but it's not recommended as college officials' first response when students engage in racist and offensive speech" (Anderson, 2020, para 1).

Colleges have, to some extent, free speech rights, too. Campus leaders may take a position on speech that it finds despicable and contrary to the institution's values. For instance, when a group of male students at a public university chants misogynistic phrases that dismiss the effects of rape, a university administrator may admonish the expressions as sophomoric and harmful to campus safety without violating the students' First Amendment rights. Similarly, when a tweet conveys disrespect to a racial group, a university leader may speak against such communication and offer institutional support to educate the campus and take further actions that advance equity and inclusion so minoritized groups feel a sense of belonging. Suffice it to say, the law, particularly the First Amendment, is designed to support provocative positions, especially when they are a matter of public concern (e.g., social, political, or community interest), but campuses also have tools, which are beyond legal recourse (e.g., communication, counseling, educational programming), to counter hateful and harmful expressions that students and other members of the community encounter.

Campus Safety and Supports

College leaders cannot protect all students or avoid all crises. Courts have previously stated that colleges are generally not the guarantors of safety for their campus community. Nonetheless, court decisions and legal mandates directed to campus safety and supports have changed significantly over the past decade, placing greater accountability on institutions to manage their campus environments, particularly when it comes to students in crisis over mental health and cases of sexual misconduct. This section introduces readers to key and emerging concerns about campus safety and supports by providing an overview of injuries from negligence, mental health, student records, and Title IX sexual harassment.

Negligence Injuries

Higher education institutions regularly face civil liability for injuries sustained from a person or entity's act or for omission leading to liability (e.g., monetary damages). In our context, these injuries most frequently involve negligence, when an injured party—whether a student, employee, vendor/contractor working on campus, or an unaffiliated community member leisurely walking on campus—typically seeks recovery of monetary damages and possibly more when harmed.

Negligence claims represent a significant category of cases within higher education. A negligence claim requires the suing party (i.e., plaintiff) to demonstrate that the college had a duty (i.e., legal obligation) to protect the injured party from harm, and the college breached its duty.[2] Examples of situations in which colleges had a duty to protect the campus community include failure to instruct students on use of specialized equipment for class, to warn and block access to a construction area, to maintain safety measures for residence halls by high-crime neighborhoods, to label and secure an electrical room in a high-traffic area of a stadium, to place signage or wipe down wet floors that are not easily visible to people who enter, or to fix dangerous ground conditions that are not open and obvious to the public. When contested, colleges or their insurance companies are more likely to argue against any duty owed to the harmed person to discharge legal obligation.

In instructional settings, the legal duty largely depends on the student's knowledge, experience, or availability of resources. For instance, a state appellate court found a public university liable when a student was kicked in the face by a horse as part of the equine studies program (*Loder v. State of New York*, 1994). The court ruled that the university was negligent in its student training and housing of the horse within the stall. It also observed that the lack of written instructions and the procedure for entering the stalls failed to support the university's defenses that it was not negligent. Similarly, a state supreme court held a college liable when a student severed his thumb from a milling machine during a die and tool class (*Garrett v. Northwest Mississippi Jr. College*, 1996). The court recognized that the college had a duty, given the type of equipment involved, to instruct, warn, and supervise students on equipment, and the college failed to do so. College leaders should ensure that students are properly trained and resourced before entering an instructional environment with foreseeable harm if not properly trained and equipped.

The duty to protect does not necessarily extend to off-campus experiences. Clubs, organizations, and Greek life activities that are not sanctioned or led by the university, such as off-campus parties in which inebriated students are walking on retaining walls and fall or are jumping in a trampoline and while doing so suffer debilitating injuries, typically do not hold the university liable for injuries. Further, colleges are also rarely liable for acts of third parties. Parties outside the college, including contractors doing business or random people on campus, cause injuries to students and other members of the campus, but courts rarely connect legal liability. Otherwise, colleges, many of which are easily accessible to the public, may create open opportunity for litigation. Thus, when an unknown shooter fired at a student, who sustained injuries outside a residence hall, the federal court concluded that the shooting was not foreseeable to the college and it did not have a legal duty to implement additional protections (*Emery v. Talladega College*, 2017; see also *Commonwealth v. Peterson*, 2013). The court also noted that the shooting was not even foreseeable to the injured student. If the incident had been foreseeable, however, the courts could have held the college liable, as it has under certain instances of students struggling with mental health.

Mental Health

Mental health is a serious concern for college leaders. College students continue to report rising levels of depression. Depending on data sources, the percentage of college students experiencing depression prior to COVID-19 ranges from 18% reporting major forms of depression (Leshner & Scherer, 2021), 22.1% suffering academically debilitating depression, and 35.7% expressing general depression states (Healthy Minds Network & American College Health Association, 2020). Studies reporting recent effects of suicide ideation range from 14.0% to 20.9% in 2018–2019 (Healthy Minds Network & American College Health Association, 2020). While COVID-19 exacerbated some mental health effects—primarily in a negative manner—data are trending toward a negative outcome. That is, no matter the source, quite consistently, data show significant rises over the prior decade, with at least 8% of college students reporting higher rates of depression and at least 6% reporting suicide ideation (Leshner & Scherer, 2021).

Adding to these concerns, mental health equity remains a concern for campuses. Students of color are significantly less likely than White students to identify their college as inclusive (28% to 45%) and are correspondingly more likely to express isolation in college (46% to 30%; Steve Fund & JED Foundation, 2017). Further, cultural and financial barriers around suicide make students of color and sexual minorities feel more vulnerable when seeking supports (Horwitz et al., 2020). Put simply, although the law provides guidance on college obligations, these guidelines are minimum standards. They require intertwining with other aspects of the college mission, adaptation, democratic partnerships, and DEI efforts.

Mental health is typically covered under Section 504 of the Rehabilitation Act (2021), the ADA, and applicable state laws. These laws prohibit discriminatory acts on otherwise qualified individuals based on the person's disability. To that end, colleges must provide reasonable accommodations or modifications in terms of policies, practices, or procedures as needed to avoid disability-based discriminatory activities. Exceptions exist to disability laws' application, however. If a college can show that making the accommodations or modifications would fundamentally alter its service, program, or activity, or the changes would lead to undue financial or administrative burden on the college, then the reasonable accommodations or modifications would not be required.

As discussed with tort claims such as negligence, colleges typically have no obligation to protect third parties from harm. That rule is not always the situation when a student struggling with mental health engages in physical violence. Privacy and confidentiality are also exempted when severe physical harm is at issue. Thus, when students visit the campus counseling center and meet with a licensed psychotherapist, the student might have a reasonable expectation of privacy—that patient records are kept confidential. In most states, however, psychotherapists have obligations to protect the patient's intended victims when the patient expresses intentions to harm another person and that event is reasonably foreseeable to take place. As one court explained, the "protective privilege ends where the public peril begins" (*Tarasoff v. Regents of the University of California*, 1976, p. 347). In such instances, the psychotherapist may notify the police, warn the intended victim, or take other reasonable steps to protect the intended victim.

Two state supreme court cases now hold colleges liable when it is reasonably foreseeable that a patient may cause violent harm to another person. In one case, a student struggling with mental health had auditory hallucinations and paranoid thoughts. He displayed numerous signs of distress as he was slowly devolving. Then, one day, he stabbed a classmate in the neck and chest. The highest court in California concluded that "universities owe a duty to protect students from foreseeable violence during curricular activities" (*Regents of University of California v. Superior Court*, 2018, p. 667) or matters that are "closely related to its delivery of educational services" (p. 674). Another state court extended higher education's duty to protect students who are struggling with mental health. Beyond protections for violence onto others, Massachusetts's highest court established a duty for colleges to protect students from violence onto oneself or self-harm (*Nguyen v. Massachusetts Institute of Technology*, 2018). This decision, which is likely to spread into other state courts, is helpful for college leaders because certain regulations under the ADA, which applies to students, exempt modifications of services when the person seeking modifications presents a threat to others, but the law does not exempt modifications of services when a person presents harm to oneself such as suicide. With this case, if a college in Massachusetts has actual knowledge of a student's suicide attempt, which would have occurred either while enrolled or recently from the time of matriculation, or the student expressed plans/intentions to commit suicide, the college has a "duty to take reasonable measures under the circumstances to protect the student from self-harm" (*Nguyen v. Massachusetts Institute of Technology*, 2018, pp. 142–143). If this case spreads to other states, colleges will be covered when they exempt modifications of services to persons who present harm to oneself, and it will initiate proper recourse. Specifically, colleges will be able to activate the college's suicide prevention protocol (if one is available) without fear of breaching confidentiality and permit psychotherapists to notify college officials, draw on supports from campus psychotherapists or clinical care from medical professionals when concerns arise, allow for notification of the student's emergency contact, and request supports from emergency personnel (e.g., police, fire, or emergency medical technicians).

These cases suggest campus leaders need to be more engaged with their students, identify warning signals, and act on foreseeable harms by implementing safety measures. A law and psychiatry expert from Columbia University described the changing court direction as a call to higher education that it will "need to be more attentive to students who are potentially suicidal or aggressive and to be more assertive about intervening before harm occurs" (Appelbaum, 2019, p. 352). Already, court opinions and U.S. Department of Education's Office for Civil Rights (OCR) determinations require individualized assessments of students with disabilities before a college exercises student conduct discipline provisions, leaves of absence, or suspension when the student displays mental health concerns (Gee et al., in press).

These assessments ensure due process protections and avoid violating disability discrimination laws (e.g., Section 504 & ADA).

Student Records

Campus safety issues often involve privacy concerns. The privacy of records that a college maintains has varying protections. A college student's "education records" are subject to a federal privacy law, the Family Educational Rights and Privacy Act (FERPA), which prohibits access to unauthorized or nonconsented persons and organizations. Education records include grades, transcripts, academic standing reports, class lists and attendance, student course schedules, student financial information, emergency contacts, and student conduct reports. The format of the education record may appear through means such as print, video file, audio file, film, microfilm, microfiche, and handwritten. FERPA gives students a right to inspect and amend their records as well as consent to disclose personally identifiable information (PII) from their education records unless an exception to consent already applies (e.g., court order, pursuant to government reporting).

Although this law is generally well known to academic advisors, faculty, and enrollment management staff as protections of education records are a privacy matter, FERPA has potential implications to housing staff, the dean of students' office, athletics, public relations/communications, and fraternity/sorority advisors, among other offices. Notably, the exceptions to the law draw implications to a wider set of audiences within a college. That is, although FERPA blocks education records, the law permits disclosure of directory information unless the student requests in writing to restrict that information. Each institution defines its directory information disclosures, which are limited to details that would typically be considered basic descriptions not violating privacy or availing one to harm, when disclosed. A college's directory information may include the student's name; email address; telephone listing; picture from student identification; major; participation in registered student organizations, fraternity/sorority life, and sports; degrees, honors, and awards received; dates of attendance; and previous educational institutions attended. These details affect other offices, not simply records on a transcript such as grades and credits awarded.

Further, a college may disclose information to the student's parents, without the student's consent, if the student is a dependent for tax purposes. Under the dependency exception, the age of the student and the custodial role of the parent/guardian are irrelevant. The sole examination is the student's status as a dependent by either parent/guardian for tax purposes, which gives any parent access to the student's education records unless there is evidence of a court order or state law indicating otherwise. Beyond consent, the law includes health or safety emergency exceptions. Notably, some exceptions concern alcohol/drug offenses or when a student is medically or psychologically impaired. This exception is particularly useful when the college has concerns over a student's physical or mental well-being, allowing the college to engage parents/guardians to collectively address the matter.

Title IX

A frequently publicized issue in higher education is on-campus sexual assault. Title IX of the Educational Amendments of 1972 is a federal civil rights law prohibiting discrimination based on sex, including sexual harassment, at any educational institution or program that receives federal funding, including colleges and universities. Specifically, the law states: "No person in the United States shall, on the basis of sex, be excluded from participation in, be denied the benefits of, or be subjected to discrimination under any education program or activity receiving Federal financial assistance." Title IX is usually referenced for two common reasons. One frequent reference is to address gender equity in educational programming, particularly athletics. For instance, do the women at a college have equity in athletic funding and sport participation with the men? The second, which is the focus here, is to address sexual harassment. Sexual harassment includes a wide range of prohibited behaviors. Sexual assaults and other forms of sexual violence represent types of sexual harassment, which have headlined in the news as a serious problem on college campuses.[3]

Campus sexual assault is a real concern. Several studies have reported alarming rates of sexual assault of women and men during their college years. Snapshot data from various sources typically report about one in four or one in five women, and one in 16 men have been sexually assaulted during their time at a four-year college (Cantor et al., 2020; Krebs et al., 2007). For the past 2 decades, the U.S. Department of Education has issued various statements and guidelines to support campuses with taking immediate action. Unfortunately, a wave of events, along with inconsistent campus approaches to addressing sexual assault, suggested a stronger guidance was needed. For instance, in 2007, the media reported that Eastern Michigan University had been accused of covering up information involving the rape and murder of a female student; according to reports of the incident, the school sought to avoid bad publicity (Bunkley, 2007; Lipka, 2007). Similarly, a watchdog group, the Center for Public Integrity, also revealed numerous instances in which colleges failed to take appropriate actions to stop alleged perpetrators—often by ignoring the grievance or delaying responses (Peebles & Lombardi, 2015).

Although policymakers across party lines wish to eliminate campus sexual misconduct, the two recent presidential administrations (i.e., Obama and Trump) had very different perspectives about Title IX compliance. The differences are quite stark and demonstrate how campus sexual harassment, particularly sexual assaults, have become politicized. For instance, the two administrations had conflicting views on the level of knowledge that a college had to have about any sexual misconduct matter to obligate it to respond in compliance with Title IX. The Obama administration, consistent with the Biden administration's perspective, held campuses responsible for taking appropriate action if the college "knew or should have known" of the sexual harassing conduct. The "should have known" refers to reasonable ways in which the institution should have learned about a sexual harassment incident, such as through the local newspaper's publication of a story about a sexual assault on campus that was not officially reported or through the discovery of a sexual misconduct incident during a proper investigation of another conduct violation. The Trump administration took a narrow approach, only holding campuses responsible to remedy sexual harassment if the college directly knew of the sexual misconduct and the college employee had the authority to institute corrective measures but did not.

Although the two previous presidential administrations held divergent views in several key areas regarding how to enforce Title IX and eliminate (or at least reduce) campus sexual assaults, a series of court challenges and policy briefs offer three clear lessons, regardless of the political perspective and other maneuvers, that campus leaders must consider.

First, each campus must employ a designated Title IX coordinator who oversees sexual harassment reports, examines institutional data about harassment complaints, and ensures appropriate responses to each incident and patterns of data. A designated person overseeing all Title IX claims provides a global view of the campus culture. For instance, many campuses follow national data about reported spikes in campus sexual assaults, particularly among college students (Krebs et al., 2016). Many traditional campuses see a spike of sexual assaults during September and October of the school year, sometimes dubbed as the "Red Zone," a vulnerable period for college students who are experiencing greater independence and are exposed to new outlets such as opening school year parties, fraternity and sorority rush, college sports tailgating, and return to campus events. At the national level, the total reports in September and October are usually higher than the subsequent four months combined, but a campus may reflect different data based on its student composition, residential living options, academic calendar, types of academic programming, and more. Title IX coordinators should review the data for their campus to identify patterns and present interventions (e.g., awareness programs, bystander training, community safety practices, and sexual violence resources).

Second, training is key. A comprehensive training approach identifies the multiple audiences who require training. For example, students need prevention and reporting training. Bystander training offers prosocial bystander behaviors to stand up and speak out when settings could lead to sexual assault. Consent training adopts a permission-based perspective to equip individuals with voice, including when dealing with perceived rejection. The Green Dot approach trains influential campus members, often student leaders, about antisexual harassment actions. These training programs and others seek to defy sexual misconduct or inaction as normative behaviors and empower groups to prevent and report impermissible conduct. Similarly, training options exist for investigators and adjudicators, emphasizing the vulnerable positions that both complainants and respondents undergo. Further, they should include special considerations such as supporting LGBTQ+ students, international students, and students with disabilities.

Third, parties involved in investigations and hearings must be aware of their rights. Notably, the design of any investigation or hearing must assure equitable treatment and due process. In recent cases, respondents, who have undergone campus adjudication as alleged perpetrators of sexual misconduct, have asserted unfairness in the process. Allegations include respondents who are experiencing clear biases from college employees, not well informed by the college of the charges or accusations against them, denied opportunities of either the respondent or male witnesses to testify as part of the hearing, and interpreting their charges as an outcome of external pressures from the U.S. Department of Education, and public wanting to be tough on Title IX claims. Further, a set of cases from respondents argues that campuses have selective enforcement of Title IX against male respondents. Although actions and decision points may be justified through clear explanations of the process, more court cases are asserting claims that colleges fail to provide due process to respondents, and advocacy groups and the media have drawn attention to these instances (Friedersdorf, 2019; Melnick, 2020; Poliakoff, 2021).

Student Due Process

Just as questions of fairness exists with Title IX-based claims, students' rights are important to know for any type of disciplinary action against a student, including dismissal from the college, whether for academic or nonacademic reasons. However, courts differentiate between academic and nonacademic disciplinary actions by granting greater discretion to colleges over academic matters.

Academic Deference

When students challenge academic matters in the courts, they are generally disappointed. Courts typically stay out of decisions addressing a university's mission and vision on educational matters. Moreover, private colleges have wide latitude to place restrictions on their students in both academic and nonacademic settings. Based on contract law, these restrictions are outlined in their student handbook and other resources, which serve as the "contract" between a private college and its students. The terms may also include religiously based policies and practices to govern students' actions.

By contrast, student challenges to public colleges are generally more contentious and nuanced because public institutions are subject to the 14th Amendment's due process clause. The due process clause represents a constitutional violation when a public college deprives a student of "life, liberty, or property without due process of law" or disciplines a student for protected expressions within the academic setting over political, social, ideological, religious, scientific, and artistic expressions. Nonetheless, from a legal standpoint, public colleges may place greater restrictions on academically related behaviors than student conduct matters that fall outside the academic setting. The courts have acknowledged three primary reasons for distinguishing between academic and nonacademic disciplinary matters.

First, courts recognize that the academic setting is not a public forum for students to freely express themselves, as they might in the quad of a college campus (*Hazelwood v. Kuhlmeier*, 1988). So long as the public college can show that any restrictions that it places on students within the academic setting are reasonably related to legitimate pedagogical concerns, the institution may exercise its rights without infringing on the students' constitutional rights.

Second, courts tend to recognize academic freedom regarding academic matters and attach special rights to it. That is, colleges may make legally permissible decisions about academic matters without the same level of external scrutiny as nonacademic matters. To that end, in *Regents of the University of California v. Bakke* (1978), which involved a public university's race-conscious admissions policy, the court articulated how it generally does not meddle into academic matters by recognizing that "academic freedom, though not a specifically enumerated constitutional right, long has been viewed as a special concern of the First Amendment," and that freedom includes a university's right "to make its own judgments as to education includ[ing] the selection of its student body" and how it should teach its students (p. 312). Thus, when an incident involving students could qualify as an academic or a nonacademic matter, such as behaviors in a cocurricular activity, campus leaders will have greater discretion if they can frame it as falling with the academic domain.

Third, the sophistication of academic judgments is often more difficult for a court to determine, so when courts must evaluate the sufficiency of the due process, they are often left to draw on the academic decisions. Due process rights come in two forms—procedural and substantive. Procedural due process refers to a policy or process, such as the days and type of information required to notify students of their wrongdoing or unsatisfactory progress. Courts can typically evaluate procedural due process challenges. Substantive due process includes the criteria upon which a student was judged to determine the student's wrongdoing or unsatisfactory progress, and it is significantly more difficult for courts to evaluate. Courts like to avoid decisions that are academic in nature (e.g., student evaluation on medical school performance) because those decisions fall outside the court's expertise (*Board of Curators of the University of Missouri v. Horowitz*, 1978; *Regents of the University of Michigan v. Ewing*, 1985). Professors may, pursuant to established standards, inform students about academic deficiencies during courses and other academic experiences (e.g., clinicals) and propose improvement plans. Or, through a holistic review, professors may recommend academic probation or dismissal. In both cases, the series of notifications during the academic experience would suffice, and unless otherwise committed to other obligations, a full hearing might not be required. One U.S. Supreme Court opinion even explained that "academic evaluations of a student, in contrast to disciplinary determinations, bear little resemblance to the judicial and administrative fact-finding proceedings to which we have traditionally attached a full-hearing requirement" (*Board of Curators of the University of Missouri v. Horowitz*, 1978, p. 89). Although a full hearing is not required, courts look to professors' evaluations of an academically dismissed student. To dismiss or discipline a student for academic reasons, college administrators must simply show that "the faculty's decision was made conscientiously and with careful deliberation, based on an evaluation of the entirety" (*Ewing v. Regents of the University of Michigan*, 1985, p. 225) of the student's academic career. The courts avoid any involvement to respect academic freedom.

This academic deference has limits, however. Courts do not support arbitrary or capricious decisions. Ensuring the basis of a decision was consistent and informed, courts examine a fundamental inquiry—whether the professors' decision was a "substantial departure from accepted academic norms"

(*Ewing v. Regents of the University of Michigan*, 1985, p. 227). That is, did the academic unit treat the student under review in a manner consistent with other students facing a similar academic review? If their decision were a substantial departure, in the eyes of the courts the academic ruling would be considered a failure of professors to exercise professional judgment and likely reflect a violation of the student's 14th Amendment due process rights.

Disciplinary Matters

Student conduct addresses matters outside the academic realm such as under-age drinking, belligerent behavior at the student recreation center, damage or defacing of college property, hazing of a new fraternity/sorority member, disrespectful and degrading language to a college employee (e.g., food service staff), or failure to disperse when a hostile crowd was forming. These student behaviors demonstrate inconsistencies with community values and likely violate a provision in the student code of conduct. As in academic disciplinary matters, private institutions have wide discretion to address these matters in a manner consistent with their student code of conduct. Public institutions are also subject to constitutional rights such as the 14th Amendment's due process clause and First Amendment's free speech clause. Unlike the academically related behaviors discussed earlier, however, student conduct matters have a more formal process. Courts require public colleges to present the notice of the charges against the student; an explanation of the evidence against the student; release of the evidence, including witnesses, prior to the hearing; and a chance for the student to respond in their defense (*Dixon v. Alabama State Board of Education*, 1961; *Esteban v. Central Missouri State College*, 1969; *Goss v. Lopez*, 1975). Ultimately, courts examine whether the process and the substantive basis for the conduct proceeding were fair.

To students, the campus conduct process can feel like an adversarial experience, so they present a defensive approach, although it is not intended to be a court proceeding. Nonetheless, it is outlined in many student codes of conduct in a very mechanical way to ensure the consistent exercise of students' rights and university protections. To those ends, campus leaders should consider four points about these proceedings. First, the focus of a student conduct process is to inquire as to whether the student violated the code. Violation of the code may have a range of remedies, including a restorative justice approach, which focuses on violators' taking responsibility, making amends based on that violation, and rebuilding trust in the campus community. Second, a finding of a student code violation within a university's policy does not preclude a criminal process, if warranted. That criminal proceeding would not be deemed double jeopardy because the student conduct proceeding is not a criminal trial. Third, generally speaking, an appeal is not required under case law for student conduct violations at private or public colleges, but as a matter of practice, and sometimes under state law, colleges have implemented appeals processes. An appeal is often limited to instances when the aggrieved party can show an error in the process, or new information, not previously available, comes to light. One exception to the optional appeal concerns Title IX sexual harassment claims. They require the availability of an appeal, and the appeal may be initiated from either the complainant or the respondent. Fourth, in some states, students have a right for representation by an attorney or an advocate (e.g., Arkansas, North Carolina, North Dakota; Ark. Code § 6-60-109 [2021]; N.C. Code § 116-40.11 [2021]; N.D. Cent. Code § 15-10 [2021], respectively). Although many student conduct proceedings permit advocates, typically a full-time faculty or staff member of the college, some state and college policies permit outside representation of a person of their choosing and at their own expense.

Athletics

Concerns of campus fairness extend to athletics. Title IX has been prevalent in addressing gender equity in athletics. Sex discrimination in athletics has occurred with access to sports participation, facilities, scholarships, equipment, transportation, athlete travel and meals, coaches' salaries, available athletic trainers, and medical supports. At times, to reach parity, colleges have eliminated selected men's sports or reclassified an activity. For instance, a college once tried to qualify competitive cheerleading as a sport, but the federal court treated the college's action as an attempt at roster manipulation and asserted that cheerleading failed to reflect a recognized sport (*Bidiger v. Quinnipiac*, 2012). Although there is some evidence that Title IX had an impact on changing opportunities for women in college athletics, gender equity in athletics needs much more progress and effort to meaningfully describe it as reaching "equity" (Pruitt, 2021).

Amateurism and Compensation

Beyond gender equity, college athletics has engaged with a series of issues regarding the philosophical differences between fair play with amateurism and fair market value. On the one hand, college athletics is a cocurricular activity for students, who participate in amateur sports and gain developmental benefits such as teamwork, accountability, performance improvement, and structure. On the other hand, college athletics is big business, attracting high-profile coaches, recruiting promising players, engaging millions of fans, benefiting various sports betting venues, and generating around $18.9 billion in 2019 (Parrot, 2021). Some argue that the amateur nature of college sports vanished when competition and commercialization took center stage (Garthwaite et al., 2020). Others argue that new and emerging concerns, which colleges and athletic groups such as the National Collegiate Athletic Association (NCAA) face, present efforts that move away from the amateur nature of college sports (Gurney et al., 2017).

A movement within college sports is advocating the employment of student-athletes. The employment movement was a reaction to multiple NCAA efforts to limit student-athlete compensation—arguably to protect amateurism in college sports. Two recent federal court cases even tried to challenge college athletic programs and the NCAA to categorize the players as employees under the Fair Labor Standards Act (FLSA). If they were recognized under the FLSA, student-athletes would have qualified for minimum wage, unemployment insurance, Social Security contributions, and more based on their "work" on the team. However, the courts rejected the arguments, disqualifying student-athletes from FLSA provisions (*Berger v. National Collegiate Athletic Association*, 2016; *Dawson v. NCAA*, 2019). The California legislature already disagreed. In 2012, it established a Student Athlete Bill of Rights (2021). The law qualifies college athletes who spend about 40 hours each week in their sport and generate large revenues as eligible for scholarship compensation, insurance deductibles payments, and medical expense coverage for injuries along with other resources and protections. Since then, the U.S. Congress has considered several bills on student-athlete rights. The policymakers were not acting without broad public support. According to data from the National Sports and Society Survey, approximately 51% of Americans support college athletes' receiving more financial support than cost of college attendance (Knoester & Ridpath, 2020). These data, including the legislative bills, suggest that society places significant value on college athletes, whom the public feels should be compensated.

Related to its policies regarding student-athlete employment and compensation, the NCAA has also historically limited athletes from receiving compensation for third-party endorsements, including prohibitions against payment for nonsport activities such as revenue from social media. After several lawsuits, in 2020, the NCAA attempted to relax its rules, but it planned to impose a compensation cap to ensure principles of amateurism. In 2021, however, the U.S. Supreme Court expanded name, image, and likeness (NIL) compensation so athletes could receive education-related benefits, covering such costs as technology devices, study-abroad expenses, scientific equipment, and more. Concurrent with these developments, from 2019–2021, public outcry grew. By 2021, 24 states had adopted NIL laws to permit college athletes to be compensated for their NIL on clothing, print ads, social media influences, video games, and more (with some limits depending on the state). Together, the courts and state legislation have transformed college athlete compensation possibilities. Considering these changes, the old adage that the football coach is often better compensated than the college president might now include mention of star student-athletes who could potentially profit at higher levels than the whole athletic department. Also, with increasing autonomy in amateurism and compensation rules, gender and team sports equity may emerge as a greater issue for campus leaders to address because the compensation imbalance currently favors male athletes in certain sports, while other sports programs are left with negligible resources.

Athletic Injuries, Including Concussions

College athlete injuries have also emerged as a serious concern because these injuries can significantly curb student-athletes' health and future earnings. Recently, concerns have arisen around effects of sport-related concussions. A series of studies based on college athletes examined the effects of concussions and later health effects (Guskiewicz et al., 2003; Kerr et al., 2018; Mayers, 2013). Adverse effects influenced cognitive processing (e.g., decision-making, information recall), physical motion (e.g., dizziness, sensitivity to noise and light), and psychological well-being (e.g., anxiety, depression). In 2019, the NCAA settled a class-action lawsuit on concussion injuries to college athletes for $75 million, primarily to establish a 50-year medical-monitoring program for college athletes, although nearly 7% was dedicated to concussion research. For campus leaders, discussions around student-athletes' amateurism, compensation, and injuries raise legitimate concerns about whether athletics falls within higher education or extends to semiprofessional settings. The status of college sports also presents challenges for college administrators because, in some cases, the financial rewards of intercollegiate athletics outpace salaries of full professors and even senior campus leaders, and medical insurance coverage extends beyond benefits to long-standing employees. At some point, higher education will have to balance amateurism and athletic value without the restrictive approaches that some felt the NCAA employed (Gurney et al., 2017).

Race-Conscious Admissions

Decisions about whom an academic institution wishes to admit seem like an obvious discretionary act, but affirmative action, or race-conscious admissions, has been a hotly contested approach for nearly half a century.

Opponents argue that a college may admit whomever it pleases so long as race is either limited in its evaluation or not considered at all. Given the educational benefits associated with diversity, however, campus leaders often ask whether race-conscious admissions is a viable policy approach, and in most states, the answer is yes. Generally speaking, private colleges may have a race-conscious admissions policy, also called an affirmative action admissions plan. This policy option is not the situation at all public colleges. In nine states—Arizona, California, Florida, Idaho, Michigan, Nebraska, New Hampshire, Oklahoma, and Washington—state laws ban the use of race as an admissions criterion at public institutions.

The basis on which race-conscious admissions can be implemented originates from several legal sources. The primary federal laws that contest race-conscious admission policies are Title VI of the Civil Rights Act of 1964 and the 14th Amendment of the U.S. Constitution. Title VI of the Civil Rights Act of 1964 applies to both private and public universities. It prohibits discrimination on the basis of race, color, or national origin in any program or activity that receives federal financial assistance. For public institutions, the 14th Amendment's equal protection clause applies. It requires government entities to treat persons with equal protection under the law. As discussed previously, legal issues with a constitutional application usually require separate analyses for private and public universities.

Constitutional analyses usually afford more rights to the aggrieved party, so the stakes are often significant for colleges and universities. Regarding race-conscious admission policies, however, cases that address Title VI (grounds on which both private and public institutions admissions policies can be challenged) require the same standards as 14th Amendment cases. Since constitutional provisions are restricted to governmental actors (e.g., a public institution), it is unusual that the same standards of a federal law are applied to private institutions, but the heightened standards for both public and private colleges and universities highlight the significance of this issue.

The legal standards around race-conscious admissions are rather technical. Specifically, for private and public colleges to maintain legally permissible race-conscious admission policies, the institution must show that diversity is a compelling educational interest. Also, to advance that educational interest, it must show how employing a race-conscious admission policy is narrowly tailored to achieve that interest. This policy requires an outlining of clear mission-oriented goals, and the institution may demonstrate that no workable race-neutral alternatives were available to meet those goals.

To operationalize the legal standard, the cases since the foundational ruling in *Regents of the University of California v. Bakke* (1978) offer several guideposts. Six overall lessons are required to properly construct and maintain a race-conscious admission policy. It is worth noting that these guidelines also apply to the use of race in other determinations, such as scholarship and fellowship awards and admission to an honors program.

First, an institution that uses a race-conscious admission policy must identify its educational interest for student diversity and outline the desired educational goals to be achieved through this diversity. For instance, a university might articulate that its four goals to enhance diversity through a race-conscious admission policy are to train future leaders in the public and private sectors as the university's mission statement requires; equip its graduates and the university itself to adapt to an increasingly pluralistic society; better educate its students through lived experiences of diversity; and produce new knowledge through diverse perspectives (*Students for Fair Admissions, Inc. v. President and Fellows of Harvard College*, 2020).

Second, the institution must demonstrate that its efforts do not cast an overly broad use of race as a criterion. Rather, its admissions review considers individualized factors of its applicants and does not use race as a mechanical plus factor. While seemingly obvious, in *Gratz v. Bollinger* (2003), the U.S. Supreme Court observed that the University of Michigan's undergraduate programs in the College of Literature, Science, and the Arts automatically awarded 20 points, or one fifth of the points needed to guarantee admission, to every underrepresented racial minority applicant. That approach demonstrated that this race-conscious admission policy was not narrowly tailored because its point system failed to evaluate an individual, simply awarding significant points based on race instead. In some cases, the system functioned as a "mechanical plus factor for underrepresented minorities" (*Gratz v. Bollinger*, 2003, pp. 271–272). Individualized review is challenging given that annually the University of Michigan receives over 20,000 applications for its first-year class, from which it must formulate its entering class of over 5,000 students.

Third, the institution must present evidence that it evaluated race-neutral alternatives but legitimately concluded that they were not workable, and that the race-conscious admission policy does not intentionally discriminate against applicants from any racial group as evidenced by both statistical and qualitative data.

Fourth, the institution has the burden to outline its diversity goals and demonstrate data in which its race-conscious admissions approach supports those diversity goals. The analysis of data is not a one-time event. A university must maintain a continuous review of its admissions policy and achievement of its goals. The court cases inform us that social science research around the benefits of diversity to student learning and development are essential.

For example, Roksa et al. (2017) found that students' diverse interactions contributed to their cognitive development, particularly that of White students. Also, Shim and Perez (2018) showed how planned, structural activities increase students' openness to diversity and challenge, which are important components to fostering cross-cultural interactions and preparing the future citizenry.

Fifth, the institution cannot use a quota system or racial balancing in its admission practices. These approaches presume a set number of people are automatically qualified for admission. While a selective university may easily reach target admission numbers, the courts have made clear that quotas, set asides of special application reviews based on race, and racial balancing efforts place race as a decisive factor and are impermissible. These predetermined numbers or balancing efforts are different from a race-conscious admission policy that seeks to maintain a "critical mass," which is an acceptable goal under the law. Critical mass, however, is not a set target number; it is a more qualitative analysis that aspires to reach meaningful representation so members of the underrepresented group may experience peer support, not be outcast, and be a significant enough presence that the educational benefits of diversity may be reached.

Sixth, other noncognitive factors (i.e., data beyond grade point average [GPA] and standardized test scores) such as athletic ability, musical talents, community service, and legacy status (except in Colorado, which prohibits the use of legacies as a criterion at its state institutions) may be taken into account. Socioeconomic status may also be considered, but research is clear that income-based policies are an insufficient substitute to race-conscious admissions for driving racial equity. While seemingly an effort to support college access across races, evidence suggests other factors at play—even when comparing races with high socioeconomic backgrounds (Jones & Nichols, 2020).

To conclude, race-conscious admissions has proven over time to benefit both White students and students from underrepresented minorities. Although college admission rates still reflect gaps with underrepresentation of Black, Latinx, and Native American students, race-conscious admission policies remain a topic of litigation, state policy discussions, and campus admissions debates, These lawsuits are expected to continue as the U.S. Supreme Court in 2022 granted hearing additional cases on race-conscious admission policies. although Justice Saundra Day O'Connor predicted in a key race-conscious admissions court decision in 2003, "We expect that 25 years from now, the use of racial preferences will no longer be necessary to further the interest approved today" (*Grutter v. Bollinger*, 2003,

p. 343). However, given the recent Supreme Court's pending review, we may have new rulings from the highest court before the 25th anniversary in 2028.

Employment

Higher education budgets are largely dedicated to personnel costs, so employment rights remain a key topic for administrators. Many of the employment laws that apply to other industries (e.g., life sciences, manufacturing, information technology) and sectors (e.g., governmental, private, not-for-profit) also apply to employees in higher education. Federal laws are broadly written to cover most organizations, typically with 50 or more employees, creating rights for employees based on certain characteristics or experiences. This list includes some key laws for readers to keep in mind.

- Title VII of the Civil Rights Act of 1964 (Title VII) prohibits discrimination of employees on the basis of race, color, religion, national origin, or sex—including gender identity. It also protects against employer retaliation for reporting these protected forms of discrimination in the workplace.
- The Pregnancy Discrimination Act expands Title VII so that sex discrimination includes prohibited acts on the basis of pregnancy, childbirth, or a medical condition related to pregnancy or childbirth.
- The Equal Pay Act of 1963 makes it illegal to discriminate based on sex to determine wages when employees, regardless of sex, perform equal jobs in the same workplace.
- The Age Discrimination in Employment Act of 1967 (ADEA) prohibits employment discrimination, including hiring, of persons who are 40 or older.
- The ADA prohibits discrimination against a qualified person with a disability with the private sector (Title I) and state/local government (Title V).
- Section 504 of the Rehabilitation Act of 1973 prohibits discrimination against qualified persons based on disability.
- The Jobs for Veterans Act of 2002 (also referenced as VEVRAA) is part of the Vietnam Era Veteran's Readjustment Act of 1974 (VEVRAA), makes it illegal to discriminate against veterans, and creates an affirmative action provision for eligible veterans for employers that receive federal contracts.

- Title II of the Genetic Information Nondiscrimination Act of 2008 (GINA) makes it illegal to base employment decisions on genetic information about an applicant, employee, or former employee.
- The Family and Medical Leave Act (FMLA) offers employees the right to take unpaid leave from work to care for a newborn or recently adopted child or to care for ill family member, including parents.

These laws protect special classes of people (e.g., race, veteran status, age, employees with ill family members) by providing civil rights protection from discriminatory action by a higher education institution, public or private. These protections are important when selecting potential employees, evaluating employees, and disciplining or dismissing employees.

Tenure

When it comes to employment arrangements and rights, a unique aspect of higher education is faculty tenure and academic freedom. The public, particularly certain media outlets, have been very critical of these faculty job characteristics and rights, and in some cases, they have misstated what tenure and academic freedom are and permit (June, 2018). If higher education wishes to retain these employment rights, college and university staff, regardless of their institutional role, should be familiar with these employment arrangements to understand what they do, why they are important, and what their limits are.

Tenure simply overcomes a presumption of at-will employment. It is not a practiced concept among college faculty internationally. It refers to an employment relationship in which the institution promises eligible employees, typically faculty members who are hired "on the tenure track," continued employment after a set number of years of service (e.g., 7 years) and achieved performance levels during that time. Often, the employing institution outlines (a) a set of criteria such as standards for teaching, research, and service—the "substantive" basis for due process or legal fairness—and (b) the process for review (e.g., the timeline for the candidate and anticipated steps involving various administrators and committees, including identifying the final decision maker)—which provides the "procedural" basis for due process or legal fairness. For both private and public colleges and universities, the legal basis for formation of the tenure review process typically derives from contract law (e.g., an actual contract between faculty and the institution; a faculty handbook; or at times, academic custom). For faculty with tenure, the legal protections for faculty at both private and public institutions derive from contract law. However, for faculty at public institutions, improperly removing tenure leads to constitutional deprivations such as the government's taking one's "property," which in this case is the property right of tenure. Because of its significance as a property right, it involves the 14th Amendment of the U.S. Constitution's due process clause and state laws on property.

When a faculty member seeks tenure but is denied, the appropriate grounds for denial depend on the institution's criteria, which may originate at a state university system level or rely on a college or department's established policies. As indicated, these criteria establish contractual rights. Typically, the criteria include evaluation of the tenure candidate's teaching, research, and service—without discriminating factors such as race, age, sex, or persons with disabilities or retaliation for protected acts such as free speech (although the latter applies for candidates at public institutions). Increasingly, colleges and universities have included "collegiality" as a criterion as well. Ultimately, courts usually defer to the institution about matters related to tenure denials. If a court hears a tenure denial case, for the most part it evaluates the credibility of whether the tenure denial falls into a series of illegal nondiscriminatory practices (e.g., violations of state and federal nondiscrimination laws), and it does not "grant" tenure or force an institution to grant tenure.

Tenure may be removed in certain instances. The legal rights pertaining to dismissals of faculty with tenure depend largely on whether the faculty member is at a private or a public institution. While both private and public colleges and universities typically establish "for-cause" justifications as reasons to dismiss a tenured faculty member, the elements that justify "for cause" might differ between private and public institutions. Often, the for-cause reasons involve incompetence, neglect of duty, or violations of moral turpitude.

Colleges may also reassign or dismiss a tenured faculty member based on special institutional circumstances such as financial exigency (i.e., an imminent financial crisis that requires changes to faculty appointments, such as eliminating or reassigning professors) and program discontinuance (i.e., a planned closure of a program based on mission-oriented decisions that may require reducing or reassigning faculty lines, including tenured professors). In addition, at private universities, faculty contracts outline provisions for dismissal, which could include violations of religious tenets. At public institutions, challenges by tenured faculty who have been dismissed arise from questions of discrimination for protected classes, discrimination for protected speech/expressions, failure to comply with policies or procedures, and vague or overbroad policies that cover constitutionally protected actions. In all instances, dismissal of tenured faculty at public institutions requires sufficient notice of the dismissal, a hearing, and an opportunity for an appeal process.

Tenure is important to the academic profession. Without it, college administrators could remove professors because of their research or creative activities. For instance, political pressure from the governor may lead to a professor's dismissal when the professor's research suggests a state policy that supports coal leads to greater adverse health outcomes than economic development benefits. Equally important, a more experienced professor may decide to shift their research away from pure science to examine student learning effects when instructed in different forms of science education. Although the college may value such research, the department faculty may not because they desire greater national recognition within traditional scientific research. With tenure, the faculty member has more due process rights to challenge their department's recommendation of nonrenewal or unsatisfactory performance in research. Without tenure, the college may be pressured not to renew the faculty member based on this research activity.

Academic Freedom

Although the awarding of tenure is based on certain criteria, the professoriate, as a unique profession, also possesses some form of academic freedom. Academic freedom consists of professional employment protections for faculty to freely make expressions in their areas of expertise without undue lay interferences. For professors at public institutions, those protections include constitutional protections. The application of academic freedom generally applies to all faculty regardless of tenure status, but private colleges and universities have the most flexibility in creating their policies.

As indicated, private institutions have the most flexibility in creating their policies. The legal parameters to assert and deny academic freedom largely rest on contract law (e.g., the actual contract between the faculty and the institution or a faculty handbook), but at times, private institutions establish policies that resemble (or are identical to) constitutional language, and in such cases, the courts often follow guidelines similar to constitutional analyses. Public institutions are also subject to contract law, but they are also subject to constitutional law—particularly the First and 14th Amendments.

As with tenure, academic freedom allows faculty members to express themselves based on their professional judgment. If higher education does not maintain its objectivity and freedom to investigate intellectual questions, scientific, artistic, humanistic, and other forms of inquiry will be relegated to potential biases and will be no different than business-based research, which is also influenced by external factors and entities. Thus, academic freedom is an important value to this profession if we care about uninhibited, objective research and creative works, which are the hallmarks of professors' scholarly production, and in many cases, it has application to teaching. If college leaders intend to further the academic enterprise as the principal source for uninhibited, objective learning, research, and creative works, it must understand and defend academic freedom and tenure.

Conclusion

The topics covered in this chapter are only a sampling of key and emerging legal issues for campus leaders. Higher education faces challenges from other court decisions and legal policies as well. For instance, we did not address First Amendment freedom of association concerns involved with starting a new student group or dismissing an existing group. We did not examine how a student group may be recognized, receive funds from the institution, and determine which students may be a member or leader. For instance, may a Christian serve as the president of Hillel? Nor did we discuss whether administrators may seize drugs from a car in a campus parking lot, student residence hall, or locker in the commuter lounge. Issues in higher education law also include governance rights, such as boards and merging institutions; employment rights around labor and collective bargaining and safety; faculty rights concerning special employment provisions, such as evaluating professors based on collegiality; student contracting rights related to housing, dining, and other services; academic and curricular issues including ownership of instructional products and options faculty have to change materials; and leasing agreements, building codes, and other campus physical space concerns. This chapter provided a basic overview of key and emerging concepts at the present, yet many more new topics will emerge as technological, human, economic, political, and social environments change. Although the key topics may evolve over time, legal issues will continue to inform higher education leaders' considerations of their institution's mission, adaptable approach, democratic partnerships, and commitment to social change.

Notes

1. Private colleges might be subject to federal constitutional rights in some rare instances. For instance, if the private institution were acting on the government's behalf, it would in that unusual circumstance be considered acting in the shoes of the state, not as a private organization. Another way in which private institutions may be subject to the more comprehensive rights of free speech, like public colleges, is when state law places private colleges with heightened protections of campus free speech matters. California's Leonard Law holds private colleges to that standard akin

to public colleges. This law grants students at private colleges a form of free speech rights. The state law extends the First Amendment free speech law and California Constitution's free speech clause to students at private postsecondary educational institutions in that state. It makes explicit that private colleges cannot take disciplinary actions against students for free speech activities off campus.

2. A negligence claim also requires showing the link between the alleged breach of duty and the injuries sustained, evidence of any damages, and justifications to overcome any defenses that the college may assert, such as the student assumed the risks when participating in the activity.

3. The social ills manifested in sexual harassment clearly extend beyond higher education. Media attention has more recently highlighted certain occupational roles and industries where power imbalances are pronounced and sexual harassment has been ignored or minimized.

References

Age Discrimination in Employment Act of 1967, 29 U.S.C. §§ 621-634 (2021)

Americans With Disabilities Act, 42 U.S.C. §§ 12132 et seq. (2021)

Anderson, G. (2020, June 23). When free speech and racist speech collide. *Inside Higher Ed.* https://www.insidehighered.com/news/2020/06/23/first-amendment-response-first-response-racism-campus

Appelbaum, P. S. (2019). Responsibility for suicide or violence on campus. *Psychiatric Services, 70*(4), 350–352. https://doi.org/10.1176/appi.ps.201900060

Ark. Code § 6-60-109 (2021)

Berger v. National Collegiate Athletic Association, 843 F.3d 285 (7th Cir. 2016), reh'g and reh'g en banc denied (2017)

Bickel, R. D., & Lake, P. F. (1999). *The rights and responsibilities of the modern university: Who assumes the risks of college life?* Carolina Academic Press.

Bidiger v. Quinnipiac University, 691 F.3d 85 (2d Cir. 2012)

Board of Curators of the University of Missouri v. Horowitz, 435 U.S. 78 (1978)

Bradshaw v. Rawlings, 612 F.2d 135 (3d Cir. 1979)

Brown v. Board of Education, 347 U.S. 483 (1954)

Bunkley, N. (2007, July 17). University fires officials for concealing killing. *New York Times*, p. A17.

Cantor, D., Fisher, B., Chibnall, S., Harps, S., Townsend, R., Thomas, G., Lee, H., Kranz, V., Herbison, R., & Madden, K. (2020). *Report on the AAU campus climate survey on sexual assault and sexual misconduct.* Association of American Universities. https://www.aau.edu/sites/default/files/AAU-Files/Key-Issues/Campus-Safety/Revised%20Aggregate%20report%20%20and%20appendices%201-7_(01-16-2020_FINAL).pdf

Commonwealth v. Peterson, 749 S.E.2d 307 (Va. 2013)

Dawson v. NCAA, 932 F.3d 905 (9th Cir. 2019)

Dixon v. Alabama State Board of Education, 294 F.2d 150 (5th Cir. 1961)

Donoso, S., & Zirkel, P. A. (2008). The volume of higher education litigation: An updated analysis. *West's Education Law Reporter, 232*(2), 549–555.

Emery v. Talladega College, 688 Fed. App'x. 727 (11th Cir. 2017)

Equal Pay Act, 29 U.S.C. §206(d) (2021)

Esteban v. Central Missouri State College, 415 F.2d 1077 (8th Cir. 1969), cert denied, 398 U.S. 965 (1970)

Ewing v. Regents of the University of Michigan, 474 U.S. 214 (1985)

Fair Labor Standards Act, 29 U.S.C. § 203, et seq. (2021)

Family and Medical Leave Act of 1993, 29 U.S.C. § 2612 et seq. (2021)

Family Educational Rights and Privacy Act, 20 U.S.C. § 1232g, et seq. (2021)

Farr, T., & Cunningham, L. (Eds.). (2017). *Academic advising core competencies guide.* NACADA.

First Amendment, U.S. Const. Amendment 1 (2021)

Fourteenth Amendment, U.S. Const. Amendment 14 (2021)

Friedersdorf, C. (2019). The ACLU moves to embrace due process on Title IX. *The Atlantic.* https://www.theatlantic.com/ideas/archive/2019/02/aclu-title-ix/582118/

Gallup & Knight Foundation. (2018). *Free expression on campus: What college students think about First Amendment issues.* https://knightfoundation.org/reports/free-expression-on-campus-what-college-students-think-about-first-amendment-issues/

Gallup & Knight Foundation. (2020). *The First Amendment on campus 2020 report: College students' views of free expression.* https://knightfoundation.org/reports/the-first-amendment-on-campus-2020-report-college-students-views-of-free-expression/

Garrett v. Northwest Mississippi Jr. College, 674 So.2d 1 (1996)

Garthwaite, C., Keener, J., Notowidigdo, M. J., & Ozminkowski, N. F. (2020). *Who profits from amateurism? Rent-sharing in modern college sports.* National Bureau of Economic Research. http://www.nber.org/papers/w27734

Gee, E. G., Daniel, P. T. K., Sun, J. C., & Pauken, P. D. (in press). *Law, policy, and higher education.* Carolina Academic Press.

Goss v. Lopez, 419 U.S. 565 (1975)

Gratz v. Bollinger, 539 U.S. 244 (2003)

Gregory, D. E., Broderick, J. R., & Doyle, C. B. (2020). Safety, security, risk management and legal issues in student affairs. In R. B. Ludeman & B. Schreiber (Eds.), *Student affairs and services in higher education: Global foundations, issues, and best practices* (3rd ed., pp. 74–82). International Association of Student Affairs and Services & Deutsches Studentenwerk.

Grutter v. Bollinger, 539 U.S. 306 (2003)

Gurney, G., Lopiano, D. A., & Zimbalist, A. (2017). *Unwinding madness: What went wrong with college sports and how to fix it.* Brookings Institution Press.

Guskiewicz, K. M., McCrea, M., Marshall, S. W., Cantu, R. C., Randolph, C., Barr, W., Onate, J. A., & Kelly, J. P. (2003). Cumulative effects associated with recurrent concussion in collegiate football players: The NCAA concussion study.

Journal of the American Medical Association, 290(19), 2549–2555. https://doi .org/10.1001/jama.290.19.2549

Hazelwood School District et al. v. Kuhlmeier et al., 484 U.S. 260 (1988)

Healthy Minds Network & American College Health Association. (2020). *The impact of COVID-19 on college student well-being.* https://healthymindsnet-work.org/wp-content/uploads/2020/07/Healthy_Minds_NCHA_COVID_Survey_Report_FINAL.pdf

Horwitz, A. G., McGuire, T., Busby, D. R., Eisenberg, D., Zheng, K., Pistorello, J., Albucher, R., Coryell, W., & King, C. A. (2020). Sociodemographic differ-ences in barriers to mental health care among college students at elevated suicide risk. *Journal of Affective Disorders, 271,* 123–130. https://doi.org/10.1016/j.jad.2020.03.115

Jaschik, S., & Lederman, D. (2021). *2021 Survey of college and university chief academic officers: A study by Inside Higher Ed and Hanover Research.* Inside Higher Ed and Hanover Research.

Jobs for Veterans Act of 2002, 38 USC § 4212 (2021)

Jones, T., & Nichols A. H. (2020). *Hard truths: Why only race-conscious policies can fix racism in higher education.* The Education Trust. https://edtrust.org/resource/hard-truths/

June, A. W. (2018, June 22). Frustrated faculty struggle to defend tenure before it's too late. *The Chronicle of Higher Education, 64*(36). https://www.chronicle.com/article/frustrated-faculty-struggle-to-defend-tenure-before-its-too-late

Kerr, Z. Y., Thomas, L. C., Simon, J. E., McCrea, M., & Guskiewicz, K. M. (2018). Association between history of multiple concussions and health outcomes among former college football players: 15-year follow-up from the NCAA concussion study (1999–2001). *American Journal of Sports Medicine, 46*(7), 1733–1741. https://doi.org/10.1177/0363546518765121

Knoester, C., & Ridpath, B. D. (2020). Should college athletes be allowed to be paid? A public opinion analysis. *Sociology of Sport Journal.* https://doi.org/10.1123/ssj.2020-0015

Krebs, C. P., Lindquist, C., Warner, T. D., Fisher, B. S., & Martin, S. L. (2007). *The campus sexual assault (CSA) study: Final report.* Office of Justice Programs, U.S. Department of Justice. https://www.ncjrs.gov/pdffiles1/nij/grants/221153.pdf

Krebs, C. P., Lindquist, C. H., Berzofsky, M., Shook-Sa, B., Peterson, K., Planty, M., Langton, L., & Stroop, J. (2016). *Campus climate survey validation study final technical report.* Office of Justice Programs, U.S. Department of Justice. https://www.ojp.gov/ncjrs/virtual-library/abstracts/campus-climate-survey-validation-study-ccsvs-final-technical-report

Leonard Law, Cal. Educ. Code, § 94367 (2021)

Leshner, A. I., & Scherer, L. A. (2021). *Mental health, substance use, and wellbeing in higher education.* National Academies Press. https://doi.org/10.17226/26015

Lipka, S. (2007). Eastern Michigan U. official says he is a scapegoat in murder inquiry. *The Chronicle of Higher Education, 53*(42), 35. https://www.chronicle.com/article/eastern-michigan-u-official-says-he-is-a-scapegoat-in-murder-inquiry/

Loder v. State of New York, 607 N.Y.S.2d 151 (N.Y. App. Div. 1994)

Mayers, L. B. (2013). Outcomes of sport-related concussion among college athletes. *Journal of Neuropsychiatry and Clinical Neurosciences, 25*(2), 115–119. https://doi.org/10.1176/appi.neuropsych.11120374

Melnick, R. S. (2020). *Analyzing the Department of Education's final Title IX rules on sexual misconduct.* Brookings Institution. https://www.brookings.edu/research/analyzing-the-department-of-educations-final-title-ix-rules-on-sexual-misconduct/

Nguyen v. Massachusetts Institute of Technology, 96 N.E.3d 128 (Mass. 2018)

N.C. Code § 116-40.11 (2021)

N.D. Cent. Code § 15-10 (2021)

Parrot, T. V. (2021, April 5). Profit motives make fixing college sports nearly impossible. *The Washington Post.* https://www.washingtonpost.com/outlook/2021/04/05/profit-motives-make-fixing-college-sports-nearly-impossible/

Peebles, J., & Lombardi, K. (2015, March 15). *"Undetected rapists" on campus: A troubling plague of repeat offenders.* Center for Public Integrity. https://publicintegrity.org/education/undetected-rapists-on-campus-a-troubling-plague-of-repeat-offenders/

Poliakoff, M. (2021, January 25). The Biden plan for Title IX must protect due process. *Forbes.* https://www.forbes.com/sites/michaelpoliakoff/2021/01/25/the-biden-plan-for-title-ix-must-protect-due-process

Pregnancy Discrimination Act of 1978, 42 U.S.C. § 2000e(k) (2021)

Professional Competencies Task Force. (2015). *Professional competency areas for student affairs educators.* ACPA & NASPA. https://www.naspa.org/images/uploads/main/ACPA_NASPA_Professional_Competencies_FINAL.pdf

Pruitt, S. (2021). *How Title IX transformed women's sports.* History. https://www.history.com/news/title-nine-womens-sports

Regents of the University of California v. Bakke, 438 U.S. 265 (1978)

Regents of University of California v. Superior Court, 413 P.3d 656 (Cal. 2018); rem'd 240 Cal. Rptr. 3d 675 (Cal. Ct. App. 2018)

Rhoads, R. A. (2016). Student activism, diversity, and the struggle for a just society. *Journal of Diversity in Higher Education, 9*(3), 189–202. https://doi.org/10.1037/dhe0000039

Roksa, J., Kilgo, C. A., Trolian, T. L., Pascarella, E. T., Blaich, C., & Wise, K. S. (2017). Engaging with diversity: How positive and negative diversity interactions influence students' cognitive outcomes. *Journal of Higher Education, 88*(3), 453–477. https://doi.org/10.1080/00221546.2016.1271690

Section 504 of the Rehabilitation Act of 1973, 29 U.S.C. § 794, et seq. (2021)

Shim, W.-J., & Perez, R. J. (2018). A multi-level examination of first-year students' openness to diversity and challenge. *Journal of Higher Education, 89*(4), 453–477. https://doi.org/10.1080/00221546.2018.1434277

Smith v. Tarrant County College District, 694 F.Supp.2d 610 (N.D. Tex. 2010)

Snyder v. Phelps, 562 U.S. 443 (2011)

Speech First, Inc. v. Fenves, 979 F.3d 319 (5th Cir. 2020)

Speech First, Inc. v. Killeen, 968 F.3d 628 (7th Cir. 2020)

Speech First, Inc. v. Schlissel, 939 F.3d 756 (6th Cir. 2019)

Steve Fund & JED Foundation. (2017). *The equity in mental health framework.* Authors.

Storbeck, S. W. (2021, January 25). College presidents need help lately, too. *The Chronicle of Higher Education.* https://www.chronicle.com/article/college-presidents-need-help-lately-too

Student Athlete Bill of Rights, Cal. Educ. Code § 67452 (2021)

Students for Fair Admissions, Inc. v. President and Fellows of Harvard College, 980 F.3d 157 (2020)

Sun, J. C. (Ed.). (2015). *Responding to campus protests: A practitioner resource.* Education Law Association & NASPA.

Sun, J. C., & McClellan, G. S. (2019). *Student clashes on campus: A leadership guide to free speech.* Routledge.

Tarasoff v. Regents of the University of California, 551 P.2d 334 (Cal. 1976)

Title II of the Genetic Information Nondiscrimination Act of 2008, 42 U.S.C. 2000ff et seq. (2021)

Title VI of the Civil Rights Act of 1964, 42 U.S.C. §2000d, et seq. (2021)

Title VII of the Civil Rights Act of 1964, 42 U.S.C. §2000e, et seq. (2021)

Title IX of the Education Amendments Act of 1972, 20 U.S.C. §1681 et seq. (2021)

Turk, J. M., Soler, M. C., & Ramos, A. M. (2020). *College and university presidents respond to COVID-19: 2020 fall term survey.* American Council on Education & TIAA Institute. https://www.acenet.edu/Research-Insights/Pages/Senior-Leaders/College-and-University-Presidents-Respond-to-COVID-19-2020-Fall-Term.aspx

The University of Chicago. (2015). *Report of the committee on freedom of expression.* Author.

White, L. (2015). *Top 10 campus legal issues for boards.* Association of Governing Boards of Universities and Colleges.

PART THREE

THE BOUNDARY SPANNERS

9

THE ENGAGED COLLEGE OR UNIVERSITY

The idea that institutions of higher learning should exist for the betterment of society and the promotion of democratic ideals is as old as the founding of this nation. It can be argued that the oldest college in the United States, Harvard, was founded to promote the advancement of societal goals. Evidence of this purpose is found in the earliest account of its creation, an article written in the 1643 publication *New England's First Fruits*, where it was stated, "After erecting shelter, a house of worship, and the framework of government, one of the next things we longed for, and looked after, was to advance Learning and perpetuate it to Prosperity" (as cited in Rudolph, 1962, p. 4).

Rudolph (1962) noted that the establishment of Harvard, and indeed all the colonial colleges, was born both out of necessity and a sense of community responsibility for future generations. If the colonists' communities, governments, and churches were to continue to flourish, they would need to train individuals to lead these critical institutions. The colleges' creation was not simply based on a need for vocations or a sense of order, however. As Rudolph pointed out, with the establishment of William and Mary, its founders specifically identified the need to ensure "that the youth were piously educated in good letters and manners from which the colony would draw its public servants" (p. 7). In other words, to our nation's founders, higher education was necessary to produce the next generation of citizens who would lead and be engaged in society.

The vision of a college and its graduates engaged in society was manifest in myriad ways during the colonial period and the creation of the United States. In fact, many believe that promotion of the democratic ideals that led to the American Revolution was partly fueled by the number of men of learned professions who were educated either in Europe or at one of the

colonial colleges. Berkin (2002) described those leaders who directly participated in the creation of the U.S. Constitution as "men with a near monopoly
on formal education and professional training in a predominantly agrarian
society" (p. 49), and Ellis (2007) believed the American people were the
beneficiaries of an "accumulated wisdom" (p. 4) to which the founders had
been exposed to through their formal education and training. A case can be
made that without this extraordinary collection of college-educated people,
the founding of this country may have taken a different course. Based on
the democratic foundation that was laid by these learned men, it is easy to
understand how an education—and especially a college education—came to
be viewed as part of the American ethos. By the middle of the 19th century,
there was a strong belief that colleges were essential to the promotion of
American democracy, and "a commitment to to the republic became a guiding obligation of the American college" (Rudolph, 1962, p. 61).

By the end of the 19th century, with the egalitarian nature of the land-
grant movement and the advancement of the German research university
model in the United States, the promotion of democratic ideals became intertwined with discussions on the true aims of education. Should the focus be
on liberal education, research, the advancement of industry and agriculture,
the promotion of democracy, or could it be all of the above? John Dewey
(1916), the influential educational philosopher of the late 19th and early
20th centuries, emphasized a pragmatic approach to education and described
the connection between education and democracy. Dewey believed that all
education that "develops power to share effectively in social life is moral"
(p. 360), making him one of the first commentators to identify the importance of democratic partnerships in advancing educational aims.

Dewey (1916) promoted the idea that theory and practice were not
merely compatible but highly interconnected. Moreover, he argued that
the greater aims of society could only be accomplished through participatory democracy. He emphasized that major advancements in knowledge
happened most often when the focus was on solving significant societal
issues. These advancements most often occurred, according to Dewey, when
learning in the classroom was continuous with learning outside the school in
the real world.

Virgil A. Clift (1948), a mid-20th-century author who wrote widely
on the topic of Black education in America built on Dewey's ideas. Clift
(1948) believed that democracy was the collective act of sharing the creation of common goals, as well as the collaborative application of intelligence,
to resolve conflict and promote the betterment of society through social
innovation. Clift offered seven recommendations for democratic practice in
higher education, which align directly with the four guiding principles of

this book. In his 1948 article on "transmitting democratic ideals into behavior" he promoted the idea that the curriculum of any college or university must facilitate the achievement of the "avowed purposes of the institution" (p. 138). In addition, he made the case that an institution of higher learning should seek to "exemplify democratic living at its best" and provide its students with a deeper understanding of the "nature of society and individuals who compose it" (p. 139).

A more contemporary approach to how colleges and universities should view their role in the promotion of democratic ideals was offered by Josephson (2020), who argued that, over the years, too much analysis of the role of higher education has used an economic lens. Josephson (2020) asserted that institutions of higher learning should consider their role through an egalitarian lens, which promotes democratic values and capacities as the true public good of higher education. She stated, "Those of us who know public education well must do the public work of arguing for the importance of educated citizens for the health of democratic public life, and for public investments to make this a reality" (Josephson, 2020, p. 169).

Unfortunately, in the 21st century, as was the case in Dewey's (1916) and Clift's (1948) times, the world outside the classroom is complicated, unpredictable, and difficult to control. It is filled with politics, shifting economic realities, and changing social mores, all of which influence how education institutions interact with or relate to the world outside the ivory tower. Developing mutually beneficial democratic partnerships with constituents outside the academy (whether local or global) to advance knowledge and enhance student learning is certainly challenging, but nurturing these partnerships to advance democracy is paramount if a college or university is to thrive in the 21st century.

Three Educational Movements

In this chapter we discuss the intersection of three important educational movements of the 21st century. We believe the confluence of these movements presents a unique opportunity for higher education to reassert its value to society by engaging more deeply in societal issues, particularly at the local level. First, we describe what led colleges and universities to take more seriously their role in educating responsible citizens and reaffirm the value that Dewey (1916), Clift (1948), and other early authors promoted—that educating students for democracy is a primary aim of higher education. Second, we address how service learning and community- and place-based pedagogies have grown and transformed higher education. Third, we consider the rising expectation for colleges and universities to be more engaged in their local communities as anchor institutions by focusing on democratic and reciprocal partnerships with local organizations that address the community's most pressing issues. Throughout this chapter we incorporate information on organizations and national engagement initiatives involved in this work. We also include in this chapter brief descriptions of how major global events, such as the worldwide recession and global pandemic, have challenged higher education institutions to reassess their roles in partnering with local communities to address serious inequities in society.

Educating Responsible Citizens

Evidence is abundant that U.S. citizens' participation in their democracy has been in decline since the middle of the 20th century. Data on voting participation show that while 2020 witnessed an uptick in voter turnout—66.3% of voter eligible population, the highest turnout since 1900 (Schaul et al., 2020)—the United States still lags behind other developed democratic nations (Desilver, 2020; Timsit, 2020). Numerous studies point to the alarming decrease in participation rate of Americans in civic acts such as voting or involvement in a local community organization (American Presidency Project, 2021; Putnam, 2000; Sax, 2004; Zukin et al., 2006).

As stated earlier, from its inception American higher education has been viewed as a key instrument for promoting democratic values that are essential to the health and well-being of the republic. By the end of the 20th century, however, there was broad concern that higher education had lost its focus on the greater good and its commitment to civic virtues. Specifically, a widespread debate emerged by the middle of the 1980s over what the priorities of U.S. higher education ideally should be in an ever-changing and pluralistic society. Some felt that higher education's primary aim was economic development. For example, in 1983 the National Commission on Excellence in Education appointed by President Ronald Reagan produced a report, "A Nation at Risk," that attempted to identify the knowledge, abilities, and skills high school and college graduates should possess to promote economic prosperity, but it said little about the promotion of democratic ideals as being key to prosperity. Others, however, felt colleges and universities needed to do more than fuel America's economic engine; higher education needed to support and sustain our democracy.

In response to these conversations, the Carnegie Foundation for the Advancement of Teaching sponsored a report (Newman, 1985) that called for the nation's schools to take more responsibility for educating students for citizenship. This report prompted the presidents of several leading U.S.

universities to form Campus Compact, a higher education association aimed at encouraging institutions to instill a greater sense of social and civic responsibility in their students. The response to this initiative was tremendous. The membership of Campus Compact grew quickly, and by 2021 more than 1,000 colleges and universities serving approximately 6 million students were part of this dynamic organization (Campus Compact, n.d.).

The Carnegie Foundation for the Advancement of Teaching continued to explore the priorities of U.S. higher education with the publication of a special report on the state of the professoriate (Boyer, 1990). Written by Carnegie Foundation president Ernest Boyer, the report suggested a new way of thinking about higher education. Rather than perpetuate the traditional debate about whether research or teaching should be prioritized in faculty work, Boyer (1990) focused on the larger idea of scholarship, identifying four broad categories: "the scholarship of discovery, of integration, of application, and of teaching" (p. 25).

This new way of thinking about academic work changed the nature of the debate over priorities and how faculty work should be categorized and rewarded, but it was Boyer's (1990) definition of the aim of education that ignited a broader discussion on higher education's civic role:

> The aim of education is not only to prepare students for productive careers but also to enable them to live lives of dignity and purpose; not to generate new knowledge but to channel it to humane ends; not merely to study government, but to help shape a citizenry that can promote the public good. (pp. 77–78)

Several years later, Boyer (1996) added a fifth element of scholarship, which he described as the scholarship of engagement. He added this category to emphasize the critical need for U.S. higher education to commit anew to public service.

In 1993 a group of U.S. higher education leaders known as the Wingspread Group on Higher Education proposed that college and university administrators needed to take a closer look at their purpose and ask how their entering freshman classes in the next year would become "more sensitive to the needs of community, more competent in their ability to contribute to society, and more civil in their habits of thought, speech and action" (p. 9). In an open letter, the group called on institutions of higher education to raise their sights and take difficult steps to promote national health.

Other observers also expressed concern about the United States' national health. Putnam (1995), for example, described what he perceived to be a disturbing downward trend in civic, social, and political engagement among

American citizens from the 1960s through the 1990s. Putnam had previously studied regional governments in Italy and discovered that local governments worked better—and communities were more likely to prosper—where there was "organized reciprocity and civic solidarity" (p. 2). Putnam argued that the health of a democracy depended on active participation of its citizens in everything from voting to membership in choral societies, to bowling. In the United States, however, he discovered that a large percentage of Americans were disconnected from their neighbors and their local communities. To counter this trend, he argued that development of strategies to improve social capital and reverse political apathy among citizens should be high on the American agenda.

Although Putnam (1995) never suggested that higher education was the only solution, his findings and recommendations resonated in academic circles and were part of the impetus for some national organizations and higher education associations to call for greater involvement by colleges and universities in their local communities. By the beginning of the 21st century, these discussions led to the establishment of working groups and national programs such as the Association of American Colleges and Universities' (AAC&U) Greater Expectations initiative, which articulated the aims and purposes of a liberal education and emphasized the importance of civic engagement in a diverse democracy. Despite the widespread conversation about social and civic responsibility, the term *civic engagement* was not clearly understood. Since civic engagement was not clearly defined, it was used as a catch phrase for a plethora of initiatives.

The difficulty with terminology stems from different interpretations of the word *civic*. A traditional understanding of the term is that it refers to the duties of a municipal or government worker rather than the responsibilities of all citizens. To others, it may have a political meaning and is often confused with student or political activism. Gradually, though, the term began to incorporate a more inclusive meaning. In 2003, for example, Colby et al. spelled out what they believed constituted a morally and civically responsible individual—one who sees themselves as

> a member of a larger social fabric and therefore considers social problems to be at least partly their own; such an individual is willing to see the moral and civic dimensions of issues, to make and justify informed moral and civic judgments, and to take action when appropriate. (p. 17)

In 2009 Jacoby and associates offered a simpler definition of civic engagement: "acting upon a heightened sense of responsibility to one's communities" (p. 9). Cantor & Englot (2016) suggested a more complex and expansive approach to civic engagement by calling on universities to be anchors in their own communities. Cantor (2016) further asserted that institutions of higher learning must be committed to addressing certain challenges to be truly civically engaged, such as "broadening participation in the land of opportunity" (p. 2), "improving the quality of public discourse" (p. 3), "rewarding and supporting publicly-engaged scholarship" (p. 4), and "building strong and just communities through community-based partnerships" (p. 3).

In this book, we refer to civic engagement as a college or university's development of students to serve as leaders in a democratic society and as an institution's commitment to democratic principles. First, colleges and universities have a responsibility to prepare students to be informed, active, and responsible citizens in a democratic society who are committed to work for positive social change. Second, institutions of higher learning have a duty to be role models for the promotion of democratic ideals, especially in their local communities as active partners in building a more just society.

Some of the work for positive social change may occur in a traditional educational setting under the leadership of a faculty member, or it may occur when students engage in a community-based learning experience, such as conducting research on an environmental issue tied to their course work. Other civic engagement activities, including voluntary service at a food bank or active participation in a political campaign, may have a positive impact on society and a student, but the lack of structure can prevent that experience from having a lasting impact on the student's development. The key to meaningful engagement is that experiences are structured in ways that help students reflect on their experiences and make it more likely they will continue to participate in a significant way in the future. The more support mechanisms an institution has in place for such activities, the more likely the institution and its students are civically engaged.

To recognize exemplars in the field of civic engagement, in 2006 the Carnegie Foundation for the Advancement of Teaching created an elective classification system for higher education institutions concerned with community engagement, or the

> collaboration between institutions of higher education and their larger communities (local, regional, state, national, global) for the mutually beneficial exchange of knowledge and resources in a context of partnership and reciprocity". . . [to] "prepare educated, engaged citizens; strengthen democratic values and civic responsibility; address critical societal issues; and contribute to the public good. (Public Purpose Institute, 2021, paras.1–2)

Colleges and universities can earn this recognition based on their work in three categories: curricular engagement, outreach and partnerships, or a combination of the two. By 2020, over 350 colleges and universities—public and private, large and small—had earned the Elective Community Engagement Classification by the Carnegie Foundation (Commission on Economic and Community Engagement, 2020).

Several other associations and organizations have emerged to assist colleges and universities with civic engagement. For example, Project Pericles was founded to promote social responsibility and participatory citizenship as essential elements of the educational programs at its 30 member institutions, all of which are independent colleges and universities. Two elements of Project Pericles worth noting include the high level of institutional cooperation and academic partnerships that exists among member institutions and the commitment and involvement of member presidents in the organization.

The American Democracy Project is a multicampus initiative sponsored by the AAC&U to prepare the next generation of engaged citizens. Over 200 public institutions are part of this program, which has emphasized the importance of students becoming citizens who are deeply engaged in local community issues that have global impact. Furthermore, the AAC&U, which includes public and private institutions in its membership, sponsors several initiatives involving hundreds of institutions focused on personal and social responsibility as well as civic and democratic learning.

Strong evidence exists that the civic engagement movement in higher education has affected college students' participation in our democracy in the 21st century. A 2006 report by the Carnegie Foundation for the Advancement of Teaching and the Center for Information and Research on Civic Learning and Engagement (CIRCLE) noted that current students, as well as those who recently attended college, were among the most engaged of all young people. For example, 28% of college graduates under the age of 25 reported being active in their communities, as compared to 13% of young people who did not attend college (Carnegie Foundation for the Advancement of Teaching & CIRCLE, 2006).

Voter participation by college-educated young adults in the 2020 national election was greater than that of their peers who did not attend college. According to a 2021 CIRCLE report, youth voters surged by 11% in 2020 over 2016, with 50% of eligible youth (ages 18–29) voting. Youth, regardless of their race or ethnicity, were far more likely to vote if they were currently enrolled in or had previously attended college at any level (CIRCLE, 2020). Earlier studies found that college students were far more active in their communities than their counterparts from the 1990s, although the later generation found the political system less accessible and felt traditional politics was not the best mechanism for change (Kiesa et al., 2007). Nevertheless, since the dawn of the 21st century there has been a noticeable increase in voter participation and community involvement among young people aged 18–25 who are attending or have attended college as compared to those who do not pursue higher education.

What caused this surge in engagement? In the next section we explore the community-based learning and service learning initiatives believed to have helped achieve these results.

Service Learning and Community-Based Learning

Service learning's roots can be traced to Dewey (1916) and his emphasis on the importance of school and community cooperation to address society's most pressing issues. Benson et al. (2007) argued that Dewey's commitment to community was influenced by his work at the University of Chicago and by its president, William Rainey Harper. Harper suggested that the universities must guide American democracy, and urban universities had a unique opportunity to collaborate with their cities to bring about remarkable societal transformations (Benson et al., 2007).

Dewey (1916) expanded on this idea to create a new educational paradigm that emphasized a union between the traditional contemplative approach to learning and a more vocational or applied method of learning. The experiential learning movement grew out of his philosophy and in turn led to the development of cooperative education, practicum experiences, and internships across myriad academic disciplines—especially in the professional schools that emerged in the middle of the 20th century.

Service learning also emerged from the experiential learning movement in the late 1960s. According to Giles and Eyler (1994), the term *service learning* was first coined by Robert L. Sigmon and William Ramsey in 1967. The early service learning movement rapidly gained popularity in U.S. institutions of higher education, but by the end of the 1970s it had largely disappeared because most programs were not tied to their academic institutions' missions, and the relationships between colleges and universities and their community partners were uneven or unequal (Jacoby & Associates, 1996; Kendall & Associates, 1990). Furthermore, little evidence was collected to demonstrate that this pedagogical approach truly had an impact on student learning.

By the early 1990s, service learning reemerged at colleges and universities across the country, but this time its goals were more clearly developed. Institutions could not expect learning to occur simply by arranging for students to engage in service activities. Instead, programs had to emphasize service and learning. Moreover, leaders had to assess initiatives' impact on student learning outcomes. The new generation of service learning advocates also recognized that to promote the practice of democratic principles among students, their institutions had to be more democratic in their approaches to education and relationships with community partners. Service learning initiatives were further buttressed by the growing realization that students would need to be able to work collaboratively across cultures in a global society—a skill that service learning programs were ready to develop (Spiezio et al., 2006).

As is the case with civic engagement, service learning suffers from the lack of a simple definition. Questions abound such as, "How is service learning different from community service?" and "Does a service experience have to be directly tied to a formal curriculum to count as service learning?" One of the pioneers of modern service learning, Sigmon (1994), developed a typology to answer these and other questions. In his typology, Sigmon identified four distinct forms of the service learning experience.

Sigmon's (1994) first type of service learning is service *learning* where the emphasis is on traditional classroom learning outcomes. For example, a student may be enrolled in a course on urban education, and as part of the course the student may serve as an assistant to an urban schoolteacher. In this role, however, the student functions only as an observer and does not actively engage with the teacher's students.

In contrast, Sigmon's (1994) second type is *service* learning, where the emphasis is on service. In this context, a student may learn about a particular community issue in a class, such as the rise of teenage pregnancy in rural communities, and be encouraged to do volunteer work on the issue outside the classroom. The class, however, includes limited organized reflection on that experience, and the quality of the student's service activity is not evaluated as part of the course.

Traditional community service or volunteerism would be considered service learning in the third type within Sigmon's (1994) typology because the activity is not tied directly to any learning outcomes or classroom experience. This categorization can be confusing to people unfamiliar with Sigmon's typology because this type of service learning experience is not always associated with the educational mission of the institution.

The fourth and most desirable form of service learning in Sigmon's (1994) typology is *service learning*, with equal emphasis on service and learning as they relate to academic course work. In this scenario, a marketing student might study the challenges associated with promoting a not-for-profit organization's services to indigent populations in a depressed urban environment and then volunteer at the agency to develop a marketing plan. The plan would be devised under the supervision of the agency as well as the classroom professor, and the student would be evaluated on the quality of the plan and its perceived value to the nonprofit.

For this book, an ideal service learning experience refers to the fourth type identified by Sigmon (1994). Beyond *service learning*'s equal emphasis on service and learning and its explicit understanding that course work and engagement are integrated, it also assumes a mutually beneficial partnership exists between the institution of higher learning and the community organization, and both have agreed to measurable outcomes prior to the beginning of the service learning experience.

Research on the impact of service learning on students' learning and civic involvement has grown exponentially over the years. In *How Service-Learning Affects Students,* Astin et al. (2000) discovered after studying a number of service learning programs that this pedagogical method did have a profound impact on several dimensions of student learning. They found that service learning had a positive impact on grade point averages, writing skills, self-efficacy, critical thinking, and a future commitment to community service.

Eyler and Giles (1999) have been leaders in the assessment of service learning and have advanced the field in significant ways. In a research study including over 1,500 college students, they discovered significant evidence of the effects of participating in service learning on achieving a variety of learning outcomes across disciplines. With regard to civic engagement, or the development of citizenship in students, Eyler and Giles's findings demonstrated that students who participated in service learning had an increased willingness to participate in service in the future, a stronger sense of community connectedness, an increased desire for social justice, and an interest in political change.

The research of Daynes and Wygant (2003) has also indicated a connection between service learning and civic engagement. In a study of 2,200 students enrolled in an American heritage course at Brigham Young University, they discovered that although service learning was not necessarily a better predictor of civic engagement than voluntary membership in an association or following politics in the media, it was influential in helping students shape their opinions on how citizens should act in a democracy.

Simons et al. (2010) at Widener University discovered that participation in two different service learning courses influenced student development in areas such as communications, problem-solving, and attitudes regarding social justice issues. This study was one of the largest of its kind, involving 600 students over 6 years, and reinforced the importance of the relevance of service performed to the content of the associated course as well as the significance of the cooperating community organization in helping design the service activities.

A Campus Compact report (Cress et al., 2010) also documented a clear connection between civic engagement and student academic success, particularly increased student access to college. For example, the report cited a study by Gallini and Moely (2003) that demonstrated that college students engaged in intensive service learning experiences scored higher on five key learning outcomes than peers who did not enroll in a service learning course. Several other studies included in the report found links between participation in a service learning course and an increased likelihood of persistence and graduation by students from traditionally underserved populations. Moreover, the report presented evidence that college-level civic engagement activities targeting at-risk high school students through mentoring and tutoring programs improved the likelihood that those students would pursue postsecondary education (Cress et al., 2010).

The evidence is clear that service learning has a positive influence on a wide range of student learning outcomes. Although a single definition of the practice does not seem to exist, three key elements appear to be involved in all meaningful service learning experiences: research, relevance, and reflection. The first element, research, is thoughtful preparation for learning prior to the service experience. In other words, the professor must prepare students for what they will encounter in the community, and students need to understand what the underlying societal issues are that contribute to the problems they will be addressing. This preparation requires advance research on the part of everyone involved, including research on the community partner, the university's history of community engagement, and the political realities associated with the issues to be addressed.

The second element, relevance, is a clear understanding of the relationship between the work students will be doing in the community and the academic subject they are studying. It is not enough to encourage students to commit to community service as part of a course. Rather, the faculty member must ensure that students understand the connection between the objectives of the service activity and the course. Students need to appreciate how their work in the community not only advances their subject knowledge and helps them develop skills to be active citizens, but also how it helps to achieve the objectives of the community organization.

The third element, reflection, may be the most critical for student learning. Eyler and Giles (1999) asserted that effective reflection on service learning must include "the five C's: connection, continuity, context, challenge, and coaching" (p. 183). In Eyler and Giles's model, the faculty member plays a critical role in helping students through their service learning experience. They also noted that the faculty member cannot fulfill this role without broader institutional support.

Several national organizations have been developed to support service learning efforts across the country. In addition to Campus Compact, the Corella and Bertram Bonner Foundation supports over 60 colleges and universities in a service learning network. Starting in 1990 with the Bonner Scholars program at Berea College in Kentucky, the Bonner Foundation has led several national conversations and administered federally funded programs aimed at increasing opportunities for students at its member institutions to engage in high-quality community service initiatives and service learning endeavors.

The federal government has also increased its involvement in service learning. The Clinton administration established the Corporation for National and Community Service, through which the Learn and Serve America program was specifically created to foster and encourage service learning in K–12 educational institutions across the country. The program emphasized the importance of reciprocal relationships between educational institutions and community partners as well as research and the collection of data on the impact of service learning. Under President George W. Bush, the corporation created the President's Higher Education Community Service Honor Roll to recognize colleges and universities for their promotion of community service opportunities for their students.

A number of other organizations, including the National Center for Learning and Citizenship, the National Service-Learning Clearinghouse, and the International Association for Research on Service-Learning and Community Engagement, have also been established to promote service learning. In addition, several academic journals have emerged to promote scholarship on service learning, including the *Journal of Higher Education Outreach and Engagement* and the *Michigan Journal of Community Service Learning*. The work of such organizations, agencies, and publications provides evidence that service learning positively affects student learning and longer-term civic involvement. It also suggests that service learning as a pedagogical tool as well as an educational movement will remain an important part of the higher education agenda for decades to come.

Engaging the Community Through Democratic Partnerships

A traditional way to view a college or university's engagement with society has been through the lens of town–gown relations. Despite the myriad benefits associated with the presence of a college or university in a community, colleges (gown) and their communities (town) continuously have to work to resolve the conflicts that arise when a college and its community have differing goals and interests.

Conflicts between colleges and local municipalities have existed in the United States since the establishment of the colonial colleges. Whether it is concern over the behavior of students and whose responsibility it is to monitor them or the physical growth of institutions to meet surging student demand, or the concern over intercollegiate athletic events and the thousands of spectators that flow into a community to watch their favorite college team, town–gown relations are complicated and require considerable time and effort on the part of every stakeholder to resolve difficult issues.

The literature on higher education is replete with examples of colleges and universities and their relationships with the communities where they reside (Gallo & Davis, 2008; Harris, 2011; Harris & Santilli, 2021; Hartley et al., 2006; Maurrasse, 2001). These relationships, positive and negative, have been categorized under a broad range of headings, such as community partnerships, town–gown relationships, and neighborhood collaborations. The nature of the relationship—and, therefore, the type of engagement—vary according to the history, current circumstances, and economic conditions of the institution and its community.

Many U.S. institutions of higher education have become increasingly involved in local community issues that can be placed in four broad categories: economic development, community development, public education initiatives, and programs designed to address social inequities. Economic development refers to universities' efforts to form partnerships with local municipalities, businesses, financial institutions, and federal and state agencies to encourage and promote the economic well-being of a region or city. These initiatives can take the form of workforce development, targeted purchasing, capital investments, neighborhood revitalization projects, corporate research, and the development or even creation of business incubators to encourage and support entrepreneurial ventures.

Community development typically includes efforts of college or university administrators to work with government officials and agencies as well as community-based organizations to address problems that affect the living conditions (e.g., housing, violence, homelessness) of the community where the university is located. Likewise, public education initiatives focus on how an institution can partner with the local public school district and other organizations to improve the quality of K–12 education. The aim of this work is to improve student learning outcomes and prepare a greater percentage of students from underrepresented groups for college-level study.

Programs at colleges and universities to address social inequities have existed since the early days of higher education in America. However, in 2020, in the aftermath of several high-profile incidents of police brutality against Black citizens and an increase in racially motivated acts of violence against Black, Indigenous, and people of color (BIPOC) populations across the United States, the need for community reconciliation and healing became paramount. Many institutions of higher learning became more deeply engaged in conversations with their local communities about what role they could play in addressing societal inequities stemming from generations of structural racism.

To articulate their commitment to advancing these four broad issues, leaders of colleges and universities, particularly urban and metropolitan institutions, are increasingly describing their institutions as place bound or anchored to a particular location. According to a report on university engagement by Hodges and Dubb (2012), officials of anchor institutions who wish to enhance the long-term viability of their communities can play many roles, but typically their institution follows one of three patterns: facilitator, leader, or convener.

When a college or university acts as a facilitator, the institution works to connect faculty members and students with local community organizations through academic service learning opportunities. In addition, it arranges conversations between various organizations to build capacity to address societal issues (Hodges & Dubb, 2012). Usually these institutions have supportive administrative and academic leadership but limited resources to contribute as a major investor in significant community development projects.

A college or university is considered a leader when it attempts to address a specific societal concern, such as crime or failing schools, by taking a leadership role in discussions about the issue and making a significant financial commitment to efforts to resolve it (Hodges & Dubb, 2012). In this context, the institution's administration may take a very active and visible role in addressing a particular topic. It may also use its influence to attract additional partners and resources.

An institution functions as a convener when it builds alliances with local organizations, government agencies, and other partners to set an agenda focused on long-term strategies for improvement of living conditions in particular neighborhoods, establishment of community health goals, or encouragement of economic development (Hodges & Dubb, 2012). In this situation, administrators view partnering with the community as part of their college or university's mission. The institution may invest its own resources to advance the initiative, but usually only if others are willing to work with the institution on the issue.

At any time, a college or university may be playing one or all three roles through engagement in any number of activities. Syracuse University is an example of an institution that has served as a facilitator, leader, and convener in community and economic development. Syracuse exhibited its commitment to being an anchor institution in several ways. Under the leadership of former Chancellor Nancy Cantor, Syracuse's anchor mission was articulated through its vision, "Scholarship in Action" (Hodges & Dubb, 2012, p. 141). Syracuse's vision included "forging bold, imaginative, reciprocal, and sustained engagements" locally and globally (p. 141). Members of the university community engaged in activities ranging from "participating in neighborhood revitalization projects, implementing economic inclusion principles by hiring local contractors, and changing tenure and promotion guidelines to support engaged scholarship by the faculty" (p. 98).

Hostos Community College, a two-year institution created specifically to serve the poor, mostly Latinx South Bronx community in New York City, has focused its involvement in the neighborhoods that provide the vast majority of their students. For example, in response to an identified need in the community to address issues of domestic violence and the spread of HIV and AIDS among immigrant populations, the college created a women's center to coordinate outreach by faculty and students to the community and to serve as a portal for local residents to connect to the college (Maurrasse, 2001). Years later, because of funding cuts, the college worked with local nonprofits to ensure that these efforts continued to be supported. In these ways the college served as an anchor to the community.

After years of frustration in dealing with the bureaucracy and changing leadership (four different superintendents in 6 years) of the lowest performing school district in Pennsylvania, Chester-Upland, officials at Widener University made the bold decision to open their own charter school. The Widener Partnership Charter School was the first of its kind in Pennsylvania and was the outgrowth of years of discussions and failed negotiations between Chester-Upland and the university to address educational reform issues throughout the district. When the university turned to the community for input and feedback, it found both strong support of and strong resistance to the idea of a charter school. Once the school opened and produced the best statewide testing results in the district in its first few years of existence, the school gained broader support, but it took strong and sustained commitment as well as political resolve from the university's administration and faculty to make it work (Ledoux et al., 2011).

California State University, Fresno, engaged with its community through a series of university-led initiatives and partnerships with key regional and state stakeholders. One of its largest projects was the creation of the Regional Jobs Initiative, a public–private partnership aimed at improving the economy of the surrounding eight-county region, known as the San Joaquin Valley, by connecting the university with community and business leaders to create sustainable economic growth through broad-based job creation (Welty & Lukens, 2009). The university became a leader and a convener by bringing together business, community, and government leaders to set a course of action.

One example of the results of this university collaboration was the identification of 10 industry clusters with strong potential for growth in the region. As of 2008 over 600 business leaders had been involved in the clusters and provided direction for the development of training to meet workforce needs (Welty & Lukens, 2009). It is important to note that Fresno's president, John Welty, was a driving force in this initiative, using his considerable political connections and influence to help this project succeed.

A number of national movements have emerged over the years to help colleges and universities make sense of these relationships in view of their particular mission or location. Most of these movements coalesce around specific institution types or within particular Carnegie classifications. As noted previously, some of the best examples of this work have revolved around urban universities and their efforts to deal with the changing economic, social, and political landscape of urban America. For example, the Coalition of Urban and Metropolitan Universities was established in 1990 to use the power of its campuses in education, research, and service to enhance the communities where they are located. Originally made up exclusively of public universities, today the coalition includes public and private institutions whose administrators are focused on fully understanding the distinctiveness of their institution's mission through conferences, a journal, research projects, creation of a policy agenda, and regular networking opportunities.

Another movement in the 21st century has been the growing recognition by institutions of higher education that they have a responsibility to be an anchor for their local community. The word *anchor* was originally used to describe a type of institution, typically not-for-profit, that was place-bound and could not leave a community. In 2001, the Aspen Institute published a study defining *anchor institutions* as ones with "significant infrastructure investment in a specific community and are therefore unlikely to move out of that community" (Fulbright-Anderson et al., 2001, p. 1). This definition could be applied to any long-standing not-for-profit institution in an urban community, but mostly it has been attached to universities and hospitals (known as Eds and Meds), which typically have large footprints in a community.

In 2008, a national task force of higher education scholars and practitioners from across the country was established to advise the U.S. Department of HUD on how it could have a greater impact and leverage the resources of anchor institutions in urban communities (Marga, n.d.). The task force created a toolkit for institutions that were seeking to expand their roles as anchors in their local communities. The following year the Anchor Institution Task Force (AITF) was created to support the efforts of institutional leaders, scholars, and practitioners to navigate the complex issues associated with promoting democratic ideals in such environments (Marga, n.d.).

In the following decade, several colleges and universities started identifying as place-based anchor institutions, which reframed how the institution saw its role in the community. Augsburg University, in Minneapolis, Minnesota, offers one example of this work. Under the leadership of its president, Paul C. Pribbenow, Augsburg collaborated with multiple partners, including a local medical center and other enduring community organizations, to create the Cedar-Riverside Partnership and the Central Corridor Anchor Partnership (Marga, n.d.). These partnerships focused on "neighborhood safety, transportation, workforce, youth programmes, transportation, infrastructure and place-making" (Pribbenow, 2021, p. 124). In the aftermath of the killing of George Floyd by Minneapolis police in May 2020 and the social unrest that followed, Augsburg relied on those established partnerships to help rebuild the community through greater engagement. For example, Augsburg partnered with the Minnesota Urban Debate League (MNUDL, n.d.) to bring the organization to campus so that MNUDL's limited resources could be used more effectively to provide staffing and programming to a community much in need of healing (Pribbenow, 2021).

Not all anchor universities take as comprehensive an approach as Augsburg University. Some may only focus on a few key initiatives. According to Ehlenz (2018), universities that serve as neighborhood anchors select and prioritize place-based initiatives depending on their size, mission, and available resources, but most focus on socioeconomic practices. In a study of 22 U.S. universities' approaches to their work as anchor institutions, Ehlenz (2018) looked at the action agenda of each institution and asked the universities to report on their activities in seven areas of neighborhood revitalization that were not strictly part of a campus expansion. The seven categories included "housing, commercial, economic, public amenities, public safety, K–12 public school, and community service initiatives" (Ehlenz, 2018, p. 9). Ehlenz (2018) found that "nine institutions were engaged in high diversification approaches (with six or more activities), 10 were moderately diversified in their approaches, and three had a low diversification approach to their anchor work (with two or fewer activities)" (p. 13).

The Future of the Engaged College or University in a Post-Pandemic World

Benson and Harkavy (1991) once wrote that "universities can no longer try to remain an oasis of affluence in a desert of urban despair" (p. 14). While much of the focus of this chapter has been on higher education institutions in urban communities, in the aftermath of a worldwide recession, a global pandemic, increased social unrest over structural racism, and a widening political divide in the United States, it is important to recognize that "despair" and the struggle to promote democratic ideals are also issues for institutions in rural communities and midsized cities across the country.

Harris and Santilli (2021) proposed that the major crises that emerged in 2020—particularly the global pandemic with its disproportionate impact on BIPOC communities, increased violence against AAPIs, and renewed violence against Black Americans—present higher education with a "liminal" moment (p. 129) and an obligation to reconsider its role in addressing these issues. The obligation to do this work is there for all colleges and universities, whether located in a rural community, a metropolitan suburb, or an urban environment.

The global pandemic's devastating impact on communities of color in the United States exposed severe inequities in access to health care. According to the Centers for Disease Control and Prevention (CDC, 2021), between March 1, 2020, and April 24, 2021, non-Hispanic American Indians and Alaska Natives were 3.3 times more likely to be hospitalized with COVID-19 than White Americans, and Black Americans and Latinx Americans were almost three times more likely to be hospitalized with the virus than White Americans. These disparities led many colleges and universities to consider ways they could ensure that medical treatments, access to testing, and vaccines were expanded to reach these populations. For example, the University of San Diego (USD) has partnered with local county health officials to open a community testing site for COVID-19 on its campus and deployed a mobile vaccination station to serve a predominantly Latinx community in San Diego (Harris & Santilli, 2021; A. Pulido, personal communication, April 2, 2021). Similarly, clinical faculty at the Yale School of Medicine served as frontline health-care providers, treating patients at the Yale New Haven Hospital (Maurrasse, 2021).

The pandemic has also had a disproportionately negative impact on economically challenged communities (World Bank Group, 2020). This economic downturn led to major cuts in funding for higher education, which meant there was less spending available for anchor institutions to dedicate to their work in local communities. Despite this challenge, some institutions discovered new ways to partner with the community that did not require significant funding. One example was provided earlier in this chapter, when Augsburg University shared university space with a community partner so the partner could spend its funds on programming rather than overhead costs (see MNUDL, n.d.). Another example from the pandemic was when USD faculty and students continued to provide critical support functions remotely to community partners. Services such as "marketing and communications support, data analysis and program impact, compiling court briefs for asylum seekers" (Maurrasse, 2021, p. 74), and other activities necessary to fulfill the missions of these vital community organizations were provided despite limited in-person connections during the pandemic.

Throughout this book, we have made the argument that to prosper in the 21st century, institutions of higher learning need to be mission driven; adaptable to environmental changes promote democratic ideals; and ultimately models of inclusion, equity, and positive social change. However, is it reasonable to expect that a college or university be held to a higher standard in democratic engagement and the challenges associated with coming to consensus over difficult issues in all that it does internally and externally? Given the challenges associated with community engagement due to conflicting goals and interests of a university and its myriad participating community stakeholders, it could be argued that no one should expect these institutions to act democratically in everything they do.

Truly democratic partnerships between higher education institutions and community partners are desirable, but many colleges and universities fear committing to a democratic approach to engagement because they know that sustainable partnerships take time to evolve. Over time, leaders move on, priorities change, new challenges emerge, and funding opportunities fluctuate. Within this ever-changing environment, is it realistic to expect democratic engagement with stakeholders whose priorities and visions for the future may not be consistent with those of the institution?

Authors have increasingly called for a rethinking of the approach colleges and universities take in engagement in their communities (see, e.g., Colby et al., 2003; Hartley et al., 2006; Maurrasse, 2001). Their reasoning is that it is not enough for leaders of institutions of higher learning to express their support for reciprocal, democratic alliances and then do what is in their best interest, in the end justifying such action by asserting they had no choice but to act unilaterally. Rather, colleges and universities need to make a commitment and be held accountable to do the heavy lifting necessary to build trust and true democratic partnerships because in the long run it is better for both the institution and the community. Furthermore, if college and university officials wish to encourage their students to become responsible citizens equipped to work collaboratively in a global society, it is paramount that higher education institutions model this behavior.

Hartley et al. (2010) called for a deeper examination of the implications of democratic civic engagement and what it will require of colleges and universities in the future. First, they proposed that administrators of institutions of higher learning must accept that these institutions do have "a responsibility to our democracy" (p. 292). Second, they suggested that true democratic engagement will require a change in how students are taught, so that greater emphasis is placed on demonstrating how democracy works by creating more reciprocal relationships between students and faculty. Furthermore, they argued that a new type of collaboration between an institution and the communities it serves needs to be developed. This collaboration should be one in which the future is cocreated, and all partners are viewed as bringing valuable expertise and resources to the table. This approach contrasts with the traditional view in which academic knowledge is valued over community-based knowledge (Hartley et al., 2010).

Fostering democratic partnerships to address society's most pressing issues has local and global implications. As Harkavy et al. (2021) stated in their analysis of the role of higher education in the wake of the pandemic and the ensuing global crises, "There has never been a greater need for democracy" (p. 22) or a better time for "re-emphasizing the role of higher education institutions as societal actors for the public good" (p. 21). In the United States, where less than 10% of U.S. college students study abroad at any time, the most likely place where students will have the opportunity to address societal issues and practice the skills necessary to function in a democratic society is in the community surrounding their campus. Therefore, it is the responsibility of colleges and universities to model democratic practices in their anchor work with local community partners, as well as to provide their students with opportunities to prepare for their future role as citizens by engaging them on and off campus in structured, meaningful, and truly democratic learning opportunities.

References

American Presidency Project. (2021, January 22). *Voter turnout in presidential elections: 1828–2016.* https://www.presidency.ucsb.edu/statistics/data/voter-turnout-in-presidential-elections

Astin, A. W., Sax, L. J., Ikeda, E. K., & Yee, J. A. (2000, January). *Executive summary: How service learning affects students.* University of California, Los Angeles, Graduate School of Education and Information Studies, Higher Education Research Institute. http://heri.ucla.edu/PDFs/rhowas.pdf

Benson, L., & Harkavy, I. (1991). Progressing beyond the welfare state: A neo-Deweyan strategy. *Universities and Community Schools, 2*(1–2).

Benson, L., Harkavy, I., & Puckett, J. (2007). *Dewey's dream: Universities and democracies in an age of education reform.* Temple University Press.

Berkin, C. (2002). *A brilliant solution: Inventing the American Constitution.* Houghton Mifflin Harcourt.

Boyer, E. (1990). *Scholarship reconsidered: Priorities of the professoriate.* Carnegie Foundation for the Advancement of Teaching.

Boyer, E. (1996). The scholarship of engagement. *Journal of Public Outreach*, *1*(1), 11–20. https://doi.org/10.2307/3824459

Campus Compact. (n.d.). *Members*. https://compact.org/who-we-are/our-coalition/members/

Cantor, N. (2016, April 6). *Reconnecting with a shared public mission in sharing governance* [Paper presentation]. The Roles and Responsibilities of Faculty: A Conversation with University Presidents. Philadelphia, PA. https://newark.rutgers.edu/sites/default/files/ncantor-upenn-faculty_senate-panel-april-2016

Cantor, N. & Englot, P. (2016). Expanding educational access: A critical anchor institution mission. *Journal on Institutions and Communities*, *1*, 4–10. https://www.margainc.com/wp-content/uploads/2017/05/AITF_Journal_2016_Vol_1.pdf

Carnegie Foundation for the Advancement of Teaching & Center for Information and Research on Civic Learning and Engagement. (2006). *Higher education: Civic mission and civic effects*. Carnegie Foundation for the Advancement of Teaching.

Center for Information and Research on Civic Learning and Engagement. (2020, November 25). *Election week 2020: Young people increase turnout, lead Biden to victory*. https://circle.tufts.edu/latest-research/election-week-2020

Center for Information and Research on Civic Learning and Engagement. (2021, April 29). *Half of youth voted in 2020, an 11-point increase from 2016*. https://circle.tufts.edu/latest-research/half-youth-voted-2020-11-point-increase-2016

Centers for Disease Control and Prevention. (2021, May 26). *Risk for COVID-19 infection, hospitalization, and death by race/ethnicity*. https://www.cdc.gov/coronavirus/2019-ncov/covid-data/investigations-discovery/hospitalization-death-by-race-ethnicity.html

Clift, V. A. (1948). The role of higher education in transmitting democratic ideals into behavior patterns. *The Journal of Negro Education*, *17*(2), 134–140. https://doi.org/10.2307/2966054

Colby, A., Ehrlich, T., Beaumont, E., & Stephens, J. (2003). *Educating citizens: Preparing America's undergraduates for lives of moral and civic responsibility*. Jossey-Bass.

Commission on Economic and Community Engagement. (2020, February 4). *2020 Carnegie Community Engagement Classification recipients announced*. Association of Public & Land-Grant Universities. https://www.aplu.org/news-and-media/blog/2020-carnegie-community-engagement-classification-recipients-announced#:~:text=One%2Dhundred%20nineteen%20U.S.%20colleges,for%20the%20Advancement%20of%20Teaching

Cress, C. M., Burack, C., Giles, D. E., Jr., Elkins, J., & Stevens, M. C. (2010). *A promising connection: Increasing college access and success through civic engagement*. Campus Compact. https://compact.org/resource-posts/a-promising-connection-increasing-college-access-and-success-through-civic-engagement/

Daynes, G., & Wygant, S. (2003). Service-learning as a pathway to civic engagement: A comparative study. *Metropolitan Universities*, *14*(3), 84–96. http://journals.iupui.edu/index.php/muj/article/view/20123

Desilver, D. (2020, November 3). *In past elections, U.S. trailed most developed countries in voter turnout*. Pew Research Center. https://www.pewresearch.org/

fact-tank/2020/11/03/in-past-elections-u-s-trailed-most-developed-countries-in-voter-turnout/

Dewey, J. (1916). *Democracy and education: An introduction to the philosophy of education.* The Free Press.

Ehlenz, M. M. (2018). Defining university anchor institution strategies: Comparing theory to practice. *Planning Theory & Practice, 19*(1), 74–92. https://doi.org/10.1080/14649357.2017.1406980

Ellis, J. J. (2007). *American creation: Triumphs and tragedies at the founding of the republic.* Knopf.

Eyler, J., & Giles, D. E., Jr. (1999). *Where's the learning in service-learning?* Jossey-Bass.

Fulbright-Anderson, K., Auspos, P., & Anderson, A. (2001). *Community involvement in partnerships with educational institutions, medical centers, and utility companies.* Annie E. Casey Foundation. https://staging.community-wealth.org/sites/clone.community-wealth.org/files/downloads/paper-fulbright-et-al.pdf

Gallini, S., & Moely, B. (2003). Service-learning and engagement, academic challenge, and retention. *Michigan Journal of Community Service Learning, 10*(1), 5–14. http://hdl.handle.net/2027/spo.3239521.0010.101

Gallo, R., & Davis, R. (2008). Research on the impact of HBCUs on African American communities. *Metropolitan Universities, 19*(2), 102–120. https://journals.iupui.edu/index.php/muj/article/view/20356

Giles, D. E., Jr., & Eyler, J. (1994). The theoretical roots of service-learning in John Dewey: Towards a theory of service-learning. *Michigan Journal of Community Service Learning, 1*(1), 77–85. https://digitalcommons.unomaha.edu/slceslgen/150/

Harris, J. T. (2011). How Widener developed a culture of civic engagement and fulfilled its promise as a leading metropolitan university. In M. W. Ledoux, S. C. Wilhite, & P. Silver (Eds.), *Civic engagement and service learning in a metropolitan university: Multiple approaches and perspectives* (pp. 1–12). Nova Science.

Harris, J. T., & Santilli, N. R. (2021). Higher education should embrace this liminal moment because there will be no "new normal." In S. Bergan, T. Gallagher, I. Harkavy, R. Munck, & H. van't Land (Eds.), *Higher education's response to the Covid-19 pandemic: Building a more sustainable and democratic future* (pp. 129–136). Council of Europe.

Hartley, M., Harkavy, I., & Benson, L. (2006). Building Franklin's truly democratic, engaged university: Twenty years of practice at the University of Pennsylvania. *Metropolitan Universities, 17*(3), 22–37. https://journals.iupui.edu/index.php/muj/article/view/20276

Hartley, M., Saltmarsh, J., & Clayton, P. (2010). Is the civic engagement movement changing higher education? *British Journal of Educational Studies, 58*(4), 391–406. https://doi.org/10.1080/00071005.2010.527660

Hodges, R. A., & Dubb, S. (2012). *The road half traveled: University engagement at a crossroads.* Michigan State University Press.

Jacoby, B., & Associates. (1996). *Service-learning in higher education: Concepts and practices.* Jossey-Bass.

Jacoby, B., & Associates. (2009). *Civic engagement in higher education: Concepts and practices*. Jossey-Bass.

Josephson, J. J. (2020). Higher education and democratic public life. *New Political Science, 42*(2), 155–170. https://doi.org/10.1080/07393148.2020.1773726

Kendall, J. C., & Associates. (Eds.). (1990). *Combining service and learning: A resource book for community and public service* (Vol. 1). National Society for Internships and Experiential Education.

Kiesa, A., Orlowski, A. P., Levine, P. L., Both, D., Kirby, E. H., Lopez, M. H., & Marcelo, K. B. (2007). *Millennials talk politics: A study of college student political engagement*. Center for Information and Research on Civic Learning and Engagement. https://eric.ed.gov/?id=ED498899

Ledoux, M. W., Wilhite, S. C., & Silver, P. (Eds.). (2011). *Civic engagement and service learning in a metropolitan university: Multiple approaches and perspectives*. Nova Science.

Marga. (n.d.). *What is the Anchor Institutions Task Force (AITF)?* Anchor Institutions Task Force. https://www.margainc.com/aitf/

Maurrasse, D. J. (2001). *Beyond the campus: How colleges and universities form partnerships with their communities*. Routledge.

Maurrasse, D. J. (2021). Challenges to US higher education in performing local missions during and after the Covid-19 pandemic. In S. Bergan, T. Gallagher, I. Harkavy, R. Munck, & H. van't Land (Eds.), *Higher education's response to the Covid-19 pandemic: Building a more sustainable and democratic future* (pp. 67–77). Council of Europe.

National Commission on Excellence in Education. (1983). *A nation at risk: The imperative for educational reform*. http://www2.ed.gov/pubs/NatAtRisk/index.html

Minnesota Urban Debate League. (n.d.). *Home page*. https://www.augsburg.edu/urbandebateleague/

Newman, F. (1985). *Higher education and the American resurgence: A Carnegie Foundation special report*. Princeton University Press.

Pribbenow, P. C. (2021). Public work and reclaiming the democratic impulse of higher education in these pandemic times. In S. Bergan, T. Gallagher, I. Harkavy, R. Munck, & H. van't Land (Eds.), *Higher education's response to the Covid-19 pandemic: Building a more sustainable and democratic future* (pp. 121–127). Council of Europe.

Public Purpose Institute. (2021). *Community engagement classification (U.S.)*. https://public-purpose.org/initiatives/carnegie-elective-classifications/community-engagement-classification-u-s/

Putnam, R. D. (1995). Bowling alone: America's declining social capital. *Journal of Democracy, 6*(1), 65–78. https://doi.org/10.1353/jod.1995.0002

Putnam, R. D. (2000). *Bowling alone: The collapse and revival of American community*. Simon & Schuster.

Rudolph, F. (1962). *The American college and university: A history*. Random House.

Sax, L. J. (2004). Citizenship development and the American college student. In J. C. Dalton, T. R. Russell, & S. Kline (Eds.), *Assessing character outcomes in college* (New Directions for Institutional Research, no. 122, pp. 65–80). Wiley. https://doi.org/10.1002/ir.110

Schaul, K., Rabinowitz, K., & Mellnik, T. (2020, November 5). 2020 turnout is the highest in over a century. *The Washington Post.* https://www.washingtonpost.com/graphics/2020/elections/voter-turnout/

Sigmon, R. L. (1994). *Linking service with learning.* Council of Independent Colleges.

Simons, L., Fehr, L., Blank, N., Connell, H., DeSimone, R., Georganas, G. M., & Thomas, D. (2010). A comparative analysis of academic service-learning programs: Students' and recipients' teachers' perspectives. *Metropolitan Universities, 20*(3), 77–92. https://journals.iupui.edu/index.php/muj/article/view/20403

Spiezio, K. E., Baker, K. Q., & Boland, K. (2006). General education and civic engagement: An empirical analysis of pedagogical possibilities. *Journal of General Education, 54*(4), 273–292. https://doi.org/10.1353/jge.2006.0012

Timsit, A. (2020, November 9). *2020's record voter turnout in the US is still lower than many other countries.* Quartz. https://qz.com/1926959/2020-us-record-voter-turnout-is-still-lower-than-other-countries/

Welty, J. D., & Lukens, M. (2009). Partnering with state government to transform a region. *Metropolitan Universities, 20*(1), 59–74. https://journals.iupui.edu/index.php/muj/article/view/20380

Wingspread Group on Higher Education. (1993). *An American imperative: Higher expectations for higher education.* Johnson Foundation.

World Bank Group. (2020). *The COVID-19 crisis response: Supporting tertiary education for continuity, adaption, and innovation.* http://pubdocs.worldbank.org/en/621991586463915490/WB-Tertiary-Ed-and-Covid-19-Crisis-for-public-use-April-9.pdf

Zukin, C., Keeter, S., Andolina, M., Jenkins, K., & Delli Carpini, M. X. (2006). *A new engagement? Political participation, civic life, and the changing American citizen.* Oxford University Press.

IO

TRUSTEESHIP AND
LAY GOVERNANCE

T he theme of this book is that the adoption of four essential principles
contributes significantly to a college or university's success: adherence to institutional mission; skill at adapting to environmental
changes; seeking to promote democratic ideals; and becoming models of
inclusion, equity, and positive social change. These themes collectively
represent a fundamental pursuit of an alignment of organizational goals
and values with educational purposes and the consequential benefits to
society for which the institution was originally created. Colleges and universities serve the public good as influential centers of intellectual, social,
cultural, and economic development. The importance society ascribes to
higher education and the benefits derived from it cannot be overstated, yet
the ultimate responsibility for the operation, growth, and success of our
nation's colleges and universities falls not to professionally trained administrators but to a special group of volunteers: the individuals who make up
each institution's (or a system's) board of trustees.

Boards of trustees hold in trust the financial, physical, and intellectual
assets of the institution, a responsibility that cannot be delegated to others.
Boards must approve and execute the institution's mission, interpret the
institution to its publics, and span boundaries between and among internal and external constituencies served by the organization. As Novak and
Johnston (2005) explained:

> Trustees are guardians of the public trust in that boards of trustees, rather
> than government officials, govern our colleges and universities. They are
> responsible for ensuring that the institutions will serve the purpose for
> which they were designed, that they will fulfill their missions and serve the
> public good by creating an educated citizenry, contributing to the crea-
> tion of knowledge, and preserving cultural heritages. [Trustees] serve as the
> bridge between higher education and society. (p. 89)

That we have entrusted the welfare of these complex and highly professional-ized organizations to a group of volunteers who quite often lack the academic credentials or administrative experiences in education to render informed judgment over the affairs of the academy strikes some as inappropriate. For example, Brown University President Francis Wayland asked in 1855, "How can colleges prosper, directed by men, very good men to be sure, but who know about every other thing except about education?" (as cited in Rudolph, 1962, p. 172). Despite such doubts, this model of governance is based in centuries-old tradition and utilitarian purpose that have actually reinforced and nurtured the unstated social contract that exists between colleges and universities and the society they serve.

A board must adhere to its institution's mission, interpret the environ-ment to the institution, and ensure strategic linkages to the many constitu-encies it serves. It is unrealistic, however, to assume that volunteer board members—who often lack intimate knowledge of the nuances of shared governance, most often are not educators themselves, and convene in board meetings only infrequently—can fully understand and execute decisions in the best interests of the college or university they serve without some mecha-nism of expert support. That support is most often manifested through the institution's president.

The central relationship for effective lay governance and institutional operation, therefore, is found between the board and the institution's (or system's) chief executive officer (CEO). One way to view this relationship is through the lens that a board has only one employee—the president or chancellor whom they select. This relationship represents the fulcrum on which institutional governance primarily hinges, and the literature on boards of trustees is replete with references to the criticality of the symbiosis between the two. Any discussions of lay governance and the service that volunteer boards render to higher education are essentially also discussions of presiden-tial leadership and the interaction that exists, or in some cases does not exist, between a board and a president.

This chapter provides an overview of trusteeship and the unique and important role lay governance plays in U.S. higher education. This review deals primarily with the role of volunteer boards in independent and public not-for-profit institutional settings rather than corporate board structures and issues associated with proprietary and for-profit institutional models. We begin with an overview of the historical foundations on which lay governance in U.S. higher education was built, from the earliest colonial col-leges through the emergence of public institutions. Key differences between private and public boards are addressed, along with the role of multicam-pus coordinating boards. Contemporary board models and characteristics are also explored briefly, as are typical roles and responsibilities of trustees. We then address the issue of board effectiveness, especially relationships that exist between a board and its institution's president. Finally, we review challenges facing governing boards today, as higher education adapts to changing economic and governmental conditions.

Historical Foundations of Lay Governance

The concept of lay governance is a societal and organizational manifestation of the value that people have placed on education over the ages. It answers this fundamental question: If education serves as the primary mechanism to advance humankind, then who should be responsible for ensuring the fulfillment of that purpose? The answer to this question has varied, depending on the specific goals of education over the millennia, the types of organizations created to achieve those goals, and the historical contexts that have shaped human intellectual expression.

The importance of educational institutions to the advancement of society required a body charged with performing fiduciary oversight of them, entrusted with the responsibility of perpetuating human progress through these institutions. The presence of a fiduciary implies there is also a beneficiary. Throughout the history of higher education, that beneficiary has been society itself, while the role of the fiduciary has been ascribed to an institution's governing board. The terms *governing board*, *board of trustees*, *directors*, *regents*, *visitors*, or *overseers* are often used interchangeably to denote fiduciary groups who are legally responsible for lay governance. The term *lay* is derived from the Greek word *laos*, which means "people" and refers to individuals who are not clergy or professionally trained in a specific discipline. Lay governance, therefore, involves a group of nonprofessionals performing a public responsibility.

Lay governance originated in the early Middle Ages in Europe and was developed to provide a system of checks and balances to thwart the formation of an intellectual monopoly and to preserve the public's interest as a counterbalance to faculty self-interest. The period following the Protestant Reformation of the 16th century was most noteworthy in the development of educational governance structures that served as future models in the North American colonial colleges of the 17th and 18th centuries. Prototypes of early American colonial boards emerged in Italy, the Netherlands, and Scotland following the Reformation, when lay leaders replaced clergy in the control and exercise of religious policy (Zwingle, 1980). Dutch Protestants in Leyden created governance mechanisms that were important precursors to modern lay boards. According to Duryea and Williams (2000),

> In effect, Leyden and three subsequent Dutch universities set a pattern of organization that anticipated much of the organization later employed in American higher education. The curators represented the government and, at the same time, conveyed to it the interests of the colleges. They were chosen from the higher official ranks, renowned lawyers and members of parliament, not unlike the American pattern. (p. 74)

The U.S. pattern of lay governance emerged with the founding of Harvard College in 1636 and served as a precedent for governance structures at subsequent colleges and universities. Hofstadter (1955) noted three factors that contributed to this development. First, strong Roman Catholic clerical influence over medieval society and its institutions was supplanted by greater lay control with the rise of the Protestant Reformation, a trend that carried over to the New World when European settlers first arrived. Just as authority in the fledging churches of the colonies was shared between laypeople and clerics, the early Protestant-formed colleges also followed this model. Second, the very limited resources of that era required the colonial colleges to embrace the involvement of wealthy merchants and people of societal prominence to support their educational mission and growth. Third, unlike the established universities of Europe, which enjoyed an influential and highly learned faculty, early American colleges employed relatively young people as teachers, and they viewed teaching as a means of ascension to more lucrative and influential positions in society. Oversight of these young teachers was thereby relegated to laypeople of greater maturity and stature, in cooperation with a college's president.

Central to any discussion of the history of lay governance is the nexus between public and private purposes and the exercise of authority in the oversight of an academic institution. It was emphasized earlier that societal benefits served as the impetus for the founding and growth of higher education institutions in the American colonial period, and the earliest trustees were empowered to ensure that colonial colleges fulfilled this role. These institutions operated within a broader societal context despite their decidedly sectarian affiliation:

> Neither the colonial governors nor the legislators looked upon the colleges as private associations removed from control by the state; rather, they considered them to be public agencies. Leaders of that time had no basis for thinking otherwise; English law had yet to recognize a distinction between public and private corporations. (Duryea & Williams, 2000, p. 64)

That distinction effectively changed in 1819 when the U.S. Supreme Court handed down a landmark decision in *Dartmouth College v. Woodward* (1819), better known as the Dartmouth College Case. The Supreme Court ruled in favor of Dartmouth, affirming the authority of its independent governing board in overseeing the institution. That seminal decision established a distinction between not-for-profit private corporations (e.g., private colleges and universities) and public sector institutions, which had been created and funded by state governments (Hendrickson, 1999). The case also supported the legitimacy, and ultimately the permanent and subsequent practice, of lay governance in both private and public U.S. higher education.

Since the Dartmouth case, the practice of lay governance has evolved substantially as higher education itself has changed. This evolutionary process has been marked by periods of significant tension as boards and their members have adjusted to monumental changes to U.S. higher education, such as the rise of the public university; the maturation and changing role of the faculty in institutional decision-making, with its subsequent challenges to lay authority; and the demise of the doctrine of *in loco parentis* as a more consumerist and pluralistic society supplanted older, more traditional norms of authority on campus. A major consequence of these changes has been a shift in the scope of interactional relationships required of boards of trustees. Early boards largely served in an authoritarian manner, unencumbered by challenges or demands from others within and beyond their institution. Today's boards of trustees must be adept boundary spanners in the context of shared governance, responding to constant internal and external challenges to an institution's mission, direction, and fiscal viability—over which trustees hold final control. The consequent increasing difficulty of trusteeship has prompted greater attention and devotion to the understanding and improvement of the role in recent decades. Whereas the earlier literature on lay governance appeared to center on a board's roles and responsibilities, later scholarship has demonstrated greater concern for issues of practice and effectiveness. In addition, unlike earlier lay boards, which were often viewed as honorific, college and university boards today are held to a higher level of scrutiny and personal accountability for the overall success of the institutions entrusted to their care.

Public, Private, and Coordinating Boards

Three primary types of governing boards are predominant. They include single-campus boards that oversee an individual public or private institution. Other boards govern multicampus systems in a state, often in conjunction with a single systemwide executive.[1] Finally, most states now also maintain coordinating boards or councils that serve a broader state policy function and operate above or alongside individual or system governing boards. As their name implies, they play an organizing, rather than governing, role and are linked to a state's legislative and/or gubernatorial educational agenda. A relatively recent addition to higher education governance (largely emerging in the 1960s and 1970s), coordinating boards differ significantly between the states in terms of their purpose, responsibility, structure, and authority, but most share in some budgeting and resource oversight, especially in matters of implementing budget policy to meet specific state purposes. (See chapter 7, this volume, for an extended discussion of public boards and state oversight of higher education, including community colleges.)

Some significant differences exist between boards of private, independent institutions and public institutions. Most notable is the selection method for board members:

> Self-perpetuating boards (those that select themselves) govern most independent, private institutions of higher education. Trustees determine the structure and stature of the board and select individuals to fit institutional or system-wide needs. Most public college or university boards, on the other hand, serve explicitly for and at the request of an external public constituent or set of constituents. (Longanecker, 2006, pp. 95–96)

The greatest challenge for public board members is the political environment in which they operate, which often influences their selection to the board in the first place. Appointment to a public board is most often either via public election by the citizens of the state (or subunit) or through the state governor's office, which may be based on the meritorious qualifications of an appointee or as a function of political patronage. Community colleges, which in some states are affiliated with counties or local taxing districts, may have governing board members who are elected or appointed by local officials.[2]

"Publicly appointed governing boards serve multiple masters, but the expectations of those different masters are not always clear" (Longanecker, 2006, p. 106). For appointees, difficulties arise when

> boards are beholden to the governor as the appointing authority but legally and ethically beholden to their institution or system. This is a complex role, for two reasons. First, many governors are uncomfortable with their relationship with their state's higher education system. . . . Second, higher education often is not a high priority for governors. (p. 105)

This discomfort was confirmed by Dorman (1990), who measured higher levels of role stress in trustees who were appointed to board service than in those serving on a self-perpetuating board. Similar sorts of tensions exist for those elected to their positions by the state's citizens. As elected officials, these trustees represent their electors as well as the interests of their institutions. Some individuals see the board membership as a steppingstone to other political ambitions (see Calvert, 2012).

Another difference between private and public boards rests with the institutional agenda. During times of fiscal stability, all types of boards may have relative autonomy in serving the fiduciary function of the institution. As resources for higher education diminish, concerns about college affordability rise, and budgets tighten in the wake of the United States' growing national debt and recessionary times, public board decision-making is becoming more constrained and susceptible to external constituent and legislative pressures. These challenges will be particularly prominent as colleges and universities work to recover from the destabilizing effects of the pandemic. The environmental circumstances facing public boards today are increasingly calling their institutions' missions and identities into question: "One of the biggest challenges resulting from decreased state funding for public universities is to what extent they will remain public" (Novak & Johnston, 2005, p. 91).

Although private college and university boards are less susceptible to the state policy vagaries faced by public institutions, they also face challenges in governance in times of economic uncertainty. According to an AGB survey (2009b), private boards' operational effectiveness and ability to recruit new board members for service is increasingly compromised as resources become more constrained. Generally speaking, governance differences between public and private boards are based "on the size of their institutions' annual budgets. Often those with the smallest budgets reported fewer of the best practices the survey covered" (AGB, 2009b, p. 2).

Roles and Responsibilities of Governing Boards

That a group of laypeople serving on a volunteer basis possesses ultimate control over an enterprise as vital to society as higher education introduces a set of organizational dynamics that has challenged college and university administration since the doors of Harvard College opened in the 17th century. These challenges have frequently originated from the ambiguity of board members' roles—to exercise legal responsibility over an organization that requires expertise they often do not hold, engage with campus power structures they often do not understand, and take actions on management decisions in which they often did not participate. Board members rightly question the value and impact they as individuals bring to their board's operation, and how they conduct themselves separately or with their colleagues as a corporate body serves as the basis for the majority of scholarship about boards of trustees.

What is often confusing to observers outside higher education is that, unlike corporate boards where individual directors are compensated for their roles and can wield greater power depending on the amount of shares they possess, lay board members of colleges and universities are volunteering their time, treasure, and talent. What complicates their role even further is that no single member of a lay board possesses any authority to make decisions on behalf of the institution (with the possible exception of the president if that individual is a voting member). However, the lay board (acting as a whole) possesses the full authority (in most cases) to make any decision on behalf of the institution if it chooses to act on a particular issue. Most of the time, boards delegate authority to make decisions to the president and others within the institution—most notably the faculty with regard to certain academic matters. This practice is what Johnstone (2013) referred to as the apportionment of authority and autonomy in higher education. How and when a board decides to delegate or cede its authority is determined by various factors including its mission, history, traditions, norms, and current financial circumstances.

The notion of "role" is more than a set of job descriptors or responsibilities. Rather, Banton (1965) defined a role as "a set of norms and expectations applied to the incumbent of a particular position" (p. 29). These norms and expectations can be assigned by the incumbent in the position, by others related to the position, or both. A lack of agreement between an incumbent and others related to their position can inhibit optimum board function, a subject explored by Dorman (1990) as it related to trusteeship at four major research universities. Though this study was described as an initial examination of board perceptions of the trustee role as it related to role effectiveness, subsequent research has suggested that enhanced efforts to articulate and orient trustees to their appropriate role significantly enhances board effectiveness (see, e.g., AGB, 2009b; Dika & Janosik, 2003; Kezar & Tierney, 2006).

The scope of a trustee's role is best addressed at the outset of the selection process, with reinforcement through a comprehensive orientation prior to the start of board service. At USD, a full-day board orientation program includes an extensive examination of the trustee role with particular attention to how trustees (most being businesspeople) must adapt to a shared governance environment and the significant differences between higher education organizations and other organization types. After the orientation, new board members are assigned an experienced trustee mentor who has served on the board for a few years. This mentor has the responsibility to help the new trustee understand their role and identify ways they can be more deeply engaged. Since understanding one's role requires an understanding of the context in which that role is exercised, trustee understanding of the nuances of the academic enterprise with all its constituencies and competing interest groups provides new trustees with a richer experience during their tenure on the board.

An individual's decision to volunteer for a college, university, or system-governing board carries with it, ideally, the obligation that the person will suspend individual self-interest in favor of what is best for the institution as a whole. Colleges and universities are among the most enduring organizational creations, and an important role of the trustee is to perpetuate that endurance:

> Whether a board serves public or private higher education or governs a single or a multi-campus system, trustees often lack continuity of perspective—that is, the recognition that they are not simply individuals but part of an ongoing process of institution-building. (AGB, 2002, p. 379)

Too often, individual trustees bring to their board their personal or political predispositions on how an organization should be run; focus on only one or two issues that inspire personal or political passion; or, as is frequently the case among alumni who serve on their alma mater's board, approach the oversight of the institution through the prism of their own collegiate experience. These trustees perform a disservice to the institution because they neglect the fiduciary responsibility of trusteeship entrusted to them. "Many trustees understand neither the concept of service on a board as a public trust nor their responsibilities to the entire institution" (AGB, 2002, p. 376). It is imperative, therefore, for trustees to be sensitized to this possibility so they may better serve the entire institution and not undermine the work of its president.

A useful list of the main responsibilities of boards of trustees, in an order that approximates the priorities highlighted in subsequent literature on trusteeship (AGB, 2009b; Kezar, 2006), was offered by Nason (1980):

- appointing the president,
- supporting the president,
- monitoring the president's performance,
- clarifying the institution's mission,
- approving long-range plans,
- overseeing the educational program,
- ensuring financial solvency,

- preserving institutional independence,
- enhancing the public image,
- interpreting the community to the campus,
- serving as a court of appeal, and
- assessing board performance. (pp. 27–46)

These responsibilities represent five broad governance domains: leadership, mission, finances, external relations, and self-assessment. Of these responsibilities, the selection, support, and evaluation of the president are the most critical.

Ensuring Outstanding Leadership

The articulation of an institution's mission (and ensuring that it has the resources necessary to fulfill that mission) is a fundamental role of the institution's board, while the execution of policies and practices to achieve that mission is the responsibility of the institution's president. As noted earlier in this chapter, the board–president relationship is the fulcrum on which an institution's performance ultimately hinges. Consequently, selection of the right individual for a college, university, or system's presidency cannot be overstated as the single most important role of a board. This process must be conducted with the greatest care and attention, beginning with board members' understanding and acceptance of their organization's unique qualities and personality as well as the challenges and aspirations that it faces. It is not enough for a board to hire a strong leader with the diverse skills necessary to handle the complex challenges inherent in today's academic presidency; a board must also ensure that the presidential candidate's personality is a good fit with the institution's organizational and operational ethos. Members of the entire board, therefore, must be clear and unified in their thinking about the type of leader who will be able not only to advance the institution but reflect the values and norms that distinguish it from its academic peers.

Once a new president is hired, a board must integrate the new president into the life of the institution and monitor progress to ensure a smooth transition and optimum cooperation between the board and the president. Rita Bornstein (2006), president emerita of Rollins College and consultant and writer on the president–board relationship, has placed strong emphasis on the processes that must occur for successful synergy between presidents and their boards: "Strong relationships between presidents and boards are built on communication, education, transparency, and accountability" (p. 1). These relationships are crucial to the long-term success of college and university presidents. Bornstein (2006) warned there are reports of presidents who undermine their own leadership and sometimes lose their jobs because of errors of omission or commission they make with their boards. These presidents tend to treat their boards in one of two ways: They "protect" trustees and maximize their own authority by providing limited screened information about institutional problems or they overwhelm trustees with excessive, nonessential information and involve them in inappropriate decisions about operations. The first option leads to disengaged and inattentive boards, the second to boards that micromanage. (p. 1)

While the primary responsibility for maintaining a sound board–president relationship falls to the president as the compensated professional responsible for the overall health of the institution, the role of the board's leadership—and particularly the board chair—in fostering a constructive working relationship between the board and the president is also important. Developing and maintaining such a relationship is no easy task, especially for one who serves as a volunteer with only a tangential comprehension of the key issues and challenges the president faces daily. Despite this tenuous understanding, board chairs serve multiple roles in relation to institution presidents. The chair is the primary spokesperson for and representative of the board and functions as the president's de facto direct supervisor. At the same time, the chair must also serve as a colleague to the president in the mutual task of advancing the mission of the institution, and as friend and confidant when the president needs informed counsel, support, or just a sympathetic ear. In short, the board chair must work equally hard on building a relationship with the president as the president does with the board chair.

Boards also hold an important responsibility for monitoring the president's annual performance, preferably against preestablished, mutually agreed-on benchmarks or goals. Presidential performance is directly correlated to the health and improvement of the institution of which the executive leader is responsible, and a board must monitor not only the professional behavior of the president but the organizational metrics that are a product of the president's leadership. Several glaring failures of proper board oversight of presidential actions in the past 2 decades are illustrative of the damage that can befall an institution when a board does not fulfill this responsibility. Eckerd College in Clearwater, Florida, experienced a two-thirds decline in its endowment—from $34 million to $13 million—in the 1990s, a time of substantial market gains, because of administrative mismanagement and a lack of proper board supervision. Trust and overconfidence in Eckerd's entrepreneurial president at the time resulted in a failure by the board to question the administration's actions and reports until the financial and reputational damage had become overwhelming (Pulley, 2000). In Washington DC, actions by American University's board of trustees were the subject of a 2005 U.S. Senate investigation into abuse of the institution's not-for-profit status when its president was found to have charged hundreds of thousands of dollars of personal expenses to the university and was subsequently granted millions in a severance package upon his termination (Williams, 2005).

Another high-profile case that illustrates a lack of appropriate board oversight and engagement, and required other state agencies to get involved, is the 2019 revelation that a former The Ohio State University team doctor had sexually abused 177 students during his tenure (Mather, 2019). The case became public after an investigation by an outside law firm in which over 500 people were interviewed. The investigation revealed that the doctor had likely been sexually assaulting students as far back as 1979, and when Ohio State's director of sports medicine was informed in 1996, he did not take appropriate action. At the time the director described the accusations as without merit. In 2019, Ohio's governor and the State Medical Board conducted their own investigations. In the end, Ohio State settled a lawsuit with the victims for over $40 million. This example demonstrates how boards must have in place appropriate internal audit functions as well as established whistleblower policies that report directly to the board. Although the Eckerd College, American University, and Ohio State examples are among the more newsworthy illustrations of board inattention to presidential and university performance, such instances are avoidable with proper board oversight mechanisms. A more complete discussion of presidential performance issues can be found in chapter 11, this volume.

Articulating the Institution's Mission

Regardless of institution type and public or private status, the definition and maintenance of institutional mission are the responsibility of the board of trustees, not the administration or the faculty. As the institution's fiduciaries, trustees must ensure that alignment exists between the historical purposes of the institution, the programs it offers, and its academic and other outcomes. The process of institutional accreditation focuses on this alignment to ensure that a college or university's stated purposes, as found in its legal and public documents, are in fact being fulfilled. Careful attention is given by accrediting bodies to an institution's mission statement and the degree to which congruence exists between the written statement and the policies, procedures, and practices that support it.

Instances may occur when the trustees, administration, or faculty wishes to pursue a new and different institutional direction to meet a programmatic desire or a financial imperative. Such changes should occur following a significant review by the board as part of the institution's overall planning process. Failure to accommodate change through deliberate planning can cause an institution to drift from its stated mission. When the mission statement of an institution requires updating or alteration out of institutional or external necessity, a board should direct its president to engage the entire campus community in that process to ensure general acceptance of any change. Although a board owns its institution's mission, the campus community must execute it. It is therefore prudent to enter such a process with full deliberation and care to guarantee that the practice of shared governance is respected.

Moreover, throughout any deliberations over institutional mission, a college or university's board and broader community should remain mindful of the notion that higher education exists to serve the public good and advance society. Novak and Johnston (2005) described how trustees can maintain this traditional role in their institution's mission:

> It is appropriate for the board both to promote and to oversee the institution's commitment to public service through the mission. Conversations at the board level can make a significant difference in how institutions serve the public good by adhering to and fulfilling their missions or adapt their missions when appropriate. (p. 93)

Maintaining Financial Solvency

Trustees bear responsibility for the financial stability of their institution, which they execute in three ways: setting tuition and fee rates; approving the budget, including establishing revenue and philanthropic giving expectations; and providing oversight of the institutions financial policies, practices, and reporting. Increased scrutiny of not-for-profit organizations' finances by the federal government in recent decades has added an additional layer of responsibility for boards in the area of audits and compliance. Revised federal Form 990, which requires colleges and universities to provide a level of documentation of annual financial operations heretofore unseen, has vastly increased the reporting burdens of institutions and has yielded unprecedented transparency within the financial operations of academic institutions.[3] These new requirements were prompted, in part, by not-for-profit organizations whose elaborate management and spending practices violated the normative behaviors generally associated with organizations that serve the public good.

In addition to federal financial reporting, college and university board members' annual completion of disclosure statements that outline potential conflicts of interest has also become accepted practice. The impetus behind this activity and other efforts to provide greater transparency in college and university governance can largely be attributed to the enactment of the Sarbanes–Oxley Act (2002), which placed new and more restrictive standards on for-profit corporate boards and accounting firms in the wake of a series of high-profile corporate management and governance malfeasance scandals. Although the law did not extend to not-for-profit entities, certain practices and policies stemming from the legislation have been voluntarily adopted by a majority of not-for-profit boards as a preventative measure to improve governance and avoid future controversies.

Since higher education's adoption of these new governance principles, several existential threats to colleges and universities have emerged, which we have enumerated elsewhere in this book. Several authors have identified the fragility of the U.S. higher education sector and correctly predicted massive changes and disruptions in the market that have threatened the financial viability of institutions. Christensen and Eyring (2011) went as far as to predict that most colleges and universities would face bankruptcy by 2030 if they did not make significant changes in their operating models. Bills and Pond (2021) asserted that the responsibility for avoiding such a dire future falls on an institution's board of trustees to have the courage to "use its authority to take action" (para. 16). Bills and Pond also placed blame for the failure of colleges and universities to avoid this fate on the boards themselves for not taking a more active role in their institutions' governance structures. They suggested that boards need to accept that the problems facing higher education are "structural, not episodic" and that they need to hire the "right leaders with the right profiles" and "quickly align expenses with revenues" (para. 15).

External Relations

A board of trustees has a special obligation to the various constituencies, internal and external, served by its institution. As fiduciaries, trustees must serve as the campus community's interpreters of the institution's environmental context to ensure consistency between the institutional mission and the educational outcomes required by the environment. Likewise, board members must serve as boundary spanners between their institution and the broader society by representing the institution to its various publics.

These interpretive roles require trustees to be accountable in their duties. According to the AGB (2007),

> boards are accountable to (1) the institution's mission and cultural heritage, (2) the transcendent values and principles that guide and shape higher education, (3) the public interest and public trust, and (4) the legitimate and relevant interests of the institution's various constituencies. (pp. 2–3)

The scope of institutional accountability has grown as higher education has been scrutinized over challenges of decreasing affordability, diminishing access, and increasing questions over the assessment of educational outcomes. Boards have been forced to assume greater prominence in understanding and confronting these issues as part of their routine governance responsibilities. These conditions have convinced some trustees to assume a more activist position in fulfillment of their duties.

The rise of trustee activism as a reaction to perceived ills in higher education was examined by Bastedo (2006), who argued that "activist trustees see themselves as protectors of a public trust, one that must be reconceptualized in light of what they see as declining academic standards and broad failures of shared governance" (p. 128). Often associated with a conservative political agenda or a desire to implement corporate governance models to counter alleged liberal faculty self-interest, trustee activism is a recent phenomenon that has emerged to diminish the perceived excessive control of faculty members over their own conditions of employment and evaluation of performance (Bastedo, 2006, p. 133). At issue is the balance between institutional and public interests, a debate that requires trustees to assume an uncomfortable but necessary boundary-spanning role. This dialogue is important, and it must be conducted in a manner that acknowledges and respects the various spheres of authority that exist on campus. As Bastedo (2006) explained,

> if the concept of the public interest remains contested, the real issue of activist trusteeship is not academic standards or tenure or any other specific policy problem. The issue is how these preferences are expressed by activist trustees and what these preferences mean for the power dynamic among faculty, administrators, and trustees. (p. 137)

If institutions are to promote greater inclusion, equity, and social justice, the board of trustees must take an active role in cultivating such an environment. Most boards primarily view their role as diversifying their membership so that they more accurately reflect the constituents whom their institutions serve, through the lens of their mission. While the diversity of the board matters, boards that take a more active stance on social justice issues—such as how and with whom they will invest their institution's endowment funds— find themselves more actively engaged in discussion about the importance of mission, their institution's values, and what it means to be an effective board.

By the 2020s some boards had begun discussing the importance of environmental, social, and governance (ESG) principles and how best to assess how these factors affect the college or university they serve. The most visible examples of this work include institutions' decisions to divest from fossil fuels and other companies that they believe have a detrimental impact on the environment. January (2019) found that it can often be challenging for corporate boards to connect to global issues that have a long-term positive impact on society, such as climate change, water scarcity, and human rights issues. The same is true for colleges and universities, but many governing board members are discovering that moving in this direction connects their board's policies more closely with the mission and values of the institution that they are serving. In the past many institutions were reluctant to move in such a direction for fear of losing potential revenue, but a 2020 study suggested that institutions that followed an ESG approach to investing their endowments and adjusting board practices did not sacrifice financial returns as a result of promoting sustainability (Dyer et al., 2020; Toner, 2020). ESG goes well beyond divesting from certain funds and industries; it also is a call to ensure that the boards of corporations in which colleges and universities invest their endowments have appropriate representation from traditionally underserved populations. What this priority has meant for higher education governing boards is that they too must take a careful look at their own practices regarding whom they recruit to serve on their own boards and the ways in which they make decisions.

Self-Assessment

The ambiguities and tensions inherent in service on a board of trustees suggest that mechanisms need to be in place to promote ongoing introspection. These practices ensure that the roles and responsibilities of the board in general, and its members in particular, are being fulfilled. Board self-assessment serves numerous functions, including building cooperation and coherence among and between board members who share in this unique and highly rewarding experience. In addition to examining the functional aspects of a board, self-assessment provides a board with the opportunity to reflect on its organizational culture, which represents the sum of its many diverse personalities. Board self-assessment seeks to answer these open-ended questions:

- In what ways are we performing our roles and responsibilities most effectively?
- What functions of the institution require further understanding?
- How well are we working collectively as a board?
- In what ways can our meetings be more productive and substantive?
- How can we improve our overall effectiveness as a board?
- How can communication between and among board members as well as with the president improve?

- How can the board better reflect the diversity of society and the constituents served by the institution in alignment with its mission?
- What mechanisms exist to measure our progress as a board?
- How effective are we in setting and meeting annual goals for the board?
- In what ways can board leadership be enhanced?

Board self-assessment should occur on a periodic basis. The frequency of such assessments varies by board and can be conducted in association with a standing meeting or at a special board activity such as a retreat. The AGB maintains an extensive library of reference materials at its Washington DC, headquarters and provides consulting services to assist boards in planning and conducting self-assessment exercises. According to AGB (2009b), two thirds of boards assess their overall performance, with public boards doing so more frequently than private boards.

Assessments are not limited to boards in their entirety. Boards are also encouraged to conduct periodic reviews of individual board members or invite members to participate in individual self-assessments of their service, often in conjunction with completion of a term and in consideration of extension of their appointment on the board. Inherently more delicate and personal a process, individual assessments can take many forms and are highly useful and instructive in isolating issues and concerns so that board members may focus on improving their participation on the board. Altogether, the combination of assessment activities for an entire board and its individual members serves an important purpose in enhancing the quality and effectiveness of trusteeship and is considered a best practice.

Board Effectiveness

The challenges facing U.S. higher education today are among the most acute in our nation's history and will require informed and inspired decision-making in the days and years ahead. Arguably, at no time in the history of higher education has the need for effective board leadership been greater. The increasing price of a college education, decreasing availability of public resources, expanding regulatory requirements, rising cybersecurity concerns, burgeoning competition from the for-profit higher education sector, and emerging artificial intelligence technologies that affect communications and learning modalities are examples of issues facing higher education. It is also imperative that boards listen and respond accordingly to the growing public outcry over racial and economic disparities in society, access to higher education for diverse populations, and the overall worth and effectiveness of higher education. Effective responses to these challenges depend on the success of governing boards to understand and address such issues in a societal context vastly altered from what it was at the beginning of the 21st century.

A recurring theme in discussions of board effectiveness is collaboration between an institution's president and board and among board members themselves (see Bowen, 2008; MacTaggart, 2011). Such collaboration must take into account an appreciation and understanding of the specific roles of the board and the president, and both parties must be adept at executing those roles consistently. When these fundamental relationships perform in harmony, board functionality—and, ultimately, effectiveness—is enhanced. The responsibility for achieving this positive relational state among board members and between the board and the president rests with three governance entities: the president, the board chair, and the trustee committee responsible for board membership and orientation (often referred to as the committee on trustees, the membership committee, or the governance committee). It is axiomatic that the selection of the right president, board chair, and individual board members is the most crucial first step in creating an effective board.

Wilson (2005) affirmed the value of a collaborative environment by noting the importance of creating a culture of interconnectedness among board members and the president. Wilson offered 10 governance habits that distinguish a highly effective board from its more typical counterparts: select the right president, select the right board chair, empower the committee on trustees, insist on a strategic vision, set goals and assess performance, understand and monitor academic policy, develop future board leaders, structure the board strategically, embrace board education, and make trusteeship enjoyable. It is important to note Wilson's 10 habits emphasize the composition of a board and the roles of its members, not board processes. This distinction is important because insufficient care and attention to building a collaborative board culture can undermine the board's operational effectiveness overall. The president and board chair must devote sufficient time to this task. A board's collaborative and positive working dynamic can be seriously compromised by the presence of rogue board members or an autocratic chair.

Collaboration between the president and the board, and among the board members themselves, is achieved when it is accompanied by a collective sense of ownership in governance decisions, respecting the roles and responsibilities of both parties:

> Trustees must make a conscious decision to create a governance partnership with the president. Moreover, the board's leadership must organize and motivate the trustees as strategic contributors by creating an environment in which the work of the board is integrated. (Wilson, 2007, p. 10).

According to Wilson (2007), it is important that this sense of partnership be embedded into the culture of the board.

> The partnership begins to take on character and strength when the president's strategic vision moves from an owned and approved plan to active implementation. The trustees owe the president four things:
>
> 1. A commitment to generate the strategic resources
> 2. Active, assertive and constructive oversight
> 3. Alignment of the work of the board with the president's goals and objectives
> 4. A fair and supportive process of presidential performance appraisal as part of an institutionalized culture of accountability. (p. 12)

The success of this partnership rests in board members' shared commitment to involve, inform, and commit one another to the operational success of their board's strategic vision. Some partnerships fail, Wilson (2007) notes, because insufficient effort is applied by either the president or the board to identify and reconcile differences or to adjust individual styles to accommodate the greater good of the partnership relationship.

Harvard's Richard Chait (2006), perhaps the United States' best-known authority on lay governance, has observed that the greatest cause of poor board effectiveness centers on how board members interact with the president and with one another. He identified two "culprits" that most often account for substandard governance: boards that are "orchestras of soloists" and boards that "either lionize or trivialize the president" (pp. 10–11). Regarding board members who operate in a noncollaborative fashion, Chait argued that "difficulties ensue not because trustees think independently, a hallmark of effective boards, but because trustees proceed independently, based on a self-declared role and a self-determined scope of authority" (p. 10). On how boards conceptualize the president, Chait noted,

> When a board perceives a president as an indispensable, heroic leader, then trustees disengage from governance or accord the chief executive undue deference—tendencies that some presidents are keen to reinforce. In short order, the trustee's overestimation of presidential importance leads to over-dependence on the chief executive and underperformance by the board. (p. 11)

Both these conditions reinforce the aforementioned need to exercise great care in the selection of a president and board members. These individuals' personal operating styles should value and support the collaborative behaviors that will encourage enhanced board effectiveness.

An example of a relationship between a board and a president in which the board relinquished some of its responsibility for oversight is the controversy that erupted at Pennsylvania State University in late 2011. At that time a retired assistant football coach was indicted on charges of child molestation, some of which were alleged to have taken place on university grounds. Penn State's president, Graham Spanier, had been a long-term, successful leader and had the complete support and trust of the board of trustees. However, when two senior university officials were indicted for perjury in the case, Spanier failed to keep the board fully apprised of the seriousness of the situation and publicly stated his unconditional support for the administrators in question. When the grand jury findings were made public, questions arose regarding who was aware of the allegations and what and when they knew—including the revered head football coach, Joe Paterno. Under great pressure from the public and the media, the board called an emergency meeting and decided to fire Spanier and Paterno, leaving the university without a leader or a recognized spokesperson. Based on reports at the time, our understanding is that the chaos that ensued may have been partly avoided if the board had a better line of communication with the president and had made clear their expectations for full disclosure about pending legal issues. Likewise, if the board had in place an emergency management plan for handling such a crisis, the university may have avoided the serious damage that was done to its reputation.

The necessity of having the right people in place was noted by Rogers (2005), who emphasized that creating exceptional boards requires exceptional people. It is essential for the president and the board to actively cultivate positive, supportive relationships and act as partners while being sensitive to each other's roles. The importance of institutional leadership as it relates to the special relationship that exists between a college or university's president and its governing board was further highlighted by a report of the AGB (2006) Task Force on the State of the Presidency in American Higher Education titled "The Leadership Imperative." The report acknowledged the increasingly challenging and complex environment facing U.S. higher education and asserted that a more symbiotic leadership partnership must characterize future relationships between presidents and their boards. A heightened level of "support, candor, and accountability" (pp. vi–vii) between both entities was viewed as essential for colleges and universities to effectively address the challenges before them. Substandard or dysfunctional governance practices will interfere with the process of resolving the educational and institutional shortcomings that face our nation's colleges and universities.

"The Leadership Imperative" offered a clarion call to strengthen the board–president relationship: "A president's ability to foster integral leadership . . . inescapably depends upon the board's support and effective oversight. The Task Force is concerned that too few presidents receive from their governing boards the degree of support necessary for courageous and visionary leadership" (AGB, 2006, pp. 9–10).

In light of the enormous challenges facing higher education today and the growing responsibility of fiduciaries to navigate their institutions through them, Chait et al. (2005) argued that institutional leadership should reframe how governance and lay leadership are viewed. Though the concepts of leadership and governance have different meanings, the authors linked the two to assert that lay leaders traditionally empowered with governance responsibilities can assume important roles as institutional leaders without undue encroachment on traditional executive authority. Whereas previous governance literature focused on best practices with an emphasis on process, Chait et al. (2005) asserted that we should divide the role of governance into three domains: fiduciary, strategic, and generative. The first two are traditional roles of lay leaders, as described earlier. The third suggests that lay leaders adopt practices that anticipate future issues and organizational directions by considering emerging challenges and environmental change. In the past, boards have used committee structures to address organizational operations that are largely managerial in nature, while chief executives have focused on more visionary and planning activities. The authors observed:

> While non-profit managers have gravitated toward the role of leadership, trustees have tilted more toward the role of management. The shift has occurred because trusteeship, as a concept, has stalled while leadership, as a concept, has accelerated. The net effect is that trustees function, more and more, like managers. (Chait et al., 2005, p. 4)

A more generative function for trustees refocuses their time and energy on issues relative to the broader context in which their college or university operates, thereby emphasizing their unique place as objective but informed fiduciaries whose primary interest is in the long-term viability of, and vision for, their institution.

In 2014, after 20 years of service as the leader of the AGB, Rick Legon wrote a piece on trusteeship in which he offered his observations on effective boards over the previous 2 decades. Legon (2014) stated that "most boards of colleges and universities don't reach their fullest potential for effective governance" (p. 8). In addition to advocating for many of the same principles of effective governance mentioned earlier (mission focus, fiduciary responsibilities, hiring and supporting a talented leader) Legon added that boards need to be sure they select the right board chair, provide appropriate oversight for academic quality, and consider more serious long-term issues such as enterprise risk management.

Trustee effectiveness can best be achieved when a collaborative environment for governance exists and when trustees themselves are confident and secure in knowing and acting appropriately in their roles. Presidents and board leaders, therefore, must ensure that trustees understand the answer to one fundamental question: What is our purpose as a board? A shared understanding of that answer—along with a team identity resulting from careful selection of board members and leaders who operate in a collective, not individual, manner—will significantly contribute to stronger leadership and governance of the institution.

Future Challenges

Numerous conditions challenge U.S. higher education today. In the AGB's (2019) periodic review of major higher education policy issues facing governing boards, it noted several conditions that will have a profound effect on the character and viability of higher education institutions going forward, such as immigration policy, international student recruitment, national security issues, college affordability, accountability, poor funding outlook, and unresolved federal education and tax policies. As fiduciaries responsible to their institutions and the publics they serve, boards of trustees will assume heightened importance in years to come as they address these environmental challenges within the context of their institutions' missions. Fulfillment of the four main principles woven throughout this book—adherence to institutional mission; skill at adapting to environmental change; seeking to promote democratic ideals; and shepherding their institutions to become models of inclusion, equity, and social justice—depends on the preservation of good governance, and effective governance rests within each trustee.

Notes

1. Most public four-year institutions are part of multicampus systems. Discussion of these dynamics are discussed in more depth in chapter 7 (this volume) on state government. In this chapter, readers will note that the discussion primarily focuses on the board and the relationship between the board and a single institution. We do note that system boards may have different arrangements in that they may have a primary relationship with a system head, who oversees campus presidents, or

they may have parallel relationships with the system head and campus presidents. There is also a growing interest among multicampus governing boards to increase coordination among their constituent campuses, and this approach will affect the board–institution relationship (Gagliardi & Lane, 2022; Lane & Johnstone, 2013).

2. In New York, for example, the community college board is comprised of members appointed by the governor and the county leadership.

3. The information provided on these forms can be accessed by the public at https://www.guidestar.org

References

Association of Governing Boards of Colleges and Universities. (2002). The role of governing boards: Issues, recommendations, and resources. In R. M. Diamond (Ed.), *Field guide to aademic leadership* (pp. 375–387). Jossey-Bass.

Association of Governing Boards of Colleges and Universities. (2006). *The leadership imperative: The report of the AGB Task Force on the state of the presidency in American Higher Education.* Author.

Association of Governing Boards of Colleges and Universities. (2007). *AGB statement on board accountability.* https://agb.org/sites/default/files/agb-statements/statement_2007_accountability_0.pdf

Association of Governing Boards of Colleges and Universities. (2009a). *AGB top public policy issues for higher education in 2009 and 2010.* Author.

Association of Governing Boards of Colleges and Universities. (2009b). *The AGB survey of higher education governance.* Author.

Association of Governing Boards of Colleges and Universities (2019). *The AGB top public policy issues for higher education 2019–20.* Author.

Banton, M. (1965). *Roles: An introduction to the study of social relations.* Basic Books.

Bastedo, M. N. (2006). Activist trustees in the university: Reconceptualizing the public interest. In P. D. Eckel (Ed.), *The shifting frontiers of academic decison making: Responding to new priorities, following new pathways* (pp. 127–141). Praeger.

Bills, M., & Pond, W. (2021, January 14). Colleges in peril can be rescued. *The Chronicle of Higher Education.* https://community.chronicle.com/news/2470-colleges-in-peril-can-be-rescued-but-only-if-governing-boards-transform

Bornstein, R. (2006). *The president's role in board development.* Association of Governing Boards of Universities and Colleges.

Bowen, W. G. (2008). *The board book: An insider's guide for directors and trustees.* Norton.

Calvert, K. (2012, November 9). *School board a political stepping stone for Tuesday's winners.* KPBS. https://www.kpbs.org/news/2012/nov/09/school-board-political-stepping-stone-tuesdays-win/

Chait, R. P. (2006). Why boards go bad. *Trusteeship, 14*(3), 8–12. https://doi.org/10.1097/01.mib.0000246785.21496.ad

Chait, R. P., Ryan, W. P., & Taylor, B. E. (2005). *Governance as leadership: Reframing the work of nonprofit boards.* Wiley.

Christensen, C. M., & Eyring, H. J. (2011). *The innovative university: Changing the DNA of higher education from the inside out.* Jossey-Bass.

Dartmouth College v. Woodward, 17 U.S. 518 (1819)

Dika, S. L., & Janosik, S. M. (2003). The role of selection, orientation and training in improving the quality of public college and university boards of trustees in the United States. *Quality in Higher Education, 9*(3), 273–285. https://doi .org/10.1080/1353832032000151139

Dorman, R. (1990). *Perceptions of role conflict and role ambiguity held by members of boards of trustees of four research I-type universities* [Unpublished doctoral dissertation]. Pennsylvania State University.

Duryea, E. D., & Williams, D. (Eds.). (2000). *The academic corporation: A history of college and university governing boards.* Falmer.

Dyer, G., DonnaSelva, A., & Bowen, H. (2020). *Financial performance of sustainable investing: The state of the field and case studies for endowments.* Intentional Endowments Network. https://www.intentionalendowments.org/financial_ performance_of_sustainable_investing

Gagliardi, J., & Lane, J. E. (Eds.). (2022). *Higher education systems redesigned: Shifting from perpetuation to innovation to student success.* State University of New York Press.

Hendrickson, R. M. (1999). *The colleges, their constituencies and the courts.* Education Law Association.

Hofstadter, R. (1955). *Academic freedom in the age of the college.* Columbia University Press.

Jan, O. (2019, February 25). *The board and ESG.* Harvard Law School Forum on Corporate Governance. https://corpgov.law.harvard.edu/2019/02/25/the-board- and-esg/

Johnstone, D. B. (2013). Higher educational autonomy and the apportionment of authority among state governments, public multi-campus systems, and member colleges and universities. In J. E. Lane & D. B. Johnstone (Eds.), *Higher education systems 3.0: Harnessing systemness, delivering performance* (pp. 75–99). State University of New York Press.

Kezar, A., & Tierney, W. G. (2006). 7 elements of effective public-sector boards. *Trusteeship, 14*(6), 29–32.

Kezar, A. J. (2006). Rethinking public higher education governing boards performance: Results of a national study of governing boards in the United States. *Journal of Higher Education, 77*(6), 968–1008. https://doi.org/10.1353/jhe.2006.0051

Lane, J. E., & Johnstone, D. B. (Eds.). (2013). *Higher education systems 3.0: Harnessing systemness, delivering performance.* State University of New York Press.

Legon, R. (2014). The 10 habits of highly effective boards. *Trusteeship, 22*(2), 8–13. https://agb.org/trusteeship-article/the-10-habits-of-highly-effective-boards/

Longanecker, D. A. (2006). The "new" new challenge of governance by governing boards. In W. G. Tierney (Ed.), *Governance and the public good* (pp. 95–115). State University of New York Press.

MacTaggart, T. (2011). *Leading change: How boards and presidents build exceptional academic institutions.* AGB Press.

Mather, V. (2019, May 17). Ohio State finds team doctor sexually abused 177 students. *The New York Times.* https://www.nytimes.com/2019/05/17/sports/ohio-state-sexual-abuse.html

Nason, J. W. (1980). Responsibilities of the governing board. In R. T. Ingram (Ed.), *Handbook of college and university trusteeship* (pp. 27–46). Jossey-Bass.

Novak, R., & Johnston, S. W. (2005). Trusteeship and the public good. In A. Kezar, T. C. Chambers, & J. C. Burkhardt (Eds.), *Higher education for the public good: Emerging voices from a national movement* (pp. 87–101). Jossey-Bass.

Pulley, J. L. (2000, August 18). How Eckard's 52 trustees failed to see two-thirds of its endowment disappear. *The Chronicle of Higher Education,* A31–A33.

Rogers, B. (2005). View from the board chair: Moving beyond oversight to active board engagement. *Trusteeship, 13*(5), 7.

Rudolph, F. (1962). *The American college and university.* Knopf.

Sarbanes–Oxley Act, Pub. L. 107-204, 116 Stat. 745 (2002)

Toner, M. (2020, February 20). *Good grades: Higher ed's ESG investments match or beat returns of peers, study says.* Karma. https://karmaimpact.com/good-grades-higher-eds-esg-investments-match-or-beat-returns-of-peers-study-says/

Williams, G. (2005, October 31). U.S. Senate to investigate board of American U. over Ladner's compensation. *The Chronicle of Higher Education.* http://chronicle.com/article/US-Senate-to-Investigate/121437

Wilson, E. B. (2005). It all boils down to this . . . *Trusteeship, 13*(5), 8–13.

Wilson, E. B. (2007). Row, row, row the same boat. *Trusteeship, 15*(3), 8–13.

Zwingle, J. L. (1980). Evolution of lay governing boards. In R. T. Ingram (Ed.), *Handbook of college and university trusteeship* (pp. 14–26). Jossey-Bass.

II

THE ACADEMIC PRESIDENCY

I t can be argued that no single individual in a college or university is more important to the advancement of the institution's mission, its adaptation to environmental changes, the development of democratic partnerships, or the diversification of its campus than its president. Given these and myriad other expectations of a college or university president, few people can fulfill the role successfully. Clark Kerr (1964), the 12th president of the University of California system and first chancellor of the University of California, Berkeley, made these observations about the academic presidency:

> The university president in the United States is expected to be a friend of the students, a colleague of the faculty, a good fellow with the alumni, a sound administrator with the trustees, a good speaker with the public, an astute bargainer with the foundations and the federal agencies, a politician with the state legislature, a friend of industry, labor, and agriculture, a persuasive diplomat with the donors, a champion of education generally, a supporter of the professions (particularly law and medicine), a spokesman to the press, a scholar in his own right, a public servant at the state and national levels, a devotee of opera and football equally, a decent human being, a good husband and father, an active member of a church. Above all he must enjoy traveling in airplanes, eating his meals in public, and attending public ceremonies. No one can be all of these things. Some succeed at being none. (pp. 29–30)

The role of the academic president has changed dramatically over the centuries. Indeed, it is doubtful that a president of a colonial college would even recognize his modern counterparts. Whereas in the early years presidents would have played a significant and direct role in the education and training of their institutions' students, guided the curriculum, and had great latitude in the selection of tutors and faculty, today's presidents may never teach a single class, engage in the development of academic curricula, or have a direct role in the recruitment of faculty members. A contemporary college or university president is expected to be first among equals with the faculty; an institutional ambassador to the world; an institution's principal fundraiser; and most of all, CEO of a complex enterprise.

Scholars have written widely about the changing role of the academic presidency over the years (Bensimon, 1989; Ikenberry, 2010; Thwing, 1926). Based on the economic, political, and social environments that all colleges and universities are confronting in the 21st century, however, higher education faces a major dilemma. During a time when the need for strong leadership has never been greater, the ability to attract, support, and prepare the next generation of academic presidents has never been more difficult.

The increasing complexity of the job and the enormous stress placed on the people who hold these roles has gained greater public recognition in recent years. One high-profile example was when the departing chancellor of the University of Texas System, William H. McRaven, stated, "The toughest job in the nation is the one of an academic- or health-institution president" (Thomason, 2018, para. 1). While McRaven's assertion could be taken as a hyperbolic comment from an academic leader under stress, what made his comments so telling was that McRaven had spent most of his career in the military as a decorated commander and four-star admiral who had led troops into battle; he had served as a corporate executive as well. When a leader of his caliber and with his experience claimed that a university president was the "toughest job," he brought to light that these jobs may just be as challenging as any in the nation.

The difficulty of the role has likely contributed to the reduction in the average number of years a college or university president serves at a single institution. In a 2017 survey conducted by the ACE, the average tenure for a president was 6.5 years in 2016 as compared to 8.5 years a decade earlier (ACE, 2017; Thomason, 2018). According to the ACE survey, chief executives' top worries concerned a lack of financial resources and issues surrounding free speech (ACE, 2017; Thomason, 2018). By the fall of 2020, in the middle of the global pandemic, a survey conducted by *The Chronicle of Higher Education* found that the top issues identified by presidents were the mental health of students, faculty, and staff; decreasing enrollments; and dwindling resources (Vasquez, 2020).

Increasing Demand and Diminishing Interest

ACE's 2017 survey of United States college and university presidents indicated that the academic presidency will face a major crisis in the coming years. Based on the data collected for this study, the average age of an academic president in the United States has increased. In 2017, 58% of presidents were over age 60 (average age 62), as compared to an average age of 52 years in 1986. The survey found that other senior leaders of academic institutions are of a similar age (ACE, 2017). This shift in the average age of college and university executive leaders suggests that between 2025 and 2030 higher education will experience a surge in retirements and a demand for professionals who are prepared to fill these vacancies. Beyond professional preparation, college and university stakeholders will likely seek diverse candidates (i.e., those who resemble the rapidly changing demographics of the students whom they are serving) to lead their institutions. As reported by the ACE (2017) study, women and minorities constituted a higher percentage of presidents in 2016 than in 1986, but the pipeline of diverse candidates for the next generation of leaders is not growing at a pace to keep up with the expected demand. One positive indicator for more gender diversity in the future was that the percentage of CEOs who are women had increased from 21% in 2001 to 30% in 2016 (ACE, 2017). For women of color, however, the appointments to CEO positions had grown by less than 3% during the same timeframe (ACE, 2017).

The position that most academic presidents hold prior to becoming the CEO of an institution is provost or chief academic officer (CAO; ACE, 2017). Although a higher percentage of presidents, particularly at smaller independent colleges and regional public universities, are coming from nontraditional backgrounds (e.g., advancement, business, or student affairs) including from outside of the academy, the traditional route remains the most likely pathway to an academic presidency (ACE, 2017). A study released by the Council of Independent Colleges (CIC) reported, however, that fewer provosts are interested in pursuing presidencies than in years past (Hartley & Godin, 2010). According to the CIC study, less than 25% of current CAOs at smaller independent colleges and 30% of provosts overall were planning to seek an academic presidency in the future (Hartley & Godin, 2010). Their lack of aspiration to the academic presidency seems to stem from "the unappealing nature of the president's work, including fundraising, board relations, and financial management" (p. 2).

Even among individuals who have prepared for and successfully achieved an academic presidency, the demands of the job often overwhelm the ablest among them. McLaughlin (1996) found that new presidents are often shocked by the expectations of the position, the exhausting pace they are expected to keep, and the range of issues they are required to address. Because of their close proximity to their presidents, provosts and CAOs experience a taste of what it is like to be the CEO of a college or university, and they increasingly say that the job is not appealing. What has changed over the years to bring about such a negative response from those individuals who historically were most likely to fill the role of president, and what are the implications of this change? What can be done to reverse or slow this trend?

The Changing Nature of the Academic Presidency

Academic presidents have been described in a variety of ways over the years. Kerr (1964) referred to them as "giants in the groves" (p. 31) and others have gone so far as to suggest that the academic presidency is an "illusion" (Cohen & March, 1974, p. 2), and that presidents are the "most universal fakers"" (Sinclair, 1923, p. 382) who at best might become good bureaucrats. Clearly there exists a panoply of views about the academic presidency, but most agree that the role of the president has changed over the years, and the pace of change has accelerated.

The evolution of the academic presidency parallels major shifts in the academy over the centuries. By the middle of the 19th century, the typical institution of higher education was religiously affiliated, and its leader could be best described as a learned clergyman. In contrast, by the turn of the 20th century, the rise of the secular research university required a new type of leader—an individual who could deal with an increasingly complex organization with broader goals and enlarged responsibilities (Kerr, 1964; Rudolph, 1962). The transition from a religious focus to a secular orientation, coupled with the increasing desire for new sources of financial support, led to a demand for academic leaders who were financially astute and able to convince foundations and wealthy benefactors that their institution was worthy of investment.

These new responsibilities required an academic leader who could keep one foot on campus to deal with student and faculty concerns and the other foot in the world outside the academy, a world that demanded the university be more relevant to the times. As the university grew more complex, a greater need for organization, standardization, and centralized control emerged. These changes necessitated more administrative oversight and required a new, more sophisticated type of academic leader (Rudolph, 1962).

This reorientation came at a cost, however. Whereas earlier academic presidents could be expected to be deeply engaged in the daily life of the institution they served, this new administrative model gave way to the type of leader Rudolph (1962) described as someone "whose remoteness from the students would be paralleled by his remoteness from learning itself" (p. 418). The remoteness described by Rudolph became the sine qua non of the 20th-century academic president, a leader academically prepared but professionally detached from the daily work of the academy, instead addressing the pressing matters of enrollment, finances, and fundraising.

By the end of the 1920s the academy had changed dramatically again. The growth of specialized academic departments and the increasing expectation for faculty research productivity were changing the relationship between institutions and their faculties, as well as between their faculties and their students. Universities were being asked to advance knowledge through the use of more sophisticated research techniques and to address global events precipitated by the Great Depression and World War II, such as expanding international commerce and national aspirations.

The societal needs and economic prosperity of the second half of the 20th century in the United States created another set of expectations for higher education. After World War II, U.S. colleges and universities witnessed an unprecedented increase in enrollments as veterans returned from the conflict eager to earn a degree and pursue the American dream (Trow, 2007). This new national interest in pursuing a college degree, prompted by the GI Bill and perpetuated by changing workforce expectations, produced a growth in student demand that could not be accommodated by existing higher education institutions. This trend led to new models of state and federal funding for student aid and research and expansion of colleges and universities across the nation.

Kerr (1964) described what developed from this changing landscape as a new model of higher education, something he called the "multiversity." To Kerr, this new entity was governed in a fashion similar to "a system of government, like a city or a city-state: the city-state of the multiversity" (p. 20). He went on to state that this organization may "be inconsistent but it must be governed—not as the guild it once was, but as a complex entity with greatly fractionalized power. There are several competitors for this power," including students, faculty, administrators, and public authorities (p. 20).

This competition for power led to the need for a new type of academic leader who was agile enough to deal with emerging changes in institutional structure and governance—a leader who had the skills and abilities to work with government officials, handle the changing nature of faculty relations, and respond to the increasing demands of students. At the same time, this new academic leader had to possess the financial and managerial skills necessary to deal with the greatest period of expansion in the history of higher education.

The remarkable growth of higher education that marked the middle of the 20th century gave way to more austere times during which increasing demands on state and federal funding caused a reduction in the resources available for higher education. This reduced support coincided with an increasing call for greater institutional transparency and accountability. In addition, during this period colleges and universities experienced increased competition for faculty, funding, and students from sectors outside the academy, including corporations, foundations, and government agencies, as well as a growing for-profit higher education sector. This new competition, coupled with an explosion in technological innovations and communication tools, created a new set of expectations for colleges and universities to remain current and to adapt new ways of meeting the demands imposed by the changing environment, but in alignment with the mission of the institution. When set against a backdrop of a progressively more complicated legal environment, a whole new era for higher education had emerged by the turn of the 21st century.

In light of these rapid changes, it is perhaps not surprising that in the 21st century the nature of the academic presidency has changed once again. Twenty-first-century presidents, as an extension of the institutions they serve, face far more demands than their predecessors did, including greater competition, increased accountability, and an expectation to be visibly connected to their constituencies, all of which complicates the role. The remoteness of a president's relationship to their institution described by Rudolph (1962) in the middle of the last century has been replaced with a new type of president, one whose connectivity to their institution is beyond anything envisioned in past generations. By the 3rd decade of the 21st century, connectivity had taken on an expanded meaning, as higher education leaders confronted emerging social media outlets that required a more nuanced and sophisticated approach to communications.

Ikenberry (2010) provided a great example of the new level of connectivity expected of a president. After a highly successful tenure as president of the University of Illinois from 1979 to 1995, and as president of ACE for 6 years, Ikenberry returned to the faculty in 2001. In 2010, after the unexpected departure of the new president of the University of Illinois, he was asked to serve as interim president for 1 year. At that time, Ikenberry described how the academic presidency has changed in the 15 years since he had last served in that role. He said the greatest change he experienced upon his return to the presidency was the "unrelenting tsunami of electronic communication that now floods the president's office and personal life" (p. 26).

Unlike previous generations, today's presidential communications are often unfiltered, and given public expectations for a response, the need to react is immediate (Ikenberry, 2010). Ikenberry also cited a more constrained environment in which presidents and governing boards face more ambiguous and daunting challenges than he experienced during his first term in office. Though the challenges are greater and the demands have grown, in

Ikenberry's eyes, the most important role of the president has not changed, which is to "help the institution find itself, articulate and embrace its mission and mobilize others toward that vision" (p. 27).

The Role of the Academic President

If we are to understand the role of an academic president in advancing the mission of an institution, we need to understand the limits and uses of presidential power and influence. In the words of Ikenberry (2010), can an academic president really play a major part in helping a college or university find itself? Or is a president only one of many players in a complex web of institutional governance whose impact on the future success of the institution is predicated on how well they manage the interests of competing constituent groups?

Several authors have weighed in on this subject. For example, Robert Birnbaum (1988), who studied the academic presidency and then served as chancellor of the University of Wisconsin Oshkosh, has asserted that academic leaders, while important as a group, may have far less influence than most believe. Birnbaum suggested viewing the academic president's role through Burns's (1978) theory on leadership, which says that leaders approach power in two ways, transformational leadership or transactional leadership. Burns described transformational leadership as contexts in which "leaders and followers raise one another to higher levels of motivation and morality" (p. 20), while transactional leadership occurs when a person makes "contact with others for the purpose of an exchange of valued things" (p. 19).

Birnbaum (1988) viewed transformational academic leaders as being able to "significantly change the institution they serve—if the circumstances are right" (p. 205). He believed that those circumstances often occur when an institution is facing a crisis and is willing to allow the president to "exert extraordinary influence over the decision-making process" (p. 205). This type of leader is characterized by self-confidence and an ability to remain aloof from others in the institution, so as to be able to make tough decisions when necessary. In contrast, Birnbaum (1999) said that transactional academic leaders emphasize the principle of approaching their work with others as a "fair social exchange" (p. 17) in which there is mutual regard and influence. Leaders who use this approach also demonstrate respect for institutional culture and history and recognize that only after fostering a collegial approach to governance can their institution make significant progress (Birnbaum, 1999). While Birnbaum was open to the idea that an academic president could be a transformational leader, he believed that this approach is the exception rather than the rule, and that true institutional transformation in academia usually occurs through good transactional leadership.

Kerr (1964) viewed the academic presidency in a similar fashion. He agreed that as the nature of universities changed over time, the presidency followed suit, with presidents needing to establish a balance of power between their institutions' constituencies, including the board, faculty, and students (p. 34). Unlike Birnbaum (1988, 1999), however, Kerr believed that academic presidents could and do have great influence over the institutions they serve. He preferred to see the successful academic president as a highly functional "mediator-initiator," an individual who can "keep the peace and further progress" (p. 38). He promoted the ideas that an academic president should use power delicately, and that the "opportunity to persuade" (p. 40) constituent groups should be commensurate with the responsibility each group possesses.

Kerr (1964) acknowledged that each institution has its own unique history and set of circumstances. Moreover, he recognized that various groups inside and outside an institution wield power over it. In Kerr's eyes, successful presidents foster an environment in which no single constituent group has too little or too much power, and none uses that power unwisely. In the end, according to Kerr, "effective presidents must encourage cooperation among constituent groups in the hope of moving the whole enterprise forward, while reconciling themselves to the harsh realities of a job in which failures are highlighted more often than successes" (pp. 40–41).

One of the best ways academic presidents can persuade others to follow their vision for their institution is to surround themselves with a team of executives, often known as a cabinet, who agree on the institution's direction and work collaboratively to promote it. In a study of higher education senior management teams, Bensimon and Neumann (1993) discovered that effective teams view leadership as a collective and collaborative process. Too often in higher education administrators join a group and subsequently assert "their independence from it" (p. 107). In highly functioning teams, the leader creates "an environment in which members open each other's eyes to new realities, make connections across administrative and academic functions, and forge new understandings about the organization" (p. 102). In other words, members of effective collegiate cabinets or teams learn from each other and use that collective knowledge to advance their institution.

Beyond their function as a team leader, academic presidents play several roles, real and perceived. One of the most important roles a president can play is to become a personal symbol of an institution's mission, goals, and aspirations, or at least understand how to use appropriate symbols to advance the mission of the institution. Pfeffer (1977) believed all leaders are, in part, actors who need to learn how to manipulate symbols if they wish to have their roles legitimized by others in the organization. Dill (1982) also found symbolic leadership to be critically important in nourishing and maintaining the culture of an academic organization. The idea that leaders need to act symbolically is important for understanding the role of academic presidents in their institutions, where power and influence must often be shared to advance institutional goals (Dill, 1982; Pfeffer, 1977).

The actions of leaders in an academic environment are open to interpretation by others (Tierney, 1989). Successful leaders understand that everything they do (or do not do) may have meaning to some constituent group, intended or not (Tierney, 1989). In this environment, academic presidents can become the personification of institutional goals and objectives by using structural and personal symbols that demonstrate what they value (Tierney, 1989). The difficulty, however, is that " leaders must interpret the institutional culture correctly, because if they fail to do so the symbols they use may not make sense to organizational participants, which could send the wrong message and be detrimental to the leader's intended outcome" (Tierney, 1989, p. 387).

Demonstrating Respect for Mission and Culture Through Democratic Partnerships

If the essential role of an academic president is to foster democratic partnerships with key constituents to achieve organizational goals that align with and ultimately support the core mission, then it makes sense that a leader in this context would need to possess certain skills to succeed. Chief among these skills are the ability to demonstrate respect for the college or university's mission and culture, use personal and structural symbols to advance and achieve the collective institutional vision, and share governance effectively and responsibly.

Whenever an academic president makes a decision, the mission and values of the institution should be reflected in that decision. This requirement can appear to complicate matters and even make decision-making more difficult, but in reality, leaders who understand their institution's mission and can demonstrate that they are living it in their words and deeds are more likely to gain support for the choices they make. When academic presidents align their actions with institutional values, it can have a powerful and lasting impact on those they serve. Deal and Kennedy (2000) found that corporate leaders who better understand an institution's "culture and core values" (p. 24) are able to create greater unity and a sense of purpose among constituents. Multiple studies of college and university presidents have found that academic leaders are able to accomplish comparable results if they use similar approaches (Bensimon, 1989; Birnbaum, 1988; Padilla, 2005).

William G. Bowen, former provost and president of Princeton University, provided an exceptional example of this type of academic leadership when he guided that institution through its transformation from a single-gender to a coeducational institution. According to Padilla (2005), Bowen was able to accomplish so much because of his ability to articulate and position any proposed change within the context of the university's established values. For example, he created a priorities committee of various stakeholders (faculty, staff, students, and administrators) to clarify the university's goals and set priorities to move forward (Padilla, 2005).

The act of establishing such a committee demonstrated to the Princeton community that Bowen appreciated collegiality and academic excellence, two values that were widely shared by the Princeton academic community. Ultimately, his approach was interpreted by many members of the Princeton community as visionary thinking, whereas he viewed it as simply creating a structure to encourage discourse within the university, which in turn produced better results (Padilla, 2005).

Another example of a leader's demonstration of understanding an institution's values and mission is Judith Rodin, former president of the University of Pennsylvania. An Ivy League research university, Penn long ignored its surrounding neighborhood of West Philadelphia. According to Maurrasse (2001), the horrible socioeconomic conditions of the neighborhood—including poor public education, deteriorating housing, rampant violence, and a lack of economic development—made university officials question the institution's relationship with and responsibility to the local community. By the 1990s Penn had established itself as one of the world's greatest research universities through its federally funded scientific research. The importance of engagement with the local community, however, was not an institutional priority and thus was never fully valued (Maurrasse, 2001).

Recognizing this disconnect, Rodin worked with the university community to create an "urban agenda" (Maurrasse, 2001, p. 31) for Penn, making that agenda one of the six top priorities for the institution. To build consensus among key constituents for this plan, Rodin appointed Ira Harkavy, a Penn graduate and respected university employee who was nationally recognized as a leader in the field of community engagement, to be the public face of this effort. She also reminded the academic community of Benjamin Franklin's original vision for Penn: for the university to serve the city of Philadelphia.

This call for a return to the original purpose of the university, coupled with a new interpretation of the part of Penn's mission that addressed the merging of theory and practice into teaching and research, helped stakeholders see that the university had a responsibility to its local community, and that by becoming more engaged, the institution would emerge stronger in the long run (Maurrasse, 2001). A decade later, Penn had established itself as a national leader in civic engagement and had enhanced its reputation as one of the world's leading research universities. In addition, West Philadelphia has become the focus of a good deal of Penn's research activities and outreach efforts, and the community and the university are stronger for it.

In the midst of creating this urban agenda, Rodin demonstrated her respect for the culture and mission of the University of Pennsylvania in several ways. First, she never suggested that Penn should reduce its emphasis on research to pursue an urban agenda focused on creating democratic and reciprocal partnerships in the local community. Instead, she recognized the importance of research and argued that Penn's research activities could be enhanced by focusing more resources on the local community. Second, she encouraged the support of internal constituents and community leaders by hiring someone who was trusted by both groups to direct Penn's efforts. These actions demonstrated her understanding of Penn's mission and values while simultaneously advancing a more democratic agenda while adapting to a challenging urban environment.

Using Symbols to Advance Institutional Objectives

Rodin and Bowen came to symbolize important advancements at their institutions because they understood that their actions spoke louder than their rhetoric. Examples of how academic leaders have used symbols to promote their work are important reminders of how powerful this approach can be in advancing institutional goals. For example, William C. Friday, former president of the University of North Carolina system, declined pay raises later in his career because he believed the president of the system should not earn more than the governor of the state, as it would send the wrong message to North Carolinians about the university's priorities (Padilla, 2005).

In another illustration of symbolic action related to institutional finances, Gerald "Carty" Monette, former president of Turtle Mountain Community College in North Dakota, assumed the leadership of a college facing enormous challenges, including a student body that could not afford college tuition payments (Colby et al., 2003). To help the college overcome its financial difficulties, Monette worked diligently to raise funds and served without an academic dean until the school had enough money to support the position (Colby et al., 2003). This action was an important symbolic gesture because it demonstrated that his priority was to use the institution's limited resources to keep student costs low and enhance classroom instruction rather than hire more administrators.

Moving an institution strategically toward greater inclusion, equity, and social justice was on the mind of Miguel A. Nevárez when he took over as the president of Pan American University (PAU) in Texas in 1981, after serving as PAU's vice president for student affairs. During his vice presidency, Nevárez put in place several initiatives that allowed him to advance the university's mission toward greater inclusion. It is important to note that the community surrounding PAU was majority Mexican American, and Nevárez wished to establish systems, practices, and programs to serve that population. According to Avila and Pankake (2018), Nevárez was ultimately able to use his role in student affairs to increase enrollment of Mexican American students and to improve student support systems and programs.

For example, Nevárez exercised a form of interest convergence to convince his president to remove a testing requirement from the financial aid process, which led to increased enrollment (Avila & Pankake, 2018). As the first Mexican American, Latinx president at PAU, Nevárez used his political acumen to negotiate PAU's merger into the University of Texas (UT) system in 1988, which brought new resources to the financially strapped institution. During his tenure he reinforced the university's commitment to social justice by leading multiple reform initiatives and building democratic partnerships inside the institution and with key state and local partners. By 2021, Nevárez's legacy endured, even while UT Pan American and UT Brownsville merged to become UT Rio Grande Valley, as the university remained a model HSI known for its commitment to serving Mexican Americans and promoting a social justice agenda.

Theodore Hesburgh, president emeritus of the University of Notre Dame, accepted the position of chair of the National Civil Rights Commission in the 1960s in the midst of his presidency of Notre Dame. During his tenure, he gave hundreds of speeches around the country to encourage support for civil rights legislation (Padilla, 2005). His actions symbolized the importance of inclusion and diversity at Notre Dame and across the nation.

In contrast to the exemplary efforts of Friday, Monette, Nevárez, and Hesburgh, the actions of an academic president can also serve as a negative symbol of an institution. In 2002 Mark Perkins, former president of Towson University, spent hundreds of thousands of dollars on renovations of a newly acquired presidential home and $25,000 on a medallion to symbolize the authority of the office of the president at official events. To the public these actions represented excess and an insatiable appetite to spend university money on items that served only his personal tastes and had nothing to do with his ability to perform his duties as president.

A president's harmful actions can also become a symbol of a problem within higher education more broadly. In 2005, for example, Benjamin Ladner came under national scrutiny when his personal expenses as president of American University were exposed, revealing a lavish lifestyle funded by the university. This scandal led to Ladner's dismissal by American's board, and he came to symbolize the abuse of power by leaders in higher education. His behavior led to changes in board policies at colleges and universities across the nation to promote better internal controls and greater oversight of university matters.

Even highly successful and talented presidents can become symbols of controversy, even while enjoying the support of many at their institution. For example, in 2009 a group of over 100 college and university presidents joined a national movement called the Amethyst Initiative to call for a review of the national issue of underage drinking. The presidents hoped their action would open the debate on the range of options that could be pursued to address the epidemic of underage drinking on college and university campuses. Unfortunately, no real debate occurred because of powerful organizations such as Mothers Against Drunk Driving, which argued that the presidents were out of line in suggesting that the minimum drinking age might be lowered.

The Amethyst Initiative quickly came to symbolize a movement to lower the drinking age rather than a national conversation about how to deal with a serious social issue. Those who supported the initiative were quickly besieged with negative messages from public interest groups, and pressure was placed on boards to make their presidents rescind their support of such a debate. In the end, no serious national discussion about the issue of underage drinking occurred, as the presidents backed away because of the negative publicity the initiative generated for their institutions and the pressure they received from various groups.

In 2017 U.S. President Donald J. Trump announced that his administration would formally end the Deferred Action for Childhood Arrivals (DACA) program initiated by his predecessor, President Barack Obama, in 2012 (Romo et al., 2017). In response to this action, a group of college and university presidents decided to take a political stance against President Trump's edict by creating the Presidents' Alliance on Higher Education and Immigration (n.d.). The purpose of the alliance is to increase public awareness of how immigration policies and practices impact college students and university communities. To the presidents who joined the alliance, President Trump's decision to end DACA was a direct attack on the mission of higher education institutions that specifically claim diversity and inclusion as core values. On the surface, the establishment of the alliance may appear to be an expected response to a policy change that would dramatically impact DACA students and their institutions, but to those who agreed with President Trump's decision, the creation of the alliance was viewed as an attack on the president's policies. To them, the alliance was a violation of what many people thought should be the proper role of college and university presidents—to remain strictly neutral on national political issues.

Unlike the Amethyst Initiative, however, the alliance stood firm and did not back down from the political rhetoric and pressure that alumni, donors, and others placed on the organization and its members to follow the U.S. president's lead on this issue. In 2020, the U.S. Supreme Court rejected the Trump administration's attempt to end DACA and provided limited but substantial legal protection to the "Dreamers," as DACA students had become known (Totenberg, 2020).

These examples demonstrate that the actions of an individual president or group of presidents can become powerful symbols that unite people and lead to significant consequences, both positive and negative. Despite the inherent risks associated with taking a stand on important national issues, college and university presidents are in a unique position to lead. They argue that presidents should take on leadership roles through formal state and national higher education associations as well as on commissions and task forces established by elected officials to deal with specific societal issues.

Hesburgh's role on the National Civil Rights Commission exemplifies the potential positive influence that an academic president can have. It is important to note that many of the leaders we have mentioned have served in other important national roles. Most of the presidents mentioned in this chapter (especially Bowen, Friday, Kerr, Monette, and Nevárez) used their positions to advance important national and regional issues that affected their institutions and the country. Whether it was advocating for improvement of living conditions for Native Americans in North Dakota (Monette) or chairing ACE (Friday), these leaders used their positions on a broader stage to symbolize the positive role higher education can play in addressing important societal issues and to go even further to become advocates for social justice and democratic ideals.

Shared Governance: The Creation of Democratic Partnerships

The idea that academic leaders can significantly influence the nature and course of an institution is as old as higher education itself. Unfortunately, much of what has been written about leaders who led successful change initiatives focused on the personal characteristics and traits of the leaders themselves. Scholarship has rarely approached these change efforts from the perspective that leaders collaborate with their followers to achieve organizational objectives. Some authors, however, do believe that leadership is best exercised when all parties share common values and goals. For example, in 1850 Ralph Waldo Emerson developed the idea that certain leaders are "representative; first of things, and secondly of ideas" (p. 7). He proposed that the best type of leader did not proceed until securing the consent of the followers through actions or words. Coles (2000) had a slightly different way of framing this connection between leaders and followers, believing that "leaders, by definition, have to come to terms with followers . . . whose deeds will confirm the reality of what has been sought as an ideal" (p. 194).

Coming to terms with those being led is a tough task for any leader, but in higher education it is a particularly challenging endeavor. Colleges and universities operate through a complex and often confusing system of governance and decision-making processes, commonly referred to as *shared governance*, which frequently is perplexing to people from outside the academy. The idea of shared governance is widely accepted in higher education, and the role of the president is critical to its success. Several authors have argued that academic leaders, especially presidents, need to be collegial in their approach to shared governance and must seek to maintain the delicate balance of authority between constituent groups (Birnbaum, 1988; Kerr, 1964; Mortimer & McConnell, 1978). Mortimer and Sathre (2007) expanded on this idea by suggesting that effective shared governance does not occur only between constituent groups. Instead, the president must also personally engage campus constituents to establish a collegial environment. This individual approach to creating a collegial atmosphere relates to the president's relationship to the governing board as well (AGB, 2006).

Tierney and Minor (2003) found that over 90% of all four-year colleges and universities have some form of faculty governance that works within a broader framework of institutional decision-making. Kezar and Holcombe (2017) found evidence that leaders/institutions who embrace shared governance had overall better outcomes in student learning, innovation, and institutional performance than institutions that did not embrace shared governance. What is often difficult for people who are unfamiliar with higher education's shared governance model to understand is that no two systems of faculty or institutional governance are exactly alike. On the surface, the vast majority of institutions follow generally accepted practices outlined by national bodies such as the AAUP, which helps define professional standards for faculty members, and the AGB, which shares best practices in board work. Such organizations bring some uniformity to governance across institutions, but just as every college and university has its own history and culture, each institution has its own unique decision-making processes. This diversity presents an interesting challenge to the academic president, who is expected to mediate differences between myriad constituent groups while recognizing their individual sovereignty over certain decisions.

College and university presidents are expected to create democratic partnerships with all constituents, be collegial good listeners, and follow the unique governance traditions already established at their institutions, all the while remaining strategic in their thinking and bold in their decision-making. Unfortunately, many decision-making processes, and the role of each constituent group in those processes, are often poorly defined and appear contrary to democratic principles of governance. This ambiguity is especially prevalent surrounding issues that affect one constituent group but are not solely that constituent group's matters to decide, such as setting the cost for tuition.

At public or state-related institutions, setting tuition is often a complicated matter. Lacking the autonomy independent institutions have to set their own pricing, public colleges and universities are often restricted by state governments or coordinating boards on how much tuition they can charge. Presidents and chancellors of public institutions spend significant time dealing with elected officials on a wide range of issues, among which setting tuition often causes the most conflict. The most successful public university leaders are often those who have built long-term relationships with government officials and have included them in the strategic planning and vision-setting processes of their institutions.

The issue of college affordability has become a particularly potent political issue in recent years, given rising college student debt and concerns about college accessibility. Historically, state governments urged or required public colleges and universities to limit or pause increases in their tuition rates. More recently, efforts at the state and federal levels have sought to "make college free" for at least some students through a combination of student aid programs. At the same time, many state appropriations have not kept pace with the cost of higher education, leaving many public institutions in difficult financial situations and looking to rethink their economic models. Presidents play an important role in these discussions to educate legislators and government officials about the important roles that colleges and universities play in not just in educating students, but also in advancing various public policy agendas, such as economic and workforce development. Moreover, they should be at the table, working to address the issues of affordably while also ensuring the financial stability of their institutions.

In the case of independent institutions, the amount of tuition revenue they collect has a direct impact on their ability to spend on different priorities, which in turn has consequences for institutional success. For example, if administrators desire to increase faculty salaries to attract and retain more competitive candidates, increasing tuition may be the only mechanism to generate the necessary funds. Current and prospective students, however, may have difficulty affording these tuition increases and may advocate for lower tuition or decide not to enroll at all. Lower enrollment would leave fewer dollars available to advance the strategic objective of competitive faculty salaries, even though more competitive salaries could attract and retain the very best faculty, thus improving student satisfaction and institutional prestige.

Most presidents of public and independent institutions quickly recognize the ambiguity inherent in the issue of tuition and understand that for shared governance to succeed, greater investment is needed up front about common goals and objectives before decisions about setting tuition costs can be finalized. Achieving buy-in requires a governance system that respects the authority of each constituent group in the decision-making process as well as a leader with specific skills and competencies who can navigate such a complex structure and create a sense of harmony in a chaotic environment.

Creating harmony in an everchanging environment is complicated by the nuances of shared governance on each campus. We believe that decision-making is tied to four key principles: authority, responsibility, expertise, and accountability (known as AREA principles; see Figure 11.1). Many college and university communities often experience confusion as to who should be making particular decisions on campus. In the case of strictly academic matters pertaining to faculty and curricular decisions, decision-making is more easily defined. For most institutions or systems, the governing board, through its mission and bylaws, delegates control over the implementation and delivery of the curriculum to the academic units through the deans and faculty. Within this structure faculty members have very clearly defined roles regarding their individual rights, such as academic freedom, and their responsibilities around delivery of academic content to students. They are also held accountable for student learning outcomes and other accountability measures, which are typically defined through accreditation standards.

Confusion often occurs when a decision needs to be made that may have some impact on faculty or students, and certain faculty members believe they should have the authority to make the decision or at least participate in the decision-making process. In these cases, the four AREA principles should be applied. Who has the right to make the decision is based on the answers to these four questions: Who has been given authority to make the decision? Who has the responsibility for implementing the decision? Who has the necessary expertise to make a wise decision? Who will be accountable for the success or failure of the decision? Regarding an academic matter pertaining

Figure 11.1. AREA principles for decision-making in shared governance.

Colleges and universities operate in an environment of shared governance. Understanding who has the ability to make a decision can be unclear at times. Following are four principles to help understand where decision-making might rest in the shared governance environment.

AUTHORITY:
Who has been given authority by the board to make the decision?

RESPONSIBILITY:
Who has the responsibility for implementing the decision?

EXPERTISE:
Who has the necessary expertise and knowledge to make a well-informed decision?

ACCOUNTABILITY:
Who will be accountable for the success or failure of the decision?

to the delivery of academic content, the answers to these four questions all point to the faculty and the academic deans. For most other decisions on campus, the answers typically point to the president or a member of the president's senior leadership team. For example, the building of an academic building may require the expertise and counsel of the end users of the building, mainly the faculty, but the responsibility to oversee the project from its inception to its completion and to ensure it is delivered on time and on budget falls primarily to the president and the senior leadership team. Once again, a president must decide how and when to engage the faculty in decision-making, and wise presidents understand that they should consult faculty on most major institutional decisions. There should be no confusion, however, as to who is ultimately responsible for decision-making around issues that are not strictly academic in nature, and that is the president and the governing board.

Integral Leadership and Emotional Competency

In *The Leadership Imperative* (AGB, 2006), a group of distinguished scholars, trustees, and presidents proposed that "no person comes to personify an institution the way the president does" (p. vi). The reports goes on to recommend that 21st-century higher education leaders must embrace a collaborative but decisive leadership style called integral leadership, which is supported by an institution's board and includes the faculty in pursuit of a shared and distinctive vision for the college or university.

The philosophy of integral leadership is that leaders need to have a broad worldview if they are to make decisions that are in the best interest of the institutions they serve. To acquire this broad perspective leaders are required to be collaborative yet resolute in their approach and willing to make appropriate changes in direction when the environment demands it. As the AGB (2006) report explained,

> Integral leadership is where a president exerts a presence that is purposeful and consultative, deliberate yet decisive and capable of course corrections as new challenges emerge—aligns the president, faculty, and the board together in a well-functioning partnership purposefully devoted to a well-defined, broadly affirmed, institutional vision. (p. vii)

In other words, the practice of integral leadership calls for a special set of competencies in leaders that enables them to put aside their personal agendas for the greater good of the organization.

According to the AGB (2007), an institution's board of trustees is ultimately responsible for creating an environment where a president can exert such leadership. In its "Statement on Board Accountability" the AGB (2007) identified two of the major responsibilities for boards: to "approve and support the mission" and to "recruit, appoint, support and evaluate the chief executive officer" (p. 10). These tasks can be accomplished by working closely with the president and key constituents through an inclusive, evergreen planning process to articulate a clear vision for the institution. Once a vision is articulated and agreed on, boards must encourage the president to be decisive while respecting institutional shared governance traditions. Using this approach, boards can ensure a smooth transition for new academic presidents as they take on their responsibilities and assist experienced presidents in their effort to move an institution toward its stated vision for the future.

It is apparent that for an academic president to exercise integral leadership, the president must possess a unique combination of professional experiences and expertise as well as an ongoing commitment to personal growth and development. To succeed in such a challenging role, academic presidents need to cultivate and develop leadership qualities that help them build consensus among diverse groups by creating an environment based on mutual respect and trust. This type of leadership quality is often referred to as EQ or emotional competence.

The idea that intelligence could be measured in different ways was formally recognized in the last quarter of the 20th century through the work of several scholars who popularized the idea of EQ, or "the ability to monitor one's own and others feelings and emotions, to discriminate among them and to use this information to guide one's thinking and actions" (Salovey & Mayer, 1990, p. 189).

One of the early writers on the subject was Howard Gardner. In his 1983 book, *Frames of Mind*, he refuted the idea that a monolithic approach to intelligence, such as IQ, was the only way to view how smart or capable someone might be at handling different situations. Gardner proposed a wide range of intelligences and developed seven different prototypes. His groundbreaking work led to the discovery of a link between the emotional skills or competencies that some people possess, such as self-awareness, exhibiting empathy, and developing rapport with others, and the ability to accomplish personal and organizational goals.

In his 1995 book, *Emotional Intelligence: Why It Matters More Than IQ*, Goleman built on the ideas of Gardner and others to develop a framework and a method to measure someone's EQ. Goleman (1995) discovered that while IQ and technical skills were important "threshold capabilities" (p. 3), EQ was the most essential component of leadership. He reported that 90% of the difference between star performers and average performers was "attributable to emotional intelligence factors rather than cognitive abilities" (p. 3). Furthermore, Goleman found that EQ increases with maturity, and, most importantly, it can be learned through dedication and concentrated effort, such as by working with a personal coach or seeking feedback about one's own performance.

One of the nation's leading corporate executive coaches, Karol Wasylyshyn, has worked with senior executives from around the world and has drawn conclusions about emotional intelligence based on observations about their behaviors. A strong advocate for the cultivation of emotional competency skills, Wasylyshyn (2012) has found that leadership types fall on a continuum, moving from remarkable to perilous to toxic. She believes that how a leader behaves at any point is influenced by "the confluence of personal history and organizational factors" (p. 8). The key difference in a leader who is remarkable versus one who is toxic is that a remarkable leader demonstrates strong EQ, including being attuned to others, practicing adaptive behaviors, adjusting better to change, and scoring significantly higher on extraversion and conscientiousness domains.

Possessing and cultivating strong emotional competency skills are essential for an academic president to exercise integral leadership. The idea that leaders could be decisive and inclusive, putting their own personal needs aside so that institutional goals can be achieved, seems to be an improbable combination. Yet several studies have found that this combination does exist in successful executives.

In a landmark study on why some corporations exceed expectations and move from good to great, Collins (2001) described the type of leadership necessary for organizations to achieve enduring success. He identified the executives of the highest-achieving corporations as level 5 executives—people who, in his words, are "a study in duality" (p. 22). Level 5 executives are characterized by personal humility and a strong will to succeed and do whatever has to be done to make a corporation great. Level 5 leaders confront the reality of a situation and successfully navigate challenges by focusing first on attracting a team of high performers and then imparting a sense of discipline to any change process. It is also important to note that in Collins's (2001) study, executives of great companies had a deep understanding of why they existed (i.e., a sense of mission) and were able to clarify that focus through a simple but carefully executed plan.

In 2011, Collins and Hansen published a follow-up study on successful organizations. In their book, *Great by Choice*, Collins and Hansen (2011) wrote that successful leaders, now called 10x leaders, share three core behaviors: "fanatic discipline, empirical creativity, and productive paranoia" (p. 19). They described these leaders as "passionately driven for a cause beyond themselves" (Collins & Hansen, 2011, p. 33). This drive for a cause "beyond themselves" (i.e., commitment to the mission) could very well be the reason academic presidents such as Hesburgh, Rodin, Nevárez, Friday, and Monette were so successful in their roles as leaders of their institutions.

U.S. higher education is challenged by the lack of an adequate pipeline of qualified candidates to fill the demand for academic presidents in the next decade. There is, therefore, an urgent need for boards, associations, nonprofit organizations, and individual colleges and universities to find ways to cultivate the next generation of academic leaders while continuing to support the successful presidents who are already in place. This task can be accomplished through AGB's integral leadership model, but it will necessitate the adoption of a different mindset by college and university boards. That is, boards must move beyond filling one of the most demanding jobs in the world with a qualified candidate, then letting that person go at it essentially alone, left to sink or swim. Instead, boards will have to approach institutional growth and renewal by recognizing the central importance of the academic president to their institution's success and take steps to train, nurture, and develop certain competencies in those leaders (as well as in those rising administrators who aspire to the presidency).

Developing and Retaining Academic Presidents

As we discussed earlier, the typical career path for a college or university president is to rise through the academic ranks, with some part of the individual's career having been dedicated to teaching and research. The skills necessary to be a successful teacher and scholar may not, however, translate into the skill set needed to be a successful academic president. The same is true for academic presidents who emerge from nontraditional career paths. They may possess the knowledge and experience to understand very clearly one aspect of the academy but perhaps not grasp the complexity of the enterprise they will ultimately lead.

We strongly encourage colleges and universities to seriously consider ways to develop future generations of academic leaders. We recommend the adoption of best practices to help new presidents get off to a good start and help experienced presidents maintain their enthusiasm and commitment to advancing the institutions they serve. One of the basic ways to accomplish these goals is to continue to support leadership development initiatives by identifying and cultivating individuals with leadership potential early in their careers and help them navigate the often confusing options they face for career advancement. Numerous programs for midlevel to senior-level individuals can help these professionals prepare for administrative roles and develop a support network that will help them throughout their career.

For example, ACE sponsors a fellows program for faculty members and administrators with leadership potential. Fellows spend a year working with a sitting college or university president and their management team at another institution (ACE, n.d.). Obviously, this program requires a great amount of time, money, and energy from the host institution, the mentor president, the fellows themselves, and their home institutions, but program alumni achievements suggest that it is well worth the investment. By 2021 the ACE fellows program had served nearly 2,000 higher education administrators and faculty members, with over 80% of participants having "served as chief executive officers, chief academic officers, other cabinet-level positions, and deans" (ACE, n.d.). Some presidents and boards may view this initiative as a tremendous drain on their institution (due to the loss of a talented colleague for a year) as well as on the mentor president. However, most presidents who have served as a mentor have reported that it is a valuable way to reflect on their own leadership style and to promote their own institution.

Some institutions have developed their own internship and leadership training opportunities for their faculty and staff, while others regularly send colleagues with leadership potential to other development programs. These programs, lasting from a few days to several weeks, are now being offered at such institutions as Harvard University, Bryn Mawr College, and Pennsylvania State University, as well as by national organizations such as the AGB, the CIC, and the American Association of State Colleges and Universities (AASCU). AGB's program, the Institute for Leadership and Governance, approaches the role of the presidency through the dual lenses of leadership and governance—two key issues emphasized in this book. In addition to programs focused on the development of individual leaders, other programs focus on developing leaders' alignment with their institution's mission and values, such as the mission integration program offered by USD. Similar programs and training opportunities also exist for newly appointed presidents and provosts in their 1st year on the job.

Once an academic president has been hired, it is incumbent on the board of trustees to ensure that the president has the support and resources necessary to be successful. Too often presidents are selected and then left to their own devices to figure out their institution's key players and to learn the culture and nature of the institution they have just agreed to lead. A board can play a major role in supporting a new president by creating a transition team of key constituents who are charged with introducing the new president to other people who can influence the president's success, such as senior faculty and staff members, elected officials, benefactors, student leaders, and alumni.

The board should also have its own process to get to know the president through formal meetings and casual gatherings. The most important thing a board can do, however, is be clear in its expectations of the new president. Ideally, within the first few months of a president's arrival, board members and the president should meet to discuss and reflect on the mission, values, and vision of their college or university and establish a clear path to move forward that is respectful of the established shared governance model.

Experienced presidents also need support and direction from their board as well as opportunities for growth and renewal. As we have stated before, the demands of the presidency are many, and the fact that the average tenure of a president is about 6.5 years speaks to the enormity of the responsibilities and the toll the job takes on individuals and their families. The issues that academic presidents face in their first few years on the job may be very different from what they encounter years later. Board members of academic institutions that have successfully retained presidents seem to understand the changing nature of the academic presidency and have adjusted the ways in which they support their leaders. For example, some institutions have invested in executive coaches to help excellent presidents continue to grow, reflect on their leadership style, and discover new ways to enhance their emotional competency skills. Many institutions have built in sabbaticals or extended vacations to allow presidents to remain current in their academic field, pursue personal interests, seek additional training, or simply take time to renew their energy.

Ultimately, boards are responsible for the hiring, support, reward, and evaluation of their institution's president, and periodically they must make the difficult decision that new leadership is necessary. The success of an academic president requires an engaged board that focuses on the mission, strategic direction, and achievement of an agreed-on vision of the institution rather than on management issues that should be left to the administration. The best relationships between boards and presidents are those that develop trusting, reciprocal, and democratic partnerships focused on the ultimate success of the institution they mutually serve.

One key part of developing a democratic partnership between the board and the president is the evaluation process. Once the board and the president have agreed on a set of objectives and the means for evaluating the president, it is critically important that the executive committee of the board or some other appropriate board committee establish a formal annual review of the president's performance and share those results with the rest of the board. This assessment of the president is a crucial way in which a board strengthens its institution's president (AGB, 2006).

Public and independent institutions differ in their requirements for reporting the board's assessment, but in either context, the evaluation should be fair and consistent with what is done for other employees, and the review process should be transparent. After the board assesses the president's performance and provides feedback to strengthen individual and institutional performances, it is the board's responsibility to set a fair and competitive compensation package for the president, taking into consideration experience, success in the role, years of service, institutional norms, and national benchmarks. Once again, independent and public institutions differ in their public reporting responsibilities about executive compensation, but both settings the process for determining compensation should be fair, consistent with institutional values, and as transparent as possible. These practices are germane when dealing with new and experienced presidents alike.

The Future of the Academic Presidency

The idea that an academic president is or should become the personification of the mission and vision of the institution they serve is controversial and will continue to be debated for years to come. Most higher education stakeholders believe there will be no more important role in the advancement of any college or university in the 21st century (and in fact the future of U.S. higher education) than that of the academic president, while others believe the president will remain just one of many important players in a complex system of shared governance. No matter where one stands in this debate, however, consensus exists that the role of the president will continue to be demanding, changing, and critically important if shared governance is to work and an institution is to advance its mission; adapt to environmental changes; promote democratic ideals; and become a model for inclusion, equity, and social justice.

In the future the academic presidency will demand that the individuals who assume these roles possess strong emotional competency skills, appropriate experience, exceptional communication skills, and the expertise to handle the rigors of the work. The ability to create democratic partnerships and work in harmony with key constituents, especially the faculty, students, elected officials, alumni, and board members, will be essential if presidents are to succeed in the 21st century. The responsibility for developing the next generation of academic leaders should be a national priority because the future of the academy, our nation, and our democracy may depend on it.

References

American Council on Education. (n.d.). *ACE fellows program.* https://www.acenet. edu/Programs-Services/Pages/Professional-Learning/ACE-Fellows-Program.aspx

American Council on Education. (2017). *American college president study.* https:// www.acenet.edu/Research-Insights/Pages/American-College-President-Study .aspx

Association of Governing Boards of Universities and Colleges. (2006). *The leadership imperative: The report of the AGB Task Force on the State of the Presidency in American Higher Education.* Author.

Association of Governing Boards of Universities and Colleges. (2007). *AGB statement on board accountability.* https://agb.org/sites/default/files/agb-statements/ statement_2007_accountability_0.pdf

Avila, R., & Pankake, A. (2018). President Emeritus Miguel A. Nevárez: An agent for social justice in higher education. *Journal of Hispanic Higher Education, 17*(4), 294–316. https://doi.org/10.1177/1538192716670995

Bensimon, E. M. (1989). The meaning of good presidential leadership: A frame analysis. *Review of Higher Education, 12*(2), 421–431. https://doi.org/10.1353/rhe.1989.0024

Bensimon, E. M., & Neumann, A. (1993). *Redesigning collegiate leadership: Teams and teamwork in higher education.* Johns Hopkins University Press.

Birnbaum, R. (1988). *How colleges work: The cybernetics of academic organization and leadership.* Jossey-Bass.

Birnbaum, R. (1999). Academic leadership at the millennium: Politics or porcelain? *Academe, 85*(3), 14–19.

Burns, J. M. (1978). *Leadership.* Harper & Row.

Cohen, M. D., & March, J. G. (1974). *Leadership and ambiguity: The American college president.* McGraw-Hill.

Colby, A., Ehrlich, T., Beaumont, E., & Stephens, J. (2003). *Educating citizens: Preparing America's undergraduates for lives of moral and civic responsibility.* Jossey-Bass.

Coles, R. (2000). *Lives of moral leadership.* Random House.

Collins, J. (2001). *Good to great: Why some companies make the leap . . . and others don't.* HarperCollins.

Collins, J., & Hansen, M. T. (2011). *Great by choice: Uncertainty, chaos, and luck—why some thrive despite them all.* Harper Business.

Deal, T. E., & Kennedy, A. A. (2000). *Corporate cultures: The rites and rituals of corporate life.* Perseus.

Dill, D. D. (1982). The management of academic culture: Notes on the management of meaning and social integration. *Higher Education, 11*(3), 303–320. https://doi.org/10.1007/BF00155621

Emerson, R. W. (1850). *Representative men: Seven lectures.* Hurst.

Gardner, H. (1983). *Frames of mind: The theory of multiple intelligences.* Basic Books.

Goleman, D. (1995). *Emotional intelligence: Why it can matter more than IQ.* Bantam.

Hartley, H. V., III, & Godin, E. E. (2010). *A study of chief academic officers of independent colleges and universities.* Council of Independent Colleges. https://www.cic.edu/resources-research/charts-data/reports/cao-report-2019

Ikenberry, S. O. (2010). The changing demands of presidential leadership. *Trusteeship, 18*(6). http://agb.org/sites/default/files/legacy/u16/Ikenberry%20NovDec%202010_copyrighted.pdf

Kerr, C. (1964). *The uses of the university.* Harvard University Press.

Kezar, A. J., & Holcombe, E. M. (2017). *Shared leadership in higher education: Important lessons from research and practice.* American Council on Education. https://www.acenet.edu/Documents/Shared-Leadership-in-Higher-Education.pdf

Maurrasse, D. J. (2001). *Beyond the campus: How colleges and universities form partnerships with their communities.* Routledge.

McLaughlin, J. B. (Ed.). (1996). *Leadership transitions: The new college president.* Jossey-Bass.

Mortimer, K. P., & McConnell, T. R. (1978). *Sharing authority effectively: Participation, interaction, and discretion.* Jossey-Bass.

Mortimer, K. P., & Sathre, C. O. (2007). *The art and politics of academic governance: Relations among boards, presidents, and faculty.* Praeger.

Padilla, A. (2005). *Portraits in leadership: Six extraordinary university presidents.* Praeger.

Pfeffer, J. (1977). The ambiguity of leadership. *Academy of Management Review, 12*(1), 104–112. https://doi.org/10.5465/amr.1977.4409175

Presidents' Alliance on Higher Education and Immigration. (n.d.). *Our mission.* https://www.presidentsalliance.org/about/mission/

Romo, V., Stewart, M., & Naylor, B. (2017, September 5). *Trump ends DACA, calls on Congress to act.* National Public Radio. https://www.npr.org/2017/09/05/546423550/trump-signals-end-to-daca-calls-on-congress-to-act

Rudolph, F. (1962). *The American college and university: A history.* Random House.

Salovey, P., & Mayer, J. D. (1990). Emotional intelligence. *Imagination, Cognition and Personality, 9*(3), 185–211. https://doi.org/10.2190/DUGG-P24E-52WK-6CDG

Sinclair, U. (1923). *The goose-step: A study of American education.* Author.

Thomason, A. (2018, May 1). Is the college president "the toughest job in the nation"? *The Chronicle of Higher Education.*

Thwing, C. F. (1926). *The college president.* Macmillan.

Tierney, W. G. (1989). Symbolism and presidential perceptions of leadership. *Review of Higher Education, 12*(2), 153–166. https://doi.org/10.1353/rhe.1989.0027

Tierney, W. G., & Minor, J. T. (2003). *Challenges for governance: A national report.* Center for Higher Education Policy Analysis. https://pullias.usc.edu/download/challenges-for-governance-a-national-report/

Totenberg, N. (2020, June 18). *Supreme Court rules for DREAMers, against Trump.* National Public Radio. https://www.npr.org/2020/06/18/829858289/supreme-court-upholds-daca-in-blow-to-trump-administration

Trow, M. (2007). Reflections on the transition from elite to mass to universal access: Forms and phases of higher education in modern societies since WWII. In J. J. F. Forest & P. G. Altbach (Eds.), *International handbook of higher education* (pp. 243–280). Springer. https://doi.org/10.1007/978-1-4020-4012-2_13

Vasquez, M. (2020, October 30). As the pandemic grinds on, here are 5 big worries of college presidents. *The Chronicle of Higher Education, 67*(5).

Wasylyshyn, K. M. (2012), *Behind the executive door: Unexpected lessons for managing your boss and career.* Springer.

12

ENGAGING THE
EXTERNAL ENVIRONMENT

The vast number of colleges and universities in the United States pales in comparison to the number of organizations that exist to support, represent, and evaluate them. Today's colleges and universities are associated with a host of ancillary organizations that reflect the myriad interests, missions, and aspirations they represent. Some serve the academic disciplines as represented by the faculty or members of a particular professional field. Others provide grants and philanthropy in support of institutional priorities or directions. Still, others perform quasi-governmental functions by coordinating educational services of multiple institutions to meet specific regional educational needs. Many play policy and programmatic support roles to administrators or aid in governmental relations, and others perform the important function of evaluating the quality of education and its effectiveness in meeting an academic organization's stated educational purposes. Regardless of their purpose, these external organizations significantly influence institutional direction and outcomes and serve as a fluid and dynamic web linking the United States' diverse universe of colleges and universities.

Three primary reasons account for the existence of these external organizations. First and most important, the U.S. Constitution is silent on the matter of education, which by default refers the issue to the states. In the absence of centralized governmental control and authority, more decentralized mechanisms of supervision and influence emerge and proliferate. This diffused system permits multiple external groups to assume roles of varying importance in the life of an academic institution. A second reason rests in the nature of professionalism and the autonomy it demands. (See chapter 4 for a full discussion of this topic.) Given the multiple goals and various constituencies served by higher education, individuals who possess personal expertise for meeting specific goals will demand primacy in how those goals are fulfilled, and they will collectively affiliate with peers with similar expertise and interests to provide support and leverage to realize their collective interests. The third reason relates to resources. Numerous funding entities, be they private or public, have a vested interest in ensuring that their agendas are realized. As important organizations of societal and individual change, colleges and universities benefit significantly from individuals and funding entities that recognize how valuable their resources are to the financial well-being and programmatic growth of institutions of higher education—while simultaneously fulfilling their own organizational missions or philanthropic interests.

External organizations that hold influence over colleges and universities can be understood in different ways. Harcleroad and Eaton (2005) broadly classified them into three sectors, providing an excellent overview on the role of influential external organizations. First, they identified the voluntary enterprise sector, which comprises thousands of independent not-for-profit organizations that serve higher education and its multiple constituencies in varied and important ways. All local, state, and federal government agencies constitute the second sector, the public enterprise group. Third, the private enterprise group includes all for-profit entities, such as corporations, that exercise influence through donations and sponsored research to meet specific goals of mutual benefit to themselves and the colleges and universities to which they provide funding. Together these entities wield an enormous, yet often unseen, influence over academia, which led Harcleroad and Eaton (2005) to refer to as "the hidden hand" (p. 253).

Another way of categorizing these external groups is by function, and this chapter examines external influential organizations accordingly. First, some organizations serve an evaluative role, meaning that their responsibility is to ensure higher education institutions' compliance with standards of educational quality. Accrediting bodies constitute the largest group in this sector. Second, some associations serve an affiliate role that allows the collective professional interests and values of the membership to be expressed and acted upon. Many hundreds of professional membership organizations, consortia, and compacts exist to serve colleges and universities, the various constituencies within them, or governments seeking regional solutions to educational needs. Third, external entities serve a funding role, allocating resources to meet programmatic or societal outcomes. Because they are discussed in chapters 6 and 7, government agencies and the role they assume in funding higher education are not discussed here. Rather, in this chapter we primarily focus on private organizations that provide funding to colleges and universities. Together, these three roles provide a framework for understanding the vast network of organizations that influence, support, and sustain U.S. higher education and why colleges and universities have developed internal controls and institutional offices to manage these complex relationships.

The diversity of functions that these influential external organizations represent mirrors the four guiding principles of this book. Each is reflective in some way of the diverse missions of today's higher education institutions. Each is tailored in purpose to conform to the special needs and issues of the institutions or constituencies they are designed to serve, and they promote the democratic values that are the hallmark of U.S. higher education. Over the years many of these organizations have also become the standard bearers for DEI and encouraged higher education institutions to do the same. These external organizations also assist colleges and universities in adapting to their changing environments by analyzing, interpreting, and addressing the issues and challenges before them, as well as by facilitating organizational change through the allocation of targeted resources. All these efforts are pursued to maintain currency, accountability, and institutional quality. Ensuring accountability and quality is a task assigned to those organizations empowered to perform an evaluative role—the subject to which we now turn.

Evaluation and the Role of Accrediting Bodies

In the absence of any single centralized governmental authority that oversees the affairs of U.S. higher education, who or what body is responsible for ensuring that the education provided by colleges and universities meets certain minimum standards? Likewise, who defines those standards and is granted the legitimacy to establish quality benchmarks and then evaluate and enforce their attainment across the wide array of institution types?

As we see in chapter 15 in our discussion of the student experience and the role of college, divergent views exist in our society on the purpose of college, what should be taught, and how student outcomes should be measured. Such disagreement does little to guide us in terms of who should make important determinations on matters of educational content and quality. Clearly, the United States' founding fathers felt it prudent to leave such matters to others apart from federal control. Rather, the notion of self-regulation and peer review by those professionals who are experts in and responsible for education was viewed as the most appropriate means of setting and enforcing standards. How this conclusion was reached is an interesting study in the formative forces that shaped American higher education and the political struggles that accompanied it.

The term *accreditation* has a variety of meanings and resonates differently with various constituencies depending on how the term is applied. Quoting Kenneth E. Young, the first president of the former Council on

Postsecondary Accreditation (COPA), Harcleroad (1980) described accreditation as a concept, a process, and a status:

> First, it is a concept unique to the United States by which institutions of postsecondary education or professional associations form voluntary, non-governmental organizations to encourage and assist institutions in the evaluation and improvement of their educational quality and to publicly acknowledge those institutions, or units within institutions, that meet or exceed commonly agreed to minimum expectations or educational quality.
>
> Second, it is a process by which an institution of postsecondary education formally evaluates its educational activities, in whole or in part, and seeks an independent judgment that it substantially achieves its own objectives and is generally equal in quality to comparable institutions or specialized units. Essential elements of the process are (1) a clear statement of educational objectives, (2) a directed self-study focused on these objectives, (3) an on-site evaluation by a selected group of peers, and (4) a decision by an independent commission that the institution or specialized unit is worthy of accreditation.
>
> Third, it is a status of affiliation given an institution or specialized unit within an institution which has gone through the accreditation process and has been judged to meet or exceed general expectations of educational quality. (p. 12)

Harcleroad noted that numerous terms have been used to describe the process of evaluating and recognizing academic organizations, and he distinguished between the terms *approve* and *accredit*. The term *approve* connotes a qualitative judgment and may suggest that an institution is being granted an endorsement, whereas *accredit* carries a more neutral tone and has been adopted by educators as the term most frequently used to describe the concept, process, and status used in recognizing that an institution has met a certain predefined minimum standard.

The self-monitoring of educational standards is a relatively recent phenomenon given the long history of higher education in the United States. The need to introduce a structure and process to determine standards and quality emerged in the late 1800s during a profound era of change in higher education. As the United States made the transition from the age of the college to the age of the university, many new forms of institutions emerged to meet the needs of an increasingly pluralistic society and to respond to the scientific and technological developments of the day. This period in history also witnessed the decline of the classical curriculum in favor of the elective system and greater student choice in course selection. New academic disciplines and majors arose, and with them came a need to coordinate content and consistency in preparing students for the new professions required for an ascendant nation.

Minimum educational criteria for college admission also emerged as an issue during this time, as a lack of consistency in the quality of preparation for college resulted in wide disparities among the students who sought higher education. Also, the distinction between institution types and their educational rigor raised new questions on what constituted college-level work. Amid this period of enormous transition and growth, educators rapidly identified the need for a mechanism to address these vast changes and the competing standards they revealed.

The challenges educators faced transcended state boundaries and institution types. On a voluntary basis, educators in specific geographic regions came together to advocate collectively for shared goals, a process that launched the current regional accreditation structure. First came the New England Association of Schools and Colleges (NEASC) and the North Central Association of Colleges and Schools, both founded in 1885, followed soon thereafter by the Middle States Association of Colleges and Schools in 1887. Though different in small ways, these early accrediting bodies shared the goals of influencing legislation favorable to their institutions, promoting common educational interests, and especially evaluating educational effectiveness and academic preparedness at the high school level. Similar motivations led to the subsequent founding of the Southern Association of Colleges and Schools' Commission on Colleges (SACSCOC) in 1912, the Northwest Association of Schools and Colleges in 1917, and the Western Association of Schools and Colleges in 1924. These six organizations today serve as the major regional accrediting bodies responsible for ensuring the standards followed by our colleges and universities.[1]

These organizations operated in coordinative and support roles early in their histories, and their scope and importance expanded considerably after World War II, when higher education experienced profound growth because of burgeoning veteran enrollments and the U.S. response to the threats posed by the Cold War. The need for more and better instructors, coupled with the creation of many new graduate programs in a host of new disciplines and fields, prompted calls for greater professional oversight to ensure consistency in academic quality. Parallel to these developments' effects on regional accrediting bodies was the creation of scores of specialized national accrediting associations in a variety of disciplines.

Each of these developments was of significant interest to the federal government, which invested heavily in veteran education with the passage of the Servicemen's Readjustment Act of 1944 (the GI Bill). By virtue of the federal government's heavy investment in higher education through that initiative, as well as through subsequent legislation that primarily concerned financial aid issues, the government's interest in educational outcomes began to increase. In a defensive move to keep the government from encroaching too deeply into higher education affairs, educators sought to strengthen the volunteer accreditation process, but the government opted to use accreditation structures to assist in determining institutional eligibility for receipt of federal funds. This governmental policy led the six regional accrediting organizations and over 70 specialized associations in 1975 to increase coordination under the auspices of the already existing COPA, which had been established earlier to develop continuity of accreditation practices and policies nationally. An excellent history of the development of accreditation can be found in Harcleroad (1980), which also provides an illuminating overview of the issues and problems associated with it.

Accreditation is essentially a partnership between three vested interests: institutions of higher education, represented by college and university presidents and their membership associations; accrediting bodies, which represent the professional expertise to render judgment on standards of performance; and state and federal governmental entities, which allow states to charter institutions, license programs, and provide state aid, and allow the federal government to provide resources in support of legislated programs. Given the inherent tension between bureaucratic principles and professionalism, this triumvirate is bound to have struggles, and so it did with COPA. According to Bloland (1999), in the early 1990s,

> accreditation was confronting a series of conflicts and pressures: a rancorous debate on multicultural guidelines, increasing pressure by the federal government to use accreditation as a regulating device to reduce high default rates on federally guaranteed student loans, and progressive transfer of federal responsibilities to the states, which encouraged states and state governors to become more active in all things educational, including accreditation. (p. 363)

Exacerbating these problems were dysfunctions within COPA itself, whose regional accrediting commissions, specialized accrediting associations, and presidential associations representing the interests of the colleges and universities were at odds on a variety of issues:

> The national associations, led by ACE, sought to curb excessive visits and demands and unwarranted proliferation of specialized accreditors. The regional accrediting commissions complained of paying too large a proportion of the COPA dues without a commensurate voice in COPA decision making. The regionals thought the specialized and professional agencies had too much power. (Bloland, 1999, p. 364)

In short, the conflict in COPA demonstrated the challenges of balancing multiple interest groups in a highly pluralistic and democratic organization that was attempting to define and execute the difficult process of setting uniform academic standards on a national level.

What arose from the termination of COPA in 1993 was a new and restructured organization that sought to address the concerns of all parties and involve all major constituencies. More important, however, was what emerged—an organization that would be viewed as a legitimate voice on matters pertaining to higher education standards. Called the Council for Higher Education Accreditation (CHEA), its mission is to "serve students and their families, colleges and universities, sponsoring bodies, governments, and employers by promoting academic quality through formal recognition of higher education accrediting bodies and will coordinate and work to advance self-regulation through accreditation" (Eaton, 2012, para.1).

CHEA (2021) "is an association of 3,000 degree-granting colleges and universities and recognizes 60 institutional and programmatic accrediting organizations" (p. 2). The jurisdiction of CHEA extends beyond the United States to 113 other countries, where institutions and programs have chosen to be governed by CHEA's accreditation standards and processes. The organization oversees four types of accrediting organizations, including the six regional accreditors described earlier; national faith-related accreditors that focus on religiously affiliated institutions such as seminaries; national career-related accreditors that review degree-granting and nondegree, career-based, often for-profit institutions; and the many programmatic accreditors that evaluate professional schools and special programs such as those focused on business, music, medicine, law, engineering, and health professions, among others.

In 2021, 19 institutional accrediting organizations and 61 programmatic accrediting organizations were recognized in the United States (CHEA, 2021). Each accrediting body has a decision-making council known as a commission composed of faculty members, administrators, and some members of the public who review and affirm recommendations for accreditation or reaccreditation. The legitimacy of the accreditation process is granted by the participating colleges, universities, and academic programs that collectively support this peer evaluation process.

According to Eaton (2012), accreditation plays four roles. Accreditation is intended to ensure quality in the academic offerings of an institution and the fiscal stability to sustain them; provide access to federal funding, since the government will only provide student financial aid or other programmatic resources to recognized accredited institutions; engender private sector confidence by ensuring to prospective employers a proper level of credentialing; and ensure quality to facilitate the transfer of credits between institutions.

It is important to note that the government also performs an important function through the process of recognition, in that CHEA and the U.S. Department of Education collaborate to develop evaluation standards of the various accrediting organizations. This "evaluation of the evaluators" ensures a level of internal validity that helps to maintain the integrity of the entire accreditation process.

In the four-step process of accreditation, administrators of an institution first prepare a written evaluation of the institution called a self-study, based on specific standards established by the accrediting organization. Second, an evaluation team, constituted of faculty members and administrators from other institutions trained in a review protocol, conducts a peer review. Third, the evaluation team conducts a multiday site visit to the institution. The team examines the level of consistency between the self-study and actual practice as determined through personal observation and document review. Fourth, the evaluation team issues a report to the accrediting organization commission in which it cites the strengths and weaknesses of the institution under review, as well as any relevant recommendations. Periodic reviews and updates may be required of the institution prior to the next regularly scheduled review. Most evaluations occur every 10 years, often with two interim reports required (Eaton, 2012).

As with any process that involves control and influence or yields such important consequences as the continuation or discontinuation of an institution or program, accreditation can be misused. Specifically, particular social or educational agendas can be advanced through the inappropriate application of accreditation. Young et al. (1983) cited several instances when such abuse could occur:

> The groups that have most particularly attempted to use accreditation in ways that depart from generally accepted principles are (1) government bodies, both federal and state, that have seen accreditation as a potentially useful regulatory adjunct, (2) professional organizations that have viewed accreditation as a tool for association advancement, and (3) institutions of postsecondary education, or units within them, that have recognized that accreditation can be used as a lever for accomplishing certain institutional purposes. (p. 75)

Governmental entities can misuse accreditation processes to gain compliance with certain federal or state agendas or social policies. As providers of funds, usually in the form of student financial aid, governments place accrediting bodies in the position of serving a quasi-public function. Accreditors are tasked with ensuring that institutions are meeting certain legislative or administrative goals, or in the case of states, that institutions are meeting some minimum standard of institutional or programmatic quality to meet state funding or licensing requirements.

Professional organizations can advance their individual agendas through accreditation at the programmatic or disciplinary level. Faculty members and administrators can use the accreditation process to influence evaluators on certain institutional deficiencies and the need for resources to correct them, even if they are not central to the overall quality of the institution. Despite these potential areas of mistreatment, Mayhew et al. (1990) exhaustively examined accreditation and concluded that "voluntary accreditation is still the best mechanism for certifying undergraduate quality" (p. 231), despite flaws in the system and the process.

Any discussion of accreditation must mention the role of assessment, as the two concepts are interrelated. Both accreditation and assessment refer to quality assurance and speak to the requirement that each institution and program be accountable for the education it delivers. Assessment, or the measurement of success in achieving desired educational outcomes, emerged as a prominent issue in the late 1980s when former U.S. Secretary of Education William Bennett supported the creation of criteria for student outcomes in the accreditation process. Since then, the practice of assessment has gained momentum and now represents an important component of the overall accrediting process (Ratcliff et al., 2001). Building on others' research, Ratcliff et al. (2001) identified four reasons for the focus on assessment: political, economic, educational, and societal.

> Political reasons include the need of government officials to ascertain that funds allocated to higher education are being used effectively for programs and services. Assessment is seen as a tool to ensure that colleges and universities produce graduates who constitute a well-trained, competent, and competitive workforce—the economic reason. Educational reasons for assessment often come from within higher education and are reflected in the various national reports. In these reports, quality is most often the primary educational reason for implementing assessment. The societal reason refers to the broader public aspect of higher education. Society needs to understand what higher education is offering and how it meets the needs of the public. (p. 14)

The assessment process is intensive and involves professional judgments on a variety of factors. Since assessment processes are intended to collect and interpret information on how effective an institution is in realizing the stated educational outcomes desired of its students, disagreements will occur over why assessment needs to occur, what is to be assessed, how it will be done, how results will be interpreted, and what shall be done with the findings (see Rowntree, 1987). Given today's challenges to improve student outcomes, increase college graduation rates, and respond to society's demands for more accountability in a competitive world, assessment is becoming an important component of the overall accreditation process.

Accreditation organizations are held accountable by the U.S. Department of Education, which controls access to federal financial aid (Eaton, 2020; see chapter 6, this volume). In 2019, then-Secretary of Education Betsy DeVos initiated a review process of accreditation bodies' effectiveness and competence, as well as the legislation and federal law that governs them (Eaton, 2020). Federal law requires consultation with constituents in such rule-making negotiations, and the outcome of this process, with the unanimous agreement of the 15 negotiators handpicked by the Department of Education, went into effect in July 2020 (Eaton, 2020; Fain, 2019). DeVos defended the new policy, and the Council for Regional Accreditation Commissions wrote a statement in support of it, arguing that it would reduce costs and paperwork and streamline accreditation processes while still supporting student access, outcomes, flexibility, and innovation, higher education stakeholders. Democratic members of Congress criticized the new regulations, stating that they would dismantle protections for students and taxpayers and could weaken federal oversight over college quality (Fain, 2019). Specifically, the new regulations require accrediting agencies to grant more autonomy to institutions of higher education (Eaton, 2020). The updated policy also accelerates the accreditation process for higher education institutions, allows the Department of Education to recognize new accrediting organizations more quickly, extends from 2 to 4 years the timeframe during which colleges and universities may meet accreditation requirements, and permits institutions to create new academic programs and open new branch campuses without obtaining previously required approvals from their accreditors (Eaton, 2020). In addition, the new regulations have opened up what had been a strictly regional process, changing it to one in which all federally approved accreditation organizations may operate throughout the United States, a change that Eaton (2020) suggested would have both potentially positive and negative implications for accreditors and the institutions with which they work. At the time of this writing, it remains to be seen what changes to these new regulations the Biden administration may pursue.

Membership Organizations

We have noted that democratic partnerships within and among colleges and universities are a defining feature of higher education in the United States. Few entities demonstrate the breadth of those partnerships better than the thousands of representative organizations that have been created over the years to support the professional interests of the many and varied constituencies within academe and the shared educational interests of the institutions they serve. In addition to accrediting organizations, three other types of membership organizations exercise important influence over the direction of higher education: regional compacts, consortia, and voluntary individual membership organizations. Each plays a unique but important role in providing educational services, guidance, and professional development to sustain and propel the higher education enterprise.

Regional Compacts

Regional compacts were created out of a shared need by multiple states in a geographic region to provide and coordinate certain types of educational services within and across state boundaries. Compacts are legislatively created and are contracted by the states within a region to provide specific educational programs usually not available at traditional colleges or universities. These services can include, but are not limited to, research and policy studies to understand regional educational needs, seminars and workshops on topics of regional interest, and coordination and administration of interstate arrangements to meet specific programmatic goals. Each compact is supported financially by its member states along with private foundations and federal agencies. Membership is derived through acts of individual states' legislatures that are signed by their governors. Each agency maintains a small staff and is governed by a board or commission appointed by the governors of the member states. Today four such regional compacts exist. Listed in order of the dates of their creation, they are the Southern Regional Education Board, 1949; the Western Interstate Commission for Higher Education (WICHE), 1953; the New England Board of Higher Education, 1955; and the Midwestern Higher Education Compact, 1991. Only New York, New Jersey, and Pennsylvania are not affiliated with one of the four compact organizations.

States' cooperation in these compacts extends to collaboration and cost-cutting measures in a variety of areas, including research and policy studies, international education and student exchanges, graduate and professional education, cooperative purchasing programs, and many others. Though beyond the scope of this chapter, Harcleroad and Eaton (2005) have provided excellent examples of some of the more successful collaborative programs and noted the flexibility these compacts provide to their regions as they constantly adapt their educational offerings to the changes continually occurring in our society.

Consortia

Individual colleges and universities can benefit from aligning in consortia as well. Advantages may include building successful legislative lobbying efforts, entering purchasing collaboratives for utilities or campus services to reduce expenditures, linking computer services in wide area networks, generating data for institutional decision-making, sharing academic programs or faculty expertise, promoting a certain educational goal (such as service learning), enhancing faculty and administrative development, and a host of other purposes that depend on mutual support to achieve articulated shared goals.

Consortia, therefore, may assume many forms for many purposes. What they all have in common is that they are voluntary, derive most of their income from dues or fees paid by member institutions, and generally maintain a small staff headed by a director. Member colleges and universities may be of the same institution type or may align because of a shared interest in some particular purpose. The value of participation in a consortium rests in the influence the group lends to achieving collective institutional goals, be they political, economic, or programmatic.

The nature of consortia can be tenuous or concrete, depending on the goals to be achieved and the relative usefulness these institutional collectives bring to their member institutions. For example, the former East Central College Consortium in Ohio existed for several decades to promote best practices and collaborative opportunities for faculty and administrators at about 10 similar private colleges in Ohio and Pennsylvania. Disbanded in 2009 at a time of tight budget constraints, the functions of the consortium were no longer viewed by many of the member institutions' presidents as having the value they did in earlier days.

Conversely, the Association of Independent Colleges and Universities of Pennsylvania continued to enjoy strong member support during a similar time of budget constraints. Its primary mission is to serve as a lobbying organization directed at members of the Pennsylvania state legislature whose votes are essential to continued state support for student financial aid through the Pennsylvania Higher Education Assistance Agency, a program that significantly benefits enrollment figures for the association's member institutions. Though the association provides numerous other important functions for its members, its influence on state government is crucial for its member institutions. These two examples demonstrate how the success of consortia depends on the value ascribed to them by member organizations and how environmental factors can alter that value at any time.

Consortia are not new. The first consortium in higher education was the Ohio College Association, founded in 1867. Other consortia appeared throughout the early 20th century as the need for collaboration became apparent for programmatic and economic purposes. The latter half of the 20th century witnessed significant growth in these groups, coinciding with the rapid expansion of higher education in the 1960s and 1970s and the emergence of new opportunities for institutions to align on a variety of programmatic and political issues. This increase in the number of consortia prompted the creation in 1965 of an umbrella membership organization called the Council of Interinstitutional Leadership, now known as the Association for Consortium Leadership, which provides a venue for consortium leaders to share ideas, services, and projects and stimulate information sharing between consortia.

The 2020 edition of the *Higher Education Directory* listed 81 major consortia-serving organizations throughout the United States (Rodenhouse, 2020). These groups range in scope, from supporting institutions of the same type (e.g., independent colleges and universities, community colleges, elite private institutions, state-owned universities) in the same state to providing specific services to meet different individual and organizational needs. For example, in 1982 the state of Connecticut, in conjunction with Connecticut colleges and universities, established the Connecticut Higher Education Supplemental Loan Authority to provide supplemental student loans separate from student financial aid packages. The program enhances opportunities for students to complete their degrees when faced with financial challenges. The Consortium of College and University Media Centers, based at Indiana University, serves as a forum for the improvement of instructional media delivery and academic technology. In addition, the Midwest Universities Consortium for International Activities represents a consortium of three land-grant research universities: The Ohio State University, Michigan State University, and the University of Minnesota. Founded in 1964 with a grant from the Ford Foundation, its purpose is to provide a variety of educational and technical services to international students and foreign governments and universities. These are but three examples of the varied nature of consortia and the important purposes that are fulfilled through cooperation made possible by formalized relationships.

Institutional Membership Organizations

Voluntary membership organizations exist to support the missions and interests of all types of colleges and universities and their disciplines and academic programs. While compacts represent the collective interests of certain states within a region as they relate to the provision of shared educational services, and consortia tend to be alliances of a limited number of institutions benefiting from a collaborative relationship, institutional membership organizations tend to be more national in scope. They also have a broader base of participation and a more focused agenda that conforms to the specific needs and issues that confront like institutions. Consequently, these collectives mostly reflect specific institution types as well as the various constituencies that serve them. As they most often represent institutions and constituencies on a national and even international level, their influence is significant and their impact on the improvement and growth of higher education is considerable. Many of the largest and most powerful of these organizations are based in Washington DC.

The impact that these organizations have on the direction of higher education in general and their member institutions, in particular, is significant. Organizations that serve an umbrella function to represent the collective interests of all of higher education are especially powerful. For example, the ACE serves as the singular voice of over 1,800 accredited colleges and universities and provides a host of programs and services to improve U.S. higher education. Founded in 1918, ACE has sponsored numerous commissions and committees to address such issues as educational quality and access, gender equity, and institutional leadership. It plays an important role in influencing legislation on higher education and helped to pass the Post-9/11 Veterans Educational Assistance Act of 2008, otherwise known as the Yellow Ribbon Program, to provide financial aid for veterans of the Iraq and Afghanistan conflicts. ACE also developed and administers the General Education Development (GED) high school educational equivalency testing program, and in conjunction with the Carnegie Foundation and the College Board, it founded the Educational Testing Service (ETS). In addition to its role as a membership organization for so many colleges and universities nationwide, ACE also performs the role of a consortium, serving as coordinator for about 50 national higher education membership organizations that collectively meet monthly to discuss issues and policies affecting higher education nationally. Called the Washington Higher Education Secretariat, the group's work holds significant importance as Congress continues to examine the federal government's role in such matters as student financial aid, support for research, institutional accountability, student outcomes, and higher education's collective response to the policies that Congress may propose.

Numerous other major membership associations represent the interests of subsets of institutions. These organizations include the Association of Public and Land-Grant Universities, (APLU, formerly the National Association of State Universities and Land-Grant Colleges), the National Association of Independent Colleges and Universities (NAICU), the CIC, and the American Association of Community Colleges (AACC), to name a few. Occasionally referred to as *sector associations*, they exist to promote the mission and interests of the institution types they represent, including representing their sectors to legislators and policymakers, sponsoring national forums for members to exchange ideas and best practices, and representing their sectors to the public at large.

Promoting institutional mission can also be an important function of associations such as the AAC&U, which has responded to the growing national focus on vocationalism by taking an active role in highlighting the value and importance of liberal learning and the unique place liberal arts colleges have in building an educated citizenry. Most associations provide ongoing communication and updates for their membership on a host of issues and developments, and those associations whose primary purpose is influencing national higher education policy involve their members in lobbying members of Congress. These associations derive their funding predominantly through membership dues, grant support, and sponsorships by vendors whose products and services may benefit the operations of member institutions.

Professional Membership Organizations

Still, other associations focus on constituencies in higher education and support their professional interests. The AGB, for example, serves as a national resource for institutional governance issues and trusteeship, with a special focus on the relationship between trustees and presidents. In addition to producing the monthly magazine *Trusteeship*, AGB sponsors conferences and forums on effective institutional governance and provides professional experts for consulting services. NACUBO is the representative voice of chief financial officers and controllers. In addition to its regular meetings at which members can share best practices, NACUBO provides research and data on a host of topics to support institutional financial decision-making. These resources are especially useful to campus leaders who must make a variety of financial decisions but lack comparative data with other institutions that can lend a point of reference. The work of NACUBO is essential in providing these data.

The continued importance of philanthropy, alumni relations, and fundraising in higher education, along with the need to expand the marketing, branding, and communications efforts that are necessary to be competitive in the 21st century, has led to significant investments on most campuses into the field of institutional advancement. Once viewed as peripheral to the operations of an institution, most universities now recognize how vitally important it is to have trained advancement professionals in key alumni, communications, and fundraising roles on campus. According to a survey of presidents conducted by ACE in 2020, one of the top five concerns of university leaders is the financial viability of their institution and the need for more financial support for students in the form of scholarships (Vasquez, 2020). To support institutional leaders and advancement professionals as well as to monitor the important role philanthropy plays in educational institutions, the Council for the Advancement and Support of Education (CASE) has grown to become one of the largest educational associations in the world, serving over 90,000 advancement professionals.

Moreover, membership associations can be found for virtually every administrative group within higher education. Admissions professionals have the National Association for College Admission Counseling (NACAC); financial aid administrators can join the National Association of Student Financial Aid Administrators (NASFAA); and registrars often belong to the American Association of Collegiate Registrars and Admissions Officers (AACRAO). Beyond this sample of the hundreds of professional membership associations that support higher education and its administrative functions, scores of membership associations exist for faculty members and the many academic disciplines they represent. Such associations often possess strict criteria for individual membership and lend considerable influence in maintaining the currency and quality of academic content taught in the classroom.

Together, these associations represent a significant influential force on the future direction of higher education, which could not be realized without them. They provide a venue for the professional exchange of ideas, issues, and best practices among its members; they influence how governmental policy is developed; and they offer their members a variety of services and resources to support the missions and functions they represent.

The Role of Athletics at Colleges and Universities

Of all the membership organizations associated with colleges and universities in the United States the one with the most name recognition among the general public is the NCAA. The NCAA is a not-for-profit membership organization of almost 1,100 colleges and universities that supports, regulates, and helps facilitate intercollegiate athletic competition across the United States (NCAA, n.d.).

Most NCAA member schools also belong to a separate multisport athletic conference typically aligned by region, institution type, and level of competition. Competition in the NCAA is divided into three divisions: I, II, and III. The level at which a school plays is dependent on the number of sports that it sponsors and whether the institution provides financial aid to students for their participation in a sport. Unlike many of the other organizations associated with higher education, the NCAA is financed primarily from revenue generated by massive television and media contracts, primarily those associated with the Division I men's basketball tournament.

The idea of creating an association that would regulate intercollegiate athletics began early in the 20th century when there was a public outcry over the safety of intercollegiate football student-athletes. This uproar soon led to the creation of the NCAA in 1906 to reform the rules and regulations of college sports. The historian Frederick Rudolph (1962) believed that the rise of college football and intercollegiate athletics helped higher education gain more attention from the broader public. He wrote that football in particular "brought into the camp of college and university supporters, people for who the idea of supporting a team was a matter of course" (p. 385). He went even further to suggest intercollegiate athletics helped promote the democratic ideals of higher education when he stated, "If football served democracy on the campus by being an instrument of social elevation, it served off-campus democracy by creating an important agency of popular entertainment" (p. 385).

By the 21st century, intercollegiate athletics had become one of the biggest sources of revenue as well as one of the largest expenses for colleges and universities. According to the "Finances of Intercollegiate Athletics," an annual report sponsored by the NCAA (2020), in 2019 total athletics revenue reported among all NCAA Division I athletic departments was $18.9 billion, and the expenses were reported at $18.8 billion. It is difficult to calculate the full impact of athletics—and especially athletic success—on college admissions and donations from happy alumni and athletic boosters. For example, it is not uncommon for an institution to see a rise in prospective student applications after winning a national Division I football or basketball championship due to the high level of media coverage such events attract in the United States. This tendency has led many institutions to invest larger amounts of money in athletic facilities and coaching salaries in pursuit of athletic success. On many campuses with successful athletic programs, the head basketball or football coach frequently earns the highest salary at the entire institution.

Since the rise of college athletics at higher education institutions across the country, local communities where colleges and universities are located have been affected in both positive and negative ways. For some communities, athletic competitions, especially in football and basketball, can attract tens of thousands of visitors to the region and have a tremendous positive impact on the local economy. However, town–gown relations are often strained when local government services such as police and fire departments are stretched to meet the demand of thousands of people descending on the local community.

Another issue associated with intercollegiate athletics is the impact of athletics on the student-athletes themselves. The notion that intercollegiate athletics could be an avenue for young men (and, later, young women) to find their way into college has been around since the early 20th century. It can be argued that for some colleges and universities, if it were not for athletics, the campus would have a much less diverse student body, and the general student population would suffer from that lack of diversity. (See chapter 3 for a discussion on how diversity enhances learning.)

Serious concerns remain over the health and safety of student-athletes, especially those engaged in high-contact sports in which injuries are linked to long-term detrimental effects on participants. Likewise, there has been greater scrutiny regarding the use of student-athletes' names, images, and likenesses, including whether players should be more generously rewarded for their use when their college athletic program benefits from it. There has also been a push to improve graduation rates of student-athletes in high-profile college sports. While most student-athlete graduation rates are above 80% (when aggregated by sport), football student-athletes still lag slightly behind with a 2020 graduation rate of 78% (Dolan, 2020; Lapchick, 2020). The 16.3% gap between graduation rates of Black (73.4%) and White (89.7%) student-athletes on bowl-bound Division I football teams still needs to be effectively addressed (Lapchick, 2020).

The role of the NCAA in higher education is both complex and complicated, and several reform efforts have attempted to make the association more responsive to the needs of its members while continuing to tackle larger societal issues. In addition to serving as a facilitator of athletic competition, it must also be an enforcer of rules and regulations. As the central agency for intercollegiate athletics in the United States, it plays a significant role with federal and state elected officials and is often involved in major legal battles that set precedent in the courts (see chapter 8, this volume).

Over the years the NCAA has also weighed in on tough societal issues associated with DEI. For example, it was a leader in opposing the use of the Confederate flag (seen as a symbol of hate) by refusing to hold NCAA championship games in states that still incorporated that symbol in their state flags. It also took a stand to allow transgender student-athletes to participate in intercollegiate athletics at a time when many states were passing laws discriminating against transgender youth.

There is no doubt that intercollegiate athletics will continue to play a major role in higher education. Therefore, the NCAA is likely to continue to be one of the most significant and most scrutinized associations in higher education for many years to come.

Foundations and Philanthropy

Foundations are playing an increasingly important role in furthering individual, organizational, and national goals for postsecondary education that are consistent with their philanthropic purposes. Colleges and universities serve as engines of social change and therefore are a significant beneficiary of the resources that foundations provide. In 2019, foundations gave $75.69 billion, which made up over 16.8% of philanthropic donations in the United States that year (Corporate Philanthropy Report, 2020). In 2018, foundations donated $14.01 billion to institutions of higher education, which represented 30% of all gifts to higher education (Council for Aid to Education, 2019). These impressive levels of support were made possible by a variety of foundations, including independent, corporate, community, and operational foundations established to support special purposes. The funds provided to U.S. colleges and universities from these sources help institutions shape their programs and educational outcomes in meaningful ways.

Foundations have existed in the United States since its inception, but they rose in prominence and impact following the Civil War, when wealthy industrialists employed vast discretionary personal assets to meet a variety of philanthropic interests. According to Kiger (2000), Benjamin Franklin is credited with creating the earliest form of a foundation when he established two trusts, one in Boston and the other in Philadelphia, the earnings from which were to provide loans to young inventors of "good character" (p. 40). In 1829, Englishman James Smithson left a large bequest to the United States to promote the creation and dissemination of knowledge; an act of Congress established a museum and research programs with his gift. Because of Smithson's philanthropy, visitors to the Smithsonian Institute in Washington DC, enjoy free exhibits and services.

At end of the 20th and beginning of the 19th centuries, wealthy industrialists such as George Peabody, Andrew Carnegie, and John D. Rockefeller provided sizable sums of their vast fortunes to create foundations expressly intended to meet a variety of social needs, most prominent among them education and research. Carnegie is usually viewed as the father of the philanthropic foundation, having established a prototype with the Carnegie Institute of Washington in 1902 with an initial corpus of $10 million, soon followed by the Carnegie Corporation of New York in 1911–1912. Over the next 40 years, many of today's most prominent national foundations—many of which provide significant support to higher education—were established, including the Russell Sage Foundation (1907), the Rockefeller Foundation (1913), the Kellogg Foundation (1930), and the Ford Foundation (1936). Together, these earliest major foundations significantly contributed to the improvement of society in general, and colleges and universities have been among their many beneficiaries.

The four types of foundations are distinguished by their purpose and source of funds. Independent foundations represent the largest group, and most of the wealthiest and well-known national foundations are of this type, such as the Kresge Foundation, the Kellogg Foundation, and the Bill and Melinda Gates Foundation. These independent foundations possess significant assets, provide grants for a wide range of programs and purposes, and are reflective of the philanthropic interests of the benefactors who created them. Smaller family foundations that dispense fewer or smaller grants for charitable purposes can also be classified under the heading of independent foundations.

Community foundations serve an urban or regional area and derive their assets from multiple sources, most often residents and businesses in their vicinity. These foundations are repositories for philanthropic dollars intended to meet local needs in either a restricted (earmarked) or unrestricted fashion and play an important role in furthering the philanthropic climate of many communities.

Corporate foundations are established to meet corporate philanthropic interests and often do so on a quid pro quo basis, meaning that the recipient of corporate foundation funds is engaging in an activity that also benefits the company itself, either directly or indirectly. Operating or special purpose foundations are established to provide a funding stream to a single organization and occasionally may make grants to outside interests. Over the years colleges and universities have derived grant funding from all four types of foundations, often with the most influential grants coming from the large national independent foundations that share specific programmatic interests and goals.

According to McIlnay (1998), foundations are among the least understood of organizations: "Inaccessibility, secrecy, and uncooperativeness have long characterized the behaviors of foundations" (p. 6). In part, this lack of understanding stems from the personal nature of foundations since they represent the application of private funds to meet the specific interests of their benefactors. One could argue that the need for discretion and privacy by foundations results from the significant influence they exert in society and the favored tax status they enjoy, even when the government may not share the specific goals some foundations promote. This lack of transparency was particularly challenging for not-for-profit organizations that applied for foundation funding in earlier decades. However, the emergence of a grant-seeking profession in which specialists identify and seek funding for the not-for-profit sector, together with more centralized information sources about grantors and their giving priorities, has aided in fostering greater understanding and transparency of foundations. "In the 1970's the lack of information on foundations became so pronounced that a whole grantsmanship industry sprang up to provide information to grantseekers that foundations could not or would not furnish" (McIlnay, 1998, p. 7).

McIlnay (1998) identified six roles or "faces" that foundations assume as they carry out their philanthropic missions: judges, editors, citizens, activists, entrepreneurs, and partners. They are active participants in the process of social change and through their philanthropy can direct policy, shape outcomes, and improve society in important ways on global and local levels. For example, the Bill and Melinda Gates Foundation (KPMG, 2020) held over $51.9 billion in assets in 2020 and is focusing much of its significant wealth on issues of global health and economic development worldwide. The foundation's U.S. programs center on enhancing social mobility and opportunity with special emphasis on projects to improve public education.

But local and regional foundations are making enormous impacts as well. With over $21.4 million in assets in 2019 (ProPublica, 2019), the much smaller Marion G. Resch Foundation of economically depressed Youngstown, Ohio, is making enormous strides in helping underserved, inner-city children prepare for and access higher education. The Resch Foundation is a partner with several area colleges that work with elementary and high school students to provide a variety of early intervention programs designed to enhance future college matriculation (Thiel College, 2020; Westminster College, 2016). Scholarship support from the foundation is also provided for those students who successfully advance to college. As the focus on educational outcomes grows, the role of foundations will become even more important to colleges and universities, as reduced government funding places greater demands on academic institutions to secure private funding to support their varied educational missions.

Growing Importance of Advancement in Higher Education

The first college in America, Harvard College (now Harvard University), was founded by the Massachusetts Bay Colony in 1636 and obtained its name after a Cambridge-educated clergyman who had emigrated from England, John Harvard, "left half his property and all his library to the College" upon his death in 1638 (Morison, 1986, p. 9). That original act of philanthropy began a tradition in America that has continued until today. Since that beginning act of generosity, individuals, foundations, and later corporations have had an extraordinary impact on higher education. The influence philanthropy was having on colleges by the beginning of the 20th century actually made President Jacob Gould Schurman of Cornell University nervous, so much so that in 1909 he stated, "The very ambition of such corporations to reform educational abuses is itself a source of danger" (Rudolph, 1962, p. 433). He went on to assert, "Men are not constituted educational reformers by having millions of dollars to spend," (Rudolph, 1962, p. 433).

If subsequent generations of presidents and boards had similar worries in the years that followed, they were rarely expressed. Today colleges and universities realize that to meet the demands of their students and other stakeholders, institutions need a margin of excellence in the execution of their missions, and it usually can only come from philanthropy. As funding from student tuition or government support no longer fully meets the budgetary needs of colleges and universities it has become imperative that they create ways to attract philanthropic support through sophisticated advancement operations inside their institutions.

Alumni have often been the individuals most likely to support their alma maters. Some colleges and universities have long traditions of organizing alumni to help advance the mission of the institution. Most have developed internal institutional mechanisms to promote the school so it can attract more philanthropic support. Once viewed as a luxury, sophisticated advancement operations are now the norm in U.S. higher education. Most independent colleges and universities typically employ someone who leads fundraising through alumni, government relations, and communications offices and reports directly to the president. In many public universities, separate institutional foundations have been created to avoid state government interference in advancement activities.

In the 21st century, philanthropic support to colleges and universities has reached astronomical proportions considered impossible just 50 years ago. For example, in 2018, Michael Bloomberg, a highly successful international businessman, U.S. presidential candidate, and philanthropist gave a gift of $1.8 billion to his alma mater, Johns Hopkins University. At the time, it was the most given to a university by an individual in history. While high-profile gifts are important, most universities conduct fundraising "campaigns" to attract donations from alumni, foundations, corporations, and other supporters. In colonial times colleges might conduct "subscription" drives (Rudolph, 1962, p. 182) that asked potential benefactors for goods such as food to feed the students, books, or even labor to help keep a college afloat, but by the end of the 20th century, all major universities had engaged in multiyear campaigns to raise funds.

Until the late 20th century large fundraising campaigns were thought to be strictly the domain of the private sector of higher education. That perspective changed in the 1980s, however, when the Pennsylvania State University conducted the largest campaign to date for a public research university and raised $300 million. In 2020, the University of California, Berkeley, announced a $6 billion campaign—a campaign 20 times the size of the Penn State campaign just 3 decades years before.

Most college and university presidents, academic deans, and other campus leaders are expected to achieve specific fundraising goals each year, and part of their performance evaluation is based on their ability to attract funds. Fundraising requires personal skill and the ability to convince donors that the institution is worthy of philanthropic support. To accomplish such goals colleges and universities are investing more money in sophisticated advancement programs. With dwindling government support, rising costs, and the need of higher education institutions to distinguish themselves from the competition, the ability to attract funding from philanthropic sources will be crucial for institutional survival and success. While just 50 years ago advancement activities were viewed as peripheral to the work of college and university leaders, this work has now become one of their key responsibilities.

Conclusion

The diverse missions of U.S. colleges and universities; the numerous higher education constituencies that must interact in a democratic fashion; and the everchanging social, political, and economic environment in which academic institutions operate all serve as reasons for the emergence and growth of external organizations that orbit the higher education enterprise. Higher education institutions depend on these ancillary organizations for the direction, coordination, and resources they need to fulfill their educational purposes.

The very presence of these external organizations reinforces the four main principles that serve as the foundation for this book, and their influence is substantial. The many challenges confronting U.S. higher education today can be resolved not through the independent efforts of each college or university, but through collective efforts to identify those challenges, research responses, implement solutions, and assess outcomes. Ongoing concern for and commitment to ensuring access and affordability, enhancing educational quality, improving graduation rates, and producing an enlightened citizenry require ongoing attention by external organizations and stronger partnerships between them and the institutions they serve.

Notes

1. Five of the six higher education accrediting bodies became distinct entities and experienced name changes in the last several decades. In 2018 the New England Commission of Higher Education (NECHE) became an independent organization from the New England Association of Schools and Colleges, the Higher Learning Commission (HLC) grew out of the North Central Association in 2014, the Middle States Commission on Higher Education (MSCHE) was spun off the Middle States Association of Colleges and Schools in 2013, the Northwest Commission on Colleges and Universities (NWCCU) separated from the Northwest Association of Schools and Colleges in 2004, and the WASC Senior College and University Commission (WSCUC) left the Western Association of Schools and Colleges as of 2012–2013.

References

Bloland, H. G. (1999). Creating CHEA: Building a new national organization on accrediting. *Journal of Higher Education, 70*(4), 357–388. https://doi.org/10.1080/00221546.1999.11780768

Corporate Philanthropy Report. (2020). Analysis of workplace giving campaigns offers tip on employee engagement. *Corporate Philanthropy Report, 35*(8), 1, 12. https://doi.org/10.1002/cprt.30653

Council for Aid to Education. (2019, February 19). *2018 Voluntary support of education, 2018.* https://www.case.org/resources/2018-voluntary-support-education

Council for Higher Education Accreditation. (2021). *2020–2021 directory of CHEA-recognized accrediting organizations.* http://www.chea.org/2020-2021-directory-chea-recognized-accrediting-organizations-pdf

Dolan, O. (2020, December 9). *The graduation success rate of NCAA student-athletes reaches an all-time high.* Swimswam. https://swimswam.com/the-graduation-success-rate-of-ncaa-student-athletes-reaches-an-all-time-high/

Eaton, J. S. (2012). *An overview of U.S. accreditation.* Council for Higher Education Accreditation. https://eric.ed.gov/?id=ED544355

Eaton, J. S. (2020, March 17). Will regional accreditation go national? *Inside Higher Ed.* https://www.insidehighered.com/views/2020/03/17/pros-and-cons-having-regional-accreditors-go-national-opinion

Fain, P. (2019, November 1). New rules on accreditation and state authorization. *Inside Higher Ed.* https://www.insidehighered.com/news/2019/11/01/education-department-issues-new-regulations-accreditation-and-state-authorization

Harcleroad, F. F. (1980). *Accreditation: History, process, and problems.* American Association for Higher Education. https://eric.ed.gov/?id=ED198774

Harcleroad, F. F., & Eaton, J. S. (2005). The hidden hand: External constituencies and their impact. In P. G. Altbach, R. O. Berdahl, & P. J. Gumport (Eds.), *American higher education in the twenty-first century* (pp. 253–283). Johns Hopkins University Press.

Kiger, J. C. (2000). *Philanthropic foundations in the twentieth century*. Greenwood.

KPMG. (2020). *Bill and Melinda Gates Foundation consolidated financial statements: December 31, 2020 and 2019*. https://docs.gatesfoundation.org/documents/ F_151002C-1B_Bill&MelindaGatesFoundation_FS.pdf

Lapchick, R. (2020, December 23). *College football grad rates slide; gap widens between Black and White players*. ESPN. https://www.espn.com/college-football/story/_/ id/30589631/college-football-grad-rates-slide-gap-widens-black-white-players

Mayhew, L. B., Ford, P. J., & Hubbard, D. L. (1990). *The quest for quality: The challenge for undergraduate education in the 1990s*. Jossey-Bass.

McIlnay, D. P. (1998). *How foundations work*. Jossey-Bass.

Morison, S. E. (1986). *Three centuries of Harvard, 1636–1936*. Harvard University Press.

National Collegiate Athletic Association. (n.d.). *What is the NCAA?* https://www .ncaa.org/about/resources/media-center/ncaa-101/what-ncaa

National Collegiate Athletic Association. (2020). *Finances of intercollegiate athletics*. https://www.ncaa.org/about/resources/research/finances-intercollegiate-athletics

Post-9/11 Veterans Educational Assistance Act of 2008, Pub. L. 110-252, H.R. 2642 (2008)

ProPublica. (2019). *Marion G Resch Foundation*. https://projects.propublica.org/ nonprofits/organizations/341853367

Ratcliff, J. L., Lubinescu, E. S., & Gaffney, M. A. (Eds.). (2001). *How accreditation influences assessment*. Jossey-Bass.

Rodenhouse, M. P. (2020). *2020 higher education directory*. Higher Education Publications.

Rowntree, D. (1987). *Assessing students: How shall we know them?* Nichols.

Rudolph, F. (1962). *The American college and university: A history*. Random House.

Servicemen's Readjustment Act, Pub. L. 78-346, 58 Stat L. 284 (1944)

Thiel College. (2020, April 15). *Marion G. Resch Foundation awards Thiel $225,000 to expand science and other scholarships* [Press release]. https://www.thiel.edu/news-room/press-releases/detail/marion-g.-resch-foundation-awards-thiel-225000-to-expand-science-and-other

Vasquez, M. (2020, October 30). As the pandemic grinds on, here are 5 big worries of college presidents. *The Chronicle of Higher Education, 67*(5).

Westminster College. (2016, January 27). *Did you know about the Marion G. Resch Foundation Bright Futures Program at Westminster College?* [Press release]. https:// www.westminster.edu/about/news/release.cfm?id=8628

Young, K. E., Chambers, C. M., Kells, H. R., & Associates. (1983). *Understanding accreditation*. Jossey-Bass.

PART FOUR

THE ACADEMIC CORE

13

GOVERNANCE OF THE
ACADEMIC CORE

Colleges and universities are typically bifurcated organizations (Blau, 1973) in that they have an academic structure to deliver education and an administrative structure that supports the academic structure. Over the past 4 decades, the administrative structure has become quite expansive, with some institutions operating as cities within cities. Institutional governance is discussed in chapter 10; here we focus on governance of higher education institutions' academic core.

The academic core is where the essential mission of a college or university is implemented and is typically overseen by a CAO, known as a provost, vice president for academic affairs, or academic dean (at some smaller institutions). The CAO is the "first among equals," serving as the leader of the faculty and holding equal rights and privileges among them. More formally, the CAO leads (or, in some cases, coordinates) the efforts of the institution's academic units, such as schools, colleges, divisions, and academic departments, playing a pivotal role in ensuring that the institution and its academic units stay true to the institutional mission. In this way, the CAO is responsible for making certain the institution and its academic decisions are mission driven, which fulfills the first theme of this book.

This book's second theme is that an institution's adaptation to environmental change must be consistent with its core mission and values. The CAO, academic deans, departmental leaders, and individual faculty members all contribute to this process because such change needs to be reflected in curricular reform in degree programs and general undergraduate education requirements. Two examples from the recent past illustrate how environmental factors necessitate change. Following the Great Recession in 2008, colleges and universities made numerous adaptations, such as the elimination of smaller programs that served few students, the alignment of academic offerings with local workforce demands, and the restructuring of academic governance models (Jacobs, 2012; Johnstone, 2012). More recently, higher education had to rapidly adapt to environmental change in response to the COVID-19 pandemic. While the pandemic's full effects on higher education remain to be seen, early reports indicate some of the ways in which colleges and universities responded include increasing online offerings; waiving certain admissions and degree requirements; laying off or furloughing faculty and staff; reducing or eliminating employee retirement contributions; and, perhaps most alarming, altering governance processes to reduce faculty involvement (AAUP, 2021a, 2021b; Jaschik & Lederman, 2021; Smalley, 2021). The actions necessitated by the pandemic could not have happened without democratic partnerships involving key constituents, including the faculty. Further, these actions rested heavily on fairness across demographic and positional groups. The institution must model such principles with DEI as core values. Ultimately, the success of these decisions rests on examining these considerations for inclusion, equity, and positive social change so decisions and actions lead to reified impact.

Academic governance draws on and illustrates our four themes. Academic governance processes engage an institution's faculty, departments, and academic administration in decision-making that ultimately will be reviewed by the president and board of trustees. There are three primary ways in which academic governance happens within higher education: peer review, shared governance, and the corporate model of governance. We begin this chapter with a brief discussion of the different types of peer review then move to a full discussion of shared governance. Subsequently, we contrast the shared governance model with an emerging form of academic governance, the corporate model. We describe the roles of different parties within academic governance structures and the main responsibilities that fall to each of them. We conclude with issues on which academic administrators should focus to respond to a rapidly changing environment.

The Peer Review Process

The term *peer review* may conjure visions of undergraduates working in small groups and reviewing each other's assignments, but peer review happens in many ways within colleges and universities. Peer review is used for quality assurance in many aspects of higher education, from entire institutions via regional accreditation to academic programs through disciplinary accreditation and state program reviews, to individual faculty work via the promotion/tenure process or evaluation of an individual article under consideration by a journal. Figure 13.1 reflects the scope and depth in which one university, the University of Denver (2010), outlined key areas in which it engaged peer or expert evaluations to advance its work.

Figure 13.1. Example of a university-wide multilevel evaluation matrix.

Level of Analysis	Evaluation / Study Completed
Individual	Performance evaluation and development system (PEDS)
	Faculty annual reports
	Administrator evaluations
Program Department, School/College/Division	Academic assessment reports
	Multi-tier academic program review
	Discipline/field-specific external accreditation
	Balanced scorecard report
College, School, or Division	Strategic planning review and analysis (Alchemy, Corona research)
	Financial aid modeling (Noel-Levitz, Scannel & Kurz, Inc.)
	Budget review and analysis
Institutional	Profiles fact book
	UPAC environmental scanning reports
	IPEDS peer data comparison reports
	Enrollment, admission status and persistence reports
	Undergraduate market planning (Royall & Co., The Lawlor Group)
	Financial aid modeling (Noel-Levitz)
	Tuition, fees, room and board rates comparison study
	Multiyear budget modeling
	Contribution margin report
	Comprehensive campaign feasibility report (Dini Partners)
	Campaign commitment summary reports
	Moody's private college and university medians analysis
	Presentation to rating agencies and bond issuers (A.G. Edwards, 2005)
	Integrated facilities plan (Sightlines)
	Greenhouse gas inventory (Sightlines)
	Land use master plan (Shepley, Bulfinch, Richardson, & Abbott)

Colleges and Universities

At the broadest level, peer review is part of the accreditation process required of all degree-granting institutions. Colleges within universities that offer professional degrees, such as in law or medicine, undergo additional accreditation beyond that which is granted to the university as a whole. Accreditation is a method of both quality assurance and quality improvement. By measuring institutions against a set of predetermined standards, accreditors can assess institutional quality on a broad scale, then provide guidance for improvement if measures are not met. Historically, the accreditation process has involved three general steps. The accrediting agency establishes a set of parameters to measure institutional quality. These standards are provided to institutions, which then use them to perform a self-study of areas that are on target and areas that need improvement. This self-study is submitted to the accrediting agency, at which point the peer review process begins.

In regional accreditation—the most common form of accreditation in higher education—accrediting agencies are comprised of the institutions that belong to that region. For example, the Southern Association of Colleges and Schools Commission on Colleges (SACSCOC) is comprised of institutions in the southern United States (e.g., Kentucky, Florida, Virginia). Thus, when institutions submit their self-study for review, they are submitting it to faculty at nearby institutions. In this way, peer review allows for those who are most well versed in the issues and daily practice of higher education to evaluate the quality of their peers. Of course, this system is not without criticism. Critics have noted that peer review accreditation may be affected by institutional or personal biases or result in a lack of accountability that causes institutions to never push past the status quo (Manning, 2018).

Additionally, changes in federal policy and public perception of higher education have expanded stakeholders in the accreditation process beyond the institutions and peer members of the accrediting agencies. As Eaton (2018) explained, the priorities of accreditation have shifted in recent years from a focus on quality improvement to compliance, and "expectations and standards for the [contemporary accreditation] are increasingly set not by accreditors but by government, especially at the federal level, influenced by students, the public, and media" (p. vii). These changes have affected the foundational purpose of peer review (i.e., quality improvement) and led some scholars to describe accreditation as being "on the edge" of a tipping point of change (Kinser & Phillips, 2018, p. 2).

Departments and Programs

Just as universities and colleges use peers to assess quality, so do the departments and programs within these institutions. While the specific methods of departmental and programmatic peer review differ between disciplines and institutions, there are some commonalities. For example, similar to the accreditation process, departmental review consists of peer assessment of the current state of a department faculty's teaching, research, and service based on a set of predetermined criteria and, if standards are not met, provision of guidance for improvement. Also, like accreditation, this process has been met with criticism. For example, one study that compared the perceptions of departmental peer review based on seniority (i.e., senior faculty, who are typically tenured, and early career faculty, who typically are not tenured) found that senior faculty were far more favorable toward the departmental peer review process, while early career faculty widely saw the process as "intimidating, problematic, and time-consuming" (Roworth, 1997, p. 36). Early career faculty members further expressed concerns that their peer reviewers, particularly reviewers who were senior faculty members, may not understand their use of new methodologies or their work in new fields. At the same time, early career faculty explained that it would be difficult for them to evaluate their senior colleagues, who would be voting on their tenure cases, without seeming like they were "sucking up" (Roworth, 1997, p. 36). In both cases, early career faculty expressed concerns about how the peer review process could affect academic freedom, which provides faculty members with the freedom to determine their research agendas without external influence. These concerns are somewhat mediated by making peer review anonymous and by sharing evaluations with the individual under review.

At the program level, peer review works to ensure programs are meeting disciplinary standards and, in some cases, professional organizations. Perhaps the most common form of programmatic peer review occurs in programs that provide licenses or certifications. For example, teacher certification programs typically undergo peer review processes to ensure that their curriculum is aligned with state and federal teaching standards. Similarly, other programs, such as those in the sciences, may undergo peer review to be accredited through professional organizations. One such widely known organization is the Accreditation Board for Engineering and Technology (ABET). ABET uses a peer review process to accredit individual programs in the applied and natural sciences, computing, engineering, and engineering technology fields. Importantly, this type of accreditation functions in addition to, and not in place of, the regional or national accreditation that the institution holds. Although the requirements of programmatic accreditation vary between disciplines, generally this type of accreditation is seen as confirmation of the program's quality and is not necessarily a requirement that the program must achieve. That is, programs in ABET's area may still operate and award degrees without their accreditation, but programs without this accreditation may suffer losses to their reputation, have limited access to networks of engineering scholars, and miss innovations in engineering education.

Faculty

Faculty play a critical role in all aspects of peer review within higher education, as they serve as reviewers for institutional, departmental, and programmatic reviews. Yet these areas are only a small portion of the ways in which peer review shapes faculty roles. The effects of peer review are felt perhaps most strongly in the publishing process, as, typically, faculty aim to publish in peer-reviewed, or refereed, journals. The process for peer review in journals usually begins with the journal editor's receipt of a manuscript submission. The editor then sends the manuscript to faculty members who have expertise in the topic being discussed. For instance, if the journal article were on a topic in 19th-century history, the editor would select senior faculty who study 19th-century history to review the submission. This type of peer review also has a degree of anonymity through a single-blind (i.e., the manuscript author does not know who the reviewers are) or double-blind (i.e., neither the author nor the reviewers know who each other are) process. In both cases, authors receive anonymous feedback from their peers; this feedback is used to evaluate whether the manuscript submission will be accepted for publication, revised, or rejected. A similar peer review process is used for the other aspects of faculty work, including conference presentations and grant applications.

The final aspect of peer review that we consider here relates to faculty hiring and promotion. As with many hiring processes, candidates are interviewed and evaluated by a hiring committee, which includes the candidate's peers (i.e., faculty in the program for which the candidate is applying). Hiring also typically involves a presentation of research or teaching that is attended by additional peers (other faculty) who then provide anonymous reviews of the candidate's qualifications for the position. Once hired, the peer review process does not end. Rather, faculty are reviewed by their peers throughout their careers. These reviews happen annually, and on a smaller scale, during the annual review process. Perhaps the most significant type of peer review in a faculty member's career happens during the tenure process, in which the other members of the department review their pre-tenure peer's dossier of teaching, scholarship and creative activity, and service, then vote whether this person should be awarded tenure. Post-tenure reviews, including the promotion from associate professor to full professor, require additional and subsequent peer review. These reviews differ between disciplines and departments, but they may include activities such as reviewing research rigor and placement, conducting observations of teaching, and evaluating service activities. Now that we have reviewed the types of peer review within colleges and universities, we turn to the concept of shared governance.

The Concept of Shared Governance

Within the bifurcated organizational structure of higher education, the concept of and process for governance and decision-making in the academic core comes from a set of joint guidelines developed by the AAUP (n.d.), the ACE, and the AGB. The "Statement on Government of Colleges and Universities" (AAUP, n.d.) delineated the roles of an institution's board of trustees, administration, and faculty in the decision-making and governance of the academic core and established a partnership or collaborative relationship between these entities (AAUP, 2021; AGB, 2017b), commonly known as the shared governance model.

Despite having guidelines that shape shared governance, there is little agreement on its definition, and some have argued that it is one of the most misunderstood concepts in higher education (AGB, 2017b; Bahls, 2014; Bliss et al., 2020). It has even been described as an "'empty' or 'floating' signifier so devoid of determinant meaning that it takes on whatever significance a particular speaker or author gives it" (Cipriano, 2020, p. 11). Others have questioned the implications of the use of the word *shared* in shared governance, worrying that "shared could suggest that administrators and trustees are entitled to share in all decisions, perhaps including those in areas of faculty primacy" (DeCesare, 2020, p. 183). Yet these concerns may be unfounded, for as Olson (2009) explained, sharing governance does not entail equal divisions of decision-making: "'Shared' doesn't mean that every constituency gets to participate at every stage. Nor does it mean that any constituency exercises complete control over the process. . . . The various stakeholders participate in well-defined parts of the process" (para. 13).

Given the lack of consensus on a singular definition of shared governance, Bahls (2014, 2017) sought to categorize the ways in which the concept is typically viewed. He argued that there are three traditional definitions of shared governance: (a) the equal rights to governance in which faculty, staff, and administrators have equal authority in decision-making; (b) the responsibility of the decision-making party to consult with others before finalizing governance matters; and (c) a set of rules that dictate the roles, responsibilities, and relationships of those involved in governance (e.g., boards, faculty, administrators). Finding these three views inadequate for contemporary governance challenges, Bahls (2017) proposed a fourth definition based on shared accountability in which shared governance is "a system where faculty, trustees, and administrators, as integral leaders, actively engage to move past the fragmentation of traditional governance to shared responsibility for identifying and pursing an aligned set of sustainable priorities and outcomes, for which each constituency is accountable" (p. 60). For certain groups, Bahls's fourth definition was widely accepted, with one survey indicating that nearly 60% of board members at public and private institutions believed that Bahls's definition is how shared governance should operate (AGB, 2016). However, as with many issues related to shared governance, reception varies by role. For example, as a member of the faculty constituency group, DeCesare (2020) criticized this understanding of shared governance as deviating too far from the original guidelines provided by the AAUP statement.

Although there are also disagreements about who should be involved in shared governance (see, e.g., Bejou & Bejou, 2016), a commonality is that, at a minimum, shared governance involves the faculty, administration, and board. At colleges and universities that practice shared governance, the board's role is to maintain the purposes of the institution's original charter and the institution's fiscal health. The president's role is to sustain current financial resources and generate new revenue sources. The role of the CAO is to coordinate and lead the institution's academic programs. The role of the faculty is to monitor existing academic programs and develop new curricula in response to environmental change. These roles are not discrete for any of the entities. Rather, there is a great deal of overlap that necessitates collaboration.

The literature on shared governance usually focuses on institutional faculty governance committees, often called a faculty senate (Bucklew et al., 2012; Miller et al., 2016). As Tierney and Minor (2003) noted, however, shared governance is more multifaceted than the structure and processes of a faculty senate. To understand the complex structure and processes of shared governance, one needs to consider the ways an institution interacts with its environment, particularly in terms of curricular development and change. Faculty members interact directly with their environments, with the result that the curricula of many fields and disciplines have changed, and new interdisciplinary fields have emerged, particularly in the last 2 decades. As part of their academic governance structures, colleges and universities maintain processes for adding new courses and degree programs, but such changes usually emanate from faculty members' responses to environmental changes within their field or discipline. The governance and decision-making roles of departments and faculty are discussed in more detail in chapter 14, this volume.

An institution's shared governance system is also influenced by its type, size, history, and culture (Ott & Mathews, 2015), but shared governance systems vary between institutions of the same Carnegie classification and across all U.S. higher education institutions. Some generalizations, however, can be made. For example, large research, doctorate-granting, and comprehensive institutions have placed organizational units—schools or colleges—between the faculty governing body and the academic departments. Schools or colleges typically employ a governance structure for their academic programs and policies that interfaces with the institution's wider academic governance structure. In addition, larger institutions usually have a representative faculty senate that contains a designated number of representatives from each school or college.

In contrast, private liberal arts colleges, depending on the size of the faculty, may have a representative form of governance or a faculty governing body composed of all faculty members. At liberal arts institutions, faculty governing bodies typically have more control over curricular issues and academic decision-making.

Academic governance is also important at community colleges. Lucey (2002), who served as president of several community colleges, discussed the importance of shared governance, and faculty involvement in curricular development in particular. She noted the negative consequences of faculty passivity around governance and the abdication of curricular decisions to administrators. She was especially critical of deans of workforce development and career-based programs as well as their faculty members who allow these deans to make decisions based on entrepreneurial priorities rather than on the quality and depth of the curriculum. She noted the responsibility that a community college has to its larger community as its most important customer:

> We realize that our customers must be the larger civic community, whose members have a right to expect delivery of an education that prepares students for an engaged life in a democracy—as well as one that offers them the opportunity to achieve a better life. To satisfy these customers, we should be willing to take the necessary steps necessary to preserve such [faculty] engagement within our own college community. While continuing to support the goals of individuals, democracy colleges also need to support democracy. (p. 31)

Lucey's observation about the need for faculty engagement to maintain strong academic governance is applicable to all colleges and universities that value democratic partnerships, want to be responsive to their environment, and model positive social change. AGB (2017a) found, via interviews with college presidents and faculty members, that erosion of faculty participation is attributable to several factors, including the faculty's competing responsibilities; the limitations that participation plays to faculty rewards (e.g., salary increases, promotion, and tenure); faculty beliefs about their potential to enact change through participation; and the shift to more contingent faculty who may not be able to participate in governance activities.

Beyond a lack of faculty engagement, numerous other criticisms of shared governance have been presented. Indeed, shared governance has been described as operating in a way that is "either impotent and perfunctory or combative and adversarial in the vast majority of institutions of higher education" (Pearce et al., 2018, p. 641). Specific challenges associated with shared governance tend to center around three related issues: who is involved, how those involved are equipped to serve, and how their involvement affects the process. As noted earlier, there is consensus that shared governance involves the faculty, board members, and administrators. However, there is far less agreement on whether other groups should be included, such as contingent faculty (AGB, 2016; Jones et al., 2017), staff (Mathews, 2020; Miller & Murray, 2011), and students (Bliss et al., 2020; Luescher-Mamashela, 2013). Of course, merely including groups within the governing process does not necessarily give them a voice in decision-making, as many employees may not exercise their voice if they believe their viewpoint will not be respected or valued (Curnalia & Mermer, 2018). At the same time, faculty members may be reluctant to participate in academic governance if it involves making hard decisions that involve their colleagues (Ott & Mathews, 2015). Thus, discussions around the challenges of including different groups within shared governance are rooted in issues of power, engagement, and trust (Bigelow & Chaddock, 2020; Curnalia & Mermer, 2018).

Several key resources describe relational characteristics that formulate optimal conditions for shared governance over academic matters to occur. For instance, AGB (2017a) identified seven relational characteristics, which are gathered from college presidents and faculty. It listed trust, collaboration, communication, transparency, inclusiveness, honesty, and integrity as critical aspects to ensure successful shared governance. Somewhat like the AGB list, Ott and Mathews (2015) identified trust, shared sense of purpose, understanding the issue at hand, adaptability, and productivity as their ingredients for effective academic governance. They also expounded on the sub-elements of each of the major five relational characteristics. Although the five primary characteristics certainly shed light to successful academic governance relationships, the sub-elements offer greater insights into each characteristic with expanded descriptors of those relationships, including expectations of the parties. Trust, for instance, is critical in a positive working relationship, but their concept of trust also meant having clearly defined expectations for governance, practices that consistently meet community expectations, and continuous commitment to transparency. Similarly, a shared sense of purpose contained further elaboration into expressing the shared vision for the future of the institution and offering practices that foster relationships across groups. Also, understanding the issue at hand captured an overarching characteristic that was built around a relationship that demonstrated respect for diverse perspectives and practices that invited broad participation. Adaptability is an essential component for the rapidly changing environment of higher education, but it also represented the developmental approaches to leadership and governance and allowances for flexibility as sub-elements to adaptability. Finally, productivity is an important element, so there is action associated with the work. As sub-elements of productivity, they included governance practices that focused on results and a joint responsibility captured through equity and reward. These descriptions illustrate how five or seven words offer only very broad characteristics, and deeper examination of the sub-elements provides more specific expectations and design features to structure successful academic governance relationships.

Regardless of the structures in place and issues confronted, colleges and universities have strong motivations to solve the challenges associated with shared governance, as the number of decisions to be made and the expectations that these decisions will be made quickly are both increasing (AGB, 2017b; Deemer & Horvath, 2017). At the same time, the notion that institutions must act quickly and decisively is not new. In the 1990s, for instance, numerous higher education experts argued that colleges and universities of any size are no longer capable of responding to a rapidly changing environment (AGB, 1996; Benjamin et al., 1993; Cole, 1994; Kennedy, 1993; Schuster et al., 1994). They maintained that traditional shared governance systems—namely, faculty senates—are unable to act on changing societal needs in a timely manner, particularly when compared with the burgeoning for-profit higher education sector. Internal stakeholders may also take issue with delayed decision-making. Particularly when decisions relate to issues of harm or historically marginalized groups, individuals may feel as if lengthy governing processes are simply delay tactics to avoid addressing the institution's problems (Bigelow & Chaddock, 2020). Such challenges are exacerbated by the reality of the academic calendar, with many faculty participants holding 9- or 10-month contracts that make them unavailable for governance tasks in the summer months. In short, all stakeholders want decisions to be made fast, but adherence to the principles of shared governance can be at odds with speedy processes.

Unsurprisingly, then, scholars have attempted to identify which factors affect the efficiency and efficacy of shared governance so that the process might be improved. Many of the issues discussed originate in a lack of training and preparation for participating in governance, as the various stakeholders share differing values, experiences, and priorities and thus may not see eye to eye on all aspects of the decision-making process. For faculty and administrators (many of whom also hold faculty appointments), issues may stem from a lack of experience with collaboration within the academy, as the type of sharing involved in shared governance does not typically occur in disciplines or divisions (Deemer & Horvath, 2017). At the same time, many board members may come from corporate backgrounds; and therefore, may be unfamiliar with the processes and values deeply entrenched within academia (AGB, 2016; DeCesare, 2020; see chapter 10, this volume). Attempts to reconcile the differences between stakeholders in a way that allows for efficient decision-making has led some observers to recommend that not-for-profit higher education institutions make the transition from their traditional shared governance model to a corporate governance model in which decision-making is concentrated at the presidential level. Their assumption is that such restructuring will allow institutions to respond more rapidly to changes in their environments.

Shared Governance versus Corporate Governance

Birnbaum (2004) connected the rising demand for corporate governance in higher education to the evolution of and the increase in for-profit institutions. He asserted that "governance is a means to an end" (p. 24), so academic governance should be structured to meet an institution's desired ends. In his analysis, Birnbaum characterized, on the one hand, many for-profits as entrepreneurial and labeled them as "market" institutions, while he described many not-for-profit colleges and universities as "academic" institutions. His main distinction between market and academic institutions was that market institutions' focus—that is, their end—is on producing individuals with the skills and abilities necessary to seek employment and perform effectively in their chosen occupation. On the other hand, academic institutions' end is the production of educated citizens who will contribute to society through the expansion of knowledge and understanding and involvement in a democratic society. According to Birnbaum, market institutions' desired end requires them to embrace a corporate governance model, while academic institutions' desired end requires a shared governance system. Birnbaum did not argue that one structure is better than the other, though. Instead, he asserted that contemporary society needs market and academic institutions with governance structures appropriate for their type to meet specific societal needs.

The focus of this book is on what Birnbaum (2004) would generally describe as academic institutions, most of which employ shared governance structures. Many shared governance systems involve faculty senates—the scapegoat for slow institutional decision-making—but also involve many more parties and occur on many more levels than just senates. For example, at community colleges, liberal arts colleges, and research universities alike, individual faculty members interact with their specific disciplinary environments and respond to changes, which can be seen in the evolution of curricula, specific course content, and teaching methods. The corporate governance model may streamline some decision-making processes, but it also risks stifling faculty members' ability to respond to their disciplinary environments in a timely manner, debilitating decision-making, and diminishing the development of an institution's social capital (i.e., individual faculty investment in institutional innovation and change). Moreover, rapid responses to change may not be the best approach for academic institutions, where deliberate and thorough analysis may lead to more effective long-term responses to environmental challenges.

Faculty report continued declines with participation in shared governance over academic matters (AAUP, 2021c). According to the AAUP (2021c) shared governance survey, the faculty role in institution-level decision-making, such as admissions, budgeting, and dean selection, has eroded to a more corporate, administrative decision-making process. The data, however, do report some promising news. Faculty members have more decision-making authority over program curricula, promotion and tenure decisions, and department chair selection. These data suggest that faculty have greater influence over their departmental and program-level decisions, which may reflect a commitment that faculty govern the roles in which they have authority, responsibility, expertise, and accountability. That is, drawing back to the discussion in chapter 10, roles and obligations within an organizational system are crucial to define and uphold consistently. We suggested the "AREA Principles for Decision-Making in Shared Governance," which outlines four principles to guide our understanding of where various decision-making roles occur through a shared governance environment. Recapping those driving questions, we must ask the following:

Authority: Who has been given authority to make the decision by the board?

Responsibility: Who has the responsibility for implementing the decision?

Expertise: Who has the necessary expertise to make a wise decision?

Accountability: Who will be accountable for the success or failure of the decision?

While a campus community may exercise shared governance with consultation, specialized insights, and information dissemination, ultimately, a person or office has authority, responsibility, expertise, and accountability (e.g., faculty for curriculum, CAO for the academic operations, dean of students for student welfare beyond the classroom).

The Faculty Senate in Shared Governance

In a 2003 national report on academic governance in higher education, Tierney and Minor acknowledged that shared governance is a complex practice but focused their study on faculty governance structures. Specifically, they looked at faculty governance in research and doctorate-granting institutions and comprehensive universities, identifying three types of faculty governance and decision-making structures. First, they identified a "fully collaborative" decision-making model, which corresponds to notions of collegiality in which decisions are shared among the faculty and the administration. Second, they described a "consultative" decision-making model in which senior administrators and board members retain ultimate decision-making authority but seek faculty advice as part of their deliberations. Third, they observed a "distributive" decision-making model, which results in the delegation of decision-making to the faculty, administrators, or the board according to each entity's assigned responsibilities. Their investigation found that 47% of institutions were "fully collaborative," 27% were "consultative," and 26% were "distributive" (Tierney & Minor, 2003, p. 9). Tierney and Minor noted that these models of faculty governance were one venue for faculty participation in decision-making, but they also observed that there were other venues for faculty engagement, including academic departments, ad hoc committees, school/college governance units, standing faculty administrative committees, systemwide governing units, and collective bargaining/union committees.

Organizational theory can assist us in understanding the role and function of faculty senates. Birnbaum (1991) used theory to understand why faculty senates, as dysfunctional as they sometimes can be, have persisted over time. Citing Blau, Birnbaum suggested that faculty senates prevent the centralization of control of academic programs. This decentralization gives faculty members the flexibility they need to respond in a timely way to the environmental changes that affect their disciplines and fields. When these changes begin to affect multiple fields or disciplines in the institution, the matter percolates to the senate for institutional resolution. This situation is an example of one of the "manifest functions" (p. 10) of the senate as a bureaucracy, a political system. The latent functions of the senate include its role as a symbol of faculty membership and participation, commitment to institutional and professional values, and authority over some institutional functions. Another important latent function of senates is that they serve as a training ground for future academic leaders (Johnston, 2003). These manifest and latent functions explain the persistence of faculty senates over time and their positive role within institutions of higher education that promote democratic partnerships.

The composition of senates varies. Some are composed of only tenured faculty members, while others are made up of all faculty members or a collaborative structure of faculty and administrators, staff, and students. The structure of a faculty senate is heavily influenced by institution type. For example, senates in larger institutions tend to be representative bodies with elected members from individual schools, colleges, or departments who serve 2- to 6-year terms. At smaller private institutions and some community colleges, faculty governance structures are made of all tenured or full-time faculty members. As the number of contingent faculty members has grown, their role has become an issue for faculty governance. Some institutions include contingent faculty in their governance structures, while others do not.

The chair or presiding officer of a faculty senate is usually elected from the senate membership (typically a member of the faculty) and may also serve in the president's cabinet. In some cases, though, the CAO serves as the presiding officer of the senate. In either arrangement, the CAO works closely with the senate as part of the CAO's responsibility to oversee the academic governance of the institution (Tierney & Minor, 2003). Some senates contain an executive committee that sets the senate's agenda and works closely with the administration (Gilmour, 1991), while in some senates the executive committee contains administrators and faculty members.

The senate leadership should adopt an abbreviated and simplified form of Robert's "Rules of Order" to keep meetings moving toward decision-making.[1] As new members join the senate, they should participate in training to have a clear understanding of the institution's mission; the senate's constitution, bylaws, and organizational structure; the role of the faculty from departments through schools and colleges in the shared governance model of institutional decision-making; the senate's relationship with the CAO; and the utility of Robert's rules for making the senate an effective and timely decision-making body.

Senates' decision-making activities primarily affect the academic side of the institution. Issues that often fall to faculty senates include monitoring curricula, such as ensuring the integrity of existing degree programs; development of new courses and degree programs, authorization of changes to existing courses, and endorsement of the closing of existing programs; teaching evaluation processes and criteria; promotion and tenure and post-tenure review processes; minimum requirements for associate, baccalaureate, and graduate degree programs; president and CAO selection and periodic evaluations; faculty personnel policies; and sometimes strategic planning and budgeting (Tierney & Minor, 2003). Most senates maintain subcommittees to monitor these matters, as well as to provide some oversight of cocurricular topics such as student life, campus climate, and athletics. Subcommittees provide a venue for wider faculty involvement in academic governance because membership can be drawn from senate members as well as from representatives from the broader faculty. In all these activities, the senate plays a role in upholding the mission, goals, and values of its institution.

The CAO

A college or university CAO is responsible for overseeing the institution's academic mission. In today's colleges and universities, the scope of the CAO's role has expanded to that of chief operating officer, meaning that the CAO manages the internal functions of the institution, while the president's role has evolved into a concern for the institution's external relationships (Bright & Richards, 2001; Lambert, 2002). In higher education, a CAO is typically referred to as a vice president for academic affairs, vice chancellor for academic affairs, dean of academic affairs, or provost. In recent years, because of the broadened scope of responsibilities, institutions have also begun to use the titles senior vice president and provost.

Little has been written about the function of the CAO, although a few works have described the scope and roles of this pivotal position, charged with setting the academic vision for the institution (ACE, 2014; Alessio, 2017; Atnip, 2009; Bright & Richards, 2001). The CAO has responsibility for all academic programs and academic support services such as the library, technology and computing centers, faculty personnel and development, admissions and enrollment management, teaching and learning, and the registrar's office (Atnip, 2009). The CAO is also usually responsible for the largest portion of the institution's budget, plays a pivotal role in strategic planning, maintains oversight of the institution's physical facilities dedicated to academics, oversees the curriculum and complex personnel issues, and ensures that the institution upholds its mission and is responsive to environmental changes. In some smaller colleges the CAO is also responsible for oversight of research activities. The CAO must cultivate strong relationships and communication with the president and the board; the vice presidents of finance, administration, and student affairs; the deans of the colleges; and the faculty.

Lambert (2002) advocated for a strong CAO who is not only in charge of academic affairs but also serves as the chief operating officer, a designation that situates this office clearly as the second most powerful position in terms of authority and responsibility. This arrangement allows the president to focus on regional, state, and national public relations issues. The president and the CAO must share a similar understanding of their institution's mission, and their working relationship should include a joint long-term vision and close communication at all times.

For this working relationship to be successful, the president must give the CAO space to perform their roles and responsibilities and not micromanage. In addition, the CAO and vice presidents for finance, administration, student affairs, and research and graduate programs should communicate regularly and develop a team approach to collaborate as members of the president's cabinet. These collaborative relationships will allow for a more coordinated effort in the institution's academic and support areas to promote the academic goals and values of the institution (Lambert, 2002, p. 426).

The deans of the colleges and the associate/assistant provosts (and sometimes the chair of the faculty senate) form the academic affairs leadership team that reports directly to the CAO, with the advice and consent of the faculty. These academic deans often serve at the pleasure of the CAO. The relationship between academic deans and the CAO is crucial to the CAO's ability to successfully guide the institution.

The institution's budget model is critical to the CAO's performance as well. At institutions where each college is financially independent with differential tuition and functions as part of a loose federation of independent entities, the CAO is often weak and has difficulty moving the institution forward. Where the CAO has more control over the budgets of individual units, the CAO's leadership team can progress toward a common agenda and goals. In the latter arrangement, general education requirements can focus on liberal arts and sciences, and there will be less of a silo mentality across the colleges (although this mentality will linger), as well as a better understanding of the specific and unique needs of individual colleges (Lambert, 2002). The reporting relationship between the CAO and the deans will vary based on how long individuals have served in their positions and the level of trust that has developed between them. Established deans may report to the CAO monthly but communicate urgent problems as needed, while new deans may meet with the CAO weekly or biweekly. The CAO often places great trust in the deans to manage their own units and avoids micromanaging any of the colleges. When a dean repeatedly fails that trust, the CAO should discern whether it is time for a leadership change—a decision that is often made with faculty consultation—or a more hands-on approach to direct that college.

The role of the CAO in faculty governance is important from both leadership and developmental perspectives. Just as the president creates a training program for the board of trustees, the CAO should work with the senate leadership to design a training program for members of the senate. Such a program will enhance the effectiveness of the senate in decision-making and benefit the institution. We recommend that the CAO meet with the senate leadership regularly to plan the agenda for routine faculty meetings and to cultivate a sense of trust. The CAO should educate the senate leadership on the changing environment and issues faced by the institution. The CAO should also attend regular senate meetings and be open to attending subcommittee meetings where information is needed to provide advice, counsel, and forward legislation to the senate. The CAO should solicit planning and budgeting suggestions from the senate on an annual basis. The senate should be provided with appropriate data and institutional research that will facilitate its ability to make recommendations (Lambert, 2002). The strength of the senate leadership may wax and wane over the years, but the CAO cannot ignore the senate.

Academic Deans

An academic dean is usually responsible for an academic school or college, a complex unit made up of numerous disciplines or fields. An academic dean holds a midlevel academic leadership position that serves as a bridge between the faculty and the CAO. Literature that focuses on the role of the dean includes, for example, Bolton (2000), Bright and Richards (2001), Chen (2009), and Leaming (2002). Not only do deans need to cultivate relationships with the faculty and provide leadership development to department chairs, they must also pay attention to nurturing their relationship to their CAO.

Bright and Richards (2001) compared being the dean to working a crossword puzzle. The dean's work is defined by constraints that are not the administrator's creation, there are defined boundaries that will affect any solution, and academics like to keep things complex and interrelated (p. 6). They noted,

> Our work as academics is a kind of semantic and logical game, and this inevitably carries over into the way we talk. Academics take a frequently

maddening pleasure in ambiguity, wit, and other forms of verbal play. As a result, discussions of new ideas, suggestions—and even strongly stated requests—sometimes seem more like a trail of bread crumbs than a well-formed loaf of bread to chew on! (p. 7)

Bright and Richards (2001) described three types of deans: the corporate dean, who sees the enterprise as a business first and an intellectual bee-hive second; the faculty-citizen dean, who is a respected senior scholar and holds the position for a short time; and the accidental tourist dean, who rises through the ranks of academic administration to upper-level administrative responsibilities.

Deans must cultivate numerous skills. They need to be advocates to their CAO for the departments and disciplines in their units. Advocacy should not be blind, however, and deans need to understand and confront areas of weakness when improvement is needed. In collaboration with faculty members and academic administrators in a college, its dean needs to embrace a vision for the college and communicate that vision articulately to faculty, students, alumni, benefactors, administrators, and staff. The dean should possess the skills to evaluate the performance of academic administrators and staff, and in an honest but caring way identify strengths and areas for improvement. Tough love and a collaborative approach to improvement are essential in dealing with personnel, as are knowing how to develop and cultivate the leadership skills of department heads and avoiding micromanagement. Having said that, a dean also must have the strength to replace someone when it becomes obvious that the person cannot perform the job effectively. Successful deans also demonstrate budget management and planning skills and cultivate donors to build the endowment of the college and the institution.

Amid all these concerns, deans must be mindful of the idiosyncratic nature of academic departments. In a college of liberal arts or a college of arts and sciences, a diversity of disciplines and fields coexist, from the humanities to the social sciences to the hard sciences. These colleges are much more difficult to lead than a college of engineering, for example, in which disciplines and fields are more closely related. Regardless of the way schools and colleges are structured in an institution, each discipline or field in the college interacts with different external environments, which creates the unique nature of each college or school.

No matter the focus of a school or college, academic departments are idiosyncratic because of the nature of the disciplines or fields of study they house. Some departments may be a combination of several disciplines or fields. Each of these areas could have its own graduate degree programs and external environment. Grasping the distinctive nature of each department is particularly important in a time of fiscal constraint because deans may look across their college for ways to streamline resources, and what they may see as a way to operate more efficiently may not work because of departmental idiosyncrasies. For example, some departments may employ one graduate officer to oversee its single master and doctoral degree programs, while other departments may employ multiple officers to handle different types of graduate programs. To conserve resources, a dean may decide that every department only needs one graduate officer, although some departments' diverse graduate programs require unique recruitment, admissions, certification, and credentialing processes. While on the surface such restructuring may appear more efficient, it may not be the most effective way to maintain strong degree programs: The complexity of the job may harm the integrity of individual programs.

One key way to understand academic departments' distinctiveness is to maintain strong relations and communication with department heads. An advisory body of department heads, unit directors, and associate/assistant deans can assist the dean in understanding issues and intended and unintended consequences of solutions under consideration. College-level faculty governance bodies are also useful resources for deans. In most cases, a proportion of the faculty is elected from each department, and several faculty members serve in at-large positions. Such a structure provides the dean with a venue to bring pressing issues and changes to the faculty for review. It also provides the college's faculty senate representatives with a place to share issues with their colleagues for input. In times of rapid change, college-level faculty governance bodies can be especially helpful in facilitating necessary change.

Responsibilities of Academic Leaders

Academic leaders must focus on a variety of areas to ensure their institution continues to be mission driven while adapting to environmental change and pursuing equity and inclusion through democratic partnerships. First, in this age of rapid expansion of knowledge and technology, academic leaders must evaluate, coordinate, and plan curricular adaptation and change to ensure their institution's offerings remain relevant. Second, changes in research policy and practice require leaders to remain current on institutional research policy issues, as well as to develop strategies to encourage faculty research and scholarship activities consistent with their institution's mission. Third, the complex problems society faces require interdisciplinary solutions, so leaders must identify ways to promote collaboration across academic units.

Because planning and implementation work across offices, role ambiguity and communication structures present significant challenges to any organization, especially colleges and universities. To address these challenges, a responsibility assignment matrix such as the responsible-accountable-consulted-informed (RACI) matrix captures parties involved in a decision or project plan (see Figure 13.2). It presents a structured format that delineates roles and communication and should be applied to major activities or milestones for a project. For instance, if the project is hiring new faculty lines, the project leader, such as a department chair, would outline each of the major activities and identify: Who is *responsible* for executing the assigned tasks? Who is *accountable* for this assigned area making final decisions and ultimately the task owner? Who is *consulted* before a decision or action is taken? Who is *informed* about the decision or action that has taken place? This approach ensures engagement in the process and connects offices and other academic departments—especially for interdisciplinary hires.

Curriculum Coordination and Planning

Work on curriculum planning by Lattuca and Stark (2009) has provided academic leaders with a reconceptualization of the process. Specifically, they described curriculum as an "academic plan" (p. 4) that takes into account the sociocultural context in which teaching and learning occur. The academic plan model for curriculum design also considers factors internal to the institution, including its history, culture, and mission. At the department level, the backgrounds and agendas of faculty members and the nature of students influence the development of the academic plan. Lattuca and Stark identified the following elements of an academic plan:

1. Purposes: to provide knowledge, skills, and attitudes to be learned.
2. Content: subject matter selected to convey specific knowledge and skills.
3. Sequencing: an arrangement of subject matter and experience intended to lead to specific outcomes of learners.
4. Learners: how the plan will address a specific group of learners.
5. Instructional processes: the instructional activities by which learning may be achieved.
6. Resources: the materials and a setting to be used in the learning process.
7. Evaluation: the strategies used to determine whether decisions about the elements of the academic plan are optimal.
8. Adjustment: enhancements to the plan based on experience and evaluation. (pp. 4–5).

Figure 13.2. RACI model of academic decision-making.

Who is *Responsible* for executing the assigned tasks?

Who is *Accountable* for this assigned area and making final decisions, and who is ultimately the task owner?

Who is *Consulted* before a decision or action is taken?

Who is *Informed* about the decision or action that has taken place?

RACI MODEL IN ACTION				
ACTIVITY	RESPONSIBLE	ACCOUNTABLE	CONSULTED	INFORMED
Establishing a faculty line	Department chair Business officer	Dean	Department members Related departments (e.g., if line supports teaching of courses required for other majors)	Human resources Other chairs and staff
Recruiting faculty	Search committee	Chair	Department members Related departments	Academic association job boards (e.g., *Chronicle*)
Hiring faculty	Chair	Dean	Provost Human resources (e.g., background checks)	College faculty staff (e.g., identifying office and lab space)

Crucial to the plan is the feedback loop that provides assessment and evaluation of the curricular responses to environmental change.

The academic plan model is useful for the evaluation and adaptation of undergraduate general education curricula and academic programs and courses at the associate, baccalaureate, and graduate degree levels, especially as they need to adapt to an ever-changing environment. Lattuca and Stark (2009) provided detailed strategies to use this model to implement curriculum plans at the degree, program, and course levels. The model is particularly useful for undergraduate-level curricula that cover general education requirements and disciplinary majors. It can be an evaluation tool to achieve the optimization of student learning and the creation of engaged citizens in society. (For an in-depth discussion of the undergraduate curriculum, see chapter 15.)

Governance and Research Policy

In response to historical abuses of human and animal research subjects, colleges and universities whose faculty members engage in research are required to comply with research standards defined by the federal government (see chapter 6). Because of the complexity of these regulations, most institutions employ staff members who are dedicated to the development and monitoring of such on-campus research. Academic administrators and faculty leaders should also be involved in the development of research policies and the implementation of federal regulations and guidelines for good research practice.

Designating specific members of the CAO's staff to coordinate their institution's research initiatives will facilitate compliance and stimulate faculty and student research initiatives, such as research on teaching, assessment, and learning outcomes, as well as applied and basic research. The focus of an institution's research agenda will hinge significantly on the institution's mission, and as the research office staff develops internal incentives to promote research projects and the acquisition of private and federal funding resources, it should ensure these efforts are consistent with the institutional mission.

Institutions with a research mission should develop incentive programs to assist faculty research agendas. Such programs assist the faculty in developing a concept or idea into a competitive proposal ready for submission to a funding agency. Significant institutional funding—amounts will vary, with higher levels in the hard sciences—should be made available to faculty members to build their capacity to apply for external research sponsorship. These funds should be distributed through an internal review process that allows a faculty committee to issue awards based on the merit or promise of the research proposal.

An institution's research office staff should also provide information on available funding opportunities and assist the faculty in search of relevant funding sources. The office should develop policies governing budget development, course buyouts, and the indirect cost or overhead rates to be built into project budgets. Upon the award of a grant or contract, policies need to be developed for the adequate administration and oversight of all externally funded projects. In larger universities, many of these functions will be distributed to the colleges or schools, but there should be overarching institutional polices governing these subunits' operations.

The U.S. Department of Health and Human Services' (HHS) Office for Human Research Protections website provides a wealth of information on federal regulations and requirements for human subjects research. Periodically, faculty members and students who conduct research involving human participants must complete tutorials and tests to confirm they understand the protections given to human subjects involved in a research project.[2]

Laws governing the use of animals in research projects exist on the state, federal, and international levels. A resource for these regulations is the National Association for Biomedical Research (n.d.), which provides guidance from HHS, the U.S. Department of Agriculture, the Animal Welfare Act, the Office of Laboratory Animal Welfare, the Public Health Service Act, the Food and Drug Administration Good Laboratory Practices for Nonclinical Studies, and federal interagency policies that outline practices for use of animals in research and clinical practice.

Developing Interdisciplinary Collaboration

Nurturing collaboration across disciplines and fields in teaching, research, and service is an essential function of academic leaders in the 21st century. As Kezar and Lester (2009) noted,

> A variety of external organizations and sectors are encouraging higher education to become more collaborative in its approach to teaching and research, including accreditors, foundations, business and industry, and government agencies such as National Institutes of Health and the National Science Foundation. (p. 4)

Indeed, there is a growing body of literature on fostering collaboration (Bolger, 2021; Guimarães et al., 2019; Lyall, 2019). Although an interdisciplinary approach is not always met with warm reception in academic circles, the approach is an emphasis on collaboration in teaching, research, and service that emanates from the complex nature of problems facing society. Diseases such as immunology and cancer involve not only biomedical issues but also lifestyle, behavioral, economic, and environmental issues that affect prevention and cure. The challenges of poverty, war, and environmental degradation must be approached from an interdisciplinary perspective involving history, economics, political science, sociology, education, and the hard sciences, which together enhance opportunities for the development of viable solutions to improve the human condition (Bolger, 2021). Colleges and universities that seek to advance knowledge and engage with society must promote collaboration in ways consistent with their missions.

Academic administrators can use their institution's governance structure to change their organization in ways that will foster and promote collaboration in teaching, research, and service. To make collaboration part of an institution's mission, Kezar and Lester (2009) argued that one must understand the organization's structural barriers to collaboration. One barrier to collaboration is structural: Disciplines and fields are organized in departments or units in colleges or schools. These loosely coupled units have a great deal of autonomy, with each discipline interacting with its specific environment. This arrangement creates a silo effect that is hard to break down. Another barrier concerns college and university reward structures such as promotion and tenure. These systems are designed to maintain disciplinary integrity, but they result in faculty members' inclination to act as lone researchers who work as individuals, not in teams.

Administrative structures also create barriers in that they are hierarchical, with divisions such as academic affairs, student affairs, and support services all reporting upward and with little lateral communication. Responsibility-centered management, a new strategy adopted by many institutions to bring about fiscal health by setting standards to measure unit profitability and requiring all units to be profitable, places renewed emphasis on units as silos and creates another barrier to working across units (Kezar & Lester, 2009). Under responsibility-centered management, the governance structure is also designed as a hierarchy with authority centralized at the institution level. Ultimately, the academic silo effect and administrative hierarchies create minimal interactions laterally in the faculty and the administration. These barriers are further exacerbated by the general gulf that has developed between the faculty and the administration at some institutions. The question becomes how to overcome these barriers to develop into a collaborative institution.

To bring about institutional change that promotes lateral communication and collaboration in teaching, research, and service, Kezar and Lester (2009) proposed using an adapted version of Mohrman et al.'s (1995) model for business corporations. The model advocated changes in six organizational areas. The first area is adaptation of the mission to promote collaboration in teaching, research, and service. The second context is the translation of the new mission into the specific work of the institution in terms of teaching, curriculum, research, and service. The third area involves the identification of the integrating and centralizing structures that need to be put in place to change the way members of the institution communicate, work across boundaries, and break down barriers. The fourth issue concerns institution members changing goal-setting strategies, planning, management, and decision-making processes to promote collaboration. The fifth area involves the ways reward structures should be changed and collaborative research, teaching, and service incentivized. The sixth and final matter concerns the developmental programs that are required to encourage collaboration between the faculty and administrators. Changes in these six areas depend on institutional context and may be manifested in very different ways in specific colleges and universities.

Further, Moore et al. (2018) uncovered that embedding structures and developing a culture with early career faculty fosters significant development of an interdisciplinary mindset and infrastructure. Guimarães et al. (2019) added to the literature on interdisciplinary research, noting that scholars who engage in this approach tend to be motivated by real-world problems, have the tolerance for opposing/conflicting views, maintain a general inquisitiveness, can absorb and integrate complex ideas, function well on teams, and operate on societal conscience and awareness toward problem-solving. The research also supports that interdisciplinarity presents challenges to one's scholarly identity, raises questions about interdisciplinary academic training, and presents challenges within academic progression because of interdisciplinary research. Yet scholars must be prepared for these clashing viewpoints and changes in the way academic researchers operate (e.g., changes to research training) to advance interdisciplinary research.

Conclusion

The themes of this book—being mission driven; adapting to environmental change; embracing democratic partnerships; and modeling inclusion, equity, and positive social change—are essential to academic leadership, administration, and governance. Shared governance is key to the success of colleges and universities in performing as effective organizations because these structures provide higher education institutions with the checks and balances necessary to inform the academic decisions that fall to the faculty, academic administrators, the CAO, and ultimately the president and the board of trustees. Shared governance is a difficult undertaking because it involves trust, transparency, collaboration, and a shared purpose—to name a few of the common relational characteristics that make shared governance successful. Research and practice demonstrate how shared academic governance leads to thoroughly informed decisions, reduced ambiguity, and community consensus around initiatives and other decisions. Also, a holistic view of institutional mission; adaptability; democratic partnerships; modeling inclusion, equity, and positive social change support academic programs so that they are designed with careful consideration about curricular development and degree integrity. In applying this framework, we also see how promoting collaboration in teaching, research, and service helps institutions remain relevant, responsive, and informed by research and practice as well as meets societal needs in the 21st century.

Notes

1. For more information on Robert's Rules, see Robert (2011) and Susskind et al. (1999).
2. See https://www.hhs.gov/ohrp/index.html for the federal regulations governing the use of human subjects in research.

References

Alessio, J. C. (2017). *The intentional dean: A guide to the academic deanship.* Routledge.

American Association of University Professors. (n.d.). *Statement on government of colleges and universities.* http://www.aaup.org/AAUP/pubsres/policydocs/contents/governancestatement.htm

American Association of University Professors. (2021a). *Special report: COVID-19 and academic governance.* https://www.aaup.org/report/covid-19-and-academic-governance

American Association of University Professors. (2021b). *Survey data on the impact of the pandemic on shared governance.* https://www.aaup.org/report/survey-data-impact-pandemic-shared-governance#technote

American Association of University Professors. (2021c). *The 2021 AAUP shared governance survey: Findings on faculty roles by decision-making areas.* https://www.aaup.org/report/2021-aaup-shared-governance-survey-findings-faculty-roles-decision-making-areas

American Council on Education. (2014). *Chief academic officer survey: The CAO job.* https://www.acenet.edu/Documents/Chief-Academic-Officer-Survey-the-CAO-Job.pdf

Association of Governing Boards of Universities and Colleges. (1996). *Renewing the academic presidency: Stronger leadership for tougher times.* Author.

Association of Governing Boards of Universities and Colleges. (2016). *Shared governance: Is OK good enough?* Author.

Association of Governing Boards of Universities and Colleges. (2017a). *Shared governance: Changing with the times.* Author.

Association of Governing Boards of Universities and Colleges. (2017b). *AGB board of directors' statement on shared governance.* Author.

Atnip, G. W. (2009). Role of the chief academic officer. In S. Chen (Ed.), *Academic administration: A quest for better management and leadership in higher education* (pp. 39–51). Nova Science.

Bahls, S. S. (2014). *Shared governance in times of change: A practical guide for universities and colleges*. AGB Press.

Bahls, S. C. (2017). From shared governance to shared accountability. In S. F. Cramer (Ed.), *Shared governance in higher education: New paradigms, evolving perspectives* (pp. 83–120). State University of New York Press.

Bejou, D., & Bejou, A. (2016). Shared governance: The key to higher education equilibrium. *Journal of Relationship Marketing, 15*(1–2), 54–61. https://doi.org/10.1080/15332667.2015.1091630

Benjamin, R., Carroll, S., Jacobi, M., Krop, C., & Shires, M. (1993). *The redesign of governance in higher education*. RAND Corporation.

Bigelow, G., & Chaddock, N. (2020). Framing the role of faculty governance toward institutional diversity and inclusion. In S. F. Cramer & P. L. K. Knuepfer (Eds.), *Shared governance in higher education: Vitality and continuity in times of change* (pp. 36–46). State University of New York Press.

Birnbaum, R. (Ed.). (1991). *Faculty in governance: The role of senates and joint committees in academic decision making*. Jossey-Bass.

Birnbaum, R. (2004). The end of shared governance: Looking ahead or looking back. In W. G. Tierney & V. M. Lechuga (Eds.), *Restructuring shared governance in higher education* (New Directions for Higher Education, no. 127, pp. 5–22). Jossey-Bass. https://doi.org/10.1002/he.152

Blau, P. M. (1973). *The organization of academic work*. Wiley.

Bliss, D., Lathrop, R., & Steele, J. (2020). Characteristics of shared governance. In S. F. Cramer & P. L. K. Knuepfer (Eds.), *Shared governance in higher education: Vitality and continuity in times of change* (pp. 3–14). State University of New York Press.

Bolger, P. (2021). A study of faculty perceptions and engagement with interdisciplinary research in university sustainability institutes. *Journal of Environmental Studies and Sciences, 11*(1), 115–129. https://doi.org/10.1007/s13412-020-00616-7

Bolton, A. (2000). *Managing the academic unit*. Open University Press.

Bright, D. F., & Richards, M. P. (2001). *The academic deanship: Individual careers*. Jossey-Bass.

Bucklew, N., Houghton, J. D., & Ellison, C. N. (2012). Faculty union and faculty senate co-existence: A review of the impact of academic collective bargaining on traditional academic governance. *Labor Studies Journal, 37*(4), 373–390. https://doi.org/10.1177/0160449X13482734

Chen, S. (2009). Administration of academic units and shared governance. In S. Chen (Ed.), *Academic administration: A quest for better management and leadership in higher* education (pp. 83–104). Nova Science.

Cipriano, R. E. (2020). Shared governance: More than a detached signifier. *The Department Chair, 30*(4), 11–13. https://doi.org/10.1002/dch.30313

Cole, J. R. (1994). *Balancing act: Dilemmas of choice facing research universities*. Johns Hopkins University Press.

Curnalia, R. M., & Mermer, D. (2018). Renewing our commitment to tenure, academic freedom, and shared governance to navigate challenges in higher education. *Review of Communication, 18*(2), 129–139. https://doi.org/10.1080/1535 8593.2018.1438645

DeCesare, M. (2020). Back to the past: Imagining the future of academic governance. In S. F. Cramer & P. L. K. Knuepfer (Eds.), *Shared governance in higher education: Vitality and continuity in times of change* (pp. 176–191). State University of New York Press.

Deemer, R., & Horvath, V. (2017). Shared governance—From both sides of the fence. In S. F. Cramer (Ed.), *Shared governance in higher education: New paradigms, evolving perspectives* (pp. 21–35). State University of New York Press.

Eaton, J. (2018). New normal accreditation: Role, practice, and values. In S. D. Phillips & K. Kinser (Eds.), *Accreditation on the edge: Challenging quality assurance in higher education* (pp. vii–xi). Johns Hopkins University Press.

Gilmour, J. E., Jr. (1991). Participative governance bodies in higher education: Report of a national study. In R. Birnbaum (Ed.), *Faculty in governance: The role of senates and joint committees in academic decision making* (pp. 27–40). Jossey-Bass.

Guimarães, M. H., Pohl, C., Bina, O., & Varanda, M. (2019). Who is doing inter- and transdisciplinary research, and why? An empirical study of motivations, attitudes, skills, and behaviours. *Futures, 112*, Article 102441. https://doi.org/10.1016/j.futures.2019.102441

Jacobs, J. (2012). The essential role of community colleges in rebuilding the nation's communities and economies. In J. E. Lane & D. B. Johnstone (Eds.), *Colleges and universities as economic drivers: Measuring and building success* (pp. 191–204). State University of New York Press.

Jaschik, S., & Lederman, D. (2021). *2021 Survey of college and university chief academic officers: A study by Inside Higher Ed and Hanover Research.* Inside Higher Ed and Hanover Research.

Johnston, S. W. (2003). Faculty governance and effective academic administrative leadership. In S. L. Hoppe & B. W. Speck (Eds.), *Identifying and preparing academic leaders* (New Directions for Higher Education, no. 124, pp. 57–63). Jossey-Bass. https://doi.org/10.1002/he.130

Johnstone, D. B. (2012). The impact of the 2008 Great Recession on college and university contributions to state and regional economic growth. In J. E. Lane & D. B. Johnstone (Eds.), *Colleges and universities as economic drivers: Measuring and building success* (pp. 277–293). State University of New York Press.

Jones, W. A., Hutchens, N. H., Hulbert, A., Lewis, W. D., & Brown, D. M. (2017). Shared governance among the new majority: Non-tenure track faculty eligibility for election to university faculty senates. *Innovative Higher Education, 42*(5), 505–519. https://doi.org/10.1007/s10755-017-9402-2

Kennedy, D. (1993). Making choices in the research university. *Daedalus, 122*(4), 127–152. https://www.jstor.org/stable/20027202

Kezar, A., & Lester, J. (2009). *Organizing higher education for collaboration: A guide for campus leaders.* Jossey-Bass.

Kinser, K., & Phillips, S. D. (2018). Accreditation: Introduction to a contested space. In S. D. Phillips & K. Kinser (Eds.), *Accreditation on the edge: Challenging quality assurance in higher education* (pp. 251–270). Johns Hopkins University Press.

Lambert, L. M. (2002). Chief academic officers. In R. M. Diamond (Ed.), *Field guide to academic leadership* (pp. 425–435). Jossey-Bass.

Lattuca, L., & Stark, J. (2009). *Shaping the college curriculum: Academic plans in context* (2nd ed.). Jossey-Bass.

Leaming, D. R. (2002). Academic deans. In R. M. Diamond (Ed.), *Field guide to academic leadership* (pp. 437–450). Jossey-Bass.

Lucey, C. (2002). Civic engagement, shared governance, and community colleges. *Academe, 88*(4), 27–31. https://doi.org/10.2307/40252185

Luescher-Mamashela, T. M. (2013). Student representation in university decision making: Good reasons, a new lens? *Studies in Higher Education, 38*(10), 1442–1456. https://doi.org/10.1080/03075079.2011.625496

Lyall, C. (2019). *Being an interdisciplinary academic: How institutions shape university careers*. Palgrave MacMillan.

Manning, S. (2018). Quality assurance and quality improvement. In S. D. Phillips & K. Kinser (Eds.), *Accreditation on the edge: Challenging quality assurance in higher education* (pp. 13-30). Johns Hopkins University Press.

Mathews, K. (2020). *What is the role of university staff in shared governance?* Harvard Graduate School of Education, Collaborative on Academic Careers in Higher Education. https://coache.gse.harvard.edu/blog/what-role-university-staff-shared-governance

Miller, M. T., & Murray, J. W., Jr. (Eds.). (2011). *Staff governance and institutional policy formation*. Information Age.

Miller, M. T., Smith, E. A., & Nadler, D. P. (2016). Debate and discourse: The role of the faculty senate on the modern American campus. *Journal of Higher Education Theory & Practice, 16*(3). https://www.articlegateway.com/index.php/JHETP/article/view/1977

Mohrman, S. A., Cohen, S. G., & Mohrman, A. M. (1995). *Designing team-based organizations*. Jossey-Bass.

Moore, M., Martinson, M. L., Nurius, P. S., & Kemp, S. P. (2018). Transdisciplinarity in Research: Perspectives of early career faculty. *Research on Social Work Practice, 28*(3), 254–264. https://doi.org/10.1177/1049731517708033

National Association for Biomedical Research. (n.d.). *About NABR.* https://www.nabr.org/about

Olson, G. A. (2009, July 23). Exactly what is "shared governance"? *The Chronicle of Higher Education.* https://www.chronicle.com/article/exactly-what-is-shared-governance/

Ott, M. W., & Mathews, K. R. (2015). *Effective academic governance: Five ingredients for CAOs and faculty*. Collaborative on Academic Careers in Higher Education.

Pearce, C. L., Wood, B. G., & Wassenaar, C. L. (2018). The future of leadership in public universities: Is shared leadership the answer? *Public Administration Review, 78*(4), 640–644. https://doi.org/10.1111/puar.12938

Robert, H. M. (2011). *Robert's rules of order newly revised* (11th ed.). Da Capo.

Roworth, W. W. (1997). Pandora's dilemma: Some reflections on peer review. *Academe, 83*(3), 35–38. https://doi.org/10.2307/40251091

Schuster, J. H., Smith, D. G., Corak, K. A., & Yamada, M. M. (1994). *Strategic governance: How to make big decisions better*. Oryx.

Smalley, A. (2021). *Higher education responses to coronavirus (COVID-19)*. National Conference of State Legislatures. https://www.ncsl.org/research/education/higher-education-responses-to-coronavirus-covid-19.aspx

Susskind, L., McKearan, S., & Thomas-Larmer, J. (Eds.). (1999). *The consensus building handbook: A comprehensive guide to reaching agreement*. SAGE.

Tierney, W. G., & Minor, J. T. (2003). *Challenges for governance: A national report*. University of Southern California.

University of Denver. (2010). *A self-study for re-accreditation*. Author.

14

ACADEMIC DEPARTMENTS AND DEPARTMENTAL LEADERSHIP

Academic departments are the core units of colleges and universities, serving as the venues for the implementation of their institutions' academic missions (Buller, 2012; Chu, 2021; Lucas, 2000a; Wolverton et al., 2005). Departments are comprised of faculty in a designated discipline or field of study, and these faculty members are overseen by an elected or appointed colleague, known as the department chair or the department head. All three of these groups—departments, chairs, and faculty—exemplify the four themes of this book: the need to base decisions on an institution's core mission and values; the need to adapt to environmental changes in ways that are consistent with institutional mission; the critical nature of creating and fostering democratic partnerships with various consistencies; and the essential role of modeling inclusion, equity, and positive social change.

Academic Departments

Academic departments began to mature into the units we know today during the late 19th and early 20th centuries (Knight & Trowler, 2001). Departmental cultures and structures vary greatly, and these wide differences have led a number of observers to speak of the idiosyncratic nature of departments (Chu, 2021; T. M. Clark, 2007). Each academic department is grounded within an academic discipline or field of study as its unifying theme, and many of the variations between departments are a result of disciplinary traditions and cultures or mimicking structures at other institutions.

Given the differences between disciplines,[1] some scholars have attempted to systemize these fields in a way that shows how they differ and overlap.

Biglan (1973a, 1973b), for instance, developed a taxonomy to elaborate on the knowledge structures perpetuated by various disciplines and fields, which provides a framework for understanding differences in departmental cultures and structures. Biglan identified two main categories of disciplines: high paradigm (disciplines organized by clearly articulated theories, namely, the hard sciences) and low paradigm (disciplines organized around perceptions and understandings, such as the arts, humanities, and social sciences). In high-paradigm disciplines, knowledge is cumulative, theoretical frameworks are highly structured, and there are clear boundaries between disciplines. At the boundaries where two or more disciplines overlap, new interdisciplinary fields have developed (e.g., biotechnology, bioengineering, astrophysics). In contrast, in low-paradigm disciplines, a general understanding exists that there are multiple ways of knowing, which causes these fields' boundaries to be more fluid, curricula more flexible, and research methodologies more diverse.

Biglan's (1973a, 1973b) taxonomy is useful, but further specializations within disciplines and fields also affect how the members of academic departments behave. These traditions influence the ways faculty members are educated, their ways of knowing and seeking truth, their professional standards, and the environment of their field or discipline, all of which influence the structure and functions of their academic departments. Academic leaders can enhance their understanding of academic departments by conceptualizing them as systems, as well as by taking time to understand their individual cultures and climates.

Departmental Culture and Climate

Effective administration and leadership require an understanding of departmental culture and climate. Austin (1994) identified the culture of a particular department, each with a unique set of values and norms. Departmental culture is in part defined by the other cultures in which faculty members operate, and it varies across academic departments in a school or college. These differences may be accounted for based on variations in the cultures of fields, disciplines, and subdisciplines, but they also emanate from each department's unique history, membership, and leadership. At the same time, a department chair can embrace new ways of thinking about its direction, selecting colleagues and staff, and supporting students. This visioning and formation of an improved environment are crucial as departments seek to become more inclusive, develop a sense of belonging, and foster a community (Chun & Evans, 2015).

A department's climate characterizes the interpersonal relationships among faculty members. To encourage positive interactions and climate, department chairs can employ a model of shared governance in which they serve as facilitator in conjunction with faculty colleagues to resolve controversial issues (Christie, 2007; Fisher, 2007; Gmelch, 1995). The climate is more likely to be a wholesome environment when conflict is acknowledged and openly discussed, and a decision is made afterward. Experience tells us that conflict is best resolved by taking a majority rule vote after a period of open discussion. Typically, after a vote, winners and losers walk away accepting the outcome and continuing a healthy professional relationship. In contrast, unresolved conflict creates an unhealthy environment in which parties connive and foster dissent to the detriment of departmental well-being. Transforming a department that seems to thrive on conflict and controversy to a more collegial atmosphere takes time and persistence by its leader. In most cases, the leader of the department is the department chair, also known as the department head.

The Department Chair

An extensive body of literature exists concerning the role of the department chair or head (Buller, 2012; Chu, 2021; Chun & Evans, 2015; Gmelch, 1995, 2004; Gmelch & Miskin, 1995; Knight & Trowler, 2001; Leaming, 2007; Lucas, 2000b; Wheeler et al., 2008). Yet the use of the title "department chair" or "department head" is potentially confusing. Some literature defines a department chair as one who is elected by the department faculty, while a department head is appointed by a dean after consultation with the department faculty. The election of a department chair may be for a multiyear term (of 2 to 5 years) or for a single-year term, after which the chair will step down. Appointed department heads usually serve 3- to 5-year terms with the option of one or two renewals.

Regardless of appointment type, a useful way to contend with the challenges of leading an academic department is to approach situations in terms of Bolman and Deal's (2017) concept of organizational frames. They identified four frames department chairs can use to understand their role and the role of their department within the institution. The *structural* frame considers the academic structure of the institution, how decisions are made, and where the department chair fits in that structure. The *political* frame addresses where the department and its chair fit into political processes in the institution, as well as where the chair fits in the politics and culture of the department. The *human resource* frame deals with developing an understanding of interpersonal relationships within the organization; hiring processes; investment of time, effort, and resources; and how to encourage quality work and professional development. The *cultural* frame situates issues and problems in the context of the history and culture of the institution and the department to make sense of the perceptions of stakeholders. Lumpkin (2004) added a fifth frame, the *personal* frame, which is a department chair's understanding of personal strengths and weaknesses and when to rely on the strengths of other members of the department. Gmelch (2004) noted that new department chairs tend to focus on the structural and human resource frames. As they grow and develop in the position, however, they start to use the political and symbolic frames. Building on Lumpkin's idea of the personal frame, department chairs should play to their individual strengths and draw on colleagues whose strengths mitigate their weaknesses.

Using all these frames will assist department chairs in understanding their role as leaders and administrators as they strive to enable growth and adaptability and foster the academic work of the department.

Enabling Growth and Adaptability

Much has been written about departments and adaptation to change (Cheldelin, 2000; Lucas, 2000a, 2000b). The adaptive leadership model (Heifitz, 1994) requires department chairs to take a proactive role in change processes through six steps. First, a chair must identify the challenge the department faces. Second, the chair needs to identify the key issues and communicate them clearly to department faculty and staff. Third, the chair must frame and prioritize the areas in which change is required. Fourth, the chair needs to secure faculty ownership of the problem-solving process. Fifth, the chair must manage any emerging conflicts and maintain focus on the problem. Sixth, it is the chair's task to create a safe place where disparate perspectives can be aired openly and without negative repercussions (Coakley & Randall, 2006).

Following these steps may help chairs overcome conflict in their departments when it inevitably arises. Gmelch (1995) noted there are three types of conflict—institutional, positional, and interpersonal—and argued that successful department chairs need to recognize the nature and cause of conflict. While one needs to be aware of institutional conflict, it may be outside a chair's purview to resolve, so the chair must discern ways to work around such challenges. Positional conflict deals with the department chair's struggles with being caught between the administration and the faculty, with obligations to respond to the needs of both constituencies. Interpersonal conflict could occur between faculty members in the department or between the department chair and individual faculty members.

Bissell (2003) wrote about handling conflict with difficult faculty. He categorized difficult faculty members into several types:

- *Bullies* shout or use threats and intimidation to get what they want.
- *Complainers* see themselves as victims and cannot solve problems because of the perceived behavior of others.
- *Procrastinators* choose to ignore problems.
- *Guerilla fighters* use sarcasm and criticism to make others feel incompetent or inadequate for raising an issue.
- *Experts* do not listen to others' arguments and use knowledge to support their arguments and show that they have all the answers.
- *Icicles* freeze up at the first sign of conflict and have no opinion about the issue under discussion.

These difficult faculty types constantly complain, and others find them difficult to be around. They overemphasize problems and are horrible problem-solvers. As a result of these weaknesses, they consume a significant portion of a department chair's time. We also want to recognize that there are many, many productive faculty, who are good partners and collaborators with chairs to advance the needs and goals of the department.

While department chairs may never change difficult faculty members, strategies exist to assist them in confronting—not rewarding—their behavior. Bissell (2003) identified a series of steps to resolve challenging situations: discern the emotional climate and calm the situation; identify the problem and remain focused on it; resist assigning blame; avoid name calling; develop and evaluate alternative solutions, then select one; spell out procedural issues; and evaluate the solution's success. Throughout such a process, straight talk and careful listening, including reading between the lines, are important. The chair should avoid conflict triangles by becoming the third person in a dispute between two faculty members. In addition, control of body language is important so that one's words, not one's body, communicate one's position on an issue. Department chairs need to be aware of their own personalities, mannerisms, and emotions so they are in control of them rather than being controlled by problem faculty members.

Of course, dealing with conflict and difficult faculty is only a part of enabling growth, and department chairs must also ensure faculty have opportunities for professional development. Rapid changes in technology have dramatically affected the ways faculty teach. The development of more interactive technology, for example, has greatly enhanced the delivery of online courses and degree programs. As technology continues to evolve, one can only imagine the effects these changes will have on the delivery of higher education in the coming decades. As Bates (2000) noted, professional development is needed to assist faculty in employing these technological developments as effective teaching and learning tools. Enabling faculty to continually develop and grow will, in turn, allow the chair to work toward fostering the academic work of the department.

With the increase of online learning, faculty roles also have shifted in many instances to the unbundling of work. The concept of unbundling faculty roles is the disaggregation of faculty functions such as curricular development, course delivery, instructional design, assessment, and other key areas (Gehrke & Kezar, 2015). This approach changes roles and responsibilities around course and program development to more specialized, yet insular, functions that require a group design approach to be successful. Thus, while academic departments might be concerned about the knowledge base and assessments within a program, the unbundling of faculty roles, which include offices such as online learning and instructional designers, may include learning design and pedagogical techniques within and across courses in ways that higher education did not previously coordinate.

Fostering the Academic Work of the Department

Monitoring and improving the quality of a department's academic work are significant and shared responsibilities of a department's chair and its faculty, and part of this work is creating a common vision and mission (Leaming, 2007; Lucas, 2000b). When a department has no shared vision, its faculty members tend to act individualistically and in ways that may not be in concert with their departmental colleagues. Similarly, to cultivate the intellectual life of a department, a chair must encourage all department members to assume responsibility for a healthy intellectual climate. While a chair may need to initiate the first few events, such as guest lectures and faculty and student presentations of current research and findings, eventually the initiative for these sessions will come from faculty and students. One way to begin this tradition is to highlight the scholarly work of faculty members in the department. Another way is to invite faculty members from other departments with similar research interests to present their research and scholarship, which will also encourage collaboration across departments. Such gatherings can also highlight outstanding student research.

Another way to encourage research activity—if it is indeed consistent with institutional and departmental missions—is for the chair to distribute resources based on faculty research productivity or potential for productivity. Distributing resources equally across all faculty members dilutes resources and will frustrate and create deterrents for productive faculty members. If faculty members desire to pursue external funding sources, it might be helpful to conduct workshops in which faculty members with grant experience educate their colleagues in the craft of pursuing grants. In addition, it might be useful to provide travel funding to enable faculty members to meet with project officers at funding agencies of interest. These investments can be very effective in bringing external funds to departments and can help faculty accomplish their work. However, as with all this work, all efforts must be paired with careful and thorough assessment.

Evaluation and Planning

While other sections of this book address strategic planning and evaluation (see, e.g., chapter 16), it is worth emphasizing the importance of these practices at the department level, as well as the role of the department chair in these processes. Wergin and Swingen (2000) described an "ideal approach" to planning and assessment:

> The ideal approach would be to evaluate academic departments and other academic units in ways that are not too costly or time-consuming, that respect the diversity of disciplinary missions and cultures, that promote departmental self-reflection, all while rewarding collective accomplishments appropriate to larger school and institutional missions. (p. 1)

While such activities as program review, outcomes assessment, specialized accreditation, financial accounting, and internal quality control are often the responsibility of units beyond individual academic departments, chairs should initiate these evaluations and planning processes in their departments when appropriate.

Planning and assessment strategies also include curricula development and adaption to environmental change, improvement in teaching strategies that capitalize on technological innovation, assessment of learning outcomes, and fostering research and scholarship (Corey, 2007; Knight & Trowler, 2001; Lucas, 2000b; Sommer, 2008; Wergin & Swingen, 2000). Gardiner (2000) discussed curricula development and adaptation to a changing environment and their links to curricula assessment, changing teaching strategies, and assessment of learning outcomes. This process includes the assessment of the effectiveness of the curriculum in developing disciplinary or field knowledge and skills, as well as values that are consistent with department and institutional goals that prepare graduates for effective citizenship in society. This assessment further includes the development of standards of performance such as "criterion-referenced evaluations," "value-added assessment," and assessment of individual courses' learning outcomes (Gardiner, 2000, p. 176).

Wergin and Swingen (2000) built on this idea, suggesting that accountability issues drive the need for assessment. They argued that there ought to be institutional coordination of assessment, but that departments should be allowed to adapt institutional guidelines to their specific needs—a practice that will yield variation across departments in terms of "how and what" is assessed (Wergin & Swingen, 2000, p. 11). The department chair and faculty should assume shared responsibility for developing a quality educational program that adapts to environment change and develops the knowledge and skills of their students. (See chapter 16 for a discussion of academic planning.) Having discussed the structures of academic departments and the roles of chairs who lead them, we turn now to the individuals who make up these departments: the faculty.

The Faculty

The faculty in a department convert the institutional mission and vision into programs and activities such as teaching and learning, research and scholarship, and service and community engagement (Leaming, 2003; Lucas, 2000b). While conventional wisdom suggests that faculty work is a cushy job that involves spending a few hours teaching in the classroom and some time holding office hours, while professors spend the rest of their time free to do as they please, the reality could not be more different for most faculty members. Faculty work is a balancing act between the roles of teaching, research, and service. Although faculty members place greater emphasis on their different responsibilities depending on their institution's mission and type, faculty typically spend 50 hours per week on their work (Schuster & Finkelstein, 2006), though more recent reports have suggested that college professors at research universities may be working much more, around 61 hours per week (McKenna, 2018; Ziker et al., 2014). Suffice it to say, the work commitment for college faculty is much more significant than what may appear to the public, especially when we typically reference workload in terms of the number of classes one teaches.

All faculty members with teaching responsibilities spend time on course preparation and delivery (O'Meara, Lennartz, et al., 2019). For example, to ensure that course offerings remain current in the field, professors should develop new course syllabi and revise existing course syllabi prior to the term when the classes will be offered. Course development should capitalize on lessons learned from previous teaching experiences, including the use of such tools as course websites. Faculty members should make themselves available to meet with their students outside the classroom, exchange emails as appropriate, and participate in online discussions. In addition, they should share with colleagues what is working well and seek input where improvements might be needed. Ultimately, the time faculty members spend on each course will depend somewhat on their prior experience with teaching the course (such as how often they have taught it previously) and the level of the course (i.e., introductory, advanced, or graduate level), but all these tasks indicate that, in reality, effective teaching practices consume a significant portion of a faculty member's time. In addition, beyond course preparation, faculty members' teaching role includes student advising and mentoring activities, which can continue even after students graduate.

Research expectations vary by institution type and by discipline (O'Meara et al., 2009; O'Meara, Lennartz, et al., 2019). For example, faculty members in hard-paradigm disciplines at a research university are expected to support a laboratory, graduate assistants, and postdoctoral researchers. Although soft-paradigm disciplines also expect funded research, they place greater emphasis on the publication of books, book chapters, and articles in refereed/peer reviewed journals. At comprehensive colleges and liberal arts colleges that have not reformed their rewards structures, faculty members are expected to have an extensive research agenda despite the high teaching load typical of these institutions. Pressure for prestige, reputation, and national rankings drives these expectations. Further, in many cases, interdisciplinary work resides on the fringes of disciplines and fields of study, so the "value" of such work is not always consistent among universities (Klein & Falk-Krzesinski, 2017).

At comprehensive universities and liberal arts colleges whose administrators understand their teaching mission and have reformed their rewards structure to reflect this focus, faculty research agendas tend to involve keeping current in their disciplines and fields and focusing on the scholarship of teaching and the development of textbooks for college-level courses (Baker, Lunsford, & Pifer, 2017; Rice, 2002). In fact, Palmer (2002) found that tenured faculty in community colleges were in many cases involved in the scholarship of teaching and textbook authorship. As a whole, however, faculty at community and technical colleges felt least supported to engage in research activities (Baker, Terosky, & Martinez, 2017).

Faculty members' service or engagement role varies somewhat by institution type but can be divided into institutional, disciplinary, and community activities. Faculty members are involved in the governance of their institution, including making decisions surrounding hiring and determination of rank. Most faculty members participate in their national or regional disciplinary associations, serving as officers or committee chairs or members and participating in conferences. The faculty's service role continues to evolve, and civic engagement has become an important aspect of the service mission of many institutions (Terosky, 2018). (For more information on civic engagement, see chapter 9.) While many factors affect a faculty member's ability to complete their job duties, faculty success begins with solid employment practices that foster trust and a sense of fairness.

Faculty Employment Issues

As is the case with most organizations, colleges and universities must contend with staff issues. In this section, we address concerns specifically related to the employment of faculty members. With the retirement of substantial numbers of senior faculty members looming, higher education institutions should develop plans for the recruitment and hiring of new faculty members. As institutions replace faculty members, they must address diversity issues in ways that are consistent with laws prohibiting discrimination. In addition, administrators should identify ways to protect faculty members' academic freedom—an important concept in the advancement of knowledge. They also should consider how faculty members can engage in academic governance as a democratic partner with administrators and board members.

Faculty Employment Plans

In the wake of the economic downturn of 2008, institutions began to downsize their faculty and staff by not replacing lines as attrition through retirements and resignations took place. At the national level, full-time faculty growth occurred in two waves within a 20-year span. That is, from fall 1999 to fall 2011, the number of full-time college professors grew by 28%. Following the 2008 recession, the pace of full-time professors' entry into the teaching ranks declined to 9% between fall 2011 and fall 2018 (de Brey et al., 2021). During these same periods, the impact on part-time faculty was much sharper, suggesting a national movement toward more part-time faculty. Between 1999 and 2011, the number of part-time faculty increased by 72%, but the pace changed after 2011, decreasing by 7% between 2011 and 2018 (de Brey et al., 2021). Also, although the number of full-time and part-time faculty grew, student enrollments grew by even more—nearly 135% (de Brey et al., 2021). At the institutional level, campus leaders should not leave staffing decisions to fate. Rather, administrators should develop and define faculty hiring strategies for the next 5 to 10 years. Such strategic planning should be completed in light of the institution's mission, and if done properly, will positively affect its academic programs.

While efforts have been made to raise institutional consciousness about equity and inclusion, especially among college faculty, the data still suggest greater efforts are needed to improve compositional diversity, which has been shown to contribute to college students' learning and development (Espinosa et al., 2019). Students of color in particular benefit significantly from diverse faculty, especially when they can be mentored by someone who shares in their experiences (Llamas et al., 2021), yet in fall 2018, 75% of full-time college faculty were White (40% males, 35% females), 12% Asian/Pacific Islanders (7% males, 5% females), 6% Black (3% males, 3% females), 6% Latinx (3% males, 3% females), 1% Native American/Alaska Native, and 1% persons of two or more races (de Brey et al., 2021; Hussar et al., 2020). A comprehensive recruitment and retention approach is essential. In a study commissioned by the Teachers Insurance and Annuity Association to investigate the changing demographics of higher education faculty, R. L. Clark (2004) made this recommendation:

> A faculty-planning model should be based on demographic models of population growth and employment records of individual institutions. Using the planning model, academic administrators would be able to observe the changing age structure of their faculty, expected turnover rates and retirement rates, and the need for new faculty. The model will also be able to address the changing composition of the faculty between fulltime tenure track faculty and other types of faculty appointments. (p. 10)

Such a plan should consider the themes of this book: institutional mission; adaptability to environmental change; democratic partnerships; and modeling inclusion, equity, and positive social change. The plan should account for the faculty positions needed to deliver quality programs, including the ratio of contingent to tenured and tenure-track faculty members and their hiring rank. In addition, no plan should ignore the quest for diversity within the faculty. According to the College & University Professional Association for Human Resources (CUPA-HR), higher education's professional association for human resources, the median age of tenure-stream faculty (i.e., tenure-track and tenured faculty) is 49 years (McChesney & Bichsel, 2020). McChesney and Bichsel (2020) posited that the older median age "could lead to increased turnover in the coming decade and increased competition in hiring new Ph.D.s" (p. 11). Given the revolving retirement effects, now is an excellent time for colleges and universities to plan for new faculty hires who will allow them to adapt to environmental changes in ways that are consistent with their mission and values. Here are some questions that should be posed in developing a faculty staffing plan:

- Based on the institutional mission, what should be the ratio of tenure or tenure-track faculty to contingent faculty (fixed-term, full-time, and part-time faculty)?
- If hiring tenured faculty, what should be the rank of a faculty member to maintain the quality and reputation of the degree program?
- Can the quality of academic programs be maintained where we only employ contingent faculty to deliver those programs?
- Will what we know about the relationship between faculty staffing patterns and student learning be used in developing the plan?

Recruiting and Hiring

Hiring new faculty members is one of the most important tasks of an academic department. While the current economic situation may mean that occasions for hiring are rare, the imminent retirement of baby boomer faculty members will result in significant changes in the makeup of department faculties. Their exodus will provide a tremendous opportunity for departments to embrace changes in their disciplines and society more broadly, as well as to move in strategic directions. Capitalizing on this opportunity will require department chairs to embrace hiring strategies that serve their departments and institutions.

Leaming (2007) has provided excellent advice on how to orchestrate successful recruitment and hiring of new faculty members. To begin, the chair and faculty members should identify the disciplinary specializations that are inadequately covered in their department, considering any shifts in their discipline's knowledge base or changes in the larger environment. This process will help the department develop a specific position description and the specific criteria used to screen applicants. It will also help, in a time of scarce resources, justify the need to fill the vacated position.

The selection of the search committee is a critical step in the success of any hiring process. The committee chair and members should be able to navigate between their department's various philosophical and ideological camps by adhering to the agreed-on job description and selection criteria. The institution's affirmative action policies should be considered in the selection of committee membership and in the selection of candidates. Moreover, recruitment of candidates is more than just advertising in the appropriate trade journals and newspapers. That is, faculty members need to be proactive, actively contacting good prospects and encouraging them to apply. Using Leaming's (2007) recommendations as a guide, we have developed an expanded checklist for departmental leaders and committee members to follow as they recruit new colleagues:

1. Develop a job description that is consistent with the departmental and institutional missions and promotes diverse ideologies and research interests within the field or discipline.

2. Appoint search committee members who will not try to clone themselves but rather seek a rich pool of candidates with strong teaching, research, and service experiences that will contribute to the department's mission.

3. Task the committee with embracing the institution's diversity objectives and conducting a fair and honest search for the best-qualified candidate who meets diversity objectives and predetermined academic and professional criteria.

4. Develop a mechanism for applicants who are not under consideration to be notified of their status as soon as possible during the search and ensure that all applicants are personally notified by letter of the search's outcome.

5. Drawing on video conferencing tools may be a good way to screen applicants prior to deciding which candidates should be brought to campus.

6. Campus visits should be a well-organized opportunity for the department to showcase its programs and activities, as well as a chance for candidates to highlight what they would contribute to the department and the institution.

Indeed, the department chair should remind faculty members that a job interview is a reciprocal situation (Leaming, 2007). Not only are the faculty, the department, and the institution looking at the candidate as a potential colleague and employee, the candidate is considering the departmental and institutional contexts to determine whether they offer an environment in which the candidate would want to spend all or part of their professional career. It is important to be open about conditions at the institution, but it is appropriate to accentuate the positive aspects of working there and living in the community. A careful, transparent hiring process should lead to the recruitment of positive and enthusiastic additions to the department, which in turn should avoid future problems.

Discrimination in Employment

Just as colleges and universities must consider affirmative action issues as they develop new faculty positions in the coming decade and beyond, administrators must also be attentive to these concerns with current faculty members. Numerous federal laws inform these matters, including Title VII of the Civil Rights Act of 1964 (as amended by the Equal Opportunities Act of 1972), Title VI of the Civil Rights Act of 1964, the Equal Pay Act of 1963, the Age Discrimination in Employment Act of 1967, Section 504 of the Rehabilitation Act of 1973 (amended by the ADA of 1990), and Title IX of the Education Amendments of 1972. The focus of each of these race-conscious and antidiscrimination laws is discussed in chapter 8, but here we emphasize the need to be mindful of these laws in hiring, salary, promotion, and tenure decisions, and in nonrenewal, layoff, and termination for cause actions.

In faculty employment decisions, institutions must uphold the relevant federal laws and any state statutes that mirror or expand upon federal laws. Today most institutions maintain affirmative action policy statements that prohibit discrimination based on race, gender, national origin, sexual orientation, and veteran status, meeting or exceeding federal and state employment obligations. Discrimination against individuals with physical handicaps is treated somewhat differently in that a person with a physical disability must be otherwise qualified to perform the requirements of the position.

Faculty Evaluation and Reward Structures

Designing an evaluation and reward structure for faculty that reflects the mission and goals of the institution is important in maintaining a strong and vibrant faculty. Evaluation processes important to faculty growth and development include annual reviews, promotion and tenure, and post-tenure reviews.

Annual Reviews

High-quality departments contribute to high-quality colleges and universities. The annual evaluation of faculty is an important step in the promotion of a strong, vibrant department that delivers quality teaching, research, and service (Chu, 2021; Leaming, 2003; Lucas, 2000b). Many institutions have instituted annual reviews to respond to societal demands for accountability and to monitor and encourage quality performance and faculty development. When annual reviews are directly linked to salary increases or merit pay, employee motivation and directed goals are much clearer (Leaming, 2007). That is, those who perform well should receive a salary increase reflective of their good work, while those performing below expected levels should receive no merit increase until they improve their performance. This approach, however, is not always possible when state regulations/policies or collective bargaining agreements outline permissible or required salary increases based on cost-of-living adjustments or alternative determinations for merit increases.

When possible, annual review achievements or outputs should be developed collaboratively with the chair (or another designated academic leader, such as the dean) and the faculty to address the criteria and measures. Ultimately, the evaluation process should be consistent with the mission and values of the academic unit, as well as with the specific disciplines or fields in the unit. Although these general recommendations offer guidance, criteria and expectations vary widely by institution type, mission, circumstances, and discipline/field of study. For example, the measures used at a small, private liberal arts institution with a strong teaching mission may focus on student engagement, peer review of teaching, and learning outcomes. In the area of research and scholarship, measures may focus on the scholarship of teaching in the field and applied research along with engagement activities in the community and the region. Regardless of an academic unit's discipline or an institution's mission, however, review processes and criteria should be enforced consistently across the department and college.

A standardized format for annual reviews often offers a fair assessment of the strongest through the weakest faculty members in a program, identification of strategies to address weaknesses, and the ability to assign workloads to accentuate faculty strengths.[2] Of course, evaluators such as chairs and deans should be aware of biases with instruments and people (including themselves). For instance, the research has consistently raised evidence of student bias against women and faculty of color in teaching evaluations (see, e.g., Kreitzer & Sweet-Cushman, 2021). Thus, the evidentiary pieces should be taken as a whole to identify patterns and trends.

The annual review evidence is important to document one's accomplishments. Although not required at some institutions, prior to their annual reviews, faculty members should create a report of their activities during the previous year and a list of goals for the upcoming year. The format of the report should be standard across the department, with department-required and self-reported data provided by the faculty member to measure the effectiveness of teaching and advising, research and scholarship, and service and outreach.

One of the most challenging aspects of performing annual reviews is working with underperforming colleagues. While department leaders may shy away from frank evaluations of weaker faculty members, the problems these colleagues present will not disappear without constructive intervention and salary increases linked to performance. Addressing a faculty member's shortcomings in performance of teaching, research, or service roles in a thoughtful manner may have a long-term positive effect on the faculty member in question, particularly in terms of potential promotion, tenure, or faculty development issues. In addition, it should have a favorable impact on the department climate more broadly.

A department chair who ignores problems with faculty performance sends the message that the chair does not care about the faculty member's behavior, which will ultimately damage the chair's relationship with this faculty member (and potentially with the rest of the department, as colleagues may resent the chair's lack of intervention in the situation). In the process of directly addressing faculty weaknesses in the context of the annual review, the chair can employ the "we" concept. That is, the chair and the faculty member in question can identify ways in which "we" can work together to address problems and implement strategies to improve performance. In the end, however, for interventions with weak faculty members to be successful, the faculty members must be willing to appraise their performance honestly and engage in the work necessary to improve performance.

Diamond and colleagues have studied these issues since the 1990s (Diamond, 2002a, 2002b; Diamond & Adam, 2002, 2004). A key recommendation that has emerged from their scholarship is that institutions need to ensure that criteria for annual reviews and rewards are consistent with their mission and their promotion and tenure process. What faculty members reported to Diamond (2002b), however, is that their institutions' rhetoric does not reflect what is actually rewarded, nor are personnel reward policies consistent with their institutions' stated mission. In addition, Diamond (2002b) found that applied research, teaching, course and curriculum design, and community service do not receive much in the way of rewards or recognition. Aguilar-Smith and Gonzales (2021) echoed these findings in the community and technical college setting. They observed that college administrators and faculty had, at times, conflicting approaches to supporting students and improving teaching, and the college's initiatives to systematize activities such as student success efforts were less effective for students and ran counter to the professors' work. For instance, the college's technocratic systems for advising and student supports, such as the midterm evaluation, lost the faculty members' more personal, relational interactions to support student success.

Similarly, faculty expectations of research and creative activities also support the need for greater clarity and alignment of annual and periodic reviews. Stupnisky et al. (2017) found that clear expectations of pre-tenure faculty research responsibilities correlated with their extrinsic motivation. However, the data also reported a negative relationship between clear expectations and perceived success in research. These data might suggest likely optimal degrees of expectation setting and realistic checks on the environmental conditions in which the faculty work. That is, the working conditions may not include teaching loads or research evaluation considerations for faculty to achieve those end states. For instance, evidence has demonstrated that U.S. universities are increasingly placing reliance on a journal's impact factor to make determinations about academic evaluations (McKiernan et al., 2019). Impact factors are often associated with journal quality, selectivity, and usefulness to the field, yet specialty areas may not have high-impact factors because few are experts in that area, or the research topics examined may rest on the fringes of the field and lack a critical mass of literature or knowledge base. Thus, while alignment between institutional mission and strategic priorities of the college are important when conducting annual and other personnel reviews (e.g., promotion, tenure, and post-tenure periodic reviews), they must accurately reflect the realities of faculty work.

Promotion and Tenure

Promotion and tenure considerations begin at the department level and are based on peer faculty's evaluation of whether a probationary faculty member is eligible to be promoted to associate professor or receive tenure (a contract without term). Academic departments must develop promotion and tenure processes consistent with their institution's processes and criteria, but they must also tailor their standards to the needs of the specific disciplines or fields housed in the department.

Historically, teaching and advising have been the most difficult areas to assess, with performance typically based on students' instructor evaluations and faculty members' classroom observations. More recently the assessment of learning outcomes has been incorporated into the evaluation of teaching, which holds promise to improve our ability to assess teaching effectiveness (Lattuca & Stark, 2009).

The challenges of measuring teaching effectiveness have resulted in an excessive focus on research and scholarship at many institutions, including some whose primary mission is undergraduate education. Instead of emulating the research and scholarship criteria used by doctoral universities (as designated by the Carnegie basic classifications), colleges and universities whose primary mission is undergraduate teaching, and whose faculty members are expected to teach six to eight courses in an academic year, need to ensure that their research and scholarship expectations appropriately reflect their mission. Their focus ought to be on criteria such as the scholarship of teaching, applied research, and community engagement (Chu, 2006; Knight & Trowler, 2001; Leaming, 2003, 2007; Lucas, 2000b).

In terms of the development of specific promotion and tenure criteria, Diamond (2000) highlighted the following points for consideration in crafting departmental policy:

- It should clearly articulate the criteria that will be used to determine the quality of a faculty member's work, providing the candidate and faculty review committee with a clear indication of not only the review process but also the documentation required.
- It is the ideal vehicle for describing the mission and priorities of your department and how they relate to the mission and priorities of the institution. In the best of worlds this statement would be the basis on which you, your unit, and your faculty would be judged.
- It is the ideal vehicle for describing to others what scholarly, professional, and creative work is in your unit and discipline. One of the major challenges you will face as chair is communicating to those in other fields this aspect of the work done in your department.
- It can play an important role in communicating to potential and new faculty the priorities of the unit and institution. It can reduce problems associated with new faculty expecting one thing and finding another—thus increasing the potential for long-term personal growth and productivity. (p. 96)

Diamond emphasized the value of engaging the entire department in the development of promotion and tenure standards, as wide participation will create a shared vision and priorities among department members.

A chair should play a significant leadership role in promotion and tenure considerations at the department level. Hiring probationary faculty members is an expensive process and should be viewed as an investment in the development of departmental programs. The department chair should work closely with probationary faculty members to ensure they have every opportunity to successfully navigate the promotion and tenure process. For example, probationary faculty members should be assigned teaching loads that include chances to teach upper-level undergraduate courses (and graduate courses, if offered). In addition, a mentoring program should be developed to assist new assistant professors in honing their teaching, research, and service skills. Periodically throughout the year, the chair should meet collectively or individually with assistant professors to assess their progress and provide assistance as needed. Annual reviews also give probationary faculty members a timely assessment of their progress toward tenure and a context in which to develop strategies to assist them as they move toward tenure review. This combination of consultation, advice, and mentoring from the department chair and other faculty members in the department is very effective in reducing stress and resulting in strong professional growth and the development of probationary faculty.

Scholars have asserted that contracts without term, commonly known as tenure, are no longer needed because they stifle institutional adaptability (Breneman, 1997; Chait, 2005; Vedder, 2019). Others have suggested that while the inability to adapt was one of the main arguments for eliminating tenure, the transition to a mix of tenured and tenure-track and contingent faculty has provided institutions with more flexibility to adapt to change (Allen, 2000; Cater et al., 2016; Finkin, 1998; Frye, 2018). Tenure advocates also argue that while contingent faculty members are protected by academic freedom at many institutions, they lack the job security of tenured faculty members (Kezar & Bernstein-Sierra, 2016). Moreover, they lack the freedom to set their own research agendas and pursue truth wherever it leads, free from intimidation and threats.

While this debate will continue, we propose that institutions need to maintain a ratio of different types of faculty positions based on their mission. This ratio will vary by institution type and geographic location, but a cadre of tenured and tenure-track faculty should be maintained at all institutions. At the same time, institutions should be cognizant of current trends in faculty evaluation, promotion, and tenure such as qualifying a broader range of scholarly and creative works and considering equity in evaluations, especially for emerging or interdisciplinary research (see, e.g., Beauboeuf-Lafontant et al., 2019; Green, 2008; Jackson et al., 2017; Weisshaar, 2017).

In his 1990 book on the professoriate, Boyer proposed revisions to the criteria used to evaluate faculty performance in awarding promotion and tenure. Specifically, he advocated for diversification of the criteria to move away from a primary focus on research and publication productivity, a secondary concern for teaching, and a tertiary interest in service. Instead, Boyer recommended that promotion and tenure criteria include balanced consideration of the four areas of scholarship: discovery, teaching, integration (interdisciplinarity), and application (engagement). Moreover, Boyer maintained that faculty members' productivity should be based on four mandates: doing original research, staying current in their fields, maintaining high standards of performance in teaching and discovery, and improving assessment tools of faculty performance. Since then, researchers and administrators have struggled with awarding credit to interdisciplinary and collaborative work when determining what is valued and whose efforts should be counted on those research projects (Klein & Falk-Krzesinski, 2017).

Further, evidence still exists that evaluations have gendered biases and inequities (O'Meara, Jaeger et al., 2019; Weisshaar, 2017). Examinations of productivity measures cannot account for the differences, yet gender data illustrate the differences in evaluation outcomes. Thus, embedded biases and unstated assumptions likely continue to plague the promotion and tenure process.

The most prominent reform in promotion and tenure has involved the tenure clock. Traditionally, a probationary faculty member (pre-tenure, tenure-track faculty member) has 6 years to be awarded tenure. During that period, the faculty member is evaluated annually and given some indication of their progress toward the award of tenure. In recent years, many institutions have established a process to stop the tenure clock so that early career women on the tenure track can consider having children. Even with such policies in place, however, research has shown that female probationary faculty of childbearing age avoid having children because of concern that it could jeopardize their chances of being awarded tenure (Bellas & Toutkoushian, 1999; Harper et al., 2001; Ward & Wolf-Wendel, 2012). Research has also suggested that new or early stage academic fathers struggle to balance the pressures of pre-tenure expectations (Reddick et al., 2012). Work-life balance has increasingly become a central matter for professors and other professions. The demands placed on faculty across institution types seem to resonate with the mantra of "do more with less." Research has indicated that workloads and pressures are pervasive problems in higher education. For instance, Latz and Rediger (2015) observed how community college faculty face various levels of overwhelming experiences based on workflow, personal life stressors, academic calendar challenges, and service participation pressures. Also, individual circumstances—whether a faculty member is partnered—do not lessen the effects (Culpepper et al., 2021). Simply put, these work-life factors affect individuals' ability to juggle responsibilities and ensure positive performance.

Given these considerations, any institutional reform that changes the faculty evaluation and reward structure for promotion and tenure should be based on the institution's mission and the work its faculty members actually perform. Too often changes in faculty reward structures have sought to mirror those of major research universities—a trend that contributes to the phenomenon of "mission creep" (Lane, 2005). For example, institutions whose primary mission is baccalaureate education should resist the temptation to adopt research universities' traditional standards for research and publication. Calabrese and Roberts (2004) noted that the quest to publish or perish forces faculty members to prepare articles for publication that are often inconsequential and are submitted to achieve the designated number of publications required for tenure and not to contribute to the advancement of knowledge. Indeed, it is incomprehensible how an institution that requires its professors to teach six to eight courses per academic year can also expect its faculty members to produce research and publications of a quality comparable to that of faculty members at research universities where they may teach two courses each year. Rather, an institution with an undergraduate teaching mission should make teaching and the scholarship of teaching the top criteria for faculty evaluation and awards.

Post-Tenure Review

The practice of post-tenure review developed in the 1980s as part of states' implementation of accountability measures for their public colleges and universities and higher education systems. Most public institutions and many private institutions have implemented this type of review. Licata and Morreale (2002) defined post-tenure review as "the systematic evaluation of tenured faculty performance and the establishment of future goals to stimulate professional growth and development" (p. 3). Post-tenure reviews usually coincide with annual reviews and occur every 5 or 7 years. Some institutions, such as Texas A&M University, use a substandard evaluation in the annual review to initiate a post-tenure review (Licata, 2000). Licata (2000) suggested several fundamental objectives that should be incorporated into a post-tenure review:

1. Comprehensive assessment of performance utilizing multiple sources of evidence and reflecting self-reporting
2. Significant involvement of peers in review and opportunity for collective departmental perspective
3. Establishment of professional goals and consideration of career direction
4. Provision of meaningful feedback and opportunity for improvement, if necessary (p. 111)

At Pennsylvania State University and the University of Louisville, a post-tenure review is a compilation of the last five annual reviews and an articulation of goals for the next 5 years. The compilation of annual reviews is compared with the last post-tenure review goal statement. While not a panacea, if used correctly, the post-tenure review process can be helpful in keeping faculty members who have lost enthusiasm or are nearing the end of their career engaged and motivated in their work. Evidence suggests that post-tenure reviews have positive effects, particularly leading to faculty vitality. For instance, the process, if allowed, encourages faculty to try new teaching techniques, explore areas of research not previously attempted, and respond to new initiatives that support students (e.g., early warning supports to advance student success), and it sparks great interest in connecting more with students (Beauboeuf-Lafontant et al., 2019; June, 2018; Mathews, 2014; Welch et al., 2018).

Contingent versus Tenure-Track Faculty

For the past several decades, higher education institutions have been moving toward greater reliance on contingent, part-time, and fixed-term full-time contract faculty (AAUP, 2015). This practice is said to give institutions the ability to adapt to environmental, programmatic, and technological changes, as well as societal needs and demands (Frye, 2018). Specifically, institutions have moved to a contingent faculty model to gain flexibility in staffing and adaptability in academic programs, as well as to reduce costs. Given these considerations, the popularity of hiring part-time faculty has grown substantially. For instance, from fall 1999 to fall 2018, the total number of college faculty who worked at degree-granting postsecondary institutions increased by 49%, specifically increasing in actual numbers from about 1.0 to 1.5 million (Hussar et al., 2020). As mentioned previously, however, the growth rate of part-time faculty increased much more rapidly, particularly between 1999 and 2011, when it grew by 72%, but then decreased by 7% between 2011 and 2018 as the economy slightly recovered from the Great Recession (Hussar et al., 2020).

According to an AAUP (2018) report, 73% of the entire college instructional faculty in 2016 consisted of contingent faculty. These instructors are faculty members who are not eligible for tenure and teach classes based on short-term contracts. The decline in tenure-track and tenured faculty presents serious concerns for the academic profession. It compromises the student experience, weakens academic freedom, diminishes the value of tenure, harms faculty continuity in an institution, limits specialties within the profession, focuses on basic core course instruction, and alters the labor force to a less professionalized environment (AAUP, 2015; Flaherty, 2018). The characteristics of this subgroup present a lack of professional commitment. For instance, part-time contingent faculty have been described in the following way:

> Faculty in these positions are typically hired by the term and paid only for the hours they spend in the classroom, not for time spent meeting with students, evaluating student work, and class planning and preparation. They often lack access to basic tools like offices, computers, and photocopying services, and can be hired on the spur of the moment with little time to prepare—sometimes after a semester has already started. And they often receive little or no evaluation and mentoring, making them especially vulnerable to being dismissed over one or two student complaints. The high

turnover among such faculty members [means] that students in a department may never have the same teacher twice, or may be unable to find an instructor who knows them well enough to write a letter of recommendation. (AAUP, 2018, pp. 2–3)

This description of the full-time contingent faculty is equally concerning as they are vulnerable to dismissal, are often excluded from departmental and institution-wide planning, lack institutional support, and have perceived weak levels of academic freedom. Suffice it to say, the rise of the contingent faculty signals the precarious nature of the academic profession as budget cuts loom and political fears continue around rising tuition prices.

Faculty Development

In line with calls for post-tenure review, the professional growth and development of faculty members has become a pressing issue in the past several decades. Gappa et al. (2007) and O'Meara et al. (2009) have discussed the need to approach faculty growth and development individually, considering the faculty member's career stage and other issues specific to that person. For example, the needs of midcareer faculty members differ greatly from those of new faculty members (Baker, Terosky, & Martinez, 2017). Zahorski (2002) advocated for a holistic approach to faculty development to achieve this individualization, including a variety of programs such as a resource center, mentoring and orientation programs, mini grants, sabbaticals, funding for annual conference attendance and participation, topical workshops, faculty exchange programs, newsletters, faculty development networks, phased retirement, awards programs, and individual counseling for faculty members. Further, Baker, Lunsford, and Pifer (2017) recommended designing more intentional leadership trajectories beyond the role of department chair.

Faculty and Community Engagement

Expectations for faculty members to engage in development activities come from several sources, including increased calls for colleges and universities to be engaged in their communities. The old stereotype of solitary faculty members holed up in the ivory tower to pursue their individual research agendas is rapidly disappearing, particularly at institutions where the primary mission is teaching and community engagement, but also in some disciplinary units at research universities (O'Meara et al., 2009; Terosky, 2018).

Faculty members may need assistance, though, to learn how to participate in civic activities effectively.

In thinking about ways to foster faculty development and academic growth, O'Meara et al. (2009) suggested the following.

> Identify ways to foster, in faculty, the desire and will to craft themselves as teachers, researchers, and partners in service and community engagement who have actively chosen—and continue actively to choose—the academic career as a way to lead their lives. (p. 19)

Faculty engagement in the community also generates greater commitments to the area, which enhance odds of faculty retention. Further, community engagement, through faculty teaching and research, also provides a laboratory to learn, apply, and examine practical problems and offers potentially meaningful solutions.

Conclusion

The faculty is a college or university's key to the promotion of the four themes of this book: being mission driven; adapting to the environment; practicing democratic partnerships; and modeling inclusion, equity, and positive social change. To understand how faculty members fulfill their roles in their institutions, one needs to understand the different cultures in which professors operate as they seek to meet their responsibilities in teaching, research, service, and boundary spanning.

The nature of faculty appointments is changing, as contingent faculty members now constitute the majority of the professoriate. The role of contingent faculty in institutional culture and governance has become a critical issue that will affect student learning outcomes. Demands for accountability, expectations for diversity, and the anticipated retirement of over half the current faculty in the next decade are forcing institutions to be more adaptable to their environment and to develop faculty staffing plans for the future.

Meanwhile, an institution's faculty reward structure must be consistent with its mission. Faculty development programs need to assist professors in their civic work as well as in the classroom, where emerging technologies provide opportunities to improve teaching and learning. An individualized approach to faculty development should focus on the continuing acquisition of knowledge and skills that promote growth. However, the modern approach to faculty development presents a more inclusive and networked strategy where multiple stakeholders such as "libraries, teaching centers, instructional technology units, and assessment offices as well as academic departments and colleges" collaborate to support faculty development and quality learning (Beach et al., 2016, p. 13).

Equally important, academic departments are the primary units that implement the mission and goals of a college or university. Moreover, they are the main venues for higher education institutions to adapt to environmental change and perpetuate shared governance. Higher education leaders need to understand the idiosyncratic nature of departments and develop policies and processes that provide sufficient flexibility for implementation of the institution's objectives across diverse academic units. In an academic department, the chair is in a unique leadership position, situated between the administration and the faculty, each of which has very different demands and expectations. To be effective leaders, chairs must understand the environments, cultures, personalities, and traditions that influence their department or academic unit.

Leaders who contend successfully with conflict can develop a collegial department that can progress toward a shared vision. The head must play a distinctive role in developing this shared vision among department faculty. In addition, the chair must lead the faculty in the assessment of work performance, curricular development, ongoing assessment of teaching and learning outcomes, and the promotion of research and service. Departments that are stable and moving toward a shared vision enhance the quality of their institution and make significant contributions toward the achievement of their institution's mission and goals.

Notes

1. Departments are typically arranged by a discipline or field of study. Rather than articulating both throughout this chapter, we simply refer to "disciplines" to avoid continuous distinctions. While there are philosophical debates regarding the difference between a discipline and field of study, broadly speaking, a discipline is a branch of knowledge with established theories and concepts, and it has an accumulated specialized knowledge examining particular objects for research (e.g., crime, education, governmental institutions) that draws on specific terminologies or a specific technical language and research methodologies. A field of study includes branches of knowledge often in an interdisciplinary manner with a unifying object for research; it examines theories and concepts across disciplines in furtherance of the field.

2. See Leaming (2007, pp. 284–308) for examples of methods and forms to gather information on faculty members' performance in teaching and advising, research and scholarship, and service and outreach.

References

Age Discrimination in Education Act of 1967. Pub. L. 90-202 (1967)

Aguilar-Smith, S., & Gonzales, L. D. (2021). A study of community college faculty work expectations: Generous educators and their managed generosity. *Community College Journal of Research and Practice, 45*(3), 184–204. https://doi.org/10.1080/10668926.2019.1666062

Allen, H. L. (2000). Tenure: Why faculty, and the nation, need it. *Thought & Action, 16*(2), 75–88. https://eric.ed.gov/?id=EJ628188

American Association of University Professors. (2015). Contingent appointments and the academic profession. In AAUP Staff (Eds.), *AAUP policy documents and reports* (11th ed., pp. 170–185). Johns Hopkins University Press.

American Association of University Professors. (2018). *Data snapshot: Contingent faculty in US higher ed.* https://www.aaup.org/news/data-snapshot-contingent-faculty-us-higher-ed

American Council on Education. (2010). *Review of faculty retirement literature.* https://www.acenet.edu/Documents/Retirement-Literature-Review.pdf

Americans With Disabilities Act, 42 U.S.C. §§ 12132 et seq. (2021)

Austin, A. E. (1994). Understanding and assessing faculty cultures and climates. In M. Kinnick (Ed.), *Providing useful information for deans and department chairs* (New Directions for Institutional Research, no. 84, pp. 47–63). Jossey-Bass. https://doi.org/10.1002/ir.37019948406

Baker, V. L., Lunsford, L. G., & Pifer, M. J. (2017). *Developing faculty in liberal arts colleges.* Rutgers University Press.

Baker, V. L., Terosky, A. L., & Martinez, E. (2017). Faculty members' scholarly learning across institutional types. *ASHE Higher Education Report, 43*(2), 9–138. https://doi.org/10.1002/aehe.20118

Bates, A. W. (2000). Giving faculty ownership of technological change in the department. In A. F. Lucas (Ed.), *Leading academic change: Essential roles for department chairs* (pp. 215–245). Jossey-Bass.

Beach, A. L., Sorcinelli, M. D., Austin, A. E., & Rivard, J. K. (2016). *Faculty development in the age of evidence: Current practices, future imperatives.* Stylus.

Beauboeuf-Lafontant, T., Erickson, K. A., & Thomas, J. E. (2019). Rethinking post-tenure malaise: An interactional, pathways approach to understanding the post-tenure period. *Journal of Higher Education, 90*(4), 644–664. https://doi.org/10.1080/00221546.2018.1554397

Bellas, M. L., & Toutkoushian, R. K. (1999). Faculty time allocations and research productivity: Gender, race, and family effects. *Review of Higher Education, 22*(4), 367–390. https://doi.org/10.1353/rhe.1999.0014

Biglan, A. (1973a). The characteristics of subject matter in different academic areas. *Journal of Applied Psychology, 57*(3), 195–203. https://doi.org/10.1037/h0034701

Biglan, A. (1973b). Relationships between subject matter characteristics and structure and output of university departments. *Journal of Applied Psychology, 57*(3), 204–213. https://doi.org/10.1037/h0034699

Bissell, B. (2003). Handling conflict with difficult faculty. In D. R. Leaming (Ed.), *Managing people: A guide for department heads and deans* (pp. 119–138). Anker.

Bolman, L. G., & Deal, T. E. (2008). *Reframing organizations: Artistry, choice, and leadership.* (4th ed.). Jossey-Bass.

Boyer, E. (1990). *Scholarship reconsidered: Priorities of the professoriate.* Carnegie Foundation for the Advancement of Teaching.

Breneman, D. (1997). *Alternatives to tenure for the next generation of academics* (Faculty Career and Employment for the 21st Century Working Paper No. 14). American Association for Higher Education.

Buller, J. L. (2012). *The essential department chair: A comprehensive desk reference* (2nd ed.). Wiley.

Calabrese, R. L., & Roberts, B. (2004). Self-interest and scholarly publication: The dilemma of researchers, reviewers, and editors. *International Journal of Educational Management, 18*(6), 335–341. https://doi.org/10.1108/09513540410553988

Cater, B., Lew, B., & Pivato, M. (2016). The efficiency of tenure contracts in academic employment. *Journal of Public Economy Theory, 19*(2), 331–361. https://doi.org/10.1111/jpet.12201

Chait, R. P. (Ed.). (2005). *The questions of tenure.* Harvard University Press.

Cheldelin, S. I. (2000). Handling resistance to change. In A. F. Lucas (Ed.), *Leading academic change: Essential roles for department chairs* (pp. 55–73). Jossey-Bass.

Christie, V. (2007). Deciding who is in charge. *Department Chair, 18*(2), 15–17. https://doi.org/10.1002/dch.20020

Chu, D. (2021). *The department chair field manual: A primer for academic leadership.* Author.

Chun, E. B., & Evans, A. (2015). *The department chair as transformative diversity leader: Building inclusive learning environments in higher education.* Stylus.

Clark, R. L. (2004, April). *Changing faculty demographics and the need for new policies* [Paper presentation]. TIAA-CREF Institute Conference, New York, NY.

Clark, T. M. (2007). Merging departments—practical lessons in leadership: Thoughts from a chair's journal. *Department Chair, 18*(1), 10–13. https://doi.org/10.1002/dch.20005

Coakley, L., & Randall, L. M. (2006). Orchestrating change at the department level: Applying the process of adaptive leadership. *Academic Leadership: The Online Journal, 4*(2), Article 8. https://scholars.fhsu.edu/alj/vol4/iss2/8/

Corey, K. A. (2007). From the other side of the desk. *Department Chair, 18*(1), 25–26. https://doi.org/10.1002/dch.20011

Culpepper, D., Lennartz, C., O'Meara, K. A., & Kuvaeva, A. (2021). Who gets to have a life? Agency in work-life balance for single faculty. *Equity & Excellence in Education, 53*(4), 531–550. https://doi.org/10.1080/10665684.2020.1791280

de Brey, C., Snyder, T. D., Zhang, A., & Dillow, S. A. (2021). *Digest of educational statistics, 2019.* National Center for Education Statistics, U.S. Department of Education. https://nces.ed.gov/pubs2021/2021009.pdf

Diamond, R. M. (2000). The department statement on promotion and tenure: A key to successful leadership. In A. F. Lucas (Ed.), *Leading academic change: Essential roles for department chairs* (pp. 95–107). Jossey-Bass.

Diamond, R. M. (2002a). Curricula and courses: Administrative issues. In R. M. Diamond (Ed.), *Field guide to academic leadership* (pp. 135–156). Jossey-Bass.

Diamond, R. M. (2002b). The mission-driven faculty reward system. In R. M. Diamond (Ed.), *Field guide to academic leadership* (pp. 271–291). Jossey-Bass.

Diamond, R. M., & Adam, B. E. (2002). Defining scholarship for the twenty-first century. In K. H. Zahorski (Ed.), *Scholarship in the postmodern era: New venues, new values, and new visions* (New Directions for Teaching & Learning, no. 90, pp. 73–79). Jossey-Bass. https://doi.org/10.1002/tl.57

Diamond, R. M., & Adam, B. E. (2004). Balancing institutional, disciplinary, and faculty priorities with public and social needs: Defining scholarship for the 21st century. *Arts and Humanities in Higher Education*, *3*(1), 29–40. https://doi.org/10.1177/1474022204039643

Equal Pay Act, 29 U.S.C. §206(d) (2021)

Espinosa, L. L., Turk, J. M., Taylor, M., & Chessman, H. M. (2019). *Race and ethnicity in higher education: A status report*. American Council on Education. https://www.equityinhighered.org/resources/report-downloads/

Finkin, M. W. (1998). Tenure and the entrepreneurial academy: A reply. *Sociological Perspectives*, *41*(4), 729–746. https://doi.org/10.2307/40252281

Fisher, M. L. (2007). Engaging faculty: Departmental shared governance that works. *Department Chair*, *18*(1), 21–23. https://doi.org/10.1002/dch.20009

Flaherty, C. (2018, October 12). A non-tenure-track profession? *Inside Higher Ed.* https://www.insidehighered.com/news/2018/10/12/about-three-quarters-all-faculty-positions-are-tenure-track-according-new-aaup

Frye, J. R. (2018). Organizational pressures driving the growth of contingent faculty. In H. A. García, J. McNaughtan, & K. Nehls (Eds.), *Hidden and visible: The role and impact of contingency faculty in higher education* (New Directions for Institutional Research, no. 176, pp. 27–39). Jossey-Bass. https://doi.org/10.1002/ir.20242

Gappa, J. M., Austin, A. E., & Tice, A. G. (2007). *Rethinking faculty work: Higher education's strategic imperative*. Wiley.

Gardiner, L. F. (2000). Monitoring and improving educational quality in academic departments. In A. F. Lucas (Ed.), *Leading academic change: Essential roles for department chairs* (pp. 165–194). Jossey-Bass.

Gehrke, S., & Kezar, A. (2015). Unbundling the faculty role in higher education: Utilizing historical, theoretical, and empirical frameworks to inform future research. In M. B. Paulsen (Ed.), *Higher education: Handbook of theory and research* (Vol. 30, pp. 93–150). Springer.

Gmelch, W. H. (1995). Department chairs under siege: Resolving the web of conflict. In S. A. Holton (Ed.), *Faculty perspective on internationalization strategies in higher education* (New Directions in Higher Education, no. 92, pp. 35–42). Jossey-Bass. https://doi.org/10.1002/he.36919959207

Gmelch, W. H. (2004). The department chair's balancing acts. In W. H. Gmelch & J. H. Schuh (Eds.), *The life cycle of a department chair* (New Directions in Higher Education, no. 129, pp. 69–84). Jossey-Bass. https://doi.org/10.1002/he.149

Gmelch, W. H., & Miskin, V. D. (1995). *Chairing an academic department*. SAGE.

Green, R. (2008). Tenure and promotion decisions: The relative importance of teaching, scholarship, and service. *Journal of Social Work Education, 44*(2), 117–127. https://doi.org/10.5175/JSWE.2008.200700003

Harper, E. P., Baldwin, R. G., Gansneder, B. G., & Chronister, J. L. (2001). Full-time women faculty off the tenure track: Profile and practice. *Review of Higher Education, 24*(3), 237–258. https://doi.org/10.1353/rhe.2001.0003

Heifitz, R. A. (1994). *Leadership without easy answers.* Belknap.

Hussar, B., Zhang, J., Hein, S., Wang, K., Roberts, A., Cui, J., Smith, M., Bullock Mann, F., Barmer, A., & Dilig, R. (2020). *The condition of education 2020.* National Center for Education Statistics, U.S. Department of Education. https://nces.ed.gov/pubs2020/2020144.pdf

Jackson, J. K., Latimer, M., & Stoiko, R. (2017). The dynamic between knowledge production and faculty evaluation: Perceptions of the promotion and tenure process across disciplines. *Innovation in Higher Education, 42*(3), 193–205. https://doi.org/10.1007/s10755-016-9378-3

June, A. W. (2018, February 16). Most professors hate post-tenure review: A better approach might look like this. *The Chronicle of Higher Education, 64*(23). https://www.chronicle.com/article/most-professors-hate-post-tenure-review-a-better-approach-might-look-like-this/

Kezar, A., & Bernstein-Sierra, S. (2016). Contingent faculty as nonideal workers. In L. Wolf-Wendel, K. Ward, & A. Kulp (Eds.), *How ideal worker norms shape work-life for constituent groups in higher education* (New Directions for Institutional Research, no. 176, pp. 25–35). Jossey-Bass. https://doi.org/10.1002/he.20207

Klein, J. T., & Falk-Krzesinski, H. J. (2017). Interdisciplinary and collaborative work: Framing promotion and tenure practices and policies. *Research Policy, 46*(6), 1055–1061. https://doi.org/10.1016/j.respol.2017.03.001

Knight, P. T., & Trowler, P. R. (2001). *Departmental leadership in higher education.* Society for Research into Higher Education and Open University Press.

Kreitzer, R. J., & Sweet-Cushman, J. (2021). Evaluating student evaluations of teaching: A review of measurement and equity bias in sets and recommendations for ethical reform. *Journal of Academic Ethics.* https://doi.org/10.1007/s10805-021-09400-w

Lane, J. E. (2005, November). *Politics of mission creep: A framework for understanding the phenomena* [Paper presentation]. Annual Meeting of the Association for the Study of Higher Education, Philadelphia, PA.

Lattuca, L., & Stark, J. (2009). *Shaping the college curriculum: Academic plans in context* (2nd ed.). Jossey-Bass.

Latz, A. O., & Rediger, J. N. (2015). Navigating the water: Community college faculty and work-life balance. *Journal of Faculty Development, 29*(1), 13–24. https://eric.ed.gov/?id=EJ1134353

Leaming, D. R. (2003). *Managing people: A guide for department chairs and deans.* Anker.

Leaming, D. R. (2007). *Academic leadership: A practical guide to chairing the department* (2nd ed.). Anker.

Licata, C. M. (2000). Post-tenure review. In A. F. Lucas (Ed.), *Leading academic change: Essential roles for department chairs* (pp. 107–137). Jossey-Bass.

Licata, C. M., & Morreale, J. C. (2002). *Post-tenure faculty review and renewal: Experienced voices.* American Association for Higher Education.

Llamas, J. D., Nguyen, K., & Tran, A. G. T. T. (2021). The case for greater faculty diversity: Examining the educational impacts of student-faculty racial/ethnic match. *Race Ethnicity and Education, 24*(3), 375–391. https://doi.org/10.1080/13613324.2019.1679759

Lucas, A. F. (2000a). A collaborative model for leading academic change. In A. F. Lucas (Ed.), *Leading academic change: Essential roles for department chairs* (pp. 33–54). Jossey-Bass.

Lucas, A. F. (Ed.). (2000b). *Leading academic change: Essential roles for department chairs.* Jossey-Bass.

Lumpkin, A. (2004). Enhancing the effectiveness of department chairs. *Journal of Physical Education, Recreation & Dance, 75*(9), 44–48. https://doi.org/10.1080/07303084.2004.10607300

Mathews, K. (2014). *Perspectives on midcareer faculty and advice for supporting them.* Collaborative on Academic Careers in Higher Education, Harvard University. https://coache.gse.harvard.edu/publications/perspectives-midcareer-faculty-and-advice-supporting-them

McChesney, J., & Bichsel, J. (2020). *The aging of tenure-track faculty in higher education: Implications for succession and diversity.* CUPA-HR.

McKenna, L. (2018, February 7). How hard do professors actually work? *The Atlantic.* https://www.theatlantic.com/education/archive/2018/02/how-hard-do-professors-actually-work/552698/

McKiernan, E. C., Schimanski, L. A., Nieves, C. M., Matthias, L., Niles, M. T., & Alperin, J. P. (2019). Meta-research: Use of the journal impact factor in academic review, promotion, and tenure evaluations. *eLife, 2019*(8), e47338. https://doi.org/10.7554/eLife.47338

O'Meara, K. A., Jaeger, A., Misra, J., Lennartz, C., & Kuvaeva, A. (2019). Undoing disparities in faculty workloads: A randomized trial experiment. *PLoS ONE, 13*(12), e0207316, 1–15. https://doi.org/10.1371/journal.pone.0207316

O'Meara, K. A., Lennartz, C., Kuvaeva, A., Jaeger, A., & Misra, J. (2019). Department conditions and practices associated with faculty workload satisfaction and perceptions of equity. *Journal of Higher Education, 90*(5), 744–772. https://doi.org/10.1080/00221546.2019.1584025

O'Meara, K. A., Terosky, A. T., & Neumann, A. (2009). Faculty careers and work lives: Professional growth perspectives. *ASHE Higher Education Report, 34*(3). https://doi.org/10.1002/aehe.v34:3

Palmer, J. C. (2002). Disciplinary variation in the work of full-time faculty members. In C. L. Outcalt (Ed.), *Community college faculty: Characteristics, practices, and challenges* (New Directions for Community Colleges, no. 118, pp. 9–20). Jossey-Bass. https://doi.org/10.1002/cc.59

Reddick, R. J., Rochlen, A. B., Grasso, J. R., Reilly, E. D., & Spikes, D. D. (2012). Academic fathers pursuing tenure: A qualitative study of work-family conflict, coping strategies, and departmental culture. *Psychology of Men & Masculinity, 13*(1), 1–15. https://doi.org/10.1037/a0023206

Rice, R. E. (2002). Beyond scholarship reconsidered: Toward an enlarged vision of the scholarly work of faculty members. In K. J. Zahorski (Ed.), *Scholarship in the postmodern era: New venues, new values, new visions* (New Directions for Teaching and Learning, no. 90, pp. 7–17). Jossey-Bass. https://doi.org/10.1002/tl.51

Schuster, J. H., & Finkelstein, M. J. (2006). *The American faculty: The restructuring of academic work and careers*. Johns Hopkins University Press.

Section 504 of the Rehabilitation Act of 1973, 29 U.S.C. § 794 (2021)

Sommer, R. (2008). Models of departmental leadership. *Department Chair, 18*(3), 5–6. https://doi.org/10.1002/dch.20029

Stupnisky, R. H., Hall, N. C., Daniels, L. M., & Mensah, E. (2017). Testing a model of pretenure faculty members' teaching and research success: Motivation as a mediator of balance, expectations, and collegiality. *Journal of Higher Education, 88*(3), 376–400. https://doi.org/10.1080/00221546.2016.1272317

Terosky, A. L. (2018). Reciprocity and scholarly connections: Faculty perspectives about the role of community engaged work in their career vitality. *Journal of Higher Education Outreach and Engagement, 22*(3), 135–159. https://openjournals.libs.uga.edu/jheoe/article/view/1404

Title VI of the Civil Rights Act of 1964, 42 U.S.C. §2000d, et seq. (2021)

Title VII of the Civil Rights Act of 1964 (as amended by the Equal Opportunities Act of 1972), Title VI of the Civil Rights Act of 1964, 42 U.S.C §2000e, et seq. (2021)

Title IX of the Education Amendments Act of 1972, 20 U.S.C. §1681 et seq. (2021)

Vedder, R. K. (2019). *Restoring the promise: Higher education in America*. Independent Institute.

Ward, K., & Wolf-Wendel, L. (2012). *Academic motherhood: How faculty manage work and family*. Rutgers University Press.

Weisshaar, K. (2017). Publish and perish? An assessment of gender gaps in promotion to tenure in academia. *Social Forces, 96*(2), 529–560. https://doi.org/10.1093/sf/sox052

Welch, A. G., Bolin, J., Reardon, D., & Stenger, R. (2019). Mid-career faculty: Trends, barriers, and possibilities. *Journal of the Professoriate, 10*(1), 22–42. https://doi.org/10.1163/9789004408180

Wergin, J. F., & Swingen, J. N. (2000). *Departmental assessment: How some campuses are effectively evaluating the collective work of faculty*. American Association for Higher Education.

Wheeler, D., Seagren, A., Becker, L., Kinley, E., Mlinek, D., & Robson, K. (2008). *The academic chair's handbook*. Jossey-Bass.

Wolverton, M., Ackerman, R., & Holt, S. (2005). Preparing for leadership: What academic department chairs need to know. *Journal of Higher Education Policy and Management, 27*(2), 227–238. https://doi.org/10.1080/13600800500120126

Zahorski, K. J. (2002). Nurturing scholarship through holistic faculty development: A synergistic approach. In K. J. Zahorski (Ed.), *Scholarship in the postmodern era: New venues, new values, new visions* (New Directions for Teaching and Learning, no. 90, pp. 29–37). Jossey-Bass. https://doi.org/10.1002/tl.53

Ziker, J. P., Wintermote, A., Nolin, D., Demps, K., Genuchi, M., & Meinhardt, K. (2014, April 21). *Time distribution of faculty workload at Boise State University* [Paper presentation]. 2014 Undergraduate Research and Scholarship Conference, Boise State University, Boise, ID. https://scholarworks.boisestate.edu/sspa_14/22

PART FIVE

IMPLEMENTATION OF THE ACADEMIC MISSION

15

THE STUDENT EXPERIENCE

The student is at the core of the work of our colleges and universities, and for this work to be done most effectively, faculty members and administrators should understand the characteristics of their students and the myriad ways in which collegiate experiences affect student development. An extraordinary amount of research and writing has been dedicated to understanding how the curricular and cocurricular experiences of college students affect their intellectual, moral, social, and attitudinal development (Mayhew et al., 2016). Since a college education is intended as a developmental process, we examine the nature of that development and the role the curriculum and cocurricular opportunities play in it.

Over the past several decades, the student body has become increasingly heterogeneous (see also chapter 2). Consequently, it is not possible to provide one description of the modern college student. For many, the image of a college student remains the "traditional" 18-year-old high school graduate, yet today's typical college student is much older, much less White, and much less "traditional." The diversity among postsecondary students enriches the college experience, but also makes it difficult describing all the ways students are affected by that experience. This diversity also challenges academic leaders to create structures that support the varied needs of students.

In this chapter, we highlight some recent strategies to create more personalized academic engagements. Readers should be aware that researchers have not fully explored the ways in which new learning opportunities, such as online and hybrid learning modalities, affect college student development, although the pandemic will likely generate new scholarship in this area (Garrett et al., 2021). While we attempt to be inclusive in this chapter, we acknowledge that we inevitably will not be able to give full attention to all aspects of the college student experience and encourage readers to pursue additional readings.

Here we provide a discussion of the demographics, cultural views, and enrollment patterns of college students; a brief history of student development as a field of study; and an overview of various theories of student development and their relationship to the curriculum and the cocurriculum. We then offer a brief synthesis of the major themes that have emerged from decades of research on the impact of college on students in an effort to answer this fundamental question: Is college truly beneficial and worth the time, effort, and expense?

College Students in the 21st Century

College students in the 21st century are more diverse than ever, as recent decades have seen increased diversity in race/ethnicity, gender, age, and enrollment patterns. In this section, we briefly review data regarding the various types of college students of today. Throughout this discussion, it is important to remember that the heterogeneity of college students resists generalizations, and the specific degrees of diversity will vary considerably based on region and institution type. What is most important for campus leaders to remember is that today's college students are very different than students of the recent past, when these leaders were college students themselves.

Demographics

According to the NCES (de Brey et al., 2021), 16.6 million students were enrolled in approximately 4,000 undergraduate degree-granting programs in 2019, a 5% decrease from the 17.5 million who were enrolled in 2009. Most of these undergraduate students were women and attended full-time. They were predominantly non-Hispanic White; Latinx and Black students were the largest minority groups in the U.S. student body (de Brey et al., 2021). Many students also maintained some connection to the military. In the 2015–2016 academic year, 6.1% of all undergraduates, 1.19 million students, had a military affiliation (e.g., veteran, active duty) (Holian & Adam, 2020).

During this same time, 3.1 million students were enrolled in postbaccalaureate (e.g., graduate and professional) degree programs, which is an 8% increase from 2009. As with undergraduates, most of them were women, most were non-Hispanic White, and Black and Latinx students represented the largest minority populations. Between 2009 and 2019, the percentage of White graduate students decreased, while the percentage of all minorities increased (de Brey et al., 2021). In contrast to undergraduates, enrollment patterns were nearly evenly split between full-time and part-time students.

The percentage of graduate students with a military affiliation in 2015–2016 resembled that of undergraduate students, 6.7%, or about 240,200 students (Holian & Adam, 2020).

The growing diversity within the college student body may be reflective of larger trends among the generation of many current college students, Generation Z. Gen Z, also known as post-millennials, are considered the most diverse generation to date (Deloitte, 2020). Generation Z has nearly reached a non-White majority, with 48% of Gen Z-ers identifying as non-White, and one in four Gen Z-ers identifying as Hispanic (Fry & Parker, 2018). The coming years will likely see further increases in the diversity of college students, as the younger members of the Gen Z population will likely be the majority of non-White high school graduates by 2027 (Hussar & Bailey, 2019).

Not all current college students are members of Gen Z, however. College student enrollment trends are increasingly moving away from the traditional 18- to 22-year-old age range and toward post-traditional undergraduates. A recent report labeled these students, formerly referred to as "non-traditional," as "post-traditional"—a group of students who, "[w]hether because of their age, employment intensity, or other responsibilities such as caregiving, parenting, or military enlistment . . . , struggle to earn a college degree because institutions were not designed to be inclusive of them" (Soares et al., 2017, p. 1). Post-traditional students may be older than 25, have children or elderly dependents, and may balance school with full-time employment. The percentage of post-traditional students has been growing steadily since the 1970s; as of 2017, they outnumbered so-called traditional students, comprising 60% of all undergraduates (Soares et al., 2017). Of this 60%, 44% were racial minority students, and 60% were women. The majority were employed while attending college, and many were employed full-time (Soares et al., 2017).

In terms of where post-traditional students pursue higher education, surveys have shown that they are more likely to opt for two-year colleges or for-profit institutions, meaning that less than a third enroll in four-year institutions (Soares et al., 2017). These students are often in a different stage of life from their academic peers, need different types of institutional supports, and have different expectations for faculty and administrators. They tend to be focused and goal driven, seeking to balance their course demands with their other responsibilities, resulting in little time for cocurricular experiences (Soares et al., 2017). The differences in backgrounds, experiences, and goals that post-traditional students bring to campus may be contributing to shifting campus cultures.

Cultural Views

Unlike many sources of data on college student characteristics, the Cooperative Institutional Research Program (CIRP) at the University of California, Los Angeles, has conducted annual surveys that provide insight into college students' beliefs, values, and cultures. In the latest CIRP report (Stolzenberg et al., 2020), participants indicated their political beliefs as middle of the road (43.6%), liberal (32.2%), far left (4.5%), conservative (17.8%), or far right (1.9%). These figures aligned with how students responded to questions that asked their opinions on specific issues, with a vast majority agreeing with such statements as "abortion should be legal," and "global warming should be a federal priority" (Stolzenberg et al., 2020). Although the minority of CIRP survey participants expressed conservative views, other research has indicated that 42% of college students hold highly positive attitudes toward students with politically conservative beliefs (Mayhew & Rockenbach, 2020).

The CIRP survey illustrates that both men and women continue to report declines in their self-assessment of their mental and physical health, which is an issue of increasing importance to academic leaders. In 2019, 50% of men and 34% of women respondents reported their mental health to be above average (Stolzenberg et al., 2020). Respondents viewed their physical health more positively, with 66% of men and 46% of women reporting above-average levels, but these percentages are part of a multiyear decline (Eagan et al., 2016). Importantly, these data were collected prior to the COVID-19 pandemic, which has been additionally deleterious to student mental health (Son et al., 2020). While most institutions have disability resource centers, or some version thereof, awareness is growing that more members of the campus community—both faculty and staff—need to be engaged in the mental health safety net for students. In chapter 6, we explore the increasing legal expectations of college staff to protect students from harm, including self-harm that might relate to students' mental health.

As noted, in 2019 approximately 3 million graduate students were studying in the United States, pursing a range of degrees from MBAs to PhDs to MDs. Participation of minority students in graduate studies has been on the rise, though they still remain substantially underrepresented as a share of the population, particularly within STEM fields (Okahana et al., 2020). A national survey of graduate education professionals conducted in fall 2020 (Gao, 2021) revealed that around 66% of respondents believed that students of color have shown greater concern about campus culture and climate than their White counterparts. An overwhelming majority of respondents (about 82%) agreed that students overall (i.e., not only students of color) were increasingly concerned about the affordability of graduate and professional education, though few agreed that interest in graduate school was waning (Gao, 2021).

Enrollment Patterns

Throughout much of the history of higher education, college students attended one college campus for the duration of their 4 years of study. However, many factors have altered this typical enrollment pattern. Students now pursue college degrees in a variety of modalities and locations, and some students may not complete their bachelor's degree within 4 years. The National Student Clearinghouse Research Center (NSCRC)[1] reported that in spring 2021 around 27% of all students were enrolled in associate (i.e., two-year) degree programs, which are primarily offered at community colleges (NSCRC, 2021). About 65% of those students were enrolled part-time, compared to all students (undergraduate and graduate) at four-year public institutions, where more than 71% were enrolled full-time. The average age of all full-time students was 22.8 years, while the average age of part-time students was almost 5 years older (27.2). Age also varied by sector, with the average age of both full-time and part-time students at private, for-profit institutions exceeding 32 years. Of course, these numbers reflect pandemic-induced trends, including overall declines in part-time student and two-year student enrollments, but the comparisons have not changed dramatically over recent time.

An increasingly common occurrence is for students to begin their undergraduate career at one institution and graduate from another. Transfer students comprise a large percentage of the overall college student population, with 38% of students transferring between institutions during their college career (Shapiro et al., 2018). Similarly, more students are classified as "swirling" between schools and programs, meaning they accumulate credits from multiple institutions during their college career, although they might not officially leave their original institution or even graduate. The number of students who swirl between institutions is expected to continue increasing because of the pandemic (Duncan & Glover, 2020).

The pandemic necessitated an almost universal shift to online enrollment in higher education, but changing student demographics and advances in technology had already caused significant increases in the number of students who attend college fully, or partially, online. In fall 2018, nearly 7 million students enrolled in at least one online course at a degree-granting college or university. Most of these students were undergraduates (82.7%) at a public institution (71.6%). A considerably smaller portion (16.6%) attended exclusively online, indicating that a high percentage of students are completing college in a hybrid format, taking classes both on campus and online (de Brey et al., 2021). Many fully online students are returning to college after an extended break, with 87% enrolling as transfer students with credits from previous college work, and 48% indicating they have not been enrolled in college for 5 or more years (Magda et al., 2020). The majority of online students appear to be career motivated, as 86% of respondents to a recent survey indicated their primary objective for obtaining a degree was to obtain new employment or to advance in their current role (Magda et al., 2020).

The composition of the college student population in the United States is incredibly complex. Academic leaders need to keep in mind that this complexity results in having to address a wide variety of developmental challenges and expectations. In many cases, colleges and universities were established and evolved to serve a very different set of students than now attend the institution. While many of the models of student development have been based on the traditionally aged student who attends a four-year institution full-time, most students do not fit this category, having different life experiences and attending different institutions. In this chapter, we briefly explore these dynamics with the intent of helping readers frame questions and conversations to better understand their own contexts.

Theories of Student Development

Student development involves the study of change and is of central importance to higher education. Only through the knowledge and understanding of how students learn and develop as humans can institutions of higher learning create and operate academic environments that yield the type and degree of individual transformation desired. The field of student development became firmly entrenched in the culture and administration of higher education during the upheavals of the 1960s, as higher education faced enormous curricular and social challenges resulting from student demands for greater equality. Called student development or student affairs, this field was appropriately defined by Miller and Prince (1976) as "the application of human development concepts in postsecondary settings so that everyone involved can master increasingly complex developmental tasks, achieve self-direction, and become interdependent" (p. 3).

The study of student development is highly challenging because of individual differences between students themselves. Innate and formative factors, coupled with infinite differences in the personal, family, environmental, and social experiences of students, render virtually useless any broad concrete application of theoretical constructs that may provide guides to understanding this complex subject. Although each student brings to college a unique set of personal traits and backgrounds, the role of higher education is not to mold them all in similar fashion. As Bowen (1977) stated, higher education provides

> opportunities to which individual students will respond in different ways according to their talents, interests, and aspirations. College is intended to give its students a chance to work out their destiny in an environment that encourages certain ranges of outcomes, rather than specific preprogrammed outcomes. (p. 432)

Despite a significant volume of literature devoted to the subject over the last half century, student development as a concept remains fluid, lacking a universal definition. The absence of agreement on a definition is largely attributable to the challenges inherent in understanding and empirically demonstrating how human development occurs. Summarizing this point, King (1994) noted that student development refers to the growth and change that occurs in a student as a result of a specific combination of cognitive and affective stimuli. Since cognitive, social, environmental, and personal attributes vary so widely and affect individuals so differently, the concept of student development cannot be easily defined. As King stated, "There is no one set of theories or theoretical assumptions that constitute THE student development knowledge base. In light of such inconsistencies, it is not surprising that the term means so many things" (p. 413).

There is some consensus, however, among those who study student development that core theories possess three common assumptions: (a) Processes involving ways of being, knowing, or doing move from less complex to more complex; (b) individual experiences affect development; and (c) institutions of higher education promote or inhibit student development and/or learning. Renn and Reason (2021) built on these key assumptions with three additional concepts, borrowed from educational psychology and student development research, that provide a foundational understanding for learning and development. Specifically, they defined these concepts as support and readiness, a balance between challenge and support, and a concept first offered by A. W. Astin (1984) that correlates development with a student's involvement in educationally meaningful activities.

As these broad generalizations show, a vast number of theories on college student development exist. While it is beyond the scope of this introduction to the subject to enumerate the scores of theories and models of student development in the literature, a number of useful summaries of this body of literature have been offered over the years, which we highlight here.

The work by Jones and Stewart (2016) has described the evolution of student development theory as occurring in three waves. First-wave theories are foundational, are grounded in psychology or sociology, and emphasize the development of the whole student. Theories in this wave (e.g., Chickering, 1969; Kohlberg, 1981) were guided by student-focused questions such as "Who is the college student in developmental terms? What changes occur and what do those changes look like?" and "How can the college environment influence student development?" (as cited in Jones & Stewart, 2016, p. 19). Within this broad framework, theories can be seen as falling into several discrete categories, including psychosocial, cognitive-structural, person-environment, typology, and maturity. While theories from this wave have been widely used and remain popular today, it is important to remember that many of them are based on samples of students that do not reflect current college student demographics. That is, they rely on data from mostly White men from middle- or upper-class backgrounds. Perhaps as a result of the homogeneity of many of the study samples, these theories largely presume that students develop in similar ways and thus may not account for the strong effects that personal experience and identity have on development.

The second wave of theories (e.g., Baxter Magolda, 2001; Hurtado & Carter, 1997) largely sought to correct the narrow focus of first-wave theories through expanded consideration of how identity affects student development, particularly regarding race/ethnicity, gender, and sexuality. As Jones and Stewart (2016) explained:

> The hallmarks of these second wave theories are that they are generally more inclusive of the experiences and identities of all college students; they are more integrative and interdisciplinary in nature; and they provide important new pathways to understanding student development outside of developmental perspectives by considering social identities, the influence of larger contexts, and a more complex emphasis on the whole student. (p. 21)

Yet while these theories focused on the identities of marginalized groups, they largely ignored the privileged identities of the dominant student groups and how dominant values, culture, and norms shape the experience and development of all campus members (Jones & Stewart, 2016).

The third wave of theories (e.g., Garcia et al., 2017; Porter & Dean, 2015) addressed these shortcomings largely through the application of critical and poststructural theories (e.g., Butler, 2004; Delgado & Stefancic, 2017; Talburt, 2011). These theories push beyond the acknowledgment of identity and its effects, which defined the second wave, to challenge hegemonic norms, structures, and systems that influence identity development. Through this work, much of the focus has been on uncovering how systems of oppression and power differentials shape college student experiences and both inhibit and promote development in ways that differentially affect students based on their own identity characteristics (Jones & Stewart, 2016).

These theoretical discussions of student development affect students the most when theory is translated into the daily practice of student affairs professionals. Torres et al. (2019) have traced the evolution of student development theory in relation to its practical uses within the student affairs profession. This work starts from a proposition that student affairs is a low-consensus field, meaning it embraces diverse perspectives without privileging a certain way of knowing, being, or doing. They argued that this low-consensus status, paired with the proliferation of theories tailored to specialized identities (but not necessarily focused on student development), has created a situation in which it is difficult for student affairs practitioners to stay abreast of which research best informs their day-to-day work. They thus recommended that practitioners take a broad view of student development theory, understanding the evolution of these theories as a continuum, rather than seeing new theories as replacing the old. In their words, "Consideration of building on, rather than discarding, older theories allows for a greater understanding between theory and practice" (p. 652).

The broadest review of all student development research has been undertaken by Pascarella and Terenzini, and later with colleagues, in three comprehensive tomes (Pascarella & Terenzini, 1994, 2005; Mayhew et al., 2016). These volumes synthesize nearly all research in the field over the previous 5 decades into a treatise-like format. In their landmark examination of the impact of college on students, Pascarella and Terenzini (2005) grouped the predominant theories and models. They characterized the first group of theories as developmental or student-centered models, focusing on the intrapersonal changes that occur as part of human growth. The developmental perspective centers on theories of personality and psychological growth, including the formation of identity, the nature and process of change and how individuals ultimately derive meaning and understanding, typological factors that distinguish individuals from one another, and the role environment plays in affecting change within a specific individual. The second group of theories focuses on environmental factors and college impact, including how one's surroundings, and other individuals whom one encounters, contribute to the change process. This set of theories and models includes such factors as the type of higher education institution one

attends; the values and norms of the organization and its players; socioeconomic status, race, ethnicity, and age or level of maturity; and other variables. According to Pascarella and Terenzini (2005),

> The primary difference between the two families of theories lies in the rela-
> tive degree of attention they give to *what* changes in college students versus
> *how* these changes come about. Whereas student-centered developmental
> models concentrate on the nature or content of student change, college
> impact models focus on the sources of change. (p. 19)

Using the four framing questions posed by Knefelkamp et al. (1978),
Strange (1994) suggested 14 propositions, each supported by developmental
mental theories, to serve as the basis for future research and improved
student developmental practices. These propositions provide a useful, if
unproven, matrix for viewing the fluid and complex subject of student
development. (See Figure 15.1.)

These propositions are supported through existing student development theories and are intended only as a framework for examining the issue
of institutional outcomes. The key point is that the programs, policies,
and practices at colleges and universities as they relate to student development must be grounded in a theoretical and practical understanding of how
students learn, mature, and grow so that the institution is able to create
specifically defined learning experiences that will yield desired developmental outcomes.

Student Development and the Curriculum

The college curriculum represents the formal mechanism that can shape student outcomes. The content of an institution's curriculum is a formal statement by its faculty, administration, and board of trustees of its educational
values. Particularly important to this discussion is which academic content an
institution views as part of its students' general education (i.e., the prescribed
curricular offerings thought to be essential to producing learned graduates).
Most general education requirements include some combination of courses
that focus on writing, mathematics, science, social science, and the arts. The
idea is to provide students with advanced general knowledge of a range of
topics and develop their critical thinking skills before they focus more deeply
on an academic major.

It is a common misconception, however, that all colleges and universities provide the same type of general education. In fact, the type and focus

Figure 15.1. Student development.

Who is the college student in developmental terms?

- Students differ in age-related developmental tasks that offer important agendas for "teachable moments" in their lives.
- Students differ in how they construct and interpret their experiences, and such differences offer important guides for structuring their education.
- Students differ in the styles with which they approach and resolve challenges of learning, growth, and development, and such differences are important for understanding how and why students function in characteristic manners.
- Students differ in the resolution of tasks by individuation often based on their intersectional identities including their gender, culture, race, ethnicity, and sexual orientation; such differences offer important contexts for understanding the contributions as well as challenges students face in their search for personal identity.

How does development occur?

- Development occurs as individuals reach points of readiness and respond to timely and appropriate learning experiences.
- Development occurs as individuals respond to novel situations and tasks that challenge their current level or capacity.
- Development occurs as individuals evaluate a learning task to be sufficiently challenging to warrant change and sufficiently supportive to risk an unknown result.
- Development proceeds through qualitative and cyclical changes of increasing complexity.
- Development occurs as an interactive and dynamic process between persons and their environments.

How does the college environment influence student development?

- Educational environments restrict and enable individuals by the form and function of their natural and synthetic physical characteristics.
- Educational environments exert a conforming influence through the collective, dominant characteristics of those who inhabit them.
- Educational environments, as purposeful and goal-directed settings, enable or restrict behavior by how they are organized.
- The effects of educational environments are a function of how members perceive and evaluate them.

Toward what ends should development in college be directed?

- Educational systems are embedded in various contexts of select values and assumptions that shape their expectations, processes, and outcomes.

Source: Strange, C. S. (1994). Student development: The evolution and status of an essential idea. *Journal of College Student Development, 35*(6), 399–412.

of classes, the extent to which classes relate to each other (e.g., through clustering, coteaching, or living–learning communities), and the philosophy of the general education program can vary markedly. For example, associate degree programs tend to include fewer and more professionally oriented classes than their 4-year counterparts because of their shorter timeframe and more vocational orientation. Some baccalaureate institutions may require all students to take the same courses as a way of encouraging a common student experience, while large research institutions often offer dozens of different courses from which students choose.

General Education

Debate over the role of general education has persisted throughout the history of U.S. higher education. With the expansion of knowledge and the rise of student choice in selecting courses in the late 19th and early 20th centuries, proponents of the traditional general curriculum warned of the dilution of education in the hands of student choice and the more flexible curricular requirements that permitted it. Ardent defenders of general education argued for its reassertion as the central purpose of higher education based on the first two of four philosophical themes identified by Levine (1979). The first theme was *perennialism*, whereby a general education provides universal truths that are perennial or everlasting and therefore serve as a foundation for the learned person. The second was *essentialism*, whose argument was that general education should be based on a prescribed or essential body of knowledge. Redefinitions of general education emerged later in the post–Civil War period as universities developed concurrently with advances in the sciences. The two new philosophical themes to emerge were *progressivism*, which viewed general education as a preparation for life and was problem-oriented rather than subject oriented, and *reconstructionism*, which held that general education should focus on applying life's experiences to changing or reconstructing society. To this day, these four philosophical themes continue to echo throughout the debate on the essential role of higher education in our society.

One of the most prominent statements in defense of the idea of a common curriculum came from what is commonly referred to as the *Yale Report of 1828* (see Committee of the Corporation and the Academical Faculty, 1828). This report acknowledged that the college curriculum "may, from time to time be made with advantage, to meet the varying demands of the community, to accommodate the course of instruction to the rapid advance of the country, in population, refinement, and opulence" (p. 5). In response to increasing demands for moving the college curriculum toward a more vocational orientation, however, the report's authors emphasized:

> The two great points to be gained in intellectual culture, are the *discipline* and the *furniture* of the mind; expanding its powers, and storing it with knowledge. The former of these is, perhaps, the more important of the two. A commanding object, therefore, in a collegiate course, should be, to call into daily and vigorous exercise the faculties of the student. Those branches of study should be prescribed, and those modes of instruction adopted, which are best calculated to teach the art of fixing the attention, directing the train of thought, analyzing a subject proposed for investigation; following, with accurate discrimination, the course of argument; balancing nicely the evidence presented to the judgment; awakening, elevating, and controlling the imagination; arranging, with skill, the treasures which memory gathers; rousing and guiding the powers of genius. All this is not to be affected by a light and hasty course of study; by reading a few books, hearing a few lectures, and spending some months at a literary institution. (p. 7)

The concept of a general education reflected a value to impart a uniform and broad knowledge base. Topics included the study of religious doctrine, an understanding of the world, knowledge of the classics and the foundations of human culture, a common understanding of the democratic principles on which society was based, and other broad subjects, all of which together rendered a comprehensive understanding and appreciation of the competencies and capacities of humankind. This broad knowledge base and exposure to a variety of topics rooted in the humanities, arts, religion, culture, and science "liberated" the mind from parochialism and came to be referred to as the liberal arts. Against this backdrop emerged the broadening of disciplinary specialties and an expanded knowledge base in the late 19th century at institutions such as Johns Hopkins and Harvard, giving rise to free electives that provided students with latitude in determining which of the general education courses they could ultimately choose (Thelin, 2011). The history of general education, therefore, involved three distinct phases of development—core requirements, distribution requirements, and free electives.

The advent of student choice and broad elective offerings in the general education component of the curriculum yielded disagreement in the academic community over the relative value of general education's content. This debate continues and is manifested in the vast array of curricula among colleges and universities and their interpretation of how, or even if, general education requirements should be offered. Levine (1979) noted a variety of concerns and criticisms about general education, including the following:

- It is a good idea in theory, but it fails in practice.
- It is unpopular with students.
- The student clientele of U.S. colleges and universities is too heterogeneous to permit common general education programs.
- It is of little economic value to the student who is forced to study it.
- General education courses are weak in educational and philosophical integrity.
- General education is poorly timed (i.e., more appropriate to older adults).

Such criticisms remain strong today and reflect changing priorities regarding what student learning outcomes should be. This issue is especially important for colleges and universities that place a special value on the liberal arts, focusing on certain core competencies and skills that are often minimized or absent from curricula that focus on vocational preparation. Efforts led by the AAC&U (National Leadership Council for Liberal Education and America's Promise, 2007) to elevate the importance of the liberal arts in U.S. society have resulted in the identification and promotion of four essential learning outcomes: knowledge of human cultures and the physical and natural world, including the humanities and social, natural, and physical sciences; intellectual and practical skills that promote critical and creative thinking, strong written and oral communication, and teamwork and problem solving; personal and social responsibility, such as civic knowledge and engagement, ethical reasoning, and the establishment of foundations and skills for lifelong learning; and integrative learning, which involves a synthesis and advanced accomplishment across general and specialized studies.

Juxtaposed against such efforts to reaffirm the value of a liberal arts education is the increasing attention being given to the mission of community colleges. These important institutions contribute substantially to furthering educational access to broader segments of society by virtue of their lower costs and more vocational focus. Another important aspect of many community colleges is their transfer function (Lane, 2003). For some students, community colleges help prepare them for more advanced study at four-year institutions. In addition, community colleges have become increasingly used as a less expensive way for students to complete some of the coursework for their baccalaureate requirements. Finally, a reverse transfer phenomenon has emerged in which students who complete a baccalaureate degree then enroll in community college programs to obtain or update their technical skills (Townsend & Dever, 1999).

One trend in recent years has been a push by some states and multi-campus systems to create more generic general education frameworks that standardize requirements across multiple institutions. This approach has largely been undertaken in reaction to the loss of credits that many students realize when transferring between institutions (National Task Force on the Transfer and Award of Credit, 2021). These frameworks tend to establish broad categories that students at each institution in the state or system are required to fulfill. Often, an individual institution can still implement its own version of general education, although it cannot make students retake requirements in the framework fulfilled at other institutions (Lane et al., 2021). Similar concerns around transfer credits have affected change at the regional level, and regional higher education compacts (e.g., Midwestern Higher Education Compact, Southern Regional Education Board) now collaborate to create course equivalencies between their general education curricula. To streamline the transfer process, these compacts frequently focus on block transfer to meet general education requirements through agreement on common learning outcomes (National Task Force on the Transfer and Award of Credit, 2021).

While no one would dispute the role that higher education plays in preparing individuals to be productive members of society in a variety of capacities, Bowen (1977) envisioned a future in which higher education could successfully integrate liberal and vocational values:

> the overriding purpose of higher education would change from that of preparing people to fill particular slots in the economy and of adding to the GNP to that of helping them to achieve personal fulfillment and of building a civilization compatible with the nature of human beings and the limitations of the environment. Vocational education would continue to be an essential function, but it would be combined in symbiotic relationship with liberal education. (p. 459)

That our society is still debating the nexus between liberal education and vocationalism reminds us of the challenges inherent in understanding and achieving the outcomes we seek when attempting to address the complex subject of student development.

The debate over what is to be included in a college or university curriculum will be forever with us as the definition of student development remains elusive. What is important, however, is that leaders of each institution must decide for themselves what outcomes their school seeks for its students given the organization's mission and what should be contained in its curriculum in order to achieve it. In other words, the academic community must be thoughtful in creating its academic offerings. Such thoughtfulness requires a blueprint for achieving prescribed outcomes for students, the subject to which we now turn.

The Academic Plan

Just as a budget represents a college or university's managerial statement of its organizational priorities, a curriculum represents an institution's academic value statement. Lattuca and Stark (2009) conceptualized the curriculum as an "academic plan":

> The intention of any academic plan is to foster students' academic development, and a plan, therefore, should be designed with a given group of students and learning objectives in mind. This focus compels course and program planners to put students' educational needs, rather than subject matter, first. The term "plan" communicates in familiar terms the kind of informal development process recognized by a broad range of faculty members across academic fields. (p. 4)

Academic planning, also known as educational master planning or academic master planning, entails identifying the university's academic goals and then detailing how the institution will meet those goals (Society for College and University Planning, n.d.). However, academic *plans* might be more appropriate than academic *plan*, as different types of academic plans serve different purposes. For instance, state systems might have systemwide plans that cover all their institutions. Institutions might also have specific college plans for programs that are regulated by the state and additional accreditation, such as clinical health, interdisciplinary early childhood, or electrical engineering.

The importance of faculty consensus and cooperation in devising an appropriate academic plan for a specific learning environment cannot be overstated. This process is complicated, however, because multiple theories of learning exist, as do multiple definitions of learning. Additionally, the academic plan is not always left to the sole discretion of the faculty or the institution. For many degrees, such as those in education, health, and engineering, external state and accreditation requirements provide the framework of courses (if not specific courses) that students must take to be licensed in those professions.

Lattuca and Stark (2009) identified three broad traditions of learning: behavioral, cognitive, and sociocultural. Behaviorists define learning as that which can be observed and measured; learning is indicated by a change in one's behavior. The cognitive approach to learning posits that learning is a function of acquisition and understanding of knowledge, irrespective of any behavioral change that can be observed as a result of gaining that knowledge. While behaviorists understand learning to be a response to environmental stimuli, those who subscribe to the cognitive approach focus on the internal processing of information and the development of memory. The sociocultural perspective combines the first two perspectives in some ways; it recognizes the role of environment in shaping understanding as well as the importance of internally processing that information into some form of understanding. However, the sociocultural tradition emphasizes the social context and interactional relationships that provide perspective, and thus understanding.

Though many faculty members believe their role is to develop the cognitive (intellectual) abilities of students, they often neglect the importance of those aspects of learning that affect their students' attitudinal, personal, or vocational development. Lattuca and Stark (2009) warned, "Separating intellectual outcomes from others . . . is both artificial and counterproductive because intellectual development is inextricably linked to students' emotions and attitudes, that is, their affective development" (p. 153). Furthermore, a universally embraced definition of what constitutes human intelligence does not exist in the literature. Some have defined it as a combination of many capabilities in reference to Gardner's (1983) theory of multiple intelligences. "One important conclusion drawn from research on intelligence is that, as behaviors become more contextualized, measures of general intelligence become less useful for predicting and explaining achievement" (Lattuca & Stark, 2009, p. 160). Learning strategies, therefore, should differ according to the circumstances in which learning takes place. Consequently, the academic plan must be tailored specifically to the environment where it will be applied and the outcomes it seeks. This theme was advanced over 50 years ago when Chickering (1969) noted that "differences in institutional objectives and internal consistency, size, curriculum, teaching and evaluation, residences, faculty and administration, friends and student culture, make a difference to student development" (p. 157). The contextual variables of student development remain as significant today as they have for generations.

Yet for all students, one's ability to graduate is inexorably linked to one's determination to complete the requirements for a degree, which brings us to the all-important subject of student persistence.

Student Retention and Completion

Since the 1980s, student persistence has been a topic of intense discussion and debate among academic leaders, as policymakers, rankings, and accrediting agencies are increasingly interested in student success outcomes related to student retention and completion. The percentage of first-time full-time students who graduated from a public four-year college within 5 years remained around 50% for the 2 decades prior to 2010; reached 59% with the cohort that started in 2010; and saw a marked increase with the cohort that entered in 2013, which had a 63% graduation rate within 6 years (de Brey et al., 2021). Two-year colleges saw lower graduation rates. Almost 40% of first-time full-time undergraduate students who began their studies in 2010 completed their associate degree within 6 years (de Brey et al., 2021; Nadworny, 2019). Across institution types, graduation rates were higher for females than males, except at private for-profit institutions, from 2006 to 2018 (de Brey et al., 2021).

Some of these trends may be due to the completion agenda, a movement that emerged in the early 2010s in response to stagnant college completion rates in the United States. The completion agenda encompasses a variety of policy changes and state- and institution-level initiatives aimed at improving college completion (Commission on the Future of Undergraduate Education, 2017). Although the purpose of the completion agenda—to enable more Americans to complete college degrees—is something that few would criticize, the execution of this agenda has been met with substantial backlash from those involved in the study and practice of higher education. Rhoades (2012), for instance, summarized some of these issues:

> The completion agenda is incomplete. It is an unfunded mandate to do more with less. Moreover, the agenda does not address the key educational, social, and economic challenges [educators] face . . . the completion agenda is compromising the learning agenda. (p. 19)

Similarly, Anderson et al. (2015) observed that the agenda advocates for a technocratic approach that inadvertently harms poor minoritized students in community college. Levesque (2018) echoed this assertion but also pointed out that the policy promotion failed to help students navigate the system, nor did institutions make their curriculum more meaningful to students.

It is easy to see why an emphasis on college completion might inspire the type of criticism that Rhoades (2012) offered. A fixation on completion may come at the expense of quality. If colleges and universities are overly focused on ensuring that students graduate, they may reduce graduation requirements and other barriers to completion that could otherwise prevent students from becoming positive statistics for the institution (Evenbeck & Johnson, 2012).

Many factors contribute to a student's ability to complete college, and many of these obstacles cannot be addressed through completion agenda policies. Other programs, such as the College Promise, have sought to address financial barriers to completion head on. Unlike the completion agenda, which is a somewhat ambiguous call to increase graduation rates, College Promise is a nonprofit initiative that provides funding to students for the first 2 years of college. The types of promise programs vary, with the most significant difference being whether programs are last dollar or first dollar. Last-dollar programs provide funding only after state and federal financial aid funds are exhausted, while first-dollar funds are provided immediately, regardless of other funding resources (Association of Community College Trustees, n.d.). Although these programs have been popular, budget cuts caused by the COVID-19 pandemic have made their future less certain (St. Amour, 2020).

Although the future of these programs is unknown, it is certain that research into college completion will continue. Student persistence is probably one of the most thoroughly studied topics in higher education research. The early work of scholars such as Spady (1970), Tinto (1975, 1987), and Terenzini and Pascarella (1980) spurred the interest of an army of researchers. These scholars have identified a wide range of student background characteristics, precollege experiences, behaviors, and campus activities, as well as institutional polices, programs, and practices that can affect student outcomes.

In reviewing the expansive literature on persistence, Reason (2009) devised a conceptual model that highlights the factors that may affect persistence at two-year and four-year institutions. In this model, Reason argued that a student's decision to persist is influenced by a combination of personal characteristics (e.g., traits; academic preparation; and academic motivation, self-discipline, and self-confidence), organizational factors (e.g., institution size, type, and selectivity), and individual student experiences in and outside the classroom (e.g., faculty interactions, engagement in student activities, and employment). Based on these factors, Reason argued the following:

> To fully and effectively address student persistence, any intervention must consider the local organizational context and the local student peer environment. Individual student's [sic] decisions about whether to persist are made within, and influenced by, these two proximal contexts. It seems clear that no effective interventions can be devised without considering them. (p. 678)

While academic leaders cannot control all the factors that influence a student's decision to stay in school, certain programs have proven to have a positive influence in this regard. First, one of the most significant factors influencing student persistence is interaction with faculty members. Early on, A. W. Astin (1993) and H. S. Astin and Kent (1983) found that students' meaningful interactions with faculty outside the classroom (e.g., working on research projects, assisting with a lecture, being a guest in the faculty member's home) have a positive correlation with students' intellectual and social development in college. Studies on student–faculty interaction have found positive effects with small class sizes, collaborations on research projects, mentoring, and reciprocal positive benefits onto professors (Kim & Sax, 2017). Second, orientation programs have been identified as an effective way to integrate students into the collegiate experience—an important factor for increasing student persistence (Braxton et al., 2006; Fong et al., 2016; Hossler, 2006). Third, early warning systems are designed to identify potential resources needed to ensure all students are successful. Accordingly, when students with high numbers of D's and F's and course withdrawals are exposed to an environment that is not centered on their success, colleges have the opportunity to target additional academic supports. They are important interventions for keeping students from dropping out, especially with an abundance of data available (Akos & James, 2020; Devlin & Bushey, 2019).

However, a large gap often exists between knowing what factors affect student persistence and adapting the academic environment to influence students positively in this regard. For instance, although research demonstrates the effects of a growth mindset at the early schooling levels in K–12 education and somewhat in college (Dweck, 2017; Han et al., 2017), less is known about the teaching or collegiate design and environmental factors associated with a growth mindset. Further, college student development through online learning and new approaches to learning such as competency-based education and apprenticeships present wide gaps in the research, which should be examined as we continue to explore ways to improve student success and search for opportunities that bring greater equity in learning.

Because of the long-standing and growing interest in student persistence, academic leaders need to be aware of some of the ways student characteristics and institutional factors affect a student's decision to stay in college. Moreover, effective leaders should try to align their policies and practices to bolster student persistence. Faculty members, in their teaching and advising capacities, also play an important role in guiding students through the educational process, including redirecting students into more appropriate majors when interest or academic success in a chosen field of study diminishes. In addition, as Mayhew et al. (2016) observed, student involvement in college life outside the classroom through such activities as athletics, clubs, student government, and other cocurricular opportunities can contribute substantially to measures of student satisfaction and, ultimately, their persistence to graduation.

Predictive Analytics in Student Success[2]

The big data movement is transforming everything from health-care delivery systems to the way cities provide services to citizens. Lane (2014) called the movement of big data into higher education "building a smarter university," but he also cautioned, "the immense amount of data that is now being generated is only useful if it can be extracted and refined to be used to make decision[s]" (p. 17). Of course, as discussed later, the use of data can have both positive and negative outcomes.

The insights regarding student success that are being derived from data are quite varied and depend on the type of data that are available, the analytical tools available, and the individual and institutional capacity to understand the analysis and what it means for practice. Some analyses can be completed using Excel spreadsheets; others require access to more advanced machine learning capabilities. While the type of analysis will vary based on resources, the bottom line is that all institutions have the capacity to use the data they have to better understand the student experience and, in turn, use that understanding to make changes that could improve student success (Gagliardi, 2022). Historically, student development data have been used in more traditional research to develop theories over time, which are then applied to future generations. While still very much in development, the new era of machine learning represents an opportunity to create real-time interventions based on more individualized analysis, such as with propensity score matching.[3]

Data sources are quite varied. Examples include using data from a learning management system (LMS) to determine when, how often, and to what extent a student engages with a course site. A student who does not access the course LMS site until the 3rd week of class is likely not to be successful in the course without appropriate intervention (Fain, 2016). Aggregated transcript data provides insight into which courses are gateway courses, where large numbers of students tend to not be successful (Koch, 2017). As a result, a faculty member may consider how to redesign the course so that students can deepen their learning, a department may consider whether courses are offered in the appropriate sequence, or an institution may consider whether alternative and more appropriate course pathways may be available for students to reach graduation.

Early alert systems are designed to identify students who may be at risk of withdrawing from a course, receiving a nonpassing grade in a course, or dropping out of college (Lane, 2014). According to a 2018 report, over 70% of institutions that responded to a survey indicated they are using some form of early alert system with their undergraduate population (Parnell et al.,

2018). A basic approach to early alert is the "see something, say something" model that encourages faculty or staff who are concerned about a student to signal the concern to the institution so that they may initiate an intervention in time to support the student toward successful completion of a degree. Analytics platforms can also monitor various data points (sometimes in real time) and derive a profile of a student to indicate whether students have risk factors upon which institution officials should act.

While early alert systems have many potential benefits, there is also rea-son to proceed carefully. As Jensen and Roof (n.d.) warned, "While the surge in available data is reshaping the foundations of higher education, it increases the risk for 'analysis paralysis,' reckless collection/storage, and improper use of data" (p. 1). Critics have noted that unchecked use of data could lead to new forms of institutional racism if the data are used in ways that lead to false assumptions about certain segments of the college population (Marachi & Quill, 2020). One of the primary arguments has been that greater transparency is needed—in terms of how the data are used and how the data are shared with students (Marachi & Quill, 2020). Using data analytics, we can explore and reflect on what has happened in the past. Although predictive models can be used to forecast what may come, we need to recognize that there will always be students who will fall outside typical behavior patterns.

Student Development, the Cocurriculum, and High-Impact Practices

The cocurricular experience, such as participating in student organizations, living in residence halls, and engaging in faculty research projects, has long been part of the undergraduate experience. In fact, Kuh (1996) estimated that half of all learning in college takes place outside the classroom.

The organizational structure of most colleges and universities assigns responsibility for the cognitive (intellectual) component of learning to academic leaders and the faculty and allocates the affective (behavioral) component to student affairs professionals. While the classroom-based academic process has been assumed to require expertise and understanding in such matters as curriculum, pedagogy, and assessment, the out-of-class experiential learning process has been understood to entail expertise in the affective realms of counseling, psychology, and human development, although the two domains increasingly intersect.

Calls for greater integration of both developmental realms have been raised throughout the history of higher education, and over the last 20 years we have seen the development of a set of *high-impact practices* (HIPs) that mostly exist at this intersection (Kuh, 2008). (See Figure 15.2.) HIPs are teaching and learning practices that have been widely tested and found to yield beneficial results in terms of learning and completion for college students from many different backgrounds. Some of these practices, such as writing-intensive courses and collaborative assignments, speak more directly to particular course design choices. Study-abroad (diversity/global learning) programs and internships and engaging in faculty-led research often occur outside the classroom, yet they are increasingly considered important components of experiential learning, which help students to connect classroom learning with learned experiences, transforming "inert knowledge to knowledge-in-use" (Eyler, 2009, p. 2). Although not all HIPs have the same effects on all students, research has shown that some HIPs, including active and collaborative learning and participating in undergraduate research, have broad positive effects on a variety of student learning outcomes (e.g., critical thinking, intercultural effectiveness), while others, such as study-abroad programs and internships, have more narrowly focused effects (Kilgo et al., 2015). Certain HIPs, like learning communities, may be particularly advantageous for community college students (Bonet & Walters, 2016).

As mentioned earlier, the curriculum of any college or university should be approached as an academic plan (Lattuca & Stark, 2009), developed by the institution's faculty to provide intellectual content that is designed to achieve predefined knowledge and skills outcomes. If the cognitive and the affective are to be integrated, however, the desired outcomes cannot be shaped

Figure 15.2. High-impact practices.

Commonly Used High-Impact Practices in Student Success
- First-Year Experiences
- Common Intellectual Experiences
- Learning Communities
- Writing-Intensive Courses
- Collaborative Assignments and Projects
- Undergraduate Research
- Diversity/Global Learning
- ePortfolios
- Service Learning, Community-Based Learning
- Internships
- Capstone Courses and Projects

Source: Kuh, G. (2008). *High-impact educational practices: What they are, who has access to them, and why they matter*. American Association of Colleges and Universities.

exclusively by those charged with providing classroom experiences. Rather, they must be informed by the sociocultural dimension that corresponds to the behavioral and psychosocial growth that helps to shape students' total learning experience. Such learning is most effectively influenced by deliberately prescribed and optional experiences found in an institution's cocurricular programs. The nature and number of these cocurricular offerings vary considerably depending on the type of institution, as institutions that are nonresidential or primarily serve adult and working populations may have educational missions that tailor cocurricular activities to the needs of adults with significant life responsibilities and time limitations.

We define the cocurriculum as a set of required and elective noncredit student experiences provided apart from, or in conjunction with, for-credit academic offerings for the purpose of producing specific student developmental outcomes. Such experiences can range from mandatory (e.g., 1st-year student orientation programs) to elective (e.g., intercollegiate sports, Greek life, student government). Cocurricular programs exist at four-year institutions as well as at community colleges. The greatest difference, however, rests in the *relative* investment made by these institutions, reflecting the overall importance such offerings hold for the institution's mission and the needs of its students. Nearly as much as academic offerings, the cocurriculum helps shape the environment and character of an institution and serves an important role in the attraction, retention, and ultimately the development of its students.

Deliberately shaping the student experience involves not only campus programs but community activities as well. Efforts to instill a sense of civic and community responsibility in students contribute substantially to overall student growth when those activities augment the learning that occurs in the classroom through applying classroom material to real-world situations. Linking student learning to community service also fosters town–gown relationships and a spirit of cooperation between the institution and the community that transcends the academic benefits. For these reasons, community engagement has become an important component to the curriculum and cocurriculum at many institutions (see chapter 9).

The literature on cocurricular activities is replete with studies that establish their positive effect on student development, but Pascarella and Terenzini (2005) noted that studies on the impact of college on the cognitive aspects of individual change exceed those pertaining to the more affective realms of personal development: "The evidence supporting the net impact of postsecondary education on learning and cognition, moral reasoning, and career and economic returns is more extensive and consistent than the evidence concerning changes in attitudes, values, and psychosocial characteristics"

(p. 579). This inconsistency in the literature suggests the challenges inherent in measuring individual change in the affective domains as a direct result of the experiences gained through attending college.

Discussions of the cocurriculum tend to be biased toward the residential collegiate experience since the opportunities for student engagement are greater there than in nonresidential institutions. Research on the effect that living on campus has on student outcomes has demonstrated that living at college versus remaining at home increases artistic interest, liberalism, self-esteem, hedonistic tendencies, academic persistence, and higher achievement in extracurricular areas, but it reduces religiousness. Most notable of these findings is that resident students are more likely than their nonresident peers to express higher levels of satisfaction with their educational experience and have higher academic success (A. W. Astin, 1977; Rockenbach et al., 2020). In fact, Pascarella and Terenzini (2005) concluded, based on a synthesis of research on intra-college effects on student development, that "living on campus was the single most consistent . . . determinant of the impact of college" (p. 603). Such findings hold enormous implications for the future of higher education as pedagogy and communications increasingly employ technology, especially in those academic settings where educational content is delivered exclusively online, and experiential opportunities for direct, personal, face-to-face, ongoing interaction between students and faculty or among student peers are either waning or nonexistent.

How the educational experience is structured determines the manner in which student growth occurs, and educational experiences are idiosyncratic to the mission and environment of each institution. College administrators are sensitive to the issue of "fit" between students and their institution, and research supports the assertion that most students will seek out those colleges that most closely reflect their interests, skills, and values (Mayhew et al., 2016). In a similar fashion, institutions will attempt to recruit those students whose personal and academic profiles most closely mirror the institution's educational values. According to Feldman and Newcomb (1969), college selection often involves a process of accentuation—matching and mirroring values and characteristics held by the student. Within these homogeneous settings, however, lie opportunities for growth and elucidation, a departure from the normative experiences of the individual. The paradox is that while it is important to have a good fit between institution and student, the goal is to bring about individual change and growth. Apart from the academic content to which a student is exposed in the process of meeting degree requirements, structuring the cocurriculum effectively can bring about significant change. If one were to closely examine college and university budgets, it would illuminate the priorities and values institutions place on shaping the entire collegiate experience to meet a set of specified student outcomes in their academic and nonacademic offerings.

The College Experience and Student Change

We began this chapter with evidence that college students look significantly different than decades earlier with increasing racial diversity, more women, more adults, and more part-timers. As college access increases, we are witnessing rising skepticism on the overall benefits of obtaining a higher education, especially in light of the growing costs to obtain a college degree. Valid arguments support the position that higher education is losing some credibility as a sure pathway to the American dream. Some observers even adopt a cynical view that higher education is merely a partitioning tool of the social elite to perpetuate the status quo rather than change society for the better:

> College is nothing more than an elaborate and expensive mechanism for employers to identify the people who were smarter and harder workers and had all the social advantages in the first place, and those people then get the higher paying jobs. Now that it's illegal to discriminate in employment by race, ethnicity, gender, religion, or sexual orientation, judging people by where and how much they went to school is just about the only acceptable form of prejudice left. (Kamenetz, 2010, p. 35)

Though critics of today's higher education enterprise have ample reason to judge its structure and process harshly because of its adherence to traditional cultures and practices and its reluctance to adapt to new economic and pedagogical realities, the body of evidence surrounding how the college experience develops and changes students is consistent and unambiguous: The undergraduate experience changes students in significant ways that would not have occurred had they not attended college. Numerous successive and important works by Chickering (1969), Feldman and Newcomb (1969), A. W. Astin (1977), Pascarella and Terenzini (1991, 2005), and Mayhew et al. (2016), among others, have explored this subject in detail, and a broad review of their conclusions is unequivocal in asserting the developmental value the college experience can give an individual on a variety of cognitive and affective measures.

Two particularly significant points emerge, however, when one examines the evidence surrounding this important and comprehensive body of literature. First is the nature of change itself. The normal process of human maturation will naturally produce individual change on a variety of measures apart from those experiences gained while enrolled in college. Any study of

this complex subject, therefore, needs to control for intervening and normative variables so that the definitive effects of the cognitive or affective inputs
resulting from the college experience itself will emerge. Yet extant studies also
lack examination of special populations such as adult students, students who
are highly functional with mild disabilities, military/veteran students, and
students aged 18–26 who work full-time (perhaps using employer benefits). Second, the research constructs employed in many studies from which
variables of student development have been measured must account for the
enormous individual, environmental, and institutional variations that exist
among the students studied, their personal backgrounds, the experiences
they undergo, and the types and missions of the institutions they attend.
Many studies omit discussions of or have very limited participation from
for-profit colleges, non–Title IV financial aid colleges, and career and technical colleges/fields. Given these challenges, we must rely on conclusions that,
although grounded in sound methodological practices, can be synthesized
and viewed holistically in generalized summaries.

Another challenge of student development research is an apparent
bias in the types of institutions from which the authors of many studies
draw their conclusions. Traditional four-year institutions (regardless of size)
dominated the earliest studies of student change, only to be augmented
with two-year institutions in later decades as the role and importance of
the community college has grown. Today, studies on the effects of college
between institution types can now be broadly analyzed because of the richness of data that have been obtained over the past 40 years. The more recent
rise of proprietary institutions and the subsequent growth of new online
modalities have not yet realized that depth of richness, although scientific
and assessment efforts to understand how such experiences affect student
development and outcomes are emerging through data analytics, which
predict odds of additional resources needed and likely enrollment patterns
based on students' characteristics.

Conclusion

Throughout this book, we discuss the importance of being mission driven;
adaptive to environmental changes; grounded in democratic partnerships;
and committed to inclusion, equity, and positive social change. These
themes are particularly relevant when considering the student experience.
It is widely acknowledged that the experiences of college students, inside
and outside the classroom, contribute to their social, moral, and cognitive
development. However, the actual experience of individual students will

vary markedly between institutions, influenced by a combination of history, traditions, and mission. This last factor is probably the most important, as academic leaders should be careful to ensure that the opportunities for students, in and out of the classroom, reflect the mission of the institution. Academic leaders also need to be diligent in ensuring that previous decisions and legacies help, rather than hinder, the student experience. Therefore, they need to be able to adapt the college experience to changing demographics and the latest research on factors that influence student success.

We do not believe that all institutions should provide the same college experience—quite the contrary. The diversity of campus cultures is a strength of the U.S. higher education system. However, it is important to ensure that the characteristics of any college experience support the success of students, particularly in light of the changing demographics of the students many institutions now serve. Finally, academic leaders should look for ways to become partners with students to support the college experience. Students can be an important source of information about the health and vitality of a college community and should be considered as one of the key stakeholders when developing partnerships.

In this overview of student development, we are limited in our ability to discuss the vast findings of decades of research on the subject, so we highlight findings from the latest and most comprehensive review on this subject by Mayhew et al. (2016). We have selected a few conclusions that may hold the greatest interest to students and professionals new to higher education administration or to laypeople serving in volunteer governance roles, the target audiences for this book. Commentary on certain findings is also offered when such findings support or refute accepted wisdom in the higher education community.

First, the notion of "four critical years" (A. W. Astin, 1977) is an apt description of the college experience, since research confirms that college produces measurable gains in cognitive and intellectual skills along with a wide array of change in affective dimensions such as moral, psychosocial, attitudinal, and values. College also yields positive changes in self-esteem and academic and social self-concept. Cognitive dimensions of student growth such as learning, career, and skills acquisition yielded more robust findings than affective changes such as attitudes and values.

Second, the impact of college lasts far beyond the college years and contributes substantially to people's lives and the lives of their significant others, including their children. This finding confirms the wise adage once conveyed from a parent to a child when the college-educated parent said, "The most important thing that separates you from poverty is my education." These findings are also confirmed in U.S. Census data. The median economic and social benefits to college graduates far outweigh those of individuals who do not possess postsecondary degrees. Evidence is also strong that those with a higher education tend to have healthier lifestyles and live longer.

Third, where one attends college has less of a net impact than the net effect of not attending college. According to Pascarella and Terenzini (2005), "The great majority of postsecondary institutions appear to have surprisingly similar net impacts on student growth, although the 'start' and 'end' points for students differ across different institutions" (p. 590). This finding is noteworthy for it debunks the myth that one necessarily benefits more from attending a more selective institution. Rather, "little consistent evidence suggested that college selectivity, prestige, or educational resources had any important net impact in such areas as learning, cognitive and intellectual development, the majority of psychosocial changes, the development principled moral reasoning, or shifts in attitudes and values" (p. 593). Especially for those who may subscribe to academic elitist notions that institutional ranking is the only true arbiter of quality, these findings should prove revealing.

Fourth, institutional context has a substantial effect on student change. Academic environments with a scholarly emphasis stimulate learning growth. Such an emphasis can be found at any institutional type, not just at highly selective institutions. Also, a wide range of cognitive and affective growth occurs in environments that foster close student–faculty ties. The level of student learning is directly correlated to the nature of the classroom instruction, including the teaching skills of the instructor and how the course material is structured and delivered.

Fifth, college impact is significantly determined by the level of involvement by the student in curricular and cocurricular activities. It is axiomatic that what students put into their academic experience will contribute substantially to what they get out of the experience.

Sixth, service learning programs, covered in chapter 9, have been shown to have positive and lasting effects in helping students clarify their values and identities, improve their self-esteem, and enhance their sense of volunteerism and social justice during their lives beyond graduation.

In short, the value of college is irrefutable in positively affecting individual development and change. But is it worth it? In finding an answer to that question today, one can reflect on the thoughts of Bowen (1977) when he said:

> One may argue that whatever is being spent on higher education is a measure of its worth. Just as we might say that the nation's output of automobiles is worth what people individually and collectively are willing to pay for them, so one could argue that higher education is worth whatever

people are willing to pay for it. That is to say, the total expenditure on higher education would not have been made unless the students and their families, the citizenry, the philanthropic donors collectively thought the returns justified the outlays. (p. 438)

Although Bowen's remarks originated more than 4 decades ago, they still resonate with college leaders, policymakers, professors, college staff, parents, and students.

As this chapter has demonstrated, those fortunate enough to gain access to higher education will be making a personal investment that will reap lifelong dividends.

Notes

1. Due to variations in data collection methods, readers should be aware that NSCRC and NCES data differ, but collectively they help us understand the college student population.

2. Some of this section is derived from the open-access online course, "An Introduction to Data Analytics for Student Success," developed by Jason E. Lane and reused here with permission of the author.

3. Propensity score matching is a statistical methodology that seeks to apply a quasi-experimental treatment to observational data and estimate the impact of an intervention by identifying like groups of individuals within the observed population.

References

Akos, P., & James, S. (2020). Are course withdrawals a useful student success strategy? *NACADA Journal, 40*(1), 80–93. https://doi.org/10.12930/NACADA-18-34

Anderson, G. M., Barone, R. P., Sun, J. C., & Bowlby, N. (2015). The new stratification: Differentiating opportunity at community colleges by race and class in the U.S. In A. M. Martinez-Alemán, B. Pusser, & E. M. Bensimon (Eds.)., *Critical approaches to the study of higher education: A practical introduction* (pp. 257–284). Johns Hopkins University Press.

Association of Community College Trustees. (n.d.). *First-dollar vs. last-dollar promise models.* https://www.acct.org/page/first-dollar-vs-last-dollar-promise-models

Astin, A. W. (1977). *Four critical years: Effects of college on beliefs, attitudes, and knowledge.* Jossey-Bass.

Astin, A. W. (1984). Student involvement: A developmental theory for higher education. *Journal of College Student Personnel, 25*(4), 297–308. https://www.middlesex.mass.edu/ace/downloads/astininv.pdf

Astin, A. W. (1993). *What matters in college? Four critical years revisited.* Jossey-Bass.

Astin, H. S., & Kent, L. (1983). Gender roles in transition: Research and policy implications for higher education. *Journal of Higher Education, 54*(3), 309–324. https://doi.org/10.1080/00221546.1983.11778194

Baxter Magolda, M. B. (2001). *Making their own way: Narratives for transforming higher education to promote self-development.* Stylus.

Bonet, G., & Walters, B. R. (2016). High impact practices: Student engagement and retention. *College Student Journal, 50*(2), 224–235. https://academicworks.cuny.edu/kb_pubs/102/

Bowen, H. R. (1977). *Investment in learning: The individual and social value of American higher education.* Jossey-Bass.

Braxton, J. M., McKinney, J., & Reynolds, P. (2006). Cataloging institutional efforts to understand and reduce college student departure. In E. P. St. John & M. Wilkerson (Eds.), *Reframing persistence research to improve academic success* (pp. 25–32). Jossey-Bass.

Butler, J. (2004). *Undoing gender.* Routledge.

Chickering, A. (1969). *Education and identity.* Jossey-Bass.

Commission on the Future of Undergraduate Education. (2017, November). *The future of undergraduate education: The future of America.* American Academy of Arts & Sciences. https://www.amacad.org/publication/future-undergraduate-education

Committee of the Corporation and the Academical Faculty. (1828). *Reports on the course of instruction.* Hezekiah Howe.

de Brey, C., Snyder, T. D., Zhang, A., & Dillow, S. A. (2021). *Digest of education statistics 2019.* National Center for Education Statistics, U.S. Department of Education. https://nces.ed.gov/pubs2021/2021009.pdf

Delgado, R., & Stefancic, J. (2017). *Critical race theory: An introduction* (3rd ed.). New York University Press.

Deloitte. (2020). *The Deloitte global millennial survey 2020.* https://www2.deloitte.com/content/dam/Deloitte/global/Documents/About-Deloitte/deloitte-2020-millennial-survey.pdf

Devlin, M., & Bushey, H. (2019). Using data holistically to create a student success safety net. *Change: The Magazine of Higher Learning, 51*(6), 17–25. https://doi.org/10.1080/00091383.2019.1674096

Duncan, A. G., & Glover, H. (2020). *Standing up for students amid the pandemic learning "swirl."* Lumina Foundation. https://www.luminafoundation.org/news-and-views/standing-up-for-students-amid-the-pandemic-learning-swirl/

Dweck, C. S. (2016). *Mindset: The new psychology of success.* Ballantine.

Eagan, M. K., Stolzenberg, E. B., Ramirez, J. J., Aragon, M. C., Suchard, M. R., & Rios-Aguilar, C. (2016). *The American freshman: Fifty-year trends, 1966–2015.* Higher Education Research Institute, University of California, Los Angeles. https://www.heri.ucla.edu/monographs/50YearTrendsMonograph2016.pdf

Evenbeck, S., & Johnson, K. E. (2012). Students must not become victims of the completion agenda. *Liberal Education, 98*(1), 26–33. https://www.aacu.org/publications-research/periodicals/students-must-not-become-victims-completion-agenda

Eyler, J. (2009). The power of experiential learning. *Liberal Education, 95*(4). https://www.aacu.org/publications-research/periodicals/power-experiential-education

Fain, P. (2016, June 13). Logging off, dropping off. *Inside Higher Ed.* https://www.insidehighered.com/news/2016/06/13/data-student-engagement-lms-key-predicting-retention

Feldman, K. A., & Newcomb, T. M. (1969). *The impact of college on students.* Jossey-Bass.

Fong, C. J., Acee, T. W., & Weinstein, C. E. (2016). A person-centered investigation of achievement motivation goals and correlates of community college student achievement and persistence. *Journal of College Student Retention: Research, Theory & Practice, 20*(3), 369–387. https://doi.org/10.1177/1521025116673374

Fry, R., & Parker, K. (2018, November 15). *Early benchmarks show "post-millennials" on track to be most diverse, best-educated generation yet.* Pew Research Center. https://www.pewresearch.org/social-trends/2018/11/15/early-benchmarks-show-post-millennials-on-track-to-be-most-diverse-best-educated-generation-yet/

Gagliardi, J. S. (in press). *How colleges use data.* Johns Hopkins University Press.

Gao, J. (2021, April). *Impact of COVID-19 on graduate education access: Selected results from the 2020 NAGAP/CGS survey of graduate enrollment professionals.* Council of Graduate Schools. https://cgsnet.org/ckfinder/userfiles/files/CGS_ResearchBrief_Impacts%20of%20COVID_v4.pdf

Garcia, G. A., Huerta, A. H., Ramirez, J. J., & Patrón, O. E. (2017). Contexts that matter to the leadership development of Latino male college students: A mixed methods perspective. *Journal of College Student Development, 58*(1), 1–18. https://doi.org/10.1353/csd.2017.0000

Gardner, H. (1983). *Frames of mind: The theory of multiple intelligences.* Basic Books.

Garrett, R., Simunich, B., Legon, R., & Fredericksen, E. E. (2021). *CHLOE 6: Online learning leaders adapt for a post-pandemic world the changing landscape of online education, 2021.* Quality Matters.

Han, C., Farruggia, S. P., & Moss, T. P. (2017). Effects of academic mindsets on college students' achievement and retention. *Journal of College Student Development, 58*(8), 1119–1134. https://doi.org/10.1353/csd.2017.0089

Holian, L., & Adam, T. (2020). *Veterans' education benefits: A profile of military students who received federal veterans' education benefits in 2015–16.* National Center for Education Statistics, U.S. Department of Education. https://nces.ed.gov/pubsearch/pubsinfo.asp?pubid=2020488REV

Hossler, D. (2006). Managing student retention: Is the glass half full, half empty, or simply empty? *College and University, 81*(2), 11–14. https://journals.sagepub.com/doi/10.2190/CS.11.1.f

Hurtado, S., & Carter, D. F. (1997). Effects of college transition and perceptions of campus racial climate on Latinos' sense of belonging. *Sociology of Education, 70*(4), 324–345. https://doi.org/10.2307/2673270

Hussar, W. J., & Bailey, T. M. (2019). *Projections of education statistics to 2027.* National Center for Education Statistics, U.S. Department of Education. https://nces.ed.gov/pubs2019/2019001.pdf

Jensen, L., & Roof, V. (n.d.). *The ethical use of student data and analytics.* http://
ts3.nashonline.org/wp-content/uploads/The-Ethical-Use-of-Student-Data-and-
Analytics.pdf

Jones, S. R., & Stewart, D.-L. (2016). Evolution of student development theory.
In E. S. Abes (Ed.), *Critical perspectives on student development theory* (New
Directions for Student Services, no. 154, pp. 17–28). Jossey-Bass. https://doi
.org/10.1002/ss.20172

Kamenetz, A. (2010). *DIY U: Edupunks, edupreneurs, and the coming transformation
of higher education.* Chelsea Green.

Kilgo, C. A., Sheets, J. K. E., & Pascarella, E. T. (2015). The link between high-
impact practices and student learning: Some longitudinal evidence. *Higher
Education, 69*(4), 509–525. https://doi.org/10.1007/s10734-014-9788-z

Kim, Y. K., & Sax, L. J. (2017). The impact of college students' interactions with
faculty: A review of general and conditional effects. In M. B. Paulsen (Ed.),
Higher education: Handbook of theory and research (Vol. 32, pp. 85–139). Springer.
https://doi.org/10.1007/978-3-319-48983-4_3

King, P. M. (1994). Theories of college student development: Sequences and consequences. *Journal of College Student Development, 35*(6), 413–421. https://psycnet
.apa.org/record/1995-27161-001

Knefelkamp, L., Widick, C., & Parker, C. A. (Eds.). (1978). *Applying new developmental findings.* Jossey-Bass.

Koch, A. K. (2017). It's about the gateway courses: Defining and contextualizing
the issue. In A. K. Koch (Ed.), *Improving teaching, learning equity, and success
in gateway courses* (New Directions for Higher Education, no. 180, pp. 11–17).
Jossey-Bass. https://doi.org/10.1002/he.20257

Kohlberg, L. (1981). *The philosophy of moral development moral stages and the idea of
justice.* Harper & Row.

Kuh, G. (1996). *Student learning outside of the classroom: Transcending artificial
boundaries.* ERIC Digest. https://www.ericdigests.org/1996-4/student.htm

Kuh, G. (2008). *High-impact educational practices: What they are, who has access to
them, and why they matter.* American Association of Colleges and Universities.

Lane, J. E. (2003). Studying community colleges and their students: Context and
research issues. In M. C. Brown & J. E. Lane (Eds.), *Studying diverse students and
institutions: Challenges and considerations* (pp. 51–68). Jossey-Bass.

Lane, J. E. (2014). *Building a smarter university: Big data, innovation, and analytics.*
State University of New York Press.

Lane, J. E., Khan, M. I., & Knox, D. (2021). *Transfer student success: Higher education systems' five top policy levers.* National Association of System Heads. https://
ts3.nashonline.org/transfertopfive/

Lattuca, L., & Stark, J. (2009). *Shaping the college curriculum.* Jossey-Bass.

Levesque, E. M. (2018). *Improving community college completion rates by addressing
structural and motivational barriers.* Brookings Institution.

Levine, A. (1979). *Handbook on undergraduate curriculum.* Jossey-Bass.

Magda, A. J., Capranos, D., & Aslanian, C. B. (2020). *Online college students 2020:
Comprehensive data on demands and preferences.* Wiley.

Marachi, R., & Quill, L. (2020). The case of Canvas: Longitudinal datafication through learning management systems. *Teaching in Higher Education, 25*(4), 418–434. https://doi.org/10.1080/13562517.2020.1739641

Mayhew, M. J., & Rockenbach, A. N. (2020, September 4). *Does 4 years of college make students more liberal?* The Conversation. https://theconversation.com/does-4-years-of-college-make-students-more-liberal-145157

Mayhew, M. J., Rockenbach, A. N., Bowman, N. A., Seifert, T. A., Wolniak, G. C., Pascarella, E. T., & Terenzini, P. T. (2016). *How college affects students: 21st century evidence that higher education works* (Vol. 3). Jossey-Bass.

Miller, T. K., & Prince, J. S. (1976). *The future of student affairs: A guide to student development for tomorrow's higher education.* Jossey-Bass.

Nadworny, E. (2019, March 13). *College completion rates are up, but the numbers will still surprise you.* National Public Radio. https://www.npr.org/2019/03/13/681621047/college-completion-rates-are-up-but-the-numbers-will-still-surprise-you

National Leadership Council for Liberal Education and America's Promise. (2007). *College learning for the new global century.* Association of American Colleges and Universities. https://www.aacu.org/sites/default/files/files/LEAP/GlobalCentury_final.pdf

National Student Clearinghouse Research Center. (2021). *Overview: Spring 2021 enrollment estimates.* https://nscresearchcenter.org/wp-content/uploads/CTEE_Report_Spring_2021.pdf

National Task Force on the Transfer and Award of Credit. (2021). *Reimagining transfer for student success.* American Council on Education. https://www.acenet.edu/Documents/Reimagining-Transfer-for-Student-Success.pdf

Okahana, H., Zhou, E., & Gao, J. (2020). *Graduate enrollment and degrees: 2009–2019.* Council of Graduate Schools and ETS GRE. https://cgsnet.org/ckfinder/userfiles/files/CGS_GED19_Report_final2.pdf

Parnell, A., Jones, D., Wesaw, A., & Brooks, C. D. (2018). *Institutions' use of data and analytics for student success: Results from a national landscape analysis.* EDUCAUSE. https://library.educause.edu/resources/2018/4/institutions-use-of-data-and-analytics-for-student-success

Pascarella, E. T., & Terenzini, P. T. (1991). *How college affects students: Findings and insights from twenty years of research.* Jossey-Bass.

Pascarella, E. T., & Terenzini, P. T. (2005). *How college affects students: A third decade of research* (Vol. 2). Jossey-Bass.

Porter, C. J., & Dean, L. A. (2015). Making meaning: Identity development of Black undergraduate women. *NASPA Journal About Women in Higher Education, 8*(2), 125–139. https://doi.org/10.1080/19407882.2015.1057164

Reason, R. (2009). An examination of persistence research through the lens of a comprehensive conceptual framework. *Journal of College Student Development, 50*(6), 659–682. https://doi.org/10.1353/csd.0.0098

Renn, K. A., & Reason, R. D. (2021). *College students in the United States: Characteristics, experiences, and outcomes.* Stylus.

Rhoades, G. (2012). The incomplete completion agenda: Implications for academe and the academy. *Liberal Education, 98*(1), 18–25. https://www.aacu.org/publications-research/periodicals/incomplete-completion-agenda-implications-academe-and-academy

Rockenbach, A. N., Mayhew, M. J., Giess, M. E., Morin, S. M., Staples, B. A., Correia-Harker, B. P., & Associates. (2020). *IDEALS: Bridging religious divides through higher education.* Interfaith Youth Core. http://ifyc.org/sites/default/files/navigating-religious-diversity-9-27.pdf

Shapiro, D., Dundar, A., Huie, F., Wakhungu, P. K., Bhimdiwala, A., Nathan, A., & Hwang, Y. (2018). *Transfer and mobility: A national view of student movement in postsecondary institutions, fall 2011 cohort.* National Student Clearinghouse Research Center. https://nscresearchcenter.org/signaturereport15/

Soares, L., Gagliardi, J. S., & Nellum, C. J. (2017). *The post-traditional learners manifesto revisited: Aligning postsecondary education with real life for adult student success.* American Council on Education. https://www.acenet.edu/Documents/The-Post-Traditional-Learners-Manifesto-Revisited.pdf

Society for College and University Planning. (n.d.). *Academic planning.* https://www.scup.org/planning-type/academic-planning/

Son, C., Hegde, S., Smith, A., Wang, X., & Sasangohar, F. (2020). Effects of COVID-19 on college students' mental health in the United States: Interview survey study. *Journal of Medical Internet Research, 22*(9), e21279. https://doi.org/10.2196/21279

Spady, W. G. (1970). Dropouts from higher education: An interdisciplinary review and synthesis. *Interchange, 1*(1), 64–85. https://doi.org/10.1007/BF02214313

St. Amour, M. (2020, October 8). College promise programs wrestle with pandemic realities. *Inside Higher Ed.* https://www.insidehighered.com/news/2020/10/08/college-promise-programs-face-cuts-uncertainty-and-changes

Stolzenberg, E. B., Aragon, M. C., Romo, E., Couch, V., McLennan, D., Eagan, M. K., & Kang, N. (2020). *The American freshman: National norms fall 2019.* Higher Education Research Institute, University of California, Los Angeles. https://www.heri.ucla.edu/monographs/TheAmericanFreshman2019.pdf

Strange, C. S. (1994). Student development: The evolution and status of an essential idea. *Journal of College Student Development, 35*(6), 399–412. https://eric.ed.gov/?id=EJ497331

Talburt, S. (2011). Queer theory. In B. J. Bank (Ed.), *Gender and higher education* (pp. 86–93). Johns Hopkins University Press.

Terenzini, P. T., & Pascarella, E. T. (1980). Student/faculty relationships and freshman year educational outcomes: A further investigation. *Journal of College Student Personnel, 21*(6), 521–528. https://eric.ed.gov/?id=EJ236188

Thelin, J. R. (2011). *A history of American higher education* (2nd ed.). Johns Hopkins University Press.

Tinto, V. (1975). Dropout from higher education: A theoretical synthesis of recent research. *Review of Educational Research, 45*(1), 89–125. https://doi.org/10.3102/00346543045001089

Tinto, V. (1987). *Leaving college: Rethinking the causes and cures of student attrition.* The University of Chicago Press.

Torres, V., Jones, S. R., & Renn, K. (2019). Student affairs as a low-consensus field and the evolution of student development theory as foundational knowledge. *Journal of College Student Development, 60*(6), 645–658. https://doi.org/10.1353/csd.2019.0060

Townsend, B. K., & Dever, J. T. (1999), What do we know about reverse transfer students? In B. K. Townsend (Ed.), (New Directions for Community Colleges, no. 106, pp. 5–14). Jossey-Bass. https://doi.org/10.1002/cc.10601

16

PLANNING, ASSESSMENT, AND BUDGETING

Former U.S. President Dwight D. Eisenhower once stated, "I have always found that plans are useless, but planning is indispensable." In this observation, Eisenhower seems to have been suggesting that the act of planning is more useful than the plan that emerges from the process and that any organization that seeks to maximize its potential should keep this advice in mind. Too often, people believe that the outcome of planning is a written plan or another final document that clearly outlines an organization's future, whether it is a corporation seeking an advantage in the marketplace or a university seeking to fulfill its mission. A more meaningful way to think about the end result of planning is that it is a living document that necessitates constant scanning, monitoring, and acting on ever-changing variables in the environment. This notion, that a continuous loop of assessment and feedback is part of a robust strategic planning process, is the best possible way to ensure that an institution is fulfilling its mission, making decisions based on its values, and being inclusive in its decision-making processes.

This continuous loop of strategic planning, environmental scanning, and change management can be traced to ancient military campaigns and the leaders who waged them. In fact, the word *strategic* comes from the Greek words for *army* and *leading*. Leading an army into battle requires significant planning and ongoing assessment of the situation. First, leaders must understand the assets and liabilities of their own organization and attempt to discover as much as they can in advance about their enemies' strengths and weaknesses. It is also important to understand other variables such as the topography of the land where the battle will take place; the condition of the troops; and, if possible, other factors such as weather conditions, supply lines, and the abilities of leaders in the field. Once a battle commences, any number of factors can influence the outcome, and history has shown that in most cases the leaders who have been able to make adjustments in the middle of a battle prevail, while those who stubbornly stick to their original plans are defeated.

The idea of preparing for a battle or war campaign is just one metaphor for strategic planning, but no matter what organization is involved, continual assessment from the field about what is happening outside the organization—and the ability to adjust to that information—most often will decide the fate of an institution. The same is true for colleges and universities: Planning is useful and necessary, but the process of continually assessing circumstances and adjusting plans accordingly is what really has the greatest potential to advance the institution.

National Priorities and Higher Education's Response

Post–World War II U.S. higher education functioned in a time of tremendous growth and expansion of resources. Changing demographics, growing national ambitions, and the vision of a better future for the United States drove the incredible growth in U.S. higher education from 1944 until the middle of the 1980s.

One of the major motivations for the passage of the Servicemen's Readjustment Act of 1944 (better known as the GI Bill) was the United States' recognition of the challenge of assimilating into the workforce all the soldiers coming home from World War II and the need for time to accommodate them when they returned. This adjustment process led to incredible growth in enrollments at colleges and universities across the country, to which institutions often responded by expanding their missions and capacities to serve larger and more diverse populations of students. The post–World War II baby boom forecasted that the demand for higher education would continue, and individual institutions and state systems of higher education developed plans for the anticipated growth.

As the Cold War emerged, U.S. higher education was also asked to respond to other urgent issues. For example, when the Soviet Union launched the world's first satellite, Sputnik, in 1957, the U.S. response was to find new ways to prepare the next generation of citizens to be more competitive, especially in scientific fields. Among the strategies adopted by the U.S. government was the National Defense Education Act of 1958, which created federally subsidized loans for college students to finance their education as well as more funding for graduate fellowships and research.

The need to accommodate returning veterans, rapid growth in the number of college-age students, and new funding sources for education created a different paradigm for the leaders of U.S. colleges and universities. Prior to World War II, public resources for higher education were limited, and only a small percentage of the adult population attended college—primarily men from upper-class White families. Consequently, academic leaders were accustomed to incremental growth in enrollments and cautious expansion of academic offerings. They could not only afford but were encouraged to be gatekeepers who limited the luxury of a college education to a privileged few. However, the postwar era was a time of relative abundance and increased demand that required academic leaders to respond to national priorities, build new facilities, and attract the best possible talent to teach students and conduct research.

Planning during a time of growth brings about its own set of demands and stresses on institutions of higher learning. During the postwar era a number of factors remained constant and facilitated planning: Government spending on education and research increased, national high school graduation rates grew, and demand for a college education rose dramatically. Given this relative steady state, or at least steady trajectory of growth, higher education leaders could plan accordingly.

In contrast, the 21st century has emerged as an era of numerous challenges, including increasing competition for inconsistent state and federal resources for both education and research, an aging faculty population, and dropping high school graduation rates. Therefore, the competition for resources, faculty, staff, and students has never been greater. During this time of scarcity and heightened competition, government officials, accrediting bodies, and the general public have begun to demand more accountability about how public dollars are being used and how institutions measure success. In this environment, institutions of higher learning need to leverage and optimize their limited resources, and those leaders who establish continual processes of strategic planning, assessment, and institutional renewal will be better positioned for the future.

The Growing Need for Strategic Planning and Accountability

By the 1980s, U.S. higher education faced a crisis. With increasing global competition, reduced government support, growing societal wealth disparities, and tough economic times, colleges and universities were being asked to do more with less. During this period, the expectation for higher education to be more accountable for institutional results became paramount. One response to this demand was a push for colleges and universities to adopt established business practices such as strategic planning and zero-based budgeting, as well as to become more attuned to the needs of the workforce and research needs of U.S. businesses in an effort to boost the economy. There was also growing pressure for the creation of new accrediting bodies, including some that would be government sponsored, to compel higher education into meeting these demands. These forces led existing accrediting organizations to introduce new accountability metrics and resulted in an expansion in measures by governing boards and state and federal agencies to hold higher education more accountable for its expenses and outcomes.

In *Academic Strategy: The Management Revolution in American Higher Education*, Keller (1983) extolled the virtues of strategic planning and introduced a new generation of higher education leaders to the power of this idea. He proposed that "design was better than drift" (p. 118), and it was time for U.S. colleges and universities to recognize that, while they had special traditions and different cultures, they were not immune to the influences of the external environment. During the troubling economic times of the early 1980s, Keller asserted that institutions needed to "pick up management's new tools and use them" (p. 118).

Keller (1983) went further to suggest that colleges and universities had to prepare for an uncertain future, be aggressive in their competitive strategies, be more agile, and position themselves to take advantage of opportunities that came their way. His basic premise was that U.S. higher education would benefit from greater planning, assessment, and environmental scanning, and that strategic planning methods would eventually become the sine qua non of higher education management, being accepted by educational leaders at all levels, from boards of trustees and state governing organizations to presidents. However, the special culture and traditions of higher education—such as shared governance, academic freedom, and tenure— sometimes made the adoption of what were viewed as business practices difficult to implement. Over time, by engaging faculty in an inclusive process to create the best possible learning environment and assess its outcomes, colleges and universities have developed their own tools to navigate difficult times while answering increased calls for accountability.

It should not have been surprising that faculty and others in the academy would be unreceptive to new management techniques and practices. Faculty members and administrators resisted adoption of business practices in higher education for years (Birnbaum, 1988; Cohen & March, 1974). Most colleges and universities existed for decades, if not centuries, without adopting what are now considered standard business management practices. An incremental, conservative approach to change had worked well in the past, and higher education leaders widely believed these outside pressures would subside so they could return to their old ways. In the 21st century, however, most administrators and faculty members have accepted that the need to be accountable for institutional and student learning outcomes as well as other societal measurements is here to stay.

Academic leaders in the 21st century must recognize it is preferable to leverage their deep knowledge of their institution's mission and culture to plan strategically, develop their own assessment metrics, and be held responsible for those outcomes than for some external organization to impose more standardized and often artificial measurements of success across the board. This realization goes well beyond a simple understanding of the budget process and how to maximize the impact of precious resources. Rather, it involves the linkage between strategic planning, budgeting, and assessment and the recognition that this relationship is critical to strengthening and executing the academic mission of the institution.

A Sense of Purpose and a Deliberate Process

If a successful college or university is truly driven by a clear sense of purpose and a core set of values, an institution's strategic vision should answer basic questions such as what it will do—and, equally important, what it will not do—with its resources to accomplish its mission (Montgomery, 2008). This principle applies not only to academic institutions but to all successful organizations. Montgomery (2008) averred that all organizations need to learn to change and adapt over time while fully recognizing the "fluid nature of competition" (p. 33). Holding too firmly to a particular strategy for realizing its mission may not be in the best interest of an organization in the long run. Rather, an "organic conception of strategy" (Montgomery, 2008, p. 37) should be sought. In other words, organizations might develop strategies that provide them with a competitive advantage, but no single strategy is likely to provide an organization with a distinctive advantage forever. The preferable goal is to ensure that an organization can add value over time, a goal that requires continuous scanning of the environment and making small and large adjustments to adapt to changes inside and outside the organization.

In his study of corporations that made the leap from good to great, Collins (2001) found that there was no single "miracle moment" (p. 169) when these companies were transformed. Likewise, there was no real sense within the organizations that they were in the midst of radical change. Rather, he found in great companies a "quiet, deliberate process" (p. 169) of determining what steps needed to be taken to create a desirable future. This fluidity indicates that great organizations are always in the process of becoming better and maintain the discipline necessary to pay attention to what is happening around them, never fully resting on their accomplishments.

Collins (2001) also asserted that an organization's core values or fundamental reasons for being should drive its decisions, and when adapting to changes in the environment, all organizations need to preserve their core ideology. In a monograph he wrote in 2005 about nonprofit organizations in the social sector, Collins stated, "Greatness, it turns out, is largely a matter of conscious choice, and discipline" (p. 31). Changing practices or strategies and setting ambitious goals are good methods for any organization when they are done deliberately, but Collins (2001, 2005) and Montgomery (2008) seem to have suggested that what distinguishes great organizations (for-profit and nonprofit) is that in the midst of such practices, their core sense of purpose remains constant.

Whether an organization is an international corporation or a small liberal arts college, the need to develop and maintain a robust planning process is paramount. All colleges and universities are required by regional and professional accrediting bodies to demonstrate that their mission is appropriate for an institution of higher learning and that they are living out that mission in meaningful ways. For example, in a 2021 accreditation handbook for the Western Association of Schools and Colleges (WASC), the WASC Senior College and University Commission (WSCUC) along with other institutional accreditors require that an institution's mission define "institutional purposes and ensure educational objectives" (Standard 1). Moreover, WSCUC asks institutions to document ongoing assessment activities that lead to organizational renewal and to have a mechanism for "developing and applying resources and operational structures to ensure quality and sustainability" (Standard 3). The Southern Association of Colleges and Schools Commission on Colleges (SACSCOC) (2017) requires every college or university in its membership to create a quality enhancement plan and demonstrate that all stakeholders are involved in the process of developing "its ongoing comprehensive planning and evaluation processes" (p. 8). Key to the quality enhancement process is the identification of assessment measures and evidence of self-renewal. It is also important to note that accrediting bodies encourage institutions to discover ways to include a broad range of stakeholders in the planning process, which is in alignment with two of the principles of this book, as we encourage democratic participation and inclusivity in decision-making.

Accrediting bodies are not the only organizations that require colleges and universities to provide a clear statement of purpose and produce evidence that appropriate assessment mechanisms are in place. Corporations, foundations, state governing boards, and federal agencies all require documentation and accountability for the resources they provide colleges and universities. For instance, state universities periodically submit campus master plans that map their multiyear building projections along with capacity forecasts, enrollment strategies, financial projections, and alignment with institutional mission (see, e.g., Rieth Jones, 2019). With myriad demands for demonstrating a sense of purpose and establishing processes to assess institutional and student learning outcomes, institutions of higher education must develop deliberate planning and assessment processes involving all their major stakeholders. For most colleges and universities, however, the question remains as to which processes will work best in light of their unique histories, missions, and cultures.

Developing an Appropriate Planning Model

Despite assumptions to the contrary, strategic planning and documentation of outcomes in their basic forms have been around for centuries. Even in the time of the colonial colleges, institutional leaders developed strategies to attract more resources and demonstrate they were good stewards of the funding they received. Lately, colleges and universities have established more formal processes to plan and document results, especially in anticipation of regional accreditation visits (usually every 5 to 10 years). Until the last quarter of the 20th century, few institutions had robust and continuous processes for planning and assessment, although regional accrediting bodies' and government agencies' expectations for accountability necessitated institutionalization of such processes by the first decade of the 21st century.

A key element of planning and assessment is serious thought on the part of academic leaders about the mission of their institution and what it means to fulfill it. Therefore, every college and university that embarks on a planning process should start by ensuring that its mission statement is appropriate to the institution and the institutional outcomes can be tied directly to that mission. For example, officials of a regional comprehensive state university with a reputation for undergraduate teaching must carefully consider how vigorously the institution will pursue graduate degree programs and faculty research.

While institutions may certainly expand their focus or core mission, it is challenging to do so. The process of affirming or expanding an institutional mission should not be taken lightly, and in the tradition of democratic participation in decision-making in higher education, changes to mission require input from all affected stakeholders. Many college and university leaders have successfully navigated these conversations by developing a discernment process in which representatives from various constituencies gather to discuss and reflect on the mission of the institution and its relevance in moving forward.

For some institutions this process may only require a few meetings in which key stakeholders (e.g., board members, faculty members, administrators, alumni, and students) discuss the core values inherent in the mission and decide how best to chart a future course. For others (especially those with a larger or more complicated set of stakeholders), this discernment process may be more elaborate. For example, a public master's-level university that was once primarily a teachers' college may seek to expand its mission by becoming more research focused. This organizational shift may require greater input from elected state officials. Likewise, a religiously affiliated institution that seeks to move in a more secular direction may require input from its sponsoring religious organization, or a single-sex college that is considering educating anyone who is eligible and interested in enrolling may need to collect input from graduates and benefactors, before making a decision.

Regardless of institution type, this process should model the best practices of shared governance if academic leaders want to be supported as the discussion progresses. In the end, leaders, particularly board members and the president, must either affirm the current mission or decide to change it to reflect an agreed-on set of new or revised core values. Once the mission has been affirmed by the board, a continuous planning process can begin in earnest.

Widener University provides a helpful example of engagement of key stakeholders in a discussion about institutional mission. In 2003 Widener held a "visioning" summit on its main campus, at which board members, faculty members, administrators, students, community members, alumni, benefactors, and local elected officials were invited to discuss what should be included in the university's mission and vision statements (Harris, 2011). The summit was one component of a two-year process to incorporate key constituents' feedback regarding the university's core values into a long-term plan that would chart the university's direction for the next decade. Based on the planning process and feedback from the summit, Widener's leaders developed a new mission statement that was later vetted by the entire university community and approved by the Widener board of trustees.

Colleges and universities may use numerous strategies to plan for the future and collect evidence that they are achieving their mission. Chaffee (1985), for example, identified three models (linear, adaptive, and interpretive) as inherent in the vast literature about strategic planning. First, the linear model of strategic planning identifies a sequence of events an organization will undertake to achieve a particular set of goals and objectives. According to Chaffee, this model requires an organization to be "tightly coupled" (p. 432), with a top-down approach to planning and a strong belief in leaders' control. In this approach, an organization may forecast future outcomes in the external environment, but the most important outcome is the accomplishment of the stated organizational goals. One of the drawbacks with this approach is that it does not take into consideration changes in the external environment during the implementation of the plan that may alter the success of achieving the stated goal.

Second, in the adaptive model of planning, organizational leaders view the external environment as ever changing and recognize the need for constant assessment of internal and external factors that may influence the outcome of a stated goal (Chaffee, 1985). In an adaptive approach, organizational goals represent "a co-alignment of the organization with its environment" and a need for the organization to "change with" that environment (Chaffee, 1985, p. 434).

Third, the interpretive model assumes that reality is not objective and is interpreted differently by myriad players both internal and external to the organization (Chaffee, 1985). Instead of dealing with the environment as something the organization can control or change, the interpretive approach requires the organization's leaders to purposefully shape the attitudes of stakeholders toward the organization and its dealings with the outside world.

Most successful college and university planning efforts incorporate elements of all three approaches. Certainly, there needs to be some discipline in an institution's approach and a clear sense of direction that will help people, both inside and outside, understand its desired outcomes and how it plans to achieve those goals. Leaders of successful organizations also realize, however, that the environment is neither static nor always malleable to the will of the institution. Moreover, changes in direction in response to environmental factors are frequently necessary. It is also important to understand that organizational leaders can and should play a significant role in interpreting the environment and conveying its meaning to key institutional constituents (Chaffee, 1985).

Engaging Key Stakeholders

Much has been written about the best way to involve stakeholders in strategic planning and help them make sense of these processes. The options for planning are as diverse as the models for shared governance. Trainer (2004) identified what he called the "top-ten planning tools" (p. 133) for higher education, including more familiar approaches such as conducting SWOT (strengths, weaknesses, opportunities, and threats) analyses, TOWS (turning opportunities and weaknesses into strengths), and using SMART (specific, measurable, achievable, results-oriented, and time-bound) language for goals, as well as less well-known approaches. For some institutions a specific, structured approach may work best, while for others a hybrid of several different approaches might be better.

If a college or university has not previously engaged in a comprehensive planning and assessment process, there are several key elements its leaders may wish to include when developing their own procedure. Morrison et al. (1984) described the strategic planning process as a merger between scanning the external environment and long-range planning, identifying six critical stages: "environmental scanning, evaluation of issues, forecasting, goal setting, implementation and monitoring" (p. 5).

Although all planning processes are unique to the institution that employs them, most include the basic elements of scanning the internal and external environments, scenario planning, charting a course of action, implementing specific strategies, assessing desired outcomes, and continuously providing feedback for future decision-making. In addition, a formal monitoring process is important to ensure that feedback is timely and that the correct data are being collected and used. This type of monitoring is often controlled by internal processes specifically designed to examine institutional effectiveness and student learning outcomes.

Whatever process an institution develops, the need to create a planning and assessment culture within a college or university is crucial. For this culture to succeed, appropriate resources must be allocated to the institutional entities that will be responsible for it. Several researchers have discovered that one of the key reasons a planning effort fails is the lack of dedicated resources and organizational structures to support it (Keller, 1983; Taylor & Schmidtlein, 1996).

No matter which specific process an institution selects, the best option for most colleges and universities is one that is highly inclusive, fits the institution's culture, provides the necessary evidence of achievement of outcomes, and is sustainable over time. In other words, the planning process should fit the current governance structure while minimizing undue or cumbersome requirements for implementation. For example, many institutions have found ways to incorporate planning and assessment directly into the work of existing administrative and faculty committees, and boards of trustees have restructured their meetings to focus more on accountability measurements, including assessing their own performance. Evidence also suggests that for an organizational planning effort to be sustainable over time, departmental and individual staff goals and performance evaluations need to be tied directly to the institution's strategic plan (Sullivan & Richardson, 2011).

Pennsylvania State University developed an annual planning model in 1983 that was still in use in the early 21st century. Two years after reorganizing its campus college system in 1999, Penn State enhanced its annual planning model by creating what it described as an integrated planning model for the entire university to "improve alignment, reduce redundancy and streamline processes" (Sandmeyer et al. 2004, p. 91). This new, integrated approach required more coordination across the Penn State system and necessitated university-wide coordination of data collection and assessment of that information. This process helped the individual campuses in the Penn State system use their resources more effectively as well as determine more quickly the financial ramifications of the decisions their administrators make. One of the reasons this approach has worked was that Penn State did not scrap its long-term approach to planning. Rather, it worked within its established process to develop improved data-collection methods and provide evidence that the university's goals and objectives were being met.

Another positive example of incorporating existing practices into a more comprehensive approach to institutional renewal was the process used by David Ward when he became chancellor of the University of Wisconsin-Madison in 1993. Ward, who had previously served as provost, helped create a planning document to meet the requirements set forth in the North Central Association of Colleges and Schools reaccreditation process in 1989. That document, *Future Directions*, laid the foundation for future planning and was so successful in its implementation that it remained the basis for the next round of accreditation in 1999 (Paris, 2004). Instead of creating an entirely new planning model, Ward institutionalized the process used in the 1989 accreditation cycle so that there was little duplication of effort going forward. He saw the need to "infuse the plan throughout the organization" by making it part of the "routine of academic life" (Paris, 2004, p. 124). This stability was accomplished by identifying key people to champion priorities identified in the plan; requiring deans and administrators to report annual progress based on these priorities; and always basing university decisions on those priorities, even in the face of budget reductions (Paris, 2004).

Developing a Culture of Evidence: The Value of Assessment

What has emerged in the 21st century is the need to continuously plan and assess specific outcomes by developing what the Educational Testing Service has labeled "a culture of evidence" (Millett et al., 2007). The idea that an institution needs to create a culture of evidence is based on the premise that continuous cycles of assessing outcomes, analyzing data, and acting on that information will improve student learning and hold institutions more accountable for the achievement of the outcomes that they define in their stated mission.

Collecting data and using it to inform the decision-making process of a college or university is at the heart of creating a culture of evidence. This type of assessment falls into two broad categories typically found in all accreditation processes: institutional assessment and student learning outcomes assessment (MSCHE, 2015). Institutional assessment asks a college or university to demonstrate it is carrying out its stated mission and goals, while student learning outcomes assessment is concerned with the competencies, knowledge, and skills individual students possess at certain critical junctures during their time in college (Gannon-Slater et al., 2014; MSCHE, 2015). What is important to understand about these two elements is that no institution ever finishes assessing either aspect. What truly matters is a continuous improvement cycle in which data are perpetually collected; decisions informed by those data are made; and the process of scanning, planning, and implementation are reinitiated.

Unfortunately, too few colleges and universities have developed a culture of evidence that enhances student learning, leads to better teaching, and improves the functioning of departments across the institution. Most view assessment, particularly student learning outcomes assessment, as a requirement with which they must comply when their department or institution is seeking some form of accreditation or is undergoing a review by another outside entity. This idea, that assessment is useful only to satisfy the needs of organizations and agencies outside the academy, has led to what Wergin (2003) described as an "outside-in" focus or "compliance mentality" with regard to assessment (p. 37). This attitude can inhibit the development of a deeper conversation about what it means to reflect on student learning data and act on institutional findings to improve teaching and learning.

Two examples of institutions that have successfully developed an enduring culture of evidence and continuous improvement approach to student learning are Alverno College and the U.S. Air Force Academy. Both institutions have devised ways to incorporate assessment of student learning outcomes into a meaningful dialogue about how their students need to be prepared for the future.

Alverno College, a Roman Catholic liberal arts college in Milwaukee, Wisconsin, that primarily enrolls women has been a leader for decades in identifying specific learning outcomes for its students, assessing those outcomes, and making changes based on the data it has collected. This approach, called *abilities-based education*, has established Alverno as a model for assessing student learning and providing clear evidence that students are achieving desired outcomes. Although Alverno developed this reputation many years ago, it still receives recognition because of the continuous improvement process the college has integrated into the fabric of the institution. For example, whether an individual is asked to serve on the board of trustees or is hired to serve as a faculty member, that person is introduced to this process. Several support mechanisms are in place to ensure that faculty members can successfully define appropriate student learning outcomes for their courses and strategies for assessing student success, and board members are advised as to how these assessment measures are related to the mission and goals of the institution.

Since its inception, the U.S. Air Force Academy's (USAFA) curriculum has been based on the idea that a broad liberal education, coupled with professional training in specific disciplines such as engineering, is important for every student. Over the first 50 years of its existence, the USAFA followed the pattern of most universities, focusing conversations about outcomes on the accumulation of credits toward a degree. In 1993, however, the conversation changed when the dean of the faculty introduced "educational outcomes" (Enger et al., 2010, p. 17) for liberal and professional studies, which were followed by the development of comparable outcomes for other aspects of cadet training.

In 2006 a team of faculty members from the USAFA attended a summer workshop sponsored by the AAC&U. Using data they collected about USAFA graduates and their educational experiences, they decided to revamp their curriculum and develop a set of measurable core competencies for each cadet (Enger et al., 2010). Since the development of these competencies, the USAFA has been engaged in an ongoing process to determine the most effective practices regarding student learning outcomes, and mechanisms have been developed to ensure a continuous conversation about the competencies U.S. Air Force officers will need in the future. This example illustrates how an ongoing conversation about student learning can bring about meaningful change in an institution. It is also important to note that the USAFA approach takes into account that the skills and competencies needed to be an officer are ever changing, and therefore, the learning outcomes at the USAFA need ongoing monitoring and adjustment.

The most frequent question asked about assessment concerns where responsibility for it falls at an institution. The AGB (2011) statement on board responsibility asserted that fiscal accountability is not the sole responsibility of a board of trustees; rather, a board is also tasked with assessment of academic quality. Unfortunately, as prepared as most board members are to assess the financial health of an organization, they often feel ill-equipped to assess the quality of the educational and cocurricular experiences their institutions provide to students.

To help trustees to feel more confident in their ability to understand and track academic progress, many institutions have developed dashboards or metrics, similar to those they use for fiscal concerns, for assessing academic matters. These metrics can include data on retention and graduation rates, students' passage rates on state or national professional licensing examinations, or comparative data on student learning outcomes or student community engagement as measured by national surveys such as the National Survey of Student Engagement. Once again, an institution's mission, its stated learning objectives, and its vision for the future will affect which assessment tools are most appropriate for a particular institution.

Boards, however, must avoid dictating what should be taught in a specific course or classroom. Instead, their role is to determine how academic quality is to be measured and by whom. In an article published in the AGB's *Trusteeship* magazine, Allen (2007) made the case that trustees might consider certain approaches to assessing educational outcomes, such as asking faculty members to clearly articulate how certain learning goals are indicative of their institution's mission, as well as how any collected data or evidence will be used to improve students' experiences.

Developing a culture of evidence and demonstrating outcomes can help an institution in a variety of ways. For example, Allen and Durant (2009) documented how their work in bringing strategic planning, assessment, accreditation, and fundraising into a seamless process informed their institution's fundraising goals and improved the university's ability to attract resources during tough economic times. In addition, Saltmarsh and Gelmon's (2006) work on engaged academic departments suggested that departments that are able to provide evidence they are accomplishing learning outcomes in various engagement activities should be most effective in attracting resources.

Linking Planning and Assessment to Budgeting

In this book, we have made the case that the creation of an institutional vision through a comprehensive planning process, coupled with the development of measurable outcomes to assess progress, can have a tremendous impact on the future of a college or university. As important as these steps are to the success of an institution of higher education, any long-term plan requires a realistic resource allocation process that considers the institution's financial viability and the resources (e.g., personnel, IT, facilities) necessary to accomplish its stated goals (Goldman & Salem, 2015).

Colleges and universities have prepared annual budgets since the founding of the colonial colleges. The act of projecting what it will cost to provide high-quality educational offerings and appropriate auxiliary programs to attract and retain students is part of every institution's annual plan of action. In the 21st century, the focus has shifted from a simple calculation of annual revenues and expenditures to more sophisticated long-term forecasting that requires accurate data collection and an ongoing environmental scanning process. These exercises can help an institution more accurately calculate what resources it will need over the long-term to fulfill its mission.

One approach that has gained momentum at colleges and universities in recent years has been scenario planning, which includes a 360-degree scan of an institution's internal and external environments and focuses on any signals that may forecast a trend that could affect the institution negatively or positively. The data and information collected during any environmental scanning exercise is used to create a set of scenarios of how a trend may play out in the long-term, discerning its impact—with a special focus on financial impact—at the macro and micro levels. Morrison and Wilson (1997) described scenarios as "stories of possible futures that the institution might encounter" (p. 7). Some of the issues in a scenario could include economic, environmental, political, social, or technological elements. However, it is not always possible to create a scenario in advance. For example the COVID-19 global pandemic had an enormous impact on how institutions operate, but such an event was not viewed as even possible by most administrators in the past.

In its simplest form, scenario planning has always been part of the annual budgeting process at colleges and universities. All institutions plan the next year's budget by considering components such as projected enrollment, endowment returns, and anticipated fundraising. True scenario planning goes a step farther to project, for an extended period of time, elements such as the long-term demand for academic programs, state and federal funding, and potential changes to philanthropic trends (depending on economic prosperity or decline). Other scenarios might include more global issues such as environmental disasters, global pandemics, the impact of social media, or advances in artificial intelligence.

Given all these possible outcomes, many institutions have developed processes for multiple constituencies to provide feedback about the likelihood of the occurrence of certain scenarios as well as possible ways in which the college or university might respond, given its mission and vision for the future. The inclusion of diverse stakeholders provides different perspectives and can serve as an opportunity to educate people on how certain events could affect the organization and its financial health.

Once a course is charted, scenarios are analyzed, and the costs of reaching desired outcomes are determined, an institution should project a budget of three to five years, including a detailed annual budget. Determining what should be included in these budgets is one of the most important elements of successful planning and is often the determining factor on whether an organization achieves its goals in the long run.

Planning for the Unimagined

Accurate planning for the future is difficult for any college or university under the best circumstances. Even with a relatively stable external environment, no institution can plan for every possible scenario. This limitation became painfully evident in 2020 when the U.S. higher education sector faced a once-in-a-century global pandemic, its second economic recession in a decade, civil and political unrest, and a national reckoning due to centuries of unresolved racial and societal inequities. Any one of these issues would have generated a crisis, but the almost simultaneous advent of them all created a tsunami of challenges that forced colleges and universities to reconcile how they intended to fulfill their missions in a new era.

Shaker and Plater (2020) proposed that in the aftermath of such adversity, trustees and academic leaders will be called upon to ensure that any institutional responses to these crises are in "alignment with the mission of an institution and support the common good" (p. 20). Shaker and Plater (2020) requested that presidents and boards consider a series of questions when responding to future crises. The questions they proposed clearly align with the four principles that guide this book: commitment to mission, adaptation to change, forming democratic partnerships, and creating inclusive communities. For example, the authors asked boards to consider mission validity through the lens of "affordability, equitable access, and inclusive engagement for all citizens" (Shaker & Plater, 2020, p. 22). Furthermore, they suggested that boards consider reaffirming higher education's role for "employment and for citizenship" and emphasized that institutions must return to a focus that emphasizes "societal advancement" as much as "individual prosperity" (Shaker & Plater, 2020, p. 23).

Asking governing boards and academic leaders to plan for the unimaginable is a tall order, especially if such a process is to be more democratic, inclusive, and open to hearing from stakeholders who have traditionally been excluded from institutional decision-making. This new process requires greater flexibility and more inclusive planning by administrators and faculty members who traditionally have controlled these processes.

Responding to a significant crisis requires a different level of scenario planning than has taken place in the past. The Society for College and University Planning (SCUP) proposed that colleges and universities consider what they described as an "integrated approach to scenario planning" (Santilli & Wutka, 2020). According to SCUP, integrated planning is a "paradigm or framework that sets the parameters for all forms of institutional planning and builds collaborative relationships, aligns the organization and emphasizes preparedness for change" (Santilli & Wutka, 2020, p. 9).

In 2020, colleges and universities suddenly found themselves facing myriad challenges they would not have thought possible even a year before. When institutions face such unexpected challenges, they need to view these circumstances as being "volatile, unpredictable, complex, and ambiguous, or VUCA, for short" (Santilli & Wutka, 2020, p. 11). Accordingly, true "integrated planning" calls for a degree of scenario planning that includes "contradictory narratives about the future" (Santilli & Wutka, 2020, p. 11). This practice will require that institutions think carefully about the planning process, who needs to participate, and what questions need to be asked in light of an environment characterized by VUCA. Old assumptions about higher education need to be challenged, and that effort will require all stakeholders, especially the board, to engage deeply and not accept the status quo as a baseline for future strategic planning and budgeting.

Planning for the unimagined also requires new ways of thinking about budgeting and how resources are distributed. Institutions can ill afford simply to continue with an incremental budget process in which a small percentage increase in each department's budget occurs automatically. Future budgeting requires a rigorous process of prioritizing resources that align with strategic priorities and providing maximum flexibility for the institution to respond to unforeseen circumstances. It also requires the discipline to provide seed money for academic and administrative units to incubate new ideas in alignment with the strategic vision. One example of this type of approach occurred at the University of San Diego (2017), which incorporated a revolving $500,000 strategic initiatives fund so that any faculty, student, or staff member could apply for funds to pilot a new program in alignment with the university's six strategic pathways. Once a project was provided seed funding for up to two years, the project was evaluated and either placed in the queue for permanent funding or discontinued.

Much has been written over the years about the failure of planning initiatives because of a lack funding or an institution's inability to reallocate resources to support priorities identified in the strategic plan. In his analysis of great companies, Collins (2001) found that those organizations had the discipline to "stop doing" (p. 140) through what he described as unique budgeting processes. To stop doing something means that an institution chooses to move in a completely new strategic direction, and to fund that effort, its leaders may decide to drop an existing business line completely. Of course, higher education, with its shared governance tradition and often limited agility for eliminating a department or program, needs to incorporate a more democratic process to implement a new strategic vision and make tough decisions. This task will likely require even more involvement by the institution's governing board.

Bills and Pond (2021) placed on governing boards the blame for failed institutional transformation in the face of a threatening environment. Similar to the recommendations from SCUP (Santilli & Wutka, 2020), they call for boards to change institutional culture by challenging the status quo, accepting the premise that "problems are structural, not episodic," and encouraging a completely new way to view how an institution adapts to a threatening and ever-changing environment (Bills & Pond, 2021, p. 35).

One process that has worked for many institutions is an annual budgeting and planning summit for the board, administration, faculty, and staff, who together determine the priorities for the following year as well as for longer-term initiatives identified in the strategic plan. A particular benefit of this approach is that if stakeholders are involved in their institution's visioning and planning processes in meaningful ways, it is more likely that a proposal to reallocate resources from one area to fund new priorities will be better understood and potentially supported by a majority of constituents.

Conclusion

Regardless of the approach or strategy that an institution uses to plan for and gain democratic consensus on strategy and budget priorities, if a college or university lacks the discipline to require every new objective or budgetary request to demonstrate how it will advance the institutional mission and strategic goals, it is unlikely that its strategic vision will be achieved in the long run. Moreover, although planning is essential, if an institution's plan is not funded, future efforts to gain support for strategic planning are doomed to fail. Successful boards, presidents, and academic leaders in the 21st century must understand that all four elements—strategic planning, scenario planning, assessment, and budgeting—are inextricably bound, and institutional health and prosperity, not to mention accreditation, are all byproducts of that union.

References

Allen, J. (2007). Ask the right questions about student assessment. *Trusteeship*, *15*(3), 14–18.

Allen, J., & Durant, L. S. (2009). Better together: Widener University marries academic assessment and the reaccreditation process to strengthen its fund raising. *Currents*, *35*(7), 44–45.

Association of Governing Boards of Universities and Colleges. (2011). *AGB statement on board responsibility for the oversight of educational quality*. https://agb.org/sites/default/files/agb-statements/statement_2011_ed_quality.pdf

Bills, M., & Pond, W. (2021, January 14). Colleges in peril can be rescued. *The Chronicle of Higher Education*. https://community.chronicle.com/news/2470-colleges-in-peril-can-be-rescued-but-only-if-governing-boards-transform

Birnbaum, R. (1988). *How colleges work: The cybernetics of academic organization and leadership*. Jossey-Bass.

Chaffee, E. E. (1985). Three models of strategy. *Academy of Management Review*, *10*(1), 89–98. https://doi.org/10.5465/amr.1985.4277354

Cohen, M. D., & March, J. G. (1974). *Leadership and ambiguity: The American college president*. McGraw-Hill.

Collins, J. (2001). *Good to great: Why some companies make the leap . . . and others don't*. HarperCollins.

Collins, J. (2005). *Good to great and the social sectors: A monograph to accompany good to great*. HarperCollins.

Enger, R. C., Jones, S. K., & Born, D. H. (2010). Commitment to liberal education at the United States Air Force Academy. *Liberal Education*, *96*(2), 14–21. https://www.aacu.org/publications-research/periodicals/commitment-liberal-education-united-states-air-force-academy

Gannon-Slater, N., Ikenberry, S., Jankowski, N., & Kuh, G. (2014). *Institutional assessment practices across accreditation regions*. National Institute for Learning Outcomes Assessment. https://www.learningoutcomeassessment.org/documents/Accreditation%20report.pdf

Goldman, C. A., & Salem, H. (2015). *Getting the most out of university strategic planning: Essential guidance for success and obstacles to avoid*. RAND Corporation. https://www.rand.org/content/dam/rand/pubs/perspectives/PE100/PE157/RAND_PE157.pdf

Harris, J. T. (2011). How Widener developed a culture of civic engagement and fulfilled its promise as a leading metropolitan university. In M. W. Ledoux, S. C. Wilhite, & P. Silver (Eds.), *Civic engagement and service learning in a metropolitan university: Multiple approaches and perspectives* (pp. 1–12). Nova Science.

Keller, G. (1983). *Academic strategy: The management revolution in American higher education*. Johns Hopkins University Press.

Middle States Commission on Higher Education. (2015). *Standards for accreditation and requirements of affiliation* (13th ed.). https://www.msche.org/standards/

Millett, C. M., Payne, D. G., Dwyer, C. A., Stickler, L. M., & Alexiou, J. J. (2007). *A culture of evidence: An evidence-centered approach to accountability for student learning outcomes*. Educational Testing Service. http://www.ets.org/Media/Education_Topics/pdf/COEIII_report.pdf

Montgomery, C. A. (2008). Putting leadership back into strategy. *Harvard Business Review, 86*(1), 54–60. https://hbr.org/2008/01/putting-leadership-back-into-strategy

Morrison, J. L., Renfro, W. L., & Boucher, W. I. (1984). *Futures research and the strategic planning process: Implications for higher education*. http://horizon.unc.edu/projects/seminars/futuresresearch/

Morrison, J. L., & Wilson, I. (1997). Analyzing environments and developing scenarios in uncertain times. In M. W. Peterson, D. D. Dill, L. Mets, & Associates (Eds.), *Planning and management for a changing environment: A handbook on redesigning postsecondary institutions*. Jossey-Bass. http://horizon.unc.edu/courses/papers/JBChapter.html

National Defense Education Act, P.L. 85–864, 72 Stat. 1580 (1958)

Paris, K. A. (2004). Moving the strategic plan off the shelf and into action at the University of Wisconsin-Madison. In M. J. Dooris, J. M. Kelley, & J. F. Trainer (Eds.), *Successful strategic planning* (New Directions for Institutional Research: Successful Strategic Planning, no. 123, pp. 121–128). Jossey-Bass. https://doi.org/10.1002/ir.126

Rieth Jones. (2019). *University of North Carolina School of the Arts: Housing master plan*. https://www.uncsa.edu/mysa/docs/housing-master-plan-rja-study.pdf

Saltmarsh, J., & Gelmon, S. (2006). Characteristics of an engaged department: Design and assessment. In K. Kecskes (Ed.), *Engaging departments: Moving faculty culture from private to public, individual to collective focus for the common good* (pp. 27–44). Anker.

Sandmeyer, L. E., Dooris, M. J., & Barlock, R. W. (2004). Integrated planning for enrollment, facilities, budget and staffing: Penn State University. In M. J. Dooris, J. M. Kelley, & J. F. Trainer (Eds.), *Successful strategic planning* (New Directions for Institutional Research: Successful Strategic Planning, no. 123, pp. 89–96). Jossey-Bass. https://doi.org/10.1002/ir.122

Servicemen's Readjustment Act, P.L. 78–346, 58 Stat. 284 (1944)

Southern Association of Colleges and Schools' Commission on Colleges. (2017). *The principles of accreditation: Foundations for quality enhancement (6th ed.)*. https://sacscoc.org/app/uploads/2019/08/2018PrinciplesOfAcreditation.pdf

Santilli, N. R., & Wutka, S. (2020). *An integrated approach to scenario planning*. Society for College and University Planning.

Shaker, G. G. & Plater, W. M. (2020). The conversations trustees must have: Higher education after the crises of 2020. *Trusteeship, 28*(6), 18–23.

Sullivan, T. M., & Richardson, E. C. (2011). Living the plan: Strategic planning aligned with practice and assessment. *Journal of Continuing Higher Education, 59*(1), 2–9. https://doi.org/10.1080/07377363.2011.544975

Taylor, A. L., & Schmidtlein, F. A. (1996). *Issues posed by graduate research universities' change environment and their planning responses: Final technical report on*

National Science Foundation project: Strategic planning's role in establishing university research policies and plans. National Science Foundation Project.

Trainer, J. F. (2004). Models and tools for strategic planning. In M. J. Dooris, J. M. Kelley, & J. F. Trainer (Eds.), *Successful strategic planning* (New Directions for Institutional Research: Successful Strategic Planning, no. 123, pp. 129–138). Jossey-Bass. https://doi.org/10.1002/ir.127

University of San Diego. (2017). *Envisioning 2024: The strategic plan for the University of San Diego.* https://www.sandiego.edu/envisioning-2024/

WASC Senior College and University Commission. (2018). *2013 handbook of accreditation revised.* https://www.wscuc.org/resources/handbook-accreditation-2013

Wergin, J. F. (2003). *Departments that work: Building and sustaining cultures of excellence in academic programs.* Anker.

THE WRITING TEAM

T his volume is the result of the contribution of time, talent, and knowledge of multiple individuals. Many of these individuals are noted in the acknowledgments. Those listed here provided the most substantive contributions to the book. Although not actively involved in the writing of this edition, Robert Hendrickson and Richard Dorman were instrumental in the development of the first edition and this edition is grounded on their initial contributions. Sarah Fuller Klyberg, the editor, was an active part of the writing team for both editions, regularly attending author meetings, working to bring a single voice to the volume, and bringing her own expertise in higher education to raise important questions on content. The four authors of this edition, of course, remain solely responsible for the final prose, including any errors, omissions, or oversights.

The Authors

Gail F. Baker is vice president and provost of the University of San Diego. She was dean of the College of Communication, Fine Arts and Media at the University of Nebraska Omaha. At the University of Florida, she served as chair of the Department of Public Relations in the College of Journalism and Communications. She later served as vice president of public relations and special assistant to the president. At the University of Missouri-Columbia, she was chair of advertising and directed the Minority Recruiting program of the School of Journalism. She also served as president of the Association of Chief Academic Officers. Baker holds a BS degree from the Medill School of Journalism at Northwestern University, an MS degree in Marketing Communications from Roosevelt University and a doctorate in Journalism from the University of Missouri-Columbia. She held public relations positions with IBM and International Harvester (now Navistar). She was a reporter and editor for the *Chicago Daily Defender* newspaper. She has earned recognition for her work as a teacher, scholar, communications practitioner and writer. She has authored books and articles and is the winner of four Emmy awards for Excellence in Documentary Writing and Producing.

James T. Harris serves as president and professor of education at the University of San Diego. He is also president emeritus of Widener University and served as the president of Defiance College earlier in his career. Harris has served in leadership roles on several national education associations, including CASE, NCAA, Campus Compact, NAICU, and CUMU, as well as for multiple other state and local governing boards. He has received numerous recognitions for his leadership and service to higher education, including being named one of the "Top Fifty Character-Building Presidents in the Nation" by the John Templeton Foundation, receiving the Chief Executive Leadership award by CASE, and being recognized by the NAACP for his work in support of civil rights. All three of his alma maters have formally recognized him for his service to society, and the Pennsylvania State University Board of Trustees awarded him the distinguished alumnus award, the highest honor given a graduate. He remains an active scholar and teacher.

Jason E. Lane serves as dean of the College of Education, Health, and Society at Miami University in Oxford, Ohio and Professor of Higher Education Leadership and International Education. Lane leads several national efforts to strengthen and diversify leadership pipelines in higher education, including the Association of Governing Board's Institute for Leadership and Governance; the National Association of System Heads' (NASH) System Leadership Academy; and the State University of New York's (SUNY) Hispanic Leadership Institute. Lane has been director and/ or principal investigator for more than $21 million in external funding and published nearly 100 papers and more than 10 books, including *Multi-National Colleges and Universities* (Jossey-Bass, 2011), *Building q Smarter Universities* (SUNY Press, 2014), and *Universities and Colleges* (SUNY Press, 2012). His awards include being named a Fulbright New Century Scholar and the award for Outstanding Contributions to International Education Research from the Association for the Study of Higher Education (ASHE). Previous positions include dean of the School of Education for SUNY at Albany, vice provost and senior associate vice chancellor of academic planning and strategic leadership for the SUNY system, founding executive director of SUNY's Academic and Innovative Leadership (SAIL) Institute, and director of research for the Rockefeller Institute of Government. He earned a BS in political science from Southeast Missouri State University and an MA of political science and PhD in higher education from Pennsylvania State University.

Jeffrey C. Sun is professor of higher education and law, distinguished university scholar, and associate dean for innovation and strategic partnerships at the University of Louisville. At Louisville, he established the university's first competency-based education program, advanced new initiatives for career and technical education teachers, developed accelerated learning pathways for veterans, established several partnerships with the U.S. Army including cadre/faculty development and noncommissioned officer leadership development, created a college leadership development program (i.e., College Academic Learning of Leadership [CALL] Academy), and led projects that expanded his department enrollments more than 25% within 3 years during his time as department chair. In addition, he has served as project director and principal investigator for over $19 million in grants/ contracts examining professional/career education, leadership development, and higher education policy and law. He has coauthored seven books within these areas. Sun received a BBA and an MBA from Loyola Marymount University, a law degree (JD) from the Moritz College of Law at The Ohio State University, and an MPhil and a PhD from Columbia University.

Authors of the First Edition

Robert M. Hendrickson, one of the original authors of the book, served as a professor of education in higher education and senior scientist and director of the Center for the Study of Higher Education at Penn State. His research and teaching interests include legal issues, organizational theory, administration and governance, and faculty employment issues. From 2001 through 2007 he served as associate dean for graduate programs, research, and faculty development in the College of Education. During his tenure as associate dean, six graduate programs were ranked in the top 10 in the *U.S. News* rankings, and research awards grew from $4 million in 2001 to $18 million in 2007. His former students serve in faculty or administrative positions in the United States and foreign countries and several are presidents of colleges and universities.

Richard H. Dorman, one of the original authors of the book, served as the 14th president of Westminster College in Pennsylvania, a coeducational national liberal arts institution. Previously, he served in various senior administrative capacities, including vice president for institutional advancement at Otterbein College and assistant vice president at the University of Louisville, where he oversaw all development operations for the Health Sciences Center. Prior to that, Dorman was associate executive director for alumni relations at the Penn State Alumni Association. He holds a bachelor's degree in music from Susquehanna University, a master's degree in counselor education in student personnel services, and a doctorate in higher education administration, both from Penn State.

The Editor

Sarah Fuller Klyberg is a higher education professional, researcher, and writer and served as the editor of both editions of this book. Klyberg spent a decade as an international educational and cultural exchange program administrator in the United States and the Middle East. More recently she has served in editorial capacities for several academic journals and a campus climate consulting group and as an academic dean at a community college. She received a BA in from the College of Wooster, an MA from The University of Texas at Austin, and a PhD from Pennsylvania State University.

Page numbers followed by "f" and "t" indicate figures and tables.

A Guide for Leaders in Higher Education, Second Edition

Concepts, Competencies, and Tools

Brent D. Ruben, Richard De Lisi, and Ralph A. Gigliotti

Foreword by Jonathan Scott Holloway

"After an award-winning first edition, Brent Ruben, Richard De Lisi, and Ralph Gigliotti are back with a second edition of *A Guide for Leaders in Higher Education: Concepts, Competencies, and Tools*. This book could not come at a better time given the leadership challenges facing society like COVID-19 and issues of equity and social justice. The authors not only address higher education's role in meeting these challenges, but they expand their treatment of the book's core concepts and tools. As a result, they bridge theory and practice and underscore the communicative foundation of academic leadership in sophisticated fashion. The continuing importance of their work cannot be underestimated. It is a resource that all academic leaders need—and will thoroughly enjoy."—*Gail T. Fairhusrt, Distinguished University Research Professor, University of Cincinnati*

"This book is unique in providing both frameworks and vital information needed for successful leadership in higher education. I recommend it to all of our department chairs and use it in our leadership development program. Coverage of essential topics such as the changing landscape of higher education, perspectives on leadership, and communication strategies for academic leaders makes this an essential resource for aspiring and current academic leaders."—*Eliza K. Pavalko, Vice Provost for Faculty and Academic Affairs; and Allen D. and Polly S. Grimshaw Professor of Sociology, Indiana University Bloomington*

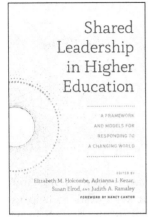

Shared
Leadership
in Higher
Education

A FRAMEWORK
AND MODELS FOR
RESPONDING TO
A CHANGING WORLD

EDITED BY
Elizabeth M. Holcombe, Adrianna J. Kezar,
Susan Elrod, AND Judith A. Ramaley
FOREWORD BY NANCY CANTOR

Shared Leadership in Higher Education

A Framework and Models for Responding to a Changing World

Edited by Elizabeth M. Holcombe, Adrianna J. Kezar, Susan Elrod, and Judith A. Ramaley

Foreword by Nancy Cantor

Today's higher education challenges necessitate new forms of leadership. A volatile financial environment and the need for new business models and partnerships to address the impact of new technologies, changing demographics, and emerging societal needs, demand more effective and innovative forms of leadership. This book focusses on a leadership approach that has emerged as particularly effective for organizations facing complex challenges: shared leadership.

Rather than concentrating power and authority in an individual leader at the top of an organization, shared leadership involves multiple people influencing one another across varying levels and at different times. It is a flexible, collective, and nonhierarchical approach to leadership. Organizations that have implemented shared leadership have been better able to learn, innovate, perform, and adapt to the types of external challenges that campuses now face and that will continue to shape higher education in the future.

Intended as a resource for leaders at the highest levels such as presidents and provosts as well as midlevel leaders such as deans, directors, and department chairs, the book is also addressed to faculty and staff who are interested in collaborating with campus leaders on institutional decision-making or creating new change initiatives. It is intended to build capacity for shared leadership across institutions and for use in leadership courses and programs.

Credentials

Understand the Problems. Identify the Opportunities. Create the Solutions.

Paul L. Gaston and Michelle Van Noy

Foreword by Peter Ewell

The credentials environment grows more complicated by the day, but key questions help us understand why we need this book to help us grapple with those complexities:

- Given the expansion in the variety of higher education credentials and in approaches to earning them, why are so many students disappointed with their postsecondary credentials?
- Despite the proliferation of credentials tailored to specific careers, why do so many employers complain that the preparation of their new hires is inadequate?
- Despite their investment in new programs meant to attract new enrollees, why are so many colleges and universities facing issues with student persistence, timely credential completion, and career success?

The plan of the book reflects the authors' practical aim. In the first of three parts, they offer a broad view of the credentials environment—how credentials work, how a proliferation in credentials has created an unprecedented array of educational choices, and why this abundance is a mixed blessing. In the second part, they focus on categories of credentials, from the associate degree to doctoral degrees to nondegree credentials. The book concludes with two chapters that consider the implications of the information the authors provide for leadership in volatile times: one discusses the importance of maintaining a priority on equity; the other offers 12 propositions for action.

To help make the book useful, each chapter begins with a paragraph that summarizes the emphases to follow, and ends with a list of initiatives, that is, "takeaways," that leaders (and those attentive to what leaders are doing) should consider.

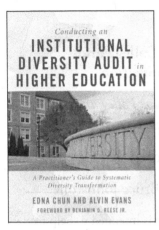

Conducting an Institutional Diversity Audit in Higher Education

A Practitioner's Guide to Systemic Diversity Transformation

Edna Chun and Alvin Evans

Foreword by Benjamin D. Reese Jr.

"This book is a *must*-read for anyone committed to diversity, particularly in higher education. Many colleges and universities have made a commitment to implementing diversity practices without a similar commitment to assessing the effectiveness of those practices. This book is a critical resource to help move institutions toward that important next step."—***Bryan Cook***, *Vice President, Data and Policy Analysis, Association for Public & Land-Grant Universities*

"Edna Chun and Alvin Evans have provided a great service through this comprehensive overview of diversity audits. Colleges and universities seeking to diversify their community, guarantee equity, and create inclusion will find this volume an excellent roadmap for organizing institutional change. I look forward to using the book!"—***Michele Minter***, *Vice Provost for Institutional Equity and Diversity, Princeton University*

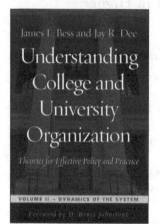